LESSONS FROM THE IDENTITY TRAIL

LESSONS FROM THE IDENTITY TRAIL

ANONYMITY, PRIVACY AND IDENTITY

IN A NETWORKED SOCIETY

EDITED BY IAN KERR, VALERIE STEEVES, AND CAROLE LUCOCK

OXFORD UNIVERSITY PRESS

Oxford University Press, Inc., publishes works that further Oxford University's objective of excellence in research, scholarship, and education.

Oxford   New York
Auckland   Cape Town   Dar es Salaam   Hong Kong   Karachi   Kuala Lumpur   Madrid   Melbourne
Mexico City   Nairobi   New Delhi   Shanghai   Taipei   Toronto

With offices in
Argentina   Austria   Brazil   Chile   Czech Republic   France   Greece   Guatemala   Hungary   Italy
Japan   Poland   Portugal   Singapore   South Korea   Switzerland   Thailand   Turkey   Ukraine
Vietnam

Library of Congress Cataloging-in-Publication Data
Lessons from the identity trail : anonymity, privacy and identity in a networked society /
Editors : Ian Kerr, Valerie Steeves, Carole Lucock.
   p. cm.
   Includes bibliographical references and index.
   ISBN 978-0-19-537247-2 ((hardback) : alk. paper)
1. Data protection—Law and legislation. 2. Identity. 3. Privacy, Right of. 4. Computer security—Law and
legislation. 5. Freedom of information. I. Kerr, Ian (Ian R.) II. Lucock, Carole. III. Steeves, Valerie M., 1959-
   K3264.C65L47 2009
   342.08'58—dc22

                                                        2008043016

1 2 3 4 5 6 7 8 9
Printed in the United States of America on acid-free paper

Note to Readers
This publication is designed to provide accurate and authoritative information in regard to the subject
matter covered. It is based upon sources believed to be accurate and reliable and is intended to be current
as of the time it was written. It is sold with the understanding that the publisher is not engaged in rendering
legal, accounting, or other professional services. If legal advice or other expert assistance is required, the
services of a competent professional person should be sought. Also, to confirm that the information has
not been affected or changed by recent developments, traditional legal research techniques should be used,
including checking primary sources where appropriate.

*(Based on the Declaration of Principles jointly adopted by a Committee of the
American Bar Association and a Committee of Publishers and Associations.)*

You may order this or any other Oxford University Press publication by
visiting the Oxford University Press website at www.oup.com

To Ejay – *"And wait for it,*
There are only two of us now
This great black night, scooped out
And this fireglow"

To David – for everything.

CONTENTS

ABOUT THIS BOOK

This book derives from the Social Science and Humanities Research Council (SSHRC) Initiative on the New Economy. Recognizing that the increased speed of technological development and the rapid growth of knowledge are contributing to major social, cultural, and personal change worldwide, SSHRC held a research competition to promote collaborative, multisectoral work on these issues. One of the research teams successful in the 2003 competition received a four-year, $4 million grant in support of a project entitled *On The Identity Trail: Understanding the Importance and Impact of Anonymity and Authentication in a Networked Society*.

With a focus on multidisciplinary dialogue and interaction, *ID Trail* brought together North American and European research talent from the academic, public, private, and not-for-profit sectors. With more than fifty co-investigators, collaborators, researchers, and partners, *ID Trail* included a distinguished array of philosophers, ethicists, feminists, cognitive scientists, sociologists, lawyers, cryptographers, engineers, policy analysts, government policymakers, privacy experts, business leaders, blue chip companies, and successful start-ups.

This book, one of four full-length volumes produced by *ID Trail*, is the outcome of two international workshops on privacy, identity, and anonymity. The first workshop was held in Paris, France, in 2006 and was hosted by the Atelier Internet, Équipe Réseaux, Savoirs, and Territoires at the École Normale, Supérieure. The second workshop was held in Bologna, Italy, in 2007 and was hosted by Dipartimento di Scienze Giuridiche at Università di Bologna.

Participants from both workshops exchanged ideas and manuscripts with the aim of creating a volume that would ultimately become an organic whole greater than the sum of its individual chapter contributions. In fulfillment of an undertaking to SSHRC to dedicate significant resources to student training initiatives, two competitions were held, and funding was provided to include ten students as full workshop participants. These and numerous other highly talented *ID Trail* student collaborators have made substantial contributions to this book, including a dozen as authors or co-authors.

In addition to the collaborative feedback that authors received at the workshops, each chapter included in this volume was subject to an anonymous peer review process prior to its submission to Oxford University Press.

ACKNOWLEDGMENTS

This book, like the *ID Trail* project itself, owes its existence to significant funding and other equally important forms of support from the Social Sciences and Humanities Research Council and a number of private and public sector partners, including the Alberta Civil Liberties Association Research Centre, Bell University Labs, the British Columbia Civil Liberties Association, Canadian Internet Policy and Public Interest Clinic, Centre on Values and Ethics, the Department of Justice, Entrust Technologies, Electronic Privacy Information Center, IBM Canada Ltd., Management Board Secretariat Ontario, Microsoft, the Office of the Information and Privacy Commission of Ontario, the Office of the Privacy Commissioner of Canada, the Ontario Research Network in Electronic Commerce, Privacy International, and the Sheldon Chumir Foundation for Leadership in Ethics. We are thankful for the support provided and could not have produced this volume or any of our other key research outcomes without the help of these organizations.

As a project that has sought to mobilize key research outputs in accessible language and across a variety of venues in order to assist policymakers and the broader public, we have worked closely with Canada's Federal and Provincial Information and Privacy Commissioners. We thank them for their invaluable time, effort, and contributions to our work and for their general interest and support. Thanks also to Stephanie Perrin, a longtime member of Canada's privacy advocacy community, for her role in putting us on the map during the early years of the project.

A number of universities and groups have collaborated with us on this book. In particular, we would like to show appreciation to Giusella Finocchiaro and the Università di Bologna, as well as Bert-Jaap Koops, Ronald Leenes, and members of the Tilburg Institute for Law, Technology, and Society for wonderful and animating discussions on the topics we all treasure so dearly. As our base of operations, the University of Ottawa has been central to everything we have accomplished. Special thanks are due to Gilles Morier and Daniel Lefebvre for their superb and supererogatory efforts in helping us run the show, and to Common Law Dean Bruce Feldthusen, for always saying, "How can I help make it happen?" With more than a hundred undergraduate, graduate, and postgraduate students working with the project over a four-year period, it is not possible to thank each by name. There are two, however, whose extraordinary involvement at the outset of the project made it possible for all of the others to participate. Our heartfelt appreciation goes to Milana Homsi and Nur Muhammed-Ally for getting the ball rolling. Similar thanks is owed to Francine Guenette, our first project administrator, for paving the road to success. Your special efforts were deeply valued.

Finding harmony among so many different voices while preserving the distinctness of each is no small task. To Amanda Leslie, our über-talented, lightning-quick, and highly reliable copyeditor, we feel privileged to have had the opportunity to work with you on this project. Thanks also to our acquisitions editor, Chris Collins, the ever-helpful Isel Pizarro, and to Jaimee Biggins and all members of the production team at Oxford University Press who have helped improve the quality of this book. We are also grateful to thirty or so anonymous reviewers for their effort and good judgment, upon which we greatly relied.

Finally, our deepest and everlasting gratitude is owed to Julia Ladouceur, our project administrator, whose playful smile and gentle manner belie her stunning ability to do just about anything. Always with kindness, always with generosity, and always with a bedazzling perfection that somehow renders invisible any remnant or recollection of the fact that the world was never that way on its own.

CONTRIBUTORS

CARLISLE ADAMS

Carlisle Adams is a Full Professor in the School of Information Technology and Engineering (SITE) at the University of Ottawa. In both his private sector and his academic work, he has focused on the standardization of cryptology and security technologies for the Internet, and his technical contributions include encryption algorithms, security authentication protocols, and a comprehensive architecture and policy language for access control in electronic environments. He can be reached at cadams@site.uottawa.ca.

JANE BAILEY

Jane Bailey is an Associate Professor at the Faculty of Law, University of Ottawa. Her ongoing research focuses on the impact of evolving technology on significant public commitments to equality rights, freedom of expression, and multiculturalism, as well as the societal and cultural impact of the Internet and emerging forms of private technological control, particularly in relation to members of socially disadvantaged communities. She can be reached at jane.bailey@uottawa.ca.

JENNIFER BARRIGAR

A doctoral candidate in the Law and Technology Program at the University of Ottawa, Faculty of Law, Jennifer Barrigar previously worked as legal counsel at the Office of the Privacy Commissioner in Canada. Her current privacy research builds on her interest in the creation, performance, and regulation of identities in online environments, focusing on the creation of the exclusively online "self" and its implications for privacy law and identity management technologies. She can be reached at jbarro72@uottawa.ca.

KATIE BLACK

Katie Black is an LLB Candidate at the University of Ottawa, Faculty of Law. Her interest in privacy rights has led her to conduct research on the human rights implications of Canada's no-fly list, the effects of battered women's support programs on personal identity, soft paternalism and soft surveillance in consent-gathering processes, and the impact of opening up adoption records on women's reproductive autonomy. She can be reached at kblac044@uottawa.ca.

JACQUELYN BURKELL

Jacquelyn Burkell is an Associate Professor at the Faculty of Information and Media Studies, University of Western Ontario. Trained in psychology, she conducts empirical research on the interaction between people and technology, with a particular emphasis on the role of cognition in such interactions. Much of her work focuses on anonymity in online communication, examining how the pseudonymity offered by online communication is experienced by online communicators and how this experience changes communication behavior and interpretation. She can be reached at jburkell@uwo.ca.

ALEX CAMERON

Alex Cameron is a doctoral candidate in the Law and Technology Program at the University of Ottawa, Faculty of Law. He was previously an associate at the law firm of Fasken Martineau Dumoulin LLP. His current studies focus on privacy and copyright with a focus on the interplay between privacy and digital rights management. He can be reached at acameron@uottawa.ca.

ROBERT CAREY

Robert Carey is a Postdoctoral Fellow at the Faculty of Information and Media Studies, the University of Western Ontario. His research at the Faculty concentrates on four different strands of anonymity-related research: conceptual and behavioral models of anonymity on the Internet; behavioral effects of anonymity in computer-mediated communication; the conceptualization of anonymity; and mass media's configuration of anonymity and information technology. He can be reached at rcarey2@uwo.ca.

JENNIFER CHANDLER

Jennifer Chandler is an Associate Professor at the University of Ottawa, Faculty of Law. She focuses on law, science, and technology, particularly the social and environmental effects of emerging technologies and the interaction of emerging technologies with law and regulation. She has written extensively in the areas of cybersecurity and cybertorts. She can be reached at jennifer.chandler@uottawa.ca.

JEREMY CLARK

Jeremy Clark is a doctoral candidate with the Centre for Applied Cryptographic Research (CACR) and the Cryptography, Security, and Privacy (CrySP) Group at the University of Waterloo. His research focuses on cryptographic voting, as well as privacy enhancing technologies, applied cryptography, the economics of information security, and usable security and privacy. He can be reached at j5clark@cs.uwaterloo.ca.

STEVEN DAVIS

Steven Davis is Professor Emeritus of Philosophy at Simon Fraser University and the former Director of the Centre on Values and Ethics at Carleton University. He researches philosophy of language and philosophy of mind, and his recent research has focused on privacy, identifying, and identification. He can be reached at davis@connect.carleton.ca.

JANE DOE

Jane Doe successfully sued the Toronto Police Force for negligence and discrimination in the investigation of her rape, a case that set legal precedent and is taught in law schools across Canada. Jane Doe is an author (*The Story of Jane Doe*, Random House), teacher, and community organizer. She is currently completing research on the use and efficacy of the Sexual Assault Evidence Kit (SEAK) and police practices of "warning" women regarding stranger and serial rapists.

GIUSELLA FINOCCHIARO

Giusella Finocchiaro is Professor of Internet Law and Private Law at the University of Bologna. She specializes in Internet law both at her own Finocchiaro law firm and as a consultant for other law firms. She also acts as a consultant for the European Union on Internet law issues. She can be reached at giusella.finocchiaro @unibo.it.

A. MICHAEL FROOMKIN

A. Michael Froomkin is Professor of Law at the University of Miami, Faculty of Law. He is on the advisory boards of several organizations including the Electronic Freedom Foundation and BNA Electronic Information Policy and Law Report, is a member of the Royal Institute of International Affairs in London, and writes the well-known discourse.net blog. His research interests include Internet governance, privacy, and electronic democracy. He can be reached at froomkin@law.tm.

PHILIPPE GAUVIN

Philippe Gauvin completed his Master's Degree in Law and Technology at the University of Ottawa and is currently working as counsel, regulatory affairs, for Bell Canada. His work consists of ensuring the company's regulatory compliance with privacy, copyright, telecommunications, and broadcasting laws. He can be reached at philippe.gauvin@bell.ca.

DAPHNE GILBERT

Daphne Gilbert is an Associate Professor at the University of Ottawa, Faculty of Law. Her privacy research focuses on the constitutionalized protection of online expression and privacy, and she has an interest in the ethics of compelling cooperation between private organizations and law enforcement and in the expectations of user privacy online. She can be reached at dgilbert@uottawa.ca.

MARSHA HANEN

Marsha Hanen is a former president of the University of Winnipeg and an Adjunct Professor of Philosophy at the University of Victoria. She was the president of the Sheldon Chumir Foundation for Ethics in Leadership from 1999 to 2006. Throughout her career, she has had a broad and deep interest in ethics, philosophy of science, and philosophy of law. Recently she has published on patient privacy and anonymity in medical contexts. She can be reached at mhanen@chumirethicsfoundation.ca.

DANIEL C. HOWE
Daniel C. Howe is a digital artist and researcher at NYU's Media Research Lab where he is completing his PhD thesis on generative literary systems. His privacy research has led to TrackMeNot, an artware intervention addressing data profiling on the Internet, which he has worked on with Helen Nissenbaum. He can be reached at dhowe@mrl.nyu.edu.

IAN KERR
Ian Kerr holds the Canada Research Chair in Ethics, Law, and Technology at the University of Ottawa, Faculty of Law with cross-appointments to the Faculty of Medicine, the Department of Philosophy, and the School of Information Studies. He is also the principal investigator of the ID Trail project. Among other things, he is interested in human-machine mergers and the manner in which new and emerging technologies alter our perceptions, conceptions, and expectations of privacy. He can be reached at iankerr@uottawa.ca.

BERT-JAAP KOOPS
Bert-Jaap Koops is Professor of Regulation and Technology and the former academic director of the Tilburg Institute for Law, Technology, and Society (TILT) at Tilburg University. His privacy research primarily focuses on cryptography, identity-related crime, and DNA forensics. He can be reached at e.j.koops@uvt.nl.

PHILIPPA LAWSON
Philippa Lawson is the former Director of the Canadian Internet Policy and Public Interest Clinic (CIPPIC), based at the University of Ottawa. Through her research and advocacy work, she has represented consumer interests in privacy issues before policy and law-making bodies. She can be reached at lawson.pippa@gmail.com.

RONALD LEENES
Ronald Leenes is an Associate Professor at the Tilburg Institute for Law, Technology, and Society (TILT) at Tilburg University. His primary research interests are privacy and identity management, and regulation of, and by, technology. He is also involved in research in ID fraud, biometrics, and online dispute resolution. He can be reached at r.e.leenes@uvt.nl.

IAN LLOYD
Ian Lloyd is Professor of Information Technology Law at the University of Strathclyde Law School. He has researched and written extensively on data

protection and has recently worked on the Data Protection Programme (DAPRO), funded by the European Union. He can be reached at i.j.lloyd@strath.ac.uk.

CAROLE LUCOCK

Carole Lucock is a doctoral candidate in the Law and Technology Program at the University of Ottawa, Faculty of Law, and is project manager of the ID Trail. Her research interests include the intersection of privacy, anonymity, and identity, and the potential distinctions between imposed versus assumed anonymity. She can be reached at clucock@uottawa.ca.

SHOSHANA MAGNET

Shoshana Magnet is a Postdoctoral Fellow at McGill University. She has been appointed as an Assistant Professor at the Institute of Women's Studies at the University of Ottawa, commencing in 2009. Her privacy research includes biometrics, borders, and the relationship between privacy and equality. She can be reached at shoshana.magnet@uottawa.ca.

GARY T. MARX

Gary T. Marx is Professor Emeritus of Sociology at MIT and recently held the position of Hixon-Riggs Professor of Science, Technology, and Society at Harvey Mudd College, Claremont, California. He has written extensively about surveillance, and his current research focuses on new forms of surveillance and social control across borders. He can be reached at gtmarx@mit.edu.

DAVID MATHESON

David Matheson is an Assistant Professor in the Department of Philosophy at Carleton University. Through his privacy-related research, he has written about privacy and knowableness, anonymity and responsible testimony, layperson authentication of contested experts, privacy and personal security, the nature of personal information, and the importance of privacy for friendship. He can be reached at david_matheson@carleton.ca.

JENA MCGILL

Jena McGill holds an LLB from the University of Ottawa Faculty of Law and an MA from the Norman Paterson School of International Affairs, Carleton University, Ottawa, Canada. She is currently clerking at the Supreme Court of Canada. She has a strong interest in equality and privacy rights, particularly as they relate to gender issues on a national and international scale. She can be reached at jena.mcgill@gmail.com.

JASON MILLAR

Jason Millar is a doctoral candidate in the Department of Philosophy at Queens University. He is interested in the intersection of ethics, philosophy of technology, and philosophy of mind. His research interests also include cryptography and personal area networks in cyborg applications, particularly their impact on the concept of identity and anonymity. He can be reached at jasonxmillar@gmail.com.

HELEN NISSENBAUM

Helen Nissenbaum is Professor of Media, Culture, and Communication at New York University and a Faculty Fellow of the Information Law Institute. She researches ethical and political issues relating to information technology and new media, with a particular emphasis on privacy, the politics of search engines, and values embodied in the design of information technologies and systems. She can be reached at helen.nissenbaum@nyu.edu.

MARY O'DONOGHUE

Mary O'Donoghue is Senior Counsel and Manager of Legal Services at the Office of the Information and Privacy Commissioner of Ontario. She is currently an executive member of the Privacy Law section of the Ontario Bar Association and her privacy research has focused on the constitutional and legal aspects of anonymity. She can be reached at mary.o'donoghue@ipc.on.ca.

DAVID J. PHILLIPS

David J. Phillips is Associate Professor at the Faculty of Information, University of Toronto. His research focuses on the political economy and social shaping of information and communication technologies, in particular surveillance and identification technologies. He can be reached at davidj.phillips@utoronto.ca.

CHARLES D. RAAB

Charles D. Raab is Professor Emeritus of Government at the School of Social and Political Studies at the University of Edinburgh. His privacy research focuses on surveillance and information policy, with an emphasis on privacy protection and public access to information. He can be reached at c.d.raab@ed.ac.uk.

VALERIE STEEVES

Valerie Steeves is an Assistant Professor in the Department of Criminology and the Faculty of Law at the University of Ottawa. Her main research focus is human rights and technology issues. She has written and spoken extensively on privacy from a human rights perspective and is an active participant in the privacy policymaking process in Canada. She can be reached at vsteeves@uottawa.ca.

ANNE UTECK

Anne Uteck is a doctoral candidate in the Law and Technology Program at the University of Ottawa, Faculty of Law. Her research is on spatial privacy and other privacy interests outside the informational context implicated by emerging surveillance technologies. Recently, she has published on the topic of radio frequency identification (RFID) and consumer privacy. She can be reached at euteco66@uottawa.ca.

SIMONE VAN DER HOF

Simone van der Hof is a Senior Research Fellow and Assistant Professor at the Tilburg Institute for Law, Technology, and Society (TILT) of Tilburg University. Her main research interests are social and legal issues with respect to identity management in electronic public service delivery, regulatory issues concerning profiling technologies and personalization of public and private services, regulation of electronic authentication, electronic evidence and information security, and private (international) law aspects of electronic commerce. She can be reached at s.vdrhof@uvt.nl.

THE STRANGE RETURN OF *GYGES' RING*:
AN INTRODUCTION

Book II of Plato's *Republic* tells the story of a Lydian shepherd who stumbles upon the ancient Ring of Gyges while minding his flock. Fiddling with the ring one day, the shepherd discovers its magical power to render him invisible. As the story goes, the protagonist uses his newly found power to gain secret access to the castle where he ultimately kills the king and overthrows the kingdom.

Fundamentally, the ring provides the shepherd with an unusual opportunity to move through the halls of power without being tied to his public identity or his personal history. It also provided Plato with a narrative device to address a classic question known to philosophers as the "immoralist's challenge": why be moral if one can act otherwise with impunity?

THE NETWORK SOCIETY

In a network society—where key social structures and activities are organized around electronically processed information networks—this question ceases to be the luxury of an ancient philosopher's thought experiments. With the establishment of a global telecommunications network, the immoralist's challenge is no longer premised on mythology. The advent of the World Wide Web in the 1990s enabled everyone with access to a computer and modem to become unknown, and in some cases invisible, in public spaces—to communicate, emote, act, and interact with *relative* anonymity. Indeed, this may even have granted users more power than did Gyges' Ring, because the impact of what one could say or do online was no longer limited by physical proximity or corporeality. The end-to-end architecture of the Web's Transmission Control Protocol, for example, facilitated unidentified, one-to-many interactions at a distance. As the now-famous cartoon framed the popular culture of the early 1990s, "On the Internet, nobody knows you're a dog."[1] Although this cartoon resonated deeply on various levels, at the level of architecture it reflected the simple fact that the Internet's original protocols did not require people to identify themselves, enabling them to play with their identities—to represent themselves however they wished.

In those heady days bookmarking the end of the previous millennium, the rather strange and abrupt advent of Gyges' Ring 2.0 was by no means an unwelcome event. Network technologies fostered new social interactions of various sorts and provided unprecedented opportunities for individuals to share their

---

1. Peter Steiner, "On the Internet, Nobody Knows You're a Dog," *The New Yorker* (July 5, 1993), http://www.cartoonbank.com/item/22230.

thoughts and ideas en masse. Among other things, the Internet permitted robust political speech in hostile environments, allowing its users to say and do things that they might never have dared to say or do in places where their identity was more rigidly constrained by the relationships of power that bracket their experience of freedom. Anonymous browsers and messaging applications promoted frank discussion by employees in oppressive workplaces and created similar opportunities for others stifled by various forms of social stigma. Likewise, new cryptographic techniques promised to preserve personal privacy by empowering individuals to make careful and informed decisions about how, when, and with whom they would share their thoughts or their personal information.

At the same time, many of these new information technologies created opportunities to disrupt and resist the legal framework that protects persons and property. Succumbing to the immoralist's challenge, there were those who exploited the network to defraud, defame, and harass; to destroy property; to distribute harmful or illegal content; and to undermine national security.

In parallel with both of these developments, we have witnessed the proliferation of various security measures in the public and private sectors designed to undermine the "ID-free" protocols of the original network. New methods of authentication, verification, and surveillance have increasingly allowed persons and things to be digitally or biometrically identified, tagged, tracked, and monitored in real time and in formats that can be captured, archived, and retrieved indefinitely. More recently, given the increasing popularity of social network sites and the pervasiveness of interactive media used to cultivate user-generated content, the ability of governments, not to mention the proliferating international data brokerage industries that feed them, to collect, use, and disclose personal information about everyone on the network is increasing logarithmically. This phenomenon is further exacerbated by corporate and government imperatives to create and maintain large-scale information infrastructures to generate profit and increase efficiencies.

In this new world of ubiquitous handheld recording devices, personal webcams, interconnected closed circuit television (CCTV) cameras, radio frequency identification (RFID) tags, smart cards, global satellite positioning systems, HTTP cookies, digital rights management systems, biometric scanners, and DNA sequencers, the space for private, unidentified, or unauthenticated activity is rapidly shrinking. Many worry that the regulatory responses to the real and perceived threats posed by Gyges' Ring have already profoundly challenged our fundamental commitments to privacy, autonomy, equality, security of the person, free speech, free movement, and free association. Add in the shifting emphasis in recent years toward public safety and national security, and network technologies appear to be evolving in a manner that is transforming the structures of our communications systems from architectures of freedom to architectures of control. Are we shifting away from the original design of the network, from spaces where anonymity and privacy were once the default position to spaces where nearly every human transaction is subject to tracking, monitoring, and the possibility of authentication and identification?

The ability or inability to maintain privacy, construct our own identities, control the use of our identifiers, decide for ourselves what is known about us, and, in some cases, disconnect our actions from our identifiers will ultimately have profound implications for individual and group behavior. It will affect the extent to which people, corporations, and governments choose to engage in global electronic commerce, social media, and other important features of the network society. It will affect the way that we think of ourselves, the way we choose to express ourselves, the way that we make moral decisions, and our willingness and ability to fully participate in political processes. Yet our current philosophical, social, and political understandings of the impact and importance of privacy, identity, and anonymity in a network society are simplistic and poorly developed, as is our understanding of the broader social impact of emerging network technologies on existing legal, ethical, regulatory, and social structures.

This book investigates these issues from a number of North American and European perspectives. Our joint examination is structured around three core organizing themes: (1) privacy, (2) identity, and (3) anonymity.

PRIVACY

The jurist Hyman Gross once described privacy as a concept "infected with pernicious ambiguities."[2] More recently, Canadian Supreme Court Justice Ian Binnie expressed a related worry, opining that "privacy is protean."[3] The judge's metaphor is rather telling when one recalls that Proteus was a shape-shifter who would transform in order to avoid answering questions about the future. Perhaps U.S. novelist Jonathan Franzen had something similar in mind when he characterized privacy as the "Cheshire cat of values."[4]

One wonders whether privacy will suffer the same fate as Lewis Carroll's enigmatic feline—all smile and no cat.

Certainly, that is what Larry Ellison seems to think. Ellison is the CEO of Oracle Corporation and the fourteenth richest person alive. In the aftermath of September 11, 2001, Ellison offered to donate to the U.S. Government software that would enable a national identification database, boldly stating in 2004 that "The privacy you're concerned about is largely an illusion. All you have to give up is your illusions, not any of your privacy."[5] As someone who understands the power of network databases to profile people right down to their skivvies

---

2. Hyman Gross, "The Concept of Privacy," *N.Y.U. L. REV.* 43 (1967): 34–35.

3. *R. v Tessling*, 2004 SCC 67, [2004] 3 S.C.R. 432, per Justice Binnie, at 25.

4. Jonathan Franzen, *How to Be Alone: Essays* (New York: Farrar, Straus and Giroux, 2003), 42.

5. Larry Ellison, quoted in L. Gordon Crovitz, "Privacy? We Got Over It" *The Wall Street Journal*, A11, August 25, 2008, http://online.wsj.com/article/SB121962391804567765.html?mod=rss_opinion_main.

(and not only to provide desirable recommendations for a better brand!), Ellison's view of the future of privacy is bleak. Indeed, many if not most contemporary discussions of privacy are about its erosion in the face of new and emerging technologies. Ellison was, in fact, merely reiterating a sentiment that had already been expressed some five years earlier by his counterpart at Sun Microsystems, Scott McNealy, who advised a group of journalists gathered to learn about Sun's data-sharing software: "You have zero privacy anyway. Get over it."[6]

To turn Hyman Gross's eloquent quotation on its head—the Ellison/McNealy conception of privacy is infected with ambiguous perniciousness. It disingenuously—or perhaps even malevolently—equivocates between two rather different notions of privacy in order to achieve a self-interested outcome: it starts with a *descriptive* account of privacy as the level of control an individual enjoys over her or his personal information and then draws a *prescriptive* conclusion that, because new technologies will undermine the possibility of personal control, we therefore ought *not* to expect any privacy.

Of course, the privacy that many of us expect is not contingent upon or conditioned by the existence or prevalence of any given technology. Privacy is a normative concept that reflects a deeply held set of values that predates and is not rendered irrelevant by the network society. To think otherwise is to commit what philosopher G. E. Moore called the "naturalistic fallacy,"[7] or as Lawrence Lessig has restyled it, the "is-ism":

> The mistake of confusing how something is with how it must be. There is certainly a way that cyberspace *is*. But how cyberspace *is* is not how cyberspace has to be. There is no single way that the net has to be; no single architecture that defines the nature of the net. The possible architectures of something that we would call "the net" are many, and the character of life within those different architectures are [sic] diverse.[8]

Although the "character of life" of privacy has, without question, become more diverse in light of technologies of both the privacy-diminishing and privacy-preserving variety, the approach adopted in this book is to understand privacy as a *normative* concept. In this approach, the existence of privacy rights will not simply depend on whether our current technological infrastructure has reshaped our privacy expectations in the descriptive sense. It is not a like-it-or-lump-it proposition. At the same time, it is recognized that the meaning, importance, impact, and implementation of privacy may need to evolve alongside the emergence of new technologies. How privacy ought to be understood—and fostered—in

---

6. *Ibid.*, Scott McNealy quote.

7. G. E. Moore, *Principia Ethica* (Cambridge: Cambridge University Press, 1903).

8. Lawrence Lessig, *Code: And Other Laws of Cyberspace, Version 2.0* (New York: Basic Books, 2006): 32.

a network society certainly requires an appreciation of and reaction to new and emerging network technologies and their role in society.

Given that the currency of the network society is information, it is not totally surprising that privacy rights have more recently been recharacterized by courts as a kind of "informational self-determination."[9] Drawing on Alan Westin's classic definition of informational privacy as "the claim of individuals, groups, or institutions to determine for themselves when, how, and to what extent information about them is communicated to others,"[10] many jurisdictions have adopted fair information practice principles[11] as the basis for data protection regimes.[12] These principles and the laws that support them are not a panacea, as they have been developed and implemented on the basis of an unhappy compromise between those who view privacy as a fundamental human right and those who view it as an economic right.[13] From one perspective, these laws aim to protect privacy, autonomy, and dignity interests. From another, they are the lowest common denominator of fairness in the information trade. Among other things, it is thought that fair information practice principles have the potential to be technology neutral, meaning that they apply to any and all technologies so that privacy laws do not have to be rewritten each time a new privacy-implicating technology comes along. A number of chapters in this book challenge that view.

Our examination of privacy in Part I of this book begins with the very fulcrum of the fair information practice principles—the doctrine of consent. Consent is often seen as the legal proxy for autonomous choice and is therefore anchored in the traditional paradigm of the classical liberal individual, which is typically thought to provide privacy's safest harbor. As an act of ongoing agency, consent can also function as a gatekeeper for the collection, use, and disclosure of personal information. As several of our chapters demonstrate, however, consent can also be manipulated, and reliance on it can generate unintended consequences in and outside of privacy law. Consequently, we devote several chapters

---

9. Known in German as "Informationelles selbstbestimmung," this expression was first used jurisprudentially in Volkszählungsurteil vom 15. Dezember 1983, BVerfGE 65, 1, German Constitutional Court (Bundesverfassungsgerichts) 1983.

10. Alan Westin, *Privacy and Freedom* (New York: Atheneum, 1967): 7.

11. Organization for Economic Cooperation and Development, *Guidelines Governing the Protection of Privacy and Transborder Flows of Personal Data,* Annex to the Recommendation of the Council of 23 September 1980, http://www.oecd.org/document/18/0,3343,en_2649_34255_1815186_1_1_1_1,00.html.

12. Article 29 of Directive EC, Council Directive 95/46/EC of the European Parliament and of the Council of 24 October 1995 on the protection of individuals with regard to the processing of personal data and on the free movement of such data, [1995] O.J. L. 281: 31; Personal Information Protection and Electronic Documents Act, S.C. 2000, c. 5.

13. Canada. House of Commons Standing Committee on Human Rights and the Status of Persons with Disabilities. 35th Parliament, 2nd Session. *Privacy: Where Do We Draw the Line?* (Ottawa: Public Works and Government Services Canada, 1997).

to interrogations of the extent to which the control/consent model is a sufficient safeguard for privacy in a network society.

Does privacy live on liberal individualism alone? Some of our chapters seek out ways of illuminating privacy in light of other cherished collective values such as equality and security. Although the usual temptation is to understand these values as being in conflict with privacy, our approach in this book casts privacy as complementary to and in some cases symbiotic with these other important social values. Privacy does not stand alone. It is nested in a number of social relationships and is itself related to other important concepts, such as identity and anonymity. We turn to those concepts in Parts II and III of the book.

IDENTITY

Although lofty judicial conceptions of privacy such as "informational self-determination" set important normative standards, the traditional notion of a pure, disembodied, and atomistic self, capable of making perfectly rational and isolated choices in order to assert complete control over personal information, is not a particularly helpful fiction in a network society. If a fiction there must be, one that is perhaps more worthy of consideration is the idea of identity as a theft of the self. Who we are in the world and how we are identified is, at best, a concession. Aspects of our identities are chosen, others assigned, and still others accidentally accrued. Sometimes they are concealed at our discretion, other times they are revealed against our will. Identity formation and disclosure are both complex social negotiations, and in the context of the network society, it is not usually the individual who holds the bargaining power.

Because the network society is to a large extent premised on mediated interaction, who we are (and who we say we are) is not a self-authenticating proposition in the same way that it might be if we were close kin or even if we were merely standing in physical proximity to one another. Although we can be relatively certain that it is *not* a canine on the other end of an IM chat, the identity of the entity at the other end of a transaction may be entirely ambiguous. Is it a business partner, an imposter, or an automated software bot?

The same could be true of someone seeking to cross an international border, order an expensive product online, or fly an airplane—assuming she or he is able to spoof the appropriate credentials or identifiers. As we saw in the extreme example of the shepherd in possession of Gyges' Ring, those who are able to obfuscate their identities sometimes take the opportunity to act with limited accountability. This is one of the reasons why network architects and social policymakers have become quite concerned with issues of identity and identification.

However, it is important to recognize that identification techniques can preserve or diminish privacy. Their basic function is to make at least some aspects of an unknown entity known by mapping it to a knowable attribute.

An identification technique is more likely to be privacy preserving if it takes a minimalist approach with respect to those attributes that are to become known. For example, an automated highway toll system may need to authenticate certain attributes associated with a car or driver in order to appropriately debit an account for the cost of the toll. But to do so, it need not identify the car, the driver, the passengers, or for that matter the ultimate destination of the vehicle. Instead, anonymous digital credentials[14] could be assigned that would allow cryptographic tokens to be exchanged through a network in order to prove statements about them and their relationships with the relevant organization(s) without any need to identify the drivers or passengers themselves. Electronic voting systems can do the same thing.

In Part II of the book we explore these issues by investigating different philosophical notions of identity and discussing how those differences matter. We also address the role of identity and identification in achieving personal and public safety. We consider whether a focus on the protection of "heroic" cowboys who refuse to reveal their identities in defiance of orders to do so by law enforcement officers risks more harm than good, and whether unilateral decisions by the State to mandate control over the identities of heroic sexually assaulted women as a protective measure risk less good than harm. We examine the interaction of self and other in the construction of identity and demonstrate in several chapters why discussions of privacy and identity cannot easily be disentangled from broader discussions about power, gender, difference, and discrimination.

We also examine the ways in which identity formation and identification can be enabled or disabled by various technologies. A number of technologies that we discuss—data-mining, automation, ID cards, ubiquitous computing, biometrics, and human-implantable RFID—have potential narrowing effects, reducing who we are to how we can be counted, kept track of, or marketed to. Other technologies under investigation in this book—mix networks and data obfuscation technologies—can be tools for social resistance used to undermine identification and the collection of personal information, returning us to where our story began.

ANONYMITY

We end in Part III with a comparative investigation of the law's response to the renaissance of anonymity. Riffing on Andy Warhol's best known turn of phrase, an internationally (un)known British street artist living under the pseudonym "Banksy"[15] produced an installation with words on a retro-looking pink screen

---

14. David Chaum, "Achieving Electronic Privacy," *Scientific America* (August 1992): 96–101; Stefan A. Brands, *Rethinking Public Key Infrastructures and Digital Certificates: Building in Privacy* (Cambridge, MA: MIT Press, 2000).

15. Banksy, "By Banksy," http://www.banksy.co.uk/- (accessed September 10, 2008).

that say, "In the future, everyone will have their 15 minutes of anonymity."[16] Was this a comment on the erosion of privacy in light of future technology? Or was it a reflection of Banksy's own experience regarding the challenges of living life under a pseudonym in a network society? Whereas Warhol's "15 minutes of fame" recognized the fleeting nature of celebrity and public attention, Banksy's "15 minutes of anonymity" recognizes the long-lasting nature of information ubiquity and data retention.

Although privacy and anonymity are related concepts, it is important to realize that they are not the same thing. There are those who think that anonymity is the key to privacy. The intuition is that a privacy breach cannot occur unless the information collected, used, or disclosed about an individual is associated with that individual's identity. Many anonymizing technologies exploit this notion, allowing people to control their personal information by obfuscating their identities. Interestingly, the same basic thinking underlies most data protection regimes, which one way or another link privacy protection to an identifiable individual. According to this approach, it does not matter if we collect, use, or disclose information, attributes, or events about people so long as the information cannot be (easily) associated with them.

Although anonymity, in some cases, enables privacy, it certainly does not guarantee it. As Bruce Schneier has pointed out[17] and as any recovering alcoholic knows all too well, even if Alcoholics Anonymous does not require you to show ID or to use your real name, the meetings are anything but private. Anonymity in public is quite difficult to achieve. The fact that perceived anonymity in public became more easily achieved through the end-to-end architecture of the Net is part of what has made the Internet such a big deal, creating a renaissance in anonymity studies not to mention new markets for the emerging field of identity management. The AA example illustrates another crucial point about anonymity. Although there is a relationship between anonymity and invisibility, they are not the same thing. Though Gyges' Ring unhinged the link between the shepherd's identity and his actions, the magic of the ring[18] was not merely in enabling him to act anonymously (and therefore without accountability): the real magic was his ability to act invisibly. As some leading academics have recently come to

---

16. Banksy, interviewed by Shepard Fairey in "Banksy," *Swindle Magazine*, no. 8 (2008), http://swindlemagazine.com/issue08/banksy/ (accessed September 10, 2008).

17. Bruce Schneier, "Lesson From Tor Hack: Anonymity and Privacy Aren't the Same," *Wired* (September 20, 2007), http://www.wired.com/politics/security/commentary/securitymatters/2007/09/security_matters_0920?currentPage=2 (accessed September 10, 2008).

18. Arthur C. Clarke's famous third law states, "Any sufficiently advanced technology is indistinguishable from magic." See Arthur C. Clarke, http://www.quotationspage.com/quotes/Arthur_C._Clarke/, *Profiles of the Future; An Inquiry Into the Limits of the Possible* (Toronto: Bantam Books, 1971).

realize, visibility and exposure are also important elements in any discussion of privacy, identity, and anonymity.[19] Indeed, many argue that the power of the Internet lies not in the ability to hide who we are, but in freeing some of us to expose ourselves and to make ourselves visible on our own terms.

Given its potential ability to enhance privacy on one hand and to reduce accountability on the other, what is the proper scope of anonymity in a network society?

Although Part III of the book does not seek to answer this question directly, it does aim to erect signposts for developing appropriate policies by offering a comparative investigation of anonymity and the law in five European and North American jurisdictions. How the law regards anonymity, it turns out, is not a question reducible to discrete areas of practice. As we shall see, it is as broad ranging as the law itself.

Interestingly, despite significant differences in the five legal systems and their underlying values and attitudes regarding privacy and identity, there seems to be a substantial overlap in the way that these legal systems regard anonymity, which is not generally regarded as a right and certainly not as a foundational right. In the context of these five countries, it might even be said that the law's regard for anonymity is to some extent diminishing.

When one considers these emerging legal trends alongside the shifting technological landscape, it appears that the answer to our question posed at the outset is clear: the architecture of the network society seems to be shifting from one in which anonymity was the default to one where nearly every human transaction is subject to monitoring and the possibility of identity authentication. But what of the strange return of Gyges' Ring and the network society in which it reemerged? And what do we wish for the future of privacy, identity, and anonymity?

Let us begin the investigation.

---

19. Hille Koskela, "'In Visible City': Insecurity, Gender, and Power Relations in Urban Space," in *Voices from the North. New Trends in Nordic Human Geography*, eds. J. Öhman and K. Simonsen (Burlington: Ashgate, Aldershot, 2003): 283–294; Julie Cohen, "Privacy, Visibility, Transparency, and Exposure," *University of Chicago Law Review* 75, no. 1 (2008); Kevin D. Haggerty and Richard V. Ericson, *The New Politics of Surveillance and Visibility* (Toronto: University of Toronto Press, 2005).

PART I

PRIVACY

In the 1970s, Western countries began to grapple with the social implications of new information technologies. Mainframe computers enabled a very few large institutions to collect vast amounts of data about individuals. Many began to worry that these databases would inexorably erode our privacy and subject us to increasingly totalitarian methods of social control. As a corrective, American legal scholar Alan Westin articulated a set of fair information practices to give individuals some level of procedural control over their personal information.

Almost forty years later, these fair information practices have become the standard for privacy protection around the world. And yet, over that same time period, we have seen an exponential growth in the use of surveillance technologies, and our daily interactions are now routinely captured, recorded, and manipulated by small and large institutions alike.

This section begins with a critical examination of the crux of the fair information practices paradigm, the notion that individuals will be able to protect their privacy if their information can only be collected, used, and disclosed with their consent. Ian Kerr, jennifer barrigar, Jacquelyn Burkell, and Katie Black examine the ways in which the consent-gathering process is often engineered to skew individual decision-making, in effect creating an illusion of free choice that helps to legitimatize surveillance practices. Drawing on interdisciplinary work in psychology and decision theory, these contributors argue that the current threshold for consent with respect to the collection, use, and disclosure of personal information is not high enough to protect us from corporate initiatives that invade our privacy.

Philippa Lawson and Mary O'Donoghue examine the same question from a legal perspective, by canvassing the use of consent in Canadian privacy laws in both public sector and private sector contexts. Although private sector legislation provides more scope for negotiation between collectors and individuals, the authors caution that our current reliance on consent as the gold standard for privacy protection may be misplaced because the exercise of that consent is often more notional than real.

Alex Cameron looks at the unintended consequences of fair information practices in the context of digital rights management (DRM) software. He begins with the hypothesis that DRM impedes the individual's right to enjoy creative works in private. He then concludes that the consent provisions in data protection laws may be ineffective in constraining the surveillance capacities of DRM-protected works, in effect making it harder to create an appropriate balance between property rights and privacy rights in digitized spaces.

Rob Carey and Jacquelyn Burkell approach the consent question from a different perspective. They examine the privacy paradox: although people maintain that they are concerned about lack of privacy in digital social networks, they nevertheless reveal information about themselves to relative strangers. Through a heuristics-based analysis, they demonstrate that people are more likely to protect their privacy in the context of their personal relationships and less likely to protect it when they interact with unknown others, because their assessment of risk in the latter scenario is stripped of the social markers upon which we rely in personal interactions. Accordingly, a heuristics approach helps to explain both aspects of the paradox and suggests that we should be cautious about assuming that the online disclosure of personal information serves as a proxy for consent to its collection, use, and disclosure.

Anne Uteck takes a similar look at the assumptions that are embedded in our enjoyment of spatial privacy. As we move to an age of ubiquitous computing, the signposts we use to negotiate our sense of space, visibility, subjectivity, and privacy are subtly reconstructed. She suggests that we need to develop a more nuanced understanding that can account for our everyday experience of privacy and the expectation that the spaces in which we interact will be protected from unwarranted intrusion.

In like vein, Jason Millar posits that we should revisit our assumptions about knowledge creation in the context of predictive data mining. He argues that the network society has given rise to new forms of knowledge about persons because it enables others to extract data about us from disparate sources and to use that data to create a representation of our beliefs, intentions, and desires even when we did not mean to disclose that information. Millar concludes that policymakers must go beyond mere procedural protections or fair information practices because the context of the original disclosure of the information is lost when it is matched for predictive purposes.

Jennifer Chandler also suggests that our notions of privacy must be reframed in the context of national security. She argues that the traditional juxtaposition of privacy versus security in a zero sum game closes down debate in favor of security before we can fully examine the impact that a given reduction of privacy will have. By accounting for the ways in which privacy enhances our security, she concludes, we will be better able to articulate an appropriate balance that will advance both security and privacy interests.

Daphne Gilbert suggests that part of the problem may be the narrow legal treatment of privacy in constitutional law as part of the legal right to be free of unreasonable search and seizure. She argues that seeking to protect privacy rights through substantive equality guarantees instead of through due process protections may create a foundation for the protection of privacy as an inherent element of human dignity. In doing so, she sets out a useful framework for addressing the original concerns of the 1970s and reconnecting the privacy debate to human rights discourses that seek to protect private life.

Jena McGill advances a similar approach through her examination of the experience of a specific equality-seeking community, abused women. Like Gilbert, she seeks to broaden the scope of the privacy debate by interrogating the feminist rejection of privacy as a means of shielding abusive men from legal sanctions. Grounding her analysis in a deep concern for the lived realities of abused women, she argues that women who are able to establish and defend boundaries that reflect their needs and desires will be better able to achieve the privacy they require to protect themselves from a battering partner.

Marsha Hanen and Valerie Steeves apply a different lens to the privacy discourse by examining the relationship between privacy and identity. Hanen provides an overview of the ways in which new genetic technologies challenge our traditional understanding of these key concepts. She argues that genomics has the potential to redefine our sense of who we are. We accordingly need to think through the implications of new technologies from a more holistic perspective that accounts for the interaction between people's genomes, the environment, and human dignity.

Steeves returns to the starting point of fair information practices and revisits Westin's theory of privacy as informational control. Incorporating the insights of social theorists, she proposes a new model that defines privacy as a dynamic process of negotiating personal boundaries in intersubjective relations. This may potentially move the policy debate beyond the current impasse of fair information practices, by placing privacy at the heart of the social experience of identity. That experience of identity is the subject of the next section of the book.

1. SOFT SURVEILLANCE, HARD CONSENT
The Law and Psychology of Engineering Consent[+]

IAN KERR, JENNIFER BARRIGAR,

JACQUELYN BURKELL, AND KATIE BLACK

Most contemporary liberal democracies continue to pay lip service to John Stuart Mill's famous *harm principle,* which he articulated as follows:

> [T]he only purpose for which power can be rightfully exercised over any member of a civilized community, against his will, is to prevent harm to others. His own good, either physical or moral, is not sufficient warrant. He cannot rightfully be compelled to do or forbear because it will be better for him to do so, because it will make him happier, because, in the opinion of others, to do so would be wise, or even right . . . The only part of the conduct of anyone, for which he is amenable to society, is that which concerns others. In the part, which merely concerns him, his independence is, of right, absolute. Over himself, over his own body and mind, the individual is sovereign.[1]

The harm principle privileges liberty over self-security. It is Mill's antidote against a state-induced paternalism that would protect people from themselves by treating them as though their personal safety mattered more than their individual liberty.[2] In this sense, one can understand Mill as saying that

> coercion can only be justified to prevent harm to unconsenting others, not to prevent harm to which the actors competently consent. The harm principle creates a 'zone of privacy' for consensual or 'self-regarding' acts, within which

---

+ This chapter is adapted from the article "Let's Not Get Psyched Out of Privacy: Reflections on Withdrawing Consent to the Collection, Use and Disclosure of Personal Information," *Canadian Business Law Journal* 40 (2006): 54.

1. John Stuart Mill, *On Liberty* (Boston: Collier and Son, 1909), 13.

2. Peter Suber, "Paternalism," in *Philosophy of Law: An Encyclopedia*, ed. Christopher B. Gray (Garland: Garland Pub. Co, 1999), 632, http://www.earlham.edu/~peters/writing/paternal.htm.

individuals may do what they wish and the state has no business interfering, even with the benevolent motive of a paternalist.[3]

Benevolent paternalism has spurred a number of social and educational programs in various jurisdictions. One well-known example is the increasingly aggressive anti-smoking campaigns across Europe and North America. No stranger to tobacco, one wonders how Mill might feel if he were living in the United Kingdom today and saw a picture of an impotent "cig" on his "pack o' smokes?"[4] While it is true that the British government is not forcing him to quit smoking outright, its paid consultants do provide a rather strong disincentive by suggesting that smoking will lead to undesirable conjugal consequences. If Mill were still kicking around, how long would it take him to sniff out this new brand of paternalism?[5]

Libertarian paternalism, as it has recently been labeled,[6] purports to have Mill's cake and eat it too. The oxymoron is this: while people are "free to choose," they are concurrently provided with cognitive escorts that lead them to do the right thing. *Soft* or *asymmetrical paternalism,*[7] as it is more often called, seeks to invoke self-conscious efforts of public or private institutions to steer peoples' choices in directions that will improve their own welfare. Does the government think its workers should save a portion of their earnings for retirement? No need to ram it down their throats with controversial legislation. Simply change the default rules for a pension program from non-enrollment to automatic enrolment.[8] Human nature (read: inertia) will do the rest. This rather new style of regulating citizens' behavior has emerged

---

3. *Ibid.*

4. "Impotence Warning for Cigarette Packs," *BBC News*, April 20, 2000, http://news.bbc.co.uk/1/hi/health/720359.stm.

5. Gerald Dworkin defines paternalism as "the interference of a state or an individual with another person, against their will, and justified by a claim that the person interfered with will be better off or protected from harm" in Gerald Dworkin, "Paternalism," *The Stanford Encyclopedia of Philosophy*, ed. Edward N. Zalta, November 6, 2002 (Revised December 2005), http://plato.stanford.edu/entries/paternalism.

6. Cass Sunstein and Richard Thaler claim that libertarian paternalists should "steer people's choices in welfare promoting directions . . . and might select among the possible options and to assess how much choice is offered" in Cass Sunstein and Richard Thaler, "Libertarian Paternalism Is Not an Oxymoron," *The University of Chicago Law Review* 70, no. 4 (2003): 1159.

7. "The Rise of Soft Paternalism", *The Economist*, April 6, 2006, http://www.economist.com/opinion/displaystory.cfm?story_id=6772346; C. Camerer, et al., "Regulation for Conservatives: Behavioral Economics and the Case for 'Asymmetric Paternalism,'" *University of Pennsylvania Law Review* 1151, no.3 (2003): 1211–1254.

8. "The New Paternalism: The Avuncular State," *The Economist*, April 6 2006, http://www.economist.com/displaystory.cfm?story_id=6768159. Opt-out protocols (where consent is assumed unless explicitly withdrawn) lead to greater rates of consent than do opt-in protocols (where the default is no consent). See E. J. Johnson, S. Bellman, and G. L. Lohse, "Defaults, Framing, and Privacy: Why Opting in ≠ Opting Out," *Marketing Letters* 13, no. 1 (2002): 5. ("Defaults, Framing, and Privacy").

from decades of research suggesting that people are not quite as rational[9] as classical economists once hoped. According to many behavioral economists, people are only *boundedly rational*[10]—an academic term used to articulate and examine human limitations in decision making.

Claiming to know our fallibilities better than we do, soft paternalists do not bother with objectionable prohibitions. Instead, they seek to aid us in making "correct" decisions through persuasion; they guide us toward the alternatives that we would have chosen had we been exercising willpower and foresight.[11] Calling themselves *"choice architects,"* they merely organize "the context in which people make decisions."[12] Emphasizing the social benefits of soft paternalism, the supporters of this approach favor government initiatives that *engineer* peoples' decision making toward a particular outcome while, at the same time, preserving the possibility of choice for those supererogatory actors willing and able to buck the psychological norm.[13] They say this form of paternalism is justified (or at least "softened") by virtue of consent—or, at very least, *a lack of dissent.*

Soft paternalists are not the only ones to have learned from the behavioral sciences. Many businesses and governments involved in the information trade have recently recognized that a kinder and gentler approach to personal information collection works just as well as, if not better than, old-school surveillance. They too are exploiting people's cognitive tendencies in order to persuade them to willingly part with their personal information. Echoing the recent shift in popularity from hard to soft paternalism, both public and private sector surveillance are increasingly relying on what Gary Marx refers to as "soft" measures[14] which "nudge" people toward disclosure.

---

9. Richard Posner defines rationality as "choosing the best means to the chooser's ends" in Richard Posner "Rational Choice, Behavioral Economics, and the Law," *Stanford Law Review* 50 (1997–1998): 50; Edward Glaeser, "Paternalism and Psychology," *University of Chicago Law Review* 73 (2006): 133.

10. Herbert Simon wrote that "boundedly rational agents experience limits in formulating and solving complex problems and in processing (receiving, storing, retrieving, transmitting) information," cited in Oliver Williamson, "The Economies of Organization: The Transaction Cost Approach," *American Journal of Sociology* 87 (1988): 553; the 'bounded' nature of rationality, as per Simon, refers to the fact that people are working with limited time and limited cognitive resources. To be completely rational would require unlimited amounts of at least one of those, if not both. See Christine Jolls, Cass R. Sunstein, and Richard Thaler, "A Behavioral Approach to Law and Economics," *Stanford Law Review* 50 (2004): 1477–79, 1471.

11. "Soft Paternalism: The State Is Looking After You," *The Economist*, April 6 2006, http://www.economist.com/opinion/displaystory.cfm?story_id=6772346.

12. Richard Thaler and Cass Sunstein, *Nudge: Improving Decisions about Health, Wealth, and Happiness* (New Haven: Yale University Press, 2008), 3.

13. *Ibid.*, 5.

14. Gary Marx defines traditional surveillance as "the close observation, especially of a suspected person" and new surveillance as the "scrutiny through the use of technical

This article investigates the nature of soft surveillance and the manner in which organizations are using certain cognitive tendencies to dissuade people from fully actualizing various rights otherwise afforded by data protection and privacy legislation that are based on fair information practice principles (FIPPs). Through an examination of recent interdisciplinary scholarship in the fields of psychology and decision theory, and using Canada's Personal Information Protection and Electronic Documents Act (PIPEDA)[15] as a model, we illustrate how the consent-gathering process is often engineered to quietly skew individual decision making while preserving the *illusion* of free choice. After contemplating the importance of setting a high legislative threshold for consent in the collection, use, and disclosure of personal information, we highlight the inadequacies of current privacy laws in dealing with the consequences of soft paternalism and soft surveillance. Through an analysis of the typical decision-making process that occurs when an individual trades personal information in exchange for "free" online services, we suggest that PIPEDA's perceived remedy—the "withdrawal of consent" provisions—will generally provide ineffective relief.[16] Consequently, we articulate the need for a much higher original threshold of consent in privacy law than in the law of contract.

I. SOFT SURVEILLANCE

When one considers the global uptake of the information trade, it is not unreasonable to expect that informational privacy will be to this century what liberty was in the time of John Stuart Mill. Our ability to control the communication of our personal information is globally recognized as an important aspect of personal liberty and self-determination.[17] Yet despite this fact, the data-gathering

---

means to extract or create personal or group data, whether from individuals or contexts" in Gary Marx, "Surveillance and Society", *Encyclopedia of Social Theory*, ed. George Ritzer (Thousand Oaks, CA: Sage Publications, 2005), 817 ("Soft Surveillance and Society"); Soft surveillance, Marx writes, is the use of "persuasion to gain voluntary compliance, universality, and... utilizing hidden or low visibility information collection techniques" in Gary Marx, "Soft Surveillance: The Growth of Mandatory Volunteerism in Collecting Personal Information—'Hey Buddy Can You Spare a DNA,'" *Surveillance and Security: Technological Politics and Power in Everyday Life*, ed. T. Monahan, (London, Routledge, 2006), 37. ("Soft Surveillance")

15. Personal Information Protection and Electronic Documents Act SC 2000 c.5 ("PIPEDA")

16. *Ibid.*

17. See, for example, Alan F. Westin, *Privacy and Freedom*, (New York: Athenaeum, 1970), 322; Privacy has historically been conceptualized as a right and has been linked with notions of dignity and autonomy. In 1948, for instance, the United Nations included privacy protections under Article 12 of the Universal Declaration of Human Rights,

process has nevertheless increasingly incorporated itself into people's daily routines, and has therefore become more obfuscated and harder to control.

One reason for this is the increasing engagement of governments and corporations in what Gary Marx has called *mandatory volunteerism*—"disingenuous communications that seek to create the impression that one is volunteering when that really isn't the case."[18] For example, Canadian airports announce:

> Notice: Security measures are being taken to observe and inspect persons. No passengers are obliged to submit to a search of persons or goods if they choose not to board our aircraft.[19]

Empowered by *self-determination*, the passengers can *choose* between volunteering to be searched and not taking their flight, which, in most cases, is not really an option. In other contexts, consumers are asked to "volunteer" their name, address, telephone number, e-mail, and postal code if they want access to online services. Other examples of typical soft surveillance include: recording help-line conversations for "quality assurance purposes"; creating free interactive online characters that play with or teach children by asking them questions about the products their families use;[20] seeking customers' phone numbers when they sign up for a new service in case there are any problems; offering downloads to anyone willing to click "I Agree" to an unending string of boilerplate legalese in an End User License Agreement.

The previous examples present the sharing of personal information as either necessary for improved customer services or as an opportunity to gain the positive feelings associated with "volunteering." Either way, information subjects are led to believe that they can only benefit by providing their data. This illustrates how the architects of soft surveillance, like the architects of other forms of soft paternalism, aim to steer people's choices. However, they do not

---

UNGA, Res 217 A (III) (December 10, 1948), http://www.un.org/Overview/rights.html. Similarly, Article 17 of the 1966 International Covenant on Civil and Political Rights refers to privacy, UNGA, Res. 2200A (XXI) (March 23, 1976), http://www.hrweb.org/legal/cpr.html. Specific data protection regimes include: Council of Europe Directive (EC) ETS No. 108, Convention for the Protection of Individuals with Regard to Automatic Processing of Personal Data [1981], http://conventions.coe.int/Treaty/en/Treaties/Html/108.htm; Organisation for Economic Co-operation and Development, "OECD Guidelines on the Protection of Privacy and Transborder Flows of Personal Data", http://www.oecd.org/document/18/0,2340,en_2649_34255_1815186_1_1_1_1,00.html; and Council Directive (EC) 95/46 on the protection of personal data [1995] OJ L 23/31, http://www.cdt.org/privacy/eudirective/EU_Directive_.html.

18. Marx, "Soft Surveillance," 37 (n. 14).

19. *Ibid.*, 37.

20. Ian Kerr and Valerie Steeves, "Virtual Playgrounds and BuddyBots: A Data-Minefield for Tinys and Tweenies," *Canadian Journal of Law and Technology* 4, no. 2 (2005): 91, http://cjlt.dal.ca/vol4_no2/pdfarticles/steeves.pdf.

necessarily do so with regard to improving general social welfare. In many instances, they do it merely as a means of improving their own ability to collect personal information.[21]

Compared to traditional Soviet watchtowers or London's omnipresent CCTV cameras, soft surveillance techniques often have relatively "low visibility, or are invisible."[22] As Marx notes, "With the trend towards ubiquitous computing, surveillance and sensors in one sense disappear into ordinary activities and objects [such as] cars, cell phones, toilets, buildings, clothes, and even bodies."[23] In-car GPS systems transmit information about a person's whereabouts and credit card companies collect data about type, time, and location of purchases via credit card purchases.[24] A person can "volunteer" his or her DNA via a mouth-swab in order to help solve a local crime.[25] These examples illustrate how the employment of universal and automated information collection strategies make it easier for people to "volunteer" comprehensive personal information. Corporations have made the conscious volunteering of personal information more palatable by universalizing the practice. Being asked by a cashier for your phone number is now a common shopping experience.

The universalization of such data collection processes tends to reduce the need for organizations to use coercive measures. Although people often say that they value privacy,[26] their actions seldom reflect this belief.[27] With increasing

---

21. Where surveillance is for purposes unrelated to increasing the welfare of those being monitored it cannot, strictly speaking, be understood as a form of paternalism (soft or otherwise), since the very justification offered by proponents of paternalism is that it is done for the good of those upon whom it is inflicted. Of course, there are many corporations and governments that try to claim that aggressive surveillance *is* a form of paternalism in that regard. Consider, for example, the following pronouncement by George W. Bush responding to questions about the NSA warrantless surveillance controversy:

> I can fully understand why members of Congress are expressing concerns about civil liberties. I know that. And it's—I share the same concerns. I want to make sure the American people understand, however, that we have an obligation to protect you, and we're doing that and, at the same time, protecting your civil liberties. George W. Bush, (press conference, Washington D.C., December 19, 2005), http://www.whitehouse.gov/news/releases/2005/12/20051219-2.html.

22. Marx, "Soft Surveillance and Society," 817 (n. 14).
23. *Ibid.*
24. *Ibid.*, 818.
25. *Ibid.*, 37 (n. 14). For example, in 2004 male residents in Truro, Massachusetts, were asked in a "non-threatening" manner by police to provide a mouth swab of their genetic material in order to solve a local murder. Citing social responsibility as their main reason for complying, people voluntarily placed their genetic identification into the police dragnet.
26. For example, see Ekos Research Associates, *Privacy Revealed: The Canadian Privacy Survey* (Ottawa, ON, Ekos Research, 1993), 10.
27. According to a recent PEW survey, 60% of all Americans are "very concerned" about privacy, while at the same time 54% have shared personal information in order to

regularity, people are complacently parting with their personal information, readily consenting to its collection regardless of purpose.[28] As data gathering is increasingly incorporated into people's daily routine, it is becoming taken for granted.[29]

While the sway of soft surveillance is superficially innocuous, it is crucial to underscore that most people are oblivious to the influences that they are under, and those who are aware of these influences are easily made to forget them. Though people do in fact retain the freedom to reject the choice that is being *softly* promoted, psychological barriers predictably discourage them from doing so. As Edward Glaeser writes, "[t]he literature on self-control[30] and hyperbolic discounting[31] argues that people would want to refrain from certain actions if they only could. The bounded rationality literature argues that people face severe cognitive limitations and often make bad decisions."[32] The *magic* of soft surveillance (and soft paternalism) is in its *misdirection*: it encourages compliance by co-opting cognitive constraints, all the while maintaining the illusion of choice. While the prevalence of "hard" surveillance remains unchanged, the "culture and practice of social control is changing"[33] as these softer measures become more effective.

---

gain access to a Web site, and an additional 10% are willing to provide this information if asked, cited in: S. Fox, et al., "Trust and Privacy Online: Why Americans Want to Rewrite the Rules," *The PEW Internet and American Life Project*, http://www.pewinternet.org/pdfs/PIP_Trust_Privacy_Report.pdf. (Hereafter called PEW survey). As Oracle C.E.O. Larry Ellison famously said, "Well, this privacy you're concerned about is largely an illusion. All you have to give up is your illusions, not any of your privacy." Larry Ellison, interview by Hank Plante, September 21, 2001, *KPIX-TV News, CBS*.

28. S. Fox, "PEW Survey," *ibid.*

29. Marx, "Soft Surveillance and Society," 817 (n. 14).

30. H.M. Shefrin and Richard Thaler, "An Economic Theory of Self-Control," *The Journal of Political Economy* 89, No. 2 (1981): 392–406, http://ideas.repec.org/a/ucp/jpolec/v89y1981i2p392-406.html.

31. The term *hyperbolic discounting* refers to empirical research demonstrating that people will choose smaller over larger rewards when the smaller reward comes sooner in time. People will choose the larger over the smaller reward when they are to be given in the distant future. For example, "when offered the choice between $50 now and $100 a year from now, most people will choose the immediate $50. However, given the choice between $50 in five years or $100 in six years most people will choose $100 in six years. In addition, given the choice between $50 today and $100 tomorrow, most people will choose $100 tomorrow." See A. Raineri and H. Rachlin, "The Effect of Temporal Constraints on the Value of Money and Other Commodities," *Journal of Behavioral Decision-Making* 6 (1993): 77–94, and David Laibson, "Golden Eggs and Hyperbolic Discounting," *Quarterly Journal of Economics* 112 (1997): 443, 445, and 446.

32. Glaeser, "Paternalism and Psychology," 136 (n. 9).

33. Marx, "Soft Surveillance," 37 (n. 14).

II. THE APPROPRIATE THRESHOLD FOR CONSENT IN PRIVACY LAW

If behaviorists are correct and human choice can indeed be so easily manipulated, the notion of consent becomes privacy's linchpin. Consent is a kind of nexus; it is the interface between human beings and our increasingly automated information-gathering systems. Except where it is unreasonable to require or otherwise inappropriate to obtain, privacy law requires the "knowledge and consent" of individuals for the collection, use, or disclosure of their personal information. Recognizing this, the current Privacy Commissioner of Canada, Jennifer Stoddart, has described consent as "the fundamental principle on which PIPEDA is based."[34]

Although data protection laws around the globe generally require consent prior to the collection, use, or disclosure of most personal information, it is our contention that FIPPs-based privacy laws must be understood as setting higher thresholds for obtaining consent than would otherwise be afforded by way of private ordering.[35] A number of the provisions of PIPEDA illustrate the legislative creation of this higher threshold. Principle 4.3 of Sch. I requires knowledge and consent; the data subject must be said to have *knowingly* consented to the collection, use, or disclosure of personal information, except where inappropriate.[36] This differs markedly from the private law where a party to a contract can be held to its terms even if it has neither read nor understood them. A further provision[37] requires consent to be "obtained in a *meaningful* way, generally requiring that organizations communicate the purposes for collection, so that the person will reasonably know and understand how the information will be collected, used, or disclosed."[38] PIPEDA also creates a higher threshold for consent

---

34. Jennifer Stoddart, Privacy Commissioner, "An Overview of Canada's New Private Sector Privacy Law: The *Personal Information Protection and Electronic Documents Act*," (speech, Ottawa, ON, April 1, 2004), http://www.privcom.gc.ca/speech/2004/vs/vs_sp-d_040331_e.asp; FIPPs-based law is equally founded upon the principle of consent.

35. For an elaboration of this claim, see generally Ian Kerr, "If Left to Their Own Devices," *In the Public Interest: The Future of Canadian Copyright Law*, ed. Michael Geist, (Toronto, Irwin Law, 2005), 167–211; Ian Kerr, "Hacking at Privacy," *Privacy Law Review*, ed. Michael Geist (Toronto: Butterworth's, 2005), 25–34.

36. PIPEDA, Sch. I, cl. 3 (n. 15).

37. *Ibid.*, cl. 3.2.

38. Kerr, "If Left to their Own Devices," *supra* note 36. See, for example, Case Summary #97, PIPEDA: Bank Adopts Sweeping Changes to Its Information Collection Practices, (2002), [September, 2002], Commissioner's Findings, http://www.privcom. gc.ca/cf-dc/2002/cf-dc_020930_e.asp; It is crucial to note that a substantial number of limits on the high threshold of consent have been placed in s. 7 of PIPEDA. For example, s. 7(1)(b) states that an organization may collect personal information without the knowledge or consent of the individual if "the collection is reasonable for purposes related to investigating a breach of an agreement or a contravention of the laws of Canada or a province." This provision was cited in the *Eastmond v Canadian Pacific Railway*,

by contemplating different forms of consent depending on the nature of the information and its sensitivity.[39] Information said to be "sensitive" will generally require more detailed reasons justifying its collection and, in some instances, express consent.[40] Moreover, unlike the law of contracts, where consent is seen as a single transactional moment... typically signaling a 'state change' that cannot be 'undone', s. 4.3.8 of Sch. I of PIPEDA generally allows the information subject to withdraw consent at any time.[41] On the basis of these provisions, PIPEDA's consent model is best understood as providing *an ongoing act of agency* to the information subject, and is much more robust than the usual model for consent in private law, which treats consent as an isolated moment of contractual agreement during an information exchange.

Although the collection, use, and disclosure of personal information pursuant to PIPEDA generally require "knowledge and consent,"[42] the notion of consent is nowhere defined in the Act. In its broader common law context, consent is often characterized as "freely given agreement."[43] More specifically, consent is described as

> voluntary agreement by a person in the possession and exercise of sufficient mental capacity to make an intelligent choice to do something proposed by another. It supposes a physical power to act, a moral power of acting, and a serious, determined, and free use of these powers. Consent is implied in every agreement. It is an act unclouded by fraud, duress, or sometimes even mistake.[44]

Because the "voluntary agreement" aspect is so central, consent is often linked to the legal paradigm of contract. The notion of an agreement, contractual or otherwise, usually presupposes some particular aim or object. One never agrees in a vacuum; rather, one agrees *to* something, or *with* something. In private law, certainly in contract law, consent is understood as inherently transactional. It is a definable moment that occurs when the parties crystallize the terms and conditions upon which they agree. Contractual consent is determined at the moment parties

---

2004 F.C. 852 (Cda) 3 regarding Principle 3, where video surveillance was said to be appropriate by Lemieux, J. A factor in the decision was that the camera was minimally invasive and was only looked at if there was a triggering incident. The video was deleted after 96 hours. See paragraph 188.

39. PIPEDA, Sch. I, cl. 3 (n. 15).

40. *Ibid.*; Kerr, "If Left to their Own Devices," (n. 36).

41. "An individual may withdraw consent at any time, subject to legal or contractual restrictions and reasonable notice." PIPEDA, (n. 15).

42. *Ibid.*, s. 7.

43. Daphne A. Dukelow and Betsy Nuse, *The Dictionary of Canadian Law*, 2nd ed. (Scarborough, ON, Carswell, 1995), 232.

44. *Black's Law Dictionary*, 5th ed. (Eagan, MN, West Publishing, 1979), 276, s.v. "Consent."

communicate their intention to be bound by that agreement.[45] Whether executed or executory,[46] contractual consent is expressed in an instant. Once the parties have achieved *consensus*, the contract is in place and the obligations become fixed.

Unlike the law of contracts, where consent is seen as a single transactional moment, PIPEDA generally allows the information subject to withdraw consent at any time.[47] PIPEDA is predicated on the notion that individuals have a *right* to control personal information about them. This ongoing right of control is reinforced in law by the corollary requirement of ongoing consent codified in Principle 4.3.8 of PIPEDA.[48] Consequently, unless they surrender it, individuals retain ultimate control over their personal information and can withdraw consent at any time, subject to legal or contractual restrictions and reasonable notice. [49] Organizations wishing to use personal information must obtain the *ongoing consent* of the information subject for continued use. In other words, the *continued use* of personal information must be understood as a necessary consequence of the information subject's *continuing consent* to its use, and not merely as a consequence of the initial consent to collect the information.

Overall, the consent provisions in PIPEDA strongly suggest that consent acts like a "license" that permits some *limited* collection, use, or disclosure.[50] Thus, the consent given to an organization to use an individual's personal information is necessarily restricted and *does not* give the organization ultimate control over personal information in perpetuity. PIPEDA's Principle 4.5 buttresses this view by disallowing an organization from retaining personal information indefinitely.[51]

---

45. Gerald H. L. Fridman, *The Law of Contract in Canada*, 4th ed. (Scarborough, ON, Carswell, 1999), 16–17; Stephen Waddams, *The Law of Contracts*, 4th ed. (Toronto, Edmond Montgomery Publications, 1999), 66–67.

46. An executory contract is one that has not yet been completely fulfilled by one or more of the parties. Gerald H. L. Fridman, *The Law of Contract in Canada*, 3rd ed. (Scarborough, ON, Carswell, 1994), 108.

47. "An individual may withdraw consent at any time, subject to legal or contractual restrictions and reasonable notice." PIPEDA, Sch. I s.4.3.8 (n. 15).

48. PIPEDA, *ibid.*

49. A question arises as to whether this right is alienable; see, for example, James Rule and Lawrence Hunter, "Towards Property Rights in Personal Data," *Visions of Privacy: Policy Choices for the Digital Age*, eds. Colin J. Bennett and Rebecca Grant, (Toronto, University of Toronto Press, 1999).

50. Under PIPEDA Principle 4.2.2, consent is only given for the purposes specified. Under Principle 4.4, these purposes must be appropriately limited, and under Principle 4.5, all uses or disclosures require consent and should be documented as *per* Principle 4.5.1. Almost any new purpose beyond those already specified requires new consent, as set out in Principle 4.2.4. PIPEDA. (n. 15).

51. *Ibid.* PIPEDA Principle 4.5.3 states that personal information that is no longer required to fulfill the identified purposes should not be retained, and requires organizations

This provision, in conjunction with others mentioned previously,[52] is meant to place the individual in control of his or her personal information at all times, signaling that his or her consent is an *ongoing act of agency*. PIPEDA's framework supports this contention as exemplified by the Sch. I Principles. Organizations are to be open about their information management practices,[53] presumably in order for individuals to make informed initial decisions and revisit those decisions when and if necessary.

The ability to withdraw consent is but one of the possible responses available to an individual managing his or her personal information. Individuals also have a right of access to their personal information,[54] and a corresponding right to challenge the accuracy or completeness of that information. Furthermore, individuals have the power to challenge an organization's compliance with the requirements of PIPEDA.[55] They can do this via a complaint to the Privacy Commissioner[56] and, if necessary, by proceeding to Federal Court after the Privacy Commissioner releases a report of her findings on the matter.[57]

III. PSYCHOLOGICAL BARRIERS TO MEANINGFUL CONSENT

Like Mill's harm principle, the theory of consent-as-ongoing-agency articulated above would seem to be a promising antidote to the erosion of individual privacy rights in the age of ubiquitous computing and soft surveillance. Certainly this is what former Privacy Commissioner of Canada Bruce Phillips thought when he proclaimed that Canada's private sector privacy law

> constitutes the first determined effort to place a check upon, and ultimately to reverse, the massive erosion of individual privacy rights brought about by the application of computer and communications technology in the commercial world.[58]

That said, the full potential of the consent model may be compromised in practice due to predictable psychological tendencies that prevent people from giving fully considered consent, and withdrawing it once given. As companies

---

to develop guidelines and implement procedures to govern the destruction of personal information.

52. *Ibid.*
53. PIPEDA, Principle 4.8 (n. 15).
54. *Ibid.*, Principle 4.9 and s. 8.
55. *Ibid.*, Principle 4.10.
56. *Ibid.*, s.12.
57. *Ibid.*, s. 14.
58. Bruce Phillips, "Foreword" in Stephanie Perrin, et al., *The Personal Information Protection and Electronic Documents Act: An Annotated Guide* (Toronto, Irwin, 2001), ix.

and governments become increasingly adept at automating the consent process, it will be important to understand how psychological factors affect:

(i) A person's ability to consent to the release of his or her personal information
(ii) A company's ability to ensure ongoing consent
(iii) An individual's ability to meaningfully choose to withdraw consent.

Such an investigation, thus far absent in the Canadian privacy law and policy literature, is essential. It is important because a systemic failure in the consent process, not to mention the failure to provide a meaningful opportunity to exercise the right to withdraw consent, reduces the consent principle to little more than the transactional moment of private ordering, thereby rendering the interpretation and application of PIPEDA's new, robust, ongoing consent provisions practically useless.

To illustrate the kind of psychological constraints that people face, let's consider a hypothetical situation that addresses the following question:

Why do people consent to an organization's demand for personal information and then, generally, not review, revise, or withdraw their consent?

To answer this question, let's construct a hypothetical model citizen named Jijk. Jijk is representative of the majority of North Americans who are "very concerned about privacy."[59] Recently, Jijk's friend recommended that she follow a breaking story in the *Globe and Mail* by setting up a "keyword alert" on the *Globe* website that automatically sends her relevant stories by email.[60] The website offers this service for free—*with one catch*: Jijk has to register as a member by providing and consenting to the *Globe*'s use of her personal information. Jijk faces a common dilemma. In order to gain the immediate benefit of the alerting service, she must accept the loss of control over her informational privacy. Having a basic understanding of privacy law, Jijk knows that if she chooses to consent to the use of her personal information, she can, at any time, withdraw her consent. Presumably, Jijk will provide the required personal information and offer her consent if the perceived benefits of the alerting service outweigh the perceived costs. If Jijk later decides to reconsider her initial decision, she will undertake a new comparison of gains and losses, evaluated from her status as a *Globe and Mail* member.

Will Jijk provide her personal information and consent to its use in order to have the *Globe and Mail* alert her to relevant articles? If she does, will she ever withdraw her consent? Much will depend on various psychological factors influencing how Jijk makes these decisions. Our analysis suggests that in the context of privacy decisions such as this, psychological factors combine to increase

---

59. See Marx, "Soft Surveillance," (n. 14).
60. *Globe and Mail*, http://www.theglobeandmail.com. (Hereafter *Globe*)

the likelihood that consent will be offered initially, and reduce the likelihood that, once given, it will be withdrawn.[61]

In considering her initial consent, Jijk wants, and stands immediately to gain, the value associated with the alerting service. Against this benefit, she must weigh the subjective value of the loss of control over her personal information. Although the ramifications of this loss are significant, these consequences will occur only in the future. For example, Jijk is likely to receive targeted marketing materials as a result of her consent, but these materials will not arrive immediately upon consent, and they are likely only to *add* to the other materials that Jijk receives on a regular basis. In contrast, if Jijk is considering the withdrawal of consent, she knows that the result of this decision would be the immediate *loss* of the alerting service provided by the *Globe and Mail* and the temporally distant, ephemeral, and potentially partially illusory *gain* of control over her personal information.[62] The consequences of regaining control of personal information will be, for the most part, invisible to Jijk, manifesting in the future *absence* of some (obviously not all) of the targeted marketing materials that she regularly receives.

It is well known in decision theory that *subjective utility*—that is, the personal value of an outcome—changes depending on *when* the outcome will be experienced.[63] In particular, the subjective value of a benefit or loss that will be experienced today is *greater* than the subjective value of that same benefit or loss if we know that it will be experienced some time in the future. While the exact form of this discounting function is the subject of much debate,[64] the existence of discounting is universally accepted. Furthermore, and critically for the current discussion, the literature on decision making also suggests that although both gains and losses lose value as they are moved into the future, the *rate* of change is faster for gains than for losses: losses become less bad the further away they are in time, while gains become *much* less good.[65] In considering her initial consent, Jijk is evaluating an immediate gain against a temporally distant loss of privacy, rendered less negative precisely because it occurs in the future. As a result, she is *more* likely to offer her consent than if both outcomes occurred at the same time. In contrast, when considering withdrawal of consent, Jijk is

---

61. E. J. Johnson, S. Bellman, and G. L. Lohse, "Defaults, Framing, and Privacy," (n. 8).

62. The benefit could be partially illusory if her information has already been provided, with consent, to a third party.

63. See G. F. Loewenstein and J. Elster, *Choice Over Time*, (New York, Russell Sage Foundation, 1992).

64. U. Benzion, Y. Schachmurove, and J. Yagil, "Subjective Discount Functions: An Experimental Approach," *Applied Financial Economics*: 14, no. 5 (2004): 299.

65. See, for example, M. Ortendahl, and J. F. Fries, "Time-Related Issues with Application to Health Gains and Losses," *Journal of Clinical Epidemiology* 55 (2002): 843; R. H. Thaler, "Some empirical evidence on dynamic inconsistency," *Economic Letters* 8 (1981): 201.

weighing an immediate loss against a temporally distant gain whose value is *much* reduced because it occurs in the future. In this case, Jijk is *less* likely to withdraw her consent than she would be if loss and gain both occurred immediately.

Other aspects of the situation could have the similar effect of biasing Jijk's decisions *against* withdrawing consent. Bias arises from what is, essentially, a re-weighting of the gains and losses associated with consent after the initial decision has been made. It is a direct result of the decision itself. According to *prospect theory*,[66] decisions are made in a context where losses loom larger than gains, and outcomes are evaluated against an anchor point or implicit comparator. If the decision under consideration is whether to offer consent in the first place, Jijk's potential immediate outcome is a gain: currently, Jijk *does not* have benefit of the alerting service that she wants, and by consenting she gains that service. By contrast, if her decision is whether to withdraw consent, Jijk's potential immediate outcome is the loss of the alerting service that she currently enjoys. Prospect theory states that losses are weighted more heavily in decision making than are gains. By extension, the negative value of the loss of the alerting service if consent were withdrawn would be greater than the positive value of the service gained when consent was initially offered. Such an outcome is also known as the *endowment effect*. It is reflected in the tendency to value an object more when one owns it.[67] In Jijk's case, it results in an increased subjective value of the alerting service once she has activated it by becoming a *Globe* member. As the subjective value of the service increases, Jijk becomes more loathe to lose it by withdrawing her consent.

Another psychological factor known as *cognitive dissonance*[68] will also cause Jijk to re-weigh the gains and losses associated with her initial consent. This, in turn, will affect her decision whether to later withdraw her consent. According to the theory of cognitive dissonance, having inconsistent beliefs or acting in a way that is inconsistent with one's beliefs can give rise to an uncomfortable psychological state. Jijk likes to think of herself as a consistent person, making careful and considered choices based on her values. Yet, if she has consented to the sweeping use of her personal information in return for the alerting service offered by the *Globe* online, she has acted in a way that is inconsistent with her own values. She is not alone in this inconsistency. According to a recent PEW survey, 60% of all Americans are "very concerned" about privacy, while at the

---

66. D. Kahneman and A. Tversky, "Prospect Theory: An Analysis of Decision under Risk," *Econometrica* 47, no.2 (1979): 263.

67. Daniel Kahneman, Jack L. Knetsch, and Richard H. Thaler, "Experimental Tests of the Endowment Effect and the Coase Theorem," *Journal of Political Economy* 98, no. 6 (1990): 1325.

68. L. Festinger, *A Theory of Cognitive Dissonance* (Palo Alto, CA, Stanford University Press, 1957); L. Festinger, *Conflict, Decision, and Dissonance* (Stanford, CA, Stanford University Press, 1964).

same time 54% have shared personal information in order to get access to a web site, and an additional 10% are willing to provide this information if asked.[69] Therefore, at least one quarter of those surveyed have acted or are prepared to act with inconsistency similar to Jijk's.

Such inconsistency can be psychologically uncomfortable: people generally don't enjoy feeling like hypocrites. Moreover, Jijk finds herself in a situation that has all the hallmarks of one that is likely to cause this discomfort:[70]

(i) Jijk feels personally responsible for her own decision to consent, and thus cannot blame her actions on someone or something else.

(ii) Jijk understands that, as a direct result of her decision, her privacy, which is something she values, has been compromised.

(iii) The justification for her decision is relatively weak since she could, with little effort, have followed the breaking news story through other means.

(iv) She has clearly made a free choice to release her personal information.[71]

In the context of information privacy, cognitive dissonance becomes problematic in the way people seek to alleviate the discomfort they experience. Psychological research suggests that people resolve cognitive dissonance through one of three mechanisms.[72] Jijk might trivialize some of her competing cognitions by convincing herself that the privacy violation in this case is not important, or that privacy itself is overvalued.[73] Alternatively, Jijk could selectively seek information consistent with her decision.[74] In the current situation, this might mean that Jijk would selectively search for and attend to information suggesting that the collection and use of personal information by the *Globe* does *not* constitute a privacy violation, since the *Globe* has a privacy policy and therefore they *must* be privacy compliant.[75] As a third possibility, Jijk might decide to change her

69. See Ekos, *Privacy Revealed*, (n. 27).

70. J. Cooper and R. H. Fazio, "A New Look at Dissonance," *Advances in Experimental Social Psychology* 17 (2004): 227.

71. E. Harmon-Jones, J. W. Brehm, J. Greenberg, L. Simon, and D. E. Nelson, "Evidence That the Production of Aversive Consequences Is Not Necessary to Create Cognitive Dissonance," *Journal of Personality and Social Psychology* 70, no. 1 (1996): 5.

72. See J. W. Brehm and A. R. Cohen, *Explorations in Cognitive Dissonance* (New York: Wiley, 1962); L. Festinger, *A Theory of Cognitive Dissonance*, (Stanford, CA: Stanford University Press, 1957).

73. L. Simon, J. Greenberg, and J. Brehm, "Trivialization: The Forgotten Mode of Dissonance Reduction" *Journal of Personality and Social Psychology* 68 (1995): 247.

74. D. Ehrlich, I. Guttman, P. Schonbach, and J. Mills, "Post Decision Exposure to Relevant Information" *Journal of Abnormal and Social Psychology* 54 (1951): 98.

75. Jacquelyn Burkell and Valerie Steeves, "Privacy Policies on Kids' Favourite Web Sites," (paper, 6th Annual Privacy and Security Workshop, Privacy and

attitude, opinion, or behavior.[76] She could, for example, modify her attitude toward information privacy by considering privacy to be less important, or she could perhaps place less value on her privacy with regard to the particular information she disclosed to the *Globe*.

Each of these resolutions would mitigate the psychological discomfort associated with offering consent. At the same time, each reduces the likelihood that Jijk will later withdraw her consent. In fact, once she has successfully resolved the dissonance, there is little reason for her to go back and revisit her original decision: after all, she now perceives the initial consent as consistent with the only value that would lead her to revoke it (that is, her valuing of privacy). This is not to say that she *couldn't* withdraw her consent. She *could*. However, the principle of cognitive dissonance suggests that she may not be motivated to do so. It is safe to assume that the architects of soft surveillance are generally aware of this and exploit it.

IV. CONCLUSION

Cognitive dissonance, prospect theory, and discounted subjective utility have been shown to apply to decision making in a wide variety of contexts, and there is every reason to think that they are also applicable to decisions about giving or later withdrawing consent.[77] These theories predict a variety of decision biases that would facilitate the *social engineering of choice*: leading individuals in a particular direction when making an initial decision and encouraging them thereafter to maintain the status quo.[78] Together, these theories illustrate how psychological factors tend to *increase* the likelihood of initial consent and form cognitive barriers to the later withdrawal of consent.

Acquisti and Grossklags argue, "we need to incorporate more accurate models of users' behavior into the formulation of both policy and technology."[79] In the privacy

---

Security: Disclosure, University of Toronto, November 3, 2005), http://idtrail.org/content/blogcategory/21/72/.

76. A. Elliot and P. Devine, "On the Motivational Nature of Cognitive Dissonance as Psychological Discomfort," *Journal of Personality and Social Psychology* 67 (1994): 382.

77. C. Camerer, "Prospect Theory in the Wild," *Choices, Values and Frames*, eds. Kahneman and A. Tversky, (Cambridge, Cambridge University Press, 2000), 288–300.

78. This is reflected in the endowment effect.

79. A. Acquisti and J. Grossklags, "Privacy Attitudes and Privacy Behavior," *The Economics of Information Security: Advances in Information Security, vol. 12*, eds. J. Camp and S.R. Lewis, 12, (Massachusetts, Norwell, and Kluwer, Springer, 2004), 176; For an article which explores the wisdom of government attempts to debias people's decision making via the law, see Christine Jolls and Cass R. Sunstein, "Debiasing through Law," *Working Paper No. 225* (working paper, University of Chicago Law and Economics, November 2005), http://ssrn.com/abstract=590929.

context, this point cannot be overemphasized. Decision biases, created by the psychological factors discussed in this chapter, have obvious implications for any theory of meaningful consent and necessarily affect consent-based policy. If privacy legislation is aimed at providing people with meaningful control over their personal information, it must employ a model of consent formation that accurately reflects people's behavior. The following reasons illustrate why such legislation cannot force people to behave according to a theoretical model of consent. First, it is difficult to disabuse decision makers of the biases and heuristics that influence their decision making. Second, one cannot expect individuals who are unaware of the implications of consenting to the collection, use, or disclosure of personal information to recognize, let alone remedy, their tendency to "stick with" their initial consent. Third, many people currently share a general impression that consenting to the use of personal information is an all-or-nothing, take-it-or-leave-it, instantaneous transaction; an offer that they cannot refuse.

The consent model for PIPEDA and similar FIPPs-based legislation, properly understood, has some ability to respond to these concerns. Recognizing privacy law's higher threshold for consent provides the fulcrum for understanding data protection regimes as more than just default contracting rules in the information trade. By providing a regime premised on the notion of consent-as-ongoing-agency, FIPPs-based privacy laws require that organizations revise many of their current practices and policies. Unfortunately, most organizations continue to treat consent as a transactional moment, using standard-form, click-wrap agreements as a means of obtaining overarching "consent" (read: assent) to excessive collection, use, and disclosure of personal information. This archaic, nineteenth-century, laissez-faire, freedom-to-contract mentality fails to recognize the higher threshold assigned to consent in the privacy law context.[80] It also fails to recognize the unique role that consent is meant to play as the nexus between people and information technology.

Information-seeking institutions engaged in soft paternalism and soft surveillance will obviously prefer consent to be conceived of as a transactional moment. This approach allows them to engineer the consent-seeking process so that individuals are steered toward automatically offering up their consent to the collection, use, and disclosure of their personal information without further reflection. The increasing use of soft surveillance indicates that governments and corporations have begun to realize the behavioral consequences of the psychological tendencies discussed in this chapter. Whether soft paternalism is used to increase pension contributions or soft surveillance is employed in the interests of airport security, corporations and governments are becoming *psych-savvy*. They are increasingly adept at harnessing people's cognitive tendencies to further their own ends.

---

80. For an articulation of this thesis in the context of consent to the collection of personal information in digital rights management situations, see Kerr, "If Left to Their Own Devices" and Kerr, "Hacking at Privacy," (n. 36).

Although there have been a number of complaints about the limitations of PIPEDA resulting from the compromises that were made during its enactment,[81] the Act does inspire the possibility of a much more robust and meaningful threshold for consent. The Government of Canada's statutory review of PIPEDA[82] provided an important opportunity to examine what further improvements, and what additional institutions, are required to more fully articulate and enforce privacy law's higher threshold of consent so that it lives up to the Privacy Commissioner of Canada's claim that it is "the fundamental principle on which PIPEDA is based."[83]

---

81. The recognition of the need for PIPEDA sprang, in part, from concern about maintaining and facilitating Canada's international trading relationship. It was enacted under the federal trade and commerce power and focused primarily on commercial activities. The CSA Model Code for the Protection of Personal Information which forms Schedule 1 of the Act was the result of a process in which business was intimately involved. See Christopher Berzins, "Protecting Personal Information in Canada's Private Sector: The Price of Consensus Building," *Queen's Law Journal* 27 (2002): 623 for a discussion of these tensions; Michael Geist, for example, criticizes the ombudsman's approach to the enforcement of PIPEDA. He argues that the Privacy Commissioner's inability to issue binding decisions means that there is insufficient incentive for companies to comply. See Michael Geist, "Canada's Privacy Wakeup Call," November 27, 2005, http://michaelgeist.ca/component/option.com_content/task,view/id,1025/Itemid,70; see also, Canadian Internet Policy and Public Interest Clinic, "Five Year Review: An Opportunity to be Grasped", July 2005, http://www.cippic.ca/en/action-items/pl_article_for_cplr_july_2005.pdf.

82. Mandated to be held five years after its introduction, as required by PIPEDA s.29, *supra* note 15 and completed in May 2007. In preparation for the review, the Commissioner released a PIPEDA Review Discussion Document that raised many questions about consent, including what she termed blanket consent where she addressed various understandings of consent's duration and intent, including a reading of the Act that argues that "informed consent is a dynamic process that involves keeping individuals actively aware—on an ongoing basis, using understandable language, and in a transparent manner—of what an organization intends to do with their personal information and for what purpose. They may see consent as giving them the opportunity to receive further explanations and to ask questions or challenge assumptions—particularly in relationships of unequal bargaining power." Office of the Privacy Commissioner of Canada, "Protecting Privacy in an Intrusive World," section f, July 2006, http://www.privcom.gc.ca/parl/2006/pipeda_review_060718_e.asp#005. Although the Commissioner did indicate in her PIPEDA Review submission to Parliament that Blanket Consent was an area in which she was open to receiving guidance, neither the ETHI Committee Report "Standing Committee Review of the Personal Information Protection and Electronic Documents Act (PIPEDA)," May 2007, http://cmte.parl.gc.ca/Content/HOC/committee/391/ethi/reports/rp2891060/ethirp04-e.html nor the consultation initiated in the "Government Response to the Fourth Report of the Standing Committee on Access to Information, Privacy and Ethics," 2007, http://www.ic.gc.ca/epic/site/ic1.nsf/vwapj/ETHI-e.pdf/$file/ETHI-e.pdf have addressed this issue.

83 "An overview of Canada's new private sector privacy law: The *Personal Information Protection and Electronic Documents Act,*" see note 35.

2. APPROACHES TO CONSENT IN CANADIAN DATA PROTECTION LAW

PHILIPPA LAWSON AND MARY O'DONOGHUE*

I. INTRODUCTION

Recognizing the dangers to privacy posed by new technologies, Canada has enacted legislation designed to protect individuals from inappropriate and unwanted uses of their personal information. Public sector privacy laws were enacted in the 1980s, followed by private sector laws in the 1990s. Since 2004, all government and commercial activity in Canada is subject to data protection legislation.

Although all the statutes rely to some degree on consent for valid collection, use, and sharing of personal information, the role of consent varies significantly by sector: public sector laws rely on consent as a *justification* for data collection,

* We would like to thank Louisa Garib, James Wishart, Janet Lo, Tara Berish, Catherine Thompson, and Martin Saidla for their excellent research support, without which this paper could not have been written. Thanks also to David Matheson, Charles Raab, Marsha Hanen, George Tomlinson, Jena McGill, Jocelyn Cleary, Michael Froomkin, and Teresa Scassa for their helpful comments on a draft version of this paper.

use, or disclosure, while private sector laws treat consent as a *requirement* for valid collection, use, or disclosure. Private sector statutes provide more scope for individuals to negotiate privacy protection, although the effectiveness of this control is questionable. The role of consent is further differentiated in the employment and health contexts, neither of which is examined here.

In this chapter, we describe approaches to consent in public and private sector Canadian data protection law. We note the markedly different role played by consent in each sector's laws, and the rationale for that difference. Although we accept that context (citizens vs. consumers) is a consideration in developing data protection rules, we suggest that a more nuanced understanding of government-citizen relationships might result in a greater role for consent in that context. Nevertheless, we caution against too much reliance on consent, given that its exercise is often more notional than real.

II. TWO COMPETING APPROACHES: HUMAN RIGHTS VS. FAIR INFORMATION PRACTICES

Privacy is treated as a human right in many international covenants, including the Universal Declaration of Human Rights (1948), the European Convention for the Protection of Human Rights and Fundamental Freedoms (1950), and the International Covenant on Civil and Political Rights (1966).[1] Under the human rights approach, privacy is a moral imperative and covers more than data protection.

Canada signed the UN Declaration, but like other common-law jurisdictions, it neither provided strong constitutional privacy protections, nor sited privacy protection statutes in the human rights arena. In contrast, the Quebec Charter of Human Rights and Freedoms (1975) enshrines a right to privacy for residents of Quebec, and amendments to the Civil Code (1991) provide extensive privacy rights.

An alternative and pragmatic approach to privacy focuses on data protection. Privacy law in Canada tends toward this approach, reflecting "Fair Information Practices" promulgated by Alan Westin and adopted by the Organisation for Economic Co-operation and Development (OECD) in its 1980 Guidelines on the Protection of Privacy and Transborder Flows of Personal Data. Under this

---

1. Universal Declaration of Human Rights (1948), art. 12; International Covenant on Civil and Political Rights (1966), art. 17 states, "No one shall be subjected to arbitrary interference with his privacy, family, home or correspondence . . . Everyone has the right to the protection of the law against such interference or attacks"; European Convention, art. 8, states, "Everyone has the right to respect for his private and family life, his home and his correspondence."

approach, consent is a central requirement but may be qualified by a broad and undefined notion of "appropriateness." However, important elements of the human rights approach have been incorporated into Canadian private sector data protection statutes, establishing certain non-waivable rights while also deferring to business "needs." This straddling of approaches is awkward and has led to a sometimes-confused jurisprudence.

Both the OECD Guidelines and the Canadian privacy enactments discussed here confine their ambit to data protection ("recorded information" about identifiable individuals) rather than privacy protection at large. Excluded from data protection law, and thus from the scope of this paper, are privacy issues such as spatial privacy, bodily privacy, search and seizure, and surveillance.

III. CONSENT IN PUBLIC SECTOR PRIVACY LEGISLATION

A. Development of Public Sector Privacy Legislation in Canada

Beginning in the 1980s, Canadian jurisdictions enacted statutory rules for handling personal information, regulating initially only the public sector, and following the voluntary OECD guidelines. The guidelines set a minimum standard of Fair Information Practices, attempting to balance competing interests between privacy protection and business-related transborder data flow; the protection of privacy is always qualified by the need "to avoid undue interference with flows of personal data between Member countries."[2]

The federal Privacy Act[3] was passed as a companion piece with the federal Access to Information Act[4] in 1982. These statutes provide for two separate oversight bodies: the Information Commissioner of Canada and the Privacy Commissioner of Canada. Ontario and the other provinces followed, generally incorporating both privacy protection and access to information in a single statute with a single overseeing Commissioner. Later provincial statutes mirror in significant ways the Ontario access and privacy scheme, with very similar structure and exemptions.[5] The Acts apply to a wide range of federal, provincial, and municipal bodies.

---

2. Colin J. Bennett, *Prospects for an International Standard for the Protection of Personal Information: A Report to the Standards Council of Canada*, August 1997. (Unpubl.) http://web.uvic.ca/~polisci/bennett/research/index.htm.

3. Privacy Act, R.S.C. 1985 c. P-21.

4. Access to Information Act, R.S.C. 1985 c. A-1.

5. The Freedom of Information and Protection of Privacy Act (FIPPA) R.S.O. 1990 c. F.31; and the Municipal Freedom of Information and Protection of Privacy Act (MFIPPA) R.S.O. 1990 c. M.56.

B. Legislative Purposes

Privacy statutes in Canada generally include an explicit purpose clause.[6] The Supreme Court of Canada has stated that the purposes of access to government information and protection of privacy are linked to important democratic values, including accountability and citizen participation in government, and the citizen's fundamental right to privacy.[7] Indeed, the Court has characterized the Privacy Act as a quasi-constitutional enactment:

> The *Privacy Act* is also fundamental in the Canadian legal system . . . Its aims are, first, to protect personal information held by government institutions, and second, to provide individuals with a right of access to personal information about themselves . . . The *Official Languages Act* and the *Privacy Act* are closely linked to the values and rights set out in the Constitution, and this explains the quasi-constitutional status that this Court has recognized them as having. However, that status does not operate to alter the traditional approach to the interpretation of legislation . . . The quasi-constitutional status of the *Official Languages Act* and the *Privacy Act* is one indicator to be considered in interpreting them, but it is not conclusive in itself. The only effect of this Court's use of the expression "quasi-constitutional" to describe these two Acts is to recognize their special purpose.[8]

Exceptions from the Privacy Act rights should therefore be interpreted narrowly and should not be used to undermine the broad purpose of the legislation. Strict construction requires that the objective not be frustrated except in the clearest of cases, and the onus lies on those asserting the exception.[9]

The Ontario Freedom of Information and Protection of Privacy Act (FIPPA)[10] is largely based on the recommendations in the 1980 Williams Commission Report.[11] The Report expressed the importance of privacy in human rights language, observing that privacy "is linked to fundamental concerns for the

---

6. Privacy Act s 2 (n. 3): "The purpose of this Act is to extend the present laws of Canada that protect the privacy of individuals with respect to personal information about themselves held by a government institution and that provide individuals with a right of access to that information."

7. *Dagg v Canada (Minister of Finance)* [1997] 2 S.C.R. 403.

8. *Lavigne v Canada (Office of the Commissioner of Official Languages)* 214 D.L.R. (4th) 1, para 24; see also *Heinz, infra* para 28: "The importance of this legislation is such that the *Privacy Act* has been characterized by this Court as 'quasi-constitutional' because of the role privacy plays in the preservation of a free and democratic society."

9. *Lavigne, paras 30–31 (n. 8); Canada (Information Commissioner) v Canada (Immigration and Refugee Board)* [1997] F.C.J. No 1812, paras 34–35 (Federal Court Trial Division); *Reyes v Secretary of State* (1984), 9 Admin. L.R. 296, 299, para 3 (Federal Court Trial Division).

10. Freedom of Information and Protection of Privacy Act (n. 5).

11. *Public Government for Private People*, Report of the Commission on Freedom of Information and Individual Privacy/1980.

preservation of human dignity and personal freedom," identifying "the essential concern of the individual," which is to maintain the right to limit the disclosure and subsequent use of information concerning himself.[12] The Report adopted Alan Westin's definition of informational privacy: "the claim of individuals . . . to determine for themselves when, how and to what extent information about them is to be communicated to others."[13] The Commission recommended provisions to promote individual control over personal information held by government but acknowledged that "the collection of personal information by government is not likely to occur in circumstances in which the individual has an effective choice in refusing to supply the information in question."[14] The Commission recommended balancing individual privacy interests against the legitimate needs of government:

> Important as the informational privacy value is, it is but one of a number of potentially conflicting values competing for attention. The government must gather personal information if it is to successfully and efficiently administer the social and economic programs adopted in response to its perceptions of the public interest; if we are to have a government-operated medical insurance scheme, for example, it is inevitable that some personal information gathering activity will occur. Similarly, concern about the use of surveillance technology by law enforcement authorities must be measured against the need for effective law enforcement. The potential dangers in the use of numerical identifiers such as the Social Insurance Number must be weighed against the desirability of accurate identification of records concerning individuals and the possible benefits of personal data for medical research purposes.[15]

Consent is not the primary mechanism suggested for delivering control. Rather, the Commission recommended that individual control be achieved through the following:

- Notice to the individual of collection of personal information
- Direct collection from the individual
- Access to one's personal information and right of appeal to independent review body
- Right to correction or attachment of statement of disagreement
- Onward disclosure of corrections to those to whom the personal information has already been disclosed
- Right to notice of FOI request, to object or to appeal

---

12. *Ibid.*, 500, 502.
13. *Ibid.* n. 11.
14. *Ibid.* n. 11.
15. Commission on Freedom of Information, *Public Government*, 505 (n. 11).

- Opportunity to refuse consent to:
  - ° disclosure of personal information pursuant to FOI request
  - ° inconsistent uses and disclosures
  - ° early destruction of personal information

Other enacted recommendations include limitations on government collection; restrictions on use and disclosure; standards of accuracy and currency; and secure keeping and disposal of personal information.

Statutory permission to derogate from some rules ensures government flexibility.[16] To better protect personal information, however, governments may be required to undertake Privacy Impact Assessments (PIAs), described by the Privacy Commissioner of Canada as a risk mitigation tool.[17] The federal government issued a directive requiring all federal agencies to conduct a PIA of proposed and revamped projects and programs that may impact privacy. The Privacy Commissioner may review and comment on the PIA and make recommendations, but the decision regarding adoption of the recommendation lies with the government department.[18]

A debate about the proper level of individual control over government processing of personal information arose in 2003. The Saskatchewan Government developed a Framework for handling personal information that made more room for consent.[19] The Information and Privacy Commissioner issued a report criticizing the Framework for going beyond the requirements of the Freedom of Information and Protection of Privacy Act. He noted that under the Act "consent is not usually required for collection, use, or disclosure provided the government institution is only collecting, using, or disclosing for purposes directly related to its core purpose... we are aware of no Canadian jurisdiction that has elected to codify a consent-driven approach for its public sector privacy regime."[20] In his highly critical report, Commissioner Dickson stated that while the Privacy Assessment and Framework were predicated on the CSA Model Code, the latter is "voluntary, consent driven, and not designed for government."[21] "Public sector realities" militate against a consent-based system. In delivering programs, government requires vast amounts of personal information, and the efficient delivery of services would be impaired by a consent requirement and increase

---

16. See for example, Ontario FIPPA, ss. 39 to 43.

17. Privacy Impact Assessment Fact Sheet, Privacy Commissioner of Canada http://www.privcom.gc.ca/fs-fi/02_05_d_33_e.asp.

18. Treasury Board guidelines for applying the Privacy Impact Assessment Policy.

19. *An Overarching Personal Information Privacy Framework for Executive Government*, 2003.

20. *Report on the Overarching Personal Information Privacy Framework for Executive Government*, June 15, 2004 (Saskatchewan) Response of Information and Privacy Commissioner, CA2 SA IPC A04 R25.

21. *Ibid.*

costs. Other mechanisms ensured that government activity was limited to that necessary for government programs. "As a consequence, public sector privacy rules are not consent based."[22]

C. The Role of Consent in Public Sector Legislation

Public sector consent arises in two distinct contexts: consent to disclosure of personal information in response to access to information (FOI) requests from third-party members of the public; and as a justification for government collection, use, disclosure and retention—just one of many possible justifications. (In certain circumstances the head has a duty to disclose personal information without consent where necessary in relation to a grave health, safety, or environmental hazard.)[23]

Individual consent plays a relatively minor role in public sector data protection law. While it can be relied upon for data uses and disclosures, it is rarely if ever *required*. Consent is only *one* of the statutory factors permitting government to derogate from the basic rules, and it will not usually be sought if government may act under another listed factor. Generally, government will seek or rely on individual consent when it cannot fit a transaction within one of the other derogations, or where it wishes to emphasize the "consensual" nature of a transaction.[24]

Although the Supreme Court has ruled that the federal *Privacy Act* has "quasi-constitutional" status,[25] the Ontario FIPPA lacks explicit language confirming that the privacy rights it creates cannot be bargained away.[26] Some provisions contain prescriptive language, including those for collection, use, and disclosure—"no person shall collect"—indicating that the rules must be followed despite consent.[27] The Ontario Court of Appeal has found that consent is not a substitute if the statutory conditions for collection are not present.[28]

---

22. *Ibid* n. 20.

23. See Ontario FIPPA s 11.

24. For example, where police are requested to provide an employment background check, they usually require the individual being checked to sign a consent form, even where background check is statutorily mandated.

25. *Lavigne* (n. 8).

26. See Preamble to Ontario Human Rights Code: "Whereas recognition of the inherent dignity and the equal and **inalienable** rights of all members of the human family is the foundation of freedom, justice and peace in the world and is in accord with the *Universal Declaration of Human Rights* as proclaimed by the United Nations." See also section 9 of Code: "No person shall infringe or do, directly or indirectly, anything that infringes a right under this Part."

27. E.g., Ontario FIPPA s. 38(2) collection; s 40 retention and accuracy; s 41 "shall not use"; s 42 "shall not disclose" (n. 5).

28. "It is conceded on the appeal that the application judge erred in law by finding that s. 28(2) does not apply where the information is collected on consent. Consent is not one

Conditions for valid collection include that collection be expressly authorized by statute, collected for law enforcement, or *necessary* to the proper adminis-tration of a lawfully authorized activity.[29] Additional personal information with limited relevance may not be collected, regardless of consent.[30] Given the remedial nature of the Act, derogation with consent from the protections is likely unlawful, and the government should not be permitted to rely on consent.

In practice, citizens often volunteer additional unnecessary information to government in communications that include necessary information. So perhaps the rule should focus on use, and volunteering the information should be insufficient to permit the use or retention of the additional information.

D. Rights to Withhold or Withdraw Consent

Public sector enactments are largely silent on the right to withhold or with-draw consent. Withholding depends on factors such as statutory or legal requirements compelling compliance, the common law, the ability of the individual to negotiate, and the importance of the government program that may be withheld if consent is not granted. The Ontario Commissioner has said about bargaining with government:

> Any discussion of "choice" must include an analysis of an individual's relative "bargaining power," or range of options available in various situations. When interacting with public sector (government) organizations, an individual is typically faced with a situation in which he or she has asymmetrical bargaining power (i.e., limited, if any, choice).[31]

---

of the three conditions set out in s. 28(2) that allow the collection of personal information by or on behalf of a municipality . . . I also agree with the appellants that contrary to the observation of the application judge, there is evidence in the record that some people who sell second-hand goods require the proceeds to meet their daily needs and therefore, when faced with the choice of providing the information or not selling the goods, cannot confi-dently be said to be giving their consent freely." See *Cash Converters v City of Oshawa* 2007 ONCA 502, para 34 (Ontario Court of Appeal).

29. Ontario FIPPA s 38(2) (n. 5).

30. Ontario adjudicator held economic duress a factor in requiring welfare recipients to disclose welfare status to potential employers; enforced disclosure **not** necessary to administration of welfare program. See Investigation I94–085P, *Ministry of Housing*, [1995] O.I.P.C. No. 315, 2–3 (Ontario Office of the Information and Privacy Commissioner); Privacy Complaint MC-030044-1, *Toronto Community Housing Corporation*, [2004] O.I.P.C. No. 196, 3–5 (Ontario Office of the Information and Privacy Commissioner).

31. Ann Cavoukian and John Eichmanis, *Privacy as a Fundamental Human Right vs. an Economic Right: An Attempt at Conciliation*, (IPC, Toronto, 1999 p. 1). http://www.ipc. on.ca/images/Resources/up-1pr_right.pdf.

As indicated in the following, a refusal to consent to disclosure is not determinative:

> In general, under the privacy protection provisions of the Act, the mere fact that someone has requested confidentiality with respect to certain information does not, in itself, provide an absolute prohibition on the disclosure of that information. This principle is reflected in the wording of the Act (which does not require consent for all disclosures of personal information) and is supported by compelling public policy considerations. To conclude otherwise would unduly restrict the ability of government institutions, faced with a request of confidentiality from an individual, to disclose personal information where a legal requirement or some other consideration makes it prudent, and correct, to do so.[32]

Requiring individuals to supply unnecessary personal information constitutes an unlawful collection.[33] In practice, where an individual wishes to resist collection, there is usually no prior necessity ruling on point, the discretion as to scope lies with the administrator so the individual may have to "comply now and grieve later."

E. Notice

Notice of collection is one of the most important public sector rights. Along with a default requirement for direct collection of information, it provides transparency regarding content and scope of collection, enabling access and correction rights and aids in knowledgeable consent. The Ontario FIPPA requires that notice must include the legal authority to collect the information, the purposes for which it will be used, and name and contact information for an official who can answer questions.[34]

Government standard consent forms offered as evidence of both knowledge (notice) and consent to collection, use, and disclosure may describe in the broadest and most general terms the information to be collected, the collection sources, the uses, and disclosures. Concerns about standard forms include knowledgeable consent, scope of consent, ability to vary or modify the consent form, and freedom to withhold consent. Where government relies on consent to disclose under FIPPA, consent is explicitly required to be knowledgeable— the individual must identify the "information in particular" and consent to its disclosure. A standard consent form may therefore be too general to enable the person to "identify the information in particular."[35]

---

32. Ontario Investigation Report MC-050017-1.

33. Alberta Information and Privacy Commissioner Investigation Report P2005-IR-007, [2005] A.I.P.C.D. No. 45, 3–4 at paras. 10, 17.

34. *Ontario* FIPPA, s 39(2) (n. 5).

35. See Ontario Investigation Reports I96–119P; I96–071P; Investigation Reports MC-050045-1 and MC-050047-1. The form of consent to employment-related police

F. Conclusions—Public Sector Consent

Given that governments may collect, use, and disclose information without individual consent, it is not contemplated that the individual can negotiate to block or modify transactions. Instead, public sector legislation provides a set of rules (with multiple derogations) that are more in the nature of obligations of government and public servants than a set of individually enforceable "privacy rights."[36] To the extent that individual control is a central aspect of data protection, this results in relatively weak privacy protection.

Governments could give much greater recognition to the sensitivity of the personal information they hold, and to the constitutional dimension of personal privacy rights,[37] by developing a more nuanced approach to individual consent and control respecting personal information.

IV. CONSENT IN PRIVATE SECTOR PRIVACY LEGISLATION

Quebec introduced the first Canadian private sector data protection laws in 1994, with the Act Respecting the Protection of Personal Information in the Private Sector, (Québec Act).[38] The federal Personal Information Protection and Electronic Documents Act (PIPEDA)[39] was enacted in 2001, followed by the Alberta Personal Information Protection Act (Alta PIPA),[40] and British Columbia Personal Information Protection Act (BC PIPA)[41] in 2004. These laws focus on the collection, use, and disclosure of personal information by organizations. The federal law applies only to commercial activities, whereas the three provincial

---

criminal background checks resulted in police disclosing to potential employers information about mental health police records. It was held that the form language was "too broad" and "d[id] not adequately describe the type of information that lead to the disclosure."

36. Ontario's legislation does not provide for individual enforcement of rights (except the right of access to own personal information) or for individual remedies for privacy breaches. See Ontario FIPPA Part III (n. 5) and *Lawrence J. M. David v Robert Binstock, Registrar, Information and Privacy Commissioner/Ontario*, Tor. Doc. 494/04 (Toronto Divisional Court); *Rita Reynolds v Robert Binstock, Registrar, Information and Privacy Commissioner/Ontario*, Tor. Doc. 485/04 (Toronto Divisional Court). The federal *Privacy Act* provides individual access to the Federal Court.

37. See Ontario Superior Court decision regarding the constitutionality of statutory disclosure of adoption information, Charter s. 7 Principle of Fundamental Justice articulated "Where an individual has a reasonable expectation of privacy in personal and confidential information, that information may not be disclosed to third parties without his or her consent." See *Cheskes, Patton et al. v Attorney General of Ontario* docket 06-CV-319936PD2, September 19, 2007 (Belobaba J.).

38. R.S.Q. ch.P-39.1.
39. S.C. 2000 c.5.
40. S.A. 2003 c.P-6.5.
41. S.B.C. 2003 c.63.

laws extend to noncommercial activities. All four laws cover employment relationships,[42] and all four exclude certain kinds of activities such as journalism, art and literature,[43] and historical or genealogical material[44] from their scope.[45]

A. Legislative Purposes

There is an interesting divergence among the statutes with respect to statutory purposes. The Québec Act is explicitly designed to particularize the informational privacy rights set out in articles 35–40 of the Civil Code, which establish that "every person has a right to the respect of his reputation and privacy." In contrast, PIPEDA and its two provincial offspring contain purpose clauses referring not only to individual privacy rights but also to "the need of organizations to collect, use, or disclose personal information for purposes that a reasonable person would consider appropriate in the circumstances."[46] This reference to business needs has led to the application of an uneasy "balancing test" when assessing reasonableness/ appropriateness under the Act.[47] Rather than focusing on the individual's right to privacy and considering legitimate business needs as one of many potential limits on this right, the assessment of legality treats "legitimate" business needs as a primary consideration. The Federal Court of Appeal has held that "the need for balancing is clear from the purpose clause which is section 3 in *PIPEDA*,"[48] stating that:

> even though Part 1 and Schedule 1 of the Act purport to protect the right of privacy, they also purport to facilitate the collection, use, and disclosure of personal information by the private sector. In interpreting this legislation, the Court must strike a balance between two competing interests.[49]

This explicit recognition of the context in which the rights arise—indeed, of the very threats that led to the legislation of those rights—is unusual.

---

42. Although differently: PIPEDA (n. 37) and the Québec Act (n. 36) apply the same rules to employment and consumer relationships; Alberta and BC apply separate rules in the employment context.

43. PIPEDA s 4(2)(c) (n. 37); Alta PIPA s 3(b) (n. 38); BC PIPA s 3(2)(b) (n. 39); Québec Act (n. 36).

44. Québec Act s 1 (n. 36).

45. Such exemptions are broader than, and in addition to, specific exceptions to the general consent rule.

46. PIPEDA s 3 (n. 38); Alta PIPA s 3 (n. 38); B.C. PIPA s 2 (n. 39).

47. *Wansink v Telus Communications Inc.*, 2007 FCA 221 (CanLII), para 10 (Federal Court of Appeal); *Englander v Telus Communications Inc.*, 2004 FCA 387 (CanLII), para 46 (Federal Court of Appeal); *Eastmond v Canadian Pacific Railway* 2004 FC 852 (CanLII), para 129 (Federal Court Trial Division). See also PIPEDA Case Summaries # 14, 39, 279.

48. *Eastmond*, para 129 (n. 45).

49. *Englander*, para 46 (n. 45).

Public sector statutes, in contrast, do not give explicit recognition to governments' legitimate need to use personal information—it is simply implied.

B. The Role of Consent in Private Sector Data Protection Laws

The requirement for consent to the collection, use, and disclosure of personal information is a cornerstone of all three common-law regimes.[50] Such consent must be informed and voluntary: all statutes include notice requirements[51] and a "refusal to deal" provision, prohibiting organizations from requiring, as a condition of the transaction, consent to unnecessary collection, use, or disclosure of personal information.[52] Under all regimes, use or disclosure of the information for different purposes requires additional consent.[53] In some cases, companies have failed the consent test by using overly vague or otherwise inadequate notice regarding their intended uses.[54]

Consent plays a less central but still critical role in Quebec, where it is required for uses and disclosures not relevant to the original stated purpose of collection, but not for the initial collection, which is instead subject to notice obligations, rights of refusal, and a "necessity" requirement.[55] Under the Alberta and B.C. laws, consent plays a limited role in the employment context, where "reasonableness" is more often the test applied.[56]

The consent requirement is accompanied in all four regimes by other obligations derived from the OECD Principles and "Fair Information Practices," including security safeguards, data accuracy, accountability, openness, and individual access to information. Moreover, consent is heavily qualified: each statute includes a long list of law enforcement, emergency, research, and other

---

50. Quebec law's requirement for consent to collection of personal data is implicit in obligation to inform and individual's right to refuse. See Québec Act ss 8 and 9 (n. 36).

51. PIPEDA Sch.1, Principle 4.3 (n. 37); Québec Act s 8 (n. 36); Alta PIPA s 13 (n. 38); BC PIPA s 10 (n. 39).

52. PIPEDA's refusal to deal provision is slightly different from Alta PIPA and BC PIPA, referring to "the explicitly specified and legitimate purposes" rather than "what is necessary to provide the product or service," but has been interpreted as meaning the latter. Quebec's provision covers employment contracts as well as consumer contracts, and allows exceptions where "authorized by law" or where the request is unlawful.

53. PIPEDA Sch.1, Principle 4.3.1 (n. 37); Québec Act ss 13, 18 (n. 36); Alta PIPA s 8(4) (n. 38); BC PIPA s 8(4) (n. 39).

54. *Englander* (n. 45). See also PIPEDA Case Summaries # 24, 97, 152, 180, 203, 244, 250, 296, 349, and Report on the Investigation into Collection, Use and Disclosure of Customer Information Re: EPCOR [2004] A.I.P.C.D. No. 15; Investigation Report P2004-IR-001 Alberta Information and Privacy Commissioner, (July 26, 2004).

55. Québec Act ss 5–13 (n. 36).

56. Alta PIPA ss 15, 18, 21 (n. 38); BC PIPA ss 13, 16, 19 (n. 39).

exceptions for which nonconsensual collection, use, or disclosure is considered socially desirable.[57]

Less recognized are statutory rights and obligations that apply *regardless* of consent. All statutes include nonconsent-based limits on collection. PIPEDA and the Quebec statute require that collection of personal information be limited to that "necessary" for the specified purposes.[58] (In all regimes, consent must be for specified purposes.) The Quebec law further provides that "in case of doubt, personal information is deemed to be non-necessary."[59] The Alta PIPA requires that collection be "reasonable" for the specified purposes,[60] while the BC PIPA requires simply that the collection must fulfill the specified purposes.[61] Although this suggests a lower standard of protection in the western provinces, such does not appear to be the case in practice. Alberta's "reasonableness" requirement has been interpreted as "necessary,"[62] while the issue appears not yet addressed in B.C. Numerous PIPEDA and Quebec cases have found noncompliance because of unnecessary collection of personal information for authentication, employee checks or other purposes.[63]

All regimes also require that the specified purposes and/or practices meet a test based on reasonableness/appropriateness or fundamental rights.[64] These rights operate regardless of consent, and thus complement the consent-based analysis. Subsection 5(3) of PIPEDA limits the purposes for which organizations can legitimately collect, use, or disclose personal information to those purposes "that a reasonable person would consider are appropriate in the circumstances." This clause has been relied upon in numerous PIPEDA findings, both as an inquiry separate from consent[65] or conflated with the consent analysis, as a basis on which to find that consent was or was not present.[66]

---

57. PIPEDA s 7 (n. 37); Alta PIPA ss 14, 17, 20 (n. 38); BC PIPA ss 12, 15, 18 (n. 39). Some of these exceptions have been the focus of fierce debate among stakeholders, while others are widely accepted.

58. PIPEDA Sch.1, Principle 4.4 (n. 38); Québec Act, s 5 (n. 36).

59. Québec Act, s 9 (n. 36).

60. Alta PIPA s 11(2) (n. 38).

61. BC PIPA s 11(a) (n. 39).

62. In Alberta Report P2005-IR-007, the Alberta Commissioner wrote, "If the collection of D/L number is not necessary for a business purpose, it cannot, as required by section 11(2), be reasonable for meeting the purposes for which the information is collected."

63. See PIPEDA Case Summaries # 22, 97, 257, 288; *X. c. Ameublements Tanguay*, [1995] C.A.I. 377 (Inquiry Report); *Pleins Droits de Lanaudière inc. et Oeurvres du Toit de Bethléem inc.* [1996] C.A.I. 399.

64. PIPEDA s 5(3) (n. 37); Alta PIPA ss 11(2), 16(2), 19(2) (n. 38); BC PIPA s 14 (n. 39); Quebec CCQ, Art.3, 37; Québec *Charter of Human Rights and Freedoms*, R.S.Q. c.C-12, s.5.

65. E.g., PIPEDA Case Summaries # 48, 94, 152, 193, 256, 280.

66. E.g., PIPEDA Case Summaries # 24, 40, 99, 104, 127, 152, 232, 245, 281, 287, 288.

Although apparently limited to "purposes," the provision has been interpreted as extending to practices.[67] For example, overly invasive debt collection practices have been found to violate PIPEDA, although the purpose of debt collection is clearly legitimate.[68] This broad interpretation of Subsection 5(3) recognizes the limits of consent as an effective data-protection principle. Without it, PIPEDA would fail to protect against excessive disclosure and other inappropriate practices, even where consent is not required. In recognition of this gap, both Alberta and B.C. supplement their consent-based regimes with rules requiring that the *practices* of collection, use, and disclosure, as well as the *purposes* behind them, be reasonable.[69]

While the Quebec statute does not include a "reasonableness" standard, per se, its express purpose is to establish rules "for the exercise of the rights conferred by articles 35 to 40 of the Civil Code."[70] Article 37 of the Code mandates "serious and legitimate reason[s]" for the creation of a file on another person, and states that one must not, "when establishing or using the file, otherwise invade the privacy or damage the reputation of the person concerned."[71] Moreover, the Québec Charter of Human Rights and Freedoms establishes privacy as a human right, stating, "Every person has a right to respect for his private life."[72] These provisions have been referenced in cases involving alleged breaches of the Québec Act,[73] as grounds for applying a reasonableness/proportionality test similar to that developed by the Supreme Court of Canada in *R. v. Oakes*.[74]

It has been argued that as a result of over-emphasis on consent, "a robust reasonable purposes test has not been developed" under PIPEDA.[75] If this is true, we submit that it is less a result of "over-emphasis on consent" per se, and more a result of conflation by some decision-makers of consent and reasonable purposes. In any case, our review suggests that a surprisingly robust "reasonable purposes" test has in fact emerged from the PIPEDA case law to date.[76] The test has been applied in a manner akin to the test for justification of otherwise

---

67. *Eastmond* (n. 45). See also PIPEDA Case Summaries #61, 99, 130, 232, 245, 282, 317.

68. PIPEDA Case Summaries #61, 130, 282, 317.

69. Alta PIPA, ss 2, 6, 11(2), 16(2), 19(2) (n. 38); B.C. PIPA, ss 4(a), 11, 14, 17 (n. 39).

70. Québec Act, s.1 (n. 36).

71. Civil Code of Québec, R.S.Q. c.C-1991.

72. Québec Charter of Human Rights s 5 (n. 62).

73. *St-Amant c. Meubles Morigeau ltée*, [2006] R.J.Q. 1434 (Québec Superior Court); *Pitre v Industrielle Alliance, compagnie d'assuances générales* (6 November 1995) Québec 200-32-000046-952, J.E. 96-19 (C.Q. civ. Pet. Cré.) (Azimut); *Pouliot c. Biochem Pharma Inc.* [1996] R.J.Q. 1845; *Duchesne v La Great-West, Compagnie D'Assurance-Vie* (14 December 1994) Alma 160-05-000129-867 (C.S.) (Azimut).

74. [1986] 1 S.C.R. 103, 1986 CanLII 46 (S.C.C.).

75. Lisa Austen, "Is Consent the Foundation of Fair Information Practices? Canada's Experience under PIPEDA," *University of Toronto Law Journal* 56 (2006): 181.

76. *Wansink* (n. 45); *Eastmond* (n. 45); PIPEDA Case Summaries #279, 290, 351.

Charter-infringing activity established by the Supreme Court of Canada in *R. v. Oakes*.[77] It has been set out in a clear and logical manner, with four criteria:

i) Demonstrable necessity to meet a specific need
ii) Likely effectiveness in meeting that need
iii) Proportionality between loss of privacy and benefit gained
iv) Absence of a less privacy-invasive means of achieving the same goal

It has been most clearly and convincingly articulated in the context of employee monitoring and surveillance,[78] but also in the context of employer use of biometric[79] and GPS[80] systems.

A similar balancing test has been applied under the Quebec law.[81] Quebec jurisprudence also separates the requirements of consent and necessity: both criteria must be met for valid collection, use, or disclosure.[82]

C. Limits on Contracting Out of Privacy Rights

In addition to these important complements to consent-based data protection, some statutes include explicit provisions invalidating attempts by organizations to contract out of their statutory obligations. The Alta PIPA provides that any waiver or release from the protections of the Act is against public policy and therefore void.[83] Although the B.C. Act expressly prohibits only those contractual waivers relating to withdrawal of consent,[84] the B.C. Privacy Commissioner has expressed "serious reservations about any suggestion that one can validly derogate from [any of] PIPEDA's minimum standards or protections by contract."[85]

Similarly, although the Québec Act has no explicit provision invalidating contractual waivers, Article 8 of the Civil Code of Québec states that "no person may renounce the exercise of his civil rights, except to the extent consistent with public order," and Quebec courts and Privacy Commissioners have found that the "necessity" criterion cannot be overridden by individual consent.[86]

---

77. *Oakes* (n. 72).
78. *Eastmond* (n. 45); PIPEDA Case Summaries #279, 290.
79. *Wansink* (n. 45); PIPEDA Case Summary #281.
80. PIPEDA Case Summary #351.
81. *Pouliot* (n. 69); *Laval (Ville) v X.* (21 February 2003) Montreal 500-02-094423-014 (Cour du Québec, Chambre civile).
82. *Laval* (n. 77).
83. Alta PIPA s 4(7) (n. 38).
84. BC PIPA s 9(3) (n. 39).
85. Order P05–01 (May 25, 2005); *K.E. Gostlin Enterprises Limited* [2005] B.C.I.P.C.D. No. 18 (QL).
86. *Laval* (n. 77); *Tremblay v Caisse populaire Desjardins de St-Thomas*, [2000], CAI 154 (Inquiry Report); *Julien v Domaine Laudance*, [2003] CAI 77; *A. v C.*, [2003] CAI 534; *Agyemang v Ipex Inc.*, [2001] CAI 201.

In contrast, PIPEDA not only lacks a "non-waivability" provision, but expressly permits the waiver of one's right to withdraw consent. Principle 4.3.8 states:

> An individual may withdraw consent at any time, subject to legal or contractual restrictions and reasonable notice. The organization shall inform the individual of the implications of such withdrawal.

Although an outlier with respect to other data protection regimes, the existence of this specific permissive provision suggests that other rights under PIPEDA cannot be so waived.[87] Moreover, as the B.C. Privacy Commissioner has found,[88] the public policy nature of privacy rights argues strongly for the invalidation of contractual waivers from those rights, especially in the context of contracts of adhesion. A finding that rights set out in data protection laws cannot be surrendered by individuals other than in exceptional circumstances would be consistent with Canadian common law on statutory illegality.[89]

D. Forms of Consent—Criteria for Validity
The Quebec law requires that consent be "manifest" in order to be valid. Thus, unless it can be logically inferred from the actions of the individual, consent must be positively communicated through an "opt-in" process.[90] However, s.17 of the Act sets out a significant exception to this rule: in the case of "nominative lists" (names and contact information), enterprises may communicate the information to third parties for commercial or philanthropic prospection, as long as they give individuals on the list a "valid opportunity to refuse" such use of their personal information.[91]

In contrast, the three common-law statutes allow for opt-out consent generally, provided that certain conditions are met. The Alberta and B.C. statutes permit opt-out consent only where the individual is notified, given a reasonable opportunity to decline, and does not decline after a reasonable period of time; and where the collection, use, or disclosure in question is reasonable given the sensitivity of the information.[92] PIPEDA gives only general guidance, stating that "an organization should generally seek express consent when the information is likely to be considered sensitive."[93] However, the federal Commissioner has articulated criteria for valid opt-out notice, including limited and well-defined purposes; clear notice, brought to the individual's attention at the time of collection;

---

87. This issue does not appear to have been addressed in PIPEDA case law.
88. *Order P05-01* (May 25, 2005).
89. Waddams, *The Law of Contracts*, 5th ed. (Aurora: Canada Law Book, 2005) 396, para 560; *Still v M.N.R.* (C.A.), (1997), [1998] 1 F.C. 549 (Federal Court of Appeal).
90. *Bedard v Robert*, J.E. 2003-589 (S.C.).
91. *Deschenes c. Groupe Jean Coutu* et al. PV 98 08 42.
92. Alta PIPA s 8(3) (n. 38); B.C. PIPA s 8(3) (n. 39).
93. Principle 4.3.6 (n. 37).

and a convenient procedure for opting out of secondary purposes.[94] Disturbingly, a 2006 CIPPIC study of online retailers found that, while the vast majority of companies rely upon opt-out consent for secondary uses and disclosures, most fail to meet one or more of these criteria for valid opt-out consent.[95]

A key criterion for valid opt-out consent is notice. Yet, none of the four statutes specifically requires that notice be *brought to the attention of* the individual. PIPEDA merely requires "a reasonable effort to ensure that the individual is advised of the purposes for which the information will be used."[96] The Alberta and B.C. PIPAs merely require that notice be "in a form that the individual can reasonably be expected to understand" and that "gives the individual a reasonable opportunity to decline."[97] Although courts and commissioners have interpreted these provisions as requiring that notice of purposes and opt-out options be brought to the attention of individuals at the time of collection,[98] studies indicate that many businesses are not doing so.[99] Without a clear requirement for *effective* notice (and enforcement of it), opt-out consent becomes meaningless. Even then, theoretical and empirical studies in psychology and economics suggest that opt-out consent protocols will always result in a large number of cases in which consent is wrongly assumed.[100]

E. Rights to Withhold, Negotiate, and Withdraw Consent

All three common-law statutes give individuals the right to withhold consent to unnecessary purposes,[101] while Quebec's Act requires that consent be "free,"[102] and that organizations relying on opt-out consent "grant the persons concerned a valid opportunity to refuse."[103]

---

94. PIPEDA Case Summary #207.

95. Canadian Internet Policy and Public Interest Clinic (CIPPIC), *Compliance with Canadian Data Protection Laws: Are Retailers Measuring Up?* (April 2006).

96. Schedule 1, Principle 4.3.2 (n. 37).

97. Alta PIPA s 8(3)(a) (n. 38); B.C. PIPA s 8(3)(a) and (b) (n. 39). The B.C. PIPA also requires that the organization "disclose to the individual verbally or in writing . . ."

98. See *Englander* (n. 45); PIPEDA Case Summaries #24, 244, 263, 273; *Marbre c. Clearnet SCP* C.A.I., Doc # 99 01 29.

99. CIPPIC, *Compliance* (n. 91); EKOS Research Associates Ltd., *Business Usage of Consumer Information for Direct Marketing: What the Public Thinks* (Public Interest Advocacy Centre, 2001).

100. Ian Kerr et al., "Soft Surveillance, Hard Consent," *Personally Yours* 6 (2006): 1–14; Eric Johnson, Steven Bellman and Gerald Lohse, "Defaults, Framing and Privacy: Why Opting in ≠ Opting Out," *Marketing Letters* 13, no. 1 (2002): 5–15.

101. PIPEDA, Schedule 1, Principle 4.3.3 (n. 37); Alta PIPA s 7(2) (n. 38); BC PIPA s 7(2) (n. 39); see also Québec Act s 9 (n. 36).

102. Québec Act s 14 (n. 36).

103. Québec Act s 232(2) and s 23 (n. 36).

In addition, Alberta's Act includes an unusual provision allowing individuals to *negotiate* the terms of their consent. Subsection 7(3) states:

An individual may give a consent subject to any reasonable terms, conditions or qualifications established, set, approved by or otherwise acceptable to the individual.

This appears to validate individual consumer revisions to standard form agreements regarding data collection, use, or disclosure, as long as they are reasonable.[104]

PIPEDA includes a right to withdraw consent at any time upon reasonable notice, but subject to "legal or contractual restrictions."[105] Alberta and B.C. include more robust and detailed withdrawal rights that can be overridden if withdrawal would frustrate the performance of a legal obligation.[106] In contrast to PIPEDA, B.C.'s provision expressly forbids organizations from prohibiting the withdrawal of consent, and as noted, the Alta PIPA includes a general prohibition on contractual waivers. The Québec Act includes no general right to withdraw consent,[107] but does give individuals the right to remove their names from "nominative lists,"[108] and is subject to the Quebec Civil Code, which includes a non-waivability clause.[109]

Rights to withdraw are an essential component of consent rights if, as we posit, the purpose of such rights is to give individuals control over their personal information. However, they may be more illusory than real, given human tendencies to accept the status quo.[110]

F. Conclusions—Consent in Private Sector Data Protection Law

Although different in important respects, all four private sector data protection laws in Canada treat consent as one part of a two-part test to determine validity of data collection, use, or disclosure. A baseline reasonableness test applies, regardless of whether consent is required or was obtained. This ensures, at least in theory, that individuals remain protected from inappropriate uses and disclosures of their personal information even when consent is not required or was given without full awareness. Moreover, consent cannot, in general, be used to

---

104. We could find no case law interpreting this provision.

105. Principle 4.3.8 (n. 37).

106. Alta PIPA s 9 (n. 38); BC PIPA s 9 (n. 39).

107. This was confirmed in the case of *X. v Equifax*, in which the Commission found that there is no general right to withdraw consent or to have one's information deleted from a file: CAI File No.03 21 10 (27 May 2005).

108. Québec Act ss 17(2), 25, 26 (n. 36).

109. Quebec CCQ Article 8.

110. Kerr et al., "Soft Surveillance, Hard Consent" (n. 96).

vitiate statutory privacy rights.[111] It is designed to enhance, not to diminish, established rights.

The role of consent in this context is, clearly, to provide individuals with greater *control* over their personal information, above and beyond those protections against privacy invasions that they enjoy as a result of reasonableness-based limits on corporate data activities. That consent is designed to provide control is demonstrated by, for example, Alberta's provision allowing individuals to set conditions on their consent,[112] Quebec's time limit on consent,[113] Alberta, B.C., and PIPEDA's rights to withdraw consent,[114] and all three provinces' limits on collection from third parties.[115]

But there is reason to question the effectiveness of the control that these consent provisions actually provide to individuals—less because of the numerous exceptions to consent in each statute, and more because of the explicit recognition of business "needs" and sanctioning of opt-out consent under each regime.[116] Theoretical and empirical studies have questioned both the validity and the effectiveness of opt-out consent.[117] Indeed, one could argue that the validity of opt-out methods eliminates the very control that consent is meant to provide. Consent is meaningless without awareness of that to which one is being assumed to consent. For this reason, we believe that informational privacy may ultimately be protected less by consent requirements and more by rights-based reasonableness tests incorporated in each statute.

V. CONCLUSIONS

Consent is a critical component of data protection, providing individuals with some control over their informational privacy. However, it offers insufficient protection on its own, given the realities of human, government, and marketplace behavior. This is so in both the public and the private sectors, where consent requirements need to be supplemented with reasonableness standards for effective data protection.

---

111. The clear exception to this rule is PIPEDA's clause allowing individuals to contract out of their right to withdraw consent.

112. Alta PIPA s 7(3) (n. 38).

113. Québec Act s 14 (n. 36).

114. Alta PIPA s 9 (n. 38); B.C. PIPA s 9 (n. 39), PIPEDA Schedule 1 Principle 4.3.8 (n. 39).

115. Québec Act s 6 (n. 38); Alta PIPA ss 7(1)(b), 13(2), (3) (n. 38); B.C. PIPA s 12(2) (n. 39).

116. Albeit more limited under the Quebec law, which permits opt-out consent protocols only with respect to name, address, and telephone number ("nominative lists"): see Québec Act s 22 (n. 36).

117. CIPPIC *Compliance* (n. 91); EKOS (n. 92); Kerr et al., "Soft Surveillance, Hard Consent" (n. 96).

The most striking difference between the public and private sector regimes is the relative importance and role of consent. Although central to private sector regimes, consent plays a minor role in public sector privacy protection

Despite their flaws, the four private sector data protection statutes establish a sensible regime in which consent plays an important but not determinative role. Their greatest flaw is, arguably, the explicit recognition of business needs and consequent sanctioning of opt-out consent, without effective notice requirements. Consent requirements should be accompanied by stronger notice requirements as well as more effective enforcement regimes in these statutes.

In contrast, public sector data protection laws rely less on consent and more on privacy protective rules and processes required of government. Yet, the technological capacity of government to track and surveil citizens is beyond anything contemplated at the time of enactment of these laws. Privacy laws have simply not kept pace with advances in technology.[118] In this context, public sector deprivation of individual control may go too far in protecting government interests and it is disrespectful of individual autonomy and dignity. It is also disrespectful of the sensitive nature of the personal information collected and the constitutional aspects of privacy protection. Although individual consent is clearly inappropriate in some circumstances (such as tax administration), it is not always inappropriate in the public sector context. A case-based analysis would, in our view, indicate areas in which more choice on the part of the individual is warranted.

In a liberal democracy, values of participatory democracy and citizen autonomy should lead to greater control by citizens over their personal information. However, such control must be real, not illusory. Experience with private sector data protection laws suggests that consent is not completely effective. Any reforms designed to give citizens more control over their government-held information should take heed of that experience.

---

118. Uwe Hessler, *Harsh Words from German Commissioner on Data Protection: Who's in the Driver's Seat Concerning Data Privacy?* Deutsche Welle 24.04.2007, http://www.dw-world.de/dw/article/0,2144,2456060,00.html.

Privacy Commissioner of Canada, *Annual Report to Parliament*, 2004–2005, http://www.privcom.gc.ca/information/ar/200405/200405_pa_e.asp.

3. LEARNING FROM DATA PROTECTION LAW AT THE NEXUS OF COPYRIGHT AND PRIVACY

ALEX CAMERON

I. INTRODUCTION

This chapter is a small part of a broader project[1] aimed at formulating principles and rules to account for intellectual privacy—individuals' freedom to access and enjoy creative works anonymously or in private—within the legal concept of copyright. The broader project argues that such principles and rules have heretofore been wanting in copyright, and that they are an essential component of copyright as a consistent and unified whole.

This chapter contributes to the goals of the broader project in two specific ways. First, the section entitled "Intellectual Privacy under Strain" describes some of the challenges posed by the use of digital technologies in association with copyright works. Second, in the section entitled "Lessons from Data Protection Law," this chapter considers whether data protection laws may stimulate important questions and provide guidance in governing digital copyright practices that involve monitoring individuals' access to and use of creative works. This chapter concludes with a look ahead to further work to be done in the area.

---

1. The broader project is the subject of the author's doctoral dissertation, in progress at the time of writing.

II. INTELLECTUAL PRIVACY UNDER STRAIN

A. The Analogue World

For nearly three centuries following the enactment of the world's first modern copyright statute,[2] neither copyright law nor copyright holders interfered with individuals' privacy. Neither *Rights of Man*[3] nor *The Clockmaker*[4] were delivered to readers on condition that they provide detailed personal information to the author, publisher, or bookseller; nor were readers monitored in their enjoyment of the works.[5]

Until relatively recently, individuals accessed and enjoyed creative works—including books, magazines, newspapers, scholarly periodicals, films, and music—almost exclusively in tangible form by purchasing a copy of the work at a retail store, visiting a library, or attending a public performance. These forms of "analogue" access to creative works usually afforded individuals a high degree of intellectual privacy. Once an individual had purchased or otherwise accessed a copy of a work, his or her relationship with the copyright holder or the distributor of the work ended; it was normally up to the individual to determine how, when, and under what conditions he or she enjoyed the work, subject of course to the terms of copyright law.

Even if copyright holders or others had been interested in monitoring individuals' access to and use of creative works, they had no practical means to do so; nor did they have any practical means to control individuals' activities or to enforce an ongoing license arrangement with them to govern use of the works. In light of these realities of the pre-digital world, copyright law and copyright holders were traditionally concerned exclusively with the activities of competing publishers, not individuals; the former group directly threatened copyright holders' economic interests, whereas individual consumers did not.

---

2. Copyright Act 1710 8 Ann c 19 [hereinafter Statute of Anne]. The Statute of Anne is sometimes referenced as originating in 1709. For an explanation of the reason for this historical discrepancy, see L. R. Patterson and Stanley W. Lindberg, *The Nature of Copyright: A Law of Users' Rights* (Athens, Georgia: University of Georgia Press, 1991), Chapter 2, note 22.

3. Thomas Paine, *Rights of Man* (London: J.S. Jordan, 1791).

4. Thomas Chandler Haliburton, *The Clockmaker, or, The Sayings and Doings of Samuel Slick, of Slickville* (Halifax: J. Howe, 1836).

5. In the case of the *Rights of Man*, the British government might very well have wished to have records of who purchased and who read the book. Paine was tried and convicted in absentia as author of a "seditious and libellous" work. See generally Thomas Paine, *The Political Writings of Thomas Paine: To which is Prefixed a Brief Sketch of the Author's Life, Volume I* (Charlestown: G. Davidson, 1824), xi. It should also be noted that both *Rights of Man* and *The Clockmaker* have been digitized and are available for download on the Internet—this point is revisited in section D(3) of this chapter.

Contrasted against this historical backdrop, late in the twentieth century and continuing into the twenty-first century—concurrent with the rise and spread of digital networks and the increasing digitization of copyrighted works—the centuries-old relationship between copyright holders and individuals became strained. More particularly, the relationship between copyright law, copyright holders, and individuals' intellectual privacy came into tension.[6] This tension is not altogether new; librarians, for example, traditionally respected the value of intellectual privacy and enforced strict protections against the disclosure of patrons' borrowing records. However, libraries are no longer the only source, or even a primary source, of information about individuals' access to creative works and other information products; far from it. We cannot rely on only our libraries to protect our intellectual privacy; we must decide more broadly whether and how to preserve the value of intellectual privacy in the digital age.[7]

B. The Digital Age

With the advent of the digital age, individuals were eager to explore new ways of using digital technologies, especially computers, to access and enjoy creative works. Many copyright holders were eager to meet the demand for digital works, to reap the benefits of digital distribution, and to pursue new business models for exploiting works. At the same time, however, they were wary of the fact that digital technologies offered "the man on the Clapham omnibus"[8] a virtually effortless means, for example, to make and manipulate perfect copies of digital works and share them with millions of other individuals, without the knowledge or permission of the copyright holder and often in violation of copyright law. The most widely-known example of this activity is peer-to-peer file sharing of music using the products and services offered by, among others, the original Napster service.[9]

---

6. The "digital age" or the "information age" could be considered to have started with the invention of the first digital computers during World War II. It was not, however, until the 1990s and into the twenty-first century that the "digital age" became truly relevant and revolutionary for copyright, particularly with the explosive growth in mainstream popularity of personal computers and the Internet which occurred during this period.

7. Lessig puts a closely related question as follows: "In a world where this monitoring could not effectively occur, there was, of course, no such right against it. But now that monitoring can occur, we must ask whether the latent right to read anonymously, given to us before by imperfections in technologies, should be a legally protected right." Lawrence Lessig, *Code Version 2.0* (New York: Basic Books, 2006), 191.

8. "The man on the Clapham omnibus" refers to an ordinary, average person. The term is a legal fiction of the "average" and "reasonable" citizen, first adopted in legal circles in *McQuire v Western Morning News* [1903] 2 KB 100 (CA) 109.

9. For a description of how the original Napster service operated, see *A&M Records, Inc. v Napster, Inc.*, 239 F.3d 1004 (9th Cir. 2001).

Many copyright holders thus legitimately perceived and continue to perceive the digital realm as both an opportunity and a threat; it is in the responses to the characteristics of the digital realm that the relationship between copyright and privacy has been most profoundly implicated. For example, in order to pursue the opportunities and to mitigate the threats of digital networks, many copyright holders and others who distribute copyrighted works turned to technological means to attempt to control individuals' access to and enjoyment of copyright works, and to prevent copyright infringement. Such technological means include digital rights management (DRM) and related technology systems.

In general terms, DRM technologies are embedded in software, hardware, or both, and travel with digital works in order to regulate access to and use of the works. DRM is a kind of "digital lock." DRM technologies used to control a song, for example, might enforce a "listen but don't share" permission, restricting the ability of individuals to copy the song to more than one computer or portable device, such as a mobile phone or iPod.[10] DRM technologies continue to evolve and are used by contemporary copyright holders and others across many different forms of works.[11]

It is perhaps not surprising that DRM technologies have sparked controversy on a number of fronts.[12] DRM technologies are relevant for the purposes of this chapter because they are emblematic of the strain in the relationship between copyright and privacy experienced to date in the digital age. In ostensibly exploiting copyrighted works and preventing copyright infringement, many DRM technologies and the licensing practices that they enable depend in part on identifying and tracking copyrighted works, as well as the individuals who access and use them.[13]

---

10. Conditions that could potentially be enforced through such technologies are limited virtually by the imagination, including, for example, "Do not copy more than 5 times," "Do not modify," "Do not print," and "Do not save as a different file format."

11. For a review of privacy-implicating DRM in use in the Canadian market, see Canadian Internet Policy and Public Interest Clinic (CIPPIC), "Digital Rights Management and Consumer Privacy: An Assessment of DRM Applications under Canadian Privacy Law" (2007) <http://www.cippic.ca/uploads/CIPPIC_Report_DRM_and_Privacy.pdf> [CIPPIC Study]. The author of this chapter contributed to the CIPPIC study.

12. Among other issues, one of the important issues raised by DRM relates to competition law and policy. See, e.g., Alex Cameron and Robert Tomkowicz, "Competition Policy and Canada's New Breed of 'Copyright' Law" (2007) 52 McGill LJ 291.

13. See, e.g., Ian R. Kerr, Alana Maurushat, and Christian S. Tacit, "Technological Protection Measures: Part I—Trends in Technical Protection Measures and Circumvention Technologies" (2003) at s 5.2.2, http://www.pch.gc.ca/progs/ac-ca/progs/pda-cpb/pubs/protection/5_e.cfm ("In order to carry out their proper function, DRMs collect, process, and in some cases, store personal information. DRMs may also closely monitor and track the use of digital content. In effect, DRMs can identify consumers and create profiles that identify individual consumer consumption patterns. While the proper use of such personal information can be positive for those consumers who wish to receive customized

Many forms of DRM use a monitoring mechanism as a component of controlling access to and use of creative works.[14] In many cases, DRM operation is fundamentally premised on a diminishment of individuals' intellectual privacy since, through the collection of information about individuals' access to and use of copyrighted works, DRM reduces or eliminates individuals' freedom to access and enjoy copyrighted works anonymously or in private. Although there are many examples of this diminishment, it is worth briefly noting one for demonstrative purposes.

eReader offers a catalog of over 17,000 electronic books for sale on its Web site.[15] An individual downloads the purchased book, installs the eReader software, enters his or her password—which is in fact his or her credit card number[16]—to unlock the book, and is then able to read it.[17] In its privacy policy, eReader candidly states that it profiles its customers:

> We store information that we collect through your stated preferences, cookies, log files, clear gifs, and/or third party sources to create a "profile" of your preferences. We tie your personally identifiable information, and your activity history, to information in the profile, in order to provide tailored promotions and marketing offers and to improve the content of the site for you.[18]

Although it is not clear whether this profiling is directly linked to the operation of the software controlling access to the e-books, it is clear that eReader collects profiling information as part of its interactions with its customers, and that it transmits data during operation of the eReader software.[19] Data collected could include a list of book searches or book titles purchased. Additionally, an appreciation for the full scope of information that the software could be collecting and

---

services, the tremendous potential for acquisition of personal information also gives rise to serious privacy concerns." (footnotes and citations omitted)). See generally L.A. Bygrave, "Digital Rights Management and Privacy—Legal Aspects in the European Union," in *Digital Rights Management-Technological, Economic, Legal and Political Aspects*, Eberhard Becker et al., eds. 418–446 (Berlin: Springer-Verlag, 2003). See also Deirdre K. Mulligan, John Han and Aaron J. Burstein, "How DRM-Based Content Delivery Systems Disrupt Expectations of 'Personal Use'" in *Proceedings of the 2003 ACM Workshop on Digital Rights Management* (New York: ACM Press, 2003) 77.

14. See, e.g., Kerr and others "Technological Protection Measures: Part I," 5.2.2 (n. 13).

15. eReader http://www.ereader.com/.

16. eReader, "Frequently Asked Questions" http://www.ereader.com/help/faq. The use of the credit card number as a password was criticized in the CIPPIC Study. See CIPPIC Study 35 (n. 11).

17. eReader, "An eBook Primer" http://www.ereader.com/help/intro.

18. eReader, "Privacy Policy" http://www.ereader.com/ereader/privacy.htm. CIPPIC Study 47 (n. 11).

19. CIPPIC Study 61 (n. 11).

reporting back to eReader can be gained by considering that the software "eReader Pro for Windows" is capable of the following functions:

> . . . while reading your book you can select any word and easily look it up using your included Merriam-Webster's Pocket Dictionary . . .
>
> . . .
>
> Create detailed notes about your reading and share them with others.
>
> . . .
>
> Highlight key words to remember them later.
>
> . . .
>
> Add and organize book marks with the click of a mouse.[20]

Subject to considerations about whether meaningful consent was obtained from affected individuals, privacy interests would naturally be implicated if, in its customer profiling, eReader is collecting, using, or disclosing the forms of detailed information identified in this passage.

C. The Broad Questions

eReader provides one example of the kinds of conflict that can arise between copyright and privacy.[21] Although this specific example and others like it may be resolved or rectified, their resolution is not determinative of the overarching questions that they raise about the intersection between copyright and intellectual privacy. To use a traffic analogy, the resolution of specific cases of conflict between copyright and intellectual privacy can be likened to two cars crashing at an intersection: the cars may be towed away after the accident, but the intersection itself may be dangerous and in need of repair.

Through the use of many forms of DRM, individuals are increasingly unable to experience creative works anonymously or in private; knowingly and unknowingly, they routinely disclose their personal information and are technologically monitored when searching for, accessing, and enjoying copyrighted works. These conditions are the norm facing individuals wishing to access and enjoy many modern forms of digital works. Indeed, conflict between copyright and intellectual privacy has reached a point where some of the most fundamental questions about the appropriate limits of copyright holders' rights are virtually synonymous with questions about the appropriate limits of intellectual privacy in connection with the enjoyment of creative works. To date, the consequence of this conflict has been a diminishment of individuals' intellectual privacy. Should this conflict continue on its current path, we may be left with little or no room to travel our vibrant copyright kingdoms anonymously or in private.

---

20. eReader, "eReader Pro for Windows Software" http://www.ereader.com/ereader/software/product/15009_pro_win.htm.

21. For other examples, see CIPPIC study (n. 11).

It is possible that the increasing diminishment of intellectual privacy will be halted or reversed. Any number of changes in technology, markets, and regulation may influence the course of intellectual privacy in one direction or another.[22] There are, for example, a number of recent indications that DRM has been dropped in connection with some music downloads[23] and audio books[24] (though it is not clear that enhanced intellectual privacy will result from these developments).[25] Further, from time to time, specific privacy-invasive practices of copyright holders are brought to light, found to be illegal, and redressed. Copyright holders are among the first to acknowledge that, where applicable, data protection laws of general application operate to restrict some activities that diminish individuals' intellectual privacy. The application of such laws is discussed in the next section of this chapter. Commentary and debate over these questions continues.

Yet, predicting the future state of copyright, technology, the market, or intellectual privacy is not object of this chapter. We may end up in a world where we "tap into the beam"[26] and have digital access to every book ever published—then again, we may not. Irrespective of what the future may hold, the presently observable diminishment of intellectual privacy has, per se, brought to the fore some critical, previously unexplored questions about the relationship between copyright and intellectual privacy. The time is ripe to consider questions that have floated, ignored and obscured, through copyright and privacy discourses for centuries. Central among these questions is the domain of the broader project—the value and role of intellectual privacy *within* the legal concept of copyright—of which this chapter is a part.

The next section of this chapter reviews how data protection law may contribute to, or otherwise inform, a broader analysis of the potential role of intellectual privacy within copyright.

III. LESSONS FROM DATA PROTECTION LAW

A. Background

Privacy regulators and policy makers are aware of the mounting tension between copyright and intellectual privacy, and have focused increased attention

---

22. Daniel Gervais introduced this "technopolicy triangle." See Daniel J. Gervais, "The Price of Social Norms: Towards a Licensing Regime for File-Sharing" *Journal of Intellectual Property Law* 12, no. 1 (2005): 39–74.

23 See Yinka Adegoke, "Sony BMG to Drop Copy Protection for Downloads" *Reuters* (January 7, 2008).

24 See Richard Wray, "Penguin Audiobooks to be Free of Copyright Protection" *The Guardian* (March 4, 2008).

25 See Bill Rosenblatt, "What Does "DRM-Free" Mean?" *DRM Watch* (June 7, 2007).

26 David Gelernter, "Tapping into the Beam," in *The Next Fifty Years: Science in the First Half of the Twenty-First Century*, John Brockman ed. (New York: Vintage Books, 2002) (offering a prediction of the state of computer technology in or about the year 2050).

on the matter. The European Union Data Protection Working Party, for example, recently expressed concern about "the fact that the legitimate use of technologies to protect works could be detrimental to the protection of personal data of individuals."[27] Canada's privacy community has voiced similar concern regarding DRM, particularly in the context of possible legislation that would protect the use of DRM.[28] A number of Canada's privacy commissioners have echoed this concern.[29]

There is also a developing contemporary literature and body of law at the intersection of copyright and intellectual privacy. Leading academics, public interest groups, business leaders, policy makers, regulators, courts, and others are increasingly engaged in a global dialogue on the topic. Courts, for example, are increasingly faced with, and must decide, cases where copyright interests are seen as pitted against privacy interests.[30] In addition, concerned about the

---

27. Article 29 Data Protection Working Party, "Working Document on Data Protection Issues Related to Intellectual Property Rights" WP104 (18 January 2005), http://ec.europa.eu/justice_home/fsj/privacy/docs/wpdocs/2005/wp104_en.pdf (accessed March 7 2008).

28. See Canada's Privacy Community, "Letter from Canada's Privacy Community to Ministers Bernier and Oda" (May 17, 2006) http://www.intellectualprivacy.ca/documents/open_letter.pdf; Canada's Privacy Community, "Background Paper: Critical Privacy Issues In Canadian Copyright Reform" (May 17, 2006) http://www.intellectualprivacy.ca/documents/background_paper.pdf.

29. See Letter from Jennifer Stoddart, Privacy Commissioner of Canada, to Ministers Prentice and Verner (January 18, 2008), http://www.privcom.gc.ca/parl/2008/let_080118_e.asp; Letter from Jennifer Stoddart, Privacy Commissioner of Canada, to Ministers Oda and Bernier (May 17, 2006), http://www.privcom.gc.ca/media/let/let_ca_060517_e.asp; Letter from David Loukidelis, Information and Privacy Commissioner of British Columbia, to Ministers Oda and Bernier (May 17, 2006), http://www.oipcbc.org/publications/Comm_Public_Comments/F06-28751.pdf; Open Letter from Ann Cavoukian, Information and Privacy Commissioner of Ontario, to Ministers Oda and Bernier (May 12, 2006), http://www.ipc.on.ca/docs/drmletter.pdf; Letter from Frank Work, Information and Privacy Commissioner of Alberta, to Ministers Oda and Bernier (May 26, 2006), http://www.oipc.ab.ca/ims/client/upload/Copyright_ltr_May_26_06.pdf. The Office of the Privacy Commissioner of Canada has also since issued a Fact Sheet regarding DRM that includes the following statement: "The use of TPMs, however, can seriously affect the privacy rights of individuals, and by invading their privacy and reporting on their behaviour, impact other civil liberties such as freedom of association and freedom of expression. While rights holders have a perfectly legitimate view of the matter, it is also reasonable to expect them to enforce their rights only in a way which respects individual privacy rights." See Office of the Privacy Commissioner of Canada, "Fact Sheet: Digital Rights Management and Technical Protection Measures" (November 2006), http://www.privcom.gc.ca/fs-fi/02_05_d_32_e.asp.

30. See *BMG Canada Inc. v Doe* [2005] 252 DLR (4th) 342; 2005 FCA 193 (CanLII) ("Although privacy concerns must also be considered, it seems to me that they must yield to public concerns for the protection of intellectual property rights in situations where infringement threatens to erode those rights." paragraph 41); *Society of Composers, Authors*

potential consequences of yielding individuals' intellectual privacy where it conflicts with copyright holders' interests, academic commentators have conducted widespread reconnaissance for support of intellectual privacy; these inquiries have spanned, among others, freedom of expression,[31] data protection,[32] human rights,[33] and ethics.[34] It is only a matter of time before a complaint is brought under data protection law.

B. Surveillance and Related Jurisprudence under Canada's Data Protection Law

This section briefly reviews surveillance and related monitoring cases under a well-known data protection law based on fair information practices and approved by the European Community[35] as providing adequate protection: Canada's federal data protection law, the Personal Information Protection and Electronic Documents Act.[36]

Except in situations where provincial laws apply, PIPEDA regulates the collection, use, and disclosure of personal information in the private sector in Canada. The Act contains a number of obligations to which organizations must adhere in

---

and Music Publishers of Canada v Canadian Assn. of Internet Providers, [2004] 240 DLR (4th) 193; 2004 SCC 45 (CanLII) [*SOCAN v CAIP*].

31. See Julie Cohen, "A Right to Read Anonymously: A Closer Look at 'Copyright Management' in Cyberspace," *Conn. L. Rev* 28 (1996): 981 (evaluating the import of diminished intellectual privacy for traditional notions of freedom of expression and freedom of thought).

32. See Graham Greenleaf, "IP, Phone Home: Privacy as Part of Copyright's Digital Commons in Hong Kong and Australian Law" in *Hochelaga Lectures 2002: The Innovation Commons*, ed. Lawrence Lessig (Hong Kong: Sweet & Maxwell Asia, 2003) (asserting that amendments to copyright law and data protection law may be needed to protect intellectual privacy); Ian Kerr, "If Left to Their Own Devices . . . How DRM and Anti-circumvention Laws Can Be Used to Hack Privacy" in *In the Public Interest: The Future of Canadian Copyright Law*, ed. Michael Geist (Toronto: Irwin Law, 2005) 167–210.

33. See P. Bernt Hugenholtz. "Caching and Copyright," (2000) 22 European Intellectual Property Review 482, 485–486.

34. See Ian Kerr, "DRM & the Automation of Virtue" (Keynote presentation to Identity and Identification in a Networked World, September 2006) http://idtrail.org/content/view/542/42/.

35. In December 2001, the Commission of the European Communities issued Decision 2002/2/EC pursuant to Article 25(6) of Directive 95/46/EC of the European Parliament and of the Council of 24 October 1995 on the protection of individuals with regard to the processing of personal data and on the free movement of such data, OJ L 281, 23.11.1995, p. 31. Decision 2002/2/EC states that Canada is considered as providing an adequate level of protection of personal data transferred from the European Community to recipients subject to PIPEDA.

36. Personal Information Protection and Electronic Documents Act SC 2000 c. 5 (Canada) [PIPEDA].

their handling of personal information, organized roughly around the following ten principles listed in the Act:

(1) Accountability
(2) Identifying Purposes
(3) Consent
(4) Limiting Collection
(5) Limiting Use, Disclosure, and Retention
(6) Accuracy
(7) Safeguards
(8) Openness
(9) Individual Access
(10) Challenging Compliance

Subsection 5(3) of PIPEDA contains an over-arching requirement under the Act that cannot be waived by consent or any other exception—it requires organizations to collect, use, and disclose personal information "only for purposes that a reasonable person would consider are appropriate in the circumstances."[37] This section is central in surveillance cases under PIPEDA, which are among the most frequently occurring and contentious cases.

Section 7 can also arise in surveillance cases. This section contains a number of exceptions to the general requirement to obtain consent for the collection, use, and disclosure of personal information. For example, paragraph 7(1)(b) permits the collection of information without consent if

... it is reasonable to expect that the collection with the knowledge or consent of the individual would compromise the availability or the accuracy of the information and the collection is reasonable for purposes related to investigating a breach of an agreement or a contravention of the laws of Canada or a province.[38]

Organizations often rely on this exception when using surveillance to investigate or deter crime or to investigate employee misconduct.

The leading surveillance case under PIPEDA is *Eastmond v. Canadian Pacific Railway*.[39] In this case, employees filed a complaint after their employer, Canadian Pacific Railway (CPR), installed video cameras in a rail yard where the employees worked. The cameras captured fixed areas of the yard and had no

---

37. PIPEDA, s. 5(3) (n. 36).
38. PIPEDA, s. 7(1)(b) (n. 36).
39. Office of the Privacy Commissioner of Canada, "PIPEDA Case Summary #114: Employee Objects to Company's Use of Digital Video Surveillance Cameras" (November 6, 2003) http://www.privcom.gc.ca/cf-dc/2003/cf-dc_030123_e.asp; *Eastmond v Canadian Pacific Railway* [2004] 16 Admin LR (4th) 275 (FC). The author was a member of the legal team acting for Canadian Pacific Railway in this case.

ability to pan or zoom. CPR retained the recordings for a short time in a locked cabinet. The tapes were overwritten and never viewed if no incidents were reported. The recordings were not monitored or reviewed by CPR for any other purpose.

CPR claimed that it had a legitimate need to install the cameras for the following purposes: deterring incidents of theft, vandalism, and trespassing, improving employee security, and aiding in the investigation of incidents.

The Commissioner applied a four-part test under subsection of 5(3) of PIPEDA in determining whether a reasonable person would find CPR's stated purposes to be appropriate. The Federal Court agreed to be guided by the test in this case and made the following findings, summarized after each item of the test:

(i) *Is camera surveillance and recording necessary to meet a specific need?*
CPR had established a legitimate need to install the cameras based on a history of incidents at the yard, and acceptance of the cameras' deterrent effects.

(ii) *Is camera surveillance and recording likely to be effective in meeting that need?*
The lack of incidents since the cameras had been installed showed that the cameras were effective.

(iii) *Is the loss of privacy proportional to the benefit gained?*
Security benefits were tangible and privacy loss was minimal (1) the recording took place where individuals had a reduced expectation of privacy and (2) CPR had taken a number of steps to ensure that the invasion of privacy was minimal.

(iv) *Is there a less privacy-invasive way of achieving the same end?*
CPR had considered and rejected other more costly alternatives, including fences and security guards.

The court upheld CPR's installation of the cameras under PIPEDA. The *Eastmond* four-part test has also been applied in subsequent cases; other leading cases include a case where the Commissioner held that a credit card company can monitor individuals' purchasing history in order to detect fraud and for other purposes.[40] A similar finding was issued in the copyright context where the Commissioner upheld the use of a continuous telephone connection to a satellite television unit for billing purposes and for the specific purpose of detecting and acting on unauthorized use of copyrighted works.[41] In doing so, however,

---

40. Office of the Privacy Commissioner of Canada, "PIPEDA Case Summary #296: Language of Consent and Monitoring Activity Challenged" (April 20, 2005) http://www.privcom.gc.ca/cf-dc/2005/296_050314_02_e.asp.

41. Office of the Privacy Commissioner of Canada, "PIPEDA Case Summary #276: The Privacy Implications of Pay Per View and Piracy Prevention Measures" (September 27, 2004) http://www.privcom.gc.ca/cf-dc/2004/cf-dc_040902_01_e.asp.

the Commissioner was careful to note that the system was not collecting information about individuals' viewing habits.

Finally, in a landmark 2007 case involving violations of PIPEDA by TJX, operator of Winners and HomeSense stores,[42] the Commissioner agreed to permit TJX to collect drivers' licenses and other information for fraud prevention in the context of receipt-less merchandise returns. In past cases, the Commissioner had stated that collecting this information was inappropriate and unnecessary in this context.[43] In this case, however, the Commissioner deviated from past findings and accepted that TJX could collect the information on condition that it immediately convert the information to unique numbers using a cryptographic hashing function. This technique would convert the license numbers into a unique new number referred to as a "hash value," therein rendering the drivers' license numbers unreadable to TJX employees. The drivers' license information would be retained only temporarily for this purpose.

C. Preliminary Questions

Before turning to the elements of the four-part test under PIPEDA, it is important to briefly note that the question of whether a reasonable person would find DRM monitoring appropriate is only one of the questions that would need to be assessed in determining whether such practices are in compliance with data protection law.

Personal Information First, under PIPEDA or another data protection law, DRM monitoring would have to involve a collection, use or disclosure of "personal information"[44] or "personal data"[45] in order for the law to apply. The answer to this question depends on precisely what information a DRM system collects and whether it can be linked to an identifiable individual, even if the individual is not actually identified by the information. The answer is highly contextual—for example, a name may be personal information if it is linked to other records; however, if it is not linked to other records, then it may not be

---

42. Office of the Privacy Commissioner of Canada, "Report of an Investigation into the Security, Collection and Retention of Personal Information—TJX Companies Inc./ Winners Merchant International L.P." (September 25, 2007) http://www.privcom.gc.ca/ cf-dc/2007/tjx_rep_070925_e.asp.

43. Office of the Privacy Commissioner of Canada, "PIPEDA Case Summary #361: Retailer Requires Photo Identification to Exchange an Item" (February 23, 2007) http:// www.privcom.gc.ca/cf-dc/2006/361_20061114_e.asp. See also, Office of the Privacy Commissioner of Canada, "Settled Case Summary #16: Personal Information on Receipts Removed, Return Information Limited" (February 13, 2006) http://www.privcom.gc.ca/ ser/2005/s16_051121_e.asp.

44. PIPEDA, ss. 2(1) & 4(1) (n. 36).

45. See U.K., Data Protection Act 1998 c. 29 s. 1(1) (definition of "personal data").

personal information.[46] The Federal Court of Canada has adopted the following definition of "personal information" developed by the Commissioner:

> Information will be about an identifiable individual where there is a serious possibility that an individual could be identified through the use of that information, alone or in combination with other available information.[47]

There are indications that DRM monitoring would often involve personal information. For example, in *SOCAN v. CAIP*, Justice LeBel of the Supreme Court of Canada lent support to the idea that the kind of information processed by DRM is sensitive personal information:

> . . . [an individual's surfing and downloading activities] tend to reveal core biographical information about a person. Privacy interests of individuals will be directly implicated where owners of copyrighted works or their collective societies attempt to retrieve data from Internet Service Providers about an end users downloading of copyrighted works.[48]

This statement, that privacy is implicated where copyright holders attempt to gather data from ISPs, suggests that privacy is implicated where the same or even more detailed information is gathered directly from individuals through DRM monitoring. The lack of judicial process in the collection of information through DRM may aggravate potential privacy violations: in keeping with good public policy,[49] this kind of information has typically only been available to copyright owners through a judicial process.[50]

To make use of another example, there is a series of findings under PIPEDA holding that Internet protocol (IP) addresses are personal information.[51]

---

46. Office of the Privacy Commissioner of Canada, "PIPEDA Case Summary #205: What Is in a Name?" (November 6, 2003) http://www.privcom.gc.ca/cf-dc/2003/cf-dc_030805_03_e.asp.

47. *Gordon v Canada (Health)*, 2008 FC 258 (CanLII) ¶34. This case arose under the Privacy Act, R.S.C. 1985, c. P-21 and the Access to Information Act, R.S., 1985, c. A–1.

48. *SOCAN*, 155 (n. 30).

49. *Irwin Toy Ltd. v Doe* [2000] O.J. No. 3318 (S.C.J.) ("In keeping with the protocol or etiquette developed in the usage of the internet, some degree of privacy or confidentiality with respect to the identity of the Internet protocol address of the originator of a message has significant safety value and is in keeping with what should be perceived as being good public policy.").

50. See *BMG*, 37 (n. 30).

51. Office of the Privacy Commissioner of Canada, "PIPEDA Case Summary #25: A Broadcaster Accused of Collecting Personal Information via Web Site" (November 6, 2003) http://www.privcom.gc.ca/cf-dc/2001/cf-dc_011120_e.asp (accessed March 7, 2008); Office of the Privacy Commissioner of Canada, "PIPEDA Case Summary #315: Web-Centred Company's Safeguards and Handling of Access Request and Privacy Complaint Questioned" (August 31, 2005) http://www.privcom.gc.ca/cf-dc/2005/315_20050809_03_e.asp; Office of the Privacy Commissioner of Canada, "PIPEDA Case Summary #319:

The European Union Data Protection Working Party has also concluded that IP addresses are personal data:

> The Working Party wishes to emphasize that IP addresses attributed to Internet users are personal data and are protected by EU Directives 95/46 and 97/66. . .

> In the case of IP addresses the ISP is always able to make a link between the user identity and the IP addresses and so may be other parties, for instance by making use of available registers of allocated IP addresses or by using other existing technical means.[52]

Since DRM will almost always involve the collection of IP addresses as part of its operation, along with other information that specifically identifies individuals (e.g., name, credit card information), DRM will in many cases almost certainly be subject to the application of data protection laws.

Consent Second, a host of questions arise around the issue of consent, a cornerstone of data protection laws. Subject to some exceptions, PIPEDA requires organizations to obtain consent from individuals for the collection, use, and disclosure of their personal information.[53]

It may be difficult to reconcile the operation of DRM with the requirement to obtain consent under data protection law. Consent provisions are typically included in privacy policies or in licenses managed by DRM. There is some question as to whether such consents are meaningful and adequate, as in other e-commerce contexts where standard-form licenses arise. The following statement appeared in a recent study of actual DRM-enabled content delivery systems:

> The ways that information is collected and processed during use of the services examined is almost impenetrably complex. It is difficult to determine exactly what data a service collects, and merely discovering that separate monitoring entities sit behind the services requires a careful reading of the services' privacy policies.[54]

Others have conducted exceptional analyses on the issue of consent and concluded that there are good reasons to believe that standard-form consents

---

ISP's Anti-Spam Measures Questioned" (February 13, 2006) http://www.privcom.gc.ca/cf-dc/2005/319_20051103_e.asp.

52. Article 29 Data Protection Working Group, "Opinion 2/2002 on the Use of Unique Identifiers in Telecommunication Terminal Equipments: The Example of IPV6" (May 30, 2002), http://ec.europa.eu/justice_home/fsj/privacy/docs/wpdocs/2002/wp58_en.pdf: 3.

53. PIPEDA, Principle 4.3 (n. 36).

54. Mulligan et al., "How DRM-Based Content Delivery Systems Disrupt Expectations of 'Personal Use,'" 84 (n. 13).

may be inadequate in connection with the operation of DRM, both as a broader public policy matter and as a matter of compliance with data protection law.[55] Kerr put the issue as follows:

> Like copyright, privacy law's compromise between the needs of organizations and the right of privacy of individuals (with respect to their personal information) will also be put in serious jeopardy if, irrespective of privacy rules, content owners are able to impose their terms and conditions through standard form contracts with complete impunity.[56]

Irrespective of the critical issue of consent, however, is the over-arching question of whether, despite a standard-form consent, an organization's use of DRM is an appropriate purpose under subsection 5(3) of PIPEDA.

D. Would the Man on the Clapham Omnibus Find DRM Monitoring Appropriate?

Is Monitoring Necessary to Meet a Specific Need? The question of need is an empirical matter weighed by the evidence submitted in support of or against a measure that diminishes privacy. In the *Eastmond* case, for example, CPR provided evidence of a history of incidents at its rail yards and argued that the surveillance was necessary to respond to those incidents.

In the case of DRM, there is conflicting broad-based evidence as to whether there is a need for monitoring access to and use of copyrighted works in order to prevent, deter, or investigate copyright infringement. Proponents of DRM assert that it is needed in order to protect copyrighted works against infringement in the digital realm, often pointing to economic studies about the losses of revenues that some copyright holders suffer as a result of infringement.[57] Opponents of DRM point to other studies which indicate that copyright infringement in the digital age has not had a net-negative economic impact on certain copyright holders.[58] Thus, on a macro level, there may be some question as to whether there is a specific need for DRM at all. Further, given that many copyright holders do not utilize DRM, and given that some copyright holders that have

---

55. See Kerr, "If Left to Their own Devices," (n. 32).

56. Kerr, "If Left to Their Own Devices," 192 (n. 32).

57. See Stan J. Liebowitz, "Economists Examine File-Sharing and Music Sales"in *Industrial Organization and the Digital Economy*, eds. G. Illing and M. Peitz (Cambridge: MIT Press, 2006) 145–174.

58. See Birgitte Andersen and Marion Frenz, "The Impact of Music Downloads and P2P File-Sharing on the Purchase of Music: A Study for Industry Canada" (October 30, 2007) http://strategis.ic.gc.ca/epic/site/ippd-dppi.nsf/en/h_ip01456e.html (accessed March 7, 2008); Felix Oberholzer-Gee and Koleman Strumpf, "The Effect of File Sharing on Record Sales An Empirical Analysis," *Journal of Political Economy*, 115 (2007): 1–42.

utilized DRM in the past have backtracked and dropped DRM,[59] the question of need is certainly an unsettled one.

On a micro level, however, a specific copyright holder may be able to show that it is in a unique situation that differs from industry-wide reports. For example, assume for the sake of argument that non-CPR rail yards in Canada typically do not have any security problems and in fact are 100% incident-free. All else being equal, one would assume that the result in *Eastmond* would nevertheless have been the same if CPR had been able to show, as it did, that *it* had a specific need at its rail yard.

The first element of the *Eastmond* test is difficult to apply to DRM monitoring, and is highly fact-specific. Despite the fact that there is broad-based disagreement as to whether alleged copyright infringement in the digital age has on the whole had a negative impact on copyright holders' interests, some organizations will likely be able to demonstrate a specific need—a specific history of copyright infringements—that they will be able to claim under PIPEDA necessitates adopting a monitoring solution.

Is Monitoring Likely to be Effective in Meeting That Need? Just as there is disagreement about whether there is a broad-based need for DRM monitoring, there is disagreement about whether DRM is effective in protecting copyrighted works against infringement. Some suggest that DRM monitoring is not and cannot ever be effective.[60]

Some copyright holders appear to conditionally agree with this conclusion, claiming that DRM technology will be ineffective if it is not protected by additional legal protections—called anti-circumvention laws: "As no technological measure can permanently resist deliberate attacks, a TPM is only as good as its legal protection."[61] Ineffectiveness of DRM may also be one of the reasons why many copyright holders who have experimented with DRM have recently reduced or discontinued its use.

As in the case of establishing a specific need for monitoring, the question of effectiveness is also highly fact-dependent. Specific organizations may be able to demonstrate that as a result of their market, works, technology, or other factors, their DRM monitoring would be effective. They may also be able to demonstrate that infringements declined or ceased following implementation of a DRM system.

---

59. See (n. 23–25) and accompanying text.

60. See Peter Biddle, Paul England, Marcus Peinado, Bryan Willman, "The Darknet and the Future of Content Distribution" in *Digital Rights Management* (Heidelberg: Springer, 2003) 155–176; Cory Doctorow, "Microsoft Research DRM Talk" (June 17, 2004) http://craphound.com/msftdrm.txt.

61. International Federation of the Phonographic Industry, "The WIPO Treaties: Technological Measures" (March 2003) http://www.ifpi.org/content/library/wipo-treaties-technical-measures.pdf.

The court in *Eastmond* was persuaded by CPR's evidence that no incidents had been reported since it had implemented its video surveillance system.[62]

Is the Loss of Privacy Proportional to the Benefit Gained? Proportionality is likely the single most important and controversial element of the test in the case of DRM. This element raises important questions about the value of intellectual privacy and how we ought to measure its loss. Recall that in Eastmond, the court considered relevant the fact that the cameras were in parking lots and other locations where there was a lower reasonable expectation of privacy, and that CPR had otherwise minimized the privacy impact of the cameras (including by not viewing the recordings unless incidents were reported). Proportionality thus depends in part on the interests of stake on both sides of the equation—it is both the value of the benefit and the value of the loss of privacy that must be considered.

In the context of DRM, it is possible that public and policy discourse regarding copyright in the digital age has disproportionately focused on the single issue of peer-to-peer (p2p) file-sharing of popular music and movies.[63] As a possible consequence, questions surrounding the resolution of digital copyright matters in general, including questions regarding intellectual privacy, may be viewed by some as being relatively trivial.[64] Some might conclude that activities such as listening to "Top 40" music and watching Hollywood movies, for example, like the parking lots in *Eastmond*, do not attract a strong expectation of privacy. For some, these categories of creative works might not *prima facie* implicate deeply-held notions regarding the importance of intellectual privacy in the same way that political or religious writings might.

As copyright works are increasingly disseminated in digital form, however, the stakes undeniably increase in the way that copyright's relationship with intellectual privacy is addressed. There are already signs that these stakes are increasing. Consider, for example, that the two books referenced at the outset of this introduction—*Rights of Man* and *The Clockmaker,* originally published in the eighteenth and early nineteenth century, respectively—have since been digitized

---

62. *Eastmond,* 179 (n. 39).

63. See Laura Murray, "Copyright Talk: Patterns and Pitfalls in Canadian Policy Discourses" in *In the Public Interest: The Future of Canadian Copyright Law,* ed. Michael Geist (Toronto: Irwin Law, 2005) 15–60, 27–28 (". . . music file-sharing is commonly taken to be the predominant Internet activity and policy problem that sets the tone for or even trumps all others.").

64. Murray "Copyright Talk" 30 (n. 63) (". . . the emphasis on music file-sharing may also make copyright reform seem less than earth-shaking: Members of Parliament might well wonder how important a bunch of teenagers ripping off music can be in the grand scheme of pressing government issues. This trivialization is unfortunate given the serious repercussions of the numerous details of copyright legislation for a growing range of economic and educational sectors.").

and are available for download on the Internet.[65] Indeed, as of early 2007, at least tens of thousands of books from libraries around the world were being digitized each week. Reports indicate that Google, one of the leaders in book digitization, "intends to scan every book ever published, and to make the full texts searchable, in the same way that Web sites can be searched on the company's engine at google.com."[66] Libraries and archives around the world are engaged in similar projects, as are publishers and book distributors.[67]

Using digitization to increase access to the information contained in books is certainly laudable; however, it does not come without risk. If DRM or other means of diminishing intellectual privacy were used in association with access to and use of *Rights of Man, The Clockmaker*, or "every book ever published," then the traditional relationship between copyright and intellectual privacy would be entirely rewritten. It is in access to books, newspapers, magazines, journal articles, and other media that questions of intellectual exploration, access to information, and intellectual privacy intuitively seem most sacred. Thus, far from being a problem circumscribed by interests at stake in "Top 40" music and Hollywood movies, the question of intellectual privacy is all the more patently pressing in light of the potential for the increasing digitization of literary works. The digitization of books is offered as an example here because it provides an easy insight into reasons why questions at the nexus of copyright and intellectual privacy are important.

Further, consistent with Justice LeBel's view that information about enjoyment of copyrighted works tends to reveal core biographical information about individuals,[68] there are good reasons to reject distinctions between various forms of copyrighted works when it comes to the application of the *Eastmond* test. Differences between "Top 40" music and Hollywood movies on the one hand, and political or religious writings on the other hand, ought not to bear to any

---

65. Both of these works have been digitized by Project Gutenberg and by Google. They are available for download at the following URLs: *Rights of Man* Project Gutenberg edition http://www.gutenberg.org/dirs/etext03/twtp210.txt, Google Books edition http://books. google.com/books?id=FKlNmiM4GJwC&pg=PA1&dq=rights±of±man, and *The Clockmaker* Project Gutenberg edition http://www.gutenberg.org/dirs/etext04/clckm10.txt, Google Books edition http://books.google.com/books?id=804lAAAAMAAJ&pg=PA1&dq=the±clo ckmaker&as_brr=1.

66. Jeffrey Toobin, "Google's Moon Shot: The Quest for the Universal Library" *The New Yorker* (February 5, 2007) 30–35, 30.

67. See University of Michigan Library, "One Million Digitized Books" (February 2, 2008) http://www.lib.umich.edu/news/millionth.html, (in partnership with Google); Cristina Jimenez, "British Library Books Go Digital" *BBC News* (September 28, 2007) http://news.bbc.co.uk/2/hi/technology/7018210.stm. The example of eReader was discussed earlier in this chapter. See also Reuters, "Report: Random House to Sell Book Chapters" (February 11, 2008) http://www.news.com/2110-1026_3-6229985.html.

68. *SOCAN*, 155 (n. 30).

significant degree—if at all—on whether an individual has an expectation of privacy in his or her enjoyment of the work. Anyone who has grown up with rock-and-roll music, for example, can attest to the importance that such music had on their identity and cultural development. Foucault offers the following view of the significance of rock music:

> Not only is rock music (much more than jazz used to be) an integral part of the life of many people, but it is a cultural initiator: to like rock, to like a certain kind of rock rather than another, is also a way of life, a manner of reacting; it is a whole set of tastes and attitudes.[69]

Is the loss of privacy proportional to the benefit gained in the case DRM? This is a difficult question. It may be inappropriate under PIPEDA to engage in such a broad-based consideration of the loss of privacy and proportionality. Perhaps the "loss" and the "benefit" ought to be confined to the specific case at issue. As in other elements of the test, there is a tension between focusing narrowly on the case at hand and focusing more broadly on the public policy ramifications of finding one way or another.

The loss of privacy may also be mitigated by other factors. For example, if an organization were to adopt the *Eastmond* "locked cabinet" approach to collecting personal information in DRM, then that would likely weigh in favor of it being found appropriate. Adopting an encryption approach along the lines described in the TJX case might also minimize privacy loss, making it more likely that the loss would be proportional to the benefit gained by the monitoring.

Is There a Less Privacy-Invasive Way of Achieving the Same End? Like the proportionality analysis, the final element in the *Eastmond* test is critical. Although *Eastmond* held that organizations are entitled to reject less privacy-invasive alternatives if they are more costly, alternatives must be properly considered.

In the case of DRM, there do appear to be less privacy-invasive ways of achieving the same end; DRM need not be inherently privacy-invasive. A number of commentators have noted that DRM design need not involve constant monitoring or the collection of personal information.[70] Ensuring that individuals are authorized to access or use particular content, which is a central purpose of DRM, does not necessarily require monitoring and the collection of personal information.

---

69. Michel Foucault, Pierre Boulez, "Contemporary Music and the Public" John Rahn Perspectives of New Music 24 no. 1 (1985), 6–12.

70. For a discussion of these proposals, see Alex Cameron, "Infusing Privacy Norms in DRM—Incentives and Perspectives from Law" in *Information Security Management, Education and Privacy, IFIP 18th World Computer Congress, TC11 19th International Information Security Workshops, 22–27 August 2004, Toulouse, France,* eds. Yves Deswarte, Frederic Cuppens, Sushil Jajodia and Lingyu Wang (Berlin: Kluwer, 2004): 293–309; Kerr "If Left to Their Own Devices," 183–185 (n. 32).

These alternative solutions may render privacy-invasive DRM inappropriate in most cases under the *Eastmond* test.

IV. CONCLUSIONS

The use of digital technologies to create, enjoy, and disseminate copyrighted works has highlighted tensions that have long existed between copyright and intellectual privacy. As part of a broader project aimed at reconciling those tensions within the copyright system, this brief chapter has crystallized some of the challenges posed by the use of digital technologies in association with copyrighted works. It is hoped that this discussion contributes to a clearer understanding of the issues between copyright and intellectual privacy, as well as what is ultimately and more broadly at stake.

This chapter also considered the application of data protection law to DRM practices. This jurisprudence is important for many reasons. For example, data protection laws are influential in shaping the future course of privacy in general. Through the repeated application of principles developed in the cases, including the *Eastmond* case, PIPEDA helps to guide the genesis of new technologies and practices. In other words, the DRM monitoring systems that PIPEDA helps to shape are the very systems that this author's broader project must account for in reconciling tensions between copyright and intellectual privacy within copyright.

The analysis under data protection law is also suggestive of possible questions that copyright might ask itself in designing principles and rules for addressing intellectual privacy within copyright. As suggested in some of the analysis in this chapter, however, there may be something of a disconnect under the data protection law analysis between results in particular cases and results that more broadly address the proper balance between competing copyright and intellectual privacy interests.

In other words, the *Eastmond* test might produce results in particular cases that may be at odds with a broader or higher-level balancing between copyright and intellectual privacy. Further, if certain forms of "lowbrow" copyrighted works were understood to be the equivalent of the parking lots in *Eastmond*—"places" where an individual's expectation of privacy is low or nonexistent—then the *Eastmond* test would fail to adequately recognize the biographical nature of copyrighted works and the potentially invasive profiling and diminishment of intellectual privacy that can result from monitoring individuals' activities in that context. Austin puts this potential shortcoming of the *Eastmond* test more generally as follows:

> . . . this test will not adequately protect privacy unless it includes, as a first step, an inquiry into the nature and extent of the privacy interest at stake.

Without this, the test . . . [misses] the important initial step of defining the right in question and the manner in which it is being violated. Because of this, the danger is that this test for reasonable purposes will become a test for limiting privacy rather than enhancing it. To counter this danger, what is needed is a return to the very difficult questions involved in defining privacy and its value. In other words, fair information practices must grapple with, rather than avoid, the same challenges facing other regimes of privacy protection such as constitutional law.[71]

When applied at the nexus between copyright and privacy, data protection laws such as PIPEDA thus stimulate a number of questions and areas for future work. This work is needed especially if principles and rules to account for intellectual privacy within the legal concept of copyright are to bear any resemblance to the *Eastmond* test. For example, further work is needed in defining intellectual privacy and its broader social value, perhaps informed in part by intellectual privacy's value to the objectives of copyright.

---

71. Lisa M. Austin, "Is Consent the Foundation of Fair Information Practices? Canada's Experience under PIPEDA" (November 2005) *University of Toronto, Legal Studies Research Paper No. 11–05* Available at SSRN: http://ssrn.com/abstract=864364: 43.

4. A HEURISTICS APPROACH TO UNDERSTANDING PRIVACY-PROTECTING BEHAVIORS IN DIGITAL SOCIAL ENVIRONMENTS

ROBERT CAREY AND JACQUELYN BURKELL

I. INTRODUCTION

In this chapter, we consider ways that perceptions of harm and risk influence privacy-protecting behaviors in digital social environments (DSEs), with particular emphasis on Web logs and online social networks. By way of introduction, we would like to contrast two incidents from the world of online social networking that demonstrate how such perceptions may provoke very different responses to apparently similar privacy threats.

In 2006, Facebook introduced to its site a seemingly innocuous feature called an RSS news feed, which ensured that any changes a Facebook member made to his or her profile would be automatically disseminated to those members listed in his or her network. Since information of this sort was already evident to other Facebook users, the company supposed that the new feature was merely a convenient way to enhance information sharing among its members. Almost immediately, however, many Facebook users began to complain that the new feature was unacceptably invasive: "[T]he RSS feed publicizes potentially embarrassing developments including romantic breakups, friendships going sour, professional setbacks, and the like. Even though this information was available before, Facebook's active spreading of it via RSS feeds offended hundreds of thousands of the site's users."[1] Indeed, the feature became so unpopular among users that the company eventually capitulated and made the feature optional.

---

1. Erik Sass, "Users Throw Book at Facebook," *Online Media Daily*, http://publications.mediapost.com/index.cfm?fuseaction=Articles.san&s=47811&Nid=23107&p=316563.

Almost exactly one year later, MySpace announced plans to collect and analyze the personal information members publish in their profiles. Fox Interactive intended to use these data to craft customized advertising specifically tailored to the individual enthusiasms and appetites of MySpace members. Unsurprisingly, privacy advocates argued that social network users should not be enrolled in a de facto surveillance campaign: "People should be able to congregate online with their friends without thinking that big brother, whether it is Rupert Murdoch or Mark Zuckerberg, are stealthily peering in," said Jeff Chester, Executive Director at the Center for Digital Democracy in Washington.[2] Interestingly, however, anecdotal reports suggested that users themselves were relatively phlegmatic about the matter. To our knowledge, there has been no concerted effort among MySpace users to stop the data collection.

These anecdotes suggest that DSE users are capable of remarkable ambivalence regarding their online privacy. Social networkers who believed that Facebook's news feed was publicizing intimate details about their personal lives were sufficiently angered to engage in a successful mass protest against the feature, yet MySpace's plans to scour its users' profiles for marketing purposes was greeted with comparative indifference. Considering that both situations involved exactly the same type of publicly-available personal information that users of the networks publish voluntarily, the contradictory behavior seems puzzling. We suggest, however, that the different responses can be explained by considering the way DSE users perceive various risks associated with their privacy, and the way such perceptions influence privacy-protecting behaviors. As the example above suggests, Facebook members had little trouble imagining likely harms if certain forms of personal information—changes to their occupational or relationship status, for example—were broadcast to all the people in their networks. From their perspectives, it mattered little whether the information was already evident on their profiles; the primary harm envisioned was embarrassment that the varied collection of people who constitute a Facebook network—including casual acquaintances who may not often visit their sites—would all be notified of consequential changes to one's life.

As several researchers have shown, DSE users often expend a great deal of effort to manage and protect certain aspects of their privacy, while remaining relatively unconcerned about other kinds of privacy threats. Accordingly, the purpose of this paper is to explore why users seem to be more highly attuned to certain kinds of risks associated with privacy in the context of DSEs. Our primary contention is that when people face complex or uncertain situations regarding privacy, they tend to rely on mental shortcuts to simplify their decision-making processes. We suggest that such shortcuts strongly influence both the way people

---

2. Brad Stone, "MySpace Mining Members' Data to Tailor Ads Expressly for Them," *New York Times*, September 18, 2007, C1.

envision the risk of harms occurring to them as a consequence of their privacy being violated, and the consequent enacting of privacy-protecting behaviors. After reviewing relevant literature on the "privacy paradox" in online behavior—that is, the relationship between individuals' intentions to disclose personal information and their actual personal information disclosure behaviors[3]—we consider ways in which privacy is important to DSE users, and how these might be consequential for their understanding and assessment of privacy risks. Specifically, we examine heuristics, the mental shortcuts or "rules of thumb" that decision makers employ to make judgments under uncertainty. We review three heuristics—affect, representativeness, and availability—and speculate how each may contribute to risk judgments about privacy. Finally, we offer testable predictions regarding heuristic reasoning and privacy-related decision making in the context of DSEs.

II. THE PRIVACY PARADOX AND DIGITAL SOCIAL ENVIRONMENTS

Behavioral scientists have for some time been intrigued by the extent to which anticipatory self-reports—that is, statements of intention, attitude, or opinion—can be relied upon to predict behavior. After reviewing the relevant literature, O'Keefe, for example, noted that intention-behavior correlations were at best moderate, indicating that much of the time there is a fair or better-than-fair chance that people will behave in ways that belie their declared intentions.[4]

This disparity is so manifest in studies of privacy-protecting behaviors in online settings that Norberg, Horne, and Horne have called it the "privacy paradox."[5] As they put it, "for all the concern that people express about their personal information, which could be expected to drive one's intended and actual disclosure, our observations of actual marketplace behavior anecdotally suggest that people are less than selective and often cavalier in the protection of their own data profiles."[6] Although they were specifically referring to disclosure in the context of consumer marketing, researchers from various disciplines have made similar observations.[7] In short, although Internet users generally profess

3. Patricia A. Norberg, Daniel R. Horne, and David A. Horne, "The Privacy Paradox: Personal Information Disclosure Intentions Versus Behaviors" *Journal of Consumer Affairs* 41, no. 1 (2007): 100–126.

4. Daniel J. O'Keefe, *Persuasion Theory and Research* (Thousand Oaks, CA: Sage Publications, 2002).

5. Norberg, Horne, and Horne, "The Privacy Paradox," (n. 3).

6. *Ibid.*, 101.

7. See, for example, Alessandro Acquisti and Jens Grossklags, "Privacy and Rationality in Individual Decision Making," *Security and Privacy Magazine, IEEEE* 3, no. 1 (2005): 26–33; Joseph Turow, *Americans and Online Privacy: The System is Broken* (Philadelphia: Annenberg Public Policy Center, 2003); Mark S. Ackerman, Lorrie F. Cranor, and Joseph Reagle,

to be concerned about their privacy, they actually do little to protect it. One way in which this intention-behavior disjuncture is evident is the generally low level of knowledge about, and adoption of, privacy-protecting technologies in various online contexts.

A great deal of research suggests that many users exhibit functional illiteracy where privacy-protecting technologies are concerned. Milne, Bahl, and Rohm found that less than half the Internet users they studied set up their browsers to reject unnecessary cookies, cleared their computer memories after browsing, encrypted their e-mail, used anonymous re-mailers, or used anonymizers while browsing.[8] Jensen, Potts, and Jensen found most of their study subjects vastly overestimated their knowledge of privacy-related technologies and practices.[9] Slightly more than 90% of their study subjects, for example, claimed to understand Internet cookies, but only 14% could actually demonstrate such knowledge. Other investigators have found that users ignore or misunderstand privacy policies and privacy seals;[10] they are unaware of the amount and origin of spyware installed on their computers; and they do not realize that peer-to-peer file sharing programs—such as Kazaa—make sensitive data evident to others.[11] These and other studies support Turow's observation that "the overwhelming majority of U.S. adults who use the Internet at home have no clue about data flows . . . Even if they have a sense that sites track them and collect individual bits of their data, they simply don't fathom how those bits can be used."[12]

It is tempting to attribute the presumed privacy paradox to guilelessness about technology—in other words, to suggest that users who are deeply concerned about their online privacy are somehow stymied by their own ignorance of privacy-protecting technologies. Other studies, however, have shown that even in situations where technical expertise is irrelevant, people are easily induced

---

"Privacy in E-Commerce: Examining User Scenarios and Privacy Preferences" (paper presented in the ACM Conference on Electronic Commerce, 1999), http://www.eecs.umich.edu/~ackerm/pub/99b28/ecommerce.final.pdf.

8. George R. Milne, Andrew J. Rohm, and Shalini Bahl, "Consumers' Protection of Online Privacy and Identity," *The Journal of Consumer Affairs* 38, no. 2 (2004): 217–232.

9. Carlos Jensen, Colin Potts, and Christian Jensen, "Privacy Practices of Internet Users: Self-Reports Versus Observed Behavior," *International Journal of Human-Computer Studies* 63, (2005): 203–227.

10. Turow, *Americans and Online Privacy*; Anthony D. Miyazaki and Sandeep Krishnamurthy, "Internet Seals of Approval: Effects on Online Privacy Policies and Consumer Perceptions," *Journal of Consumer Affairs* 36, (2002): 28–49; Robert LaRose and Nora Rifon, "Your Privacy Is Assured—of Being Invaded: Websites with and without Privacy Seals," *New Media and Society* 8, no. 6 (2006): 1009–1029.

11. Nathaniel S. Good and Aaron J. Krekelberg, "Usability and Privacy: A Study of Kazaa P2P File-Sharing," in *Proceedings of the SIGCHI Conference on Human Factors in Computing Systems, CHI'03*, 2003, http://www.hpl.hp.com/techreports/2002/HPL-2002-163.pdf.

12. Turow, *Americans and Online Privacy*, (n. 10).

to give up personal information.[13] As Norberg, Horne, and Horne suggest, "Perceptions of risk and trust are activated differently when intention measures are taken as compared to actual disclosure settings. . . . It appears that, in the realm of privacy, behavioral intentions may not be an accurate predictor of actual behavior."[14]

The importance of disclosure settings is illustrated in a study conducted by Berendt, Gunther, and Spiekermann, who investigated how privacy concerns relate to actual self-disclosing behavior.[15] They set up a laboratory experiment in which 206 participants took a virtual shopping trip in an online store. At the start of the trip, an anthropomorphic "bot" named Luci introduced herself. Luci's ostensible purpose was to provide product information and to guide participants through the virtual store; her actual purpose, however, was to ask questions of the shoppers. Researchers found that rates of disclosure, even to inappropriate questions, were "alarmingly high,"[16] concluding that "given the right circumstances, online users easily forget about their privacy concerns and communicate even the most personal details without any compelling reason to do so. This holds true in particular when the online exchange is entertaining and appropriate benefits are offered in return for information revelation."[17]

This observation has particular resonance for DSEs, which are almost entirely predicated on the beneficial consequences of personal disclosure. By its nature, social networking requires participants to reveal personal information—without at least some degree of disclosure, social networks cannot be cultivated or maintained.[18] Similarly, most blogs (short for Web logs) fall into the category of personal journals, whose chief purpose is to reflect the thoughts, feelings, and everyday details of their authors' lives.[19]

---

13. See, for example, Norberg, Daniel R. Horne, and David A. Horne, "The Privacy Paradox," (n. 3); Acquisti and Grossklags, "Privacy and Rationality," (n. 7).

14. Norberg, Daniel R. Horne, and David A. Horne, "The Privacy Paradox," (n. 3).

15. Bettina Berendt, Oliver Günther, and Sarah Spiekermann, "Privacy in E-Commerce: Stated Preferences vs. Actual Behavior," *Communications of the ACM* 48, no. 4 (2005): 101–106.

16. Berendt, Günther, and Spiekermann, "Privacy in E-Commerce," (n. 15), 104.

17. *Ibid.*, 103.

18. Judith Donath and Danah Boyd, "Public Displays of Connection," *BT Technology Journal* 22, no. 4 (2004): 71–82; Roya Feizy, "An Evaluation of Identity on Online Social Networking: MySpace," in *Eighteenth International ACM Conference on Hypertext and Hypermedia, Manchester, Sept 2007,* http://www.informatics.sussex.ac.uk/research/groups/softsys/papers/feizy-hypertext07.pdf 2007.

19. Susan Herring, Lois Ann Scheidt, Sabrina Bonus, Elijah Wright, "Bridging the Gap: A Genre Analysis of Weblogs," in *Proceedings of the 37th Annual Hawaii International Conference on System Sciences (HICSS'04),* http://www.ics.uci.edu/~jpd/classes/ ics234cw04/ herring.pdf; Fernanda, B. Viégas, "Bloggers' Expectations of Privacy and Accountability: An Initial Survey," *Journal of Computer-Mediated Communication* 10, no. 3 (2005): article 12; Bonnie Nardi, Diane Schiano, Michelle Gumbrecht, and Luke Schwarz, "Why We Blog," *Communications of the ACM* 47, no. 12 (2004a): 41–46.

Given the centrality of self-revelation to DSE productions, it is not surprising that they constitute rich troves of personal information. Many profiles on social networking sites, for example, have been shown to include identifying information such as full or partial name, sex, birth date, phone number, high school, or current residence.[20] Some research has verified that much of the personal information culled from samples of network profiles is indeed accurate.[21] Many bloggers, too, provide full or partial names, contact information, and demographic information such as age, address, or occupation.[22] Personal photographs are another common feature of blogs and social network profiles; indeed, the majority of MySpace and Facebook profiles include an image,[23] and many of these are photographs suitable for direct identification.[24]

The revelation of such detailed personal information through blogs and social network profiles obviously invites a range of privacy threats. Marketers, for example, are interested in non-identifying personal information reflecting attitudes, beliefs, desires, and preferences, to support research agendas,[25] identify market

20. Amanda Lenhart and Mary Madden, *Teens, Privacy, & Online Social Networks* (Washington, DC: PEW Internet and American Life Project, 2007); Ralph Gross and Alessandro Acquisti, "Information Revelation and Privacy in Online Social Networks (the Facebook Case)," in *ACM Workshop on Privacy in the Electronic Society (WPES)*, 2005, http://www.heinz.cmu.edu/~acquisti/papers/privacy-facebook-gross-acquisti.pdf; Cliff Lampe, Nicole Ellison, and Charles Steinfield, "A Face(book) in the Crowd: Social Searching vs. Social Browsing," in *Proceedings of the 2006 20th Anniversary Conference on Computer Supported Cooperative Work*, http://delivery.acm.org/10.1145/1190000/1180901/p167-lampe.pdf?key1=1180901&key2=0211721911&coll=GUIDE&dl=GUIDE&CFID=371 88441&CFTOKEN=27270162; Harvey Jones and José Hiram Soltren, "Facebook: Threats to Privacy," *Massachusetts Institute of Technology*, http://www-swiss.ai.mit.edu/6805/student-papers/fall05-papers/facebook.pdf.

21. Alessandro Acquisti and Ralph Gross, "Imagined Communities: Awareness, Information Sharing and Privacy on the Facebook" (paper presented at PET 2006), http://privacy.cs.cmu.edu/dataprivacy/projects/ facebook/facebook2.pdf.

22. Herring et al., "Bridging the Gap"; David A. Huffaker and Sandra L. Calvert, "Gender, Identity, and Language Use in Teenage Blogs," Journal of Computer-Mediated Communication 10, no. 2, article 1 (2005), http://jcmc.indiana.edu/vol10/issue2/huffaker. html; Bonnie A. Nardi, Diane J. Schiano, and Michelle Gumbrecht, "Blogging as Social Activity, or, Would You Let 900 Million People Read Your Diary?" in *Proceedings of the 2004 ACM Conference on Computer Supported Cooperative Work, CSCW'04*, http://home.comcast.net/~diane.schiano/CSCW04.Blog.pdf; Viégas, "Bloggers' Expectations," (n. 19).

23. Catherine Dwyer, Starr Roxanne Hiltz, and Katia Passerini, "Trust and Privacy Concern within Social Networking Sites: A Comparison of Facebook and MySpace," in *Proceedings of the Thirteenth Americas Conference on Information Systems, Keystone, Colorado August 09-12 2007*, http://csis.pace.edu/~dwyer/research/DwyerAMCIS2007.pdf; Lenhart and Madden, *Teens, Privacy, & Online Social Networks*, (n. 20).

24. Gross and Acquisti, "Information Revelation and Privacy," (n. 20).

25. Mike Thelwall, "Blog Searching: The First General-Purpose Source of Retrospective Public Opinion in the Social Sciences?" *Online Information Review* 31, no. 3 (2007): 277–289.

trends,[26] select potential customers who are likely to influence others,[27] or target ads to specific consumers who are likely to respond based on their profile information.[28] Traditional concerns about online identity theft, fraud, and stalking have been exacerbated by the inclusion of personal photographs in various DSE applications, compromising visual anonymity,[29] and new applications allow for sophisticated data mining of blogs and social network profiles.[30] Additionally, archiving renders even deleted data accessible for analysis for an extended period.

Despite these threats, the privacy paradox appears to be just as operative in the DSE context as it is in more traditional online settings. A survey of Facebook users, for example, found a strong discrepancy between subjects' stated privacy attitudes and their actual privacy-protecting behaviors.[31] The researchers "detected little or no relation between participants' reported privacy attitudes and their likelihood of providing [personal] information" online. Even among the students who claimed to be very concerned about privacy, 40% provided their class schedule on Facebook, 22% published their address, and 16% posted both. Along similar lines, a 2006 survey suggests that some DSE users may have difficulty envisioning possible harms arising from publishing personal information online. The survey found that "40% of employers say they would consider the Facebook profile of a potential employee as part of their hiring decision, and several reported rescinding offers after checking out Facebook."[32] And yet, when students were informed of this, 42% thought it was a violation of privacy for employers to investigate their profiles, and "64% of students said employers should not consider Facebook profiles during the hiring process."[33]

26. Qiaozhu Mei, Chao Liu, Hang Su, and ChangXiang Zhai, "A Probabilistic Approach to Spatiotemporal Theme Pattern Mining on Weblogs," in *Proceedings of the 15th international Conference on World Wide Web (WWW 2006)*, http://sifaka.cs.uiuc.edu/czhai/pub/wwwo6-blog.pdf; Gilad Mishne and Maarten de Rijke, "Capturing Global Mood Levels Using Blog Posts," *American Association for Artificial Intelligence 2006 (www.aaai.org)*, http://staff.science.uva.nl/~gilad/pubs/aaaio6-blogmoods.pdf.

27. Pedro Domingos and Matt Richardson, "Mining the Network Value of Customers," in *Proceedings on the Seventh ACM SIGKDD International Conference on Knowledge Discovery and Data Mining, 2001*, http://www.cs.washington.edu/homes/pedrod/papers/kddo1a.pdf. 2001.

28. Hugo Liu and Patti Maes, "Interestmap: Harvesting Social Network Profiles for Recommendations," in *Workshop: Beyond Personalization 2005, IUI'05*, http://ambient.media.mit.edu/ assets/_pubs/BP2005-hugo-interestmap.pdf 2005.

29. Hua Qian and Craig R. Scott, "Anonymity and Self-Disclosure on Weblogs," *Journal of Compuer-Mediated Communication* 12, no. 4 (2007): 1428–1451.

30. Gross and Acquisti, "Information Revelation and Privacy," (n. 20).

31. Acquisti and Gross, "Imagined Communities," (n. 21).

32. University of Dayton, "Facing the Consequences of Facebook," *UD News*, http://universityofdayton.blogs.com/local/2006/11/facing_the_cons.html.

33. *Ibid.*

III. A STUDIED MINUET: PRIVACY BEHAVIORS IN DSES

Some researchers have, intriguingly, painted a more complex portrait of privacy-protecting behaviors in DSE environments than the foregoing suggests. Nardi et al. described blogging as a "studied minuet" between author and reader— many bloggers are aware that at least a portion of their audience consists of people with whom they have some offline connection.[34] Since bloggers are concerned that their writings could impinge on these relations, they expend a great deal of effort tailoring their entries to accommodate the sensitivities of their readers.[35] One survey found that bloggers were most sensitive to privacy implications when blogging about friends and family.[36] The same survey results also indicated that 62% of respondents had considered that some topics were "too personal" to write about. Indeed, several respondents explained "that they had encountered trouble with acquaintances in the past because they had disclosed their names on blog entries. After having gotten in trouble, respondents became more sensitive to the issue of identification."[37] The primary response to such concerns is to modify content or to limit the blog audience by using filters.[38]

Participants in social networking sites demonstrate similar concerns, insofar as their productions are also directed toward an audience of family, friends, and acquaintances. In one study of Facebook, for example, more than half the subjects identified friends, acquaintances, classmates, fellow students, and family as their target audience, while fewer than half intended their profiles to be viewed by strangers, professors, administrators, or those in law enforcement.[39] In unpublished interviews we conducted with users of online social networks, we found that most participants were primarily attuned to privacy concerns arising from their immediate social relations, rather than unknown others. The following comment is illustrative:

> I'm not really concerned what random third parties think. I mean, it doesn't affect my life. They're never going to affect my life. It's those middle people, like the ex-boyfriends and the friends who you are not friends with anymore. Then it would affect your life because they're out to get you.

---

34. Nardi, Schiano, and Gumbrecht, "Blogging as Social Activity," (n. 22).
35. Qian and Scott, "Anonymity and Self-Disclosure on Weblogs," (n. 29).
36. Viégas, "Bloggers' Expectations of Privacy and Accountability," (n. 19).
37. *Ibid.*
38. Qian and Scott, "Anonymity and Self-Disclosure on Weblogs," (n. 29); Nardi, Schiano, and Gumbrecht, "Blogging as Social Activity," (n. 22).
39. Nicole B. Ellison, Charles Steinfield, and Cliff Lampe, "The Benefits of Facebook "Friends:" Social Capital and College Students' Use of Online Social Network Sites," *Journal of Computer-Mediated Communication* 12, (2007): 1143–1168.

Like bloggers, social network users have developed a repertoire of informal privacy-protecting tactics intended to avoid causing embarrassment to themselves, friends, or family, and foremost among these is content modification.[40]

It appears, then, that DSE users exhibit ambivalence where privacy-protecting behaviors are concerned. As the foregoing research suggests, even those who profess to be concerned about their privacy publish a great deal of revealing personal information about themselves. Users appear to be unaware or unmindful of possible harms arising from profligate disclosures, particularly harms visited upon them by unknown others. Indeed, when users are moved to enact privacy-protecting behaviors, these efforts consist primarily of modifying the stylistics or content of their communications so as to be less revealing to known others. In general, bloggers and social network participants seem most sharply attentive to the constellation of concerns surrounding what DeCew has called expressive privacy,[41] which Goldie summarizes as "one's ability to freely choose, act, self-express and socially interact."[42] For Goldie, the protection of expressive privacy—an actor's efforts to control the degree to which he or she is known by preferred others—is central to the development of close relationships: "Because intimacy is based on the self-disclosure of information, if we were unable to choose or control what information we give out or the degree to which we allow other people to know us, intimate relationships would cease to exist, and essentially everyone would know everything about everyone."[43]

As several researchers have suggested, however, users who are attuned solely to violations of their expressive privacy remain at risk for other sorts of privacy-related harms. Gross and Acquisti point out that the fragile privacy protection afforded to social network users can be circumvented through social engineering or search techniques, such that "one may conclude that the personal information users are revealing even on sites with access control and managed search capabilities effectively becomes public data."[44] Thus, we return to the central question that animates this chapter: why do many users appear to be attuned to certain harms associated with privacy in the context of DSEs, but not to other types of harms? In the remainder of this chapter, we examine the cognitive techniques that decision makers commonly employ to make judgments about risks, and we speculate about ways these may be consequential for DSE users.

---

40. Lenhart and Madden, *Teens, Privacy, & Online Social Networks*, (n. 20).

41. Judith Wagner DeCew, *In Pursuit of Privacy: Law, Ethics & the Rise of Technology* (Ithaca: Cornell University Press, 1977).

42. Janis L. Goldie, "Virtual Communities and the Social Dimension of Privacy," *University of Ottawa Technology and Law Journal* 3, no. 1 (2006): 139.

43. *Ibid.*, 140.

44. Gross and Acquisti, "Information Revelation and Privacy," (n. 20).

IV. HEURISTICS, BIASES, AND THE ESTIMATION OF RISK

Decisions about whether to make personal information evident to others require some sort of calculation regarding the relative costs and benefits of disclosure. In the context of DSEs, this imperative is complicated by the uncertain nature of many harms. For example, while it is certainly possible that a potential employer might view one's compromising Facebook photographs, this outcome is far from certain. In weighing the costs of disclosure, therefore, it is not enough to imagine what might happen—the harm—since this may or may not actually transpire. The decision maker must also come to some reckoning of the harm's likelihood—in other words, the risk.

The central problem of risk assessment, however, is that risks are often unknown. From the decision maker's limited perspective, there may be no way to find out how frequently certain harms occur. In many situations, therefore, it seems there is no reliable way for users to evaluate their own risk of negative outcomes. Kahneman and Tversky called this situation "judgment under uncertainty" and suggested that, when faced with the task of assessing the unknown likelihood of an uncertain event, decision makers are forced to rely on heuristics to make their judgments.[45] These cognitive shortcuts are designed to assist decision makers when information, along with other cognitive resources such as time and attention, is limited.[46]

Heuristics are helpful for risk assessment insofar as they allow the decision maker to bypass complex calculations regarding probability. Often, the result of heuristic reasoning is a response that "satisfices,"[47] meeting the decision maker's immediate need without necessarily being the optimal or exact response. In some cases, the use of heuristics to make decisions has been shown to produce better results than those generated by a fully rational approach.[48] Heuristics may also lead to biases, in which case the decision maker's best guess results in estimates that are predictably biased. In the following section, we consider ways in which three heuristics—affect, availability, and representativeness—might influence DSE users' apprehension of privacy-related risks.

A. The Affect Heuristic

As we have suggested, conventional approaches to the study of risk management have often configured actors as rational decision makers capable of applying

---

45. Daniel Kahneman and Amos Tversky, "Judgment under Uncertainty: Heuristics and Biases," *Science* 185, (1974): 1124–1131.

46. Herbert Simon, "Rational Choice and the Structure of the Environment," *Psychological Review* 63, (1956): 129–138.

47. *Ibid.*

48. Gerd Gigerenzer and Daniel G. Goldstein, "Reasoning the Fast and Frugal Way: Models of Bounded Rationality," *Psychological Review* 103, no. 4 (1996): 650–669.

logic to situations requiring self-protection. Protection motivation theory (PMT), for example, suggests that actors invoke protective behaviors after having appraised the advantages and disadvantages of responding to a perceived threat. This and cognate approaches—such as the theory of reasoned action (TRA) and subjective expected utility (SEU) theory—share "a cost-benefit analysis component in which the individual weighs the costs of taking the precautionary action against the expected benefits of taking that action."[49] These theories assume that the actor possesses sufficient ability to calculate the probabilities of harms or rewards arising from any action.

Increasingly, however, the notion of bounded rationality[50] has become consequential for studies of risk perception. The concept of bounded rationality is consonant with a growing belief among researchers that most risk analysis is performed expediently by what Slovic et al. have called the "experiential" mode of thinking, which is "intuitive, fast, mostly automatic, and not very accessible to conscious awareness."[51] Heuristic processing is central to the experiential system in that it operates quickly and intuitively to make crucial information salient to the decision maker.[52]

One such type of processing is the affect heuristic. "Affect" refers to a feeling of goodness or badness arising from perceptions of a positive or negative stimulus. Researchers argue that such feelings are crucial for the apprehension of risk: if a person's feelings toward an activity are favorable, they are inclined to judge the risks as low and the benefits as high; if their feelings are unfavorable, they tend to judge the opposite—high risk and low benefit.[53] In this sense, affect precedes and directs the individual's judgment of risk and benefit. Finucane et al. examined this hypothesis by presenting decision makers with information designed to influence affect without directly influencing perception of risks or benefits.[54] The researchers demonstrated that when study subjects were given information indicating that nuclear power was highly beneficial—for example,

49. Donna L. Floyd, Steven Prentice-Dunn, Ronald W. Rogers, "A Meta-Analysis of Research on Protection Motivation Theory," *Journal of Applied Social Psychology* 30, no. 2 (2000): 408.

50. Simon, "Rational Choice and the Structure of the Environment," (n.46).

51. Paul Slovic, Melissa L. Finucane, Ellen Peters, and Donald G. MacGregor, "Risk as Analysis and Risk as Feelings: Some Thoughts about Affect, Reason, Risk, and Rationality," *Risk Analysis* 24, no. 2 (2004): 311.

52. Ellen Peters, Kevin D. McCaul, Michael Stefanek, and Wendy Nelson, "A Heuristics Approach to Understanding Cancer Risk Perception: Contributions from Judgment and Decision-Making Research," *Annals of Behavioral Medicine* 31, no. 1 (2006): 45–52.

53. Slovic, Finucane, Peters, and MacGregor, "Risk as Analysis and Risk as Feelings," 311–322 (n. 51).

54. Melissa L. Finucane, Ali Alhakami, Paul Slovic, and Stephen M. Johnson, "The Affect Heuristic in Judgments of Risks and Benefits," *Journal of Behavioral Decision Making* 13, no. 1 (2000): 1–17.

that it does not depend on fossil fuel—they judged its overall risk to be low. Conversely, when subjects were given information suggesting that nuclear power was of minimal benefit—that it produces only a small percentage of the nation's electricity—they judged the risk from nuclear power to be high. Thus, the experiment supports the theory that risk and benefit judgments are influenced, at least in part, by affective evaluation.

We suggest that the affective and experiential nature of risk perception may be relevant to decision making regarding privacy in digital social environments insofar as there is abundant evidence that the kind of revelatory self-writing these media entail effect a positive affect—in other words, that writing about oneself to a real or imagined audience makes one feel good. Much research indicates that writing about life events reduces both negative mood and stress symptoms,[55] by reducing negative mood after traumatic events,[56] and decreasing symptoms of worry, anxiety disorder, and depression.[57] Some research suggests that the expressive self-writing implicit in blogging and social networking affords the same benefits. Finding that many of the bloggers they studied wished to "work through" difficult, traumatic, or personal matters, Nardi et al. state, "[t]he format of frequent post, diary-style, is both outlet and stimulus for working through issues. Often, bloggers turned to the blog as a welcome relief valve, a place to 'get closure out of writing.'"[58]

The affective nature of blogging and social networking may explain why users are sometimes unmindful of certain kinds of privacy risks when they write about themselves. Bloggers and participants in social networking sites are aware of privacy threats, and yet they continue to provide extensive personal information.[59] Research has shown that attention to salient affective cues can

---

55. E.g., Stephen J. Lepore, Melanie A. Greenberg, Michelle Bruno, and Joshua M. Smyth, "Expressive Writing and Health: Self-Regulation of Emotion Related Experience, Physiology, and Behaviour," in *The Writing Cure: How Expressive Writing Promotes Health and Emotional Well-Being*, ed. S. J. Lepore & J. M. Smyth (Washington, DC: American Psychological Association, 2002), 99–117; James W. Pennebaker, "The Effects of Traumatic Disclosure on Physical and Mental Health: The Values of Writing and Talking about Upsetting Events," *International Journal of Emergency Mental Health* 1, (1999): 9–18; Denise M. Sloan and Brian P. Marx, "Taking Pen to Hand: Evaluating Theories Underlying the Written Disclosure Paradigm," *Clinical Psychology: Science and Practice* 11, (2004): 121–137; Joshua M. Smyth, "Written Emotional Expression: Effect Sizes, Outcome Types, and Moderating Variables," *Journal of Consulting and Clinical Psychology* 66, (1998): 174–184.

56. Laura A. King, "The Health Benefits of Writing about Life Goals," *Personality and Social Psychology Bulletin* 27, (2001): 798–807.

57. Natalie Goldman, Michael J. Dugas, Kathryn A. Sexton, and Nicole J. Gervais, "The Impact of Written Exposure on Worry: A Preliminary Investigation," *Behavior Modification* 31, no. 4 (2007): 512–538.

58. Nardi et al., "Why We Blog," 8 (n. 19).

59. Gross and Acquisti, "Information Revelation and Privacy," (n. 20).

lead to a neglect of the probabilistic information necessary to estimate risk accurately.[60] Along similar lines, DSE users whose activities provide them with strong positive feelings may underestimate the harms arising from the disclosure of personal information.

B. The Availability Heuristic

The availability heuristic makes it possible for decision makers to gauge the likelihood of an outcome by retrieving relevant examples from their memories. Outcomes are judged probable if instances of analogous phenomena can be readily brought to mind. This cognitive shortcut allows the decision maker to estimate probabilities expediently by avoiding time-consuming calculations. In one experiment, subjects were asked to estimate which occurs more frequently in the English language: words beginning with the letter "k," or those in which the letter "k" appears in the third position. Specific instances of the first category easily come to mind, while recalling words that fit the second category is an effortful process.[61] The common conclusion, therefore, is that there are more words that start with "k." In fact, the opposite is true.

Several factors influence the application of this heuristic. One of these is retrievability. As we have noted, categories of events or objects that are easy to recall are judged to be more probable. Consequently, events that are more recent, salient, or familiar to the decision maker tend to be judged more likely because they are easily retrievable. There are numerous situations, however, in which decision makers are required to judge the probability of events for which they can recall no specific instances. In these situations, decision makers judge an event to be more likely if it is easier to imagine or construct.

One consequence of the availability heuristic is that the perception of risk increases with direct experience of negative outcomes. In other words, if a person's experience of a negative outcome is memorable, he or she will be more attuned to risk in comparable subsequent situations because examples of negative outcomes are readily available to him or her. Researchers have shown, for example, that there exists a tendency to overestimate cancer risk among people who have friends or acquaintances (not relatives with whom they might share a genetic risk) with cancer.[62] Along similar lines, direct experience with natural disasters has been shown to increase the perception of risk for similar disasters,[63]

60. Yuval Rottenstreich and Christopher K. Hsee, "Money, Kisses, and Electric Shocks: On the Affective Psychology of Risk," *Psychological Science* 12, (2001): 185–190.

61. Amos Tversky and Daniel Kahneman, "Availability: A Heuristic for Judging Frequency and Probability," *Cognitive Psychology* 5 (1973): 207.

62. K. Fiandt, C.H. Pullen, and S.N. Walker, "Actual and Perceived Risk for Chronic Illness in Rural Older Women," *Clinical Excellence for Nurse Practitioners* 3 (1999): 105–115.

63. Michael Siegrist and Heinz Gutscher, "Flooding Risks: A Comparison of Lay People's Perceptions and Experts' Assessments in Switzerland," *Risk Analysis* 26, (2006): 971–979.

while products are viewed as more likely to fail in the future if past failures have been memorable.[64]

The availability heuristic may account for the fact that DSE users often expend a great deal of effort to manage elements of their expressive privacy while remaining indifferent to other kinds of privacy violations. Bloggers and social networkers demonstrate ambivalent behavior in this respect. Although they express concern about socially distant individuals accessing their personal information, much of their actual privacy-protecting behavior tends to be organized around more intimate relations.[65] The mass protest against Facebook's news feed and MySpace users' relative indifference to the data mining of their profiles are illustrative. We suggest that one reason DSE users appear to be more attuned to violations of expressive privacy is the result of the associated harms that are more readily available to them; in other words, it is easier for them to recall uncomfortable consequences of the release of "destructive information" simply because these sorts of episodes are commonplace.[66] Conversely, data mining may excite little interest from DSE users because the harms resulting from this activity are not readily available.

The media are also a source of information about privacy risks, which may be consequential for risk assessments regarding privacy. Since availability may be influenced by emotionally compelling and vivid information,[67] highly publicized events are likely to be more salient and, therefore, more readily remembered. An example is the publicity surrounding "To Catch a Predator," a 2004 series on the NBC news magazine program *Dateline*. The series included three programs in which hidden cameras captured men meeting teenagers, who turned out to be volunteers with a group dedicated to policing Internet stalking. Anecdotal reports describe the series as a "tipping point" that sparked a wave of concern about social networking sites that some experts described as overreaction:

> "Everyone is freaked," said Parry Aftab, the director of Wired Safety, a nonprofit group of volunteers who conduct safety meetings for parents. "They are convinced the Internet Bogeyman is going to come into their window," she said. "To date that has not happened."[68]

Indeed, the *New York Times* story quoted above noted that the U.S. Department of Justice's Internet Crimes Against Children task forces made 600 arrests in 2005, but few of these were for actual assaults. It would seem that if the *Dateline*

---

64. Valerie S. Folkes, "The Availability Heuristic and Perceived Risk," *Journal of Consumer Research* 15, no. 1 (1988): 13–23.

65. Janis L. Goldie, "Virtual Communities and the Social Dimension of Privacy," *University of Ottawa Technology and Law Journal* 3, no. 1 (2006): 135–166.

66. Erving Goffman, *The Presentation of Self in Everyday Life* (New York: Doubleday, 1959), 144.

67. Peters, McCaul, Stefanek, and Nelson, "A Heuristics Approach," (n. 52).

68. A. Bahney, "Don't Talk to Invisible Strangers," *New York Times*, March 9, 2006, G1.

series did heighten parental concern about social networking sites, it did so by providing parents with highly imaginable examples of negative outcomes. Interestingly, some research suggests that although media representations can influence availability, they do so only in the absence of personal experience.[69] This may account for the fact that social networkers may underestimate potential privacy threats. Indeed, a 14-year-old social networker interviewed by the *New York Times* noted, "[p]arents are going to panic. They are going to overreact. Suddenly somebody, some random person in Illinois or somewhere, gets kidnapped, and then it's a problem."[70] This user's personal experience of social networking may provide him with a different basis with which to calculate the probability of negative outcomes.

C. The Representativeness Heuristic

The representativeness heuristic allows a decision maker to estimate probability by relying on mental models or stereotypes, thereby circumventing more complex calculations. It is sometimes used to estimate likelihoods associated with group or category membership. If, for example, a decision maker wanted to know how likely it is that object A is a member of category X, he or she might first recall specific traits he or she believes to be characteristic of typical category X members. If object A also possesses these traits, then, in the decision maker's estimation, it is likely to be a member of category X.

The representativeness heuristic was first articulated by Kahneman and Tversky, who devised an experiment in which subjects were required to determine whether an individual was more likely to be a lawyer or an engineer.[71] Subjects were told that the target individual was drawn from a larger group of whom 70% were lawyers and 30% were engineers. Subjects were also given a list of traits possessed by the target individual (these traits were carefully chosen to represent stereotypes associated with either lawyers or engineers). Rather than considering the actual base rate of the two occupations in the group from which the target individual was drawn, subjects tended to rely instead on the stereotypical traits to make their judgments. Thus, if the description of the target individual fit the stereotype of a lawyer, he was judged more likely to be a lawyer; if his description fit the stereotype of an engineer, he was judged more likely to be an engineer.

The representativeness heuristic has been shown to have wide application in everyday risk assessments. For example, the logic of the heuristic may explain why certain individuals underestimate their risk of disease if they feel that they

---

69. Rick W. Busselle and L.J. Shrum, "Media Exposure and Exemplar Accessibility," *Media Psychology* 5, no. 3 (2003): 255–282.

70. Bahney, "Don't Talk to Invisible Strangers," G1 (n. 68).

71. Kahneman and Tversky, "Judgment under Uncertainty," (n. 45).

do not resemble someone with the disease.[72] As Kahneman and Tversky's experiment demonstrates, over-reliance on stereotypes often causes people to ignore other information when making risk judgments.[73] Researchers have speculated that because heart disease is more stereotypic of men, women incorrectly view their risk of breast cancer as greater than the risk of heart disease.[74]

In the realm of privacy, this heuristic may operate when DSE users underplay the possibility that they may be vulnerable to harms because they do not identify themselves with someone who is stereotypically at risk. A 23-year-old social networker, in an unpublished interview we conducted, claimed not to be concerned about stalkers, even though she acknowledged that she had divulged a great deal of personal information in her profile: "I don't know. I think that's kind of an early, twelve-year-old kind of fear, that stalkers are looking for you on the Internet. And I don't think it's anything other than just creepy people that are looking to find information about you." According to this user's schema, she does not belong to the category of users at risk for stalking, and, therefore, she concludes that her probability of experiencing this threat is low.

It is also possible that the way users conceptualize privacy threats makes it easier for them to invoke the representativeness heuristic. Experts and non-experts differ in the mental models they use to conceptualize computer security risks.[75] Another DSE user we interviewed claimed, "I guess I'm not really adventurous, I just go into the same sites I'm familiar with, for the most part. I do think Internet activity should be private, other than if it's being used for criminal intent or anything like that. But I'm not doing that." This user equated threats to privacy with the surveillance of Internet traffic for criminal justice purposes; since she was not engaged in criminal activity, she believed she was not at risk for privacy violation.

V. CONCLUSION

We began this paper by reviewing the privacy paradox and its relevance to DSEs. We also suggested that the paradox takes on a more complex character in these environments. Users of DSE applications claim privacy concerns, yet continue to reveal personal information. At the same time, they demonstrate different responses to two types of privacy concerns: they are more likely to enact behaviors

---

72. Mark Parascandola, Jennifer Hawkins, and Marion Danis, "Patient Autonomy and the Challenge of Clinical Uncertainty," *Kennedy Institute of Ethics Journal* 12 (2001): 245–264.

73. Kahneman and Tversky, "Judgment under Uncertainty," (n. 45).

74. Peters, McCaul, Stefanek, and Nelson, "A Heuristics Approach," 47 (n. 52).

75. Farzaneh Asgharpour, Debin Liu, and L. Jean Camp, "Mental Models of Computer Security Risks," in *The Sixth Workshop on the Economics of Information Security–WEIS, 2007,* http://weis2007.econinfosec.org/papers/80.pdf.

to protect privacy in their personal relationships, and less likely to act to protect their privacy in relation to unknown others. Following Goldie and DeCew, we have used the term expressive privacy to refer to the former.[76]

Under models of protective behavior or market exchange, decisions about the release of personal information involve a weighing of the risks and benefits associated with such release. In DSEs, the risks are uncertain. In fact, it is difficult to specify the precise chance that negative privacy outcomes will occur. Faced with the estimation of uncertain risks, decision makers are forced to rely on cognitive heuristics—shortcuts that allow them to establish some reasonable estimate of risk in the absence of specific information about actual risk levels.[77] We suggest that the application of these heuristics in the estimation of privacy risks in DSEs could account for both aspects of the privacy paradox observed in these environments.

The analysis presented in this chapter is largely speculative, and four specific predictions emerge that invite empirical investigation. Research on these questions will help to identify whether perceived risk, and the heuristics involved in that assessment, can account for the privacy paradox evident in DSEs.

Prediction 1: Participants in DSEs will be most attuned to expressive privacy risks. Our speculations rest on the initial assumption that DSE participants have different perceptions of risks associated with various privacy hazards. In particular, we predict higher perception of risks associated with expressive privacy, compared to other privacy hazards. One way to assess these risk perceptions is to have participants generate lists of privacy concerns, rating their perceived risk of experiencing each negative outcome. This approach avoids cuing respondents to specific privacy issues, and instead focuses on those that are salient. We would make two specific predictions in this work: first, that the list of concerns generated would be primarily related to expressive privacy; and second, that among those concerns identified, expressive privacy concerns will receive higher ratings of perceived risk.

Prediction 2: To the extent that DSE participants enjoy their online experience, they will have decreased overall privacy risk perceptions. According to our analysis, the use of the affect heuristic should lead to reduced privacy concerns in DSEs. Two approaches can be used to investigate this prediction: a descriptive approach, and an experimental approach. If affect influences perceived privacy risk, then users of DSEs who feel positive about their participation should also perceive lower risk of privacy breaches. If this association is observed among DSE users, then an experiment could determine whether different risk evaluations can be produced by affect manipulations. Specifically, we would predict that users who are

---

76. Goldie, "Virtual Communities," (n. 42); DeCew, *In Pursuit of Privacy*, (n. 41).
77. Kahneman and Tversky, "Judgment under Uncertainty," (n. 45).

induced to have positive affect regarding their DSE use through informational or other interventions will show decreased perceptions of privacy risks.

Prediction 3: To the degree that DSE participants can easily recall specific instances of privacy violations, they will have an increased perceived risk of that type of privacy violation. If the availability heuristic is responsible for different perceptions of expressive and non-expressive privacy risks in DSEs, then instances of expressive privacy breaches should be more available to users of these applications. Asked to recall or generate instances of negative consequences of privacy breaches, they should offer more examples of expressive privacy breaches, claim more direct knowledge of those breaches (e.g., personal experience rather than media reports), and offer a more detailed report of such breaches. Furthermore, measures of the accessibility of such instances (e.g., number recalled, reported ease of recall, amount of detail provided) should be positively associated with perceived risk of expressive privacy breaches. The same association is expected to hold for breaches of non-expressive privacy, although the overall availability of such outcomes is predicted to be lower.

Prediction 4: To the extent that DSE participants view themselves as different from those likely to experience privacy violations, they will evaluate their risk as lower. We suggest that the representativeness heuristic could explain depressed risk perceptions associated with non-expressive breaches, precisely because DSE participants view themselves as different from those at risk. If true, DSE participants should associate different qualities with individuals at higher risk for expressive versus other types of privacy breaches. Moreover, they should see themselves as more similar to the profile of those at risk for expressive privacy breaches. Finally, perceived risk of breaches of non-expressive privacy should be positively related to the perceived similarity between oneself and the "at-risk" group.

5. UBIQUITOUS COMPUTING AND SPATIAL PRIVACY

ANNE UTECK

I. INTRODUCTION

In 1991, Mark Weiser envisioned a world in which computing would become an integral part of our everyday experience.[1] This vision assumed a paradigmatic shift, not only in computing, but also in society. Enabling technologies would be everywhere,[2] embedded in everyday things, people, and places. As they are combined, integrated, and connected, invisibly and remotely to networks, we move toward a society characterized by ubiquitous computing (ubicomp).[3]

Emerging location, communication, and mobile technologies, such as Global Positioning Systems (GPS), Radio-Frequency Identification (RFID), and advanced wireless devices enhance and extend the ability to locate and track people and things in the real physical world *anywhere, anytime, accurately, continuously, and in real time.* There are compelling advantages to such capabilities that are important to serving the public interest, as for example, more effective emergency services, security applications by law enforcement, and child safety. The privacy implications, however, are profound. The seamless integration of

---

1. Mark Weiser, "The Computer for the 21st Century," *Scientific American* 265, no. 3 (1991), http://www.ubiq.com/hypertext/weiser/SciAmDraft3.html.

2. Adam Greenfield, *Everyware: The Dawning Age of Ubiquitous Computing* (Berkeley, CA: New Riders, 2006).

3. Gordon A. Gow, "Privacy and Ubiquitous Network Societies," background paper prepared for International Telecommunication Union, March 2005, http://www.itu.int/osg/spu/ni/ubiquitous/Papers/Privacy%20background%20paper.pdf.

these technologies into the spaces and places of our everyday lives, more directly and more pervasively, compromises physical and social boundaries in private and public spheres. This potential to be caught within a web of constant accessibility, visibility, and exposure challenges our fundamental ideas about personal space and boundaries, and the privacy expectations that accompany them.

The predominant emphasis on the data protection model of information privacy does not address the central spatial threats to privacy implicated by ubicomp technologies. While this next generation of technologies certainly adds a new dimension to data collection, its use also implicates the interests we have in limiting intrusions into our space, movements, and activities so as to be free from observation. While privacy has both spatial and informational dimensions, "linking privacy to informational transparency tends to mask a conceptually distinct privacy harm that is spatial."[4] Without an assessment that more broadly considers people and their spaces, we risk privacy interests with a spatial dimension being collapsed into the informational paradigm, further marginalizing core interests that individuals have in sustaining physical and personal space.

This chapter begins to examine spatial privacy, its nature and scope, and its viability for legal protection. While geospatial technologies create new concerns for consumers, the focus of this chapter is in the context of government conduct and surveillance activity. Section II briefly describes the technologies that are enabling and driving the development of ubicomp, highlights the main features of this new era of computing in everyday life, and identifies the surveillance issues that potentially threaten our noninformational privacy interests in the spaces of our daily lives. These interests and the spaces in which we seek to protect privacy are explored in Section III. Section IV assesses the extent to which law acknowledges and protects spatial privacy under the Section 8 search and seizure provision of the Canadian Charter of Rights and Freedoms.[5] This analysis demonstrates that while Section 8 purports to recognize a reasonable expectation of spatial privacy, it has been narrowly interpreted and fails to take into account the nature of changing technologies and the plurality of realms in which we engage in activities that we seek to protect from ubiquitous surveillance. This chapter concludes by suggesting that we need to develop a construct that better reflects the spatiality central to our experiences of everyday life and our expectations that the spaces in which we live those experiences are protected from unwarranted intrusion.

---

4. Julie Cohen, "Privacy, Visibility, Transparency and Exposure," *University of Chicago Law Review* 75, no. 1 (2008), http://ssrn.com.abstract=1012068.

5. Part I of the *Constitution Act, 1982*, being Schedule B to the *Canada Act, 1982* (U.K.), 1982, c. 11.

II. THE TECHNOLOGICAL DIMENSIONS AND IMPLICATIONS

A. Enabling Technologies

Mainstream technology, such as credit and affinity cards, closed-circuit television (CCTV), red-light cameras, biometric systems, tracking software, thermal imaging, and infrared devices, are all forms of surveillance technologies to varying degrees, but have inherent limitations. GPS, RFID, and advanced wireless technologies overcome many of the limitations of the mainstream technologies because they can point to the exact location of a person, and follow movement—in real time—on an ongoing, uninterrupted basis. In effect, these technologies create the potential for directed surveillance throughout the environment of our every-day lives with the ultimate, albeit unstated, goal of monitoring or observing all people in all places all of the time.[6]

GPS[7] has been transformed from a technology used solely for military purposes to a viable real-time, multisatellite network supporting a host of non-military, civilian, and consumer applications. For example, GPS is being used for traffic engineering for the purpose of crash reporting and traffic system performance.[8] Additionally, GPS is being increasingly marketed as a tracking device in vehicles,[9] and for monitoring both employees[10] and parolees.[11]

RFID technology is essentially a microchip, which acts as a transmitter that is embedded in an object or implanted in a person, and is generally used to describe any technology that uses radio signals to identify specific objects.[12] RFIDs, like

---

6. Martin Dodge, Michael Batty, and Robert Kitchin, "No Longer Lost in the Crowd: Prospects of Continuous Geosurveillance," Association of American Geographers Conference, March 2004 http://www.casa.ucl.ac.uk/martin/aag_geosurveillance.pdf.

7. GPS is a radio navigation system that allows land, sea, and airborne users to determine their exact location, velocity, and time in all weather conditions, anywhere in the world. Mark Monmonier, *Spying With Maps, Surveillance Technologies and The Future of Privacy* (Chicago: The University of Chicago Press, 2002); Waseem Karim "The Privacy Implications of Personal Locators: Why You Should Think Twice Before Voluntarily Availing Yourself to GPS Monitoring," *University of Washington Journal of Law & Policy* 14 (2004) 485; and April Otterberg "GPS Tracking Technology: The Case for Revisiting Knotts and Shifting the Supreme Court's Theory of the Public Space Under the Fourth Amendment," *Boston College Law Review* 46, no. 3 (2005) 661.

8. Monmonier, *Spying With Maps* (n. 7).

9. See for example, Solutions Into Motion Limited Web site, http://www.trackem.com; Fleetboss Global Positioning Solutions Inc. Web site, http://www.fleetboss.com; AirIQ Web site, http://www.airiq.com.

10. J. K. Peterson, *Understanding Surveillance Technologies: Spy Devices, Privacy, History and Applications* 2nd ed., (Boca Raton: Taylor & Francis, 2007), 337.

11. See for example, Pro-Tech Web site, http://www.ptm.com.

12. Simson Garfinkel & Beth Rosenberg, eds., *RFID: Applications, Security, and Privacy* (New Jersey: Pearson Educational, Inc., 2005), 3–36.

GPS systems, are not new, but are being refined and developed for current and potential use in a wide range of contexts.[13] The potential for government use of RFIDs is very broad, in part because of the many roles that governments play in society. Governments may seek to use RFIDs as part of regulatory schemes, in the delivery of service, supply chains, health care systems, or in relation to government employees, such as police officers or military personnel. On Canadian highways RFIDs are used in a prepaid system of highway or bridge tolls,[14] and some RFID systems measure the travel time of motorists.[15] In public transit systems, users pay by waving an RFID-equipped card before a reader at a subway turnstile.[16] With an overriding interest in security and public safety, as issuers of identity and other official documents, governments are contemplating deployment of larger and more powerful RFIDs, including driver's licenses,[17] health cards,[18] passports,[19] and boarding passes.[20] Public libraries are already looking to track their books by embedding chips that will communicate the book's title, the library to which it belongs, and to whom it is signed out.[21]

In the United Kingdom, law enforcement tagged over 600 adults and close to 6,000 juveniles—some as young as twelve—to ensure compliance with bail conditions.[22] Offenders released from prison are also subject to electronic monitoring either as a condition of early release from prison under the Home Detention Curfew Scheme[23] or as a condition of being released on parole.[24] At five Canadian and Mexican borders, RFID-enabled border smart cards are currently being tested to record the entry and exit of visitors who are required to carry the smart card and enroll in the US-VISIT program.[25] And, people are

---

13. In the consumer context, see Teresa Scassa et al., "Consumer Privacy and RFID Technology," *Ottawa Law Journal* 37, no. 2 (2006): 215.

14. See for example, 407 ETR Web site, http://www.407etr.com; see also Katherine Albrecht & Liz McIntyre, *Spychips* (Nashville: Nelson Current, 2005) 135–143.

15. RFID Journal "RFID Drives Highway Traffic Report," http://www.rfidjournal.com/article/articleprint/1234/–1/1/.

16. Albrecht & MacIntyre, *Spychips* (n. 14).

17. Albrecht & MacIntyre, *Spychips*, 143 (n. 14).

18. Kenneth Fiskin & Jay Lundell, "RFID in Healthcare" in Garfinkel & Rosenberg, *RFID*, 211 (n. 12).

19. United States Department of Homeland Security E-Passports Initiative, http://www.dhs.gov/xnews/releases/pr_1160497737875.shtm.

20. David Fraser, Canadian Privacy Law Blog, http://www.privacylawyer.ca/blog/2006/05/q-what-could-boarding-pass-tell.html.

21. Information and Privacy Commissioner of Ontario, *Guidelines for Using RFID Tags in Ontario Public Libraries,* June 2004, http://www.ipc.on.ca/docs/rfid-lib.pdf.

22. National Probation Service Bulletin, (2006) Electronic Monitoring 6, http://www.probation.homeoffice.gov.uk/output/Page137.asp#Current%20Programmes.

23. In 2005–2006, some 19,000 people were released early under this scheme, *ibid.*

24. *Ibid.*

25. United States Department of Homeland Security Fact Sheet, June 5, 2006, http://www.dhs.gov/xnews/releases/pr_1160495895724.shtm.

opting for RFID implantation. In the United States, some individuals with degenerative brain conditions have also been implanted so that they can be more easily tracked.[26] In another instance, a company chipped two of its employees for workplace access control.[27]

Increasingly important in a world of high mobility, communication is no longer limited while in transit to fixed line. Today, advanced cellular devices do not have to be in use and within range for the location to be identified, but now have tracking capabilities using Automatic Location Identification (ALI) without the necessity that they even be turned on.[28] Wireless Fidelity (Wi-Fi)[29] has also emerged as viable technology for wireless access. This technology is evolving with nodes, or hotspots, as they are known, appearing in locations such as coffee shops, hotels, libraries, educational institutions, and airports. With a Wi-Fi base station, routed to a broadband connection, devices equipped with Wi-Fi wireless network cards can share the Internet connection emanating from the base station. As the number and variety of hotspots grow, wireless Internet service providers hope to create meshed networks of hotspots with the potential to observe and track the physical movement of those connected to the Wi-Fi network. Bluetooth[30] uses similar technology for the purpose of providing interconnection between a wide variety of devices—mobile telephones, PDAs, laptops, even Internet-ready refrigerators or washing machines.[31] Organizations deploy Bluetooth-based locational surveillance systems.[32]

The convergence of the enabling technologies offers complementary strategies to the limitations of each in determining instantaneous location and tracking of people, vehicles, and objects. An RFID system can record location when a subject with an RFID tag passes within range of a compatible reader. An RFID chip with read-write memory and the ability to record location identifiers from transmitters along its path can be debriefed by a system design to reconstruct the subject's route. RFID tracking requires readers positioned at appropriate choke points in

26. See Verichip Corporation, http://www.verichipcorp.com.

27. Richard Waters, "US group implants electronic tags in workers" *Financial Times*, February 12, 2006 http://www.ft.com/cms/s/ec414700-9bf4-11da-8baa-0000779e2340.html.

28. Colin Bennett and Lori Crowe, "Location-Based Services and the Surveillance of Mobility: An Analysis of Privacy Risks in Canada," (2005) *A Report to the Office of the Privacy Commissioner of Canada*, http://web.uvic.ca/polisci/bennett/pdf/lbsfinal.pdf.

29. Colin Bennett and Priscilla Regan, eds, "Mobilities," *Surveillance & Society* 1, no. 4 (2004) http://www.surveillance-and-society.org/journalv1i4.htm; see also Ontario Information and Privacy Commissioner Web site, "Privacy in a Wireless World," 2001, http://www.ipc.on.ca/scripts/index_.asp?action=31&N_ID=1&P_ID=11263&U_ID=0.

30. "Bluetooth and Wireless Technologies," *Intel Technology Journal* 4, no. 2 (2002) http://intel.com/technology/itj/archive/2000.htm.

31. Albrecht & MacIntyre, *Spychips*, 85–95 (n. 14).

32. Pius Uzamere, Simson Garfinkel & Ricardo Garcia, "Bluejacked" in Garfinkel & Rosenberg, *RFID*, 323 (n. 12); See also Bluetooth SIG, Inc. Web site, http://bluetooth.com/bluetooth/.

the circulation network. GPS, on the other hand, allows for continuous tracking, especially if linked in real-time to a wireless mobile system, but because of signal attenuation and multipath corrupted signals in certain areas, GPS does not guarantee reliable uninterrupted tracking.[33] These technical difficulties are diminished with the amalgamation or convergence of RFID, GPS, and mobile technologies because RFID extends GPS tracking capabilities, and mobile devices add the real-time component. This integration of mobile computing devices and communication services means more powerful location-based systems because they can pinpoint coordinates more precisely—continuously and in real time.

Location-based services (LBS) combining location technologies are producing a number of new applications designed to assist government, consumers, employers, parents, and others to "locate" individuals and objects in real time. The telecommunications industry intends to use LBS in order to improve public safety through the E-911 Initiative,[34] to aid law enforcement through the lawful access initiative,[35] and to develop LBS commercial applications.[36] Potential future uses include a networked GPS system right in the home which could pinpoint the whereabouts of people, things, and animals.[37] Currently, many of the individual nodes behind the location systems exist as objects that surround the individual—car, clothing, mobile phones, transit systems, and walls with tag readers. Embedding chips, however, in a wider range of objects—identification documents for example, or even implanted under the skin,[38] especially when coupled with GPS—will further refine and enhance location-based services.

B. Ubiquitous Computing (Ubicomp)

Ubicomp has been defined as "the method of enhancing computer use by making many computers available throughout the physical environment, but

---

33. While GPS operates on a continuous basis, it is limited to the extent that satellites cannot be transmitted through physical barriers, as for example, underground, in buildings or as a result of topography.

34. Bennett & Regan, "Mobilities" (n. 29).

35. CIPPIC Report, "Lawful Access: Police Surveillance," http://www.cippic.ca/en/projects-cases/lawful-access/.

36. For example, mapping and directory services, fleet management, protection of goods, and shipping management: Bennett and Crowe, "Location-Based Services and the Surveillance of Mobility," (n. 28); see also David Phillips & Michael Curry, "Privacy and the Phenetic Urge: Geodemographics and the changing spatiality of local practice" in David Lyon, ed., *Surveillance as Social Sorting: Privacy, Risk and Digital Discrimination* (New York: Routledge, 2003), 137.

37. Bennett and Crowe, "Location-Based Services and the Surveillance of Mobility," (n. 28).

38. Angela Long, "Implanting Dignity: Considering the Use of RFID for Tracking Human Beings" ID Trail Mix, March 27, 2007, http://www.idtrail.org/content/view/656/42/; Thomas C. Greene, "Feds Approve Human RFID Implants," *The Register* (2004) www.theregister.co.uk/2004/10/14/human_rfid_implants/.

making them effectively invisible."[39] Intelligent, intuitive interfaces will make computer devices simple to use and unobtrusive. Communication networks will connect these devices to facilitate and build on the anywhere, anytime paradigm by adding access for all persons and things creating an anytime, anywhere, for anyone, and anything paradigm.

Ubiquitous computing will be everywhere. This is its essence, its explicit goal.[40] Consequently, a ubiquitous system will affect a large—if not every—part of our lives, from crossing a street to sitting in the living room or entering an office building. A key feature of ubicomp is its *invisibility* in the design of everyday living and work spaces.[41] It is, literally, visible (you can physically see and touch a device), yet effectively invisible in everyday spaces and as we go about our activities within those spaces. It is then, difficult for individuals to be aware of the surveillance possibility. The technology not only hides the possibility of surveillance, but it also hides the signs of what is being monitored. Individuals are not always aware of what is being observed, even if they are aware of the installed technology. Apart from hiding the existence of surveillance, the embedded technology also makes it difficult to know what exactly is being observed and monitored. This creates, in effect, an embedded panopticon—pervasive surveillance hidden in the environment. As the technology shrinks and processing power increases, so will the ability of sensors to refine perception of the environment. Thus, observation and tracking will result in a greater degree of accuracy, which translates into greater visibility and exposure of objects and people. This will enable government to interact with devices more naturally and more casually than they do currently, and in ways that suit whatever location or context in which they find themselves, some operating with our expressed permission, others without our permission or our knowledge.[42]

Interestingly, there is no longer the need anymore to surreptitiously install tracking devices on persons, vehicles, or objects because increasingly people carry or use tracking devices voluntarily in their everyday lives. For example, location-determining technology is routinely installed in cell phones and cars. Electronic toll systems, such as the MAC Pass in Nova Scotia,[43] register the presence of each driver who has chosen to install a tag or transponder in her windshield so there is no need for the driver to stop and pay. Such electronically facilitated transactions make driving less burdensome, but at the cost of making

---

39. Weiser, "The Computer for the 21st Century," (n. 1).

40. Greenfield, *Everyware: The Dawning Age of Ubiquitous Computing*, (n. 2); Marc Langheinrich, "Privacy by Design—Principles of Privacy-Aware Ubiquitous Systems," http://guir.cs.berkeley.edu/pubs/ubicomp2002/privacyworkshop/papers/uc2002-pws.pdf.

41. Langheinrich, *ibid.*

42. It is predicted, in the United States, that by 2014 there will be increasing numbers of arrests based on this kind of government surveillance: Pew Internet and American Life Project, http://www.elon.edu/e-web/predictions/expertsurveys/2004_embeddednetworks.xhtml.

43. Halifax Bridge Commission Web site, http://www.macpass.com.

it less anonymous. This trade-off characterizes numerous other features of evolving "intelligent transportations systems."[44] The same technologies that allow lost drivers to find out where they are, what services are nearby, and how to get where they are also going to potentially allow unseen government observers to watch, learn, and record information.

Radio transmitting devices may also allow officials to observe and trace the paths not only of our phones and cars, but also numerous other tag-embedded products we cannot do without, or choose not to do without. Some people have even voluntarily installed RFID chips into their own bodies or those of their children.[45] And with networked cameras commonplace in many cities, authorities can more easily watch and track people as they walk down a street, even if they are not equipped with a device that emits or receives signals.

The cumulative effect of the emerging technologies and the move toward a world of ubiquitous computing will make it increasingly difficult to evade surveillance. The expansive nature of surveillance made possible by location and tracking technologies "defies the contextualization of life: the workplace, store, and home are no longer separate places in which one is surveilled, but instead each becomes a point on the flow of surveillance."[46] As each of these points becomes increasingly connected to others as a result of technological convergence, more of our everyday lives are exposed. From home, to work, to shop, to take a walk down the street, all these movements and "flows" are subject to scrutiny. The objects we use or carry with us, in turn become tools for surveillance. Movement is no longer a means by which we can evade surveillance, but rather, becomes the subject of surveillance. Such technological transformations bring to physical space many of the same concerns that were raised about tracking movements in virtual space through the use of cookies or Web-click trails. Indeed, "the street itself seems to have evolved into a sensory apparatus."[47]

There is no right not to be observed, but surveillance, regardless of whether or not it is technologically assisted, assaults human dignity and changes behavioral patterns, thereby reducing self-determination.[48] Further, being under the public gaze impairs aspects of individuality that are, or should be, protected in a

44. ITS refers to emerging products, services, and systems, which are based on advanced technologies with enhanced sensory, memory, communication, and information processing capabilities: Transport Canada, http://its-sti.gc.ca/en/what-is-its.htm.

45. Long, "Implanting Dignity," (n. 38); Greene, "Feds Approve Human RFID Implants," (n. 38).

46. Bennett & Regan, "Mobilities," 453 (n. 29).

47. William Gibson, "The Road to Oceania," New York Times, June 25, 2003, http://www.nytimes.com/2003/06/25/opinion/25GIBS.html?ei=5007&en=d57cc2565eb4ec57&ex=1371960000&partner=USERLAND&pagewanted=print&position.

48. Jeffrey Reiman, "Driving to the Panopticon: A Philosophical Exploration of the Risks to Privacy Posed by the Highway Technology of the Future," *Santa Clara Computer & High Technology Law Journal* 11 (1995) 27, 30.

free and democratic society.[49] And, now well documented, Jeremy Bentham's "Panopticon" as interpreted by Michel Foucault[50] demonstrates the psychological repercussions of being observed and monitored. More recently, the "panoptic geolocator" has been used to describe today's context of surveillance.[51] This may result, for example, in a person being fearful of visiting someone at an AIDS hospice out of concern over being tagged in that location. A chef may worry about bringing a new tag-embedded knife purchased on the way to work on a transit system. Or a student may avoid passing government buildings with research materials on terrorism that have been checked out of the library.

However, even when the observer will not use what is observed in any harmful way or whether anyone is actually watching, there are systemic risks to surveillance. Ubiquitous surveillance alters the experience of space and places producing greater transparency and exposure.[52] In turn, "[e]xposure alters the capacity of places to function as contexts within which identity is developed and performed."[53] As Julie Cohen reminds us, technologies do not exist in a spatial vacuum. These things affect the "lived embodied spaces of real people."[54] We do not give up all expectation of privacy "simply by venturing into a public area"[55] because "privacy results not from locked doors and closed curtains, but also from the way our publicly observable activities are dispersed over space and time."[56] Intrusions into one's life in nontraditional environments "disturbs the victim's daily activities, alters her routines, destroys her solitude, and often makes her feel uncomfortable and uneasy."[57] The question then is what are the privacy interests at risk and what are the spaces in which we expect these interests to be protected?

49. Lisa Austin, "The Privacy Interests at Stake in Public Activities" Centre for Innovation, Law & Policy, *Innovate* (Spring 2006): 18, http://www.law.utoronto.ca/documents/publications/Innovate06.pdf.

50. Michel Foucault, *Discipline and Punish: The Birth of the Prison*, A. Sheridon, trans. (New York: Vintage, 1979).

51. Jonathon Weinberg, "RFID, Privacy and Regulation" in Garfinkel & Rosenberg, 83 (n. 12).

52. Julie Cohen, "Privacy, Visibility and Exposure," abstract from conference, *Unblinking, New Perspectives on Visual Privacy in the 21st Century*, Berkeley, November 3–4, 2006, http://www.law.berkeley.edu/institutes/bclt/events/unblinking/unblinking/cohen-unblinking-abstract.htm.

53. *Ibid.*

54. Cohen, "Privacy, Visibility and Exposure," (n. 52).

55. Anita Allen, *Uneasy access: Privacy for women in a free society* (New Jersey: Rowman and Littlefield, 1988), as cited in Gary Marx, "Murky conceptual waters: The public and the private," *Ethics and Information Technology* 3 (1995) 157, 163.

56. Jeffrey Reiman, "Driving to the Panopticon: A Philosophical Exploration of the Risks to Privacy Posed by the Information Highway Technology of the Future" in B. Rossier, ed., *Privacies: Philosophical Evaluations* (Stanford CA: University of Stanford Press, 2004), 194, 196.

57. Daniel Solove, "A Taxonomy of Privacy," *University of Pennsylvania Law Review* 154 no. 3 (2006) 477, 549.

III. PRIVACY AND SPACE

A. Characterizing the Privacy Interest

Many formulations of privacy rest on the assumption that there is a "zone" or "realm" into which government may not encroach. A privacy interest in limiting these intrusions is characterized by language of inaccessibility. The concept of limited access recognizes that privacy extends beyond merely being apart from others, to more broadly embracing freedom from scrutiny and intrusions by others.

A number of theorists have advanced limited access conceptions as the underlying basis for protecting privacy.[58] For philosopher Sissela Bok, privacy is "the condition of being protected from unwanted access by others—either physical access, personal information, or attention."[59] According to Ernest Van Den Haag, "[p]rivacy is the exclusive access of a person to a realm of his own. The right of privacy entitles one to exclude others from watching, utilizing, invading, or intruding upon his private realm."[60] And for Ruth Gavison, privacy as limited accessibility concerns "the extent to which we are known to others, the extent to which others have physical access to us, and the extent to which we are the subject of others' attention."[61] The extent to which we are known to others refers to the extent of others' knowing information about us. Physical and visual invasions occur when others obtain access to us or when we are the subject of others' attention. Gavison explains what constitutes limited access, which consists of "three independent and irreducible elements: secrecy, anonymity, and solitude."[62] Similarly, under Alan Westin's typology, reserve, anonymity, and solitude are identified as states of privacy.[63] Reserve refers to the creation of a psychological barrier against intrusion. According to Westin, reserve means that you wish to limit accessibility to yourself or communication about yourself to others.[64] Or as Irwin Altman defines, "privacy is selective control of access to the self," including over one's territory and one's personal space.[65] Solitude is being free from observation by others.[66]

---

58. Anita Allen, *Uneasy access* (n. 55); Jeffrey Reiman, "Driving to the Panopticon," (n. 56);. Ruth Gavison, "Privacy and the Limits of Law," *Yale Law Journal* 89 (1980): 421; Sissela Bok, *Secrets: On the Ethics of Concealment and Revelation* (New York: Random House, 1989); Ernest Van Den Haag, "On Privacy" in J. Roland and J.W. Chapman, ed., *Nomos XIII: Privacy* (New York: Atherton Press, 1971).

59. Bok, *Secrets*, 10 (n. 58).

60. Van Den Haag, "On Privacy," 149 (n. 58).

61. Gavison, "Privacy and the Limits of Law," 423 (n. 58).

62. *Ibid.*, 433.

63. Alan Westin, *Privacy and Freedom* (New York: Atheneum, 1970).

64. *Ibid.*, 32–39.

65. Irwin Altman, *The Environment and Social Behaviour: privacy, personal space, territory and crowding* (Monterey, CA: Brooks/Cole, 1975), 18.

66. Solove, "A Taxonomy of Privacy," (n. 57); Judith Wagner DeCew, *In Pursuit of Privacy: Law, Ethics and the Rise of Technology* (Ithaca: Cornell University Press, 1997).

Recently, Julie Cohen has formulated a variation of accessibility privacy by advancing a theory that characterizes the spatial dimension of privacy as an interest in avoiding or limiting exposure—in other words, a privacy interest against exposure. Under this formulation, "privacy encompasses an interest in the structure of experienced space, and this interest is threatened under conditions of visual or informational exposure."[67]

B. Anonymity

As identified by Gavison and Westin, anonymity is also a key component of privacy. Anonymity is the form of privacy desired when one wishes, or needs, to be among others, but does not want to be personally identified or be the subject of scrutiny or observation.[68] This depiction would typically include an individual's activities in public places or as an individual moves through public spaces, seeking to merge into the "situational landscape."[69] Often even when an individual is in a public place and can be observed by others, the individual does not expect to be "identified and held to the full rules of behavior and role that would operate if he were known to those observing him."[70] The knowledge, or even the apprehension, that one is under observation in public places "destroys the sense of relaxation and freedom that men seek in open spaced and public arenas."[71] An individual is not defending a defined physical, territorial space, but arguably, the intangible personal space within which they wish to limit access to the self.

Anonymity, from another point of view, can also be understood as a positive urban value, even essential to the idea of urbanity. A "society of strangers" is the classical Simmelian[72] interpretation of the urban condition in which urban anonymity equates with freedom. In urban space, people actually expect to remain anonymous.[73] Indeed, as Jacobs points out, "[p]rivacy is precious in cities."[74] Anonymity and privacy in public may actually be a peculiar consequence of modern living in large urban environments. In small communities, one would have little space for being free from surveillance by other community members

---

67. Cohen, "Privacy, Visibility, Transparency and Exposure," (n. 4).

68. Westin, *Privacy and Freedom*, 32 (n. 63).

69. Melvin Gutterman, "A Formulation of the Value and Means Models of the Fourth Amendment in the Age of Technologically Enhanced Surveillance," *Syracuse Law Review* 39 (1998) 647, 706.

70. Westin, *Privacy and Freedom* (n. 63).

71. Westin, *Privacy and Freedom* (n. 63); Richard Posner, "The Right to Privacy," *Georgia Law Review* 12 (1978) 393.

72. Georg Simmel, "The Metropolis and Mental Life" in D. Levine, ed., *On Individuality and Social Forms* (Chicago: University of Chicago Press, 1971), 71.

73. Nick Taylor, "State Surveillance and The Right to Privacy," Surveillance and Society 1, no. 1 (2002): 66, 74, http://www.surveillance-and-society.org/articles1/statesurv.pdf.

74. Jane Jacobs, *The Death and Life of Great American Cities* (New York: Random House Inc., 1961); Reprinted: (New York: Vintage Books, 1992), 58.

or government agents wandering around the town. In urban spaces, however, pervasive public surveillance has serious consequences for the "anonymity in public [that] promotes freedom of action and an open society."[75] Exercising anonymity in a library, a classroom, in a park, or even in a crowded space such as a bus depot, airport, or a bench on a busy street was created by surrounding walls, distances from prying eyes, or by social conventions. However, embedded networked technologies potentially obliterate the spaces and places in which to be anonymous, and also diminish the ability to carry out private activities in public.

C. Conceptualizing Space

Space is a concept that is central to many different areas of study and has varied meanings across a multitude of disciplines. The great variety of possible "types" of space make any definition of space difficult. My aim here is not to construct a theory of space, but, rather, to provide the relevant dimensions of space that are under surveillance and those that implicate privacy interests. Thus, for the purposes of examining spatial privacy in the current technological and legal context, three key categorizations are described here: territorial space, personal space, and urban public space.

Territorial Space The term "territory" generally refers to a particular or indeterminate geographical area. Territorial space is the physical manifestation of something, namely, a physical location.[76] A primary territorial space is one owned by an individual, controlled on a relatively permanent basis and central to daily life. Territoriality is the means of exercising control over this defined physical space.[77]

Territoriality, in its most basic forms, has been defined as a pattern of behavior and attitudes held by an individual that is based on perceived, attempted, or actual control of a definable physical space that may involve habitual occupation, defense, personalization and marking of it.[78] *Marking* means placing an object or substance in a space to indicate one's territorial intentions, and *personalization* means marking in a manner that indicates one's identity.[79] Although a territory is not synonymous with property, territoriality works to control defined spaces and physical places. Thus, territorial space finds architectural and geographical expression whereby control over access serves as a defensible shield to protect privacy.

---

75. Christopher Slobogin, "Public Privacy: Camera Surveillance of Public Places and the Right to Anonymity," *Mississippi Law Journal* 72 (2002) 213, 240.

76. Bryan Lawson, *The Language of Space* (Oxford: Architectural Press, 1999).

77. Julian Edney, "Human Territoriality," *Psychological Bulletin* 81 (1974) 959.

78. *Ibid.*

79. *Ibid.*

Personal Space Spatial dimensions of our lives involve not only constructions of territory anchored in physical space, but also establishing personal zones of privacy.[80] People often expect space from others, even when they are with other people or when in public. We need "personal space" for our psychological well-being.[81] Personal space has been defined as "an area with invisible boundaries surrounding a person's body into which intruders may not come."[82] Personal space differs from other territories in that it is portable, but emphasizes distance for the purposes of exclusion of others.[83] Spatial boundaries are upheld by rules of civility and social respect.[84] We each have certain "territories of the self," and norms of civility require that we respect others' territories.[85]

The Supreme Court of Canada has spoken about a personal zone of privacy, articulating personal privacy as spatial: a person is deemed to be surrounded by a space, but, unlike physical property, this space is not necessarily bounded by tangible barriers.[86] Its realm transcends "the physical and is aimed at protecting the dignity of the human person."[87] Personal privacy can be said to relate to a sphere of the self—a zone of privateness surrounding the individual, which should not be invaded without justification by either unwarranted physical contact or by unwarranted observation.

Public Urban Space Public spaces of cities are the collusion of physical space with the everyday world and have temporary quality in which an individual has occupancy rights.[88] They are multipurpose, accessible spaces which are distinguishable from, and mediate between, demarcated exclusive territories of homes and individuals. These spaces have been described as the surface not in private ownership and are ubiquitous, neutral, and a contingent carrier of urban functions.[89] These areas, sometimes referred to as "in-between" spaces,[90]

---

80. Simmel, "The Metropolis and Mental Life," 71 (n. 72); Robert Sommer, *Personal Space: The Behvourial Basis of Design* (Englewood, NJ: Prentice-Hall, 1969); E.T. Hall, *The Hidden Dimension* (Garden City, NY: Doubleday, 1966).

81. Altman, *The Environment and Social Behaviour*, 52 (n. 65).

82. Sommer, *Personal Space* (n. 80).

83. *Ibid.*

84. Robert Post, "The Social Foundations of Privacy Community and Self in the Common Law Tort," *California Law Review* 77 (1989) 957, 966.

85. Erving Goffman, *The Presentation of Self in Everyday Life* (New York: Doubleday, 1959).

86. *R v Dyment* [1988] 2 S.C.R. 417 citing *Report of the Task Force established by the Department of Communciations and Department of Justice: Privacy and Computers*(Ottawa: Communication Group, 1972), 428.

87. *Ibid.*

88. Altman, *The Environment and Social Behaviour*, 118 (n. 65); see also, Hille Koskela, "The Cam Era: The Contemporary Urban Panopticon," *Surveillance and Society* 1, no. 3 (2003): 292.

89. Lyn Lofland, *The Public Realm: Exploring the City's Quintessential Social Territory* (IL: Waveland Press, 1998).

90 Eric Paulos, Ken Anderson, and Anthony Townsend, "Ubicomp in the Urban Frontier" conference abstract, September 7, 2004, http://www.paulos.net/intel/pubs/

include, for example, streets, parks, transit routes, libraries, and airports. They are the spaces of everyday lived experience where people work, travel, relax, and interact, hence, both physical and social.[91] Public urban space, then, is a socio-spatial landscape open to, accessible by, and shared among society's members in their multiple roles as individuals, community members, consumers, employees, parents, friends, and citizens. Not only do we spend a significant amount of time in such urban landscapes, but these spaces contribute to our formulation of identity, community, and self.[92]

Public urban space takes on greater significance as new technologies are moving out of structured and enclosed physical environments into urban spaces. The technological embeddedness shifts "the emphasis from abstract information processing to concrete physical space, from clothing and cars to the entire urban landscape."[93] As such, everyday actions and behaviors no longer belong to particular places, and because there is no place—no arena of life which is truly public,[94] private activities can occur in these urban spaces that we may not want or expect to be observed.

IV. LEGAL PROTECTION

The highest legal authority for providing protection of privacy in Canada is the Charter of Rights & Freedoms.[95] While not explicitly granting a right of privacy, the Charter has been interpreted to protect dignity, autonomy, and privacy under sections 7 and 8. Section 7 provides that "Everyone has the right to life, liberty and security of the person and the right not to be deprived thereof except in accordance with the principles of fundamental justice." The Supreme Court of Canada has held that the Charter protects a reasonable expectation of privacy as an element of the right to liberty and security of the person.[96] These rights have been taken to guarantee a degree of personal autonomy over decisions affecting an individual's life and protection of the psychological or mental integrity of the individual.[97]

papers/Urban%20Frontier%20Workshop%20(UbiComp%202004).pdf.

91. Spiro Kostof, *The City Assembled: The Elements of Urban Form through History* (London: Thames & Hudson, 1992); Rob Krier, *Urban Space* (London: Academy Editions, 1979).

92. Paulos, Anderson, and Townsend, "Ubicomp in the Urban Frontier," (n. 90).

93. Jerry Kang and Dana Cuff "Pervasive Computing: Embedding the Public Sphere," *Washington & Lee Law Review* 62 (2005) 62.

94. Helen Nissenbaum, "Protecting Privacy in an Information Age: The Problem with Privacy in Public," *Law and Philosophy* 17 (1998):559.

95. Part I of the *Constitution Act, 1982*, being Schedule B to the *Canada Act, 1982* (U.K.), 1982, c. 11 [hereinafter the *Charter*].

96. *R v O'Connor* [1995] 4 S.C.R. 411.

97. *R v Morgentaler* [1988] 1 S.C.R. 30.

While a privacy right has not been fully developed under Section 7, given the potential for increasingly sophisticated surveillance technologies to be used all around us, wider application of its scope and content may take on greater importance.[98] Similarly, the Section 15 equality guarantee provision under the Charter may prove useful to protecting privacy in public. Daphne Gilbert considers privacy in the context of Section 15 in which she proposes the equality provision as "another home" but not "new" home for constitutional protection of privacy interests.[99]

The principal basis for legal recognition of the protection of privacy interests in the context of government activity is Section 8 of the Charter, which provides that "Everyone has the right to be secure against unreasonable search and seizure." The fundamental objective of Section 8 is "to protect individuals from unjustified State intrusion upon privacy"[100] by ensuring them a "reasonable expectation of privacy."[101] It is only where "state examinations constitute an intrusion upon some reasonable privacy interest of individuals does the government action in question constitute a 'search' within the meaning of s.8."[102] Section 8 then guarantees a right to be secure from unreasonable search where the person has a reasonable expectation of privacy. If a person cannot establish that she had a reasonable expectation of privacy, Section 8 will not be engaged. To qualify, a privacy expectation must meet both subjective and objective criteria, the individual must have an actual expectation of privacy, and that expectation must be one that society recognizes as reasonable.[103] Section 8 purports to protect a reasonable expectation of territorial or spatial privacy as one of the zones articulated by the Supreme Court of Canada.[104] This zone of privacy protects physical privacy, but has been de-physicalized so that its protection, at least in theory, extends beyond a property analysis.[105]

Section 8 protection has been characterized as a "broad and general right" to privacy.[106] And in *R v Plant*, the Court confirmed that it is not necessary for a person to establish a possessory interest to attract Section 8 protections.[107] Determining

---

98. A thorough analysis in this regard is beyond the scope of this chapter.

99 Ian Kerr, *Lessons from the Identity Trail: Anonymity, Privacy, and Identity in a Networked Society* (New York: Oxford University Press, 2009), Chapter 8.

100. *Hunter v Southam Inc.* [1984] 2 S.C.R. 145.

101. *R v Evans* [1996] 1 S.C.R. 8.

102. *R v Tessling* [2004] 3 S.C.R. 432.

103. *Hunter*, 159 (n. 100).

104. The other two zones identified are personal privacy (invasions into the body *R v M (M.R.)* [1998] 3 S.C.R. 393; and informational privacy (protects against the collection of intimate, core biographical information, *R v Plant* [1993] 3 S.C.R. 281; *R v Tessling* (n. 102).

105. *Katz v United States*, 389 U.S. 347 adopted by *Hunter*, 107 (n. 100).

106. *Hunter* (n. 100).

107. *Ibid.*

whether individuals have a reasonable expectation of privacy in a given context is a nuanced, contextual and fundamentally normative exercise. This assessment must be made in light of all the circumstances.[108] All of which envisions that an individual's reasonable expectation of privacy is protected not only within certain well-marked zones or enclaves, but everywhere that circumstances might give rise to such an expectation. This interpretation is supported by *Hunter* in which the Supreme Court of Canada sought to remedy the trespass theory of privacy by linking Section 8 to the protection of "people not places."[109] Such language accords with powerful intuitions about privacy. Many people would probably object to the idea that they relinquish an expectation of privacy simply because they are in a public area. As Jeffrey Reiman points out, "privacy results not from locked doors and closed curtains, but also from the way our publicly observable activities are dispersed over space and time."[110]

If Section 8 then does not protect the privacy of places, but the privacy of the people in those places, it suggests that its protections can move with people as they leave their homes and move from place to place. Section 8 then could be said to protect privacy anywhere that people reasonably expect to have such privacy. Since some people may reasonably expect to be free from ongoing government surveillance even on sidewalks, parks, streets, or coffee shops, Section 8 should have force in these public urban environments as well as in the home or office. This kind of justification has been offered by former Justice LaForest of the Supreme Court of Canada who advised that courts should dispense with "rigid, formalistic borders between private and public spatial domains" and instead attend to what constitutes a "reasonable expectation of privacy in a given context."[111]

Helen Nissenbaum's "contextual integrity" model follows similar reasoning.[112] Rejecting the broadly defined public/private distinction, Nissenbaum's benchmark theory of contextual integrity recognizes that all of the activities people engage in take place in a "plurality of distinct realms."[113] Within each of these realms, or contexts, norms exist, either implicitly or explicitly, which both shape and limit roles, expectations, actions, and practices.[114] Indeed, an emphasis on norms is already at the heart of the reasonable expectation of privacy test because one cannot tell what expectations society is prepared to recognize as reasonable unless one looks at society's practices and specifically privacy norms.[115]

---

108. *R v M (M.R.)*, para 31 (n. 104); *R v Edwards* [1996] 1 S.C.R. 128, para. 30; *R v Wong* [1990] 3 S.C.R. 36, 62; *R v Colarusso* [1994] 1 SCR 20, 54.

109. *Hunter* (n. 100).

110. Reiman, "Driving to the Panopticon," 196 (n. 56).

111. Legal Opinion to then Privacy Commissioner of Canada, G. Radwanski, April 5, 2002.

112. "Privacy as Contextual Integrity," *Washington Law Review* 79, no. 1 (2004) 119.

113. *Ibid.*, 137

114. *Ibid.*

115. Lisa Austin, "Privacy and the Question of Technology," *Law and Philosophy* 22 no. 2 (2003): 119.

The Supreme Court of Canada, however, has yet to strongly reaffirm that Section 8 protects people not places. The *Hunter* framework has only extended to spaces that are in some sense enclosed or marked off by clear boundaries from the outside world. The spatial privacy analysis has largely remained tied to its territorial roots by focusing on the location or place under government surveillance. The persistent tendency toward the territoriality construct is certainly understandable. After all, both property and privacy are inextricably linked to concepts of spatiality and exclusion.

The home—a primary territorial space—remains the dominant place that has attracted a significant privacy interest under Section 8,[116] including nonphysical intrusions through observations by law enforcement agents.[117] However, in *Tessling*, the Supreme Court of Canada found that the privacy of the home extended no further than its external walls.[118] While Binnie J. acknowledged that the territorial privacy interest was implicated, the privacy interest was characterized as "essentially informational" that led to a significantly different result than that of the lower court decision.[119]

The Supreme Court has ventured out to include other locations under Section 8 protection finding that a person is likely to have a reasonable expectation of privacy in hotel rooms,[120] toilet stalls in public washrooms,[121] an apartment,[122] or the perimeter search of a home.[123] However, on the current assessment of spatial

---

116. *R v Silveira* [1995] 2 SCR 297, per Cory J. "[t]here is no place on earth where persons can have a greater expectation of privacy than within their 'dwelling-house'."

117. *R v Sandhu* (1993) 28 B.C.A.C. 203, 82 C.C.C. (3d) 236, which held that eavesdropping on conversations from outside the home on conversations taking place in a home was an unreasonable search.

118. In *Tessling*, the RCMP arrested a man for running a marijuana growing operation out of his house, which they discovered by using thermal imaging technology to measure the heat emanating from the house. The police did not obtain a warrant for their surveillance activities and the accused brought a s.8 challenge.

119. *R v Tessling*, (2003) 63 O.R. (3d) 1 (CA). The Ontario Court of Appeal followed *R v Kyllo* 533 U.S. 27 (2001), which directly addressed the question of the use of thermal imaging technology by police to photograph patterns of heat escaping from the surface of the home, finding that the warrantless use of FLIR technology violated the Fourth Amendment protection against search and seizure because it was a device not in general public use and it allowed exploration into the home.

120. *R v Wong* (n. 102). But note Lamer's dissent that the hotel room ceased to be a private space when the defendant invited others, including strangers, into the room thus eliminating any reasonable expectation of privacy in that space.

121. *R v O'Flaherty* (1987), 63 Nfld. & P.E. IR 21 (Nfld. CA); *R. v Silva* (1995), 26 O.R. (3d) 554 (Gen. Div.), but note in *R v LeBeau* (1988), 25 O.A.C. 1 (CA) that there is no reasonable expectation of privacy outside the closed toilet cubicles of a public washroom.

122. *R v Pugliese* (1992), 52 O.A.C. 280, but not in common hallways of an apartment building, *R v Laurin* (1997), 98 O.A.C. 50.

123. *R v Kokesch* [1990] 3 S.C.R. 3; *R v Wiley* [1993] 3 S.C.R. 263.

privacy interests, you can still point to barriers that are sustaining its protection, even if law enforcement did not actually trespass. It is, consistently, a tangible barrier that clearly delineates a boundary crossing triggering Section 8. Even in *Tessling*, the Court made clear that this was "off the wall" technology and not "through the wall" technology further reinforcing the tangible barrier basis for sustaining privacy protection. Technologies that enable law enforcement to locate and observe an individual anywhere, at any time operate across all spaces and places without necessarily crossing any tangible boundary, thus, presumably outside the scope of Section 8 protection.

Moreover, within the territorial model of spatial privacy, there is a sliding scale of the level of expectation and degree of privacy the law protects. Hence, a person is entitled to an extremely high expectation of privacy in relation to her residence,[124] and to a much lower expectation in relation to a vehicle in which she is merely a passenger,[125] or an apartment to which one is a visitor.[126] Where the expectation of privacy will fall on the spectrum of places is unclear and difficult to reconcile from a theoretical and practical perspective. If a person has a higher expectation in one physical location and lower in another, then potentially a person who enters, leaves or re-enters physical places or spaces will move up and down the scale during any given period, but potentially being surveilled continuously through those spaces. Observation, tracking, or monitoring made possible by new technologies does not necessarily stop or change because of where you are, but the level of protection may.

The requirement that society recognizes an expectation as reasonable appears to focus less on a person's actions or activities and more on the place in which she acts. In other words, under the current reasonable expectation of privacy test, particular attention is given to the nature of the place in which a person is being observed because this will bear directly upon whether there was a justified expectation of privacy. This is problematic in the context of new technologies that are not always or necessarily deployed or tied to particular places. Clearly, in ubicomp environments technologies are embedded everywhere, thus fluid, mobile, rather than fixed and defined.

Therefore, while the reasonable expectation of privacy standard contemplates the possibility that privacy protection under Section 8 might be made portable and taken with people, it has not been so broadly interpreted. Arguably, the effect has been to further entrench a property analysis, rendering the *Hunter* aspiration unfulfilled. This difficulty is compounded by the ambiguity of the phrase itself, "people, not places." What this phrase actually means remains a mystery and it would, perhaps, have made more sense if this phrase had read "people *and* places." It remains unclear how Section 8 protects people, or rather,

---

124. *R v Feeney* [1997] 2 S.C.R. 13.
125. *R v Belnavis* [1997] 3 S.C.R. 341.
126. *Edwards* (n. 108).

how it protects people's spatial privacy interests. Does it protect only their physical persons, their words, or activities in enclosed spaces or traditionally private places or does it protect more? Privacy protection encompassed under Section 8 protects "people, not places" but courts have not defined the "space" or the dimensions of privacy that people occupy beyond that which is bounded by traditional perceptions of time and space. Moreover, "people not places" is a problematic foundation because people do rely heavily on the place of an activity in determining whether it is private or not. Deprived of the boundary lines provided by place, courts often resort to factors that weaken privacy protection rather than bolstering it. Courts examine, for example, whether the activity is sufficiently "intimate" to warrant Section 8 protection,[127] a decision that in turn requires controversial judgments about what activities people should and should not have a right to shield from others.

V. CONCLUSION

The powerful new wave of technologies is now being adopted for mainstream use in a variety of contexts. As the full geo-location and tracking capabilities materialize, we are at risk of being more visible and more exposed as we move through the spaces of our everyday lives. The surveillance and privacy implications are profound. However, the current constitutional regime for protecting privacy is less effective in an environment of ubiquitous computing where traditional dichotomies for space, person, and time are easily deconstructed. The parameters of Section 8, namely the territorial spectrum, have been narrowly interpreted by the Supreme Court of Canada. This approach is problematic. As more of our lives and activities are subject to observation by government, the current spatial privacy construct does not take into account all of the spaces in which we carry out private activities nor the nature and effect of the changing technologies rendering irrelevant protections afforded by traditional analysis. The problem is particularly acute where there are no clearly defined tangible barriers to secure protection. The challenge of preserving the privacy interests we have come to enjoy and expect without the fear of being watched and exposed is compounded as the ubiquitous computing agenda moves forward. Central to a ubiquitous networked society is the anytime, anywhere paradigm further contributing to the perception, real or imagined, that we are living in a surveillance society within which the spaces and places for privacy are increasingly vulnerable.

A privacy analysis for the ubiquitous computing age must focus on something other than physical location. This next generation of technology holds vast implications for all of the spaces in which we expect some level of privacy. Indeed,

---

127. *Tessling* (n. 102); *Plant* (n. 104).

these new forms of ubiquitous systems challenge some of our fundamental ideas about subjectivity, visibility, space, and the distinction between public and private. Together, these challenges necessitate formulating a more nuanced spatial privacy construct that more adequately protects the entire array of privacy interests.

6. CORE PRIVACY
A Problem for Predictive Data Mining

JASON MILLAR[*]

I. INTRODUCTION

Data mining technologies are pervasive in our society.[1] They are designed to capture, aggregate, and analyze our digital footprints, such as purchases, Internet search strings, blogs, and travel patterns in an attempt to profile individuals for a variety of applications. Knowledge of the full scope of data mining often leaves people feeling as though it is intuitively wrong. On the one hand, this feeling is written off just as an unreflective expression of unease toward the technology, the potential harms of data mining (assuming any can be identified) outweighed by its potential benefits. On the other hand, the feeling is often explained by an appeal to more academic conceptions of privacy. Built primarily on surveillance technologies, data mining is implicated as a potential violation of individuals' privacy. People's unease with data mining might best be understood as the expression of some intuitive understanding that their privacy is at stake.

Nissenbaum and Tavani address the privacy threats associated with data mining, and analyze them based largely on contextual accounts of privacy.[2]

* The author would like to thank Jacquie Burkell, Jeremy Clark, Carole Lucock, David Matheson, Val Steeves, and Ian Kerr for valuable insight and feedback regarding this article. Ian Kerr, Canada Research Chair in Ethics, Law and Technology at the University of Ottawa, deserves special thanks for providing countless students an opportunity to cut their academic teeth in distinguished company.

1. Andy Clark, *Natural-born Cyborgs: Minds, Technologies, and the Future of Human Intelligence* (New York: Oxford University Press, 2003); David Lyon, "Facing the future: Seeking ethics for everyday surveillance," *Ethics and Information Technology* 3, no. 3 (2001): 171–181; Helen Nissenbaum, "Protecting Privacy in an Information Age: The Problem of Privacy in Public," *Law and Philosophy: An International Journal for Jurisprudence and Legal Philosophy* 17, no. 5–6 (1998): 559–596.

2. See Nissenbaum "Protecting Privacy in an Information Age: The Problem of Privacy in Public," (n. 1).; H.T. Tavani, "Informational Privacy, Data Mining, and the Internet,"

But a privacy analysis of predictive data mining underpinned by contextual arguments is unable to fully analyze the unique privacy threats posed by the technology. The reason is that contextual accounts of privacy are open to two objections that predictive data miners can exploit in defense of their technology. As a result contextual accounts of privacy suffer in trying to describe what is problematic with predictive data mining where profiling individuals is the goal.

In order to better understand what *feels* wrong about data mining to many people, I will focus on some unique characteristics of predictive data mining. In particular, I will argue that current technology allows datasets to be analyzed with a level of sophistication that results in the emergence of new types of data. Fully analyzing the privacy implications of the new data requires first, an evaluation of what types of data count as *core private information* and second, an evaluation of what constitutes a *core privacy violation*.[3] By viewing data mining in this new light, I hope to explain, and overcome, one of the theoretical barriers to a full privacy analysis of predictive data mining, while providing a methodology for use in assessing, on a case-by-case basis, whether or not particular instances of predictive data mining constitute a privacy violation.

II. PREDICTIVE DATA MINING AND PROFILING THE INDIVIDUAL

It is impressive to think of the number of digital footprints each of us will have left behind during the course of our lives. Every swipe of an electronically readable document (e.g., credit cards, ATM cards, student cards, library cards, passports, etc.), every search string entered into a Web browser, every blog entry and email, any Electronic Product Code (EPC) identified by a reader, all phone calls and connections between an individual's digital hardware and a network, and every other interaction between an individual or her possessions and a computer of some sorts, is logged and time stamped in an electronic database for possible future reference.[4]

Ethics and Information Technology 1 (1999): 37–145.; and H. T. Tavani, "KDD, Data Mining, and the Challenge for Normative Privacy," *Ethics and Information Technology* 1 (1999): 265–273.

3. Within the Canadian legal system the notion of "a biographical core of personal information" has been used to determine whether or not an individual has a reasonable expectation of privacy with respect to certain information (see *R. v Plant*, [1993] 3 S.C.R. 281.). Though there may be overlaps between what counts as core private information or as a core privacy violation (i.e. those concepts I intend to develop) and the legal notion found in Canadian jurisprudence, they are not intentional. My intentions are philosophical, directed at understanding how to think of privacy in light of particular data mining technologies. If there are legal implications buried in my account, I leave it to those better versed in the law to decide what they may be, and elucidate (or import) them accordingly.

4. EPCs are currently in the advanced stages of development by EPCglobal, Inc (see http://www.epcglobalinc.org/home). They will be deployed in the form of Radio Frequency

A great majority of those footprints are either explicitly associated with identifiable individuals or were designed to make the process of identification relatively painless. That means that the databases collecting the footprints can contain identifying information about the individuals alongside the footprint data. Exceptions to this are health care information, which is intentionally "anonymized," and some personal data sold to third parties that, depending on the legal jurisdiction, must be "anonymized" prior to release.[5] In a given year, a conservative estimate of twenty digital transactions a day means that more than 7,000 transactions become associated with a particular individual—upwards of a half million in a lifetime. Capturing and storing this information is becoming easier and cheaper—the number and detail of our daily transactions is increasing. Actual numbers need not be calculated in order to get the sense that the resulting datasets represent a source of great potential value to anyone interested in analyzing, or *mining*, them.

The field of data mining is burgeoning. There are no fewer than thirty major technical conferences held internationally each year.[6] According to the Institute of Electrical and Electronics Engineers (IEEE) International Conference on Data Mining official Web site, the number of paper submissions for the conference's proceedings more than doubled to 776 in its first six years of being held.[7] Various topics are discussed at these technical conferences including new algorithms for use in solving specific problems and Knowledge Discovery in Databases (KDD), which is defined as the nontrivial extraction of implicit, previously unknown, and potentially useful information from data.[8] Despite the growing size of the literature and increasing sub-specialization, data mining can generally be understood as the search for patterns within a given dataset.

Identifier Tags capable of uniquely identifying each individual product (as opposed to a box or flat containing several of the same product) that rolls off an assembly line, by means of a 96-bit number.

5. This should not give the impression that the so-called "anonymous" data cannot be used to re-identify individuals. B. Malin, L. Sweeney, and E. Newton, "Trail Re-Identification: Learning Who You Are From Where You Have Been," in *Carnegie Mellon University, School of Computer Science, Data Privacy Laboratory Technical Report, LIDAP-WP12* (Pittsburgh: Carnegie Mellon University, Laboratory For International Data Privacy, February 2003), point to the ease with which most such data can be re-associated with the individuals they belong to.

6. IEEE International Conference on Data Mining, http://www.kmining.com/info_conferences.html (accessed March 5, 2008).

7. Last year of data was the 2006 conference at the time of writing. IEEE International Conference on Data Mining, http://www.cs.uvm.edu/~icdm/ (accessed June 17, 2008).

8. W. J. Frawley, G. Piatetsky-Shapiro, and C. Matheus, "Knowledge Discovery In Databases: An Overview," in *Knowledge Discovery In Databases*, eds. G. Piatetsky-Shapiro and W. J. Frawley (Cambridge, MA: AAAI Press/MIT Press, 1991): 1–30.

There are two broad categories of data mining tasks: *descriptive data mining*, where the goal is to describe the general properties of the existing data, and *predictive data mining*, where the goal is to predict based on inference from the original data.[9] Descriptive tasks might include comparing the features of two datasets as in determining that they are identical or similar to some degree, or can involve simple characterizations like "dataset x includes fifty-two instances of doughnut purchase activity." Predictive tasks, on the other hand, include activities like *profiling*. Inferences can be drawn from the regularities and patterns found in datasets, which allow certain predictions to be made. For example, data from hospital emergency room visits is mined such that potential outbreaks of diseases can be effectively predicted during the early stages of the outbreak. On a more personal level, individuals' Web browsing patterns can be predictively mined in order to glean the types of information that are of particular interest to those individuals. Based on the resulting dataset, predictions can be made about them including the types of music that they may like to purchase, political or religious affiliations they may have, or illnesses from which they may suffer.

A diverse group of individuals currently applies predictive data mining techniques during the course of its business. Law enforcement and intelligence agencies have long relied on data mining techniques to develop detailed profiles of individuals (political leaders, criminals, etc.) in an attempt to better predict the behavior patterns of those individuals based on past behavior patterns. They, and militaries, are increasingly making use of data mining techniques to identify potential threats. Credit card companies use data mining techniques to better detect fraudulent activities. Cross-referencing each transaction request with models of regular versus irregular activity, and flagging potential irregular activity have resulted in fewer losses due to fraudulent activity. Security companies use data mining to monitor and analyze the information captured on video cameras and other monitoring devices (swipe cards, etc.) in order to identify potential security threats or breaches. Businesses use data mining to profile customers and understand their potential purchasing preferences. Web sites use data mining techniques to better serve up information, such as search results and advertising, to those browsing their sites.

These descriptions of data mining underscore the important role that surveillance technologies play in the overall data mining scheme. Surveillance typically involves the targeted collection of seemingly disparate bits of information, via the application of various technologies, for potential use in some sort of post hoc analysis. Cameras collect data for analysis after some interesting activity has taken place; swipe card readers log the comings and goings of people in some

---

9. O. R. Zaiane, J. Lia, and R. Hayward, "Mission-Based Navigational Behaviour Modeling for Web Recommender Systems," in *Advances in Web Mining and Web Usage Analysis: Lecture Notes in Artificial Intelligence*, eds. B. Mobasher, O. Nasraoui, B. Liu, and B. Massand, (Springer Verlag, LNAI 3932, 2006): 37–55.

secure area; phone logs are recorded for use in billing or potentially for use in criminal investigations. Surveillance technologies can be seen as the backbone of data mining, providing the seemingly disparate pieces of information that populate datasets. Those datasets are then fed into the various data mining algorithms and the search for patterns begins.

III. ASSESSING THE PRIVACY IMPLICATIONS OF DATA MINING

Data mining, both descriptive and predictive, carries privacy implications. An individual's privacy, in the most general terms, turns on the status—known versus unknown, public versus private—of particular kinds of information about an individual. When a certain piece of information deemed private by some theory, say theory *A*, becomes known about an individual, the individual is said to have suffered a privacy loss according to theory *A*. Data mining technologies provide a means of discovering information about individuals. So determining whether or not the process or results of data mining are privacy invasive is the crux of the problem at hand.

Before outlining some assessments of the privacy implications of data mining, a word about the public-private dichotomy of personal information is in order. The particular version of it that I will offer here conflicts with some theories of privacy. However, I mean only to expound what may be a typical version of the dichotomy for clarity; my overall argument does not depend on the correctness of this account, only on the fact that the public-private dichotomy of personal information is commonly the focus of privacy theories.

Given the above generalization of privacy theories we can say that bits of information about an individual may be considered public or private. An example of a public piece of information could be that person X was walking down Main Street last night; person X was in a public space and had no expectation of privacy with respect to his whereabouts. If another individual came to know that person X was on Main Street last night then person X would not suffer a privacy loss with respect to that piece of information. An example of a private piece of information could be that person X is secretly in love with person Y and expresses this love in the form of letters hidden in X's closet. If another person were to stumble across the cache of love letters and proceed to read them, person X would have suffered a loss of privacy with respect to the information about her feelings toward Y. One of the main problems that a theory of privacy needs to address is expounding what qualifies a particular kind of information as public or private.[10] Generally speaking, public information is considered to be

---

10. See Judith Jarvis Thomson, "The Right to Privacy," *Philosophy and Public Affairs* 4 (1975): 295–314, and T. Scanlon, "Thomson on Privacy," *Philosophy and Public Affairs* 4 (1975): 315–322, for good examples of this approach to theorizing about privacy.

public full stop, and private information is considered to be private full stop, in other words the status of information about an individual is not vague.

How do we assess the privacy implications of data mining? Nissenbaum and Tavani have focused largely on problems related to the public versus private status of the data that is included in the original dataset used for data mining, and construct a contextual account of why data mining can violate privacy norms. In this section, I will argue that this has the effect of preventing them from fully assessing the privacy implications of predictive data mining, especially with regard to the resulting data, or knowledge, that is unique to predictive data mining.

A brief sketch of Nissenbaum's and Tavani's arguments is in order to properly assess their approach to the problem. Both of their arguments adopt a contextual conception of privacy; they focus on the importance of an individual's control over the flow of personal information because that information can have different privacy implications from one social context to another. Rachels's account of why privacy matters points to the root of their theories. He argues that privacy matters because it is the mechanism we use to maintain the integrity of our relationships with one another.[11] He says,

> Because our ability to control who has access to us, and who knows what about us, allows us to maintain the variety of relationships with other people that we want to have, it is, I think, one of the most important reasons why we value privacy.[12]

The claim that a contextual control over information is essential to privacy is echoed in a roughly equivalent form in each of Nissenbaum's and Tavani's arguments, which are explicit attempts to understand the privacy implications of data mining. Nissenbaum rejects the traditional public-private dichotomy of information (described above), arguing instead that certain bits of information relating to a person can be public in one context and private in another.[13] For example, knowledge that person X was walking down Main Street last night could be public with respect to a certain set of X's friends, but deeply private with respect to X's co-workers if, for example, Main Street happened to be in the heart of the local gay district and X was aware that his co-workers would interpret his mere presence there as cause for discrimination. According to Nissenbaum this dual nature of information is problematic where public surveillance and data mining are concerned because of the inherent potential for data to be taken out of context. Data mining is of particular concern because it frequently involves the

---

11. James Rachels, "Why Privacy is Important," *Philosophy and Public Affairs* 4 (1975): 323–333.

12. Rachels, "Why Privacy is Important," (n. 11).

13. Nissenbaum, "Protecting Privacy in an Information Age: The Problem of Privacy in Public," (n. 2).

buying, selling, and trading of so-called public data for use in new contexts—contexts in which the data was not explicitly divulged and in which that data is private.

Tavani offers reasons for considering data mining a new threat to privacy, above and beyond traditional data retrieval techniques.[14] Though he appears to be analyzing the unique features of predictive data mining tasks (i.e., the discovery of unknown, nontrivial information), in assessing their privacy implications he seems to emphasize the contextual implications similar to those raised by Nissenbaum. Consider the privacy implications he draws from a scenario involving Lee, an individual who has divulged information to his bank while applying for a car loan. Lee's information is mined by successive algorithms, which in turn determine that Lee is part of a high credit-risk group of executives that is likely to declare bankruptcy within five years, despite current gainful employment. Tavani notes the following:

> Why does the mining of data about Lee by the bank raise concerns for privacy? While Lee voluntarily gave the bank information about annual salary, previous loans involving vacations, and the type of automobile he intended to purchase, he gave each piece of information for a specific purpose and use. Individually, each piece of information was appropriately given in order that the bank could make a meaningful determination about Lee's request for an automobile loan. However, it is by no means clear that Lee authorized the bank to use disparate pieces of that information for more general data mining analyses that would reveal patterns involving Lee that neither he nor the bank could have anticipated at the outset.[15]

Although Tavani focuses specifically on the particular strengths of data mining to uncover unknown patterns in a dataset, the example he uses suggests that the discovered knowledge is problematic from a privacy perspective because it shifts the context within which the data is considered. The implication seems to be that Lee would consider the data public with respect to his application for a car loan, but private with respect to a determination of his future credit risk.[16] Even though the data resulting from the predictive data mining is considered problematic, the privacy implications remain in relation to the dual public-private nature of the data in the original dataset.

---

14. Note that those techniques are essentially traditional methods of surveillance in which the main activity is the collection and aggregation of physically observable data for future analysis; Tavani, "Informational Privacy, Data Mining, and the Internet," (n. 2).

15. Tavani, "Informational Privacy, Data Mining, and the Internet," 141 (n. 2).

16. There is an additional implication that the resulting risk profile is also problematic because it could be false. This is a common argument against data mining in general, and it, too, fails to allow for a full analysis of predictive data mining, which I will address shortly.

So Nissenbaum and Tavani each describe the privacy implications of data mining with a focus on analyzing the contextual aspects (i.e., the public-private status) of the original dataset. The data itself is described as moving from a broadly public kind, as in the information divulged by X during his walk down Main Street, or from a narrowly public kind, as in the information divulged by Lee during his car loan application, to a private kind owing to some shift in the context of analysis.[17]

If our goal is to fully assess the privacy implications of predictive data mining, then I think we face a theoretical difficulty if we limit our arguments to the contextual nature of information. There are at least two problems with this approach. First, both Nissenbaum and Tavani mention how contextual arguments seem to be open to a normative "knock-down" objection, namely that profiling is acceptable because the individuals whose privacy is supposedly at stake publicly divulged all of the information in the original dataset.[18] This is a formidable objection that Nissenbaum and Tavani attempt to address in each of their arguments; if individuals have publicly divulged information that is subsequently mined, how can they make a post hoc claim to privacy with respect to information *gleaned only from that dataset*? As I have pointed out, Nissenbaum and Tavani both offer useful arguments how this can be possible. In addition, Nissenbaum claims that contextual norms are violated during profiling, which places the public at risk of manipulation and signals a loss of control of their personal information. These two factors, she suggests, are part of the reason that data mining (and public surveillance) is ill received by the public. However, even in the wake of their analyses, the objection remains formidable against their (and any other) contextual account of privacy.

A second problem arises with a contextual analysis of data mining. It is the possibility of a scenario in which data mining is performed that raises no contextual privacy concerns of the kind that may result from a shift in context of analysis, and in which the results turn out to be accurate. One could imagine that even in that scenario knowledge resulting from predictive data mining could be privacy invasive, a fact that would depend only on the nature of the resulting knowledge, though not on its being false. A thorough privacy analysis of predictive data mining must account for these scenarios in addition to those covered adequately by contextual analyses.

Though they certainly provide important insight into privacy problems associated with the flow of information due to data mining, Nissenbaum's and Tavani's arguments each seem to fall short of allowing a full assessment of the unique aspects of predictive data mining associated with the discovery of

---

17. "Broadly" and "narrowly" referring to the relative expectation of privacy that X has with respect to the divulged information.

18. Nissenbaum, "Protecting Privacy in an Information Age: The Problem of Privacy in Public," 587 (n. 1).

new knowledge. Focusing on the nature of the knowledge discovered through the process of predictive data mining, rather than on the contextual (public-private) status of the data in the original dataset, might add to our understanding of privacy in a way that allows us to further explain the bad taste that data mining leaves in so many of our mouths.[19] To this end, the unique characteristics of predictive data mining technologies, as well as the unique nature of the data that is produced by it, must be directly addressed.

IV. THE EMERGENT DATA OF PREDICTIVE DATA MINING

Focusing on the contextual nature of data in a privacy analysis of predictive data mining only tells us part of the story. What can be said of the kinds of data that are the results of complex predictive analyses where the goals include such things as psychological profiling?

Predictive data mining tasks, including those related to the psychological profiling of individuals, rely on KDD for their resulting data. Recall that KDD is characterized as the nontrivial extraction of unknown information from datasets. In the case of psychologically profiling individuals, the types of resulting knowledge that are of most interest are those offering the best predictions about the individuals' underlying psychological properties (i.e. the individuals' beliefs, desires, or intentions). This is because those kinds of psychological properties are typically seen as the causal roots of action production. Thus individuals' underlying beliefs, desires, or intentions combine to motivate their purchases, crimes, or mouse clicks. Discovering the kinds of knowledge—from seemingly disparate pieces of information in a dataset—that most accurately reflect an individual's psychological properties is therefore the holy grail of psychological profiling via predictive data mining.

Is it reasonable to expect that a computer algorithm could somehow provide accurate representations of an individual's psychological properties? It is beyond our current theoretical landscape to answer in the affirmative as we lack the scientific and philosophical knowledge of the mind that would allow us to clearly delineate beliefs from desires from intentions, or to give an accurate account of what those properties consist of from a physical or psychological perspective. But this does not preclude us from articulating the privacy implications of algorithms that attempt to discover knowledge about an individual's beliefs, desires, or intentions. Describing the precise relationship between the knowledge resulting from predictive data mining and our mental properties may not be

---

19. Nissenbaum, "Protecting Privacy in an Information Age: The Problem of Privacy in Public," (n. 1), argues that proof of the bad taste can be found in a 1990 poll, which showed that consumers felt that they were being asked to provide "excessive personal information."

necessary in order to begin articulating a theory of privacy that accounts for predictive data mining activities. Any talk of data representing psychological properties from here on in should therefore not be interpreted as a statement about an identity relationship between the two. By considering specific examples where psychological profiling is applied, I will argue that we can identify cases where predictive data mining is practically successful in its attempt to represent an individual's beliefs, desires, or intentions. I will also provide a means for gauging the success of a psychological profiling algorithm that is meant to address the underlying unease that may be felt concerning predictive data mining.

Consider an example in which predictive data mining is applied to Web browsing activity to determine what particular kind of information an individual is searching for. Predictive data mining here is applied in an attempt to satisfy her informational *intentions or desires*. A dataset composed of the content of Web pages she has visited, her Web access history and the connectivity between resources in a Web site can be used to predict the particular kind of information she is currently looking for.[20] Resulting data, namely the predictions about what she might currently be looking for, can be typologically distinguished from the data contained in the original dataset—the new data is meant to reflect her intentions or desires, whereas the original dataset contained seemingly disparate pieces of information divulged by virtue of her Web browsing activity. The dataset used in the prediction could theoretically be composed not only of an individual's current sessional data, but also of her entire Web browsing history, as well as knowledge of her blogging activity and any other piece of information about her that is made available to the algorithm. An example of this kind of predictive data mining project is Google's Web History (formerly Google Personal Search), designed to deliver personalized search results based on search string input and the individual's entire Web search and click history.[21] In addition to recommending information, data mining could be performed on such a dataset to try to predict a host of other information, the individual's religious beliefs and political beliefs among others.

This account demonstrates how psychological profiling differs from descriptive data mining in an important respect: the resultant dataset emerging from this kind of predictive data mining contains new data items that are not mere aggregations or simple characterizations of the original dataset. Those new data

---

20. This particular kind of dataset is described in O. R. Zaiane, J. Lia, and R. Hayward, "Mission-Based Navigational Behaviour Modeling for Web Recommender Systems," (n. 9), as a useful dataset for use in Web recommender systems (i.e., those systems that recommend particular options to users based on previous Web activity).

21. See http://www.google.com/psearch for Google's own description of the product. Andy Clark, *Natural-born Cyborgs: Minds, Technologies, and the Future of Human Intelligence*, (n. 1) also describes in detail the kind of qualitative difference between this kind of technology and the more traditional search-string-based information recommender system.

items are better characterized as non-trivial representations of an individual's beliefs, intentions, or desires. Hence, the resultant dataset includes emergent data that must be considered in its own right if we are to properly characterize predictive data mining and the privacy implications of it.

Understanding the nature of the emergent data contained in the resulting dataset can be aided by a trivial case of predictive data mining, one that may be carried out by any attentive individual. Imagine your coworker, Jon, shows up for work every day eating a chocolate doughnut. Based on the dataset including only the information, 1) that Jon walks by every day with the same thing in his hand, and 2) that the thing is always a chocolate doughnut, one could descriptively conclude that "Jon eats a chocolate doughnut every work day." However, being human and knowing that Jon is also human, one may also use the data to draw the predictive conclusion, "Jon likes chocolate doughnuts," thus attributing a desire, or preference, to Jon that is not a mere description of the original dataset since the original dataset does not contain any data about Jon's preferences or desires. A statement about Jon's desires is qualitatively different from the data in the original dataset, and that qualitative property is one that emerges by virtue of a trivial yet complex prediction about Jon's psychology.

Recall that my concern is to address the scenario where contextual accounts of privacy fail to provide an adequate means of dealing with the resulting knowledge discovered by a predictive data mining algorithm. It would help to have a methodology capable of dealing with the scenario in which a predictive data mining algorithm produces highly accurate results about an individual. Some privacy arguments claim that it is the falsity or incompleteness of the predictions that prove problematic, and they are easily refuted by those claiming to have accurate results.[22] So an account of how we might gauge the success of predictive data mining algorithms is in order. In the Web browsing case, partial success of the profiling might be gauged by the individual's willingness to click on a link to the recommended information. Complete success, however, could be gauged by her complete satisfaction with that recommendation. In other words, if an individual has a particular informational intention that is completely satisfied by the data resulting from the predictive algorithm, we could say that the profile correctly represented her intentions in the form of a recommendation.

It could be objected that the emergent data are superficially coincident with psychological properties at best. For example, a Web recommender application might mine an individual's music collection and browsing habits (e.g., on an online music store) to pick out similarities between artists that an individual likes in order to recommend artists the person *might* like. But the assertion that those recommendations are anything like a person's beliefs, intentions, or

---

22. David Lyon, "Facing the future: Seeking ethics for everyday surveillance," (n. 1), seems to use this argument in the way that he claims an individual can become alienated by the "faceless" profiles resulting from data mining.

desires remains unfounded. If it turns out that the individual does like the recommendations, then the recommendations are a statement about the predictability of his listening habits, or some other mere statistical fact about musical purchase trends in general. A person's beliefs, desires, and intentions need not be inferred in order to predict, or suggest with high rate of success, his purchases. Therefore, the psychological assertion is spurious.

What counts for an analysis of the success of predictive data mining is the *psychological resemblance* between the prediction and the individual's underlying psychological properties. If the emergent data of predictive data mining psychologically resembles an individual's beliefs, intentions, or desires, then we can gauge the data mining a success and put the objection to rest. Psychological resemblance between an output of a psychological profiling algorithm and an individual's beliefs, intentions, and desires, is something we can assess empirically. Our means of accomplishing this borrows from a well-known example in artificial intelligence—the Turing test.

Turing proposed his test as a means of recognizing intelligence in a machine.[23] In order to tell if a machine is intelligent, he suggested, an interrogator poses a series of questions to one of two potential respondents: a human or a machine. The interrogator is unaware which he is questioning; the identity is somehow hidden. His task is to determine if he is interrogating the machine or the human. If he is unable to correctly identify the respondent (with some statistically significant reliability), then the machine is said to be as intelligent as a human being. In the Turing test, the inability to distinguish between artificial intelligence and human intelligence counts toward asserting the machine's intelligence even though it is *not a statement about the identity between the kind of mental activity common to human intelligence and that activity occurring in the machine.*[24] A similar distinction can be exploited to provide a means of gauging the success of a predictive data mining task whose goal is to psychologically profile an individual by means of producing data resembling his beliefs, desires, or intentions.

Turing's test can be modified to test for psychological resemblance between the emergent data of predictive data mining and psychological properties, thus gauging the success of a predictive data-mining task. Turing's approach is a good candidate for our purposes particularly because the interrogator, in our case, has first person access to the comparison class against which the emergent data of predictive data mining is tested, namely his own beliefs, desires, and intentions. We can define the test as an attempt to determine whether the emergent data is considered *synonymous* to his corresponding psychological properties.

Our interrogator, in this test, would approach a prediction from data mining in a self-reflective inquisitive mode. Take a predictive data mining algorithm

---

23. Alan M. Turing. "Computing machinery and intelligence," *Mind.* 59, no. 236 (1950): 433–460.

24. Daniel Dennett, "The Age of Intelligent Machines: Can Machines Think?" KurzweilAI.net, http://www.kurzweilai.net/articles/art0099.html.

designed to determine political beliefs as an example of how the test would run in determining the psychological resemblance of a data mining prediction to a belief. Our interrogator is submitted to whatever surveillance method is required to populate the dataset used by the algorithm, say by turning over his entire Web browsing and search history. The interrogator is then asked to describe, in as much detail as possible, whatever political beliefs he possesses in accordance with whatever beliefs the data mining algorithm will target as predictions. The algorithm then predicts his political beliefs or more particular political beliefs, maybe in relation to one or several particular hot button issues. If the prediction matches the interrogator's own description of the belief (i.e., if the interrogator is satisfied to a sufficient degree that the prediction is what he believes) then it qualifies as synonymous to his actual belief.

I will refer to this as the *synonymy test*: if an interrogator is unable to distinguish the emergent data from a self-generated description of the target psychological property of the prediction (e.g., the particular belief, intention, or desire) to a sufficient degree, then the data and psychological property qualify as synonymous. Cases satisfying the synonymy test would be cases where the emergent data *psychologically resemble* the interrogator's psychological properties, the upshot being that they are cases of successful predictive data mining.

Why is this kind of synonymy sufficient for gauging the psychological resemblance between emergent data and a psychological property? Let us suppose that an interrogator produces a self-generated description of whatever the target of the data mining algorithm is. Let us suppose, then, that she is reasonably convinced that some particular set of emergent data is such that her best self-generated description of her beliefs, desires, or intentions represented by those data is synonymous with them. For the interrogator to then claim that they do not resemble one another would seem to be a case of incredulous question begging. At the very least, she would need to provide some description of how they do not resemble one another to support her rejection of their resemblance, especially since she has already agreed that they are synonymous according to the test. Of course, if such a description were then produced it would presumably qualify as self-generated, and would provide descriptive information individuating it from the emergent property, meaning that she was initially mistaken about the synonymy.

This approach to gauging success could be considered problematic because of a well-documented psychological phenomenon known as the Forer Effect (or Barnum Effect, or the Fallacy of Personal Validation). According to the Forer Effect, people tend to consider vague statements about personality, such as those found in horoscopes, to be highly accurate and unique to them, even though they could apply to almost anyone.[25] Given that the synonymy test relies on the individual's own evaluation of whether or not the prediction relates to her to a satisfactory degree, the systematic nature of the Forer Effect could render every

---

25. D. H. Dickson and I. W. Kelly, "The 'Barnum Effect' in Personality Assessment: A Review of the Literature." *Psychological Reports*, 57 (1985): 367–382.

prediction highly synonymous, thus rendering the test useless. In addition, it could have a similar force to the objection raised above, in that the Forer Effect would limit our statements about synonymy and psychological resemblance to statements about mere statistical facts, thus undermining the stronger psychological claim.

There is a problem with this objection. The Forer Effect describes how an individual incorrectly believes that a vague descriptor (like a typical description contained in a horoscope) uniquely applies to him.[26] As such, horoscope-like descriptions might actually pass the synonymy test, as would a host of other trivial descriptions—that X likes to read a good book now and again, or that X believes murder is wrong—but this does not pose a significant problem to the synonymy test in the context of predictive data mining. Practically speaking, it would be unusual for anyone to question the privacy implications of a horoscope. Regardless, a predictive data-mining algorithm that provided vague, horoscope-like descriptors as output would likely be considered a failure, especially since the goal of KDD is to discover *nontrivial* knowledge. Nontrivial information—an individual's voting intentions, sexual history, or health profile—is not attributable to broad swaths of the population, making it unlikely that a random individual would incorrectly adopt it in self-description. Indeed, the less trivial the descriptor, the less likely it seems that the Forer Effect would obtain and invalidate the synonymy test.

By focusing on the unique results of predictive data mining designed for the discovery of nontrivial knowledge for psychological profiling, we are faced with assessing the privacy implications of a new kind of data. We can understand the relationship between emergent data and the target individual's psychological properties in terms of their psychological resemblance. Psychological resemblance can be used as the relevant test in assessing the success of a predictive data mining task aimed at psychological profiling. Psychological resemblance finds its natural ethical implications under the rubric of *core privacy*.

V. CORE PRIVACY

There is much more going on inside us than we are willing to express, and civilization would be impossible if we could all read each other's minds.[27]

If it is possible to identify a kind of information that is essentially private, the emergent data of predictive data mining is a good place to start looking. Despite our intuitions that we often have something like a right to privacy regarding such information, the public nature of the original dataset provides for a formidable

---

26. Forer reportedly constructed his personality descriptors from horoscopes.

27. Thomas Nagel, "Concealment and Exposure," *Philosophy and Public Affairs*, 27, no. 1 (1998): 3–30, 4.

objection to privacy claims—how could someone who rightfully obtained the information subsequently use it and pose a threat to privacy in doing so? In addition, accuracy in the resulting data further complicates objections to data mining based on the emergence of false positives. Contextual accounts of privacy go a long way in describing some of the privacy issues related to data mining, but they fail to fully address how emergent data that is both obtained and used in the same context, and is highly accurate, could threaten privacy. Providing a test for assessing the psychological resemblance between emergent data and an individual's target psychological properties allows us to gauge the success of a predictive data mining algorithm. In this section, I will outline the privacy implications of emergent data. In doing so, I will argue that we can construct an understanding of *core privacy*, and that certain information counts as *core private information*. By focusing on how emergent data potentially violates core privacy, I hope to provide an argument for understanding why predictive data mining is intuitively, and practically, problematic.

Nagel's claim suggests a point of departure for assessing the privacy implications of emergent data. Each of us entertains a great number of thoughts (psychological properties) that we choose not to divulge for some reason or other. Whether they are fleeting observations, beliefs, or intense desires, they typically remain inaccessible to everyone but the individual with first-person access to them. Based on Nagel's observation, we can define *core private information* as an individual's unexpressed psychological properties to which only the individual has first-person access, and that are not knowable by anyone else, except by the individual's prior divulgence of them, or by an unreasonable inference based on other facts already known about the individual. *Core privacy* can be defined in relation to core private information as follows: A person, P, has core privacy in relation to a piece of core private information, I, and any other person, O, so long as I remains unexpressed by P, such that O can neither observe nor reasonably be expected to infer I.

The notion of reasonable inference is likely to raise objections, primarily because it may be considered too vague to underpin a theory of privacy. But in the case of data mining, what one can reasonably be expected to infer plays an important role in balancing claims to privacy. Generally speaking, any inference that an average unassisted person is capable of making given a set of data (about another individual) to which he has access via first-person observation, that is, a person who is not using a data mining algorithm, or working with a trained team of investigators, or referencing a database, etc., is a reasonable inference. This is intuitively compelling because by claiming that the gold standard for reasonable inference is an inference that could be made based on first-person observation, one maintains the social aspect of privacy as articulated by Rachels.[28] In addition,

---

28. James Rachels, "Why Privacy is Important," (n. 11).

settling the question of reasonableness can be accomplished on a case-by-case basis—a requirement that mirrors the fundamental claims of the contextual approach.

Take our prediction about Jon's doughnut preference as a test case. Applying the synonymy test between the target property, namely Jon's desires regarding doughnuts, and our prediction, (i.e., an inference regarding Jon's doughnut preference) we would likely consider them synonymous. However, we would also conclude that it was reasonable to expect that any observer (one of his coworkers in this case) would have a good chance at inferring Jon's preference for chocolate doughnuts. So an application of the definition of core private information would lead us to conclude that Jon's doughnut preference was not, in fact, a private matter with respect to his colleagues. However, the inference might be unreasonable if it were made by an employee of Jon's credit card company, who would never be in a position to make the inference if not for her special access to vast quantities of data collected about Jon's and every other customer's purchases. So Jon's preference for chocolate doughnuts could be construed as core private information with respect to the employee, and Jon could have a reasonable claim to privacy with respect to that information. For cases in which the target predictions were less trivial, we would expect the determination of reasonableness to be less controversial.

Core privacy, as I have defined it, might strike some as too obvious to be worth discussing. *Of course* some of our unexpressed beliefs, intentions, and desires are private, maybe even "core" private; what of it? But if my description of emergent data is compelling, the current (and future) technological reality of data mining prompts the definition of core privacy; emergent data is nontrivial data obtained by O that has not been expressed by P, and that could not have been reasonably inferred by O. The corollary is that core privacy, once defined, can be used to assess the privacy implications of predictive data mining where a contextual analysis cannot. If the goals of predictive data mining are to produce emergent data that passes the synonymy test, then we need a methodology for assessing the privacy implications of those goals. Successful emergent data potentially contains core private information that *may not have been expressed by the individual in any context*. The upshot is that we have a way of describing how predictive data mining can violate core privacy.

Another way of interpreting the obviousness of core privacy is to say that it packs an intuitive punch, which goes a long way toward explaining peoples' intuitive objection to data mining. Explaining how predictive data mining can violate core privacy strikes a nerve in the same way that the fictional prospect of mind reading, as expressed by Nagel, would be intuitively problematic.[29] The use of far less credible technologies said to provide rudimentary mind-reading capabilities— fMRI scans touted as providing a visual means to predicting behavior or as

29. Thomas Nagel, "Concealment and Exposure," (n. 27)

proving guilt in a crime, and polygraphs said to discern lies—has met with real criticism despite the limited success rates.[30] A concept like core privacy allows us to move beyond expressions of the intuitive unease we feel toward data mining practices, by providing a theoretical framework with which to identify and addresses some specific problems associated with the unique aspects of the technology.

VI. CONCLUSION

Predictive data mining differs from descriptive data mining in its use of KDD to discover nontrivial knowledge in datasets. KDD can produce emergent data when applied to datasets about individuals, the privacy implications of which contextual accounts of privacy fail to fully address. Assessing some of the unique privacy threats posed by predictive data mining can be helped by understanding the relationship between an individual's core private information and the predictions resulting from predictive data mining technology. If we are to better account for peoples' intuitive aversion to data mining, our focus should be on the emergent data—those properties that are meant to resemble an individual's beliefs, intentions, or desires. This shift in focus draws our attention to the unique potential that predictive data mining has for violating our core privacy. If "a *prima facie* case for caring about public surveillance is that it stirs popular indignation," then core privacy points to a *prima facie* argument that explains why that is the case.[31]

---

30. J. Adler, "Mind Reading: The New Science of Decision Making. It's Not as Rational as You Think," *Newsweek*, August 9, 2004, http://www.newsweek.com/id/54762?tid=relatedcl.

31. Nissenbaum, "Protecting Privacy in an Information Age: The Problem of Privacy in Public," 579 (n. 1).

7. PRIVACY VERSUS NATIONAL SECURITY
Clarifying the Trade-off

JENNIFER CHANDLER

After the September 11 attacks, the idea that civil liberties had to be reduced in favor of national security emerged with renewed vigor. Many have noted the paradox that security measures intended to protect a liberal democracy can end up eroding the civil liberties at the heart of that liberal democracy.[1] It is common to view this problem as one of striking the appropriate balance or trade-off between security and civil liberties.[2] The focus of this chapter is on an aspect of this general problem, namely the trade-off between privacy and national security.

---

1. See Jef Huysmans, "Minding Exceptions: The Politics of Insecurity and Liberal Democracy," *Contemporary Political Theory* 3 (2004): 321 at 322.

2. Richard Posner, *Not a Suicide Pact: The Constitution in a Time of National Emergency*, (New York: Oxford University Press, 2006); Eric A. Posner and Adrian Vermeule, *Terror in the Balance: Security, Liberty and the Courts* (New York: Oxford University Press, 2007); Kent Roach, "Must we trade rights for security? The choice between smart, harsh or proportionate security strategies in Canada and Britain," *Cardozo Law Review* 27 (2005–2006): 2151; Bruce Schneier, *Beyond Fear: Thinking Sensibly about Security in an Uncertain World* (New York: Copernicus Books, 2003); Jeremy Waldron, "Security and Liberty: The Image of Balance," *Journal of Political Philosophy* 11 (2003): 191; K. A. Taipale, "Technology, Security and Privacy: The Fear of Frankenstein, the Mythology of Privacy

The need for a trade-off between privacy and security is likely true in certain contexts and with respect to certain aspects of the right to privacy. However, framing the issue as a contest between privacy and national security tends prematurely to shut down the debate in favor of security.[3] Security has been described as the "trump of trumps," outweighing civil and political rights.[4]

However, the danger with prematurely permitting the needs of national security to trump competing values is that important questions may not be adequately considered. These include

1. Whether the contemplated security measure actually delivers any security
2. Whether there is a less privacy-invasive manner to achieve the same level of security
3. Whether the gains in security are worth the total costs of the security measure, including privacy costs and the opportunity costs of security-enhancing spending on health, education, poverty, and the environment
4. Whether the costs are distributed fairly so that the increased security of the majority is not purchased by sacrificing the interests of a minority

If the security versus privacy trade-off is biased in favor of security, particularly in times of public insecurity, there is reason to fear that we may too easily sacrifice rights and freedoms such as privacy. One of the difficulties is in trying to balance two different values against one another. As a result, this chapter proposes a reframing strategy designed to highlight some of the ways that privacy-reducing counterterrorism measures also reduce security. In this way, at least some measure of protection for privacy may be achieved by analyzing the trade-off as one of security versus security.

I. THE MEANING OF "PRIVACY" AND "SECURITY" IN THE PRIVACY VERSUS SECURITY TRADE-OFF

The privacy versus security trade-off is often asserted to be an unavoidable, if lamentable, necessity. It is rare that the meaning of the terms is made clear, or that the process of balancing them is explained. Below, I sketch out the meaning of the terms "privacy" and "security," with emphasis on the points that will shed light on the nature of the trade-off between the two.

---

and the Lessons of King Ludd," *Yale Journal of Law & Technology* 7 (2004–2005): 123; Amitai Etzioni, *The Limits of Privacy* (New York: Basic Books, 1999); Jeffrey Rosen, "The Naked Crowd: Balancing Privacy and Security in an Age of Terror," *Arizona Law Review* 46 (2004): 607.

3. Peter P. Swire, "Privacy and Information Sharing in the War on Terrorism," *Villanova Law Review* 51 (2006): 101 at 124–125.

4. Conor Gearty, "Reflections on Civil Liberties in an Age of Counterterrorism," *Osgoode Hall Law Journal* 41 (2003): 185 at 204–5.

A. Security

Security has been defined as an "absence of threats to acquired values"[5] or a "low probability of damage to acquired values."[6] A distinction is often drawn between objective and subjective security. Objective security refers to the low probability of damage, while subjective security refers to the feeling of security, or the absence of fear that acquired values are threatened.[7] The subjective component of security is highly relevant in the context of terrorism, which works primarily by inducing fear rather than by posing a real physical threat to most people.

While one can have objective without subjective security (or the reverse), the two are related. It is possible that an incorrect subjective perception of risk may become an actual threat to objective security. This is because fear may produce counter-productive risk avoidance or destabilize society. On the other hand, an absence of justified fear may cause a person to run greater objective risks, with the same holding true at the national level. Security may thus require that one be objectively free from risk and also subjectively feel free from risk.

The above-mentioned definition of security is very general. It does not specify the entity whose security is at issue (e.g., the individual, a group, the state, the international system, or the biosphere[8]) or the types of values amenable to being secured. During the 1980s, the concept of security in political science was broadened beyond a concern with the security of the state (national security), which entailed a focus on international relations and military issues, toward the security of people as individuals or as collectivities.[9] The security of people ("human security") is understood to extend beyond national security, also including economic welfare, the health of the environment, cultural identity, and political rights.[10] Thomas suggests that human security incorporates both quantitative and qualitative aspects. The quantitative aspect refers to the satisfaction of the basic material needs essential for survival, including food, shelter, and health care, while the qualitative aspect refers to "the achievement of human dignity which incorporates personal autonomy, control over one's life, and unhindered participation in the life of the community."[11]

5. Arnold Wolfers, "National Security as an Ambiguous Symbol," *Political Science Quarterly* 67, no. 4 (1952): 481 at 485.

6. David A. Baldwin, "The Concept of Security," *Review of International Studies* 23 (1997): 5 at 13.

7. Wolfers, "National Security," (n. 5) at 485; Lucia Zedner, "The Pursuit of Security," in *Crime Risk and Security*, eds. Tim Hope and Richard Sparks (London: Routledge, 2000) 200 at 202.

8. Emma Rothschild, "What is security?" *Daedalus* 124, no. 3 (1995): 53 at 55; Baldwin, "Concept of Security," 13 (n. 6).

9. Ole Waever, "Securitization and Desecuritization," in *On Security*, ed. Ronnie D. Lipschutz, (New York: Columbia Univ. Press, 1995), 47.

10. *Ibid.*, 47.

11. Caroline Thomas. Global Governance, Development and Human Security. (London: Pluto Press, 2000), 6–7.

When we are considering the trade-off between "privacy" and "security," should we adopt a narrow or broad concept of security? Most discussions of the trade-off after September 11 have contemplated security in a narrower sense than that meant by "human security." The pursuit of security in this context has most often been understood to be counterterrorist efforts intended to defend the physical security of people and property as well as the stability of the state, and the following analysis will adopt this concept of security.

B. Privacy

The nature and moral significance of "privacy" are difficult questions that have attracted significant philosophical attention.[12] There is disagreement over whether "privacy" actually refers to something fundamental and coherent or simply groups together diverse issues that have a superficial connection.[13] Accepting that the concept of privacy is a coherent and useful one, various writers have proposed definitions of privacy. It has been variously described as a person's claim to determine what information about him or herself is communicated to others, a person's measure of control over personal information and over who has sensory access to him or her, and a state or condition of limited access to the person.[14]

Although these descriptions assist in identifying the nature of privacy, it is still necessary to explain why it should or should not be protected. Here again, there are various explanations of why privacy is important. Privacy is said either to promote or to be a necessary component of human interests of inherent value such as human dignity, autonomy, individuality, liberty, and social intimacy.[15] A person who is completely subject to public scrutiny will lose dignity, autonomy, individuality, and liberty as a result of the sometimes strong pressure to conform to public expectations.[16] In addition to freedom from the pressure to conform, privacy also protects the individual from another party's use of his or her information to manipulate, out-compete, or otherwise exploit the individual.

The value of privacy takes on another dimension as a result of modern information technologies. A certain measure of privacy with respect to personal information used to be ensured by the technological limits on its storage,

---

12. Allan Westin, *Privacy and Freedom* (New York: Atheneum, 1967); Ruth Gavison "Privacy and the Limits of Law," *Yale Law Journal* 89 (1980): 421 at 424.

13. Ferdinand Schoeman, "Privacy: Philosophical Dimensions of the Literature," in *Philosophical Dimensions of Privacy: An Anthology*, ed. F. Schoeman (New York: Cambridge Univ. Press, 1984) at 5.

14. *Ibid*, at 2–3; Gavison, "Privacy," 428 (n. 12).

15. Schoeman, "Privacy: Philosophical Dimensions," (n. 13) at 8; Gavison, "Privacy," 448–55 (n. 12); James Rachels, "Why Privacy is Important" *Philosophy and Public Affairs* 4, no. 4 (1975): 323.

16. Schoeman, "Privacy: Philosophical Dimensions," 19 (n. 13); Gavison, "Privacy", 448 (n. 12).

communication, and cross-referencing with other information. However, as information technology has become more sophisticated and efficient, it has become possible to collect and integrate large quantities of personal information. "Data surveillance" or "dataveillance" refers to "the systematic use of personal data systems in the investigation or monitoring of the actions or communications of one or more persons.[17] The systematic collection, from multiple sources, of large quantities of personal information creates risks for individuals. While the risks mentioned in the preceding paragraphs flow from the disclosure of true and relevant information about an individual, dataveillance creates the additional risk that incorrect or unreliable data may come to be used to make judgments about whether to apply benefits or sanctions to individuals. In addition, as databases are integrated, data that was sufficiently reliable and relevant in one context may come to be used for inappropriately sensitive purposes.

Westin suggests that there are two main sources of social pressure against individual privacy. The first is human curiosity or the seemingly universal "tendency on the part of individuals to invade the privacy of others."[18] Second, and more applicable in this context, is the use of surveillance "to enforce the rules of the society."[19] Since terrorism (particularly suicide terrorism) is not easily deterred by punishment after the fact, the pressure to detect and preempt terrorist plots is strong. Increased surveillance is therefore a predictable response to a dramatic terrorist attack.

II. EXPLAINING THE "WEIGHT" OF SECURITY

The purpose of this section is to consider why security is so powerful, and why it seems fairly easily to trump competing values such as privacy. The reasons suggested for security's rhetorical power are first that security in the sense of physical survival is a prerequisite for the enjoyment of other values such as privacy.[20] Second, human risk perception may be subject to cognitive biases that cause us to overestimate the risk of terrorism and to have difficulty perceiving the harm of reduced privacy. Third, we are apt to think that it is better to have more rather than less security, while this is not true for privacy. Fourth, to the extent that national security is obtained at the expense of the privacy of a minority,

---

17. Roger Clarke, "Dataveillance: Delivering '1984'" in *Framing Technology: Society, Choice and Change* eds. L. Green and R. Guinery (Sydney: Allen & Unwin, 1994), available at www.anu.edu.au/people/Riger.Clarke/DV/PaperPopular.html.

18. Westin, *Privacy and Freedom*, 19 (n. 12).

19. *Ibid.*, 20.

20. Although some values may be protected beyond death (e.g., autonomy rights dictate respect for an individual's expressed wishes with respect to the use of his or her remains), the full enjoyment of these values exists during life.

the majority is more likely not to perceive or care about the privacy costs and thus will regard the security measures as reasonable. Fifth, social-psychological reactions of solidarity following an external attack may cause people to be more willing to set aside individual rights claims such as privacy for a perceived collective benefit in terms of national security. Finally, judges tend to defer to governments on matters of national security.

A. Is Security the Prime Value?

Security is privileged over values such as liberty and autonomy in various strands of political philosophy, with an important role of the state being the protection of the physical security of people and property. This is so in competing individual-istic and communitarian accounts of the state. The idea of the social contract has been an important part of western political philosophy for centuries, serving to justify political authority. Classical social contractarians emphasized the danger-ousness of life in the "state of nature."[21] The social contract was the means by which people voluntarily surrendered a certain measure of their individual freedom in exchange for the security and protection provided by a legitimate political authority. According to these views, security is a primary obligation of the state since that is what individuals have contracted for in submitting to state authority. The communitarian perspective also privileges security over individual privacy.[22]

Baldwin refers to this approach to valuing security as the "prime value" approach, and challenges it by suggesting that it is logically and empirically indefensible.[23] The prime value approach would suggest that all societal resources should be poured into the pursuit of absolute security. As an empirical matter, we do not behave in this way. It is unfortunately clear that even affluent societies do not value the survival of their members above all else. For example, no society puts all of its resources into health care, and the resulting underfunding indi-rectly takes lives. Instead, each society chooses a level of basic security, which may not entail survival for all its members, and allocates the remaining resources to other values according to the relative importance of those values to that society.

If we pursue neither absolute security, nor the level of security required to ensure basic survival for everyone, it does not make sense to say that security is the prime value or that it ought necessarily to trump values such as liberty or privacy. One response to this argument is that we may be willing to make compromises between the various values essential to survival, but that we would not trade a survival requirement for a nonsurvival value such as privacy. In other words, we would spread resources between health care, housing, nutrition and

---

21. David Boucher and Paul Kelly eds, *The Social Contract From Hobbes to Rawls* (London: Routledge 1994), 2–10.

22. Etzioni, *The Limits of Privacy*, 42 (n. 2).

23. Baldwin, "Concept of Security," 18 (n. 6).

counterterrorism (for example), even though we could not assure a basic level of any of these goods for all members of society, but we would not underfund any of these survival requirements in order to obtain liberty or privacy.

In the end, it is probably true that, up to a point, we view survival as more important than the protection of fundamental rights and freedoms that we feel are essential to a good life. This cannot be taken so far that the life being secured is no longer felt to be worth living because it is without liberty, privacy, or other rights. However, the sacrifice of privacy for security in the context of counter-terrorism measures has not reached this stage for the general public. As a result, it is possible that the view that survival is indispensable for the full enjoyment of civil liberties is partly responsible for the greater weight accorded to security over privacy after September 11.

B. Human Perception of Risk

Research in the psychology of risk perception suggests that people employ a set of heuristics to assess probabilities, and that these heuristics can produce serious and persistent biases.[24] Some of these tendencies lead people to overestimate the risks of terrorism. At the same time, they cause people to be relatively unconcerned about the risks to privacy caused by counterterrorist security measures.

The "availability heuristic" refers to the tendency of people to assess the probability of an event by the ease with which occurrences can be brought to mind by recall or imagination.[25] Familiar, recent, or salient events seem more probable because they are more available to the mind than the less famous, older, or less dramatic events.[26] Similarly, whether a risk can be easily imagined or not also affects assessments of its probability.[27] An important consequence of the availability heuristic is that repeated discussion, for example in the media, of a low-probability hazard will increase its perceived riskiness regardless of the actual probability of harm.[28] The harms of terrorism are famous, dramatic, recent, vividly imaginable, and repeatedly covered in the media. On the other hand, the consequences of counterterrorism measures for civil liberties are much less available to the mind and so tend not to evoke as much concern.

---

24. Paul Slovic, "Perception of Risk" (1987) reprinted in Paul Slovic, *The Perception of Risk*, (London: Earthscan Publications Ltd, 2000) 220, at 221–222; Amos Tversky and Daniel Kahneman, "Judgment Under Uncertainty: Heuristics and Biases," (1974) reprinted in *Judgment Under Uncertainty: Heuristics and Biases*, eds. Kahneman, Slovic, and Tversky (Cambridge: Cambridge Univ. Press 1982), 3.

25. Tversky and Kahneman, "Judgment Under Uncertainty," 11 (n. 24).

26. *Ibid.*, 11.

27. *Ibid.*, 12–13.

28. Paul Slovic, Baruch Fischhoff, and Sarah Lichtenstein, "Facts Versus Fears: Understanding Perceived Risk," in *Judgment Under Uncertainty: Heuristics and Biases*, eds. Kahneman, Slovic, and Tversky (Cambridge: Cambridge Univ. Press 1982), 463.

In addition to the consequences of the "availability heuristic," terrorism also pushes "all the risk perception hot buttons" since it has "vivid and dreadful consequences; exposure is involuntary and difficult to control (or avoid); and it is unfamiliar, often catastrophic, and caused by human malevolence."[29] Risks of this type are termed "dread risks."[30] People are more apt to avoid dread risks than risks in which a similar or greater number of people are killed over a longer period of time.[31]

People also tend to be insensitive to probability with respect to strongly positive or negative events.[32] They tend to react to the possibility rather than the probability of the event, which causes very small probabilities to carry great weight.[33] Slovic suggests that this cognitive distortion is particularly at issue with terrorism.[34]

C. Inherent Limits to the Value of Privacy

Another reason why security seems to be a more compelling value than privacy is perhaps that privacy is an inherently limited value, while security is not. As a result, we are more likely to always want more security, but unlikely to feel the same way about privacy.

Most individuals want an intermediate level of privacy, rather than complete exposure to or complete isolation from others.[35] As Gavison writes, "Privacy thus cannot be said to be a value in the sense that the more people have of it, the better."[36] Indeed, some of the justifications for privacy inherently contemplate that privacy is not to be an absolute insulation of the individual from all others. For example, it is said that without privacy we would be unable to form close relationships since the relinquishment of some privacy to selected people is a critical aspect of how we form closer and deeper relationships.[37] If everyone knew everything about us, these gradations of closeness would be more difficult to establish. However, if everyone knew nothing about us, we similarly would be unable to establish close relationships.

---

29. Paul Slovic, "What's fear got to do with it? It's affect we need to worry about." *Missouri Law Review* 69 (2004): 971 at 985.

30. Slovic, "Perception of Risk" (n. 24) at 225.

31. Gerd Gigerenzer, "Out of the Frying Pan into the Fire: Behavioral Reactions to Terrorist Attacks," *Risk Analysis* 26, no. 2, (2006): 347 at 347.

32. Slovic, "What's fear got to do with it?" (n. 29) at 982.

33. *Ibid.*

34. *Ibid.*, 987.

35. Westin, Privacy and Freedom, 7 (n. 12).

36. Gavison, "Privacy," 440 (n. 12).

37. Emanuel Gross, "The struggle of a democracy against terrorism—Protection of human rights: The right to privacy versus the national interest—The proper balance," *Cornell International Law Journal* 37, (2004): 27 at 32.

The goal of security is not subject to the same type of inherently desirable limits. It may be that we unconsciously have an ambivalent attitude toward privacy, while we are more certain that more security is a good thing.

D. The Distributive Implications of Counterterrorism

Another of the reasons why security may trump privacy in the context of counterterrorism is that the security improvement is sometimes bought at the expense of a minority. To the extent that this is true, the majority will either fail to perceive the costs of that security or they will not care sufficiently. As will be discussed further below, the "war on terror" exposes Muslims and those of Arab ethnicity to increased risks of being falsely suspected of terrorism and mistreated.[38]

To the extent that we obtain objective or subjective security at the expense of a minority, there is distributive injustice. However, the distributive implications of counterterrorism measures are not so clear. One must consider both who is at greater risk because of counterterrorism measures, as well as who is at greatest risk of harm from terrorism if an effective counterterrorism measure is not adopted.

The groups most at risk from a terrorist attack vary according to the type and location of the attack. It may be that the failure to take effective counterterrorism measures may disproportionately harm disadvantaged minorities within the population. If this is true, counterterrorism efforts may disproportionately both help and harm different vulnerable minorities.

The majority of the victims in the September 11 attack on the World Trade Center were Caucasian men living in the United States.[39] Other types of terrorist targets may disproportionately affect other groups of people. The population at risk of an attack on public transportation in the United States is different, where users of public transport are less than 50% Caucasian and male, and are likely to have a lower than average household income.[40] Industrial plants are another type of potential target for terrorist attacks,[41] and members of disadvantaged

---

38. CAIR-Canada, "Presumption of Guilt: A National Survey on Security Visitations of Canadian Muslims," (8 June 2005), http://www.caircan.ca/downloads/POG-08062005.pdf at 3.

39. "Demographic Data on the Victims of the September 11, 2001 Terror Attack on the World Trade Center, New York City," *Population and Development Review* 28, no. 3 (2002): 586.

40. John Neff and Larry Pham, American Public Transportation Association, "A Profile of Public Transportation Passenger Demographics and Travel Characteristics Reported in On-Board Surveys" (May 2007), http://www.apta.com/government_affairs/policy/documents/transit_passenger_characteristics_07.pdf.

41. Thomas C. Beierle, "The Benefits and Costs of Disclosing Information About Risks: What do We Know about Right-to-Know?" *Risk Analysis* 24, no. 2 (2004): 335.

groups disproportionately live near hazardous industrial installations.[42] To the extent that terrorism targets these industrial plants, the victims would come disproportionately from within the disadvantaged groups within society.

Disadvantaged segments of the community are also more vulnerable to harm in the event of a disruption of critical public infrastructures. In the aftermath of Hurricane Katrina, it was seen that poor and racialized persons suffered the most from the disruption.[43]

Terrorism also poses the risk of revenge attacks and discrimination, depending upon the nature of the terrorist attack. After September 11, many people of Arab (and Arab-appearing) ethnicity were subject to a sharply increased level of hate crimes.[44] Unfortunately, this community might suffer a disproportionate risk of being targeted for revenge attacks should counterterrorism measures not successfully stop further attacks or should the public's feeling of security significantly deteriorate.

In sum, one of the reasons why some counterterrorism measures that trade privacy for security might appear to be reasonable is that the majority's security is being purchased at the expense of the minority. However it is possible that a decision to abandon otherwise effective counterterrorism measures that dispro-portionately endanger a minority might expose other disadvantaged communities to greater actual risk of harm from terrorism. This does not necessarily mean it is acceptable to obtain security at the expense of a minority. Alternative measures or safeguards may be available to ensure that the minority is not sacri-ficed for the perceived security of the majority. The point here is that the majority is unlikely to perceive the costs that are borne by a minority, or, if they do perceive them, may not be sufficiently concerned with the costs visited upon people other than themselves.

---

42. See Andrew Szasz and Michael Meuser, "Environmental Inequalities: Literature Review and Proposals for New Directions in Research and Theory," *Current Sociology* 45, no. 3 (1997): 99; M.R. Elliott et al., "Environmental Justice: Frequency and Severity of US Chemical Industry Accidents and the Socioeconomic Status of Surrounding Communities," *Journal of Epidemiology and Community Health* 58 (2004): 24.

43. Kristin E. Henkel, John F. Dovidio and Samuel L Gaertner, "Institutional Discrimination, Individual Racism and Hurricane Katrina," *Analyses of Social Issues and Public Policy* 6, no. 1 (2006): 99 at 105–108.

44. Michael Welch, *Scapegoats of September 11th: Hate Crimes & State Crimes in the War on Terror* (Piscataway, NJ: Rutgers Univ. Press, 2006) at 66; Debra L. Oswald, "Understanding Anti-Arab Reactions Post-9/11: The Role of Threats, Social Categories and Personal Ideologies," *Journal of Applied Social Psychology* 35, no. 9, (2005): 1775 at 1776; American Arab Anti-Discrimination Committee, "ADC Fact Sheet: The Condition of Arab Americans Post 9/11" (20 November 2001), http://adc.org/terror_attack/9-11af-termath.pdf; BBC News, "11 September revenge killer guilty," 3 April 2002, http://news.bbc.coc.uk/1/hi/world/americas/1909683.stm.

E. A Social Psychological Need for a Reaction

In times of perceived breakdown in order and security, the social and psychological pressures to react in some way are very powerful. Jeremy Waldron suggests that this psychological reaction largely explains the willingness to trade liberty for an apparently security-enhancing measure.[45] When attacked, people want their government to inflict reprisals and they are less interested in their effectiveness than that "something striking and unusual is being done."[46]

There is also a tendency for a society to display increased solidarity and patriotism following an external attack. The so-called "rally effect" refers to the sudden and substantial increase in public trust in and approval for political leaders after a dramatic international event.[47] The September 11 rally effect was the largest of all recorded rally effects in the United States, producing the highest ever recorded approval rating for any U.S. president, and it lasted longer than any other recorded rally effect.[48]

The surge of patriotism and the desire for social unity may contribute to the willingness with which people sacrifice individual liberties for a perceived collective security improvement.

F. Courts and the Security Versus Privacy Trade-off

It is likely that judicial deference to government also accounts for the extent to which governments are able to curtail liberties including privacy in the name of national security. In recent years, there has been great debate over the institutional competence of judges to deal with questions of national security. Some argue that the courts are not institutionally competent to assess security measures, [49] while others argue that the courts routinely balance competing interests in a wide range of complicated policy domains and that the review of security policies should not be an exception.[50]

Whether or not judges are institutionally competent to consider national security measures, there may be deeper psychological factors at work in the

---

45. Waldron, "Security and Liberty," 209 (n. 2).

46. *Ibid.*

47. Marc J. Hetherington and Michal Nelson "Anatomy of the Rally Effect: George W. Bush and the War on Terrorism" (2003) 36 *Political Science and Politics* 36 (2003): 37 at 37 citing John Mueller, *War, Presidents and Public Opinion* (New York: Wiley, 1973); Richard C. Eichenberg, Richard J. Stoll, and Matthew Lebo "War President: The Approval Ratings of George W. Bush," *Journal of Conflict Resolution* 50, no. 6 (2006): 783.

48. Hetherington and Nelson, "Anatomy of the Rally Effect," 37 (n. 47).

49. Posner, *Not a Suicide Pact*, 35–36, (n. 2); Posner and Vermeule *Terror in the Balance* (n. 2).

50. Daniel J. Solove, "Data Mining and the Security-Liberty Debate" forthcoming *University of Chicago Law Review* 74 (2007–2008) available at http://papers.ssrn.com/sol3/papers.cfm?abstract_id=990030.

judicial reluctance to scrutinize them. In particular, judges may realize that, whether or not an impugned security measure would have been effective, they will be blamed should an attack occur after they have ruled it unconstitutional. If the measure is implemented and no attack occurs, those who object to the measure will find it difficult to criticize the government or the courts as it will be hard to show the measure had absolutely no benefit. If the measure is implemented and an attack occurs, the government may be criticized for ineffective security measures, but the courts will not be viewed as responsible. As a result, the obvious and attractive option for the judge who fears the weight of responsibility for national security is to defer to government expertise.

III. REFRAMING THE TRADE-OFF: SECURITY VERSUS SECURITY

Given that the security versus privacy trade-off appears to be biased in favor of security, particularly in times of public insecurity, there is reason to fear that we may too easily sacrifice rights and freedoms such as privacy. Perhaps the bias in favor of security may be resisted by examining how privacy-reducing counterterrorism measures themselves reduce security. In this way, the trade-off analysis may be reframed as one between values that are more commensurable.

Measures and programs intended to increase national security may actually reduce security in certain ways or for certain people. First, security measures may be "security theatre" in that they are reassuring rather than effective in improving actual security. As will be discussed below, this may still be worthwhile to the extent that fear itself produces other forms of harm. However, ineffective security measures may also lull people into a false sense of security, or pose opportunity costs, draining resources away from other public objectives that might improve security. Second, whether effective or not, security measures may create new vulnerabilities. Third, security measures may reduce the security of a minority of the population with unfair and counterproductive results. In the case of counterterrorism measures, the security of the Muslim and Arab population, whose willingness to assist intelligence and law enforcement could be helpful for national security, may be undermined.

A. Security Theatre
The term "security theatre" refers to the adoption of useless or nearly useless security measures in order to provide the reassuring appearance of a response to perceived risks.[51] However, security theatre is not necessarily useless or irrational when the harmful consequences of public fear are taken into account.

The losses associated with terrorism can be divided into two categories. First, a terrorist attack takes a direct toll in lives, damage to property, disruption of

---

51. Schneier, *Beyond Fear*, (n. 2).

normal life, and immediate remediation efforts. Second, there are several types of indirect harm that arise because of the effect of the attack on the minds of the members of a society. These indirect losses flow from the fear created by the initial attack and may produce a level of casualties comparable to the initial attack. It appears that for approximately one year after September 11 in the United States, there was a reduction in air travel, an increase in highway travel, and a concomitant increase in highway traffic fatalities.[52] Gigerenzer estimates that an extra 1,595 people died on the highways trying to avoid the risk of flying during the year after September 11.[53] He notes that this number is six times greater than the total number of airplane passengers who perished on September 11.[54]

Another type of indirect cost of a terrorist attack is the subsequent expense of security measures that are adopted out of fear of a future attack, such as an elaborate airline passenger screening system. These measures may save lives if they improve actual security or only the perception of security, for the reasons mentioned above. However, where these measures are not effective in achieving either, or the benefits could be achieved more efficiently, the measures impose additional opportunity costs. The resources dissipated on poor security measures should also be understood as the loss of the extra social benefits that the resources could have achieved in terms of life and well-being, for example in health care or education.

Given all of the indirect harms that are suffered as a result of the fearful reaction to a terrorist attack, measures that merely address subjective feelings of insecurity rather than improving real security may be justifiable.[55] Great care should be taken here since this is manipulative of the public, and may reduce trust in the government. Second, it may cause the public to be careless, when vigilance and precaution would be helpful to reduce actual insecurity.[56] Third, governmental attempts to visibly increase security may not be reassuring. This seems to be the case with the color-coded threat warnings in use in the United States, which create a continuous and vague sense of alarm without communicating information of any particular use.

B. Security Measures May Introduce New Vulnerabilities

In order to maintain access to private communications and stored data for surveillance purposes, governments have sought to ensure that "backdoors" or

---

52. Gigerenzer, "Out of the Frying Pan," 347 (n. 31).

53. Ibid., 350.

54. Ibid.; Michael Sivak and Michael J. Flannagan "Consequences for Road Traffic Fatalities of the Reduction in Flying Following September 11, 2001," Transportation Research Part F (2004): 301–305.

55. See Cass Sunstein, "Terrorism and probability neglect," Journal of Risk and Uncertainty 26 (2003): 121.

56. George Avery, "Bioterrorism, Fear, and Public Health Reform: Matching a Policy Solution to the Wrong Window," Public Administration Review 64, no. 3 (2004): 275.

"access points" are built into telecommunications equipment and software. While this has obvious appeal from a government perspective, this approach deliberately introduces vulnerabilities into technologies that are widely used by the public. In addition to the risk of government abuse, the public is exposed to the additional risk that a third party will figure out how to exploit the vulnerability.

This risk is vividly illustrated by the 2006 scandal over the wiretapping of the Greek government by unknown parties. The lawful interception capability built into mobile phones was hacked by unknown parties to intercept the communications of the Greek Prime Minister and other top officials.[57]

The problem of backdoors is also present in software. Backdoors are methods of gaining access to a computer by avoiding the normal authentication requirements. They are sometimes built into software to solve software design problems.[58] However, once present there is a risk that those who introduced the backdoors may misuse them. Furthermore, there is a risk that third parties may discover and use the vulnerabilities.

Although it is difficult to separate fact and legend with respect to government involvement with software backdoors, there is suspicion that some software vendors have placed backdoors into their software at the request of the government.[59] In 2001, a public outcry followed news reports about an FBI project named "Magic Lantern," said to involve a government spyware program circulated by e-mail attachment. The reports indicated that antivirus software companies had worked with the FBI to ensure that their antivirus programs would not detect the spyware.[60] In 2006, the BBC reported that Microsoft was in discussions with the British government to enable it to decrypt the BitLocker system available in some versions of the new Vista operating system.[61] Microsoft's response to inquiries about this was initially evasive, but the company eventually issued a denial.[62]

Apart from the risks of abuse by government, it is clear that the deliberate and general introduction of security vulnerabilities in information and communications technologies creates the additional security risk of outsider attack. The risks associated with vulnerable information and communications technologies are not limited to identity theft, the loss of privacy, or the loss of valuable

---

57. G. Danezis (trans.) "The Greek Illegal Wiretapping Scandal: Some Translations and Resources," translating the Greek Government Press Briefing 06-02-02, available at http://homes.esat.kuleuven.be/~gdanezis/intercept.html.

58. Kevin Poulsen, "Interbase back door exposed," *SecurityFocus.com*, 11 January 2001, http://www.securityfocus.com/news/136.

59. Declan McCullagh, "'Lantern' backdoor flap rages," *Wired News.com*, 27 November 2001, http://www.wired.com/politics/law/news/2001/11/48648.

60. *Ibid.*

61. Ollie Stone-Lee, "UK holds Microsoft security talks," *BBC News.com*, 16 February 2006, http://news.bbc.co.uk/2/hi/uk_news/politics/4713018.stm.

62. Nate Anderson, "Secret back doors? Microsoft says no, China says maybe," *Ars Technica*, 6 March 2006, http://arstechnica.com/news.ars/post/20060306-6319.html.

business information. The physical security of human rights workers and journalists operating in hostile political environments can be seriously compromised if their activities are exposed.[63]

C. Security Measures May Reduce the Security of a Minority of the Population

After the September 11 attacks, increased attention was devoted to dataveillance for national security purposes. As noted earlier, dataveillance, or the systematic acquisition and integration of multiple streams of data about things and people, poses the risk that incorrect or unreliable data may be used to make decisions about people. In the context of data mining for counterterrorist purposes, the consequences of being flagged as suspicious can be serious.

Technologies for data aggregation and data mining (the automated analysis of large datasets to extract useful information) have led to increased efficiency in gathering and using data.[64] In the context of counterterrorism, the objective is to examine a wide range of data (relating to people, places, things, activities, associations, etc.) in order to identify patterns that point to terrorist activity, and to use those patterns to identify targets for further investigation.[65]

The U.S. Government's "Total Information Awareness" system (later renamed the "Terrorism Information Awareness" system) was intended to link together separate government databases into a virtually centralized database that would permit effective data mining.[66] The eventual inclusion of data from private commercial databases was also contemplated.[67] The U.S. Congress eventually refused funding for the program amid concerns over privacy.[68] Although the Terrorism Information Awareness program has been shut down, data mining projects are continuing elsewhere within the U.S. government.[69]

Counterterrorist data mining projects have been criticized on three fronts. First, they are said to be ineffective due to the necessarily high rate of false positives.[70] Second, they are likely to impose disproportionate burdens on ethnic

---

63. Affidavit of Patrick Ball in *ACLU v. Miller,* 96-CV-2475-MHS (N.D. Ga.), 24 January 1997, available at http://www.aclu.org/privacy/speech/15525lgl20031009.html.

64. Taipale, "Technology, Security and Privacy" (n. 2) at 177.

65. *Ibid.,* 174; Wayne Renke "Who Controls the Past Now Controls the Future: Counter-Terrorism, Data Mining and Privacy," 43 *Alberta Law Review* 43 (2006): 779.

66. Defence Advanced Research Projects Agency, "Report to Congress Regarding the Terrorism Information Awareness Program," (2003), available at http://www.eff.org/Privacy/TIA/TIA-report.pdf.

67. Ron Wyden et al., "Law and Policy Efforts to Balance Security, Privacy and Civil Liberties in Post-9/11 America," *Stanford Law & Policy Review* 17 (2006): 331.

68. *Ibid.*

69. Bruce Schneier, "Why Data Mining Won't Stop Terror," Wired.com, 9 March 2006, http://www.wired.com/politics/security/commentary/securitymatters/2006/03/70357; Renke, "Who Controls the Past," 789 (n. 65).

70. Schneier, *Beyond Fear,* 253 (n. 2).

and religious minorities. Third, centralized databases of personal information offer a more enticing target for outsider attack and insider abuse, and the compromise of a centralized and comprehensive database is likely to do more harm than the compromise of one of many decentralized and limited databases.

Even if the profiling and data mining efforts are highly accurate and subject to a low rate of errors, the volume of data being collected and mined is so large that there are likely to be many errors. Indeed, the U.S. National Security Agency's controversial communications surveillance program is reported to have produced an unmanageable flood of tips virtually all of which were false alerts.[71]

While the harms associated with the misuse of centralized databases of personal information fall on everyone, it is possible that the dangers of data mining will fall disproportionately along racial, ethnic, or religious lines. Data mining programs based on profiles thought to be correlated with terrorism will generate false positives unless the profile is perfectly predictive of terrorism. If the profiles are based partly on race or religion, the risk of false positives is likely to fall disproportionately on people of the profiled groups.

One of the concerns with the aggregation of data from various sources and its use in data mining projects is that information that is reliable for one purpose may come to be used for much more sensitive applications.[72] The case of Maher Arar illustrates this type of danger. In his case, through a lack of care by the Canadian RCMP with respect to the characterization and handling of information that linked him to an al-Qaeda suspect, Arar came to be suspected of being a terrorist himself, leading to his deportation by the United States to Syria where he faced torture.[73]

One contributing element to Arar's terrible experience was lax data handling by the RCMP. Maher Arar came to the attention of the RCMP because of a connection to Abdullah Almalki, who was suspected of involvement with al-Qaeda.[74] In the subsequent inquiry into the case, the Inquiry Commissioner found that it was reasonable for the RCMP to have investigated Arar, but that the RCMP had provided inaccurate and quite prejudicial information about Arar to U.S. agencies.[75] This information was provided in contravention of RCMP policies that required information to be screened for relevance, reliability, and personal

---

71. Lowell Bergman et al., "Spy Agency Data After Sept. 11 Led F.B.I. to Dead Ends," *New York Times*, 17 January 2006.

72. Marcus Wigan and Roger Clarke, "Social Impacts of Transport Surveillance," *Prometheus* 24, no. 4, (2006): 389 at 400.

73. Commission of Inquiry into the Actions of Canadian Officials in relation to Maher Arar, "Report of the Events Relating to Maher Arar: Analysis and Recommendations," (2006) available at http://www.ararcommission.ca/eng/AR_English.pdf.

74. *Ibid.*, 18.

75. *Ibid.* at 18, 28.

information before being shared, and that written caveats be attached to the information to control the uses to which it is put.[76]

The case of Maher Arar illustrates the grave dangers that can face those who find themselves flagged for further terrorism investigation. It also illustrates the manner in which information gathered into databases can be used for purposes to which it is unsuited, with results that are catastrophic to the individual. To the extent that data mining projects are based on a terrorist profile that specifies young, Muslim males of Arab ethnic background, and to the extent that data mining creates a large number of false positives, this minority group will find itself more frequently flagged for further groundless investigation. This elevated level of inter-action between the suspect group and the security community increases the chances that mistakes will be committed as in the case of Maher Arar.

In this way, national security is pursued in a manner that reduces the security of a minority within the population. Not only does this reduce the security of individual members of the minority group, it may reduce overall national security. This is because the minority group may justifiably come to feel alienated and defensive, as well as fearful of contact with intelligence and law enforcement officials. Their assistance and insight in fighting terrorism might be partly forfeited as a result.[77]

IV. CONCLUSION

In the aftermath of the September 11 attacks, it was widely accepted that it would be necessary to trade some personal privacy in order to obtain improved national security through greater government surveillance. The concept of an inevitable trade-off or balance between the two is longstanding, but tends to emerge with renewed vigor at times of national insecurity. This was certainly the case after September 11, as numerous governments including Canada moved to strengthen their counterterrorism efforts through increased surveillance and to implement various data-gathering and data mining programs. The harms associated with this erosion of privacy were often ignored or those who raised them were denigrated.[78]

For various reasons, the value of security tends to trump that of privacy. Perhaps one way to ensure that the debate is not prematurely ended in this way

---

76. *Ibid.*, 18.

77. Michael P. O'Connor and Celia M. Rumann, "Into the Fire: How to Avoid Getting Burned by the Same Mistakes Made Fighting Terrorism in Northern Ireland," *Cardozo Law Review* 24 (2003): 1657 at 1737.

78. Testimony of John Ashcroft. Preserving our freedoms while defending against terrorism. Hearings before the Senate Committee on the Judiciary, 107th Congress, 1st Session, 2001, 316.

is to focus on the ways in which a privacy-reducing measure actually reduces security. In this way, values of similar weight may be considered in the trade-off. Counterterrorism measures may imperil the physical security and lives of individuals by introducing new vulnerabilities or by sacrificing the security of a minority for a *feeling* of security for the majority.

This paper has not sought to answer the difficult question of the justice of specific counterterrorism measures. However, it is clear that the justice of the trade-off is a complex matter. Actual harm may flow from mass panic, so that measures to address the *feeling* of insecurity may be justified. Furthermore, certain types of terrorist attacks may disproportionately harm a minority such that a refusal to employ an effective counterterrorism measure might leave them bearing greater risks.

8. PRIVACY'S SECOND HOME
Building a New Home for Privacy Under Section 15 of the Charter

DAPHNE GILBERT[*]

In Canada, any constitutional "right"[1] to privacy has been housed in section 7[2] or section 8[3] of the Charter of Rights and Freedoms.[4] Located as such, privacy is grounded and protected within the Legal Rights portion of the Charter, the provisions of which set out the rights of people in dealing with the justice system and law enforcement.[5] Although sections 7 and 8 of the Charter guard recognized "zones" of privacy in certain, primarily criminal contexts, the positioning of privacy in the Legal Rights section alone neglects privacy's relevance to other Charter guarantees. This is an impoverished interpretation of what privacy could offer to human rights protections in Canada. Privacy can be viewed as more than simply a legal interest, and finding a home for it, outside of the Legal Rights section of the Charter, opens new possibilities for expanding its constitutional protection and its utility as a tool in advancing other Charter rights.

---

   * My thanks to Jena McGill for superb research assistance and to Ian Kerr for helpful suggestions

   1. There is no specific guarantee of or right to privacy enumerated in the Canadian constitution; however, the Supreme Court of Canada has interpreted guarantees in the Canadian Charter of Rights and Freedoms, Part I of the Constitution Act, 1982, being Schedule B to the Canada Act 1982 (UK) 1982 c 11 (Canada), as implicitly including a right to privacy, as will be explored here.

   2. Canadian Charter (n. 1) s 7 reads "[e]veryone has the right to life, liberty and security of the person and the right not be deprived thereof except in accordance with the principles of fundamental justice."

   3. Canadian Charter (n. 1) s 8 guarantees, "[e]veryone has the right to be secure against unreasonable search or seizure."

   4. Canadian Charter (n. 1).

   5. The Legal Rights section of the Canadian Charter (n.1) encompasses s 7–s 14.

In this paper, I contend that in addition to the protections offered by sections 7 and 8, a constitutional interest in privacy could be housed in the section 15 equality rights provision of the Charter.[6] I argue that privacy could be interpreted as an aspect of the human dignity interest that forms the foundation of section 15, and protected within the existing legal framework for adjudicating equality rights, outlined by the Supreme Court of Canada in *Law v. Canada (Minister of Employment and Immigration)*.[7] The *Law* framework for equality analysis asks, in part, whether an impugned legislative provision harms the human dignity of the claimant and the group to whom the claimant belongs. Understanding privacy as a component of human dignity would allow privacy to find a home outside of the Charter's Legal Rights provisions, breathing new life into constitutional protections for this important value.

The paper begins in Part I with an overview of privacy's legal personae and its current home in the Legal Rights section of the Charter. Part II reviews the concept of human dignity protected by section 15 of the Charter and then locates privacy as an aspect of the dignity interest. Finally, Part III offers two brief case study examples demonstrating the potential of a constitutionally protected privacy interest under section 15 for furthering the human dignity of two equality-seeking groups: women and the (dis)abled community.

I. PRIVACY

Privacy as both a legal and philosophical idea is mutable and highly contested.[8] There are numerous scholarly debates over the definition of privacy[9] and its role as a value in the social and legal fabric of our society. One of the earliest

---

6. Canadian Charter (n. 1) s 15(1) reads: "Every individual is equal before and under the law and has the right to the equal protection and equal benefit of the law without discrimination and, in particular, without discrimination based on race, national or ethnic origin, colour, religion, sex, age or mental or physical disability."

7. *Law v Canada (Minister of Employment and Immigration)* [1999] 1 S.C.R. 497.

8. This paper focuses on the legal approach to privacy in Canadian Common Law, and does not explore the multiple philosophical theories on privacy. For philosophical explorations, see Steven Davis, "Privacy, Rights and Moral Value," *University of Ottawa Law and Technology Journal* 3, no. 1 (2006): 109–131; William Prosser, "Privacy: A Legal Analysis," *California Law Review* 48 (1960): 338–423; Anita Allen, *Uneasy Access: Privacy for Women in a Free Society* (Totowa: Rowman and Littlefield, 1988); and Judith Jarvis Thomson, "The Right to Privacy," *Philosophy and Public Affairs* 4, no. 4 (1975): 295–314, who begins from the observation (at 295) that "the most striking thing about the right to privacy is that nobody seems to have any very clear idea what it is."

9. The "right to be let alone" is the most prevalent conception of privacy, coined by Samuel D. Warren & Louis D. Brandeis in their influential article, "The Right to Privacy," *Harvard Law Review* 4, no. 1 (1890) 193–220.

and best-known theorists on privacy argued that the concept has been "the subject of . . . vague and confused writing by social scientists,"[10] and legal academics and jurists[11] are similarly perplexed at how to describe, define, and protect privacy. Despite competing visions of the concept and significance of privacy, the Supreme Court of Canada has recognized that "privacy is essential for the well-being of the individual [and] [f]or this reason alone, it is worthy of constitutional protection . . . "[12] In Canadian jurisprudence, privacy has found a constitutional home within sections 7[13] and 8[14] of the Charter, two parts of the Legal Rights portion of that document.

I begin with section 8 because it is here that Canadian courts have had the most opportunities to engage with privacy interests. The Supreme Court has interpreted the section 8 right to be free from unreasonable search and seizure in a broad fashion, describing the purpose of section 8 as the protection of a reasonable expectation of privacy in respect of government action.[15] Section 8 encompasses three general categories of privacy claims: (1) personal privacy (most often concerned with bodily integrity[16]); (2) territorial privacy (including strong protections for the home as "the place where our most intimate and

---

10. Alan Westin, *Privacy and Freedom* (New York: Atheneum, 1967), 7.

11. In the Supreme Court of Canada's most recent pronouncement on privacy in *R. v Tessling* [2004] 3 S.C.R. 432 at 25, Binnie J. characterized privacy as a "protean concept," and noted the difficulties inherent in balancing privacy with countervailing considerations like safety, security, and the suppression of crime.

12. *R. v Dyment* [1988] 2 S.C.R. 417 at 17. The strong privacy-protective language in *Dyment* reflects the egregious nature of the privacy violation in that case. While treating Dyment following a motor vehicle accident, a doctor collected a blood sample for medical purposes without Dyment's knowledge or consent and then turned the blood sample over to a police officer, though the officer had not requested a blood sample and had no search warrant. Following analysis of the sample, Dyment was convicted of impaired driving. At issue was whether the police officer's taking of the sample amounted to an unreasonable seizure for the purposes of section 8 of the Canadian Charter (n. 3). The Supreme Court found that an unreasonable seizure had taken place, and that Dyment's spatial, physical, and informational privacy interests had been violated, stating at 38, "[t]he Charter breach . . . was a very serious one . . . The sense of privacy transcends the physical. The dignity of the human being is . . . seriously violated when use is made of bodily substances taken by others for medical purposes in a manner that does not respect that limitation."

13. Canadian Charter s 7 (n. 2).

14. Canadian Charter s 8 (n. 3).

15. See *Dyment*, 426 (n. 12). The limits of a "reasonable expectation of privacy" are contentious and subject to considerable judicial interpretation in any section 8 case. See *Tessling* (n. 11). See also Ian Kerr & Jena McGill, "Emanations, Snoop Dogs and Reasonable Expectations of Privacy," *Criminal Law Quarterly* 52, no. 3 (2007): 392–432.

16. See *R. v Golden* [2001] 3 S.C.R. 679 at 90–92; *R. v Stillman* [1997] 1 S.C.R. 607; and *Dyment*, 431–32 (n. 12).

private activities are most likely to take place"[17]); and (3) informational privacy ("how much information about ourselves and activities we are entitled to shield from the curious eyes of the State"[18]). Claims to each of these kinds of privacy first require a claimant to establish the existence of a reasonable expectation of privacy[19] in order to trigger the application of section 8, because the "guarantee of security from *unreasonable* search and seizure only protects a *reasonable* expectation [of privacy]."[20] The privacy protections that section 8 offers are therefore available to claimants in a limited number of circumstances, and are of primary significance in the criminal law context.

Although section 8 is the major source of privacy protections under the Charter, the Supreme Court has also recognized privacy interests within the section 7 guarantees of liberty and security of the person. The Court generally uses section 7 to describe a residual right to privacy, apart from the more specific categories protected by section 8,[21] and often looks to section 7 to protect "decisional privacy" or an individual's ability to make fundamental decisions free from state scrutiny.[22] Specifically, the Court has found that the liberty guarantee, " . . . properly construed, grants the individual a degree of autonomy

---

17. *Tessling*, 22 (n. 11). See also *R. v Silveira* [1995] 2 S.C.R. 297 at 144 where Cory J. states, "[t]here is no place on earth where persons can have a greater expectation of privacy than within their 'dwelling-house.'"

18. *R. v B. (S.A.)* [2003] 2 S.C.R. 678.

19. A reasonable expectation of privacy is established using the two part "totality of the circumstances" test, first described by the Supreme Court in *R. v Edwards* [1996] 1 S.C.R. 128, which focuses on the existence of (1) a subjective expectation of privacy; and (2) the objective reasonableness of that expectation. The latter half of the test includes a consideration of contextual factors including the place where the alleged search or seizure occurred and whether the information obtained exposed core biographical or intimate details of an individual's life. The Supreme Court has noted that the "objectively reasonable" aspect of the section 8 analysis is particularly troublesome, describing it in *Tessling*, 43 (n. 11) as "a major battleground in many of the section 8 cases."

20. *Hunter v Southam* [1984] 2 S.C.R. 145 at 159 (emphasis in original).

21. See *Thomson Newspapers Ltd. v Canada (Director of Investigation and Research, Restrictive Trade Practices Commission)* [1990] 1 S.C.R. 425 at 178, where the Supreme Court held that "section 7 may, in certain contexts, provide residual protection to the interests protected by specific provisions of the Charter." Similarly, in *Re: B.C. Motor Vehicle Act* [1985] 2 S.C.R. 486 at 28 the Court explained, "[s]ections 8 to 14 of the Charter address specific deprivations of the right to life, liberty and security of the person in breach of the principles of fundamental justice and, as such, violations of s.7. They are designed to protect, in a specific manner and setting, the right to life, liberty and security of the person. It would be incongruous to interpret s.7 more narrowly than the rights in ss. 8 to 14."

22. See *R. v O'Connor* [1995] 4 S.C.R. 411 at 487, where L'Heureux-Dubé J. concludes that the right to privacy is a significant aspect of the right to liberty in a free and democratic society; and *R. v Beare* [1988] 2 S.C.R. 387 at 58 where LaForest J. for the Court voices "considerable sympathy" for the proposition that "section 7 includes a right to privacy such as that inhering in the guarantee against unreasonable searches and seizures in s. 8 of the *Charter*."

in making decisions of fundamental personal importance,"[23] and security of the person has been similarly interpreted as including a right to privacy with respect to one's physical body, its well-being, and decisions about one's body.[24] The Supreme Court has further suggested that the principles of fundamental justice, the cornerstone of the Charter's Legal Rights guarantees, include a right to privacy.[25]

Despite these well-established (though still controversial) protections for privacy in the Charter, the interpretive framework and availability of sections 7 and 8 are narrowly circumscribed. There are two main constraints, one internal to these two sections and the other a structural limitation of the Charter. Internally, the Supreme Court has developed fairly rigid "tests" that a claimant must satisfy in order to access sections 7 and 8. Before a privacy-related claim can succeed under section 7 or 8 of the Charter, an applicant must establish that a breach of section 7 is contrary to a principle of fundamental justice, or, in the case of section 8, that a reasonable expectation of privacy exists with regard to the subject matter of a search or seizure, and that the search or seizure in question was unreasonable.

Structurally, situating privacy within the Legal Rights section of the Charter entails inherent restrictions on the nature and scope of privacy interests protected. In *Gosselin v. Quebec (Attorney General)*,[26] a majority of the Supreme Court of Canada affirmed that the guarantees under the Legal Rights section of the Charter are triggered by state action involving the administration of justice. This means that the Legal Rights guarantees are usually triggered in the criminal law context, though they may also apply in administrative contexts,

---

23. In her concurring decision in *R. v Morgentaler* [1988] 1 S.C.R. 30 at 299, Wilson J. concluded that "the right to liberty contained in section 7 guarantees to every individual a degree of personal autonomy over important decisions intimately affecting their private lives."

24. See the dissenting opinion of McLachlin J. (as she then was) in *Rodriguez v British Columbia (Attorney-General)* [1993] 3 S.C.R. 519 at 91, arguing that the right to security of the person under section 7 of the Charter protects "the dignity and privacy of individuals with respect to decisions concerning their own body." The majority in *Rodriguez* concurred with McLachlin J.'s conclusion that by interfering with an individual's ability to make autonomous choices about his or her own bodily treatment, the prohibition on assisted suicide violated the right to security of the person under section 7.

25. See *Winnipeg Child and Family Services v K.L.W.* [2000] 2 S.C.R. 519 at 96, where the Court reiterated the value of privacy, stating: "[t]his Court has suggested . . . . that the principles of fundamental justice include a right to privacy given its great value to society . . . In particular, this Court has recognized that it may be necessary, in certain contexts, to balance one individual's right to privacy against another individual's competing rights and interests . . . The privacy interest underlies and informs the content of this right [security of the person]."

26. *Gosselin v Quebec (Attorney-General)* [2002] 4 S.C.R. 429.

as was the case in *New Brunswick (Minister of Health and Community Services) v. G.(J.)*,[27] involving a challenge to child protection processes.

Although *Gosselin* left open the question of whether an adjudicative context is strictly required for the Legal Rights guarantees to apply, the majority of the Supreme Court insisted that it was appropriate to restrict the applicability of the Legal Rights protections to the administration of justice.[28] On the facts of *Gosselin*, this meant the section 7 guarantee to life, liberty, and security of the person was useless in challenging an inadequate welfare regime. If privacy as a legal value is located only in sections 7 and 8 of the Charter, the nature of the interests protected is unavoidably limited. This is, in my view, an incomplete and inadequate vision of a constitutional privacy interest, and of unnecessarily limited utility for the protection of this important value.

II. BUILDING ANOTHER HOME FOR PRIVACY: SECTION 15 OF THE CHARTER

My basis for advocating a home for privacy interests in section 15 of the Charter rests on my understanding of the concept of human dignity. Human dignity is a fundamental constitutional value underlying almost every right protected under the Charter.[29] It has found special protection as the touchstone of the section 15 equality guarantee. The leading Supreme Court of Canada pronouncement on section 15, *Law v. Canada (Minister of Employment and Immigration)*,[30] makes human dignity the fundamental inquiry in cases of discrimination, with the Court defining the purpose of section 15 in the following manner:

> to prevent the violation of essential human dignity and freedom through the imposition of disadvantage, stereotyping, or political or social prejudice, and

---

27. *New Brunswick (Minister of Health and Community Services) v G.(J.)* [1999] 3 S.C.R. 46. See also *Blencoe v British Columbia (Human Rights Commission)* [2000] 2 S.C.R. 307 at 45, where the Supreme Court acknowledged that section 7 has some applicability outside of the legal rights or criminal context, stating, "[t]here is no longer any doubt that s. 7 of the *Charter* is not confined to the penal context. Section 7 can extend beyond the sphere of criminal law, at least where there is state action which directly engages the justice system and its administration."

28. It is notable that in her dissenting opinion in *Gosselin*, 305 (n. 26), Arbour J. took a different and radical approach to section 7, interpreting the guarantees broadly and without the limitations imposed by its location in the Legal Rights section of the Charter. She left the Supreme Court soon after the *Gosselin* decision and her views on section 7 have not gained further traction at the Court to date.

29. See *Morgentaler*, 288 (n. 23), where Wilson J. states, "[t]he idea of human dignity finds expression in almost every right and freedom guaranteed in the Charter." See also *Blencoe*, 76–77 (n. 27).

30. *Law* (n. 7).

to promote a society in which all persons enjoy equal recognition at law as human beings or as members of Canadian society, equally capable and equally deserving of concern, respect and consideration.[31]

Connections between privacy and human dignity have long been acknowledged and explored by theorists,[32] and the Supreme Court of Canada has declared, "a fair legal system requires respect at all times for the complainant's personal dignity, and in particular his or her right to privacy, equality, and security of the person."[33] It seems natural, then, that privacy should find a home outside of the Legal Rights portion of the Charter, within human dignity as it is understood and protected under section 15.

I anticipate two practical and legal benefits to interpreting section 15 to include a privacy interest. First, protecting privacy as part of the Charter's equality guarantee will provide new opportunities for the advancement of privacy-related claims that do not fall within the boundaries of Legal Rights. A claimant whose privacy interests have been violated in situations that do not trigger the application of section 7 or 8, could have an avenue under section 15 to bring forward the claim, expanding the Charter's range of privacy protections. Second, understanding privacy as an equality issue could present more expansive possibilities for safeguarding a range of different kinds of privacy interests, over and above those protected under section 7 or 8.[34] Whatever the content of

---

31. *Law*, 59 (n. 7).

32. A number of philosophers have connected privacy to human dignity, and explained the relationship between the two as harmonious and even symbiotic in nature. See Edward J. Bloustein, "Privacy as an Aspect of Human Dignity: An Answer to Dean Prosser," *New York University Law Review* 39, no. 6 (1964): 962–1007; Jeffrey H. Reiman, "Privacy, Intimacy and Personhood," *Philosophy and Public Affairs* 6, no. 1 (1978): 26–44; Helen Nissenbaum, "Privacy as Contextual Integrity," *Washington Law Review* 79, no. 1 (2004): 119–158; David Matheson, "Dignity and Selective Self-Presentation," *Lessons from the Identity Trail* eds. Ian Kerr, Carole Lucock, & Valerie Steeves (New York: OUP, 2009), Chapter 18.

33. *O'Connor*, 154 (n. 22).

34. It is beyond the scope of this chapter to theorize on what the precise content of privacy is, could, or should be; however, as noted previously, section 8 has been interpreted by Canadian courts as protecting three specific "classes" of privacy interests: personal, territorial, and informational, and the residual interest embodied in section 7 is often interpreted as a decisional privacy interest. This is not an exhaustive list of privacy-related interests that deserve protection. A number of theorists have argued persuasively that a robust understanding of privacy includes more than simply protecting individuals from government interference, and may include recognition of values such as solitude and anonymity, and features such as positive obligations on the state to provide the conditions necessary for true private choice to be exercised. Although these and other privacy interests do not fall strictly within the boundaries of section 7 or 8, it is possible that understanding privacy through a lens of equality could provide a forum for such arguments to be made. See Allen, *Uneasy Access*, (n. 8); Linda McClain, "Reconstructive Tasks for a Liberal Feminist Conception of Privacy," *William and Mary Law Review* 40, no. 3

privacy is understood to include, there is general agreement in law and society that privacy is worth protecting, as a requirement both of "inviolate personality"[35] and human dignity.[36] Expanding the possibilities for protecting privacy by including it within the ambit of the section 15 equality guarantee recognizes the foundational role that privacy plays in society and its contribution to ensuring equal respect for the dignity of all persons.[37]

In imagining a new home for privacy within section 15, I begin by briefly outlining the relevant interpretive framework for assessing claims of unequal treatment under the Charter: the *Law* test. In *Law*,[38] the Supreme Court of Canada outlined three broad inquiries to be made when assessing a claim under section 15:

(1) Does the law, program, or activity impose differential treatment between the claimant and the applicable comparator group,[39] creating a distinction between the groups in purpose or effect?

(2) Is the differential treatment based on enumerated or analogous grounds?[40]

(1999): 759–794; Dorothy Roberts, "Punishing Drug Addicts who Have Babies: Women of Colour, Equality, and the Right of Privacy," *Harvard Law Review* 104, no. 7 (1991): 1419–1482.

35. Warren & Brandeis, "The Right to Privacy," 194 (n. 9).

36. See Bloustein, "Privacy as an Aspect of Human Dignity," (n. 32).

37. While I define here two distinct benefits of a section 15 privacy interest, I acknowledge that they will inevitably overlap and intersect in any number of ways.

38. *Law* (n. 7).

39. The choice of comparator groups is integral to any equality claim. The Supreme Court has held, in cases including *Corbiere v Canada (Minister of Indian and Northern Affairs)* [1999] 2 S.C.R. 203, that the comparator group must possess all the characteristics of the claimant except for the personal characteristic at issue. The Court has further held, in cases including *Hodge v Canada (Minister of Human Resources Development)* [2004] 3 S.C.R. 357, that a court may reject a claimant's choice of comparator group, and that choosing a comparator group deemed "incorrect" by the court may cause an equality claim to fail. See *Auton (Guardian ad litem of) v British Columbia (Attorney-General)* [2004] 3 S.C.R. 657. The comparator group model has received a great deal of criticism. See Daphne Gilbert & Diana Majury, "Critical Comparisons: The Supreme Court of Canada Dooms Section 15," *The Windsor Yearbook of Access to Justice* 24, no.1 (2006): 111–142; Dianne Pothier, "Equality as a Comparative Concept: Mirror, Mirror, on the Wall, What's the Fairest of Them All?" in *Diminishing Returns: Inequality and the Canadian Charter of Rights and Freedoms*, eds. Sheila McIntyre & Sanda Rodgers (Toronto: LexisNexis Butterworths, 2006), 135.

40. The concept of enumerated and analogous grounds originated in *Andrews v Law Society of British Columbia* [1989] 1 S.C.R. 143. There are nine enumerated grounds stated in the Canadian Charter's section 15 provision (n.6), and to date the Supreme Court has recognized analogous grounds including sexual orientation (see *Egan v Canada* [1995]

(3) Does the differential treatment discriminate, by imposing a burden upon or withholding a benefit from the claimant in a manner that reflects the stereotypical application of presumed group or personal characteristics, or that otherwise has the effect of perpetuating or promoting the view that the individual is less capable or worthy of recognition or value as a human being or as a member of Canadian society, equally deserving of concern, respect, and consideration? For discrimination to be established under the final step of the *Law* framework, it must be shown that the burden or denial of a benefit harms an individual's human dignity.[41]

I propose that it is within the dignity analysis of the *Law* framework that privacy interests could be recognized and protected, though I acknowledge that the dignity step of the section 15 test has proven arguably problematic.[42] The concept of dignity has been accused of being "vague to the point of vacuous and, therefore [it] . . . can be used as an empty place-holder for other less presentable reasons for finding or refusing to find a violation of equality."[43] Indeed, although there is considerable judicial and academic consensus on the importance of human dignity as a measure of equality, there is considerably *less* agreement about the nature or content of the dignity interest itself. The Supreme Court has made human dignity the central feature of equality analyses, but has yet to offer any defining characteristics to make the concept more concrete, intelligible,

---

2 S.C.R. 513), off-reserve Aboriginal status (see *Corbiere* (n. 39)), and marital status (see *Miron v Trudel* [1995] 2 S.C.R. 418).

41. *Law* (n. 7). The Supreme Court in *Law* set out a nonexhaustive list of four contextual factors to be considered in determining whether a claimant's dignity has been infringed: (1) preexisting disadvantage, stereotyping, prejudice, or vulnerability experienced by the individual or group at issue; (2) the correspondence, or lack thereof, between the ground or grounds on which the claim is based and the actual need, capacity, or circumstances of the claimant or others; (3) the ameliorative purpose or effects of the impugned law upon a more disadvantaged person or group in society; and (4) the nature and scope of the interest affected by the impugned law.

42. Criticisms leveled against the dignity aspect of section 15 include the fact that the concept is too imprecise to ground equality jurisprudence. I am included amongst those who have concerns about using human dignity as the central focus of section 15. For elaboration of my position on this issue see Daphne Gilbert, "Time to Regroup: New Opportunities for the Supreme Court and Section 15 of the *Charter*," *McGill Law Journal* 48, no. 4 (2003): 627–649; and Daphne Gilbert, "Substance without Form: The Impact of Anonymity on Equality-Seeking Groups," *University of Ottawa Law and Technology Journal* 3, no. 1 (2006): 225–247. See also Sophia Moreau, "The Wrongs of Unequal Treatment," in *Making Equality Rights Real: Securing Substantive Equality Under the Charter*, eds. Fay Faraday, Margaret Denike, & M. Kate Stephenson (Toronto: Irwin Law, 2006), 31 at 34–35.

43. Denise G. Réaume, "Discrimination and Dignity," in *Making Equality Rights Real: Securing Substantive Equality Under the Charter*, eds. Fay Faraday, Margaret Denike, & M. Kate Stephenson (Toronto: Irwin Law, 2006), 124.

or identifiable. In *Law*, Iacobucci J. for a unanimous Supreme Court attempts to define human dignity for the purposes of a section 15 analysis stating,

> There can be different conceptions of what human dignity means . . . [T]he equality guarantee in s.15(1) is concerned with the realization of personal autonomy and self-determination. Human dignity means that an individual or group feels self-respect and self-worth. It is concerned with physical and psychological integrity and empowerment. Human dignity is harmed by unfair treatment premised upon personal traits or circumstances which do not relate to individual needs, capacities, or merits. It is enhanced by laws which are sensitive to the needs, capacities, and merits of different individuals, taking into account the context underlying their differences. Human dignity is harmed when individuals and groups are marginalized, ignored, or devalued, and is enhanced when laws recognize the full place of all individuals and groups within Canadian society.[44]

The way that human dignity is currently framed in law offers section 15 claimants and Canadian judges few, if any, guidelines as to its content, and dignity's amorphous nature has caused difficulties for equality claimants in a number of post-*Law* decisions.[45] Despite its ambiguity, human dignity remains, for the time being, the fundamental consideration in assessing equality claims under the Charter. A number of legal commentators continue to theorize on ways to work within the confines of the *Law* framework, arguing that human dignity can be rehabilitated to provide important contours to equality analyses under section 15.[46] I take a similar approach here, and work with the *Law* framework to contend that the ongoing project of defining and interpreting the section 15 dignity interest should include recognition of, and protection for, privacy interests.

Legal scholar Denise Réaume has developed a defense of human dignity that offers a useful departure point for incorporating privacy into the section 15 concept of dignity.[47] The core of Réaume's defense is that dignity protects agency and self-determination and a recognition that humans are choosers and planners, "beings with projects and dreams who make commitments and attachments and at least partly measure their own sense of worth according to

44. *Law*, 53 (n. 7).

45. See *Gosselin* (n. 26) and *Auton* (n. 39).

46. See Moreau, "The Wrongs of Unequal Treatment," 35 (n. 42), who proposes that a model of the kinds of treatment that violate human dignity is necessary in order to give "[t]he abstract ideal of equal concern and respect for dignity of all . . . content by a substantial conception of what kinds of treatment violate human dignity."

47. Though she defends human dignity, Réaume, "Discrimination and Dignity," 124 (n. 43), acknowledges that the process of giving dignity some meaningful content "stands as perhaps the most significant challenge facing the Court in the coming years."

their ability to exercise their capacities and realize their dreams."[48] Réaume's description of dignity's contribution to equality analysis includes many of the same ideas that underlie the legally dominant conception of privacy under section 7 of the Charter,[49] evidencing the relatedness of the two concepts. The value of privacy in the human dignity context is that it is an enabling tool for persons to be self-determining individuals, which, according to Réaume, is one of, if not *the* goal that human dignity seeks to further and protect under section 15. Although privacy and dignity may remain conceptually imprecise, accepting Réaume's defense of dignity illustrates that both concepts are directed toward the same, or similar goals—the valuing of individual persons through respect for their autonomy—and that privacy and dignity intersect in ways that may offer guidance in interpreting each of them individually.

Commentators have noted a similar connection between human dignity and the nebulous value of liberty arguing,

> [a] fully fleshed out concept of dignity should help explain a range of, if not all of, the human rights typically entrenched in constitutions, just as the value of liberty does. Different rights will reflect different aspects or dimensions of the concept . . . [W]e need to be looking for the dimensions of dignity that help with the work of s.15 in particular.[50]

A comparable relationship exists between dignity and privacy, and in this way my argument here dovetails with that of Réaume. Like liberty and dignity, privacy can be considered a meta-concept that may support increasingly sophisticated and layered interpretations of other concepts that inform Charter values. Privacy may be a companion tool to dignity, furthering the "work" done by section 15[51] and contributing to the realization of equality through human dignity.[52] If dignity is concerned with the promotion or safeguarding of

---

48. Réaume, "Discrimination and Dignity," 144 (n. 43).

49. See Part I, above.

50. Réaume, "Discrimination and Dignity," 109 (n. 43). Wilson J. made a similar connection in *Morgentaler*, 289 (n. 23), stating " . . . an aspect of the respect for human dignity on which the *Charter* is founded is the right to make fundamental personal decisions without interference from the state."

51. According to the Supreme Court in *Law*, 51 (n. 7), the "work" of the section 15 equality guarantee is aimed at preventing the "violation of essential human dignity and freedom through the imposition of disadvantage, stereotyping, or political and social prejudices, and to promote a society in which all persons enjoy equal recognition at law as human beings or as members of Canadian society, equally capable and equally deserving of concern, respect and consideration."

52. The Supreme Court has acknowledged the contribution of privacy to the realization of human dignity in cases including *Dyment*, 27 (n. 12), where the Court stated, "the use of a person's body without his consent to obtain information about him, invades an area of privacy essential to the maintenance of his human dignity."

the conditions necessary for the realization of full personhood, privacy is the tool that may, in some instances, help to accomplish this end. I turn now to examine briefly two contexts where section 15-based privacy protections could contribute to the furtherance of human dignity for equality-seeking groups.

III. CASE STUDIES: EMPLOYING PRIVACY UNDER SECTION 15

I have outlined two broad benefits of situating and protecting privacy interests within human dignity under section 15.[53] This model, used both as a new avenue for privacy claims that do not fall within the spectrum of Legal Rights, and as the basis for protecting new kinds of privacy beyond those recognized under sections 7 and 8, presents possibilities for equality-seeking groups to argue for the privacy they require to realize their human dignity. I foresee at least two possible ways in which these privacy-related arguments under section 15 could be used by equality-seeking groups. The first argument is that equality-seeking groups must have equal access to privacy,[54] understood here as the right to be left alone, to lead one's life and make decisions free from scrutiny or interference by the state. The argument favoring privacy presumes a context within which privacy is desirable and must be protected in order for human dignity to be realized. In *Falkiner v. Ontario (Ministry of Community and Social Services)*,[55] the Ontario Court of Appeal implicitly recognized this argument in its section 15 analysis of a social assistance regime that presumed that once persons of the opposite sex began living together, they were "spouses" and their eligibility for social assistance was less than that of a single person. The Court noted that single people not on social assistance were free to have "try-on" relationships without suffering any adverse financial consequences, whereas those on social assistance were penalized as a result.[56] Although it did not use the language of privacy, in my view, the Court accepted the idea that the claimants should have the privacy to define their relationships as they

---

53. See page 8 of this chapter.

54. Equality-seeking groups are generally afforded less privacy and are subject to greater levels of surveillance than those occupying more privileged positions in society. For instance, individuals are often required to divulge a great deal of personal information in order to access social support services, as is required by the United States' Department of Housing and Urban Development's Homeless Management Information Strategies, which tracks homeless persons and the services they access by collecting names, Social Security Numbers, dates of birth, race, gender, health status information including HIV status, and income information. See Electronic Privacy Information Centre, *Poverty and Privacy*, http://www.epic.org/privacy/poverty/.

55. *Falkiner v Ontario (Ministry of Community and Social Services)* [2002] 59 O.R. (3d) 481.

56. *Falkiner*, 73 (n. 55).

deemed fit, without being subject to state-imposed labels and the resulting financial consequences.

Although it is true that government nonintervention may be a necessary condition for individuals to realize dignity, merely shielding a sphere of decision-making from the reach of government may be insufficient to ensure meaningful privacy for everyone in all contexts. The second privacy-related argument under section 15 begins from the premise that the privacy an equality-seeking group may appear to enjoy is often a consequence of neglect; in other words, being "let alone" by government does not categorically translate to a meaningful state of privacy for everyone. Simply removing the state from the equation of choice leaves a claimant with only the abstract freedom to choose, which "is of meager value without meaningful options from which to choose and the ability to effectuate one's choice."[57] Human dignity may demand that positive steps be taken in order for an equality claimant to access privacy and enjoy its benefits.[58] This second argument shifts the focus of the privacy construct away from state nonintervention toward an affirmative guarantee of the resources necessary to make privacy meaningful in the particular context of an equality-claimant's life.[59]

These two arguments evidence the dual nature of privacy—a dual nature that may be uniquely accommodated within a section 15-based understanding of privacy. Interpreting privacy within the section 15 pursuit of human dignity illustrates that for dignity to be realized, privacy may take on a different meaning or character in different circumstances. Infringements to human dignity may require a remedy with either a negative or a positive approach to privacy, in accordance with the demands of a particular case. I outline here two examples where equality-seeking groups could utilize a privacy interest under section 15

---

57. Roberts, "Punishing Drug Addicts," 1478 (n. 34).

58. The "positive obligations" notion of privacy acknowledges that privacy must be understood within the broader societal context within which it is employed. Feminist critiques of conventional privacy doctrine have noted that in the context of our patriarchal society, privacy does not benefit men and women equally. See Anita Allen, "Coercing Privacy," *William and Mary Law Review* 40, no. 3 (1999): 723–757, where she notes that "[t]o the extent that the government is infused with patriarchal, heterosexual ideals, men's and women's privacy rights are likely to reflect patriarchal, heterosexual ideals of a [privacy]."

59. Current privacy jurisprudence under sections 7 and 8 is overwhelmingly based on an understanding of privacy as a negative right—the ability to live one's life free from state intrusion—and the assumption that this kind of privacy is accessible and desirable for all. See *Tessling*, (n. 11). Canadian courts have given little, if any, formal acknowledgment to the fact that in some instances, privacy may do more harm than good, or that some individuals may not be able to access the conditions necessary to truly exercise private choice.

to further their human dignity: (1) access to abortion services for women; and (2) (dis)ability rights.

A. Abortion Access

Abortion was decriminalized in *R. v Morgentaler*[60] on the basis that the procedural requirements imposed by the Criminal Code[61] to access a legal abortion violated women's security of the person interest under section 7 of the Charter. Although privacy was not explicitly relied upon by the Supreme Court in *Morgentaler*,[62] privacy-related language featured prominently in many of the judgments, particularly that of Wilson J. She emphasized the importance of protecting private decisions affecting the physical body, including choices about health care, sexuality, and procreation, from unwanted intrusions, and stressed the importance of such decisions to personal autonomy and maintaining a sense of control over one's body. All of these ideas speak to the concept of human dignity, and implicitly recognize the importance of privacy in a woman's decision to abort a pregnancy. Section 15 provides a new avenue for privacy-based claims similar to those implicitly acknowledged in *Morgentaler*, to protect a woman's private decision to abort. Understanding the role that privacy plays as an aspect of human dignity in the context of abortion accepts that reproductive control is "essential to women's full personhood and participation in all spheres of life,"[63] and that dignity demands decisions about procreation be "let alone," free from state scrutiny or control.

Section 15 may present a new avenue to argue for a woman's right to make private choices regarding reproduction; however, the existing constitutional framework around access to health care services raises a separate but equally fundamental issue. The risk of construing abortion as a wholly private matter is

---

60. *Morgentaler* (n. 23). *Morgentaler* did not bestow a right of access to abortion upon Canadian women, but simply decriminalized the procedure. The narrow boundaries of the *Morgentaler* decision continue to circumscribe women's access to abortion services across Canada. See Sanda Rodgers, "Misconceived: Equality and Reproductive Autonomy in the Supreme Court of Canada," in *Diminishing Returns: Inequality and the Canadian Charter of Rights and Freedoms*, eds. Sheila McIntyre & Sanda Rodgers (Toronto: LexisNexis Butterworths, 2006), 271.

61. Criminal Code, RSC 2005 c C-8 (Canada) s 252 (now s 287). Section 252, the therapeutic abortion provision, stated that a woman could only access an abortion legally if it was performed in a hospital with the approval of a 3-doctor committee that must certify that continuing the pregnancy would endanger the life or health of the mother.

62. In *Morgentaler* (n. 23), three judgments concurring in the result were written by Dickson C.J., Beetz J., and Wilson J. A dissent was entered by McIntyre J.

63. Rhonda Copelon, "Losing the Negative Right of Privacy: Building Sexual and Reproductive Freedom," *New York University Review of Law and Social Change* 18, no. 1 (1990–1991): 15–50 at 49.

that the state is under no obligation to provide access to abortion services.[64] Section 15 must also act as a platform for arguing that women's dignity requires that they *not* be "let alone" when it comes to the provision of abortion services. It is "society's responsibility both to protect choice and to provide the material and social conditions that render choice a meaningful right rather than a mere privilege."[65] Privacy under section 15 in the reproductive rights context must therefore include arguments for both the negative proscription against government coercion, as well as the imposition of a positive duty on governments to facilitate the process and actualization of choice by providing the conditions necessary for all women to enjoy and exercise privacy in furtherance of their human dignity.

B. (Dis)ability Rights

Despite antidiscrimination laws and legal guarantees for (dis)abled persons in Canada, "it remains a crucial task to argue vigorously for policies that insure the full measure of equal dignity to people with all forms of disability."[66] Understanding the role of privacy in achieving human dignity is a critical part of this project, particularly in light of the fact that the Supreme Court has offered little insight into what aspects of human dignity are most pertinent to an equality-based (dis)ability rights claim.[67] Section 15 offers a new avenue for (dis) ability claimants to advance privacy-related claims that do not arise in the Legal Rights context, and also offers possibilities for arguments in favor of recognizing the unique privacy-related needs that (dis)abled persons may require in order to realize their full measure of dignity and equality.

---

64. For example, in New Brunswick, access to abortion services is limited by the province's Medical Services Payment RSNB 1973 c M-7 (New Brunswick), NB. Reg. 1984–84–20, Sched. 2(a.1), which deems abortion services ineligible for public funding except when " . . . performed by a specialist in the field of obstetrics and gynecology in a hospital facility . . . and two medical practitioners certify in writing that the abortion was medically required." This means that New Brunswick women must meet procedural requirements to access an abortion at one of only two hospitals in the province providing the service, or must pay out-of-pocket for an abortion in a clinic setting. These are serious limits to abortion access.

65. Copelon, "Losing the Negative Right," 16 (n. 63).

66. Eva Feder Kittay, "Equality, Dignity and Disability," *Perspectives on Equality: The Second Seamus Heaney Lectures*, eds. Mary Ann Lyons & Fionnuala Waldron (Dublin: The Liffey Press, 2005), 95 at 99.

67. In *Granovsky v Canada (Minister of Employment and Immigration)* [2000] 1 S.C.R. 703 at 33, the Court articulated what is to date its most progressive vision of what section 15 might offer to (dis)ability claimants, but see *Auton* (n. 39), where the Court appeared to move backwards by accepting the government's position that its decision on what treatments to fund could not be judicially challenged.

One location where the privacy interests of (dis)abled persons are routinely violated is in interactions with the medical community. (Dis)ability theorists[68] have argued that the clinical encounter is fraught for individuals with (dis) abilities, that there is a strong disconnect between the law's promise of protection for confidentiality and the actual experience of (dis)abled persons,[69] and that insufficient respect for the bodily privacy of a (dis)abled individual amounts to an insult to human dignity.[70] Employing section 15 to protect privacy in this context focuses on issues of self-determination, autonomy, bodily integrity, and free choice, all of which speak to the concept of human dignity underlying the Charter's equality guarantee.

In addition, using section 15 to protect the privacy of (dis)abled individuals may open doors for new arguments regarding the nature of the privacy interests at stake. For instance, physically (dis)abled individuals may not enjoy the benefits of privacy-related values such as solitude, seclusion, or anonymity[71] to the same degree as non(dis)abled persons as a result of the fact that they may require a higher degree of assistance in going about their everyday lives.[72] Accepting under section 15 that a range of privacy-related values over and above the right to be "let alone" can be critical to the realization of human dignity, claimants could argue for the constitutional protection of a spectrum of different privacy interests of unique importance for the realization of their dignity and therefore essential to equality.

CONCLUSION

I have argued here that privacy can be fundamental to the realization of human dignity and must therefore be understood as an aspect of equality

---

68. Including Catherine Frazee, Joan Gilmour, & Roxanne Mykitiuk, "Now You See Her, Now You Don't: How Law Shapes Disabled Women's Experience of Exposure, Surveillance, and Assessment in the Clinical Encounter," in *Critical Disability Theory: Essays in Philosophy, Politics, Policy, and Law*, eds. Dianne Pothier & Richard Devlin (Vancouver: University of British Columbia Press, 2006), 223.

69. Despite the fact that privacy's traditional constitutional home in section 8 of the Charter ostensibly maintains the privacy of one's health information, the privacy interests of the disabled community are routinely violated, as noted by Frazee, Gilmour, & Mykitiuk, "Now You See Her," 234 (n. 68).

70. Feder Kittay, "Equality," 96 (n. 66).

71. Allen, *Uneasy Access* (n. 8), terms these values "paradigmatic" privacy concepts, and explores their importance to women, arguing that a robust understanding of privacy must include acknowledgment and protection of these ideals.

72. Frazee, Gilmour, & Mykitiuk, "Now You See Her," 234 (n. 68), note the ways in which the privacy of (dis)abled women may be compromised by others out of a paternalistic desire to do "what is best."

under section 15 of the Charter. Equality is an ideal to which all individuals are entitled and a reality to which governments and societies should aspire; it is difficult to imagine denying an individual's right to privacy when it is framed as an aspect of equality. Conceptualizing privacy under section 15, therefore, presents an important "higher level" of protection, complementing the safeguards currently offered by sections 7 and 8. Building a home for privacy interests in section 15 expands the spectrum of constitutional privacy protections and acknowledges the importance of privacy in our individual lives and society as a whole.

9. WHAT HAVE YOU DONE FOR ME LATELY?
Reflections on Redeeming Privacy for Battered Women

JENA MCGILL*

The dichotomy between the private and the public is central to almost two centuries of feminist writing and struggle; ultimately, it is what the feminist movement is about.[1]

INTRODUCTION: PRIVACY IN ACTION, PRIVACY IN THEORY

Gillian Hadley was granted a protection order against her abusive estranged husband, Ralph. When Ralph breached the terms of the protection order by trespassing on Gillian's property and harassing her, Gillian's numerous calls for assistance were repeatedly given low priority by police in Durham, Ontario, with some going unaddressed for more than 24 hours. Ralph Hadley broke into Gillian's home, shot her dead, and killed himself.[2] In Colorado, Jessica Gonzales's

---

* My appreciation to Professors Elizabeth Sheehy and Kim Pate, under whose supervision the first iteration of this chapter was carried out, and to Professors Ian Kerr, Jane Bailey, Valerie Steeves, and Daphne Gilbert for their guidance in bringing it to its final incarnation. Thank you also to Julie Shugarman for her insights during countless conversations that have informed my thinking on this and other subjects in many ways.

    1. Carole Pateman, *The Disorder of Women: Democracy, Feminism and Political Theory* (Stanford: Stanford University Press, 1989), 118.

    2. See Jim Coyle, "Officer Saw Risk to Gillian Hadley," *Toronto Star*, November 8, 2001, Toronto Star Online, http://www.fact.on.ca/news/news0111/ts011108.htm. The 2002 inquest that followed Gillian Hadley's death—the third such inquest in Ontario between 1998

estranged husband, Simon, kidnapped their three young children in violation of a restraining order barring him from contact with the family. The police refused to enforce the order and retrieve the children despite Jessica's multiple requests for them to do so. Simon Gonzales eventually went to the police station and was killed in a gunfire exchange with officers, following which police found his three daughters dead in his truck. Each had been shot in the head at close range.[3]

I first faced the tragic, all-too-common realities of stories like Gillian Hadley's and Jessica Gonzales's while working at a shelter for battered women.[4] I bore witness, time and again, to the ferocity of woman abuse and the inadequacies of existing social and legal mechanisms designed to combat violence against women by their intimate partners or former partners.[5] I came to understand the

---

and 2002—resulted in more than 50 recommendations on providing better protection and services to battered women. The majority of these recommendations have yet to be implemented in the province.

3. In *Gonzales v City of Castle Rock* 545 US 748 (2005), Jessica Gonzales sued the town of Castle Rock, Colorado, for failure to enforce the restraining order, alleging that she had a property right to have the order enforced and that the police's failure to do so was an actionable deprivation. The District Court dismissed the matter. On appeal, The 10th Circuit Court of Appeals reversed the dismissal and held that the Colorado law under which the restraining order was issued mandated police enforcement and that Ms. Gonzales had a protected property interest in the enforcement of her order. Castle Rock appealed to the United States Supreme Court, and on June 27, 2005, a 7–2 opinion found that there is no property right to enforcement of a restraining order under the United States Constitution. Ms. Gonzales decided to appeal that ruling to the Inter-American Commission on Human Rights, and issues of admissibility were dealt with in *Jessica Gonzales* et al. *v United States* Case 1490–05, Report No. 52/07, Inter-Am. C.H.R., OEA/Ser.L/V/II.130 Doc. 22, rev. 1 (2007), heard on March 2, 2007, at the Inter-American Commission on Human Rights, the first hearing on domestic violence to be heard in that forum.

4. The language used to describe male violence against women is incredibly problematic, as highlighted by authors including Nancy Berns, "Degendering the Problem and Gendering the Blame: Political Discourse on Women and Violence," *Gender & Society* 15, no. 2 (2001): 262–281. The gender-free terms "domestic violence" or "partner abuse" are often used to describe violence against women in the home; however, they willingly erase the gendered nature of woman battering, see note 6. In this chapter, the terms "woman battering" or "woman abuse" will be used interchangeably, and should be understood to include systematic abuse, whether physical, sexual, psychological, emotional, financial, or other, of a woman by her intimate partner who, in the vast majority of cases, is a man. For excellent analysis of the particularities and inadequacies of the language of woman battering see Ann Jones, *Next Time She'll Be Dead: Battering and How to Stop It* (Boston: Beacon Press, 2000).

5. Even with the monumental progress made in recent decades by the feminist and antiviolence communities on the issue of domestic violence, woman battering persists at an unacceptably high rate. Measuring the prevalence of intimate violence is next to impossible as a result of exceptionally low levels of reporting. Statistics Canada reports that just over one third of spousal assaults are reported to police. Even considering

perils of attempting to escape an abusive relationship, and I saw, first-hand, how the maintenance of a sphere of privacy became a near-absolute requirement for the physical and emotional integrity of the women our shelter served: If an abusive partner or former partner could not locate a woman at our shelter, he could not stalk, harass, or kill her.[6] In attempting to secure a bubble of privacy around a woman as against her battering partner, shelter clients were not required to give their real names when seeking services at the shelter, nor were they required to disclose any other personal information. Based on my experience of "privacy in action" at the shelter, I believed that privacy equaled safety, and safety equaled life for battered women, and as a result, I became a constant advocate for quantitatively *more* privacy protections for battered women.

Some time later, I found myself steeped in the academic world of law school, where I discovered the theoretical dimensions of many of the concrete phenomena I had witnessed in my work at the shelter—theories about violence, about policing, about relationships between men and women, between individuals and the state, and theories, of course, about privacy. I dove into all of this theorizing, certain that I would uncover a wealth of literature endorsing my "more is better" stance on privacy for battered women, and doubly certain that I would discover such support among feminist scholars. What I found instead was that "privacy in theory" looked very different from the privacy that I had seen in action at the women's shelter. I discovered that the relationship between privacy and much

---

that the available statistics underestimate the extent of intimate violence in Canada, the numbers are startling. Statistics Canada reports that 7% of women living in a common law or marital relationship reported that they had been physically or sexually assaulted by a spousal partner at least once in the past five years. This number represents approximately 653,000 women. Holly Johnson, Statistics Canada, *Measuring Violence Against Women: Statistical Trends 2006* (Ottawa: Minister of Industry, 2006). It is notable that the surveys used to generate statistical profiles of abuse may focus on common law or marital relationships and thereby exclude women who are battered by boyfriends or former partners. Such surveys are also likely to focus on physical or sexual abuse, and do not capture the full ambit of woman abuse, which may include psychological, emotional, and mental abuse, as well as other mechanisms of coercion employed by batterers including economic control and threats. See Evan Stark, "Re-Presenting Woman Battering: From Battered Woman Syndrome to Coercive Control," *Albany Law Review* 58, no. 4 (1995): 973–1026.

6. Gender specificity is intended throughout this discussion and reflects the overwhelming rate at which women are battered by male partners. Although the vast majority of intimate violence is perpetrated by men against women, intimate violence does occur between partners of the same sex, and individuals who identify as transsexual, transgender, or gender queer are also subject to violence at the hands of their intimate partner. On intimate violence in same-sex relationships and the legal response to violence between same-sex partners, see e.g. Janice L. Ristock, "And Justice for All? The Social Context of Legal Responses to Abuse in Lesbian Relationships," *Canadian Journal of Women and the Law* 7 (1994): 415–430.

feminist theory is fraught with difficulties to such an extent that some feminist scholars[7] contend that privacy is not only *useless* for women, but is *detrimental* to women's lives, and should be rejected outright as antithetical to the feminist project of achieving equality for women. Catharine MacKinnon, one of the most well-known voices in feminist legal scholarship, is a leader in the "privacy-rejection" camp, arguing that privacy has never done anything for women, and there are no signs that this will change anytime soon.[8] I learned that the feminist rejection of privacy is grounded in large part on the relationship between privacy and woman battering[9]—the very context that founded my belief in the utility of privacy for women escaping situations of battering. Feminist theorizing arguing for quantitatively *less* privacy for women and *more* state intervention in the private sphere to prevent violence against women seemed incongruous with my experience at the shelter, where I saw women as requiring more privacy in order to secure their physical and emotional safety against abusive partners.

The unsettling disconnect that I encountered between much, though certainly not all, feminist theorizing on privacy and my own experience with privacy in the context of woman battering forms the inspiration for this project. In this chapter, I offer some thoughts on the connections between privacy and woman battering informed by my experiences both with "front-line" activism and work in this area, as well as "back-line" academic theorizing on privacy. My goal is to critically examine, from a feminist perspective, one particular feminist stance on privacy— that which has traditionally rejected privacy as antithetical to the project of women's lived equality—and to illuminate some of the pitfalls I see with rejecting privacy, in light of the realities of woman abuse. I do not have an answer to the problem of woman abuse, but, contrary to many feminists, I do believe that, at least in the short term, privacy may be an important part of the solution.

---

7. Rejecting privacy is only one of many responses feminists have advanced to address the problems with privacy. At the opposite end of the spectrum, a number of feminists have provided important arguments for the utility or potential utility of privacy in women's lives, including Anita Allen, *Uneasy Access: Privacy for Women in a Free Society* (New Jersey: Rowman & Littlefield, 1988); Ruth Gavison, "Privacy and the Limits of Law," *Yale Law Journal* 89, no. 3 (1980): 421–455; and Patricia Williams, *The Alchemy of Race and Rights: Diary of a Law Professor* (Cambridge: Harvard University Press, 1991), 164.

8. Catharine MacKinnon, "Feminism, Marxism, Method, and the State: Toward Feminist Jurisprudence," *Signs* 8, no. 4 (1983): 635–658 at 656–57. See also Martha C. Nussbaum, "Is Privacy Bad for Women? What the Indian Constitutional tradition can teach about sex equality," *Boston Review*, (April/May 2000), Boston Review http://bostonreview. net/BR25.2/nussbaum.html.

9. See Catharine MacKinnon, "Reflections on Sex Equality under Law," *Yale Law Journal* 100 (1991): 1281–1328 at 1311, who describes the legal inviolability of the home, celebrated under the rubric of privacy, as yielding a "sphere of sanctified isolation" that benefits men at the expense of women.

I begin by briefly reviewing the concept of privacy itself. In the second section, I examine the connections between privacy and woman battering that have historically formed the crux of the feminist rejection of privacy. The third section reevaluates the traditional relationship between privacy and woman battering by proposing a different way in which we might understand woman abuse that situates women's privacy interests at the forefront. This third section then argues that, given this new understanding of the relationship between privacy and woman abuse, the feminist position that rejects privacy outright must be reconsidered. Finally, in the fourth section, I consider the problematic ways in which privacy is deployed within the existing confines of inequality, and argue that in this context, privacy should be understood as a "stop-gap" measure to ensure battered women's safety while we work toward feminism's long-term goal of equality.

I. PRIVACY

Philosophers, legal scholars, and jurists continue to debate the definition, function, and value of privacy and to deliberate on how best to ensure and protect a right to privacy in law while striking an appropriate balance between privacy and competing interests.[10] Although the subtleties of its definition remain conflicted, privacy is perhaps most frequently described as "the right to be let alone."[11] Implied by, and encompassed within, "the right to be let alone," is the right to create and enforce boundaries[12] around the self in order to "keep out" arbitrary or unwanted intrusions by both state and nonstate actors so as to preserve a sphere of personal privacy. As such, privacy is generally understood as a negative right—a right *not* to have outside parties interfere arbitrarily in one's private life.

---

10. A full consideration of these debates is beyond my scope here; however, for philosophical explorations, see e.g. Steven Davis, "Privacy, Rights and Moral Value," *University of Ottawa Law & Technology Journal* 3, no. 1 (2006): 109–131; William Prosser, "Privacy: A Legal Analysis," *California Law Review* 48, no. 3 (1960): 338–423; Alan Westin, *Privacy and Freedom* (New York: Atheneum, 1967); and Judith Jarvis Thomson, "The Right to Privacy," *Philosophy and Public Affairs* 4, no. 4 (1975): 295–314. In a recent pronouncement on privacy by the Supreme Court of Canada, Binnie J. characterized privacy as a "protean concept," and noted the difficulties inherent in balancing privacy with countervailing considerations like "safety, security and the suppression of crime." *R. v Tessling*, [2004] 3 S.C.R. 432 at paras. 25 and 17.

11. Samuel D. Warren & Louis D. Brandeis, "The Right to Privacy," *Harvard Law Review* 4, (1890): 193–220.

12. The idea of privacy as a boundary between the self and others has been enunciated by "restricted access" privacy theorists including Gavison, "Privacy and the Limits of Law," 428, (n. 7); and Allen, *Uneasy Access*, 43, (n. 7) describing privacy as a "condition or set of social practices constituting, creating or sustaining boundaries that should be drawn between ourselves and others in virtue of our status or potential as persons."

Preserving a personal sphere of inviolability against the outside world is doubtless a valuable goal, and many privacy theorists have usefully highlighted the important role that privacy and related ideals can, in theory, play in women's lives. Privacy can contribute to providing "the literal and metaphorical space or opportunity for self-development as well as for revision of self,"[13] it may present opportunities for women to exercise their creative and intellectual capacities,[14] and can offer relief from the endless caretaking duties for which women are often responsible. Privacy can contribute to "fostering self-development and affording a space in which persons prepare themselves for roles, relationships and responsibilities, while allowing the realization of goods such as solitude, chosen intimacy and retreat."[15] At face value, then, privacy seems like it could be a pretty good idea for women—assuming women really *have* meaningful access to privacy's benefits. In actuality, however, privacy is rarely available to women in service of such worthwhile ends as self-development and personal growth, and despite its seemingly "neutral" nature, men and women do not "have" privacy, nor enjoy its benefits, equally.[16] This differential access to privacy is perhaps nowhere more evident than within the realities of woman battering.

II. THE PROBLEMS WITH PRIVACY

A. The Privacy–Woman Battering Connection
The privacy at stake in the context of woman battering is generally understood to be that that inheres in the familial home, where the "right to be let alone" is protected as sacred by law. Images of the "private" home are associated with

13. Linda McClain, "Reconstructive Tasks for a Liberal Feminist Conception of Privacy," *William & Mary Law Review* 40, no. 3 (1999): 759–794.

14. In attempting to explain why Western women have not contributed more to art, literature, and philosophy, Simone de Beauvoir argued that women need liberty and opportunities for privacy if they are to exercise their creative and intellectual capacities to the fullest. See Simone de Beauvoir, *The Second Sex*, trans. and ed. by H. M. Parshley (New York: Alfred A. Knopf, 1952), 670.

15. McClain, "Reconstructive Tasks," 771, (n. 13). Some theorists have made bold claims for personal privacy, arguing that a fundamental requirement of respect for persons presupposes conditions of privacy sufficient for personhood. See Jeffrey Reiman, "Privacy, Intimacy and Personhood," *Philosophy and Public Affairs* 6, no. 11 (1976): 26–44.

16. Differential access to privacy is also drawn along lines of race, class, disability, and sexual orientation, which interlock with and inform gender-based access to privacy. For further analysis of interlocking oppressions generally, see Sherene Razack, *Looking White People in the Eye: Gender, Race and Culture in Courtrooms and Classrooms* (Toronto: University of Toronto Press, 1998), 12; and Kimberlé Crenshaw, "Mapping the Margins: Intersectionality, Identity Politics and Violence Against Women of Colour," *Stanford Law Review* 43, no. 6 (1991): 1241–1299.

inviolability, and reflect the ". . . idea of a man's home as his 'castle' or fortress, where he is free from arbitrary intrusion by government or others."[17] Indeed, the common law tradition upholds the home as the domain of the family and of the personal, "an environment whose privacy has consistently and insistently been designated by the courts as worthy of the state's highest respect."[18] Privacy thus functions as a shield, keeping the government out of the "sanctuary" of the "private" home, and rendering the relationships and activities within virtually immune from legal scrutiny.[19] For this reason, many have charged that the "rhetoric of privacy . . . has been [and continues to be] the most important ideological obstacle to legal change and reform" on the issue of woman battering,[20] operating to make violence against women "legally and politically invisible."[21]

The "remnants of the idea that the law (and courts) should not invade the privacy of the home or 'go behind the curtain' of domestic life"[22] are used to justify state nonintervention in the private home, resulting in a lack of reliable

---

17. Linda C. McClain, "Inviolability and Privacy: The Castle, the Sanctuary and the Body," *Yale Journal of Law and the Humanities* 7, no. 1 (1995): 195–241, 202. See also Gavison, "Privacy and the Limits of Law," 464, (n. 7).

18. *R. v Tessling* (2003), 63 O.R. (3d) 1 at para. 33 (Ont. C.A.), rev'd 2004 SCC 67. The Canadian Charter of Rights and Freedoms, Part I of the Constitution Act, 1982, being Schedule B to the Canada Act 1982 (UK) 1982 c 11 (Canada), s. 8 guarantees, "[e]veryone has the right to be free from unreasonable search and seizure" and is understood in a broad fashion "to secure the citizen's right to a reasonable expectation of privacy against governmental encroachments." Section 8 has been interpreted to include a hierarchy of territorial privacy interests with the home at the top. See *R. v Tessling*, para.22, (n. 10) and *R. v Silverira*, [1995] 2 S.C.R. 297 at para.144.

19. As recently as 1983, men who sexually assaulted their intimate partners were granted legal immunity from prosecution in Canada "in order to protect the privacy of the family and to promote 'domestic harmony.'" See Reva Siegel, "The Rule of Love: Wife Beating as Prerogative and Privacy," *Yale Law Journal* 105, no. 8 (1995-96): 2117–2207 at 2118. The spousal rape immunity provision, formerly section 143 of the Criminal Code, RSC1970, c C-34 (Canada), s. 143, read: "[a] male person commits rape when he has sexual intercourse with a female person who is not his wife, without her consent." The marital rape exemption was repealed in 1983 by Bill C-127, An Act to Amend the Criminal Code (Sexual Offences), SC 1980–81–82–83 c 125 (Canada), s. 6.

20. Elizabeth Schneider, *Battered Women and Feminist Lawmaking* (New Haven: Yale University Press, 2000), 87–91 details the ways in which privacy functions to shield men's violence against women in the home, stating, "[p]rivacy says that violence against women is immune from sanction, that it is acceptable and part of the basic fabric of . . . family life. Privacy says that what goes on in the violent relationship should not be the subject of state or community intervention. Privacy says that woman battering is an individual problem, not a systemic one. Privacy operates as a mask for inequality, protecting male violence against women."

21. Sally Goldfarb, "Violence Against Women and the Persistence of Privacy," *Ohio State Law Journal* 61, no. 1 (2000): 1–87 at 2.

22. McClain, "Inviolability and Privacy," 212, (n. 17).

state protection for women subjected to violence at the hands of their partners. Even when state machinery does become involved in a "private" situation of abuse between intimate partners in the home—for instance, when a battered woman seeks a protection order[23] against an abusive partner—privacy may be used to justify police unwillingness to enforce a protection order in a serious manner. Indeed, there is an acknowledged pattern of police unwillingness to respond effectively to violence against women in the home,[24] including a marked lack of rigor when it comes to the enforcement of battered women's protection orders against abusive men,[25] resulting in tragedies like those of Gillian Hadley and Jessica Gonzales, whose stories opened this chapter.[26]

B. The Feminist Rejection of Privacy

Based on the foregoing, the rejection of privacy by some feminists is certainly justifiable. In the context of woman battering, it is evident that the ostensibly "neutral" privacy ascribed to the domain of the home is not enjoyed equally by men and women within.[27] The legal protection of privacy in the home in fact amounts to the safeguarding of men's privacy such that state nonintervention functions to preserve

---

23. Protection orders are the primary means whereby a battered woman may call upon police to protect her from an abusive partner. There are different kinds of legal orders that can include police enforcement, including a recognizance (also known as a "peace bond"), a restraining order, and conditions on bail bonds or probation orders. See George S. Rigakos, "Situational Determinants of Police Responses to Civil and Criminal Injunctions for Battered Women," *Violence Against Women* 3, no. 2 (1997): 204–216.

24. See George S. Rigakos, "The Politics of Protection: Battered Women, Protection Orders, and Police Subculture," in *Unsettling Truths: Battered Women, Policy, Politics, and Contemporary Research in Canada*, ed. Kevin D. Bonnycastle & George S. Rigakos (Vancouver: Collective Press, 1998), 82.

25. See Rigakos, "The Politics of Protection," (n. 23); and Joanne Belknap, "Law Enforcement Officer's Attitudes about the Appropriate Responses to Woman Battering," *International Review of Victimology* 4 (1995): 47–62.

26. Studies in which battered women were interviewed on their experiences with police showed that an overwhelming proportion of these women would never report to police again. See Shoshana Pollack, Melanie Battaglia, and Anke Alspach, *Women Charged with Domestic Violence in Toronto: The Unintended Consequences of Mandatory Charge Policies* (Toronto: The Women Abuse Council of Toronto, 2005), 23. In one study, women identified the reasons they would not report abuse to police as including: delayed police response, feeling that police did not see domestic abuse as a serious issue, insensitivity, and feeling like they were being blamed for staying in an abusive relationship. See Joseph Roy Gillis et al., "Systemic Obstacles to Battered Women's Participation in the Judicial System," *Violence Against Women* 12, no. 12 (2006): 1150–1168 at 1159.

27. Privacy in the home attaches not as a result of the sanctity of property rights, but because of the privacy expectations of persons (read: men) *within* the home. See *Canada (director of Investigation & Research, Combines Investigation Branch) v Southam Inc. (sub. nom Hunter v Southam)* [1984] 2 S.C.R. 145 at para. 24.

the sanctity of the home as a reality for men at the expense of women. The law's failure to go behind the "curtain" of the private home permits the home to continue to be a site of "domestic tyranny marked by violence and coercion."[28]

In light of the realities of woman abuse, feminists have argued that it is almost meaningless to speak about a woman's right to privacy in the home at all, as privacy is employed to shield the actions of men who batter women from public scrutiny so that it "imperil(s) rather than secure(s) women's inviolability."[29] Indeed, privacy's role in masking violence against women in the home confirms the general feminist charge against privacy,[30] which contends that privacy does nothing for women because it is defined and employed according to men's needs and desires. How can feminists knowingly support, in theory or practice, a concept that privileges men's needs over women's with such injurious consequences? A concept that disguises violence against women and provides justification for the ongoing victimization of women at the hands of men behind closed doors? The short answer to the question of whether privacy can be good for women is, for many feminists, a resounding "no." It is my contention here, however, that this is not the only answer possible, nor, perhaps, is it the most desirable answer in the context of woman battering. The feminist critique and ultimate dismissal of privacy that emerges from the relationship between privacy and woman battering presents an "important but incomplete" analysis of the connections between privacy and woman battering that merits further consideration.[31]

III. PUTTING WOMEN FIRST: RECONCEPTUALIZING THE PRIVACY–WOMAN BATTERING CONNECTION

A. Whose Privacy and Against Whom? Battering as an Invasion of Women's Privacy

The feminist critique of privacy detailed above clearly demonstrates that in the context of woman battering, men's privacy interests are concealed behind the misleading, seemingly "neutral" rhetoric of protecting privacy in the home, and that the legal protection of this particular "brand" of privacy serves to disguise

---

28. Heather Strang & John Braithwaite, eds., *Restorative Justice and Family Violence* (New York: Cambridge University Press, 2002), 130.

29. McClain, "Inviolability and Privacy," 207, (n. 17).

30. Feminist critiques of privacy are numerous and multifaceted. Feminists have rejected privacy for reasons including the fact that privacy is grounds for preserving private property, status, and privilege that is contrary to economic justice, and the fact that individualist privacy is antithetical to the collective values of connection and caretaking that women often value. For a comprehensive survey of these and other feminist critiques of privacy, see Allen, *Uneasy Access*, 52, (n. 7).

31. Strang & Braithwaite, *Restorative Justice and Family Violence*, 131 (n. 28).

violence against women. What remains "incomplete" on this account of the privacy–woman battering relationship, I contend, is that it fails to cast a critical gaze on the assumption upon which it is based—that is, that the only privacy interests at stake are those of men and their "right to be let alone" against state intrusion into their homes. As feminists, it is incumbent upon us to ask: What about women's privacy interests in the context of woman battering? Although some in the privacy-rejection camp of feminism might claim that women's privacy is so marginalized in the context of woman abuse as to be virtually nonexistent, I believe that if this is the case, we must endeavor to reconceptualize the privacy interests at stake in woman battering so as to put women's privacy needs front and center. In doing so, we must understand woman battering itself as an infringement of women's privacy.

At an intuitive level, it is clear that physical, sexual, and emotional abuse, as well as other forms of woman battering[32] infringe a woman's right to be "let alone" as against her battering partner, such that woman abuse may, indeed must, be understood as a violation of a woman's privacy interests. This account is further supported by an understanding of "the right to be let alone" that is concerned with the creation and maintenance of boundaries between the self and others. Clearly the coercive, abusive behaviors of woman battering, including, for example, stalking, amount to infringements of a woman's right to create and maintain privacy boundaries between herself and her batterer.[33] If we understand

---

32. Studies and statistics generally focus on physical or sexual abuse, and do not capture the full ambit of woman abuse, which includes psychological, emotional, and mental abuse, as well as other mechanisms of coercion employed by batterers including economic control and threats. See Stark, "Re-Presenting Woman Battering," (n. 5).

33. Studies estimate that 50% of women who experience domestic violence also experience stalking and harassment. M.B. Mechanic et al., "Intimate Partner Violence and Stalking Behaviour: Exploration of Patterns and Correlates in a Sample of Acutely Battered Women," *Violence and Victims* 15, no. 1 (2000): 55–72. The majority of cases involve a male accused who harasses a former female partner, with 56% of Canadian women who reported being stalked in 2002 identifying current or former partners as their stalkers. Karen Hackett, "Criminal Harassment," *Juristat: Canadian Centre for Justice Statistics* 20, no. 11 (2000) at 8, online: Statistics Canada <http://www.statcan.ca/bsolc/english/bsolc?catno=85-002-X20000118384>. This is particularly troubling since ex-intimate partner stalking is considered the most dangerous form of this crime. R.E. Palarea et al., "The Dangerous Nature of Intimate Relationship Stalking: Threats, Violence, and Associated Risk Factors," *Behavioural Sciences & the Law* 17, no. 3 (1999): 269–283. There were nine stalking-related murders in Canada between 1997 and 1999, and in *every case*, a woman was killed by a partner from whom she had recently separated. Hackett, "Criminal Harassment," 2, (n. 33). Isabel Grant, Natasha Bone, & Kathy Grant, "Canada's Criminal Harassment Provisions: A Review of the First Ten Years," *Queen's Law Journal* 29, no. 1 (2003): 175–241 at 179, note that because it is only recently that criminal harassment can form the foundation for a first-degree murder charge, it is possible that this is an underestimation of the connection between harassment and murder. Other charges, like

woman abuse as a violation of women's privacy, state nonintervention and police reluctance to seriously and reliably enforce protection orders must be seen as a privileging of men's right to be "let alone" from state interference over a woman's right to be "let alone" from a battering partner, so that for battered women, the home may be the place where they are afforded the *least* amount of privacy as a result of invasive abuse by a partner. In her landmark decision in *R. v. Lavallee*, Wilson J. for the Supreme Court of Canada noted the illusory nature of the home as a "sanctuary" for battered women, remarking, "[a] man's home may be his castle but it is also the woman's home even if it seems to her more like a prison in the circumstances."[34] A reading of woman battering that understands it as a violation of women's privacy interests invites an important reassessment of the feminist rejection of privacy in the context of woman abuse.

B. Rethinking the Feminist Rejection of Privacy

If we understand woman battering as an infringement of women's privacy by their battering partners, it follows that to combat woman abuse, women require meaningful privacy boundaries so as to be "let alone" by their violent partners.[35] Battered women must be able to draw and enforce chosen boundaries around their lives in order to "keep out" battering partners. In the context of woman battering, the simple fact of the matter is that a woman cannot be abused, raped, harassed, or stalked if she cannot be accessed or located by her batterer,[36] a truth I have seen demonstrated in practice time and again. My claim here, then, is that

---

sexual assault, break and enter, or forcible confinement might have been more common precipitators of homicide, even though there was overlap with criminal harassment.

34. *R. v Lavallee*, [1990] 1 S.C.R. 852 at para. 63. *Lavallee* was a landmark case because it was the Supreme Court of Canada's first acknowledgment of Battered Women's Syndrome and its utility for battered women accused of killing an abusive spouse or partner. In her decision, Wilson J. found that evidence of prior abuse and the effects of the abuse on a battered woman may be heard by a judge and jury when this information contributes to an argument that a woman acted in self-defense.

35. The fact that we so rarely consider the question of who we are "keeping out" with privacy boundaries is evidence of the patriarchal privileging of the relationship between the state and the individual citizen.

36. This is not to say that the abuse will necessarily end, because a partner could still be able to exert coercive control over a woman without knowing where she is physically located. Such coercive measures may include cutting off her finances, denying her access to her children, or cyberstalking. Criminal harassment is prohibited by s. 264 of the Criminal Code, s.264, (n. 19) Prohibited conduct under 264(2) includes:

(a) repeatedly following from place to place the other person or anyone known to them; (b) repeatedly communicating with, either directly or indirectly, the other person or anyone known to them; (c) besetting or watching the dwelling-house, or place where the other person, or anyone known to them, resides, works, carries on business, or happens to be; or (d) engaging in threatening conduct directed at the other person or any member of their family.

if woman battering is a privacy invasion, a battered woman may require both quantitatively *more* privacy as against an abusive partner, and qualitatively more *effective* means to create and enforce those privacy boundaries so as to ensure her safety and that of her family. Privacy is therefore fundamental to a battered woman's safety and well-being, and on these grounds, it is my contention that feminists cannot reject privacy outright. After decades of opposing privacy's role in concealing violence against women in the home, feminists may now have to fight *for* privacy rights for battered women on the understanding that privacy can be a tool to protect women from their batterers.

This assertion stands in contrast to the privacy-rejection theories advanced by many feminists as a result of the different "players" implicated in the two analyses: Although some feminists have rejected privacy on the basis that it is deployed to disguise men's violence against women in a contest between the privacy of a "man's castle" and the state, understanding woman battering as a violation of women's privacy instead sees the key privacy interests worthy of protection as those of battered women, not as against the state, but as against their battering partners. Feminists who reject privacy often assert that in order to combat woman battering, the state must intervene reliably and effectively in the private sphere of the home,[37] and indeed this strategy may have an important role to play in putting an end to woman abuse; however, if we understand woman battering as an invasion of women's privacy, then any kind of state intervention must recognize and engage with the preservation of a *woman*'s privacy boundaries as against her batterer, instead of seeing only the abstract contest between the state and the privacy of the domestic home.

Even more important than increasing the effectiveness of state intervention, perhaps, battered women must have the means necessary to access privacy in meaningful ways so that they can create and enforce their own privacy boundaries against a battering partner instead of relying on the state to do so on their behalf. The realization of true privacy for battered women may therefore involve more than simply a negative "right to be let alone."[38] Ensuring only a negative right to be free from outside scrutiny is premised on the false presumption that "the right to choose is contained entirely within the individual and is not circumscribed by the material conditions of the individual's life."[39] Although it is true that

---

37. See Jones, *Next Time She'll Be Dead*, (n. 4). But see Evan Stark, "Insults, Injury and Injustice: Rethinking State Intervention in Domestic Violence Cases," *Violence Against Women* 10, no. 11 (2004): 1302–1330.

38. Feminist critiques have emphasized the ways in which a privacy that simply proscribes state intervention exempts the state from any obligation to provide the conditions and resources necessary for privacy to be accessed, employed, and enforced by women. See, e.g., Dorothy Roberts, "Punishing Drug Addicts who have Babies: Women of Colour, Equality, and the Right of Privacy," *Harvard Law Review* 104, no. 7 (1991): 1419–1482 at 1477.

39. Roberts, "Punishing Drug Addicts," 1479, (n. 38).

nonintervention may be a necessary aspect of the "right to be let alone," in many instances, merely shielding a sphere of decision-making from coercion by outside forces will be insufficient to ensure that all women can access, create, and enforce the privacy boundaries they require in situations of battering.[40] The abstract freedom to create privacy boundaries "is of meager value without meaningful options from which to choose and the ability to effectuate one's choice,"[41] and so ensuring that battered women can access privacy and create and enforce privacy boundaries requires first that women enjoy the conditions necessary to do so.

In the context of woman abuse, it is clear that certain prerequisites must be in place for a woman to realize meaningful privacy boundaries as against a battering partner, including "educational, economic and sexual equality [as] a requirement of meaningful choice."[42] Under current conditions, however, where women's access to goods like economic security and educational or employment opportunities is circumscribed by the realities of systemic inequality, a battered woman may make the choice to leave an abusive partner only to find herself without opportunities to make significant life choices that would allow her to create and enforce effective privacy boundaries against her batterer.[43] A woman's decision to leave an abusive partner is seriously constrained by her available options once she exits the relationship, options that are limited by ". . . women's subservient position within society and the family structure, sex discrimination in the

---

40. Roberts, "Punishing Drug Addicts," (n. 38) has explored negative privacy as it relates to racialized women, concluding that a new approach to privacy must include positive obligations on the government and recognition of the connection between the right of privacy and racial equality.

41. Roberts, "Punishing Drug Addicts," 1478, (n. 38).

42. Anita Allen, "Coercing Privacy," *William & Mary Law Review* 40 (1999): 723–757 at 754.

43. Systemic factors limiting a woman's ability to exit an abusive situation may include: lack of affordable housing and available employment opportunities, concerns about child care, a deficiency in social services including women's shelters and inadequate protection from police, societal pressure and women's cultural training to "see things through" and keep the family together, fear of losing children, and conflicting personal, family, religious, and cultural loyalties. See, e.g., Ontario Association of Interval and Transition Houses, "Locked In, Left Out. Impacts of the Budget Cuts on Abused Women and Their Children" in *Violence Against Women: New Canadian Perspectives*, eds. Katherine M.J. McKenna & June Larkin, (Toronto: Ianna Publications, 2002), 413. A woman's ability to leave a battering relationship may be further constrained by intersecting oppressions of race, class, sexuality, language, and (dis)ability that "often converge in these women's lives, hindering their ability to create alternatives to the abusive relationship . . ." Crenshaw, "Mapping the Margins," 1245, (n. 16). See also Anne McGillivray & Brenda Comaskey, *Black Eyes All of the Time: Intimate Violence, Aboriginal Women, and the Justice System* (Toronto: University of Toronto Press, 1999) addressing these issues as they impact upon the lives of Aboriginal women in Canada.

workplace, economic discrimination, problems of housing and a lack of child care, lack of access to divorce, inadequate child support, problems of single motherhood, [and] lack of educational and community support."[44] Recognition that women require the material and social conditions of autonomy and equality to make real privacy possible is an important first step toward ensuring that battered women are able to exercise and employ privacy and to "police" their own privacy boundaries as against a battering partner.

Beyond recognition, creating and ensuring privacy-promoting conditions for battered women in particular, and for *all* women generally, within the current confines of our society is a daunting task. The restrictions imposed by systemic inequality continue to impede women's access to meaningful privacy. Understood within this broader context, the feminist critique and dismissal of privacy may be seen as stemming less from the particulars of the concept of privacy itself and more as a result of the conditions within which privacy is experienced and employed—that is, within the social, economic, political, and legal realities of a society that systematically privileges men and undervalues women. This analysis casts further doubt on the utility of the feminist rejection of privacy, and begs the question of whether privacy is really the problem that feminists seek to address by rejecting privacy.

IV. IS PRIVACY THE PROBLEM?

The systems of patriarchy and its interlocking systems of oppression,[45] including racism, classism, ableism, heterosexism, and neo-colonialism, dictate whether and how privacy is accessed (or rendered inaccessible), experienced (or not experienced), valued (or undervalued), and protected (or not). In the case of woman battering, it is clear that the patriarchal positioning of privacy informs the determination of whose privacy "counts," such that men's privacy rights "trump" women's, as demonstrated in the preceding section. Patriarchy situates men as the dominant, defines the "right to be let alone" with reference to men's needs and desires, and employs privacy to accomplish patriarchy's goals, which include the subordination of women. Patriarchy and its interlocking oppressions thereby permit those with power (men) to act with impunity toward those with less power (women),[46] in accordance with the systemic privileging of men that is foundational to patriarchy in all spheres of society.

Privacy is deployed along the fault lines of patriarchy to solidify existing hierarchies and bolster the project of patriarchy and its interlocking oppressions. We thereby find ourselves in a situation where "[t]o the extent that the government

---

44. Schneider, *Battered Women and Feminist Law Making*, 72, (n. 20).
45. Razack, *Looking White People in the Eye*, (n. 16).
46. See Robin West, "Reconstructing Liberty," *Tennessee Law Review* 59 (1992): 441.

is infused with patriarchal, heterosexual ideals, men's and women's privacy rights are likely to reflect patriarchal, heterosexual ideals of [privacy],"[47] which quite simply are not attuned to the needs and desires of women. The consequences are predictably detrimental to women, and include the privileging of men's privacy in the home such that woman abuse is concealed from sight. The problem, however, is not privacy itself, but the fact that privacy exists within a "constricted referential universe"[48] where existing lines of power defined by gender, race, class, disability, and sexuality dictate the form privacy will take and the ways it will be employed.

Accepting that the source of the privacy problem is not the concept of privacy itself, but the ways in which privacy is accessed, employed, and enforced within the confines of a system circumscribed by patriarchy and its interlocking oppressions leads privacy-rejection feminists to conclude that within the limits of a society characterized by inequality, it makes no sense to devote time or resources to privacy. Faced with the immensity of the ubiquitous obstacle of patriarchy, privacy-rejection feminists halt their analyses and discard privacy outright, apparently concluding that privacy might be redeemed for women only when it can be employed and accessed in the context of real equality. Conversely, I remain hopeful about privacy's present potential as a tool for the protection of battered women, even within the confines of inequality. Feminists must continue to challenge the particular limits of patriarchy that circumscribe privacy for women, and work toward affecting the kinds of systemic change required to realize equality in the long term; however, we must keep women safe and alive in order to do so. Equality may be the long-term goal, but as a "stop-gap" measure to ensure battered women's safety *right now*, privacy is worthy of our time and resources.

Feminist critiques of privacy have recognized the limits of privacy as it is currently defined and employed. Acknowledging these limits does not, however, automatically mandate a blanket negation of privacy itself, and doing so risks implied acceptance of the status quo. More importantly, perhaps, rejecting privacy simply does not reflect the realities of women's lives, for whether we love or hate it, reject or accept it, privacy matters. It can and does play an important role in battered women's lives, as demonstrated in theory and confirmed in reality by my experience working in a battered women's shelter. If and when systemic equality is realized, woman battering itself may become a relic of history, doing away with the need for strong privacy protections behind which battered women may "hide" in order to secure their safety. Ultimately, of course, this is the world I want to live in—one where systemic equality dictates that woman battering is simply unthinkable. In the meantime, however, I am willing to use all available

---

47. Allen, "Coercing Privacy," 749, (n. 6).
48. Williams, *Alchemy of Race and Rights*, 159, (n. 7).

resources, including imperfect privacy, to keep battered women safe from violent partners.

CONCLUSION

I remain committed to the belief that theory matters most when it is accessible as a tool of transformation in people's lives. This is most likely to be the case when theory is alive to the lived realities of those upon whose experiences it is based. Feminists have justifiably charged privacy with a number of offenses, among the most serious of which is its role in shielding woman abuse from public scrutiny and serving as justification for state nonintervention in the private home to prevent and protect women from abuse. The subsequent blanket rejection of privacy that has followed this critique, however, is no answer to the problem of woman battering, nor does it reflect the lives of women who may require privacy to protect themselves from a battering partner. Despite the existing limits of our patriarchal society, feminist theory and practice must remain alive to privacy's potential and work to reclaim and conscript privacy as a tool to be used in the fight against woman battering. When battered women, indeed when all women, can establish and defend boundaries in accordance with their needs and desires, privacy becomes a tool for empowerment, as opposed to an instrument of oppression.

10. GENETIC TECHNOLOGIES AND MEDICINE
Privacy, Identity, and Informed Consent

MARSHA HANEN*

I. INTRODUCTION

In the roughly ten years since the announcement of the sequencing of the human genome, we have seen an increasing number of articles in the popular press reporting various medically related genetic breakthroughs. In recent months, we have heard claims that scientists have found a gene contributing to Alzheimer's disease, a gene for spina bifida, and a gene related to long-term memory recall, among others. There are genetic tests for certain cancers, which are, in some cases, highly controversial.[1] Companies aim to match the genetic makeup of individuals with pharmaceutical nutrient formulations—nutraceuticals—to enhance health and ward off disease, leading to assertions that the science of nutrigenomics is the way of the future. And we have the announcement of the sequencing of Craig Venter's personal genome,[2] together with urgings that others do the same, so as to create a massive augmentation of the research database. In light of all this, it is understandable if people believe that the ability to tailor medical treatment to each individual is with us already. Indeed, the

* I wish particularly to thank Kenna Miskelly for her dedicated assistance with this paper. Ron Pearlman, Dan Shapiro, Bob Weyant, Shoshana Magnet, Dave Matheson, Stephanie Perrin, Philippa Lawson, and Mary O'Donohue kindly provided helpful comments on an earlier draft. George Tomlinson and I engaged in a number of fruitful discussions of approaches to this work and its implications, which we were planning to connect with his work on the development of the science underlying genetic medicine. Sadly, Dr. Tomlinson died suddenly on September 27, 2007. This paper is dedicated, with respect and admiration, to his memory.

1. See Erik Stokstad, "DNA Testing: Genetic Screen Misses Mutations in Woman at High Risk of Breast Cancer," *Science* 311 (2006): 1847.

2. See Samuel Levy, Granger Sutton, Pauline C. Ng, Lars Feuk, Aaron L. Halpern, et al., "The Diploid Genome Sequence of an Individual Human," *PLoS Biol* 5, no. 10 (2007): e254.

excitement about these developments, in the media, in the private sector, and even among researchers, universities, and funders, has been so pronounced, and exaggerated, as to be labeled "genohype."[3] And much of this "genohype" is problematic, for a variety of reasons.

The work done to date on the Human Genome Project has depended upon the development of a variety of new technologies which, although they have considerable potential for leading to beneficial results, also raise legitimate concerns, many of which were outlined in the 1997 *Universal Declaration on the Human Genome and Human Rights*.[4] In this paper, I examine the effects of some of these emerging technologies on a range of ethical issues concerning privacy, autonomy (sometimes described as "the primary ethical value in medicine in most Western countries"[5]), and related aspects of the control we attempt to exercise over our lives. Specifically, I focus on these issues in relation to "personalized medicine," commercialization, uses and misuses of information, discrimination, and informed consent. Of course, some of the concerns presented here arise in a familiar way in nongenetic medical contexts, but advances in genetics and genomics bring with them a new set of issues that are likely to multiply the concerns significantly.

II. PERSONALIZED MEDICINE AND COMMERCIALIZATION

"Personalized medicine" is the practice of sequencing a patient's genome and combining this information with new knowledge of the genetic basis of many diseases, as well as the genetic component of treatment. For example, in the future, sequencing a patient's genome might reveal a predisposition for a heart condition. This information, linked with other knowledge gleaned from the patient's genome, would allow a physician to choose the optimal prevention strategies and most effective medications for that individual. In this way, medical diagnostics and treatment might be tailored to each patient. The Personalized Medicine Coalition, an independent, nonprofit group that "works to advance the

---

3. See, for example, Timothy Caulfield and Tania Bubela, "Media Representations of Genetic Discoveries: Hype in the Headlines?" *Health Law Review* 12 (2004): 53–61; Tania Bubela and Timothy Caulfield, "Do the Print Media 'Hype' Genetic Research?: A Comparison of Newspaper Stories and Peer-Reviewed Research Papers," *Canadian Medical Association Journal* 170 (2004): 1399–1407.

4. Universal Declaration on the Human Genome and Human Rights, UNGA Res 53/152 (9 December 1998); also see Bartha Maria Knoppers, *Human Dignity and Genetic Heritage: A Study Paper Prepared for the Law Reform Commission of Canada* (Ottawa: The Commission, 1991); Deryck Beyleveld and Roger Brownsword, *Human Dignity in Bioethics and Biolaw* (New York: Oxford University Press, 2002).

5. Dorothy C. Wertz, "Patients' and Professionals' Views on Autonomy, Disability and Discrimination," in *The Commercialization of Genetic Research: Ethical, Legal and Policy Issues*, eds. Caulfield and Williams-Jones (New York: Kluwer Publishers, 1999), 171.

understanding and adoption of personalized medicine for the ultimate benefit of patients" claims that personalized medicine will transform health care by predicting likely outcomes of drug therapy and engaging in targeted drug development to improve health outcomes and increase cost-effectiveness.[6]

Many of these hoped-for outcomes involve commercialization of testing and genetic products. The practice of "genohype" often leads to unrealistic claims about the imminence of medical breakthroughs arising from genetic and genomic information; and the consequent trading on such information has been closely associated with a wide range of commercial activities, aimed at commodifying much of the rapidly expanding knowledge about connections between genetics and health.

The apparently great promise of personalized medicine, both for enhanced medical care and for substantial profit, has attracted a large number of companies into the field. The Personalized Medicine Coalition has a Board of Directors principally made up of large biotech/pharmaceutical companies, IT/informatics companies, diagnostic companies, health insurance companies, and venture capitalists.[7] And, although commercialization may lead to useful tests and treatments, it is reasonable to ask whether these companies are likely to give priority to the ethics of promoting genetic technologies or to considerations of privacy and autonomy.

These are early days for many genetic and genomic technologies, and little is known that would support the transformation of our considerable genomic knowledge into genetic therapies. Equally as important, the claims surrounding the possibilities of direct-to-consumer genetic testing for a variety of conditions bring with them little evidence that such testing is likely to provide useful results in the near term. Nevertheless, more than

> 1000 types of genetic tests are currently on the market for single-gene diseases, like cystic fibrosis and hemophilia. And the latest crop of DNA testing services, often sold directly to customers, offer to scan a person's entire genome to determine the likelihood of developing more common conditions like obesity or Alzheimer's disease.[8]

Critics, including many leading health policy advisors and geneticists, insist that the tests are both unproven and probably unnecessary in determining

---

6. "Science and Public Policy: Personalized Medicine 101," *Personalized Medicine Coalition*, 2007, http://www.personalizedmedicinecoalition.org/sciencepolicy/ personalmed-101_overview.php (accessed April 20, 2007); see also Francis S. Collins, webcast, "Personalized medicine: How the human genome era will usher in a health care revolution," *National Human Genome Research Institute*, February 10, 2005, http://www. genome.gov/Pages/News/webcasts/Personalized_Medicine_files/Default. htm#nopreload=1 (accessed April 20, 2007).

7. "About PMC: PMC Members," *Personalized Medicine Coalition*, 2007, http://www. personalizedmedicinecoalition.org/about/pmc_members.php (accessed May 27, 2008).

8. Laura Bonetta, "Getting up Close and Personal with your Genome," *Cell* 133 (2008): 753.

people's propensity to certain disease conditions.[9] And in any case, it is important to remember that genes constitute only one among many determinants of health and disease, so that the testing, even if evidence-based, still tells us little about an individual's future health.

In addition, there are numerous companies that trade on our wish to remain healthy by offering advice and products that are said to be tailored for each individual. For example, Sciona, one among many nutrigenomics companies, "provides personalized health and nutrition recommendations based on an individual's diet, lifestyle and unique genetic profile."[10]

Although commercialization of genomic information is inevitable and frequently useful, we need to examine and understand the various forces at work in developing both the science and its applications, including the rhetoric employed,[11] as a way of distinguishing possibly beneficial treatments from snake oil, and also of dealing with issues that could compromise people's autonomy and dignity.[12]

III. PERSONALIZED MEDICINE, PRIVACY, AND DISCRIMINATION

Whether involving commercialization or not, several aspects of personalized medicine are already with us. Pharmacogenomics[13]—the study of the inherited basis of differences in response to drugs—has shown that interindividual differences in the rate that individuals metabolize medications are often more than tenfold. This means that a "slow metabolizer" or "low responsive" individual might require one-tenth of the dose of a medication recommended for a "rapid metabolizer" or "high responsive" person. The slow metabolizer is therefore more likely to experience drug toxicity from the standard prescribed dosage than

---

9. For example, see United States Government Accountability Office, *Testimony Before the Special Committee on Aging, Nutrigenetic testing: Tests purchased from four web sites mislead consumers: Statement of Gregory Kutz, Managing Director Forensic Audits and Special Investigations,* U.S. Senate. July 27, 2006.

10. "About Sciona," *Sciona: Optimal Health Through Genetics,* 2006, http://www.sciona.com/ (accessed September 20, 2007).

11. Donna Haraway discusses the Human Genome Project and the claim that it is biology's equivalent to putting a man on the moon. She states "All these technoscientific travel narratives are about freedom; the free world; democracy; and, inevitably, the free market." Donna Haraway, *Modest_Witness@Second_Millennium.FemaleMan©_Meets_OncoMouse™: Feminism and Technoscience* (New York: Routledge, 1997), 167.

12. Nola Ries and Timothy Caulfield, "First Pharmacogenomics, Next Nutrigenomics: Genohype or Genohealthy?" *Jurimetrics* 46 (2006): 281–308.

13. The term "pharmacogenomics" is used more or less interchangeably with "pharmacogenetics."

a rapid metabolizer,[14] although what actually happens in individual cases is a matter of probabilities rather than certainties.[15]

Proponents of pharmacogenetics, including leaders of the pharmaceutical industry, ". . . speak of a future in which . . . comprehensive genetic testing of individuals would become routine; large arrays of genetic data would be held for each individual; genetically targeted pharmaceuticals would reduce inappropriate prescription and (supposedly) lower drug costs."[16]

However pharmacogenetics, and other genetic technologies that begin with the sequencing of a patient's genome,[17] run some significant risks. If a patient's genotype and phenotype become widely available to physicians, there is a danger that this information will be more generally disseminated, with consequent significant effects on privacy and the possibility that a variety of unauthorized or even discriminatory uses will be made of the information.

This connection between the potential for privacy violations and possible stigmatization and discrimination is a central theme of this section of the paper. A person's autonomy and ability to direct her life and to present herself in particular ways (always within constraints over which she has varying degrees of control) is closely connected with her sense of her identity, including genetic identity, her health, and her susceptibilities to diseases. Identity, autonomy, and privacy are tied to concerns about genetic discrimination because genomic information is more sensitive than "ordinary" medical information. Genomic information has the potential to provide much larger quantities and more varied types of personal data. And, given that genetic links to certain stigmatizing diseases such as mental illnesses and addictions are being sought by researchers,[18]

---

14. Daniel W. Nebert and Eula Bingham, "Pharmacogenomics: Out of the Lab and into the Community," *TRENDS in Biotechnology* 19, no. 12 (2001): 519–523; For more on pharmacogenetics, also see Tom Ling and Ann Raven. "Pharmacogenetics and Uncertainty: Implications for Policy Makers," *Studies in History and Philosophy of Science* 37, no. 3 (2006): 533–549; Abdallah Daar and Peter A. Singer, "Opinion: Pharmacogenetics and Geographical Ancestry: Implications for Drug Development and Global Health," *Nature Reviews Genetics* 6, no. 3 (2005): 241–246; Laviero Mancinelli, Maureen Cronin, and Wolfgang Sadée, "Pharmacogenomics: The Promise of Personalized Medicine," *AAPS PharmSci* 2, no. 1 (2000): E4.

15. Bonetta, *ibid.*, 754.

16. Onora O'Neill, "Informed Consent and Genetic Information," *Studies in History and Philosophy of Biology and Biomedical Sciences* 32, no. 4 (2001): 689–704, 700.

17. For example, preimplantation genetic diagnosis, certain cancer and disease screenings, and some prenatal testing can include genetic testing and may, in the near future, begin with the sequencing of a patient's genome or the genome of her fetus or embryo.

18. See for example X. Luo, H. R. Kranzier, L. Zuo, B. Z. Yang, J. Lappalainene, and J. Gelerntner, "ADH4 Gene Variation is Associated with Alcohol and Drug Dependence: Results from Family Controlled and Population-Structured Association Studies," *Pharmacogenet Genomics* 15, no. 11 (2005): 755–768.

individuals who have their genomes sequenced now may, in the future, have to confront the possibility of discrimination if they test positive for certain gene variations.

Furthermore, discoveries of the genetic basis for certain diseases, such as multiple sclerosis or Alzheimer's, will likely translate only into an increase in the *probability* of getting these illnesses for those who are found to carry the relevant genes; but misunderstandings of what an "increased probability" means could lead some to believe that carrying certain genes means that the individual *will* get the disease. In addition, genomic information from one person can imply a great deal about the genetic makeup of her blood relatives, raising privacy concerns for those who are not even being screened for the various markers of disease. As genetic discoveries advance, stronger genetic links may be found for various diseases and more individuals may face stigmatizing results, increasing the motivation to keep genetic information private. Since widespread information sharing leads to increased privacy threats, privacy protection is critical.

One privacy concern is that, once a patient's genome sequence or the results of genetic tests become part of an individual's electronic medical file, persons other than one's medical practitioner, and those who "need to know," may have access to the information. And genetic testing is already widely entrenched in medical practice, from prenatal testing to testing of "at risk" populations. If the information thus obtained becomes available to almost anyone in, say, pharmacies, or social agencies, we may experience a loss of control with respect to information about us that we consider private.

Furthermore, the ubiquitous use of information technologies, such as data mining in relation to medical information could mean that employers, insurance companies, or others have access to the results of genetic testing.[19] Although complicated analysis of medical information is not new, what *is* new are the masses of data produced by genomics and DNA studies, the extent to which these studies allow us to learn things not previously available to us, and the ease with which such information can be provided technologically and connected with other information.

These concerns lead to questions about data security.[20] Examples abound of human errors that have led to security breaches, exposing millions of people to

---

19. Data mining is a method that uses mathematical algorithms to extract implicit, previously unknown connections and patterns from large databases. The fact that the connections and patterns are largely unknown before the analysis begins can have profound ethical implications. For example, see U. Fayyad, G. Piatesky-Shapiro, and P. Symth. "Discovery in Databases: An Overview," in *Knowledge Discovery in Databases*, eds. G. Piatestsky-Shapiro and W. J. Frawley (Menlo Park, CA: AAAI Press/MIT Press, 1996).

20. N. M. Ries and G. Moysa, "Legal Protections of Electronic Health Records: Issues of Consent and Security," *Health Law Review* 14, no. 1 (2005): 18–25.

unauthorized disclosure of their personal and medical information.[21] And this issue is pressing. An announcement on April 17, 2007, indicated that British Columbia "has contracted with Sun Microsystems (B.C.) Inc. and other partners to establish a province-wide electronic system of health data aimed at improving patient care and reducing medical errors."[22] The project is said to be the largest in Canada, and one of the largest in North America. Advantages such as transcending the silos in which medical information currently resides, having patient-centric data, reducing the number of unnecessary tests being performed, bringing faster, more accurate diagnoses are cited. But what happens when incorrect information finds its way into the system, or when the information goes to the "wrong" place? Will there be legal or other consequences for careless handling of information or other failures so as to provide strong incentives not to allow this to happen? We must consider the sensitive nature of genetic information and recognize that personalized profiles make individuals more vulnerable to possible negative consequences. These concerns will likely increase if entire genetic profiles become a part of medical records.

There are ways to address these privacy concerns before such systems are put in place. Carnegie Mellon computer scientist Latanya Sweeney claims that there are accessible solutions to the privacy problems we face, but the solutions must be built into the systems *before* implementation. "If we build the right [privacy protecting] designs in up front, then society can decide how to turn those controls on and off. But if the technology is built without controls, it forces us to either accept the benefits of the technology without controls, or cripple it by adding them later."[23]

Unfortunately, many current measures aimed at protecting genetic privacy may be falling short. Advanced coding of information may still leave it vulnerable

---

21. In one instance, in March 2005, computer equipment containing the personal information of over 900,000 individuals was stolen from the American International Group (AIG), a leading international insurance organization. In January 2007, the theft of a laptop computer from a researcher's car exposed 2900 current and former patients of Toronto's Hospital for Sick Children to unauthorized release of their personal health information. News of the theft provoked the Ontario Privacy Commissioner to consider requiring that all such information be encrypted so as to make it more difficult to use, should it fall into the wrong hands. See Karen Howlett, "Information on 2,900 Patients Stolen with Laptop," *The Globe and Mail*, A7, March 8, 2007.

22. Rod Mickleburgh, "Record-keeping to Leap out of Stone Age," *The Globe and Mail*, S1. April 17, 2007.

23. Chip Walter, 2007, June 27. "Privacy isn't dead, or at least it shouldn't be: A Q&A with Latanya Sweeney." *Scientific American.com*. Retrieved Sept. 6, 2007 from http://www.sciam.com/print_version.cfm?articleID=6A2EF194–E7F2–99DF–3323DA6BA4346B0B, See also: B. Malin and L. Sweeney, "How (Not) to Protect Genomic Data Privacy in a Distributed Network: Using Trail Re-identification to Evaluate and Design Anonymity Protection Systems," *Journal of Biomedical Informatics* 37, no. 3 (2004): 179–192.

to hackers, and can, in any case, often be quite easily reconnected to its subjects.[24] A focus on coding practices aimed at protecting privacy may also ignore other important issues such as autonomy and informed consent. For example, deCODE genetics and the Icelandic government were widely criticized for coupling coding practices with policies of presumed consent when they devised biobanks for the study of population genomics.[25]

Rather than focusing narrowly on coding practices to protect privacy, we also need to consider the problem of genetic information falling into the "wrong" hands or being used in discriminatory ways. Legislation needs to be put in place to deal with such cases. Antidiscrimination laws are required to ensure that genetic information cannot be used by employers for hiring and firing purposes or by health insurers to prevent coverage; and additional legislation may be required to protect privacy more generally.[26]

The U.S. Genetic Information Nondiscrimination Act is intended to protect patients against the kind of apparent discrimination suffered by Terri Seargent in 1999.[27] Seargent discovered that she had alpha-1 deficiency, a respiratory disease that killed her brother. The discovery and early treatment probably saved Seargent's life, but she was fired and lost her health coverage when her employer learned of her costly medical condition. Likewise, the Council for Responsible

---

24. Malin and Sweeney, *ibid.*

25. Biobanks are depositories of stored genetic information and/or biological material for the purposes of current and future genetic research. deCODE's database of personal medical files is commonly referred to as the Health Sector Database (HSD) (Árnason, "Coding and Consent," 28 (n. 25)). deCODE Genetics negotiated with the Icelandic government to gain access to the medical records of Icelandic citizens, so that this information could be coded and used for research purposes. deCODE and the government argued that polls indicated that the majority of the population supported this important research and thus consent could be presumed. The personal medical information was obtained without explicit consent from patients and often without consent from medical professionals. An opt-out option was added only after citizen groups, doctors, and international organizations loudly denounced the policy. See Vilhjálmur Árnason, "Coding and Consent: Moral Challenges of the Database Project in Iceland," *Bioethics* 18, no. 1 (2004): 27–49.

26. Some such legislation is already in place. In the United States, Congress passed the Genetic Information Nondiscrimination Act (GINA) on May 1, 2008. According to the National Human Genome Research Institute, "The act will protect individuals against discrimination based on their genetic information when it comes to health insurance and employment. These protections are intended to encourage Americans to take advantage of genetic testing as part of their medical care." National Human Genome Research Institute. Genetic antidiscrimination bill clears congress. *Policy & ethics: Critical issues and legislation surrounding genetic research*. Retrieved May 15, 2008 from http://www.genome. gov/PolicyEthics/.

27. Diane Martindale, "Genetics Discrimination: Pink Slip in your Genes," *Scientific American*, January 284, no. 1 (2001): 19–20.

Genetics[28] reported that, when genetic testing revealed that a young boy had fragile X syndrome, "an inherited form of mental retardation," the family's insurance company dropped the boy's health insurance "claiming that his disability represents a preexisting condition."[29] In another reported case, a social worker lost her job within a week of mentioning that her mother had died of Huntington's disease.[30] And concerns about genetic discrimination are not unique to the United States.[31]

Genetic discrimination can have far-reaching social consequences that go beyond implications for individuals and their families. The Council for Responsible Genetics discusses a case where a lead battery manufacturing operation attempted to bar women from working for the company because lead interferes with reproductive capabilities.[32] "One of the main occupational health aspects of this is that employers would rather discriminate against prospective employees than clean up the work place."[33] Indeed, the Council argues that it is actually not acceptable to expose anyone—men, or sterilized women, for that matter—to these excess lead levels.

The Council also raises the concern that genetic susceptibilities might be seen as "preexisting conditions" that could be used to "justify" workplace discrimination. But if this is our future, they claim:

(1) We are treating those people as damaged goods. We are devaluing their personality. (2) We are discriminating in ways that are not justifiable. The employers should clean up their act.[34]

Furthermore, genetic discrimination in this area will likely serve to further disadvantage those who are already marginalized. And the issue of marginalization

---

28. Council for Responsible Genetics, "Genetic Discrimination: A Position Paper Presented by the Council for Responsible Genetics," (original version written 1997; January 2001), http://www.gene-watch.org/programs/privacy/genetic-disc-position.html (accessed April 20, 2007).

29. Ibid.

30. Ibid. In this example, the social worker has a 50% chance of carrying the gene that causes Huntington's disease. Unlike most diseases with a genetic component, Huntington's is a genetically inherited disease. It only takes one copy of the HD gene to cause Huntington's disease (it is an autosomal dominant trait). Persons who are gene carriers *will* develop the disease (assuming that they live long enough).

31. See, for example, Trudo Lemmens, Mireille Lacroix, and Roxanne Mykitiuk, *Reading the Future? Legal and Ethical Challenges of Predictive Genetic Testing* (Montreal: Les Éditions Thémis, 2007).

32. Diane Horn, interview with Phil Bereano, "Genetic Discrimination: A Primer," *Council for Responsible Genetics*, KCMU 90.3 FM-Radio, Seattle, Washington, http://www.gene-watch.org/programs/privacy/BerInterview.html (accessed April 24, 2007).

33. Ibid.

34. Ibid.

is particularly important in the context of discrimination as it is the poor, the homeless, immigrants, and aboriginal people who are most likely to be subject to discrimination.

IV. GENETIC TECHNOLOGIES, IDENTITY, AND AUTONOMY

The focus of the paper on autonomy and related issues that have an ethical dimension is crucial because of the importance of viewing persons in medical contexts as "possessing dignity and inherent worth"[35] and being able to make rational choices for their lives. But because of the problem of marginalization, our view of autonomy must go beyond the purely individualistic. We need a more contextualized, socially situated, "relational" notion, which "examines patient autonomy in the social and political dimensions within which it resides and provides us with the theoretical resources that we need for restructuring health care practices in ways that will genuinely expand the autonomy of all patients."[36] We need to take account of the factors that influence our ability to exercise our autonomy and maintain our sense of identity based on social, as well as the traditional individual understandings of health and the factors that affect it.

There are also serious ethical implications for autonomy and identity stemming from misconceptions that many diseases are "purely" genetic in origin. The focus on genetics and disease sometimes leads to a kind of reductionism—"genetic essentialism" or "genetic determinism,"[37] which holds that our genes determine almost everything about us, to the exclusion of other important influences.

Actually, genetic and environmental interactions mean that few diseases are "purely" genetic in character. For example, a person whose birth is extremely premature may develop chronic respiratory illnesses that do not show up on her genetic map; likewise, people who work in coal mines, or have been in serious car accidents may develop illnesses unrelated to their genetic makeup. Carriers of the "breast cancer genes" have an increased risk for developing breast cancer,

35. Kwame Anthony Appiah, *The Ethics of Identity* (Princeton, NJ: Princeton University Press, 2005), 61.

36. Susan Sherwin, *The Politics of Women's Health: Exploring Agency and Autonomy* (Philadelphia, PA: Temple University Press, 1998), 44.

37. There are numerous examples in the literature of the problems associated with accepting genetic determinism. See for example, Dorothy Nelkin and Susan M. Lindee, *The DNA Mystique: The Gene as a Cultural Icon* (Ann Arbor: University of Michigan Press, 2004); R. C. Lewontin, Steven Rose, and Leon J. Kamin, *Not in Our Genes* (New York: Pantheon Books, 1984); Celeste M. Condit and Deirdre M. Condit, "Blueprints and Recipes: Gendered Metaphors for Genetic Medicine," *Journal of Medical Humanities* 22, no. 1 (2001): 29–39. See also Abby Lippman, "The Politics of Health: Geneticization Versus Health Promotion," in Sherwin, *The Politics of Women's Health* (1998): 64–82.

but this does not mean that they will inevitably develop the disease, nor does it mean that those who do not carry these genes will not develop it. So, although current genetic research may appear to suggest that we are on the verge of understanding, and even eradicating many major diseases, it is important to keep in mind that "genetic status" gives us only limited prediction of future illness;[38] and overemphasizing genetic makeup could negatively affect people's view of themselves and their sense of their own autonomy.

Furthermore, and contrary to the expectations of many, information about connections between genes and particular diseases has generally not led to breakthroughs in treatment.[39] If important environmental factors and the complexity of disease are overlooked, conclusions can be seriously misleading and even damaging; it is not unreasonable to be concerned that the medical profession may pay less attention to environmental causes of disease as more information about the genome comes to light and a "geno-centric" view of disease becomes entrenched.[40]

Some have worried that genetic technologies and the push for personalized medicine could lead to a loss of autonomy or confusion about identity because we do not have a clear conception of what "disease" and "wellness" mean. As S. O. Hansson notes,

> Disease is not a biologically well defined concept but one that depends largely on social values. Some conditions previously regarded as diseases are now thought of as normal states of the mind or body. Others that were previously perceived as variations of normality are now regarded as diseases. Homosexuality is an example of the former, attention deficit hyperactivity disorder of the latter.[41]

Confusion about medical terminology is compounded by confusion about the role of genetic technologies: Will the focus be to cure, to prevent disease, to screen for and eliminate genetic "abnormalities," or will the focus switch to "enhancement"

---

38. Maxwell J. Mehlman and Jeffery R. Botkin, *Access to the Genome: The Challenge to Equality* (Washington, DC: Georgetown University Press, 1998), 25.

39. The National Human Genome Research Institute states, "It is important to realize . . . that it often takes considerable time, effort, and funding to move discoveries from the scientific laboratory into the medical clinic. Most new drugs based on genome-based research are estimated to be at least 10 to 15 years away. According to biotechnology experts, it usually takes more than a decade for a company to conduct the kinds of clinical studies needed to receive approval from the Food and Drug Administration." "A Brief Guide to Genomics," *National Human Genome Research Institute*, June 27, 2007, http://www.genome.gov/18016863 (accessed September 21, 2007).

40. Recent research suggests that there may be a stronger link between gene expression and environmental factors than previously thought. We are beginning to see a biological basis for environmental influences and social determinants of health through epigenetics—the study of the link between gene expression and environmental factors. This could eventually lead to a clearer understanding of individual genomes and individual susceptibilities.

41. S. O. Hansson, "Implant Ethics," *Journal of Medical Ethics* 31 (2005): 519–525; 522.

and creating longer, better lives for people? Much depends upon how "abnormalities" are defined and viewed, and whether these definitions will change our view of our own identities and ability to make autonomous decisions about treatment. We need also to ensure that access to new technologies will not be a function of wealth or influence rather than need, or other more egalitarian criteria.

In a context in which people are increasingly being viewed as "responsible" for many of their illnesses, because of what are viewed as poor "lifestyle" choices—inappropriate diet, lack of exercise, smoking, and the like—the belief easily develops that individuals have the power to maintain optimal health, regardless of poverty, homelessness, mental illness, or environmental toxicities.[42] Similarly, if the expectation develops that technologies available for preventing or removing genetic "abnormalities" will be used in ways advocated by professional or corporate interests, who will also determine which people "deserve" care, there is a significant risk of unfairness and dysfunction in the system.

P. J. Boyle correctly notes that genetic research is neither more "neutral" than much other scientific research, nor are researchers "mere spectators to the unfolding of the secrets of the human genome."

> We plant the seeds of the answers we will arrive at in the way we frame the questions we ask. The genetic knowledge we shape in such a manner will in turn dictate the nature of our social, legal, and ethical responsibilities.[43]

Likewise, genetic technologies give rise to questions of ethical responsibility for physicians. What should be the role of the practitioner in situations where a patient could lose her health insurance, her job, or be exposed to other forms of discrimination as a result of genetic findings? If a woman requests genetic testing for breast cancer genes and the genes are found, she may be vulnerable to genetic discrimination, whether or not she ever develops cancer. And where testing could have a negative impact on a patient's career, position in society, or relationships with other people it is reasonable to ask whether the physician has a duty to warn the patient of such potential impacts. On the other hand, we might ask whether we should assume that the patient has a right to know, and that the negative consequences to patient autonomy always tell against attempting to protect a patient from worrisome knowledge.

Medical professionals must also take account of their possible responsibilities to the patient's relatives when genetic testing is involved. Consider the example

---

42. Researchers working in epigenetics are showing how our "lifestyles and environment can change the way our genes are expressed, leading even identical twins to become distinct as they age." NOVA: Science Now. (PBS) 2007, July. *Epigenetics*. Retrieved Sept. 21, 2007 from http://www.pbs.org/wgbh/nova/sciencenow/3411/02.html. For more on the science of epigenetics, see A. Bird, "Perceptions of Epigenetics," *Nature* 447 (2007): 396–398.

43. P. J. Boyle et al., "Genetic Grammar: Health, Illness, and the Human Genome Project," *Hastings Center Report*, Special Supplement 22, no. 4 (1992): S1.

of the woman whose mother died of medullary cancer.[44] Three years later the woman was diagnosed with the same cancer, already in an advanced stage. She felt that her mother's doctor should have disclosed to her the fact that the disease is transmitted genetically as a dominant trait and sued the doctor for not passing on information about her mother's genetic makeup that affected the woman herself. "The Florida Court ruled that, in the usual doctor-patient relationship, the physician has no legal obligation to speak with other members of the family about their risks."[45] But, from a moral point of view, perhaps a different conclusion would be in order, especially in light of the effect the physician's decision may have had on the daughter's autonomy and sense of self.

Also consider instances where individuals who have had a grandparent die of Huntington's disease have chosen to be tested for Huntington's even though their asymptomatic parent has chosen not to be tested. If the individual tests positive for the Huntington's allele, then the parent is a carrier and will develop the disease. In these cases the parent is likely to find out something about his or her own genetic makeup that he or she did not want to know. Such scenarios could become more common as genetic technologies advance and more diseases with genetic origins are discovered, even in the case of diseases not as deterministic as Huntington's. Does a physician have any duty to individuals who are not patients if the information also pertains to them?

These examples highlight how the identity and autonomy of the involved parties can conflict with one another: One person's autonomous choice to learn facts about herself could change the way another person views himself. In the first of these examples, the daughter was deprived of information to which she felt entitled, whereas in the second, the parent is likely to gain information about his own genetic makeup that he does not wish to have. The physician must grapple with the ethical concerns of her patient as well as considering the ethical questions that arise from acquiring critical medical information about *another* person. These examples also help to illustrate the complexity of issues surrounding genetic testing, and point to ways in which genetic technologies complicate the informed consent process.

V. INFORMED CONSENT AND TRUST

Onora O'Neill writes,

> *Informed consent* has been seen as the key ethical requirement for medical treatment and research, to be supported by requirements for *professional confidentiality* and for *personal privacy*. Securing the informed consent of patients

---

44. Nebert and Bingham, 2001, p.521 (n. 14).
45. *Ibid.*, 521.

and respecting the confidentiality of information they provide have been seen as operationalising the ethical ideals of respecting individuals, their rights and their autonomy.[46]

Among the reasons for a systematic insistence on informed consent in medical contexts is society's belief in the importance of people's ability to make autonomous decisions about what they wish to keep private about themselves, and about the identities that they wish to project to the world. In this context, the issue of trust looms large, particularly with respect to consent to medical procedures, research, and other uses of genetic information. Trust and trustworthiness underline concerns about security of information, genetic discrimination, and even the usefulness and appropriateness of genetic testing itself, and trust is clearly tied to the practice of informed consent in that the patient needs to be able to trust that her wishes with respect to her genetic information will be honored.

Yet it is often difficult, when consent is sought, to be certain just what is being consented to. Much depends upon how procedures or research or other processes are described to the person whose consent is needed, and how much contextual information as well as overall understanding that individual possesses.

In particular, because a considerable portion of most patients' knowledge of medical matters derives from what they are told by their physicians, and people not medically trained may have difficulty understanding some of what they are told, trust becomes more necessary, but harder to sustain. In terms of informed consent, this difficulty is summarized by O'Neill:

> Consent is particularly problematical in medical practice, because it is commonplace even for patients who are in the maturity of their faculties to find themselves at a time of weakness and distress surrounded by others who seem (and may be) more knowledgeable, whose influence and power are considerable, whom they very much do not want to offend. If consent is to be a governing principle in medical ethics, we seemingly need to be ideal rational patients; but when we are patients we are often furthest from being ideally rational . . . [47]

Moreover, the more complicated the technology being brought to bear, the more likely it is that patients will have limited knowledge with which to make decisions, so it is easy to see how dependent we become on trusting the practitioner.

We must also consider that in the medical context, it is not unusual for people who live in "situations of oppression, marginality, illiteracy, poverty, or a range

---

46. Onora O'Neill, "Informed Consent and Genetic Information," *Studies in History and Philosophy of Biology and Biomedical Sciences* 32, no. 4 (2001): 689–704; 691.

47. *Ibid.*, 693.

of other"[48] circumstances to find it impossible, without the help of an advocate of some sort, to take charge of their own medical decisions in the face of physician expertise that is, frequently, experienced as intimidating. Therefore, although much of the discussion of physician-patient relationships assumes that patients are fully autonomous beings, this view is unrealistic in many cases. This is important, because informed consent is supposed to enable individuals to make autonomous decisions about what they wish to keep private about themselves, and for marginalized members of society, "sensitive information" may be even more "sensitive," as there may be more at stake if their privacy is threatened.[49]

These worries can be translated into a more general critique of the informed consent process. As O'Neill writes,

> Consent is a *propositional attitude*: it is always directed to some description of a proposal, situation or action. Its object is always some specific *propositional content*. Where a proposition consented to misdescribes a proposed action, or is economical with the truth, consent may be misdirected and so will not be legitimate. This is all too common . . . The ethical implications of the *referential opacity of propositional attitudes* are massive. We generally consent in the required, informed and freely chosen way to rather little: so rather little can be legitimated by appeal to consent.[50]

Genetic technologies compound the opacity of the informed consent process because of the immense amount of information that comprises genetic decision making. O'Neill claims that it is not merely that science has made these decisions more complex:

> We remain finite, ignorant and vulnerable agents with limited cognitive capacities, limited abilities to choose and limited time: but in medical contexts we face, and will increasingly face, vastly complex ranges of information, organised in the increasingly formalized ways demanded by increasingly intricately structured regulatory processes. Nowhere is this more evident than in those parts of medicine and of life which are most affected by the increasing complexity and availability of genetic data, and by the increasing variety of ways in which such knowledge may be collected, stored, used and disclosed.[51]

---

48. Lorraine Code, *Ecological Thinking: The Politics of Epistemic Location* (New York: Oxford University Press, 2006), 187.

49. For example, individuals in lower socio-economic situations may be more vulnerable to the genetic discrimination that could result from employers exploiting links between various environmental factors and genetics, such as the example of the battery factory. Diane Horn, interview (n. 32).

50. O'Neill, "Informed Consent and Genetic Information," 692, (n. 46).

51. *Ibid.*, 695.

Thus, O'Neill believes that our cognitive capacities are being overwhelmed and more attempts to make decisions easier and more straightforward will make the process even more opaque. O'Neill's critique highlights another important consideration. In our technological society, with genetics so often featured in the media, it is hard to know what expectations are reasonable to set with respect to becoming informed. Often we feel that we should know more about DNA, genetics, and the human genome, not to mention data mining and other information technologies. These high expectations may make patients feel responsible and inadequate in decision making situations, and they may be reluctant to ask questions or to delay consenting to procedures, particularly in clinical environments where formal consent is often sought at the last moment, when there is little time available for discussion. Furthermore, it is not just what a patient knows (or does not know) but also how much *is known*. As indicated earlier, the way that genetic technologies will shape our future and the associated privacy implications are largely *unknown* at this time. Processes based on the notions of informed consent must make these points transparent.

O'Neill notes that in a typical biomedical setting autonomy and informed consent are given center stage, while trust is pushed to the margins. But she takes the position that trust is more important than autonomy "in any ethically adequate practice of medicine, science and biotechnology."[52] As Daniel Callahan argues, autonomy "is *a* value, not *the* value," and proper medical practice requires "a search for morality in the company of others, community as an ideal and interdependence as a perceived reality, and an embracing of autonomy as a necessary but not a sufficient condition for a moral life."[53]

The use of genetic technologies may be especially damaging to the trust necessary in medicine and research. Medical care that is specific to the individual's genetic profile may appear to some to be the ultimate in personalized medicine: it may look as though the medical practitioner has come to know you intimately and is designing care with your unique characteristics in mind. However, this is more appearance than reality. It is unlikely that the intimate and individual doctor-patient relationship that appears as the paradigm of good medical practice will be realized in this genetic age. And it is reasonable to ask whether it should be. It might be more appropriate to maintain that transparency about medical procedures and informed consent processes are the only things that can

52. Onora O'Neill, *Autonomy and Trust in Bioethics* (Cambridge: Cambridge University Press, 2002), ix.

53. Daniel Callahan, "Autonomy: A Moral Good, Not a Moral Obsession," *The Hastings Center Report* 14, no. 5 (1984): 40–42; see also Willard Gaylin and Bruce Jennings, *The Perversion of Autonomy: Coercion and Constraints in a Liberal Society* (Washington, DC: Georgetown University Press, 2003).

solidify trust between individuals and the medical professionals with whom they come in contact.

Furthermore, it may be that we need to think in new ways about informed consent itself. O'Neill, for example, believes that, because of the extreme quantity and complexity of genetic information that would have to be grasped in each instance of granting consent, the emphasis in the future will have to be on constructing trustworthy institutions rather than on individual acts of consent; and such institutions will only earn their designation as trustworthy if "there are feasible procedures by which an individual can check on what is done."[54] But whether it is at all practical to create such institutions remains to be seen, so it would, at this stage, be unwise to be too sanguine about the possibility of finding techniques adequate to sustaining trust and giving voice to people's apparent need to maintain their ability to control the use of their genetic information.

VI. CONCLUSION

Genetic technologies and genomic information are rapidly evolving, and enormous changes can be expected in the next few years. Clearly, there is tremendous promise in genetic medicine—only a small part of which has been realized to date. There are also potential pitfalls, which have been much discussed, but have not been dealt with in an integrated way.

The increased use of genetic information in medical contexts raises questions about who decides on the collection of genetic material and applications of genetic technology and what safeguards need to be in place to guard against errors of fact or interpretation and poor decisions that could be harmful to individuals or groups. In the varied and rapidly changing landscape of medical knowledge, the availability of reliable sources of information to medical decision makers would go a long way toward raising people's confidence that their genetic information will be used in their best interests. In order to deal appropriately with the issues of privacy and the ways in which genomics has the potential to make us think differently about our identities, we must recognize that we need much more information, and time to think carefully, not only about people's genomes, but also about how genomic information interacts with environmental characteristics. However tempting commercial applications may be, we need to assess both their positive and negative implications, especially the possible effects on privacy, autonomy, dignity, and even people's sense of who they are. And where a need for policies or laws

---

54. O'Neill, "Informed Consent and Genetic Information," 702–703 (n. 46).

to protect privacy is identified, appropriate methods of enforcement and measures of accountability must be included.

In all of this, informed consent plays a major role, because it represents people's ability to make autonomous decisions about their lives. Such decisions may be different for different people, so it is important that the framework within which decisions are made allows for such variations, and recognizes that the groups to which people belong, whether through their choice or not, play a significant role in how their medical care will develop.

11. RECLAIMING THE SOCIAL VALUE OF PRIVACY

VALERIE STEEVES*

The protection of privacy has been on the policy agenda since Alan Westin first published his seminal work, *Privacy and Freedom*, in 1967.[1] The book was followed swiftly by a series of governmental studies in France, the United Kingdom, Canada, Sweden, and the United States,[2] and each of these countries subsequently passed data protection laws based on Westin's definition of privacy as informational control. By 2000, over forty countries around the world had passed similar legislation as part of an ongoing international effort to harmonize the legal regime governing privacy.[3]

However, critics argue that the legislative activity of the past forty years has done little to constrain the collection of massive amounts of personal information on the part of governments and corporations. Sociologists have been particularly critical of Westin's conceptualization of privacy, arguing that as "appealing and seemingly intuitive as this concept is, it plainly doesn't work."[4] Their argument

---

* The author would like to thank Jane Bailey and Marsha Hannen for their insightful comments on an earlier draft of this chapter.

1. Alan Westin, *Privacy and Freedom* (New York: Atheneum, 1967).

2. G.B.F. Niblett, ed., *Digital Information and the Privacy Problem* (Paris: OECD Informatic Studies No. 2, 1971); Great Britain, Home Office, Report of the Committee on Privacy (London, 1972); Canada, Department of Communications and Department of Justice, Privacy and Computers: A Report of the Task Force (Ottawa, 1972); Sweden, Committee on Automated Personal Systems, Data and Privacy (Stockholm, 1972); United States, Department of Health, Education and Welfare, Secretary's Advisory Committee on Automated Personal Data Systems, Records, Computers, and the Rights of Citizens (Washington, D.C., 1973).

3. Colin Bennett and Charles Raab, *The Governance of Privacy: Policy Instruments in Global Perspective* (London: Barnes and Noble, 2002), 102.

4. Felix Stalder, "Privacy Is Not the Antidote to Surveillance," *Surveillance & Society* 1, no. 1 (2002): 121. See also Mark Andrejevic, "The Kinder, Gentler Gaze of Big Brother—Reality TV in the Era of Digital Capitalism," *New Media & Society* 4, no. 2 (2002): 257; and David J. Phillips, "Ubiquitous Computing, spatiality, and the construction of identity: Directions for policy response" in this volume (Insert page number).

is supported by the fact that data protection has been unable to stop the rollout of technologies like closed-circuit television cameras in public places, remote-activated location devices in cell phones, iris scans in school cafeteria lunch lines, and security cameras in bathrooms, hotel rooms, and school buses, in spite of concerns that the surveillance these technologies enable may have deleterious effects on our social and political relationships. The conceptualization of privacy as informational control has also arguably displaced broader—and potentially more empowering—discourses rooted in a human rights model that seeks to protect human dignity and democratic freedoms in the surveillance society.[5]

My own concern that there may be something wrong with our definition of privacy as informational control was underlined a few years ago, when I was asked to give some advice regarding a hospital privacy policy. The patient admission form included a field for religious affiliation. Historically, that information had been passed on to the hospital chaplains so that a member of the appropriate clergy could visit the patient and offer support. The hospital felt that passing on that information without express written consent was a violation of data protection legislation, and they were struggling to come up with a way to satisfy the law and their patients' needs.

Interestingly, the hospital administrators were unconcerned about the fact that data protection laws do little to restrict the flow of patient data for all sorts of other secondary purposes such as research and quality control, both of which occur outside of the social context of the doctor-patient relationship. However, they felt strongly that passing on the information to the chaplain would violate the patient's privacy, in spite of the fact that the requirement of express consent in these circumstances created barriers to the normal flow of social interaction. They acknowledged that the only reason a patient voluntarily affiliates herself with a faith community while in the hospital is to get the support of that community. In fact, one could argue that the chaplain's visit is an example of community in action. If the patient does not want to talk to the chaplain, she can simply say so at the time. In other words, her desire for privacy and her need for community support can be negotiated through normal social interaction. Ironically, the patient's ability to negotiate her own privacy in this way was negated by the hospital's refusal to pass on the information to the chaplain, while her data continued to flow to government managers and the Canadian Institute for Health Information without her knowledge or consent.

The gap between the goal of data protection legislation and the reality of life in the surveillance society is not just a matter of poor implementation.

---

5. Valerie Steeves, "Under Suspicion: The Cybercrime Convention, Privacy and Canadian 'Lawful Access' Proposals," in *Social Justice and Human Rights in the Era of Globalization: From Rhetoric to Reality*, eds. James Mulvale, Stephan Parmentier, Paul Redekop, and Elmar Weitekamp, (Place: Publisher, forthcoming).

I suggest it reflects the fact that we rely upon a definition of privacy that is problematic because it strips privacy out of its social context. Accordingly, this chapter goes back to the source and revisits Westin's theory of privacy with a view to recapturing the social elements of the privacy equation. I argue that, although Westin's theory is rich in sociality, he limits his insights into the social nature of privacy by focusing on the flow of information rather than on the social interaction of persons seeking or respecting privacy. In addition, Westin equates perfect privacy with social withdrawal; from this perspective, any social interaction becomes a risk to privacy, making privacy not only asocial, but also antisocial.

As a corrective, I draw on Irwin Altman's work on territoriality and George Herbert Mead's work on social interactionism and propose an alternative framework that conceptualizes privacy as a dynamic process of negotiating personal boundaries in intersubjective relations. In doing so, I am not arguing in favor of a collective right versus an individual right. Rather, I am suggesting that by placing privacy in the social context of intersubjectivity, privacy can be more fully understood as a social construction that we create as we negotiate our relationships with others on a daily basis. This conceptualization frees the policy questions from the narrow procedural considerations of data protection, and reinvigorates our ability to question—and limit—the negative impact of surveillance on our social and democratic relationships.

I. WESTIN AND THE SOCIAL VALUE OF PRIVACY

Priscilla Regan's 1995 book, *Legislating Privacy*,[6] is the most comprehensive attempt to date to examine the weaknesses inherent in Westin's conceptualization of privacy as informational control. She argues that privacy policy has failed because it is based on a notion of privacy that is rooted in a liberal understanding of the individual and society. If privacy is a right held by an individual against the state, then, because no right is absolute, it must be balanced against competing social interests. This leads to a zero-sum game that pits the individual's interest in privacy against society's interest in competing social benefits, such as medical research and protection against terrorism.[7] However, as Regan points out, privacy

---

6. Priscilla Regan, *Legislating Privacy* (Chapel Hill: University of North Carolina Press, 1995).

7. Communitarians have long argued that privacy may promote antisocial ends. In 1949, H.W. Arndt wrote, "the cult of privacy rests on an individualist conception of society, not merely in the innocent and beneficial sense of a society in which the welfare of individuals is conceived as the end of all social organization, but in the more specific sense of 'each man for himself and the devil take the hindmost'" (H.W. Arndt, "The Cult of Privacy," *Australian Quarterly*, XXI, (1949): 69–71, 69). Similarly, Hannah Arendt's work was predicated on a rigid separation of public and private; and her interpretation of Kantian "reflective judgment"

is more than an individual right; it is also a social good in and of itself that "serves other important [social] functions beyond those to the particular individual."[8] She warns that, if the social value of privacy is not taken into account by policymakers, privacy will continue to shrink in the face of competing claims for security and convenience.

Regan's critique of Westin is a compelling one. Westin's analysis is firmly rooted in American liberal legal tradition and the Millean view that society is an aggregate of individuals who seek to establish a sphere of autonomy independent of and in tension with the collective. From this perspective, the need to restrict surveillance is part of the individual's ongoing "struggle for liberty,"[9] and technologies are problematic precisely because they erode the "libertarian equilibrium among the competing values of privacy, disclosure, and surveillance"[10] established by the framers of the American constitution in 1789. Westin argues that the role of the law is to articulate a "balance that ensures strong citadels of individual and group privacy and limits both disclosure and surveillance" in order to maintain the conditions necessary for individual autonomy and democratic governance.[11]

However, Westin's legislative prescriptions call for much more than an instrumental balancing of individual needs against social needs. Data protection is merely the last step in a five-step process that first seeks to hold surveillance up to public scrutiny. Westin writes, "[w]hat is needed is a structured and rational weighing process, with definite criteria that public and private authorities can apply in comparing the claims for disclosure or surveillance through new devices with the claims to privacy."[12] To do this, we must ask five questions:

1. How serious is the need to conduct surveillance?
2. Are there alternative methods to meet the need?
3. What degree of reliability will be required of the surveillance instrument?

---

required that private, egocentric concerns be set aside in favour of those interests that are shared in common (Hannah Arendt, *The Life of the Mind*, 2 vols. (London: Secker & Warburg, 1978)). These views resonate with the perspective of modern communitarians, who argue that a good society must seek "a carefully crafted balance between individual rights and social responsibilities" (Amitai Etzioni, *The Limits of Privacy* (New York: Basic Books, 1999), 5). Since the individual's right to be let alone detracts from the degree of participation, cooperation, and community necessary to a healthy democracy, it must be balanced against competing social interests (Amitai Etzioni, *Spirit of Community: Rights, Responsibilities and the Communitarian Agenda* (New York: Simon and Schuster, 1994); Etzioni, 1999, supra; Fred H. Cate, *Privacy in the Information Age* (Washington, D.C.: Brookings Institute Press, 1997).

8. *Ibid.*, 16.
9. Westin, *Privacy and Freedom*, 67 (n. 1).
10. *Ibid.*, 67.
11. *Ibid.*, 24.
12. *Ibid.*, 370.

4. Can true consent to the surveillance be given?

5. Do we have the capacity to limit and control the surveillance if it is allowed?

Data protection principles are only introduced if the organization seeking to use surveillance first proves to the public that the surveillance should be "allowed."

Moreover, Westin argues that some collective benefit is not a sufficient reason to invade privacy. The importance of the benefit can only be determined by honestly evaluating the effect of the surveillance on relationships of social power and the potential for discrimination in society at large.[13] From the start, Westin's full legislative program accordingly questioned whether or not surveillance should be tolerated by the public, based on its effect on social relationships. However, data protection legislation avoided those questions and focused solely on the last step in his legislative plan, the enactment of procedural protections to ensure, among other things, access to one's data file and the accuracy of the information found there.

Interestingly, just as Westin's broader legislative program has been truncated by data protection, the second part of his definition of privacy—the social part— has been dropped from policy discourses. Westin is most often quoted for the definition of privacy as "the claim of individuals, groups, or institutions to determine for themselves when, how, and to what extent information about them is communicated to others."[14] However, the definition continues:

> Viewed in terms of the relation of the individual to social participation, privacy is the voluntary and temporary withdrawal of a person from the general society through physical or psychological means, either in a state of solitude or small-group intimacy or, when among larger groups, in a condition of anonymity or reserve.[15]

The next part of this chapter revisits Westin's theoretical approach to privacy in order to identify the social elements contained in that definition.

II. SOCIAL ELEMENTS IN WESTIN'S THEORY OF PRIVACY

Privacy and Freedom is, in essence, a legal project that seeks to reinvigorate the mechanisms of democratic governance by articulating legal protections for privacy.[16] However, Westin expressly roots this project in the social psychological

---

13. *Ibid.*, 370–371.

14. *Ibid.*, 7.

15. *Ibid.*

16. Westin was tasked by the Association of the Bar of the City of New York's Committee on Science and Law with finding legal and policy responses that would maximize the

TABLE 11.1 WESTIN'S PRIVACY STATES AND FUNCTIONS

States	Functions
1. Solitude	1. Personal autonomy
2. Intimacy	2. Emotional release
3. Anonymity	3. Self-evaluation
4. Reserve	4. Limited and protected communication

literature and seeks to explore privacy's "psychological, sociological, and political dimensions . . . on the basis of leading theoretical and empirical studies."[17] He starts by drawing on Edward Hall's *The Hidden Dimension* and Robert Ardrey's *Territorial Imperative* and concludes that privacy is rooted in human evolution[18] and that privacy norms are present "in virtually every society."[19] Although these norms vary from culture to culture, "a complex but well-understood etiquette of privacy is part of [every] social scenario."[20] From this perspective, then, privacy is inherently social—it is part of the way in which social beings interact.

The social nature of privacy is evident throughout Westin's discussion of privacy states (see Table 11.1). For example, small group intimacy is essential to achieve the "basic need of human contact," which is expressed through "close, relaxed, and frank relationships between two or more individuals."[21] Anonymity is constructed socially by the recognition on the part of others that the anonymous person should not be "held to the full rules of behaviour that would operate if he were known to those observing him."[22] The state of reserve—defined as a "psychological barrier against unwanted intrusion"—is dependent upon the interaction between the individual seeking privacy and the others with whom she is interacting: "The manner in which individuals claim reserve and the *extent to which it is respected or disregarded by others* is at the heart of securing meaningful privacy in the crowded, organization-dominated settings of modern industrial society and urban life."[23]

As such, Westin's understanding of privacy is rich in sociality. But this sociality does not come out of a theoretical vacuum. Westin's work is rooted in

---

benefits of new technologies while minimizing the risks. In Westin's words, his hope was that his work "may help to guide American policy makers" (*Ibid.*, 4).

17. *Ibid.*, 3.
18. *Ibid.*, 8.
19. *Ibid.*, 13.
20. *Ibid.*, 39.
21. *Ibid.*, 31.
22. *Ibid.*
23. *Ibid.*, 32 (emphasis added).

a core group of sociologists who provide touchstones for his thought. He draws heavily on Georg Simmel, particularly in defining the privacy states of anonymity and reserve. For Westin, anonymity is an essential part of Simmel's "phenomenon of the stranger." Westin uses Simmel's insight that strangers "often received the most surprising openness—confidences which sometimes have the character of a confessional and which would be carefully withheld from a more closely related person"[24] to explain how anonymity allows a person to "express himself freely" because he knows he will not be "held to the full rules of behavior and role that would operate if he were known to those observing him."[25]

Reserve is rooted in Simmel's concept of "mental distance": the combination of "reciprocal reserve and indifference" that is exhibited during social interaction to "protect the personality."[26] Westin notes that his own conceptualization of privacy as the tension between the individual's desire to withhold or to disclose information was earlier identified by Simmel as the tension between "self-revelation and self-restraint," and between "trespass and discretion."[27]

Westin's sociological roots are also evident in his discussion of privacy functions (see Table 11.1). He expressly adopts the description of the self developed by Simmel, Robert Park, Kurt Lewin, and Erving Goffman to ground his first function, autonomy, as an aspect of the core self that interacts with others in a series of concentric circles moving outward from solitude to intimacy to general social interaction.[28] He also uses Park's and Goffman's work on social masks to explain why forced exposure is so devastating to the individual:

> If this mask is torn off and the individual's real self bared to a world in which everyone else still wears his mask and believes in masked performances, the individual can be seared by the hot light of selective, forced exposure . . . [O]nly grave social need can ever justify destruction of the privacy which guards the individual's ultimate autonomy."[29]

Westin's description of the second privacy function, emotional release, is based on Goffman's work on social roles. Westin writes,

> Like actors on the dramatic stage, Goffman has noted, individuals can sustain roles only for reasonable periods of time, and no individual can play

---

24. Georg Simmel, *The Sociology of Georg Simmel*, trans. and ed. Kurt H. Wolff (New York: The Free Press, 1950), 408.

25. Westin, *Privacy and Freedom*, 31–32 (n. 1).

26. *Ibid.*, 32.

27. *Ibid.*

28. *Ibid.*, 33.

29. *Ibid.*, 33–34.

indefinitely, without relief, the variety of roles that life demands. There have to be moments "off stage" when the individual can be "himself."[30]

Westin argues that, from this perspective, privacy is essential because it provides moments when individuals can "lay their masks aside to rest. To be always 'on' would destroy the human organism."[31] He draws on Goffman's work on total institutions to support this, and concludes that the privacy function of release allows us "respite from the emotional stimulation of daily life"[32] and space in which to manage bodily and sexual functions.[33]

The privacy function of self-evaluation is based on Park's argument that reflective solitude is necessary to provide the individual with an opportunity "to anticipate, to recast, and to originate."[34] For Park, solitude, like religious contemplation, is a time for "organizing the self."[35] Westin argues that contemplation enables the individual "to integrate his experiences into a meaningful pattern and to exert his individuality on events," and that, "[t]o carry on such self-evaluation, privacy is essential."[36]

In his discussion of the last privacy function, limited and protected communication, Westin draws heavily from the work of Simmel and Goffman. Westin begins by asserting that, "[i]n real life, among mature persons all communication is partial and limited, based on the complementary relation between reserve and discretion that has already been discussed"[37] in connection with Simmel's work on self-revelation and self-restraint. He then notes that limited communication is particularly important in the context of urban life and, in support of this, refers to Simmel's work on the role of reserved communication in preserving the self in the metropolis. Westin's argument that limited communication enables us to share confidences in relationships of trust relies on Goffman's ethnographic studies of everyday social relationships, and on Simmel's analysis of the confessional aspect of sharing confidences with strangers. His conclusion that it also "serves to set necessary boundaries of mental distance in interpersonal situations"[38] is drawn directly from Simmel's discussion of the need to create mental distance in a successful marriage, and Goffman's studies of the ways in which facial expressions, gestures, jokes, and conversational conventions (such as changing the subject) are used to signal the need to withdraw from others.

---

30. *Ibid.*, 35.

31. *Ibid.*

32. *Ibid.*

33. *Ibid.*, 36.

34 Robert E. Park and Ernest W. Burgess, *Introduction to the Science of Sociology* (Chicago: University of Chicago Press., 1921), 231.

35. *Ibid.*, 237.

36. Westin, *Privacy and Freedom*, 36 (n. 1).

37. *Ibid.*, 37.

38. *Ibid.*, 38.

III. THE DISAPPEARING SOCIAL DIMENSION

Westin is therefore steeped in the sociological literature, and his work highlights the role that privacy plays in everyday social interaction. Why, then, is the social value of privacy so isolated from the policy debate around data protection?

Regan argues that Westin fails to develop the social meaning of privacy fruitfully because he anchors the concept to a "personal adjustment process" in which the individual decides when and how information about him should be revealed to the general public, unless there is some extraordinary and exceptional social interest at play. In this way, the individual is extracted from the social and placed in conflict with the collective, as he seeks to resist social demands for exposure.

Clearly, the juxtaposition of the individual and the social was built into Westin's inquiry at an early stage, when the Association of the Bar of the City of New York's Committee on Science and Law tasked Westin with explaining the "interaction of [privacy] and the competing claims of society"[39] in the context of "their underlying, adversary values."[40] Moreover, Westin continually refers to the tension between the individual's right to privacy, on one hand, and society's interest in invading privacy on the other hand, and Regan's critique that this makes privacy vulnerable to attack is a cogent one.

However, when Westin speaks of competing interests in privacy, disclosure, and surveillance, the disclosure side of the equation is not imposed *by* the collective *on* the individual in order to obtain some social end; social control is brought about through surveillance that can, in turn, be resisted by the individual through withdrawal and reserve. Disclosure, on the other hand, is the result of the *individual's* choice to seek out and participate in social interaction, and not the result of a collective decision to invade. Westin writes, "the individual in virtually every society engages in a continuing personal process by which he seeks privacy at some times and disclosure or companionship at other times."[41] Moreover, the desires for privacy and disclosure are coequal: "[i]ndividuals have needs for disclosure and companionship every bit as important as their needs for privacy."[42]

Westin, quoting Murphy, calls the process of balancing these competing interests one of the key "dialectical processes in social life,"[43] and sets the stage for Irwin Altman's development of privacy as a boundary control mechanism discussed below. However, Westin immediately limits his insight into the social

---

39. Oscar M. Ruebhausen, forward to *Privacy and Freedom*, by Alan Westin (n. 1), xii.

40. *Ibid.*, xi.

41. Westin, *Privacy and Freedom*, 13 (n. 1).

42. *Ibid.*, 39.

43. Robert F. Murphy, "Social Distance and the Veil," *American Anthropologist* no. 66 (1964): 1257.

nature of privacy in two related ways. First, as Regan argues, he leaves it up to the individual to adjust the balance by himself, in isolation of others. He states, "Although it is obviously affected by the cultural patterns of each society, the process is adjusted in its finer degrees by each individual himself."[44] Accordingly, the individual is burdened with the sole responsibility of protecting his privacy, just when technology is permeating traditional boundaries. This leads to the result in the *Tessling* case, where individuals who wish to remain inscrutable are required to take extraordinary measures to retain their body heat within the physical limits of their dwelling house so it cannot be captured by infrared technologies.[45]

Second, by defining privacy as the opposite of social interaction, Westin shifts the focus of his inquiry to the flow of information across the boundary between private spaces and public spaces, rather than on the boundary itself. If privacy is "the withdrawal of a person from the general society,"[46] then the fullest form of privacy is social isolation. In Westin's words, "solitude is the most complete state of privacy that individuals can achieve."[47] But if this is so, then privacy is asocial, existing on one pole of a continuum in tension with social interaction on the other pole. As the individual seeks to satisfy her competing interest in privacy and in social participation, she must develop mechanisms that allow her to control the consequences of her interactions in ways that do not disclose more than she is willing to reveal as she moves out of solitude. Accordingly, as the individual moves further from "perfect privacy" through interactions with intimates to general social participation, privacy shrinks and "restricting information about himself and his emotions [becomes] a crucial way of protecting the individual in the stresses and strains of social interaction."[48] (See Table 11.2.)

Westin accordingly interprets social mechanisms to protect privacy within the context of the disclosure of information. For example, he argues that kinship rules "present individuals with a need to restrict the flow of information about themselves to others and to adjust these regulations constantly in contacts with others."[49] "Covering the face, averting the eyes, going to one's mat, or facing the wall" are seen as ways of "restricting the flow of information about oneself" in the intimacy of the household.[50] Reserve "expresses the individual's choice to withhold or disclose information—the choice that is the dynamic aspect of privacy in daily interpersonal relations."[51]

---

44. *Ibid.*, 13.
45. *R. v. Tessling* [2004] 3 SCR 432 (Canada).
46. Westin, *Privacy and Freedom*, 7 (n. 1).
47. *Ibid.*, 31.
48. *Ibid.*, 13.
49. *Ibid.*, 14.
50. *Ibid.*, 15–16.
51. *Ibid.*, 32.

TABLE 11.2 PRIVACY AS INFORMATIONAL CONTROL

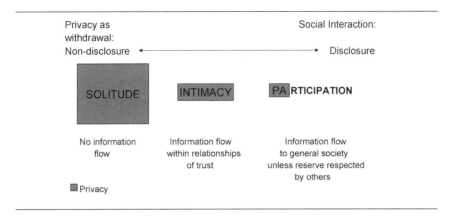

Once the focus shifts to the flow of information, privacy is no longer grounded in the social interaction of subjects, but becomes located in the individual's unilateral control over keeping information on the internal side of the boundary. As Westin states, "deciding when and to what extent to disclose facts about himself—and to put others in the position of receiving such confidences—is a matter of enormous concern in personal interaction, almost as important as whether to disclose at all."[52] From this perspective, privacy is no longer asocial—it is antisocial. Because disclosure is dependent on the trustworthiness of intimate others and the sensitivity of the general public to respect the individual's reserve, any social interaction poses a risk to privacy, and privacy can only be fully protected by a withdrawal from others. Accordingly, the social roots of Westin's conceptualization of privacy states and functions, like the social elements of his legislative program, disappear from view.

IV. IRWIN ALTMAN AND PRIVACY AS BOUNDARY

Irwin Altman was an environmental psychologist who was interested in personal space and territoriality. Like Westin, he saw privacy as a cultural universal, and located it in a variety of complex social settings. However, Altman placed special significance on Westin's insight that individuals and groups seek a balance between openness and closedness. But rather than placing privacy and

---

52. *Ibid.*, 37.

social interaction at opposite poles, Altman's dialectic juxtaposes openness and closedness to others; privacy becomes the negotiated line between the two. Altman accordingly defines privacy as:

> an interpersonal boundary process by which a person or a group regulates interaction with others. By altering the degree of openness of the self to others, a hypothetical personal boundary is more or less receptive to social interaction with others. Privacy is, therefore, a dynamic process involving selective control over a self-boundary, either by an individual or a group.[53]

In this model, privacy is not equated with social withdrawal. Instead, it is an interplay of opposing forces of being open or closed to others. Privacy is also no longer anchored to the individual's control over the disclosure of information. Instead, it is a bidirectional process that involves both inputs from and outputs to others. In Altman's words, privacy is "an interpersonal event, involving relationships among people."[54]

Altman concludes that privacy has three functions or goals:

1. the regulation of interpersonal boundaries;
2. the development and management of interpersonal roles and dealing with others; and
3. self-observation and self-identity.[55]

Interestingly, all three are tied to identity and the experience of subjectivity. For Altman, identity is the central experience of being human: so long as we can control "what is me" and "what is not me," then we can each come to understand and define who and what we are. He concludes that privacy is the boundary that enables us to do that.[56]

Accordingly, Altman's approach captures many of Westin's insights into the relationship between privacy and identity, but he theorizes them within a fully social framework. For example, Altman draws on Westin's insight that privacy is an essential part of self-evaluation because it is necessary to enable the individual "to integrate his experiences into a meaningful pattern and to exert his individuality on events."[57] However, Altman expands on this by placing it into the context of a fully social understanding of identity. He writes,

> We use other people to help label our feelings and define our perceptions. It might be said, therefore, that one function of privacy is to assist in the social-comparison process—at the interface of the self and others. As such, privacy

---

53. Irwin Altman, *The Environment and Social Behavior* (Monterey, California: Brooks/Cole, 1975), 6.

54. *Ibid.*, 22.

55. *Ibid.*, 47–48.

56. *Ibid.*, 50.

57 . Westin, *Privacy and Freedom*, 36 (n. 1).

regulation may enable the person to decide on courses of action, to apply meanings to various interpersonal events, and to build a set of norms or standards for interpreting self/other relations.[58]

Margulis suggests that Altman's work points to a theoretical framework that has the potential to subsume Westin's theory,[59] and to capture and develop Westin's insights into the sociality of privacy. However, as an environmental psychologist, Altman was primarily interested in the relationship between human social behavior and the physical environment.[60] Privacy was important to Altman because he saw it as a key link between territorial behavior and personal space.[61] He accordingly stopped short of developing a "full-blown theory" of privacy, expressly leaving that to others.[62]

To take Altman's work on privacy forward, the next part of the chapter returns to the source of Altman's conceptualization of identity, the social theory of George Herbert Mead. Interestingly, Mead drew on concepts developed by his contemporaries Park and Simmel, and his social interactionism is the foundation upon which Lewin and Goffman built. Accordingly, his work is at the base of the sociological tradition upon which Westin draws.

V. A SOCIAL THEORY OF PRIVACY—APPLYING GEORGE HERBERT MEAD TO WESTIN AND ALTMAN

Mead, like Westin, was writing at a time when technology was challenging traditional social and political relationships. At the turn of the century, industrialization and rapid growth had led to the disintegration of small communities, and liberal individualism was unable to reorient a public that was overwhelmed by the conditions of modern life. The Chicago School's critique of the technological and economic consequences of modernity, and the attendant concentrations of economic and political power that threatened the democratic project, convinced Mead and his colleagues that the social sciences should create knowledge that would make society visible to itself.[63] Accordingly, they sought to retheorize social interaction in a conscious effort to create the self-reflexive conditions necessary for the workings of modern democracy. Mead was therefore occupied

---

58. Altman, *Environment and Social Behavior*, 47 (n. 52).

59. Stephen T. Margulis, "On the Status and Contribution of Westin's and Altman's Theories of Privacy," *Journal of Social Issues* 59, no. 2 (2003): 411–430, 422.

60. Altman, *Environment and Social Behavior*, 1 (n. 52).

61. *Ibid.*, 4.

62. *Ibid.*

63. John Durham Peters, "Institutional Sources of Intellectual Poverty in Communication Research," *Communication Research* 13, no. 4 (1986): 527–559.

with the same question as Westin—how to theorize democratic relationships so new technologies do not derail the democratic project.

For Mead, the answer to this question is rooted in the social nature of the individual. He argues that individuals are reflexive, intelligent beings capable of knowing themselves and the world. However this reflexivity does not arise in a social vacuum; we become aware of ourselves as individuals only through our social interaction with others. The basic mechanism which allows us to do this is language; during any social interaction, it is language that allows for an adjustment in the actions of one actor to the actions of the other.[64]

From this perspective, there is no conflict between the individual and the social. Rather, the social is a prior condition to the emergence of subjectivity that nonetheless allows each individual to develop her own unique, autonomous personality. Mead's understanding of identity therefore accounts for both the social nature of private experience *and* the potential for individual autonomy so important to Westin: although individual identity emerges from social interaction, it is not determined by the social. Accordingly, the tension between the social and the individual—which is so problematic in Westin's theory—dissolves.

Moreover, Mead's conception of language allows us to posit a theory of privacy that accounts for both Westin's and Altman's insights into the social nature of privacy. Mead argues that the individual subject only comes to know itself if it becomes an object to itself, and that can only occur through language. As Habermas puts it, it is language that enables each social actor to see his own actions from the perspective of the other, and to see himself as the other sees him, a social object.[65] If the individual's understanding of himself as a subject emerges through the recognition of the other and the self, privacy, as the boundary between the two, is placed at the centre of identity, because privacy is what allows the self to become reflexive.

Mead sets the stage for this when he distinguishes between the "private" nature of subjective experience, which is withheld from others, and the "private" nature of reflexivity. He argues that both are private, in the sense that they are only accessible to the individual. However, this does not necessarily mean that they are the same at a conceptual level: "the self has a sort of structure that arises in social conduct that is entirely distinguishable from this so-called subjective experience of these particular sets of objects to which the organism alone has access."[66]

The first meaning of "private" resonates with Westin's understanding of privacy as the withholding of information by an isolated individual. However, the second meaning of "private" implies that privacy is a necessary condition for

64. George Herbert Mead, *Mind, Self, and Society from the Standpoint of a Social Behaviourist*, ed. C.W. Morris (Chicago: University of Chicago Press, 1934) 9.

65. Jurgen Habermas, "Individuation through Socialization: On George Herbert Mead's Theory of Subjectivity," in *Postmetaphysical Thinking: Philosophical Essays*, trans. William Mark Hohengarten (Cambridge, Massachusetts: MIT Press, 1992), 176.

66. Mead, *Mind, Self and Society*, 167 (n. 63).

reflexivity and intersubjective dialogue because it delineates the boundaries of the self. In Westin's terms, "Every individual needs to integrate his experiences into a meaningful pattern and to exert his individuality on events. To carry on such self-evaluation, privacy is essential."[67] However, by extending Mead's understanding of the self as a social construction, privacy is no longer tied to an autonomous self acting in isolation of others, as it is in Westin's theory; it is the result of a process of socialization that is mediated through language.[68] Privacy cannot, therefore, shelter the liberal ego from social interaction, as Westin posits; rather, privacy—as the line between self and others—is intersubjectively constituted through communication. Privacy is therefore possible *across* Westin's spectrum, beyond solitude through to social participation, because privacy is what enables the self to see itself as a social object and to negotiate appropriate levels of openness and closedness to others.

Moreover, Mead argues the process of coming to know ourselves requires us to play a variety of social roles. By trying on these roles and seeing them reflected back at us through our social interactions with others, we come to know who we are. Because role-taking is in essence a social phenomenon, privacy is essential because it allows us to construct lines between roles. It is privacy that allows us to perform one role—as wife or mother—separate and apart from other roles—as teacher or policy maker, for example. From this perspective, surveillance is problematic precisely because it collapses the boundaries between roles and makes the individual accountable for all her actions, independent of the context or the role she is playing.

Goffman[69] calls this "looping." During his study of mental hospitals, he noted that patients were unable to keep their various roles separate because they were always under observation—their actions in the context of one role were never separated from their actions in the context of other roles. They were, accordingly, "constantly confronted with inconsistencies in their behavior and were fully accountable to the same people for all aspects of behavior."[70] Altman concludes that this type of boundary violation "may well be a deterrent to rehabilitation, because [it] exposes the self, eliminates a number of normal self-boundary processes, and makes the person extremely vulnerable to others."[71] These are prophetic words for a society in which Facebook pictures are used by employers to decide whether or not to hire someone.

Locating privacy within Mead's social theory accordingly explains Westin's insight that privacy serves to relieve the self of emotions that build up because the self plays a multiplicity of social roles.[72] It also provides a theoretical

67. Westin, *Privacy and Freedom*, 36 (n. 1).
68. Habermas, "Individuation through Socialization," 153 (n. 64).
69. Erving Goffman, *Asylums* (New York: Doubleday, 1961).
70. Altman, *Environment and Social Behavior*, 40 (n. 52).
71. *Ibid.*
72. Westin, *Privacy and Freedom*, 35 (n. 1).

foundation for Westin's concerns about surveillance. Westin argues that placing people under surveillance is dehumanizing because "the person-to-person factor in observation—with its softening and 'game' aspects—has been eliminated."[73] Surveillance is, by definition, nonreciprocal: the actor's actions and words are captured by the watcher without any opportunity for intersubjective interpretation. Surveillance is invasive because, independent of whether or not data protection principles have been respected, the individual's social actions are removed from the intersubjectivity that grounds the identity and enables him or her to enter into social relationships with others.

Altman argued that privacy is a boundary control mechanism that externally allows social actors to negotiate the boundary between self and others. However, if one takes Mead's concept of the self into account, privacy is also internalized, because it is the dialogue between the self and others that enables the self to become visible to itself and identities to emerge. Accordingly, privacy sits at the core of self-reflection and intersubjectivity. Privacy is no longer confined to solitude or procedural control over personal information; instead, it is intersubjectively constituted through social interaction. From this perspective, privacy is the boundary between self and other that is negotiated through discursive interaction between two or more social actors. It is, accordingly, a dynamic process that is exhibited by the individual in social interaction with others, as the individual withdraws from others into solitude or moves from solitude to intimacy and general social interaction. Privacy is no longer juxtaposed against social interaction, as Westin posits, but is a potentiality throughout the full range of human experience. For example, an individual desiring low contact with others is able to obtain privacy though solitude. If others invade that solitude, the individual experiences a sense of trespass, as he or she is unable to negotiate the desired level of aloneness. On the other hand, as both Westin and Altman indicate, there is a difference between privacy and isolation—the latter is experienced when the closedness to others is not satisfying to the individual.

This conceptualization of privacy captures the dialectical nature of privacy identified by earlier theory, but does not inappropriately collapse privacy into solitude. In addition, social interaction no longer poses a risk to privacy that must be managed by individual control over the flow of personal information, because privacy can only be obtained through social interaction. The onus of privacy protection is therefore no longer carried by the individual in isolation of others. Moreover, as Westin first noted, there are a number of privacy states, such as reserve and intimacy, which the individual can negotiate as he becomes more open to others. One can also identify a number of invasive states that are experienced when the individual is unable to negotiate the desired state of privacy with other social actors. Westin's privacy states and functions, therefore, come to life, and questions of privacy protection are focused on the quality of

73. *Ibid.*, 59.

interaction between social actors (including the state and corporations) rather than on the reified flow of information.

This conceptualization also enables us to conceive of privacy in public spaces. An individual who moves through public spaces in high proximity with others but who remains relatively closed to them can achieve privacy through anonymity or reserve. Excessive crowding may impinge on these states but, as Westin's work indicates, societies that experience physical crowding develop psychological mechanisms to maintain social distance. Privacy is accordingly not dependent on physical separation but on the negotiated interaction between social actors.

Surveillance of public spaces invades the individual's sense of privacy precisely because it identifies him when he wishes to move through public space free of others' recognition. More specifically, the lack of anonymity is perceived of as invasive when the watcher does not ignore what he sees but actively seeks to manipulate or control the person being watched. Accordingly, a surveillance camera in a bank that does not seek to identify customers is more readily accepted than police who take pictures of the faces of people who gather to hear a political speech or employers who use surveillance cameras in the street to record how long people spend smoking cigarettes during the workday. What defines each incident as invasive is the social action taken by the watcher. Anonymity is achieved when *others* agree to respect the individual's wish to remain unidentified. Anonymity, like all privacy states, is dependent upon the social negotiation of a desired boundary between self and other; it cannot be achieved by the individual in isolation. In like vein, an individual who expresses reserve feels invaded by those who fail to respect the social cues he sends and rudely pursues interaction that is too personal or exposing of the self.

As the individual becomes more open to others, she more willingly enters into public activities, including forms of civic participation. However, civic participation is also contextualized by a social agreement regarding the boundary between self and other. There is an unwillingness to accept surveillance in voting booths and public fora because, even though both involve participation in a public process, being watched in these circumstances severely restricts the individual's autonomy. Surveillance of both is perceived to invade the private citizen's democratic space, even though the latter takes place in public. Accordingly, there is an inherent connection between autonomy, privacy and democratic action. On the other hand, individuals who wish to participate in public activities but are unable to negotiate the desired levels of privacy and participation are subject to feelings of alienation and anomie.

The individual who is most open to others seeks interaction within relationships of intimacy. If there is too much contact with non-intimate others in these circumstances, the intrusion into intimate space is a privacy violation because it impinges on the boundary both between the self and unwanted others and between intimates and others. In other words, the intrusion of others into intimate exchanges interferes both with the inviolability of the exposed self and with the social interaction between people who share a level of intimacy. Intimacy can be

TABLE 11.3 PRIVACY AS BOUNDARY

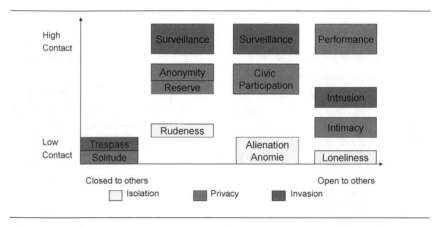

maintained within a broad range of contact levels precisely because others are willing to withdraw from intimate interaction and allow intimates social space that recognizes their closeness, much as people do when they avert their eyes when romantic couples exchange a kiss. When the other does not withdraw, the intimates feel intruded upon. On the other hand, an individual seeking intimacy who is unable to enter into intimate interactions with others feels loneliness.

Conceptualizing of privacy as a social construction therefore enables us to theorize the ways in which privacy states are negotiated throughout a range of social interactions, in situations of low to high contact with others. (See Table 11.3.) It also suggests that privacy cannot be traded off in exchange for some other benefit, such as efficiency, security, or convenience. Privacy is a flash point in the surveillance society precisely because surveillance objectifies the self, collapses the boundaries between social roles and negates the conditions necessary for inter-subjectivity.

Ironically, Westin's original legislative program sought to protect this broader social understanding of privacy. I suggest we need to reinvigorate Westin's program in its totality, and develop a definition of privacy that captures its importance as a social value. If not, surveillance will continue to grow in spite of data protection legislation, and Westin's warning that, "if all that has to be done to win legal and social approval for surveillance is to point to a social problem and show that surveillance would help to cope with it, then there is no balancing at all, but only a qualifying procedure for a license to invade privacy"[74] may come to characterize privacy policy in the future.

74. *Ibid.*, 370.

PART II

IDENTITY

As Marsha Hanen points out near the end of Part I, new technologies that have the potential to rewrite what it means to be human will raise interesting questions about who we are and how we experience privacy. Part II picks up on those questions by interrogating various aspects of identity in a network society.

Steven Davis leads off with a philosophical analysis of the concept. He sets out a framework that distinguishes between metaphysical, epistemological, and social/cultural/political identities. In doing so, he sets the stage for those authors who seek to understand the ways in which demands for identity authentication implicate questions of power.

Charles Raab addresses this directly in his chapter. Like Davis, he sets out a top-level categorization of the concept of identity that accounts for both its individual and its social nature. He then examines the ways in which the social negotiation of both forms of identity is affected by the relative power status of the parties involved in the negotiation, particularly when misrepresentations of identity are perceived as inherently threatening to national security.

Michael Froomkin examines an instance of this same negotiation in the specific context of identity cards. He argues that residual romanticized notions of the American "cowboy" and the "Englishman" as a rights-holder have limited policymakers' ability to create an appropriate set of rules to protect privacy in light of new and emerging information technologies. He warns that greater transparency is required if we are to successfully build a broad bundle of rights into the identity card regime.

Jane Doe turns the tables, examining the social construction of the identities of women who have been raped and the manner in which they experience anonymity in jurisdictions that provide "protective" publication bans during and after the criminal trials of their assailants. She argues that court-enforced anonymity has identity implications for those who have been raped, with perils particular to racialized and other marginalized women. Sexually assaulted women are often identified as defiled and suspect; their lack of agency—indeed of any activity of their own—necessitates that their identities must be hidden and subsumed in the anonymity of being a Jane Doe. Her powerful interviews with women who have lived through this experience underscore the ways in which this identity fails to reflect the lived experience of these women as vibrant, reflective, and informed persons.

Jane Bailey examines what happens when a woman's private life is similarly taken out of context through self-exposure on the Internet. Her analysis of the experiences of Jennifer Ringley, the first woman to broadcast pictures of her daily life through a webcam, is a compelling account of the tension between the advancement of the feminist project and the reassertion of dominant representations of women as sexual objects. Although Ringley's experiment provided an opportunity to transgress and resignify sexual identities, Bailey ultimately concludes that the sexual imagery that Ringley broadcast was co-opted by and helped to reify the heterosexual male fantasy found in mainstream pornography.

David Phillips continues to interrogate questions of social justice in his analysis of the ways in which ubiquitous computing will restructure the social practices that we rely upon to construct our identities. He suggests that the notion of semiotic democracy would better inform policies intended to ensure that the resources for social meaning-making are equitably distributed in the network society.

David Matheson examines what happens when automated identification systems sidestep the careful negotiation of identity to which Phillips alludes. He argues that the nonreflexive nature of identifying oneself in an automated system invades privacy in the same way that Goffman's total institution does, by transforming social interaction into exercises of nonselective self-presentation. By depersonalizing those persons who are authenticated by the system, the system itself shrinks the opportunity for us to develop a robust dignity.

Ian Kerr raises similar concerns in the context of human-implantable radio frequency identification (RFIDs). He argues that the emerging RFID-enabled Internet of Things may soon become an Internet of People, and warns that a human-machine merger will challenge our notions of identity and privacy in a profound sense. Although the current regulatory regime provides some level of protection from today's one-off RFID applications, Kerr urges us to be forward thinking and to avoid sacrificing our core values in favor of the short-term expediencies of RFID-enabled networks.

In her examination of biometric identification as a form of border control, Shoshana Magnet reminds us that the human-machine merger is not neutral but works to perpetuate inequalities. Her analysis of the U.S.-Canada border demonstrates that biometric technologies imbue bodies with racialized and gendered meanings that continue to disadvantage some people and privilege others. Like Kerr, she warns that we must go beyond simplistic narratives of technology as neutral and efficient in order to fully understand the social consequences of the network society.

Gary Marx examines countervailing narratives of social resistance in his analysis of surveillance songs. He argues that popular music is a form of soul training that provides us with a source of imagery, which works to either deconstruct or legitimize the surveillance society. He identifies two opposing trends. On one hand, proponents of surveillance—control agents and members of the surveillance industry—represent surveillance as a means of solving serious social problems. Artists, on the other hand, tend to portray surveillance as the problem, and their songs warn us that the technologies upon which we rely may profane our experience as humans.

Jeremy Clark, Philippe Gauvin, and Carlisle Adams take social resistance to the network level. In order to promote technologies that support and protect autonomous action from state interference, they have devised a method to prove that an anonymous remailer is not the original sender of illegal material and is therefore not subject to search warrants. Their system is a practical attempt to push back against the current "is-ism"—the mistake of confusing how some-thing is with how it must be—against which Lawrence Lessig warns.

Similarly, Daniel Howe and Helen Nissenbaum set out a technical method to hide one's surfing patterns from surveillance. Like Clark, Gauvin, and Adams, they argue that this kind of technology enables us to resist network surveillance on a principled basis, to protect the free inquiry, association, and expression that is an essential part of democratic citizenship. From this perspective, anonymity—the subject of the last section of the book—is a vital component of a network society that retains opportunities for individuals to enjoy privacy and to act autonomously.

12. A CONCEPTUAL ANALYSIS OF IDENTITY

STEVEN DAVIS

There are three notions of identity that must be distinguished that I shall call metaphysical identity,[1] cultural/social/political identity, and epistemological identity. I shall concentrate my discussion on the last of these and illustrate it by discussing identity theft. Because the central interest is in epistemological identity and its relation to identity theft, I shall describe the first two notions only to the extent that it is necessary to distinguish them from epistemological identity.

Let us begin with metaphysical identity and with the following question. At a particular time, t, what makes it the case that a given object, A, is synchronically identical to B? Consider a simple object, a wooden chair, which I shall call 'Alfred.' Imagine that reflected in a mirror is an image of a chair—one that I shall call 'Natalie.' Now at a given time, t, Natalie and Alfred might well be the same chair. Properties play an important role in determining the conditions under which Natalie and Alfred are identical. A property is something an object has; it is a characteristic or quality of an object that is true of the object. Red objects, for example, have the property of being red and it is true of them that they are red. Properties come in different varieties: monadic and relational and accidental and essential. A monadic property is a quality of an object that does not relate it to another object—for example, being square—while a relational property, such as being to the left, relates an object to another object. An accidental property is a property that an object has that it might not have. If it were not to have the property, it would still be that object, for example, the property of the number two that it is my favorite number. An essential property is a property of an object that it is necessary for it to have to be that object, for example, the property of the number two that it is even. Properties are characteristically exemplified or instantiated. For instance, the property of being red is exemplified by all the objects that are red, which then share the same property—being red.

---

1. H. Noonan, "Identity," *Stanford Encyclopedia of Philosophy* (2006), http://plato.stanford.edu/entries/identity/#2.

Let us call the objects that exemplify properties 'particulars' and the properties that are or could be exemplified, 'universals.'

What makes it the case that Natalie and Alfred are synchronically identical at *t* is that, at *t*, Natalie and Alfred have the same properties. For example, Natalie is brown, is reflected in a mirror, has a back, has a seat, is owned by the man next door, is in Canada, is believed by me to be different from Alfred, etc. If all these properties, and any other property that Natalie exemplifies, were exemplified by Alfred and conversely, Natalie and Alfred would then be one and the same chair a *t*.[2] Does it follow from Natalie and Alfred's being identical that they have the same properties? If Natalie and Alfred are identical, then there is only one thing that is designated in two different ways, as 'Natalie' and 'Alfred.'[3] Thus, then at *t*, any property that Natalie has, Alfred has and conversely.

The identity of our chair consists of the set of those properties that are necessary and sufficient for it to be that object, which we shall call an object's 'individual essence.' This set that individuates a particular object must pass the tests of time and possibility. Synchronic identity is not enough. Take time. Alfred is brown at t_1, but suppose that it is painted red at t_2. Its becoming red makes it qualitatively a different chair; it is now a red chair at t_2 and at t_1, it was a brown chair. But it is not numerically a different chair. We can say that, from t_1 to t_2, Alfred undergoes a qualitative change from brown to red, but numerically, it is one and the same chair. It is still Alfred. Rather, what has changed is that it loses an accidental property at t_1, the property of being brown, and at t_2, it gains another accidental property, that of being red.

Possibility is similar to time. Alfred is brown at t_1, but it is possible that it could have been red at t_1. Had Alfred another color, it would not affect its identity. Alfred would be numerically the same chair had it been red, rather than brown, its actual color. One way to describe such changes is by invoking the notion of possible worlds,[4] which is a way that the world could be. Alfred is brown in the actual world, which we shall designate as α. Given the possibility that it could have been red, there is a possible world in which Alfred is red, which we shall designate as α_1. What is possible need not, at any time in the future, become actual. Let us suppose that at no future time does Alfred become red. Thus, α_1 is not the way the world will turn out to be, but the way the world could be. Hence, there are possible ways for the world to be that are different from the way the world will turn out to be—from the future, that is.

---

2. A generalization of this is known as the identity of indiscernibles. For any object *y* and any object *x* if *x* and *y* have the same properties, then *x* = *y*.

3. This is known as Leibniz's Law. For any object, *y* and any object, *x*, if *x* = *y*, then *x* and *y* have the same properties.

4. For two views about the nature of possible worlds, see David Lewis, "Counterpart Theory and Quantified Modal Logic," *The Journal of Philosophy* 65 (1968): 113–126; Saul Kripke, *Naming and Necessity* (Oxford: Basil Blackwell, 1980).

Does anything go in a possible world? Could we have a possible world in which I can fly unassisted on earth, in which there are people with three heads, and in which everyone is over ten meters tall and weighs only one kilo? None of this is physically possible, but it is logically possible. There is no contradiction or conceptual impossibility in any of this, although it is contrary to physical laws, because they are not logically necessary. As far as we know, nothing can go faster than the speed of light, but it is not logically impossible for this to occur. A possible world then goes beyond what is physically possible; it ranges over what is logically possible. There are certain things that are not logically possible. It is not logically possible that I am a bachelor and yet a married woman over thirty.

Let us now consider how persons fare with changes across time and worlds. Clearly, we change through time and could have been different than we are. Yet despite the changes and possible changes we are or would be one and the same person. In describing ourselves, we sometimes say that we are not the same person that we were in our youth or would not be the same person if we had undergone some change. What we mean is that certain features of our character, body, and/or personality have changed or could change, characteristics that we think to be important. But despite what can or could be rather dramatic changes in character, body, and personality, we do not or would not cease to exist, nor have we become or would become numerically another person. What properties then are essential to us that guarantee our continuity through time and across worlds, properties such that if we no longer had them, we would no longer exist or there would even be a different person numerically? That is, what properties of persons are like the properties that make Alfred that chair and not another, and properties that, if Alfred were to lose them, would render Alfred nonexistent?[5]

What properties are essential for me to be the particular person that I am, that is, if I were not to have any of these properties, I would not be Steven Davis? Clearly my height is not such a property, because I would still be Steven Davis had I been two meters tall. What about my nationality? I was born in the United States, but I am now a dual Canadian/U.S. citizen. Had I been born and raised in a different country, say France, I might have been a very different person. I might not have spoken English, or have had some of the values that I currently have, but there is no reason to think that I would not have been Steven Davis, although I might not even have been called 'Steven Davis.' It could have turned out that my parents named me Didier and that they changed their last name to Dupont. But if the world had been that way, Didier Dupont would have been me. Hence, my height, nationality, place of birth, language, and name are not properties that are essential for me.

---

5. For a discussion of personal identity, see Eric T. Olson, "Personal Identity," *Stanford Encyclopedia of Philosophy* (2002), http://plato.stanford.edu/entries/identity-personal/#1.

A person's essential properties are not obvious. Some have argued that it is the person's body; others have argued that it is the person's psychological states.[6] There are problems with both of these, but what is important for our purpose is to see what sorts of things are not necessary to a person's metaphysical identity. As with Alfred, my individual essence is a set of properties that are necessary and sufficient for me to be Steven Davis. Moreover, there is no settled opinion among philosophers about the properties that constitute our individual essences. In addition, even if there were a view on which philosophers agreed, it would not be something readily available to most people, since they lack the philosophical training to understand it. Hence, what properties constitute our metaphysical identities are not epistemologically accessible to most people.

Let us turn to cultural/social/political identity. In recent years, identity politics has become increasingly important. On this view, it is not a person qua person who is part of the moral/social/political order, but a person with a particular identity. For many, it matters politically, socially, culturally and/or morally whether they identify themselves as a Canadian, a member of a First Nation, aged, disabled, a Muslim, etc. Of course, people can have multiple identities. They can be, for example, a Canadian and a Jew. Most discussions of cultural/ social/political identity concentrate on a narrow range of properties—those connected with nationality, citizenship, and religion. This however, leaves out a wide range of properties that are important to people and can play a role in their cultural/social/political identities, for example, being a dancer, a butcher, and even an alcoholic. In fact, it is possible for any property of a person to be part of his identity, if it is important to the way that he lives his life and plays a cultural, social, or political role.

What makes a property part of a person's cultural/social/political identity? I shall argue that, for a property to be a part of a person's identity, it must be a characteristic that the person has, not just one that he thinks that he has; his believing that he has the property must play an important role in his life;[7] and these beliefs must connect him to the cultural, social, and/or political order of

---

6. For views that account for personal identity in terms of our bodies, see J.J. Thomson, "People and their Bodies," *Reading Parfit*, ed. J. Dancy, (Oxford: Blackwell, 1997); and A.J. Ayer, *Language, Truth, and Logic* (London: Gollancz, 1936); and in terms of psychological states, see R. Nozick, *Philosophical Explanations* (Cambridge, Mass.: Harvard University Press, 1981); and D. Parfit, *Reasons and Persons* (Oxford: Oxford University Press, 1984).

7. It might be argued that a person's believing that he has a property is not necessary for it to be part of his social, cultural, or political identity. Imagine that someone, call him Harold, is gay, but does not believe that he is, nor does anyone else. His being gay, however, plays an important role in his life; it has an effect on his dreams and fantasies and on his relations with men and women. Although Harold does not have a conscious belief that he is gay, for it to have the effects on his life that it does, he must be in some cognitive states with respect to his being gay, unconscious beliefs or desires that play causal roles in his actions and on his dreams and fantasies.

which he is a part. Let us begin with my claim that a property is part of an individual's cultural/social/political identity only if he has the property and not merely that he thinks that he has it.[8] Consider Sally, who identifies herself as a writer, but seldom puts pen to paper. When she does, she writes a paragraph or two and then puts it in her drawer. She has never completed a poem, novel, short story, or any other type of literary work or sent anything that falls into these categories to a publisher. She talks a great deal about her plans to write this or that, but the plans come to nothing. She, however, thinks of herself as a writer and represents herself to others as being a writer. Being a writer is certainly who she thinks she is. This is not, however, who she is.[9] Rather, it is part of her self-conception. It might be claimed that a person's self-conception and her identity are one and the same, that with identity, thinking makes it so. To be a writer, however, one must write, something that Sally does not do. One's identity, I claim, is connected to who or what a person is, not who or what a person thinks that he is. If this is unconvincing, think of someone who takes himself to be part of a First Nation in Canada, the Mohawks, for example, but is not. As much as he identifies with the Mohawks and thinks of himself as a Mohawk, being a Mohawk is not part of his cultural/social/political identity. It is not part of who he is, although it might be who he thinks that he is.

Let us turn to my second claim that, for a property to be part of person's identity, not only must he have the property, but it must play an important role in his life.[10] First, it can provide an explanation for his behavior. Second, it can yield values that provide a way for him to live his life. Finally, it can yield for him something of value, either negative or positive, for his life. Let us consider each of these in turn. Suppose that Sam is a Canadian, which he takes it to be part of his identity. Sam crosses his legs by putting the ankle of one leg across the knee of the other; he eats meat by cutting it with a fork in his left hand and a knife in his right hand, placing the knife across the edge of the plate, transferring the fork from his left hand to his right, and eating the meat with his fork; when asked a question that he does not understand, he will say, "Heh?"; he prefers beer to wine, likes to eat maple sugar pies and Montreal smoked meat; and he watches hockey on television rather than American football. When asked why he

---

8. I shall make the simplifying assumption that there is only one property that is part of a person's cultural/social/political identity. Amartya Sen argues that this assumption is morally and politically distorting. I shall not take up the issues that Sen raises in his discussion of multiple identities. Amartya Sen, *Identity and Violence: The Illusion of Destiny* (New York: Norton, 2006).

9. We might say, however, that she is a would-be writer.

10. It cannot, however, be any sort of importance. Suppose that Sam is a rock climber, an activity that he does every couple of months in season and that he enjoys doing. It is thus of some importance to him. This, however, is not enough for being a rock climber to be part of Sam's identity. For it to play this role it must be an important part of his life.

behaves in these and other ways, he says that he is a Canadian and this is the way Canadians behave, offering to others and himself thereby an explanation for his behavior.

Not only can a person's identity provide for him explanations for his behavior, it can also provide him with values for the way he thinks that he ought to live his life. Suppose that Sam is a Christian, which he takes to be part of his identity. When he wonders how he ought to behave in a certain situation or whether his behaving in a certain way is justified, he might appeal to Christian values. He might say that he thinks that he ought to do X, or that his doing X is justified, because he is a Christian and it is the way a good Christian behaves, when he lives according to Christian values.

Finally, suppose Sam is not only a Canadian and a Christian, but also a journalist. Being a journalist is part of Sam's identity, and he identifies with the role of being a journalist. It gives a positive value to Sam's life. He loves being a journalist and enjoys the status that comes with it. In addition, he is accepted as a journalist by other journalists, and because of this, he has the positive emotions that arise from being a member of a group that he values and being accepted as one of them.[11] Sam has the sense of belonging to a group and being accepted by the group. A person's identity can also yield negative value for his life. Someone can have a property that he takes to be part of his identity, but rather than finding positive value in the property, he might wish that he did not have the property. Suppose that Sam was an alcoholic and that, in his society, alcoholics were despised. They were thought to be weak and of bad character. Sam, however, takes it to be part of his identity, because it is central to his life, which is filled with thinking about alcohol and consuming it.[12] Because it is despised in Sam's society, he feels ashamed about being an alcoholic and tries to hide it from others. Rather than provide him with feelings of self-esteem, it yields, for him, feelings of self-loathing.[13]

In each case in which someone's identity places an important role in his life, it does so by being connecting to the social, cultural, and/or political world of which he is a part. Sam's appealing to his being a Canadian serves as an explanation for his behavior because he has acquired his behavior by being part of Canadian culture. Being Christian provides values for him because he participates in

---

11. There is a difference between identifying with a group and identifying oneself as being a member of the group. Clearly, I can identify with the oppressed without identifying myself as being part of this group, and I can identify myself as being an alcoholic without identifying myself with alcoholics.

12. Notice that being an alcoholic could also provide Sam with a way to understand why he behaves the way that he does. Thus, Sam's identity, being an alcoholic, could play two important roles in his life.

13. For a discussion of what he calls self-esteem identity, see David Copp, "Social unity and the identity of persons," *The Journal of Political Philosophy* 10 (2002): 365–391.

Christian life and has acquired these values from the Christian community of which he is a part. Lastly, being a journalist imparts positive value to Sam's life because he is accepted as belonging to the journalist clan, and his being an alcoholic yields negative value for him because it is something that is despised in the community of which he is a part, an evaluation that Sam accepts about being an alcoholic.[14]

Let us turn to epistemological identity. Our epistemological identities are connected to first-person acts of identifying, acts that are common in everyday life. We can divide such acts into two sorts: those that arise through institutions such as banks, universities, credit card companies, governments, etc., and those that exist because of various practices connected to our culture and language. I enter a bank and request to withdraw money from my account. I am asked to swipe my bank card through a terminal and punch in a code that calls up my account on the teller's computer screen. I go to the library and ask to check out a book from the library. I am asked for my library card, which has my picture on it and my identification number. I go to a store and wish to purchase an item. I take out my bank card again, it is swiped through a terminal, and I am asked to enter my code. Or I pay with a credit card. It is swiped through a terminal, and I am asked to sign one of the terminal receipts. I am at a party and identify myself by saying, "My name is Steven Davis. I am your host." In each case, I provide someone with identifying information with the intention that he uses it to identify me as having a set of properties, a set that I shall take to be an epistemological identity.

I want to consider a case of this sort involving a passport presented at passport control for which the institutional framework is established by a government order.[15] It consists of the procedures involved in issuing passports and in using them at passport control as a means of identification. In issuing me a passport, Passport Canada assigns the passport a number, issue and expiration dates, a place at which it was issued, a type, an issuing country, and a bar code. In addition, Passport Canada specifies that the passport will include my name, sex, place and date of birth, picture, and signature. The information is propositional; it is information that my name is "Steven Davis," that the passport number is such and such, etcetera.[16]

---

14. It is possible for some characteristic of a person to play an important role in his life without its being connected to his social, cultural, or political world. Consider again Sam's being an alcoholic, and suppose that there is no social stigma attached to it and it has no particular cultural role to play in Sam's community. His being an alcoholic might play a role in Sam's being able to explain his behavior to himself, but it is not part of his social or cultural identity, because his being an alcoholic plays no social or cultural role in Sam's society.

15. *Canadian Passport Order.* SI/81–86.

16. Although it is not false in this case, I take it that information conveyed in identifications can be false.

Let us look more closely at what happens when I present my passport at passport control. Suppose that I am at Pierre Elliot Trudeau International Airport in Montreal, and I walk up to the passport control desk and hand the agent my Canadian passport, intending thereby that he identifies me as being the person described in the passport, a holder of a valid Canadian passport and a Canadian citizen who has the right to enter Canada. In doing so, I identify myself to the agent as having these properties, my epistemological identity in this situation, and intentionally convey to him identifying information about certain properties that I have that I believe will lead him to identify me as having the epistemological identity in question. In walking up to the counter, I convey to him information about how I look; in handing him my Canadian passport, I present him with information about whether I have a passport and about the information contained in the passport. In addition, in doing these things ostensibly at passport control about which the agent and I are mutually aware, I communicate to the agent my intention to have him recognize that I am a Canadian citizen.

That I convey this information to the agent does not mean that my intention in doing so will be fulfilled. For this to occur, the agent must identify me as being the holder of a valid Canadian passport, being the person described in the passport, and being a Canadian citizen. There are various steps in the agent's coming to identify me in this way. He sees that I have handed him what appears to be a Canadian passport, and he must determine whether I am the person described in it. He looks at the passport picture and at me and sees that the picture in the passport resembles me. Hence, he has good reason to believe that I am the person depicted in the passport that I handed him. Thus, he has identified me as the person described in the passport.

The next step is for the agent to determine that the passport is a valid Canadian passport. There is information in the passport that serves to determine this: the appearance of the passport, the passport number, the expiration date, and information accessible through the bar code on the passport. It is, of course, possible that, even given this information, the passport is a forgery or has been altered. Let us suppose the agent has good reason to believe that very few Canadian passports that are presented at Pierre Elliot Trudeau International airport are forged or have been altered. In addition, the agent looks at me and concludes that I do not look like the sort of person who would forge or alter a passport. The agent has identified the passport that I handed him as a valid Canadian passport.

Moreover, the agent knows that if someone has a valid passport that belongs to him, he must be a Canadian citizen. The agent then looks at the passport and the information that it contains. Since there is nothing particularly suspicious about me, nor about the passport that I handed him, utilizing the information that I conveyed, the agent concludes that I am a Canadian citizen having a right to enter the country and allows me to enter the country. We see that the epistemological identity I have in this situation is the set of properties that I intend the agent to identify me as having: my being the person depicted in the passport, my having a valid Canadian passport, and my being a Canadian citizen. I intend to fulfill this intention by providing the agent with identifying information, the way I look in presenting myself to the passport counter, and the information contained in my passport.[17]

To fill out the story of identifications and identity, let us consider a case of identifying involving a machine. Imagine an eye scanner at an entrance to a building, the purpose of which is to identify those who are authorized to enter the building. The machine is linked to a database containing the iris patterns of those who are authorized to enter the building. I intentionally present myself to the machine so that the machine can scan my eyes, gathering information about my iris patterns to determine whether they match a set of iris patterns stored in the database to which the machine is connected. If there is a match, I am allowed to enter the building. In presenting myself to the machine, I identify myself to the machine as being authorized to enter the building, and the epistemological identity that I have is being someone who is authorized to enter the building.

We see that I use information about certain of my properties, identifying information, to identify myself as having a set of properties, my epistemological identity. In turn, this identifying information can be used by a person or a machine to identify me as having this epistemological identity. In the passport example, my identity is being the person depicted in the passport, having a valid Canadian passport, and being a Canadian; in the eye scanner example, my identity is being someone who is authorized to enter the building. In presenting my library card at my university library, my identity is being someone who is authorized to use the university library. Thus, what epistemological identities I have depends on my acts of identifying myself as having particular properties for a certain purpose. We can say that I invoke different identities in identifying myself depending upon the purpose of my identifications. Any set of properties that I have, then, could constitute my epistemological identity in a particular context as long as I have the properties in the set and I can identify myself as having the set of properties to another for a certain purpose.

A person's epistemological identities fall into two kinds: standing and occasion. When I am issued a credit card, I am endowed with the potential to use it to identify myself as being authorized to make a purchase in places that accept the credit card, my epistemological identity. I have this epistemological identity as a standing identity even when I do not use my credit card and even

---

17. That is, I intend to induce in the agent an epistemic state, namely, that he believes that I have a particular epistemological identity. My having an epistemological identity in this case, however, does not depend upon his being able to identify me as having this identity. He might fail to draw the necessary conclusion or make a mistake and think that my passport is a fake. If this were to occur, I would still have the epistemological identity that I invoke in this situation.

if I never use it. This sort of epistemological identity arises through the institutional practices of banks, passport offices, libraries, license bureaus, universities, governments, etcetera that issue various sorts of identity cards and documents. We can say that these sorts of identities are potential epistemological identities of the person who has the identity card and are actualized on the occasions in which he uses the card in appropriate circumstances to identify himself.

An occasion epistemological identity is invoked in acts of identifying ourselves as having a set of properties on a particular occasion. They can be instantiations of standing epistemological identities, but they can also arise when we identify ourselves as having a certain property that is connected only to a particular occasion. For example, sides are being chosen in a game of baseball and I say, "I'll play first base." In doing so, I identify myself as someone willing to play first base—my epistemological identity in this situation. This property that I identify myself as having need not carry over to other occasions; I might be unwilling to play first base in any other game of baseball. Rather, my willingness to play first base is an occasion epistemological identity that I take on in the situation in which I say that I am willing to play first base, which marks it as being distinct from my epistemological identities connected to an identification card that I have from one occasion to the next as long as my identification card is valid.

It might be thought that, contrary to what I claim, it is not necessary that I have a property that I identify myself as having for it to be part of one of my epistemological identities. Imagine that an individual, let us call him "Al," who is not a Canadian citizen finds my passport in Paris. He copies the information from the passport and, with it, produces a fake Canadian passport with a picture of himself and information about me and my passport so that he can gain entry to Canada as a Canadian citizen. Suppose further that he then takes a plane to Montreal and, at Trudeau International Airport, presents the fake passport to an agent, conveying information to the agent about me. In doing so, he identifies himself as having properties that he does not possess. He identifies himself as having my epistemological identity, being Steven Davis, having a valid Canadian passport, and being a Canadian citizen. Al is guilty of misidentifying himself to the agent. That is, identifying himself as having properties that he does not have, and thus, having an epistemological identity that he lacks.

Let us suppose that some property can be be part of an epistemological identity of a person even though he does not have the property. It would follow, contrary to what I claim, that Al would have as his epistemological identity the properties he identifies himself as having. Consequently, there would be no misrepresentation, because Al would identify himself as having certain properties that would constitute his epistemological identity. That is, on this supposition, in identifying himself as me, Al would not misidentify himself to the agent as having an identity that he does not have. Correspondingly, if the agent were to identify Al as having my epistemological identity, being Steven Davis, having a valid Canadian passport, and being a Canadian citizen, he would not have misidentified him, since the supposition is that Al has whatever epistemological identity that he identifies himself as having. Hence, Al would not be guilty of misrepresentation and the agent would not be mistaken in admitting Al to Canada. Because it is clear that Al has misrepresented himself and the agent has misidentified him, the supposition is mistaken. Al does not have the epistemological identities that he identifies himself as having. The conclusion to be drawn is that a property is part of someone's epistemological identity, in the context in which he identifies himself as having it, only if he possesses the property.

I would now like to turn to identity theft and show how it illuminates the notion of epistemological identity. Before this can be done, we must have some idea about what identity theft is. There is no one answer to this question, because there are various uses of the term. One use requires that there is a wrongful taking of information about a person's epistemological identity and then a fraudulent use of this information for personal gain. We find this use in the Office of the Canadian Privacy Commissioner. Identity theft "is the unauthorized collection and use of your personal information, usually for criminal purposes."[18] An example of this kind of identity theft is Al's taking information about me and using it at passport control. His identity theft consists of two transgressions: stealing the information from my passport, and then using the information to identify himself as having my epistemological identity connected to my passport.[19]

The Consumer Protection Agency of the Government of Ontario however has a different take on identity theft. "Identity theft occurs when someone uses your personal information without your knowledge or consent to commit a crime, such as fraud or theft."[20] Only the second condition, using information about someone's epistemological identity fraudulently, plays a role in this account. There does not have to be a wrongfully taking of the personal information. Cases of this sort can occur when a family member uses information about a member of his family that was obtained legitimately. Consider the following example reported in the *New York Times*. A divorced mother of three used her children's Social Security numbers to take out credit cards in their names, which she then

---

18. Office of the Privacy Commissioner of Canada, "Identity Theft: What it is and What You Can Do About It," *Fact Sheet*, http://www.privcom.gc.ca/fs-fi/02_05_d_10_e.asp.

19. Public Safety Canada has a similar account. "Identity theft refers to all types of crime in which someone wrongfully obtains and uses another person's personal data in some way that involves fraud or deception, typically for economic gain." Public Safety Canada, "Identity Theft," *Advice for Consumers*, http://www.publicsafety.gc.ca/prg/le/bs/consumers-en.asp#1.

20. Ontario Ministry of Government and Consumer Services, "What is Identity Theft?," *Consumer Protection*, http://www.gov.on.ca/MGS/en/ConsProt/STEL02_045992.html. David Matheson brought this account of identity theft, and the example that follows, to my attention.

used fraudulently to rack up charges on the cards that she obtained.[21] In this case, the mother did not come by the information about the children's Social Security numbers by stealing it; it is information that she obtained legitimately. It is the unauthorized fraudulent use of the information that, on this account, constitutes identity theft. In presenting one of the cards as hers and using it to make purchases, she represented herself as one of her children, which her child presumably did not authorize her to do. In so presenting herself as someone she was not, she used the cards fraudulently.[22] The second of these accounts of identity theft should not be called 'identity theft,' because the mother did not steal the information about her children's Social Security numbers. Her transgression was in using the information fraudulently to impersonate her children. A better term for this might be "identity fraud" rather than "identity theft."

I have distinguished three types of identity that apply to persons, metaphysical, social/cultural/political, and epistemological. Each involves properties that the person has, but there is a difference among them. The characteristics that are part of a person's metaphysical identity must be essential properties that the person has across worlds and times in which, and at which, the person exists. The characteristics that constitute a person's social/cultural/political and epistemological identities can be accidental properties that he might have at one time or world, but not have at another time or world. Take being a Canadian citizen, a property that constitutes some people's social/cultural/political identities and for Canadian citizens with a passport part of their epistemological standing identities. It cannot, however, be part of anyone's metaphysical identity, since a person's citizenship is an accidental property and need not be constant across worlds and times. It follows that some social/cultural/political and epistemological identities are not metaphysical identities.

Can metaphysical identities be social/cultural/political or epistemological identities? It is possible for any property or set of properties to be a social/cultural/political or epistemological identity, as long as we have access to them. Suppose that a person's DNA constitutes his metaphysical identity. It is possible that having a particular DNA is a social/cultural/political identity. We can imagine a society in which it is socially, culturally, and politically important for people what DNA they have and it is something that for them plays an important role in

---

21. John Leland, "Stolen Lives: Identity Theft is Often Found in a Family Photo," *The New York Times*, November 13, 2006, http://www.nytimes.com/2006/11/13/us/13identity.html?ex=1321074000&en=e14f0e296f75978a&ei=5088&partner=rssnyt&emc=rss.

22. The U.S. Federal Trade Commission has a similar account. "Identity theft occurs when someone uses your personally identifying information, like your name, Social Security number, or credit card number, without your permission, to commit fraud or other crimes." U.S. Federal Trade Commission, "About Identity Theft," *Fighting Back Against Identity Theft*, http://www.ftc.gov/bcp/edu/microsites/idtheft/consumers/about-identity-theft.html.

their lives. As well, a person's DNA can be one of his epistemological identities. We can imagine a person at a police station or a doctor's office identifying himself to the police or the doctor as having a particular DNA.

That properties, which might be constitutive of our metaphysical identities, could be constitutive of our social/cultural/political or epistemological identities does not of course show that they are. Whether a certain property plays an actual role in social/cultural/political and epistemological identities is an empirical question, the answer to which is best left to sociologists and anthropologists. It is clear, however, that the actual properties that are constitutive of our metaphysical identities cannot now be constitutive of our social/cultural/political or epistemological identities, because these require that we have access to the properties that constitute these identities. It is still an open question among philosophers about what sorts of properties constitute our metaphysical identities. For this reason, we cannot be said to know what they are and thus, no one can be said to have cognitive access to them. We must know or at least have current cognitive access[23] to what our social/cultural/political identities are, because they play important roles in our lives through our cognitive states concerning them and, thus, must be in some sense accessible to us. Our epistemological identities must be avowable and thus accessible to us; we must be able to provide others with information about them so that they can identify us as having them. We present the merchant our visa card, which contains information relevant for making a purchase with the intention that the merchant comes to believe that we are authorized to do so. Thus, connected to our social/cultural/political identities and epistemological identities, we have access to information that is not available to us with respect to our metaphysical identities, because we currently have no idea what they are.

Let us look at the relationship between social/cultural/political and epistemological identities. Since any set of properties could be a social/cultural/political or epistemological identity, as long as they are accessible, it follows that it is possible that for a given individual one of the properties that constitutes his social/cultural/political identity could constitute one of his epistemological identities. For example, the property of being a Canadian is part of many Canadians' social/cultural/political identities and, if they have a Canadian passport, a constituent of one of their standing epistemological identities.

There are also properties that can be part of a person's social/cultural/political identity, but are not any of his standing or occasion epistemological identities. Imagine that Fred is an alcoholic, a property that is important to him in that it gives an explanation for his behavior and that is important in the society of which he is a part, because in this society those who are known to be alcoholics are ostracized. For this reason, Fred wishes to hide the fact

---

23. See n. 11 for a discussion of cognitive access.

that he is an alcoholic and, hence, does not identify himself to others as being afflicted with the problem. Thus, being an alcoholic is not one of Fred's epistemological identities, because there are no occasions on which he identifies himself as being an alcoholic. Consequently, there can be social/cultural/political identities that are not epistemological identities.

There are some properties that are constituents of one of a person's epistemological identities that are not part of his social/cultural/political identities. I have a department credit card that bestows on me a standing epistemological identity of being able to make purchases on credit in that store. Being able to do this, however, is not part of my social/cultural/political identity, since it is not something that plays an important role in my life. I have not even used the card to make a purchase. The conclusion is that there are some epistemological identities that are not social/cultural/political identities.

To sum up, we see that our metaphysical identities are distinct from our epistemological and social/cultural/political identities, while the latter two, although they overlap, are distinct. It follows that the notions of metaphysical identity, epistemological identity, and social/cultural/political identity are distinct notions, because they do not apply to the same sets of objects.[24] A person's epistemological identities are properties of the person that he has and that for certain purposes he can identify himself as having to others by conveying information to them. Epistemological identities are of two sorts, standing and occasion. A standing epistemological identity is connected to an identity card issued by an institution that specifies either directly or indirectly the identifying information that the person who holds the card can convey to another to identify himself as having a particular epistemological identity. An occasion epistemological identity is a set of properties of a person, which he identifies himself as having to another on a particular occasion with the intention of inducing in the other the belief that he has that epistemological identity. Identity theft is the unauthorized taking and use of identifying information that is connected to one of a person's epistemological identities. It is information about a person that the thief appropriates without permission and uses to identify himself to another as having an epistemological identity that he does not have. Identity fraud is the unauthorized use of information about a person that is connected to one of the person's epistemological identities.[25]

---

24. 'Object' is used broadly to cover anything that can be a member of a set.

25. I would like to thank Jane Bailey, Jeremy Clark, Jacquie Burkell, Michael Fromkin, and especially David Matheson for useful comments on this paper.

13. IDENTITY
Difference and Categorization

CHARLES D. RAAB

I. ABSTRACT

This paper considers the concept of identity and the two directions that it faces, denoting both the individual's difference from others, and the individual's membership of categories and groups. Some implications of this duality are explored, and propositions for further research are indicated.

II. INTRODUCTION: TWO CONCEPTS OF "IDENTITY"

Keeping one's bearings along the identity trail is a complicated matter. The trail is forked: one path ends in commonality and in identity shared by the person with others as members of certain categories or collectivities; the other ends in individuation or uniqueness, differentiating one person from another. These paths resemble what Hildebrandt, following Ricoeur,[1] articulates as two interrelated concepts of identity: one derives from *idem*, the Latin word, "meaning sameness, similarity and/or continuity;" the other "refers to the concept of *ipse* or self . . . the *sense of self* that is constitutive of the human subject (emphasis in original)."[2]

---

1. P. Ricoeur, *Oneself as Another* (Chicago: University of Chicago Press, 1992).

2. M. Hildebrandt, "Profiling and the Identity of European Citizens," in M. Hildebrandt, S. Gutwirth, and P. De Hert, *D7.4: Implications of Profiling Practices on Democracy and Rule of Law*, FIDIS Programme deliverable, 2007, http://www.fidis.net/resources/deliverables/profiling/int-d74000/doc/ (accessed September 30, 2007).

TABLE 13.1

	Identity defined by self		
Uniqueness	"I am. . ."	"I am a. . ."	**Membership**
	"You are. . ."	"You are a. . ."	
	Identity defined by others		

Idem identity has two components: sameness and similarity refer to the categories into which items are placed; and continuity refers to sameness over time. *Ipse* identity depends on continuity; the sense of self "cannot emerge without the *idem*-identity we experience (our sense of continuity) and the *idem*-identity we are attributed by others (as this is how we establish our sense of self in contrast to others)."[3] Both kinds of identity are relational in that *ipse* "is constructed in confrontation with an environment," while *idem*'s "establishment of sameness builds on comparison."[4]

Both paths on the identity trail carry traffic moving in either direction—going out from ourselves and coming toward us from others. Traffic densities vary along each path, and we have to negotiate the path's use with others. Thus, a person's individual identity may be asserted, and accepted or rejected by others; it may be attributed to the person by others, and accepted or rejected by the person. Likewise, our shared identity may be that which we adopt as groups, and is accepted or rejected by others; it may be assigned as a category by others and accepted or rejected by ourselves. These attributions or assignments may, further, be made authoritatively by powerful institutions, such as the state or companies, and not just by societal "others." Table 13.1 plots the four analytical positions heuristically, summing up the gist of each with a characteristic phrase.

The conclusion of this paper will revisit this table in suggesting some propositions that could be explored in future research that would draw attention to the factors of power and conflict that are instinct in questions of identity and identification. But in terms of the "path" imagery, we should not think of the various paths as in an M. C. Escher[5] drawing in which one person ascends and another descends the same staircase in the same direction, but between whom contact is impossible, "because they live in different worlds and therefore can have no knowledge of each other's existence."[6] The processes of identification in both our "trail" cases overlap, just as the individual's conception of who she is

3. Hildebrandt, "Profiling and the Identity of European Citizens," 17 (n. 2).
4. *Ibid.*
5. Maurits Escher, *The Graphic Work of M.C. Escher* (London: Pan/Ballantine, 1972), plate 67. Also see plates 66 and 75.
6. Escher, *The Graphic Work of M.C. Escher*, 15 (n. 5).

involves both dimensions: what she is uniquely, and what she shares with others; there is a dialectic of self-image and public image.[7] In a related way, the "lifestyle" categorization processes used in commerce, which define and predict consumers' behavior, actually bring the paths together. Pridmore explains that "[e]ach engagement of the consumer with marketing is defined by prior data processing, and though these may be articulated as singularly customized representations, . . . businesses understand 'consumers' as the accumulation of statistically defined categories."[8]

The two faces of identity are interdependent, yet they also constitute a duality. Hekman states,

> Each of us possesses a personal identity that is constituted by an array of influences and experiences that form us as a unique person. These forces are both public, the hegemonic discourses that define our social life, and individual, the character and situation of those who care for us as infants, and through whom the public concepts are transmitted to us. The result of these influences is . . . our core self. But in addition to possessing a personal identity, each of us is subsumed under an array of public identities: woman/man; white/nonwhite; middle class/working class, and so forth.[9]

If one identifies with, and acts politically as, a member of a category, this does not thereby fix one's personal identity, but represents a choice in the public realm that is rooted in the complexities of the personal identity that transcend this public category. Hekman notes, "Our personal identity makes us different from everyone else. Our public identity identifies us as the same as particular others."[10] But, in terms of Table 13.1, the public identity or identities may implicate either the upper-right or the lower-right boxes, and the political, social, and informational processes that arbitrate this need to be understood.

III. WHAT ABOUT "THE SELF"?

Whether the concept of a "core self" is helpful—or necessary—engages a far more psychological, anthropological, historical, and philosophical argument than can be considered here. We may note, however, Cohen's emphasis on the

---

7. R. Jenkins, "Categorization: Identity, Social Process and Epistemology," *Current Sociology* 48, no. 3 (2000): 8.

8. J. Pridmore, "Expert Report: Consumption and Profiling," in Surveillance Studies Network, *A Report on the Surveillance Society*, ed. D. Murakami Wood (Wilmslow: Office of the Information Commissioner, 2007), 32.

9. S. Hekman, *Private Selves, Public Identities: Reconsidering Identity Politics* (University Park: Penn State University Press, 2004), 7.

10. Hekman, *Private Selves, Public Identities* (n. 9).

self-consciousness of the "authorial self,"[11] which is overlooked in many paradigms. Our authorial selves can resist definitions imposed by organizations if we find that that "personhood" jars with the sense of self we want to assert as our identity. On the other hand, Cohen argues that, when we declare adherence to collective categories such as gender, nationality, ethnicity, or religion, we are not necessarily surrendering to alien impositions, but are reappropriating or creating our identities.[12] In Hekman's terms, the self is not just a matter of self-declaration, or something primordial and ineffable, but is amalgamated with definitions by others. This illustrates how the paths come together—the left-hand side of Table 13.1—and bears out Jenkins' insistence that "all human identities are by definition *social* identities."[13] In his analysis of the "historical sociology of the self,"[14] Rose highlights the situation in which, "Through self-inspection, self-problematization, self-monitoring, and confession, we evaluate ourselves according to the criteria provided for us by others . . . The irony is that we believe, in making our subjectivity the principle of our personal lives . . . that we are, freely, choosing our freedom."[15] Rose links identity and self-definition processes to the subtleties of both political power and the workings of a consumer society. In the case of political power, Rose describes a situation that is not a matter of crude manipulation or domination of the subject:

> The regulatory apparatus of the modern state is not something imposed from outside upon individuals who have remained essentially untouched by it. Incorporating, shaping, channelling, and enhancing subjectivity have been intrinsic to the operations of government . . . not . . . through the growth of an omnipotent and omniscient central state whose agents institute a perpetual surveillance and control . . . Rather, government of subjectivity has taken shape through the proliferation of a complex and heterogeneous assemblage of technologies . . . bringing the varied ambitions of political, scientific, philanthropic, and professional authorities into alignment with . . . the selves each of us want [sic] to be.[16]

Identity, however, is not merely an aggregate of our roles and performances. Clarke does not talk about a self, but about an underlying physical "entity":

> Individual people perform various social, economic and political functions, in roles such as citizen, consumer, sole trader, and member of

11. A. Cohen, *Self Consciousness: An Alternative Anthropology of Identity*, (London: Routledge, 1994).

12. *Ibid.*

13. Jenkins, "Categorization: Identity, Social Process and Epistemology," 73 (n. 7).

14. N. Rose, *Governing the Soul: The Shaping of the Private Self*, 2nd ed, (London: Free Association Books, 1999), vii.

15. Rose, *Governing the Soul*, 11 (n. 14).

16. *Ibid.*, 219.

partnerships . . . A person may present the same persona for every role, or different personae for each of them, or a few personae each of which is used in multiple contexts . . . It is useful to have a term available that encompasses both identities and the entities that underlie them . . . the term "(id)entity" is used for that purpose.[17]

For information systems, the practical significance of Clarke's view is that an (id)entifier is seen as the items of data concerning an (id)entity that distinguish the latter from other instances of its class and that therefore signifies this (id)entity; whereas, an "entifier," as a form of biometric, is that which signifies an entity and distinguishes it from other physical persons.[18] An entity can have several identities and several entifiers, but each of those refers to only one entity. Anonymity and pseudonymity are cases in which a "nym" is used in order to prevent the association of an (id)entifier with a specific entity. Nyms may be valuable features of information systems that are designed to allow for the authentication of a person's claims or assertions about who she is in business or governmental contexts while protecting her privacy by not revealing her identity, much less her self.

IV. NEGOTIATING IDENTITIES

The dualisms show some of the complexities of identity and identification, in terms of the criteria by which one claims to be, or is seen and authenticated, as distinctive or as part of wider collectivities. At various times and in different contexts, we may want both to be uniquely identified, and identified as a member of a group or category. The organizations, states, and other persons with whom we interact may also want to make these different attributions about us. Explanations of why, how, and when these choices are made are beyond the present scope. But the selection of criteria for asserting, assigning, or discrediting identities is political, in the broad sense that power is exercised in their application, or in their denial, and that these processes may be the sites of conflict. Jenkins writes, "whose definition of the situation *counts*? The power or authority to generate consequences, to make identification matter regardless of internalization, must be part of the equation."[19] The conclusion of this paper draws on this insight.

"Identity," therefore, is a highly intricate concept that opens up issues that technical discussions of identification and verification do not often, or perhaps

---

17. R. Clarke, "Authentication Re-visited: How Public Key Infrastructure Could Yet Prosper," paper presented at the 16th International eCommerce Conference, Bled, Slovenia, June 9–11, 2003, version of April 27, 2003, http://www.anu.edu.ac/people/Roger.Clarke/EC/Bled03.html, (accessed November 29, 2007).

18. *Ibid.*

19. Jenkins, "Categorization: Identity, Social Process and Epistemology," 9 (n. 7).

do not have to, address. It is used in everyday life, and also in connection with research on persons and selves (the "I" and the "me"), on social groups, societies, and peoples (the "we," who may be Inuit, Catholics, Manchester United support-ers, etc.), on cultural and political entities, not only including politically sovereign ones ("Scottish," "British," "Canadian," "Palestinian," etc.), on supranational aggregates ("Europeans"), and on species ("human beings"). Some identities are self-confident, while others are said to be in crisis, not only about who is inside and who is outside, but about the qualities and attributes of membership. This has given rise to public and political debate about, as well as behavioral manifes-tation of, what it means to be, for example, English or British today, and the means of collective symbolic and political expression are being refashioned, sometimes xenophobically.

Social and political change, including migration patterns, affect these conceptions and self-conceptions as well as the characteristics attributed to those seen as outsiders. Identity's stock-in-trade is certainty in a changing—some would say globalizing—world. It is asserted by the invention, discovery, or reassertion of unifying properties, symbols, memories, or traditions by collectivities; by oppos-ing the movement (as in attacks on "them," who are swamping "us"); or by deny-ing the change. But certainty must be renegotiated over time; we may—singly or consensually—move smoothly from one such settlement to another, or we may stumble or fight over it. Economic cycles, political leadership, and the media shape these routes, as they also do the apparatuses whereby unique individual identities are claimed or rejected. Bauman is insightful on this point:

> That work of art which we want to mould out of the friable stuff of life is called "identity." Whenever we speak of identity, there is at the back of our minds a faint image of harmony, logic, consistency: all those things which the flow of our experience seems—to our perpetual despair—so grossly and abominably to lack. The search for identity is the ongoing struggle to arrest or slow down the flow, to solidify the fluid, to give form to the formless . . . Yet far from slowing the flow, let alone stopping it, identities are more like the spots of crust hardening time and again on the top of volcanic lava which melt and dissolve again before they have time to cool and set. So there is need for another trial, and another—and they can be attempted only by clinging desperately to things solid and tangible and thus promising duration, whether or not they fit or belong together . . .[20]

Identities, Bauman argues, only look solid from the outside, as when we contemplate others and perceive their existence as coherent, a "work of art." From the inside, our sense of identity is precarious, so we put one on, as in adopting a fashion. Bauman states,

> Given the intrinsic volatility and unfixity of all or most identities, it is the ability to "shop around" in the supermarket of identities, the degree of genuine

---

20. Z. Bauman, *Liquid Modernity* (Cambridge: Polity Press, 2000), 82–83.

or putative consumer freedom to select one's identity and to hold it as long as desired, that becomes the royal road to the fulfilment of identity fantasies. Having that ability, one is free to make and unmake identities at will. Or so it seems.[21]

V. IDENTITY, INFORMATION, AND THE QUEST FOR CERTAINTY

These are *individual* identities, ones that differentiate each of us, and Bauman's remarks are made in a critique of the consumer society that abets our individualist fantasies, albeit with mass-produced goods. Leaving the critique aside, we may remain with the point about fragility and choice, whether real or apparent. The extent to which choices are tolerated today, in a climate of personal and state insecurity, is brought into question. This, too, is a theme in Bauman: individuals and collectivities become "the last defensive outposts on the increasingly deserted battlefield on which the war for certainty, security and safety is waged daily with little, if any, respite."[22] Current writing such as that of Monahan, and of Zureik and Salter[23], attests that it is waged through intensified surveillance and the tracking of flows of various kinds—people, goods, information—in which identifications are crucial.

These are grand themes for sociology and political science, and portraying them in apocalyptic terms is heuristically useful. If, as some argue, we are living in times of uncertainty, anxiety, and "liquid fear"[24] in the "First Life," we can expect institutional impatience with, and intolerance of, ambiguous identity. So important is it to establish the "truth" of someone's identity in a world that is perceived to be unsafe, that persons cannot be trusted to give an unquestioned account of who they are. Where trust, in general, is ebbing, trust in identities follows suit; ironically, trust in technologies and information systems designed to check or establish identities is—perhaps unwarrantably—high. Moreover, the legitimacy of anonymity is strongly challenged, and opportunities for its exercise may become restricted by the growing official and business impatience with defenses of privacy that would seek to limit, or at least regulate, the use of information systems that serve to identify individuals and collectivities.

Let us look a bit further into this matter. Information systems and processes are involved in the complex shaping and negotiation of identities; they are developed in all paths, for different purposes. Identity verification is an issue for

---

21. *Ibid.*, 83.

22. *Ibid.*, 184.

23. T. Monahan, ed., *Surveillance and Security: Technological Politics and Power in Everyday Life* (New York: Routledge, 2006); E. Zureik, E. and M. Salter, eds., *Global Surveillance and Policing: Borders, Security, Identity* (Cullompton: Willan Publishing, 2005).

24. Z. Bauman, *Liquid Fear* (Cambridge: Polity Press, 2006).

states, governments, public policy, and business, perhaps especially on the Internet. Regulating immigration, crime detection, running a welfare system, granting consumer credit, and the conduct of e-commerce and e-government all normally require verification of personal identity. But for many universal public services, an important question is whether the identification of persons, rather than simply the verification of their entitlement, is *really* necessary, for many personal identifiers may be irrelevant for particular state or business functions. In providing a service, permitting entry to places and spaces, or allowing the purchase or obtaining of a good, the agent or automatic system with whom or which the person directly interacts may need to know no more than the legitimacy of the person's claim in order to open or close the gate, produce the product, and so on. However, current programs of personalized, "citizen-focused" or "citizen-centered" public services[25] require extensive knowledge of who the citizen is, in terms of *idem* identity but going beyond this into a knowledge of needs, desires, and likely behavior. These knowledge requirements, involving profiling, adopt "customer-relations management" (CRM) from the marketing sector; this point will be revisited later. But suppose identification is in question at some of these moments: on what grounds can a person so identified contest her identification? On what grounds can she assert another one, and have it acknowledged? Related to this, what are we to make of "personal data"—a concept currently in question within systems of regulation[26]—as a concept implicated in these identifications?

In contemporary circumstances, which owe something but not everything to the events of September 11, 2001, safety and security are important, even paramount, values of the context for identity-related processes.[27] The search for safety and security is conducted in mundane, bureaucratic routines, involving technologies of identity verification, contestation, and management. It also takes place in mundane, personal-interaction routines, involving social "technologies"—for example, the manipulation of spacing, timing, appearance, and demeanor—whereby the identity of oneself and others is negotiated. This seems intrinsic to the human condition, for Goffman has shown that we are all everyday practitioners of safety- and trust-related strategies of information management and appraisal. States and organizations, on the other hand, have developed specialisms in this, investing in resources and public policy to find out things about identifiable persons and groups, to process information, and to create derivative knowledge.

---

25. M. Lips, S. van der Hof, C. Prins, and T. Schudelaro, *Issues of Online Personalisation in Commercial and Public Service Delivery* (Nijmegen: Wolf Legal Publishers, n.d.).

26. In the UK, the Durant case of 2003 in the Court of Appeal threw the accepted definition of "personal data" in data protection law into some confusion. C. Raab, "Perspectives on 'Personal Identity,'" *BT Technology Journal* 23, no. 4 (2005): 17–18.

27. C. Raab, "Governing the Safety State," lecture given in the University of Edinburgh, June 5, 2005.

Whether through sensory organs and the mind, or through materials that we refer to as "information technology," information is collected, compared, evaluated, and stored, and decisions are made on the basis of this "knowledge." Depending on the kind of decision it happens to be—for instance, whether to trust a passer-by not to accost me, or whether to trust him with a secret; whether to trust the person at the claimants' office not to be a fraudster, or whether to grant her asylum status on entry into the country—information processing ranges over several levels of intensity and extensiveness.

States may have rules regarding what is proportionate or excessive in the collection and further processing of information; persons or cultures may also have rules about these information activities; and both states and persons may run the gamut from compliance to derogation, and from paranoia to relaxation about these identity and trust judgments, and, therefore, about the way information should be processed. Both states and persons may take precautions against error, or else pay the price for errors not sufficiently anticipated. These rules and stances can be considered "policies," although that term is usually reserved for what is done by states, not persons or cultures. Both may learn from experience, or they may not if they see advantage in persisting with their chosen policy despite evidence that it has been either too careful or too lax. The consequences of such persistence with faulty information and identification policies cannot be investigated further here.

Many kinds of information may be involved. Marx considers "identity knowledge" in terms of seven types by which individuals are identified or not; non-identification involves ignorance of identity, of which anonymity is an example.[28] Social categorization is one type, and Marx enumerates a variety of categories, the membership of which a person may share with others, such as gender, religion, region, health status, and temporal or spatial co-location, however transitory.[29] Then there are people-processing categories used by states (and indeed, the commercial sector): credit-risk categories, lifestyles, and education scores. Marx points out that these may have predictive uses; thus, we may say, the identities to which these categories point are those that people are likely to acquire, and not necessarily those that they already have—criminals, the impoverished, those destined for leadership, and so on.

The private sector has led in many analytical practices. As was noted earlier, in the commercial and online world, and within the "data-informed marketing model,"[30]

---

28. G. Marx, "Identity and Anonymity: Some Conceptual Distinctions and Issues for Research," in *Documenting Individual Identity: The Development of State Practices in the Modern World*, eds. J. Caplan and J. Torpey (Princeton: Princeton University Press, 2001).

29. *Ibid.*, 314–315.

30. M. Evans, "The Data-Informed Marketing Model and its Social Responsibility," in *The Glass Consumer: Life in a Surveillance Society*, ed. S. Lace (Bristol: Policy Press, 2005).

CRM identifies, profiles, and targets individuals. Many benefits may well be realized from these ways of doing business, yet there are costs: the consumer is not only "glass" in the sense of transparency, as Lace[31] describes, but also in the sense of fragility. Yet, as Gandy, Charters, and others have illustrated, the retailing relationship can discriminate against some individuals or consumption classes and in favor of others.[32] The ability of online technologies to abet these processes through the fine-grained behavioral and personal data they collect and "mine," or analyze, implicates them in social sorting.[33] The public sector is heavily involved in this as well, not only for the purposes of security and fear-control, but also for social-policy purposes, although the line is blurred. In a climate in which the anticipation of fraud, criminal and antisocial behavior, and health risks have risen alongside punishment and treatment as policy aims, governments aim to improve the predictability of behavior in order to take preventative or precautionary action through the policy process. They proactively target certain categories of identifiable people—very young children and the unborn, frequently—for special treatment designed to avert undesirable future behavior, or perhaps to encourage certain forms of behavior, to open up beneficial opportunities to them, and to overcome social exclusion. The reliability of prognoses about people who may be at risk to themselves or to others is hotly debated. So too, is the propriety of government's anticipatory policy-making when it may serve to stigmatize groups and categories even while helping them, or aiming to help them; there are echoes of the American policy debates about "positive discrimination" some years ago.

States' targeting techniques, involving data-mining and profiling, are not unlike those of the commercial sector. They attract a similar "panoptic sort" critique to the one pioneered by Gandy, and invite questions about the privacy implications of "knowledge discovery in databases," as Tavani[34] has posed. We will see later, by reference to Vedder's work, what some of the privacy issues are in these information practices and policies. Data mining discovers patterns in collections of personal data and shapes them into categories for decision-making and action; "knowledge," however contestable, becomes potent, perhaps especially when in the hands of public authorities. How are these developments kept within bounds? Whether harmful or beneficial in terms of purposes, functions,

---

31. S. Lace, ed., *The Glass Consumer: Life in a Surveillance Society* (Bristol: Policy Press, 2005), 1.

32. O. Gandy, *The Panoptic Sort: A Political Economy of Personal Information* (Boulder: Westview Press), 1993; D. Charters, "Electronic Monitoring and Privacy in Business-Marketing: The Ethics of the DoubleClick Experience," *Journal of Business Ethics* 35 (2002): 243–254.

33. D. Lyon, ed., *Surveillance as Social Sorting: Privacy, Risk, and Digital Discrimination* (London: Routledge, 2003).

34. H. Tavani, "KDD, Data Mining, and the Challenge for Normative Privacy," *Ethics and Information Technology* 1 (1999): 265–273.

and side-effects, these processes are not adequately addressed by privacy commentators, regulators, and policy-makers. Computer ethicists such as Gotterbarn and Tavani—along with other critics such as Danna and Gandy, who do recognize the issues as serious—are, however, at a loss to suggest remedies that go beyond moral suasion, applied Rawlsianism, better laws, more guidance, codes of professional ethics, and individual self-help.[35] But these may have to do; how they integrate as regulatory tools is an under-examined question. Another problem, as Marx mentions, concerns the lack of transparency of the categories by which the state or business claims to know us, and the possible discrepancy between the way they see us and the way we see ourselves.[36] This is "a nice research question," but in just what way it is a research question, and in what way it is an "issue," needs further discussion. That discussion should begin with some exploration of "the way they see us," in which identity is established and inscribed in information systems that relate to decisions and judgments that are made concerning citizens or customers.

VI. IDENTITY CARDS: AN ILLUSTRATION

There may be a disjuncture between social-scientific perspectives on identity, whatever they may be, and the worlds of government and commerce, in which unique identities are the currency of practice, and the meaning of "identity" is not problematical, but matter-of-fact. For example, governments do not see it as problematical in their policy on identity cards, and in many identity-management schemes, in which the types of information items embedded in the processes of identification are critical for citizens' enjoyment of rights and entitlements. These items differentiate persons, insofar as they describe uniqueness, as fingerprints, iris scans, facial characteristics, and other biometrics purport to do. Another interesting example is the welter of "registrable facts" specified in the Section 1(5) of the United Kingdom's (UK) Identity Cards Act 2006 for the National Identity Register that will include every person in the country. These are as follows:

(a) His identity;
(b) The address of his principal place of residence in the United Kingdom;
(c) The address of every other place in the United Kingdom or elsewhere where he has a place of residence;

---

35. D. Gotterbarn, "Privacy Lost: The Net, Autonomous Agents, and 'Virtual Information,'" *Ethics and Information Technology* 1 (1999): 147–154; H. Tavani, "Informational Privacy, Data Mining, and the Internet," *Ethics and Information Technology* 1 (1999): 137–145; A. Danna and O. Gandy, "All that Glitters is not Gold: Digging Beneath the Surface of Data Mining," *Journal of Business Ethics* 40 (2002): 373–386.

36. Marx, "Identity and Anonymity," 315 (n. 28).

(d) Where in the United Kingdom and elsewhere he has previously been resident;
(e) The times at which he was resident at different places in the United Kingdom or elsewhere;
(f) His current residential status;
(g) Residential statuses previously held by him;
(h) Information about numbers allocated to him for identification purposes and about the documents to which they relate;
(i) Information about occasions on which information recorded about him in the Register has been provided to any person; and
(j) Information recorded in the Register at his request.

The Act stipulates that the individual's "identity" is a registrable fact, defined in Section 1(6) as:

(a) His full name;
(b) Other names by which he is or has previously been known;
(c) His gender;
(d) His date and place of birth and, if he has died, the date of his death; and
(e) External[37] characteristics of his that are capable of being used for identifying him.

Other "facts" about persons are not deemed "registrable": for example, details of employment and marital status, educational achievements, religious affiliation, diagnosed diseases, and attributes by which a person may be both well known to her friends and family and in good company with thousands of others who share certain categories of membership or affinity. These are considered irrelevant to the purposes envisaged for the identity card scheme, yet a person—and significant others—may think that these and other facts are inherent parts of the identity she constructs for herself and presents to the world (and by which that world knows her) than her other names or her fingerprints.

Schedule 1 of the Act, however, further specifies a long list of other recordable information. It construes the registrable five of Section 1(6), plus past and present residential addresses, as "personal information" separate from "identifying information" (but, confusingly, not from "identity," as indicated in Section 1) about an individual, which is described in Schedule 1 as:

(a) A photograph of his head and shoulders (showing the features of the face);
(b) His signature;
(c) His fingerprints;
(d) Other biometric information about him.

---

37. The Bill that preceded the Act said "physical." The Act's Explanatory Notes, no. 19, explains that "external" means, for example, biometric information. "Physical," one supposes, might include height, whereas biometric information does not record this.

By implication, and curiously, identification here concerns the body, and not what is otherwise labeled "personal." Other recordable information itemized in Schedule 1 involves residential status within the United Kingdom; thirteen personal reference numbers on various kinds of document; one's previously recorded details, and any changes to those; nine different forms of particulars concerning one's identity card registration and its history; a further set of validation information relating to the latter; several kinds of security information; and information about the provision (disclosure) of register information to third parties: in all, over fifty items. In addition, Section 3(6) gives government the power to modify this inventory, subject to parliamentary approval. This may require further primary legislation, because the new information system is required to be consistent with the Act's statutory purposes.

The import of the Act is to say, "you are who we say you are, on the basis of the facts registered and recorded in predetermined categories" which, taken together, identify a unique individual. This falls within the lower-left box of Table 13.1. But the person may be saying, beyond these facts, "I am who I say I am, and that is a different 'me' from the identity you have constructed about me"—the upper-left box of Table 13.1. As we have seen, social scientists, having read their Goffman,[38] their Bauman,[39] and many other writers, may say that identity is a result of interactive negotiation with others, and not just a unilateral declaration by either party. Moreover, it is more fluid and changeable than is claimed by many persons who assert a permanent self-definition, and by many organizations for which the stability of identities poses less of a threat to operational performance than would changeable ones, unless the changed identities can be linked back to stable properties: "'be' whom you wish, we know the *real* you." Identity management, according to a prominent UK review of public services,[40] will establish a "single source of truth," reinforced by identity cards, and—we can infer—abolishing the basis for rebuttal, conflict, and negotiation.

VII. IDENTIFICATION AND CATEGORIZATION: PRIVACY AND OTHER ISSUES

Social scientists have, of course, debated the relationship—if there is any—between "real" and "virtual" identities, and between personal and social identities. Writing about stigma and spoiled identity, Goffman makes these distinctions in

---

38. E. Goffman, *The Presentation of Self in Everyday Life* (New York: Doubleday Anchor, 1959).

39. Bauman, *Liquid Modernity* (n. 20).

40. HM Treasury, *Service Transformation: A Better Service for Citizens and Businesses, a Better Deal for Taxpayers* (Review by Sir David Varney), 2006, http://www.hm-treasury.gov.uk/media/4/F/pbr06_varney_review.pdf (accessed November 27, 2007), 40.

analyzing coping strategies when discrepancies between whom one "is" and who one claims to be are, or are in danger of being, exposed in face-to-face interaction.[41] But, as mentioned earlier, Jenkins sees no value in the adjective "social" attached to "identity"[42] because "Identifying ourselves or others is a matter of meaning, and meaning always involves interaction: agreement and disagreement, convention and innovation, communication and negotiation;"[43] identity is not a fixed attribute but a reflexive process. For this reason, Jenkins prefers to talk about identification rather than identity.

The social psychology of categorization or identification need not be explored here,[44] but it is germane to understanding the processes by which one of the two main identity trails is navigated. But there are other issues surrounding the categorization path. Vedder's discussion of the formation of group profiles[45]—actually, categories of persons who do not feel a common bond of loyalty or belongingness—distinguishes between distributive and non-distributive collective properties.[46] Vedder defines a distributive collective property as "a property that can be truly assigned to a group of individuals and at the same time be truly and unconditionally assigned to the individual members of the group," whereas in the non-distributive situation, the property is "only conditionally ascribable to the individual members."[47] Vedder's illustration of the latter is of a group in which the properties are a variety of different medical conditions or treatments, large percentages of unemployment or of employment types, and a significant sub-group of the over-50s. Inferences cannot be made about any one person in the group (category), so that making selection decisions about these persons on the basis of the aggregated profile risks unfair and inequitable treatment of any of them. This is a relevant source of anxiety for individuals whose categorical identities may thus be rigidified in administrative memories, and communicated throughout sectors in which decisions may be made on possibly erroneous grounds concerning individuals' probable trustworthiness, financial solvency, and other attributes. In daily social relations, we can observe similar, and often adverse, workings of stereotyping or labeling.

More narrowly, perhaps, there are also privacy implications that can be briefly touched on. Vedder aims to relate these practices to the paradigmatic, individualist

41. E. Goffman, *Stigma: Notes on the Management of Spoiled Identity* (Englewood Cliffs: Prentice-Hall, 1968).

42. R. Jenkins, *Social Identity*, 2nd ed., (London: Routledge, 2004), 73.

43. *Ibid.*, 4.

44. C. Raab, "Governing the Safety State," lecture given at the University of Edinburgh, June 5, 2005; Jenkins, *Social Identity*, 79–93 (n. 42).

45. A. Vedder, *The Values of Freedom* (Utrecht: Aurelio Domus Artium, 1995), 9–11.

46. These terms are taken from Feinberg's work on collective responsibility. J. Feinberg, "Collective Responsibility," *The Journal of Philosophy* 65, no. 21 (1968): 674–688.

47. Vedder, *The Values of Freedom*, 10 (n. 45).

concept of privacy[48] that renders that concept unfit to handle technology-related problems and practices. Among these is group profiling using information that "has been abstracted from what is usually considered to be the private life-sphere of individual persons, but had been made anonymous, generalized and statistically processed."[49] This points Vedder toward shaping a concept of "categorial privacy." This is not to be confused with collective or group privacy; it is rooted in the value of individuality that privacy protection champions, but concerns the protection of the privacy of those who, by virtue of having been placed in a category, may be injured by inferences and decisions made about them when the properties of the category are non-distributive—that is, all the members. Thus, "categorial privacy resembles stereotyping and wrongful discrimination on the basis of stereotypes."[50] This is a rather different situation from the one remarked upon by Oakes et al. in which Tom, Mary, Jane, and Harry are individuals, but they are also men and women, and they are also a string quartet, and there is no necessary distortion in our seeing them—and in their own self-definition—in categorical terms.[51] Vedder's, by contrast, is a situation in which one's particular attributes are overlooked in favor of the simplification of classifications that may satisfy the identification purposes of the sorters, and perhaps even of the sorted, but which, through a process of what we may call "identity-creep," threatens to become perpetuated and transferred to other contexts in which damage may be done.

These consequences go beyond privacy invasions, which, though important, are grounded in somewhat separate argumentation and theorizing from those that fuel critiques of surveillance. Identity, identification, and the use of personal data are implicated in both the practice of privacy invasion and protection, and the practice of surveillance and its limitation. Regulatory policies, based on human rights principles, are important in both. They have been developed in relation to privacy and data protection, and the rules, assumptions, and institutional practices have embodied particular understandings of the generalized, abstract person whose privacy, or whose information, is to be protected. They have embodied particular understandings of the purposes of states and other organizations, and they have also been predicated upon notions of the "reasonable expectation of privacy" that have become part of privacy jurisprudence (e.g., Nouwt et al.[52]). Whether this configuration of discourse, policy, and practice

---

48. *Ibid.*, 109–114; C. Bennett and C. Raab, *The Governance of Privacy: Policy Instruments in Global Perspective*, 2nd ed. (Cambridge: MIT Press, 2006).

49. *Ibid.*, 109.

50. *Ibid.*, 112.

51. P. Oakes, S. Haslam, and J. Turner, *Stereotyping and Social Reality* (Cambridge: Blackwell, 1994), 104.

52. S. Nouwt, B. de Vries, and C. Prins, eds., *Reasonable Expectations of Privacy?: Eleven Country Reports on Camera Surveillance and Workplace Privacy* (The Hague: T.M.C. Asser Press, 2005).

can be applied to the consequences of identification processes is for future consideration.

VIII. CONCLUSION: TOWARD FURTHER RESEARCH

The subject of identity is usually couched in a conceptual and descriptive mode of discussion that, while yielding information about processes and consequences, seems in need of new directions. In terms of the "identity trail" trope, we need to put fresh tracks upon the earth. Based upon some of the exploration of complexities above, one way forward in research is to move toward new rationales for, and ways of, gathering and analyzing empirical material in the contexts of novel ways of thinking about identity and identification. This paper began by depicting, in Table 13.1, four positions described by two pairs of variables: uniqueness/membership, and self-defined identity/identity defined by others. Can more be said about this configuration in terms of researchable propositions or assertions? The paper concludes by stating, and briefly elaborating, several of these for further exploration.

A. Proposition 1
Institutional and social power includes the ability of others to assign identities to individuals or groups authoritatively, and to reduce the ability of the latter to contest or reject these attributions.

This proposition invites an analysis of the means whereby such power is exerted. This would involve application of Lukes's third "face" of power, in which power can be exercised even without overt conflict and without the suppression of grievances felt by the powerless that prevents them from becoming issues on political agendas.[53] According to this approach, power can be exercised where no one questions their situation, because the latter's naturalness is so culturally and psychologically internalized that it cannot be conceived of as being different from what it is. In the case of identities, the "naturalness" of the categories of identity attribution could be so strongly entrenched that they are not questioned. The powerful have an interest in keeping it that way. But there are also situations of the first two faces of power, overt conflict and agenda-control, and these may sometimes be prevalent when people resist the way in which they have been socially sorted, as Bowker and Star have shown.[54] Research would have to examine power relations in some detail, drawing upon sociological and political science literature.

---

53. S. Lukes, *Power—A Radical View* (London: Macmillan, 1974).

54. G. Bowker, and S. Star, *Sorting Things Out: Classification and its Consequences* (Cambridge: MIT Press, 1999).

B. Proposition 2

The extent to which pairs of the four claims conflict varies according to the nature of the identification categories involved.

This proposition is related to the first one. The extent to which conflict over identities emerges, is actively suppressed, or is culturally and psychologically unimaginable, depends upon the importance of the relevant category or categories to the society, the economy, or the polity. Potential or actual conflicts can be about the individual's rejection of a socially or politically attributed identity, or about the social or political rejection of a claimed individual identity. These varied situations could be described, analyzed and compared in case studies. In turn, they would be informative about what matters to different individuals, groups, and whole societies in terms of the centrality or marginality of certain categories. Left-handedness, for example, is less fateful than ethnic origin or gender. But other examples and comparisons are less easy to make.

C. Proposition 3

Asserting or contesting identity claims depends on the nature of the supporting information that is invoked.

This proposition points to what counts as valid information in a society or in an administrative system. The difference between immediate impressions conveyed in interpersonal interactions, and the supposed hard "truth" of biometric information inscribed in databases invites exploration in terms of information management, deniability, and the relative prestige of scientific and other ways of knowing. It also invites us to investigate how much of what kinds of information is considered necessary—and with what tools and degrees of intrusiveness it is gathered[55]—for what kinds of identity verification, and to relate that to the importance of the various purposes for which identification is thought necessary. The legal and ethical principle of proportionality would be an important element on the normative side of this investigation.

D. Proposition 4

The movement of Table 13.1's configuration through time is shaped by changes in power, categories, and information.

This proposition draws attention to the probable fact that the means, rationales, and processes of asserting and denying identities today may not be those of tomorrow or of yesterday. Research into this would draw upon historical studies such as Torpey, as well as Caplan and Torpey,[56] but would also seek to discern

---

55. Hood's analysis of governance "tools" may be useful here. C. Hood, *The Tools of Government* (London: Macmillan, 1983); C. Hood and H. Margetts, *The Tools of Government in the Digital Age* (London: Palgrave Macmillan, 2007).

56. J. Torpey, *The Invention of the Passport: Surveillance, Citizenship, and the State* (Cambridge: Cambridge University Press, 2000); J. Caplan and J. Torpey, eds.,

trends in the variables that are likely to affect the salience and types of identity assertions, attributions and contestations in the future. The extent to which, for example, improvements in the reliability of certain kinds of information and its processing (e.g., biometrics) make it more difficult to dispute certain identities, would be a focus for investigation. Or, for example, the effect of emergent categories through history upon conceptions of the self and others is an important area for systematic investigation and comparison.

E. Proposition 5

The incidence and relationships of the four positions are shaped by the extent to which, and why, individuals, societies, and states are risk-averse and security-conscious to the point where misrepresentation of identity is considered problematical.

This proposition highlights the effect of personal, societal, and governmental pressures toward safety and security upon the arbitration of identity claims. Work on "risk society," as in Beck and in Ericson and Haggerty,[57] can contribute to research on this proposition by helping to focus on the implications of intolerance of ambiguity and the drive for certainty in interpersonal relations, in relations between citizens and states, and in relations between customers and business firms. The advent of online relationships and transactions, and their effect upon risk, risk-perception and risk-aversion, would be an important dimension that emphasizes the collection and communication of information.

Space does not permit anything like the investigation these propositions or assertions might deserve beyond broad-brush remarks; moreover, they are not the only ones that could be derived. As mentioned earlier, however, they seek to carry traditional political-science themes of power and conflict further into the investigation of the subject. They build upon the approaches and findings of others in a variety of relevant disciplines in order to shape new research questions that could be used to unearth new data to help us in understanding issues in which identity is implicated.

Documenting Individual Identity: The Development of State Practices in the Modern World (Princeton: Princeton University Press, 2001).

57. U. Beck, *Risk Society: Towards a New Modernity* (London: Sage, 1992); R. Ericson and K. Haggerty, *Policing the Risk Society* (Toronto: University of Toronto Press, 1997).

14. IDENTITY CARDS AND IDENTITY ROMANTICISM

A. MICHAEL FROOMKIN

"National ID cards" are scare words in the United States, in England, and to a degree throughout the common-law world. If the instinctively negative reaction to ID cards were only an American phenomenon, one might dismiss it as yet another example of American exceptionalism—or, perhaps, another example of the U.S. failure to learn from foreign experience. But this powerful popular distaste for government-issued ID cards is not limited to the U.S. Similar and powerful reactions are found in England, Australia, and Canada. Indeed, in 2000, one could say that only four common-law countries had adopted ID cards in peacetime: Cyprus, Hong Kong, Malaysia, and Singapore. Meanwhile, however, ID cards are a routine and often uninteresting fact of life in the democracies of the civil-law world. That difference deserves exploration. (Some might argue that ID cards are inescapable, and that even the U.S. has them although it does not admit it,[1] but this makes the difference in popular attitudes even more difficult to understand.)

This chapter suggests that the U.S. hostility to ID cards is based on a romantic vision of free movement, and that the English view is tied to a related concept of "the rights of Englishmen." I then suggest that these views distract from the real issues raised by contemporary national ID plans in the common and civil-law worlds. Today's issues, I suggest, involve a complex set of data protection issues that have little to do with romantic stories of cowboys and motorists talking back to policemen, and a great deal to do with data storage and access.

A discussion of mental iconography should not blind us to critical issues such as the regulation of the databases to which ID cards are linked. Even so, it pays to tarry on the *image* of cards themselves because, until we shift to a purely biometric system of identification, ID cards are likely to remain the most tangible and visible symbols of national identification regimes. As both an emotive and

---

1. See Joseph W. Eaton, *Card-Carrying Americans* (Totowa, NJ: Rowman & Littlefield, 1986), 2 ("on a *de facto* basis, the United States already has a national ID system."), 82–84.

political matter, how people feel about ID cards likely will play a large, perhaps even disproportionate, role in debates over fundamental national privacy policy.

I. WHY (SOME) PEOPLE CARE

Government-issued national ID cards evoke very different reactions around the world. The greatest cleavage is between common-law and civil-law countries. On the one hand, a very significant part of the population in the United States, England, and other common-law-based democracies seem instinctively frightened of ID cards. On the other hand, millions of people in democracies around the world carry ID cards every day and neither feel nor appear to be oppressed by them. To the extent that an organized opposition to ID cards coalesced in the civil-law world during the last few years, it seems based either on concerns about European federalism, or on new, reasonable concerns about possible misuse of modern databases linked to the cards. Some of the same arguments are found in the United States and especially England, but what is striking is how recent they are compared to the long-standing antipathy to ID cards.

A. In the United States

The United States has little tradition of identification documents before the twentieth century. With the important exception of racist legislation such as the Chinese Exclusion Acts, peacetime immigration to the United States did not require a passport for most of the period before World War I.[2] ID cards appear to be identified as tools of oppression in the U.S. popular imagination for three main reasons. First, the public strongly identifies ID cards with totalitarianism. Second, some religious groups, and at least one influential religious broadcaster, identify ID cards with the anti-Christ. Third, ID cards conflict in both principle and practice with the popular myth (but declining reality) of the right to move about freely. Notably absent from this list is any association with the manumission documents that might have been required of freed black slaves before the U.S. Civil War. This old precedent that affected only a small segment of a minority population seems to have no effect on current debates.

Citing Bentham's "Panopticon," Orwell's "Big Brother," and modern politics, opponents of ID cards routinely point to their association with totalitarianism. There are genuine grounds for this association, amplified by popular culture, for modern history is rich with examples of repressive regimes using ID cards as the cornerstone of programs designed to stifle dissent and oppress people. But the archetypical popular image—probably in black-and-white—is of a movie Nazi, perhaps with a big German Shepherd at his side, demanding "papers, please" in

---

2. See Martin Lloyd, *The Passport: The History Of Man's Most Traveled Document* (Thrupp, Stroud, Gloucestershire: Sutton Publishing, 2003), 115–116.

a movie-German accent. When I talk about ID cards with people, or read comments that people post online, this is surely the most often mentioned image even if no one can actually identify a movie in which it appears.[3] Indeed, the image of ID cards, and enumeration in general, as a technology of control is endemic in film and literature, as is the revolt against identification as part of a revolt against authority. Recent films such as *Gattaca* and *Enemy of the State* project a dystopian future in which identity cards or biometric-based controls are used to track and control.

Although fears of ID cards and enumeration are linked to film, or to an idealized vision of liberty, the concerns do have roots in reality. The census as a form of social control is an idea as old as the Romans—indeed it is a critical part of the founding story of Christianity, appearing in Luke 2:1, 3–5. And the census remains a privacy issue today. Although U.S. law protects the confidentiality of individual responses to the census, there are documented incidents of census data being turned over to other government departments for national security purposes. Despite numerous government denials that personal information had been released, there is now strong evidence that the Census Bureau provided the U.S. Secret Service with names and addresses of Japanese-Americans during World War II.[4] This extended beyond residence pattern and included "microdata"— individual names and addresses—at least in the Washington DC area. Similarly, the Census Bureau admits that it turned over data on residence patterns of Arab Americans to the Department of Homeland Security.[5]

Christianity, or at least some segments of the evangelical Protestant movement, is a further element that may fuel the modern U.S. antipathy to ID cards. Certain millenialist sects believe that mandatory IDs are a precursor to the second coming, or the end of times, foretold in Revelations 13:16–18. In this view, a national ID card is the next step toward the imposition of the biblical "mark of the beast" that they believe Christians will be forced to have to buy and sell during the "Last Days," and that it is therefore a religious duty to oppose them.

This view that enumeration is ungodly is as old as the Republic, and as contemporary as the Internet. George Washington feared that the first U.S.

---

3. *Stalag 17* (1953) has moments that come close ("Anybody asks for your papers, you're French laborers"). The film that probably launched the image is *The Great Escape* (1963), but neither film has the actual image that people seem to refer to. The real-life events on which *The Great Escape* was based certainly involved multiple encounters with German guards who demanded papers, although whether dogs were involved is less clear. See Alan Burgess, *The Three That Got Away*, http://www.pbs.org/wgbh/nova/greatescape/three.html.

4. J.R. Minkel, "Confirmed: The U.S. Census Bureau Gave Up Names of Japanese-Americans in WWII: Government documents show that the agency handed over names and addresses to the Secret Service," *Scientific American*, (March 30, 2007), http://www.sciam.com/article.cfm?chanID=sa003&articleID=A4F4DED6-E7F2-99DF-32E46B0ACI FDE0FE&pageNumber=1&catID=1.

5. See EPIC, Department of Homeland Security Obtained Data on Arab Americans From Census Bureau, http://www.epic.org/privacy/census/foia/default.html.

census in 1790 would "greatly" undercount the population because so many would refuse to be counted due to "religious scruples"—although President Washington noted that others would evade the census for fear "it was intended as the foundation of a tax."[6] Today, doubts about ID cards, and especially cards with biometrics, are found both in the leadership of the Christian Coalition and all over the wilder parts of the Internet. Religious movements, and especially Protestants, are organized political forces in the United States, and the opinions of the leaders of advocacy groups such as the Christian Coalition carry weight, especially within the Republican Party.

The most widespread source of objection to ID cards is that Americans believe that they have a constitutional, or even natural, right to move freely around the nation. They do and they do not, but the ID card mythos seems tied to an enduring, romantic, if legally debatable, version of personal freedom.

The popular vision of untrammeled freedom to move about may reflect an earlier era in which the state lacked the ability to control a very mobile population. That romantic vision also reflects something real about the law: as a formal matter, the right to travel has strong roots in the modern decisions of the U.S. Supreme Court. The word "travel" is not found anywhere in the Constitution. Nevertheless, the modern Supreme Court has been clear that "the 'constitutional right to travel from one State to another' is firmly embedded in our jurisprudence."[7] This right of movement is said to be a fundamental component of nationhood: "the nature of our Federal Union and our constitutional concepts of personal liberty unite to require that all citizens be free to travel throughout the length and breadth of our land uninhibited by statutes, rules, or regulations which unreasonably burden or restrict this movement."[8]

Today, the Anglo-Saxon ideal that in a free country a person should be able to move freely without having to justify himself to authorities—that police have no right to stop you without probable cause and that even when they do one has no obligation to speak to them—is more deeply ingrained in the national psyche than reflected in the Constitution. Many states have stop-and-identify laws that require citizens to identify themselves to police officers.[9] Often, however, these

---

6. George Washington to Gouverneur Morris (July 28, 1791), http://teachingamericanhistory.org/library/index.asp?document=389 Cf. Margot Anderson & Stephen E. Feinberg, *The History of the First American Census and the Constitutional Language on Censustaking: Report of a Workshop* (Feb 23, 1999), lib.stat.cmu.edu/~fienberg/DonnerReportsFinal/FirstCensus.pdf (quoting George Washington to Gouverneur Morris (July 28, 1791)).

7. *Saenz v Roe*, 526 U.S. 489, 499 (1999) (quoting *United States v Guest*, 383 U.S. 745, 757, (1966)).

8. *Ibid.*, 499 (quoting *Shapiro v Thompson*, 394 U.S. 618, 629 (1969), with approval).

9. Note, *Stop and Identify Statutes: A New Form of an Inadequate Solution to an Old Problem*, 12 RUTGERS L.J. 585 (1981); Note, *Stop-and-Identify Statutes After* Kolender v. Lawson: *Exploring the Fourth and Fifth Amendment Issues*, 69 IOWA L.REV. 1057 (1984).

statutes require that an officer have a reasonable suspicion of criminality before making an identity demand.[10]

That is fine as far as it goes—and it goes about as far as your feet will take you. When it comes to augmenting one's feet with mechanized transport the picture changes rather significantly and—the great American road movies notwith-standing—travel via mechanized transport is subject to ID-based controls that limit the right to travel.

The most prevalent and obvious control is the drivers' licenses required by all fifty states in order to operate a motor vehicle on public roads. Cars are a practical necessity for most Americans who live outside the largest urban areas, making a driver's license a practical necessity for most people. Today, the legal regulation of driving starts from the premise that driving is a "privilege" not a "right."[11] It was not always thus: fifty to one hundred years ago, "Courts repeatedly wrote of an individual's 'right to travel' by automobile and struck down regulations aimed at limiting the liberties of automobile drivers on constitutional grounds. In contrast, "Since 1950, no court has described driving an automobile as a 'right.'"[12]

Classifying the right to drive as a mere privilege has significant legal consequences. Although the government does not have a right to suspend privileges in a wholly arbitrary manner—the Equal Protection clause of the Constitution prevents that—the procedural guarantees for "rights" are entirely absent for "privileges." Similarly, the substantive requirements that attach to laws that may infringe on rights—means-ends rationality for example—are largely absent for the regulation of privileges.

A similar, but not identical, system of identification-based control applies to mechanized mass transit. In general, the official attitude remains somewhat ambiguous as regards domestic travel. The federal and state governments have tended to avoid taking the position that identification is an absolute requirement for access to planes and trains, while nonetheless promulgating rules that make it extremely difficult to travel without them. Similar ID requirements are being extended to intercity buses, and even local buses.[13] Although demands for ID as

---

10. See *Hiibel v Sixth Judicial Dist. Court of Nevada, Humboldt County*, 542 U.S. 177, 183 (2004).

11. Carl Watner, "Driver's Licenses and Vehicle Registration in Historical Perspective," in *National Identification Systems*, Carl Watner & Wendy McElroy eds., (Jefferson, NC: McFarland & Co., 2004), 109. This is true in both federal and state law: "Driving an automobile is a privilege, not a right, according to the prevailing laws of every jurisdiction of the United States." Roger I. Roots, *The Orphaned Right: the Right to Travel by Automobile, 1890–1950*, 30 Okla. City U. L. REV. 245, 245 (2005).

12. Roger I. Roots, *The Orphaned Right: The Right to Travel by Automobile, 1890–1950*, 30 Okla. City U. L. REV. 245, 245, 267 (2005).

13. See PapersPlease.org, *United States v Deborah Davis*, http://www.papersplease. org/davis/facts.html (recounting demands by Denver police for ID from passengers on a

a condition of boarding mass transit are increasingly common, and do not seem to be causing much in the way of resistance, their legal status remains debated.

The collision between the romantic vision of freedom of movement and the legal regulation of it took place in a recent Supreme Court case involving, of all things, a motionless cowboy. The cowboy, surely the embodiment of the romantic ideal of the wandering American, was Dudley Hiibel, and his case was *Hiibel v. Sixth Judicial Dist. Court of Nevada, Humboldt County.*[14] His legal team described him as "a 59-year-old cowboy who owns a small ranch outside of Winnemucca, Nevada. He lives a simple life, but he's his own man." In this account, Hiibel "was standing around minding his own business when all of a sudden, a policeman pulled up and demanded that Dudley produce his ID. Dudley, having done nothing wrong, declined." This refusal led to his arrested on charges of "failure to cooperate" for refusing to show ID on demand.[15]

The Supreme Court, however, noted that the arresting officer was responding to a phone tip reporting an assault, and that while Hiibel was not in his truck, there was a young woman inside it; skid marks in the gravel caused the officer to believe it had come to a sudden stop. Hiibel appeared drunk. Asked repeatedly for ID, Hiibel repeatedly refused to provide it, then "began to taunt the officer by placing his hands behind his back and telling the officer to arrest him and take him to jail." In the end he got his wish.[16]

From these facts, the Court concluded that "Here there is no question that the initial stop was based on reasonable suspicion"[17]—in other words, that its ruling would not address the more general case of suspicionless stops and requests for identification.[18] Then, in language that is already being quoted in other decisions,[19] the Supreme Court characterized the government's interest in identifying Hiibel and others subjected to valid investigative stops as one of great importance.[20]

Having defined the issue of identifying suspects in valid investigative situations as critical to police safety, it was short work to brush away contrary dicta and even to sweep aside Justice White's concurring statement in the leading investigative stop decision. Justice White had suggested that a person detained

---

municipal bus route that crosses the Denver Federal Center). Charges in the case were later dropped. See Victory, http://www.papersplease.org/davis/.

14. 542 U.S. 177 (2004).

15. PapersPlease.org, Meet Dudley Hiibel, http://www.papersplease.org/hiibel/. For the record, I did some very minor legal kibitzing with various people involved in defending Mr. Hiibel.

16. *Hiibel,* 542 U.S. at 180-181.

17. *Ibid.,* 184.

18. The earlier case of *Brown v Texas,* 443 U.S. 47 (1979) suggested that such a rule would be unconstitutional.

19. E.g., *City of Topeka v Grabauskas,* 33 Kan.App.2d 210, 99 P.3d 1125 (Kan.App.,2004); *State v Aloi,* 280 Conn. 824, 838, 911 A.2d 1086, 1095 (Conn. 2007).

20. *Hiibel,* 542 U.S. at 186.

for an investigatory stop can be questioned but is "not obliged to answer, answers may not be compelled, and refusal to answer furnishes no basis for an arrest."[21] In *Hiibel* the Supreme Court held that nothing in the Fourth or Fifth Amendments prevents a state from requiring "a suspect to disclose his name in the course of" a justified investigative ("*Terry*") stop.[22]

This holding had three theoretically important limits, although their practical significance is more debatable. First, the Court expressly noted that it did not wish to open the door to bootstrapping arrests: "an officer may not arrest a suspect for failure to identify himself if the request for identification is not reasonably related to the circumstances justifying the stop."[23]

Second, in rejecting Hiibel's claim that the sheriff's demand for identification was an attempt to extract a form of coerced self-incrimination barred by the Fifth Amendment, the Court did not hold that such claims must always fail. They failed in Hiibel's case because there was no way that the information could actually have incriminated him in the circumstances.[24] The Court thus left open the door to voiding application of an ID law if the suspect was, for example, fleeing from an arrest warrant.[25]

Third, and perhaps most importantly for our purposes, the Court carefully sidestepped the ID card issue that gave the Hiibel case so much of its public resonance. It chose to read the Nevada statute as being satisfied with *oral* self-identification, and thus read the demand for an identification document right out of the statute:

> [T]he Nevada Supreme Court has interpreted [the Nevada statute] to require only that a suspect disclose his name . . . As we understand it, the statute does not require a suspect to give the officer a driver's license or any other document. Provided that the suspect either states his name or communicates it to the officer by other means—a choice, we assume, that the suspect may make—the statute is satisfied and no violation occurs.[26]

This decision to avoid ruling on whether a demand for an identification document would be constitutional is a very significant limitation in the holding, although one that may be lost on some of the lower courts.[27]

Whether the U.S. Constitution places limits on official demands for ID is especially salient in light of legislative initiatives that seek to standardize

21. *Terry v Ohio*, 392 U.S. 1, 34 (1968) (White, J. concurring).
22. See *Hiibel*, 542 U.S. at 187.
23. *Ibid.*, 188.
24. *Ibid.*, 190.
25. *Ibid.*, 191.
26. *Ibid.*, 186.
27. See *State v Mattson*, 2006 WL 2474237 * 6 (Minn.App.,2006) (summarizing *Hiibel* as "interpreting officer's request for identification as a request to produce a driver's license or some other form of written identification").

government-issued ID cards and expand their use. Most notably, the REAL ID Act[28] of 2005 imposed a series of requirements on state issuance of driver's licenses, seeking to exploit the fault line between the easy-to-regulate privilege of holding a driver's license and the reality that this license has become a practical necessity for most people in the United States. If ever fully implemented (opposition is growing), all federal agencies will have to require state-issued credentials that comply with technical standards issued by the Department of Homeland Security. Although it will not be federally issued, the new federally defined ID card will become a practical necessity for anyone wishing to "travel on an airplane, open a bank account, collect Social Security payments, or take advantage of nearly any government service."[29]

The REAL ID Act defines how states must issue drivers' licenses and what information licenses must contain. The card will have to include physical security features as to be defined by the Department of Homeland Security designed to prevent tampering, counterfeiting, or duplication. The act also requires that states verify the applicant's documentation and keep copies. States may not accept any foreign document other than an official passport. The state also must verify the applicant's name, primary address, date of birth, and Social Security number, plus check the number's correctness and uniqueness. The license must contain the holder's address, full legal name, date of birth, gender, signature, driver's license number, and a digital photo of the person's face.[30]

Although promoted as a way to protect against terrorism, the act's most likely effect will be to make it more difficult for undocumented aliens to forge credentials for employment. The REAL ID Act specifies that states may only issue drivers' licenses to citizens, permanent residents and the holders of particular types of visas.[31] Opposition to the REAL ID Act was slow to build, but has recently become something of a bandwagon,[32] in part because states are discovering how expensive compliance may be. Several states have enacted legislation blocking REAL ID compliance and have called for the federal law to be amended. However, a number of states, including California, have already made plans to comply with REAL ID.

---

28. REAL ID Act of 2005, Pub. L. No. 109-113, div. B, 119 Stat. 231, 302. Title II of REAL ID, "Improved Security for Drivers' Licenses and Personal Identification Cards," codified in scattered sections of 8 and 49 U.S.C.A.

29. Declan McCullagh, *FAQ: How REAL ID will affect you*, C|Net News.com, http://news.com/FAQ+How+Real+ID+will+affect+you/2100-1028_3-5697111. html May 6, 2005.

30. REAL ID §§202(b), 202(c), 202(d).

31. REAL ID, §202(c)(2). The list of visa classes that qualify for a driver's license is noticeably shorter than the list of visa types that permit long-term residence and even employment in the United States. This is likely to cause serious problems.

32. See http://www.privacycoalition.org/stoprealid/; http://www.realnightmare.org/news/105/.

Whether or not REAL ID's opponents succeed in their attempt to change the statute, the underlying legal regime will remain one in which the constitutional protections relevant to ID cards are uncertain at best. The *Hiibel* case exemplifies the confused state of ID card law and practice in the United States: in theory, the United States runs a two-track system regulating the demand for identification, with car licensing as the exception to the background rule of romantic freedom of movement. But in practice the two tracks are merging into something unromantic. Although the legal system exhibits some queasiness at the margins, the de facto rules are that one must present ID to travel on most long-distance public transport, and that the issue is joined even for shorter-range common carriers. Automobile travel is heavily regulated and requires ID. Anyone stopped for the smallest offense—a broken taillight, a rolling stop—is immediately subject to a *Terry* stop, a valid investigation which routinely includes a demand for a driver's license.[33] After *Hiibel* a similar regime extends to pedestrians, and even those stationary in public: although it is unclear whether the police may demand physical ID, it is now clear that whenever the police can make out the elements of reasonable suspicion of even the most minor criminal activity, they may demand that a person identify themselves. In practice that is going to mean a driver's license far more often than anything else. Driving is only a privilege; walking is still a right, but one easily burdened in practice—dare to complain that police have no right to stop you, and a charge of resisting arrest is likely to figure in your future. Baseless charges can doubtless be beaten often, but it takes time, money, and effort—and leaves a data trail.

B. In Britain

Unsurprisingly, there are important similarities between U.S. and British attitudes to ID cards. But there are also differences. "The introduction of universal identity card systems has only been politically achievable in Britain in times of universal mobilization for war. In peacetime, partial systems gave the appearance of liberty—and therefore distance from continental models."[34] Thus, the British accepted ID cards during WWI, but abandoned them shortly after it ended.[35] After WWII, the government initially sought to keep a national ID system in place, citing first the needs of the rationing system and its utility to the national health system. The legality of the holdover from WWII came to a head in 1951, in *Willcock v. Muckle*,[36] the *Hiibel* case of its time and place, although it involved

---

33. A small number of states allow the license to be presented at a police station after the fact; most require that the driver be carrying it.

34. Jon Agar, *Modern Horrors: British Identity and Identity Cards* in *Documenting Individual Identity* (Jane Caplan & John Torpey eds.) (Princeton, NJ: Princeton University Press, 2001), 101, 102.

35. *Ibid.*, 106.

36. [1951] 2 KB 844, [1951] 2 All ER 367, 49 LGR 584, 115 JP 431, [1951] WN 381.

no cowboy but instead one Clarence Henry Willcock playing the part of the quintessential British motorist.

Mr. Willcock refused to show his national registration identity card when demanded to do so by a constable. Offered instead a citation requiring him to produce his identity card at any police station, Mr. Willcock replied, "I will not produce it at any police station and I will not accept the form."[37] (Indeed, legend has it that Mr. Willcock told the constable that "I am a Liberal and I am against this sort of thing."[38]) This stand on principle resulted in prosecution, conviction, a fine of ten shillings, and in due course an appeal to a specially constituted tribunal of seven judges of the King's Bench Division.

The court agreed with government on the primary issue, holding that emergency wartime legislation creating the ID system was still in force. But having announced that judgment, Lord Goddard went to say that courts nevertheless should not convict Britons for failing to produce their identity cards on demand: "To use Acts of Parliament, passed for particular purposes during war, in times when the war is past, except that technically a state of war exists, tends to turn law-abiding subjects into lawbreakers, which is a most undesirable state of affairs."[39] On this point, even Devlin, J, *dubitante* though he might have been on the continuance of the emergency powers acts, noted, "that I entirely agree . . . I think it would be very unfortunate if the public were to receive the impression that the continuance of the state of emergency had become a sort of statutory fiction which was used as a means of prolonging legislation initiated in different circumstances and for different purposes."[40]

Faced with this judicial disapproval, the British government abandoned the national registration system shortly after the court's decision.[41] Thanks to *Willcock v. Muckle*, the idea that the rights of Englishmen included the freedom to move about without having to carry identification, or to justify oneself to authority, was reaffirmed in England, and would survive for another half-century. (A popular version of it still survives in the idea of a right to ramble.)

The beginning of what now appears to be the end came in 2004, when the British government, citing the need to fight benefits fraud and combat terrorism, proposed legislation to bring in peacetime ID cards. At one point, British opinion seemed strongly in favor of the government's plan for a mandatory ID card, with one poll showing support as high as 80% in 2004,[42] but public support has since fallen. The British government is not only pressing on with its

37. *Ibid.*
38. See http://www.publications.parliament.uk/pa/cm200506/cmhansrd/vo051018/debtext/51018-21.htm (18 Oct 2005: Column 759).
39. *Willcock v Muckle*, [1951] 2 KB 844.
40. *Ibid.*, (opinion of Devlin, J.).
41. Agar, *Modern Horrors*, 110 (n. 34).
42. http://www.mori.com/polls/2004/detica-top.shtml.

plans for a domestic ID card, but used its presidency of the EU to push for a European-wide biometric ID card with fingerprints as well as photographs,[43] although the current EU policy appears to be to standardize for interoperability rather than to issue a centralized card.[44]

Under the new UK legislation, anyone applying for a British passport will need to have fingerprints and eye or facial scans added to a National Identity register. The first ID cards are scheduled to become available in 2009. The act remains controversial and has sparked an organized opposition movement. The creation of a massive new identity database sparked wide opposition, as did concerns over the weak legal and technical safeguards against misuse and unauthorized access. Opponents also warned of the unreliability of biometrics. Further, the shifting and vagueness of the government statements about the purpose(s) that the ID card scheme would serve led to justified fears of excessive data collection and function creep.

Academic commentary was and remains negative, notably in a series of reports from the LSE. Having seen its thoroughgoing 2005 critique[45] largely ignored, in 2007 the LSE described the government plan as "explicitly designed to maximize the surveillance capabilities of identity cards in ways that other countries find unacceptable."[46] Nevertheless, the Labor party has pledged to make mandatory ID cards part of its platform in the next general election, meaning that if it achieves another majority it will introduce legislation to make biometric ID cards compulsory for all UK citizens over sixteen, but will not require that citizens carry the card at all times.[47]

Similarly vociferous debates about mandatory ID cards are ongoing in other common-law based democracies, including Australia[48] and Canada.

---

43. John Lettice, "UK EU presidency aims for Europe-wide biometric ID card," *The Register*, July 13, 2005, http://www.theregister.co.uk/2005/07/13/uk_eu_id_proposal/. See also http://www.statewatch.org/news/2005/jul/11092-05.pdf (text of UK proposal).

44. European Union, eGovernment in the European Union: Frequently Asked Questions, (Nov. 25, 2005), http://europa.eu/rapid/pressReleasesAction.do?reference=MEMO/05/446 &format=HTML&aged=0&language=EN&guiLanguage=en.

45. See THE IDENTITY PROJECT: AN ASSESSMENT OF THE UK IDENTITY CARDS BILL AND ITS IMPLICATIONS (June 27, 2005), http://is2.lse.ac.uk/IDcard/identityreport.pdf; The Identity Project: ID Cards - UK's high tech scheme is high risk (June 27, 2005), http://www.lse.ac.uk/collections/pressAndInformationOffice/newsAndEvents/archives/2005/IDCard_FinalReport.htm.

46. London School of Economics and Political Science Identity Project, Submission to the House of Commons Home Affairs Committee inquiry into "A surveillance society?" (24 April 2007), http://identityproject.lse.ac.uk/#Home_Affairs_Committee. [hereinafter LSE Testimony].

47. BBC, Q&A: Identity card plans (Dec. 19, 2006), http://news.bbc.co.uk/1/hi/uk_politics/3127696.stm.

48. http://www.privacyinternational.org/article.shtml?cmd[347]=x-347-61882&als[theme]=National%20ID%20Cards&headline=On%20Campaigns%20of%20

C. Civil-Law Western European Democracies

Although the diversity of the European experience makes generalizations treacherous, there is no question that much of continental Europe has a long experience of ID cards and similar social registration and control documents or tokens. Perhaps because familiarity breeds content, ID cards have not widely been seen as a significant civil liberties issue, at least not until recently.

The history of identification documents in Europe would require a book.[49] Domestic identity cards as we now know them are a modern invention—nineteenth- and twentieth-century—if only because their use requires fairly general literacy not least among front-line officialdom. France required internal passports for travel from town to town from well before the French Revolution.[50] Before1800, both France (*carte d'identité*) and Russia (internal passport) had the most elaborate internal document-based travel controls in Europe; but that statement, while true, is also slightly misleading. France and Russia were among the largest states in Europe; for smaller states a partly equivalent regulation of travel could be achieved by border control. For example, historically both Germany and Italy were divided into so many different states that the role of an internal document in France was to some extent played by *laissez-passer*, passports, and various documents or insignia of authorization. Other European countries evolved their own means of controlling movement; some also used identifying documents or badges to signal the rights and stations of members of the domestic population.[51]

Leaving aside their use as a means of controlling domestic travel in Russia and France, until World War I passports were primarily documents issued to nobles and other VIPs. Their most common use was to signal to local customs officials, and not least the local constabulary, that the holder was a person of importance, and that the sending government would appreciate the holder's being given kid-glove treatment by the receiving one. As travel became more common in the eighteenth and nineteenth centuries, ordinary people crossed many borders without showing identification documents for their persons—although the treatment of their goods was subject to customs duties and regulations.

Perhaps because of this long history, in contrast to the passions that ID card proposals generate in the common-law world, in a significant fraction of the civil-law western European democracies today ID cards are routine and boring.[52]

Opposition%20to%20ID%20Card%20Schemes.

49. For a superb effort at telling many of the stories that would form the basis for any generalization, see Agar, *Documenting Individual Identity* (n. 34).

50. See Martin Lloyd, *The Passport: the History of Man's Most Traveled Document*, supra note 2; John Torpey, *The Invention of the Passport: Surveillance, Citizenship and the State* (New York: Cambridge University Press, 2000), 21–56.

51. Agar, *Documenting Individual Identity* (n. 34).

52. In France, for example, about 90% of the population carries a government-issued ID card. http://news.bbc.co.uk/1/hi/uk_politics/3127696.stm. ID cards are also required

ID cards are compulsory in many European countries, although few require that they be carried at all times. ID cards are prevalent even when not legally required in most of the rest of the continental democracies. As a result, when I've discussed this issue with civil liberties-minded European colleagues, they almost inevitably struggle to understand why anyone would care about something they carry all the time and that in their view has never hurt anyone, and probably see it as yet another sign of American, or Anglo-Saxon, mania.

That ID cards were used in very harmful ways in Nazi Germany, in occupied areas, and in Vichy France, is not doubted. Nor is their use as control documents in Eastern European, notably East Germany and the Soviet Union. It may be that western Europeans, however, tend to see these pathological uses of identification systems as just one of many results of a deeper and broader political or social pathology. Where common-law critics of ID card regimes tend to see in the cards the creation of a regime that at the very least enables totalitarians if it does not actually tempt them into being, a generation that has carried IDs with no great discernable ill effects sees them as being little more threatening than other things that totalitarians, like others, might find useful—such as cars, currency, or telephones. Although I have not seen it stated in quite these terms, one gets the sense the western European answer to common-law paranoia about ID card systems would be that if a regime is using ID cards to oppress its people, the problems are much more fundamental than the existence of the cards—and their absence will not pose much of an obstacle to oppression anyway. Plus, they would note, even those civil-law countries that claim not to have ID cards do in fact have them in practice, whether they are called driver's licenses, cheque cards, social security numbers, or national health numbers. And the sky has not fallen.

If much of Europe has been sanguine about their domestic ID regimes, that calm has been perturbed by two recent developments: European cooperation and changes in computer technology.

In what may be reflexive nationalism or may be a reasonable concern about personal information leaking out to places where it is less subject to democratic control, a number of groups have begun to express concern about plans to harmonize European identity documents.[53] The EU has announced plans to standardize national identification regimes, leading many to speculate that the EU plans to have an ID card of its own, just as there is now a common European passport. In fact, as noted above, to date the European plan (not unlike the current European passport

---

or ubiquitous in Belgium, Germany, the Netherlands, and Portugal: http://news.bbc.co.uk/1/hi/uk_politics/2078604.stm#chart. For a survey of the latest round of electronic ID card deployments, involving millions of cards in ten European countries, see Smart Cards in Europe: eID Avalanche, http://blog.negonation.com/en/smart-cards-in-europe-eid-avalanche/.

53. See, e.g., French campaign against biometric ID card, http://www.edri.org/edrigram/number3.11/biometrics.

system) is to leave member states as the front line bodies and allow a degree of local variation, while harmonizing the collection and display of key information—which will include biometrics going beyond a photograph. In addition to standardizing their data collection and display, member states will be committed to a trans-European system of data sharing, at least at police request. There may not be a centralized European repository of information about Europeans, but there will, it seems, be a reasonably well-ordered distributed database organized to allow police and other officials to access data held beyond their borders.

This concern is far from universal. Belgium, Germany, and Austria are already deploying biometric smart cards.[54] But as the European project gathers steam it has spurred resistance, particularly in the countries that do not at present have mandatory cards. In France, for example, six large human rights organizations launched a campaign in 2005 against the proposed French mandatory biometric ID card, but the French government continued with its plans for a mandatory ID card with a contactless chip containing address and civil status, plus a photograph and fingerprints. Similar data would be held in nationally centralized databases.

II. NEW CHALLENGES

Whatever their merits in the past, there is good reason to believe that neither a focus on "the rights of Englishmen" nor on the "freedom to travel" will suffice to meet the challenges presented by twenty-first-century ID card regimes. Attention to a much broader set of issues is now required in order to preserve not just the freedom of movement, and privacy more generally, but perhaps also those civil liberties that could be threatened by pervasive surveillance and record-keeping, including freedom of association, transactional freedoms, and various forms of dissent and whistle-blowing. Among the issues which urgently need attention are: (1) the regulation—if any—of both public and private databases to which the card is linked or to which it serves as a gateway; (2) the terms on which ID cards will be available; and (3) the construction of the legal regime that will define the citizen's rights and duties regarding the cards themselves once they are in circulation. The database has received the lion's share of attention, but all three are worthy of attention.

A. ID Cards and Data Protection
ID cards stand poised to become the front end of a new regime of observation and perhaps control.[55] Even when they carry a chip, the cards currently on the

---

54. http://europa.eu/rapid/pressReleasesAction.do?reference=MEMO/05/446& format=HTML&aged=0&language=EN&guiLanguage=en.

55. See A. Michael Froomkin, *The Death of Privacy?*, 52 STAN L. REV. 1461 (2000), available at www.law.miami.edu/~froomkin/articles/privacy-deathof.pdf.

drawing board only carry relatively small amount of data, but they serve as a connection to databases of unlimited size and detail. In both the United States and the United Kingdom, much remains unclear about how the governments will use the new cards, and especially the higher-quality databases that the card-creation exercise will produce. Ironically, the debate is more advanced in the United Kingdom, even though the need is even more acute in the United States because it has so little data protection legislation.

This is not the place to recapitulate the debate over the need for data protection legislation, nor of the merits and demerits of current implementations. But it is important to note that each ratchet up in an ID card regime—the introduction of a non-mandatory ID card scheme, improvements to authentication, the transition from an optional regime to a mandatory one, or the inclusion of multiple biometric identifiers—increases the need for attention to how the data collected at the time the card is created will be stored and accessed. Similarly, as ID cards become ubiquitous, a de facto necessity even when not required de jure, the card becomes the visible instantiation of a large, otherwise unseen, set of databases. If each use of the card also creates a data trail, the resulting profile becomes an ongoing temptation to both ordinary and predictive profiling.

In the United States we have already seen a disturbing tendency toward the use of "no-fly lists," "terrorist watch lists," and other secret government databases that restrict the freedom of persons who have not been charged with a crime. Some of the people caught in these lists are intended targets; others are accidental victims whose names resemble someone on the list. At present the legal system provides almost no redress for those who find their lives limited by being listed, however erroneously. And here we see the continuing attraction of the old-fashioned approach: at least until governments have a biometric database for the whole population and can do contactless identification, a centrally managed regime such as the no-fly list functions only when the rules require that IDs be tendered. The romantic version of free movement provided an acceptable formula for resistance to these almost standardless exercises of government power. As the romantic story becomes less relevant, some other autonomy-protecting principle must replace it to maintain a balance.

ID card proponents suggest that the balance is built into the system. They offer a counter-narrative: secure cards with good authentication will make accidental inclusion in watch lists less likely. With strong ID cards, the only people on these lists will be the ones that the government means to put there. Although not without its attractions, that account fails to give due consideration to the rights of the people whom the government means to target. If we are going to have ID cards, the whole relationship between a citizen and the government's use of personal data needs, especially in countries without strong data protection rules, to be brought within the reach of judicial review and due process. To do that, however, requires that we define who holds what rights, and that in turn will require a very hard-nosed, quite unromantic, conversation.

B. Issuance and Nature of the Card

The terms on which ID cards will be issued remain controversial. Much turns on who will be entitled to have one, what it will cost, who will pay for it, how secure it will be, what information citizens will be required to produce before they will be issued one, how much of that information will be inscribed on the card (and whether it will include biometrics), what sort of security the card will have, and, finally, who will be able to read from or write to the card.

Who is entitled to an ID is far from obvious, and shapes the social contexts in which IDs can be required. Including every tourist is expensive and difficult, especially if they lack documentation comparable to that required of locals. Excluding anyone—children, tourists, residents without work permits, refugees—means that systems that ordinarily require an ID must have a built-in override. Routine overrides make systems less secure. For example, an ID system will be of even less value as a way of preventing suspected terrorists from boarding airplanes if it is routine to let foreign nationals board with passports instead. Yet attempting to include everyone becomes expensive and probably impractical.

Mandatory systems, whether required by law or practice, tend to be expensive. Many state Department of Motor Vehicles oppose the United States' REAL ID because they see the program as an unfunded federal mandate—the feds make the rules, the states pay the costs. Similarly, the UK debate has been marked by a series of increasingly large estimates as to what the new IDs would cost— a burden that will fall first on passport applicants and later on everyone wanting an ID. ID cards are touted, plausibly, as a way to reduce the Chicago species of vote fraud ("vote early, vote often") although it is unclear how frequently double voting actually occurs. But if IDs are expensive and are required to exercise the franchise, they threaten to operate as a form of poll tax. Twenty-four U.S. states now require voters to show identification prior to voting. Seven of these states require a photo ID. Many of these statutes are being challenged in ongoing litigation.

More secure ID cards tend to be more expensive. Some security techniques also reduce transparency, although not all. The more secure the card, the more reasonable it will be for people to rely on it in a large variety of transactions, and the more damaging the results of identity theft if the card is counterfeited or cracked. Proper use of biometric data can enhance security by making identity theft more difficult, but it also raises more hackles and creates potential problems of its own. If the biometric data is stored centrally, that data becomes a target of its own. Using particular biometrics, especially DNA, may raise other sensitivities should it turn out that the DNA information has other uses as well.

C. Legal Regime Defining Citizens' Relationship to the Card

In the United States, almost no attention has yet been paid to the subtle but emotive issue of whether citizens will be required to carry the card, display it on demand, or even surrender it at times. Linking REAL ID to drivers licenses—a necessity for most of the adult population outside a few major cities—disguised the importance of this question. Messrs. Wilcock and Hiibel both thought they were defending an important point of principle, the right to tell a police officer to stuff it. Both Wilcock and Hiibel found this point of principleimportant enough to go to court; Wilcock vindicated it in front of a special seven-judge division of the Kings Bench. Hiibel fought it to the Supreme Court—where he lost narrowly, but in terms that presage the end of the romantic ideal. Moving to a must-carry or must-identify regime surrenders this principle and works a psychological change in the nature of a citizen's interactions with law enforcement and perhaps other state functionaries. How great a change this works is very hard to measure.

On the one hand, a demand for "papers please" is allowed in many European democracies. The harm, if there is one, does not seem to have run deep into society—the arts flourish, elections are held regularly, and the trains are occasionally late. Although one could attempt to establish the extent to which a French citizen's rights as a criminal defendant or her remedies for police misconduct are of a piece with the authority relationship established by the police's ability to demand identification, this seems an ultimately unrewarding project. The real issues are likely to be elsewhere.

On the other hand, polities differ. A more productive line of investigation might seek to correlate attitudes to authority with ID card must-carry/must-display rules. It could be, for example, that ID cards present a greater problem in societies with a greater tendency towards compliance with state authority. In these more rule-following societies there may be a greater need to have a socially sanctioned method for refusing to comply with unreasonable police requests. Certainly the *Hiibel* rule—that police can only demand that a person identify him or herself when there is some reasonable suspicion warranting an investigation—will in practice prove to be a very weak limitation on law enforcement. There is certainly ample evidence from the way that United States law enforcement approaches traffic stops that police officers will do whatever they can to game any system of rules in order to maximize their discretion to stop and question people.[56]

A related issue is the extent to which the government can condition the use of the card—who owns it, and what process is due before it is taken or its usage is burdened. This question implicates the entire data retention and access regime associated with the ID card, because the most likely "burden" will be to put some sort of annotation—setting the "no fly bit" for example—into some dossier associated with the card.

Even a less-than-ubiquitous card that strongly verifies identity will have great attraction for many private-sector applications, ranging from fraud protection to background checks to age and status verification. Whether private uses should

---

56. For a frank exposition of the police officer's view that almost anyone driving a car can be stopped, see Dale C. Carson & Wes Denham, *Arrest-Proof Yourself* (Chicago, IL: Chicago Review Press, 2007): "[T]here are thousands of mobile Easter eggs rolling down the roads." *Id.* at 235.

be regulated, and if so how, falls under general data protection law in Europe. In the United States, however, the issue of private use, in databases and elsewhere, has been all but absent in debates over REAL ID and other proposals. As one great criticism of the United States' social security card is that it was sold as for public use only but gradually became a de facto national identification number, one might have expected more on this subject. I have argued that in the United States, private uses of a public card could be conditioned on adherence to fair information practices,[57] but this counter-intuitive idea that an ID card could in any way be privacy-enhancing has not met with many takers.

III. CONCLUSION

As of 2000, only four common-law countries had recognized, centralized peacetime national ID card regimes. The picture is certain to be quite different by 2010. Driven in part by fears of terrorism, government initiatives in the United Kingdom, United States (subject to possible repeal of REAL ID), Australia, and other countries are moving forward with plans to introduce various forms of mandatory or nearly mandatory domestic civilian national identity documents. The move from patchwork systems to standardized or even centralized ID card regimes has not been without controversy. That this debate has too often relied on old bogeymen is unsurprising because those images—Germans, guns, dogs, trains—resonate with the public. But maximizing the changes of a set of rules emerging that maximize the benefits and protect against some the real—and often new—dangers requires that we focus the debate on the issues that really matter: the legal rules that will define how the card is used, and the legal rules that will regulate the databases to which the card is linked. Where the old narrative was the plucky citizen-hero standing up for his rights, the new narrative may be the puzzled citizen trapped in the coils of bureaucracy. Great transparency and the careful definition and assignment of a sufficiently broad bundle of rights need to be designed into an ID card regime from the start. This may be especially important in countries such as the United States that do not have background data protection rules on which to fall back on, but if ID cards become the key—perhaps literally—to full participation in economic and political life, not to mention part of an internal travel control system that French Kings and Russian Tsars would have envied, a healthy dose of due process and judicial review will be called for as well. The U.S. experience with the "no fly list" does not bode well in this regard.

ID cards do in fact pose real threats to privacy and freedom, threats that need to be defused before it could be safe to deploy them, especially in countries without

---

57. A. Michael Froomkin, *Creating a Viral Federal Privacy Standard*, 48 B.C.L. REV. 55 (2007), available at http://law.tm/docs/virtial-privacy-standard.pdf.

strong data protection rules, but these threats are both larger and more complex than those contemplated by the romantic visions. It is always suspect to suggest that the grass may be greener elsewhere, but one cannot help but wonder whether the European twentieth-century desensitization to ID cards—the absence of romanticism coupled with the recognition that data protection rules are necessary—might not put much of Europe in a better position to have a rational debate about the ID card issues that matter most.

The romantic accounts have value, but there is good reason to question whether they form an adequate lens through which to view the challenges posed by twenty-first-century ID card regimes. Without the shield provided by the romantic vision, those of us in the common-law world—and especially those of us outside the umbrella of European-style data protection regimes—urgently need to evolve and share not just new arguments, but new images to replace, or at least supplement, that black-and-white image of a guard with a German Shepherd on a train.

15. WHAT'S IN A NAME?

Who Benefits from the Publication Ban in Sexual Assault Trials?*

JANE DOE

I. INTRODUCTION

According to Canadian law,[1] a publication ban (also referred to as a media ban) is granted when a court official applies on a raped woman's behalf. The ban prohibits, under the threat of criminal sanction, the public use of the woman's name, likeness, or any other identifying information. If not stipulated otherwise, the pseudonym most often assigned to her is "Jane Doe."

I am a Jane Doe. I have lived with that alias and the relative anonymity it grants me since 1986. In this essay, I will investigate whether the publication ban does in fact protect the privacy of sexually assaulted women, or instead keep the crime of sexual assault private and hidden. To accomplish this, I will address the gendered nature of anonymity.

The qualitative research that I conducted was designed to elicit personal accounts that centre on the experiences of women who have been sexually assaulted and who either chose or rejected the publication ban. Through interviews with women who work in agencies that provide counseling and support to women who have been sexually assaulted, I will reflect on the dominant thinking on publication bans from the Violence Against Women (VAW) sector. Canadian case histories and transcripts further inform my content. Finally, I will draw on my own personal experience and reasoning for "staying Jane."

---

* Sections of this paper are taken from Jane Doe, *The Story of Jane Doe: A Book About Rape* (Toronto: Random House, 2007).

1. Section 486.4 of the Canadian Criminal Code is specific to publication bans in sexual assault trials and is mandatory.

A. Context and Background

Pursuant to the *Canadian Criminal Code*, section 486.4(1)(a)(i), it is stated that,

> Subject to subsection (2), the presiding judge or justice may make an order directing that any information that could identify the complainant or a witness shall not be published in any document or broadcast in any way, in proceedings in respect of . . . an offence under section . . . 271,272, 273 . . . [2]

Literature regarding the case indicates that the publication ban was enacted to

> foster complaints by victims of sexual assault by protecting them from the trauma of widespread publication resulting in embarrassment and humiliation. Encouraging victims to come forward and complain facilitates the prosecution and conviction of those guilty of sexual offences. It's ultimate objective is to favour the suppression of crime and to improve the administration of justice.[3]

But the ban and its intent were soon challenged A newspaper publisher, who appeared at a rape trial in 1986, opposed the application of the publication ban on the basis that it violated the right to freedom of the press, guaranteed by s. 2(b) of the *Canadian Charter of Rights and Freedoms*. The publisher argued that the ban denied the accused a public trial by preventing others who may have been previously falsely accused by the woman involved from coming forward. The presiding judge decided against Canadian Newspapers, stating that, although the ban did encroach on the right to freedom of the press, it is a *reasonable limitation* on that right and he subsequently issued the ban.

An appeal was heard at the Supreme Court for this case. In its decision, the court held that

> Arguments based on the possibility that publication of the complainants name in a particular case might lead to other person's coming forward who had previously been falsely accused by the same complainant had no relevance to the freedom of the press issue. As regards the accused's right to a public hearing, the mandatory ban on publication provided for in s. 442(3) does not prevent the public or the press from attending trial proceedings. Therefore [the publication ban] does not in any way infringe the accused's right to a public hearing.[4]

The Women's Legal Education Action Fund (LEAF) and a coalition of VAW community agencies intervened to reject the "spurious false allegation defense" put forth by the publisher. In addition, these groups rejected the court ruling that the ban was a mandatory right that grants the women involved control over

---

2. Criminal Code R.S.C. 1985 c. C-46.

3. *Canadian Newspapers Co. v Canada (Attorney General)* [1988] 2 S.C.R. 122.

4. *Canadian Newspapers* (n. 3).

whether their name is used or not, as this control appears to be transferred to the presiding judge (who did not comment on this matter in this ruling).[5]

Feminist activists, researchers, and scholars have examined rape and its significance regarding women's equality, agency, and choice for decades.[6] Critiques of the legislation and policies that govern the crime of sexual assault are certainly familiar with the arguments. In fact, recent studies have illustrated the deleterious effect of certain sexual assault legislation on female equality rights as protectionist[7] and even promoting harm.[8] There has been little focus, however, on the influence of the publication ban on the lives of women.

This is not to suggest that it has been ignored. In her case comment *Canadian Newspapers Co. v. Canada*, Christine Boyle[9] praises the Supreme Court for upholding the publication ban and the protection it offers raped women. She laments that the Court's reasoning did not focus on the rights of women to freedom of expression, liberty, and security by enshrining C486 under equality-seeking sections of the Charter. Instead, the Supreme Court upheld "the complainant initiated mandatory ban as the minimal *interference with freedom of the press* necessary to facilitate the prosecution and conviction of those guilty of sexual offences" (emphasis added).[10] In her conclusion, Boyle reminds us that "the contrast between the privileged

---

5. Women's Legal Education Action Fund (LEAF). (2000). *Sexual Assault Law, 2000*, http://www.leaf.ca (accessed September 30, 2007).

6. Christine Boyle, *Sexual Assault* (Toronto: Carswell, 1984); Susan Browmiller, *Against Our Will: Men, Women, and Rape* (Toronto: Bantam Books, 1975); Catherine Mackinnon, *Only Words*. (Cambridge, MA: Harvard University Press, 1993); Elizabeth Sheehy, "Advancing Social Inclusion: The Implications for Criminal Law and Policy," *Canadian Journal of Criminology* 46 (2004): 73–95; Carol Smart, *Law, Crime, and Sexuality: Essays in Feminism* (London, Thousand Oaks, New Delhi: Sage Publications, 1995).

7. Canadian Association of Sexual Assault Centres (CASAC), "Myths Mask the Facts About Rape," *Myths and Facts* (2004), http://www.casac.ca/english/issues/myths_rape. htm (accessed September 30, 2007); M. Denike, "Sexual violence and 'fundamental justice': On the failure of equity reforms to criminal proceedings," *Canadian Woman Studies* 20. (2000): 151–159; Ontario Women's Justice Network, *When a Sexual Assault Case Goes to Trial: Basic Legal Information for Women Experiencing Violence*. (Toronto: 2006); Walker (1988). "Introduction to feminist therapies," in *Feminist Psychotherapies: Integration of Therapeutic and Feminist Systems*, eds, M.A. Dutton-Douglas and L.E. Walker (Norwood, NJ: Ablex), 3–11.

8. Nora Currie and Kara Gillies, "Bound By Law: How Canada's Protectionist Public Policies in the Areas of Both Rape and Prostitution Limit Women's Choices, Agency and Activities" (forthcoming); Rita Gunn and Rick Linden, "The Impact of Law Reform on the Processing of Sexual Assault Cases," *Canadian Review of Sociology and Anthropology* 34, 2 (1997): 155–177; Sheehy, "Advancing Social Inclusion," (n. 6).

9. Christine Boyle, "Publication of identifying information about sexual assault survivors: *R. v. Canadian Newspaper Co. Ltd.*" *Canadian Journal of Women and the Law*, 3 (1989): 602–614.

10. *Ibid.*, 609.

constitutional status accorded freedom of the press and the lack of any constitutional status afforded women in complaints about sexual assault is acute."[11]

A lack of clarity remains about how the publication ban is applied, which raises the question of whether it indeed benefits women.

B. Methodology

In analyzing the publication ban, I have rejected the characterization of sexually assaulted women as fundamentally damaged and in need of paternalistic protection, and have instead used a framework that acknowledges their individual and collective agency. I do not use the popular discourse of victimization ("rape victim," "survivor," or "thriver"), and I use the terms "rape" and "sexual assault" interchangeably. My focus is not on individual stories of victimization that keep sexual assault in the realm of the normative, confessional, or depoliticized as is often reflected in what is referred to as "Survivor Discourse,"[12] or viewed through mainstream pop psychology such as that of Dr. Phil or Montel.

The term "experiential" is used in this paper to specifically identify adult women who have entered the legal system as the result of their rapes. The phrase "key informant" refers to women who work in community-based rape crisis centers.

Sexually assaulted women are an extremely hard-to-reach population in part as a result of the lack of institutional, social, and legal supports. The issue of anonymity itself makes studies about raped women's experiences difficult to design and complete.

Interviews were held with eight experiential women from three provinces who had been sexually assaulted as adults, and three key informant women who work as counselors/advocates in feminist community rape crisis centers. Of those, one was Aboriginal, (experiential) and three were women of color (two experiential, one key informant). The sample for this study also included the contributions of three reporters from one national and two local media outlets.

Interview material does not distance the voice of interviewed women from mine. I will not attempt to present recommendations for change or alternatives to the publication ban, as there are too many other fugitive pieces that must also be tracked and inspected. Instead, my goal here is to look sideways at rape, to surveil and "talk back" to the cacophony of the publication ban. Ultimately, I question the benefits of its use. I hope to identify what is not working, and, in doing so, convert, subvert, or at least give pause to what has gone under the radar as normal discourses of rape.

I was told that my success in contacting this population of women was due to my own experiential location as a Jane Doe. They understood that this was not to be the traditional positioning of raped women as emotionally traumatized

---

11. *Ibid.*, 614.

12. Linda Martin Alcoff and Laura Gray-Rosedale, "Survivor Discourse: Transgression or Recuperation?" *Signs* 18, 2 (1993): 260–290; Boyle, "Publication of identifying information about sexual assault survivors," (n. 9).

and/or intellectually incapacitated by the crime that has been committed against them. But how does an anonymous woman (myself) write about women and anonymity while respecting the stipulation of most of the women I interviewed that I maintain their anonymity?

Articulating/Voicing Jane(s) There is a research practice to assign participants numbers, which seemed like the cleanest and most symbolic approach, but it is cold and hard and, well, *anonymous*, and it does not reflect the agency and acumen of the women with whom I spoke. Then, I thought I would give them the names of fictional female heroes, (quick! name three), or saints or celebrities (sinners). Most women in those categories are already sexualized, and many use first names only or aliases. All groups hold preconceived notions of female identity and were therefore unsuitable for my purposes.

> *We are symbolic creatures and whatever name we choose would be a powerful choice. You could choose your grandmother's name as opposed to the namelessness of Jane Doe and all of its symbolism.*
>
> Key Informant Jane Doe

C. Interrogating Anonymity/Jane

Constructing Women's Identities; or, What's in a Name? Not much if it's Jane Doe. It is the sobriquet commonly used to denote the "average" woman. She is otherwise unidentified and understood as anonymous or "ordinary."

In law, and in the media, especially given the glut and popularity of crime procedurals on TV, the moniker is code for unidentifiable women who are raped, missing, or dead. Jane Doe is their epithet, and the true identities of these women are forever lost. We view their bodies as piecework, as evidence, as information. There is no power in a Jane Doe identity. The same can be said of female nomenclature generally. In the West, patriarchal institutions assume that a woman will take the family name of the man she marries.

Women are cautioned about using their full names online in phone books and other public directories, and in public space for fear of signaling female identity to sexual offenders, thieves, and any man who may harm or exploit them.[13] We are cautioned not to put our names on luggage, jewelry or other personal public space.[14] To a large extent, society demands Jane Doe-ism of all women—in the name of our own safety—as if there is safety in not being a woman and danger inherent in womanhood (especially if you take your womanhood out in public).

---

13. Ontario Women's Justice Network (n. 7).
14. Http://www.witi.com/careers/2004/travel safety tips (accessed August 8, 2007).

The construction of the "rape victim" reflects and supports feminist sociological literature about private and public women and private/public space.[15] We already think of rape as a private matter between one man and one woman versus a public, social matter that affects all men and all women. Anonymity reinforces this understanding.

In rightly preserving women's privacy, the publication ban also allocates the crime to the private realm where the overwhelming majority of sexual assaults take place.[16] Women raped in public by serial or stranger rapists are warned by the police before the fact, and then admonished afterwards that it was their very presence in public space that precipitated their sexual assaults. They did not do as they were told. The message to all women is to regulate their movements and/or "stay home" as prevention.[17]

The publication ban reinforces the current understanding of rape as blight on the perceived goodness or the quality of the woman involved, and one that she has brought on herself.[18] The theme in both publication bans and rape warnings seems to be that privacy/safety for women can only be accomplished if women withdraw from public life into the private realm.

The publication ban's stated purpose to "foster complaints by victims of sexual assault by protecting them from the trauma of widespread publication resulting in embarrassment and humiliation" is confirmation of the disgrace and dishonor we attach to a raped woman, and the manner in which her virtue and body are understood to be sullied and defiled.[19] The second proposition that the ban would "encourage victims to come forward and complain to facilitate the prosecution and conviction of those guilty of sexual offences" is dubious, particularly in nonurban areas where women's identity quickly becomes common knowledge.[20] There is no research to prove the ban's efficacy in this regard.

Embodying Jane Doe: Who Does "Jane" Erase? I asked all of the women I interviewed to tell me what they imagined Jane Doe looked like when they read or heard of "her" in the news. Elements of their reply were always the same. They said she was white, relatively young, and middle-class.

---

15. Tamara Myers, *Caught: Montreal's modern girls and the law, 1869–1945* (Toronto: University of Toronto Press, 2006); Mariana Valverde, *The Age of Light, Soap, and Water: Moral Reform in English Canada, 1885–1925* (Toronto: McClelland & Stewart, 1991).

16. Statistics Canada, "Crime statistics in Canada, 2000," *Juristat* 21 (Ottawa: Canadian Centre for Justice Statistics, 2001).

17. Ontario Women's Justice Network (n. 7).

18. Franca Iacovetta and Mariana Valverde, *Gender Conflicts: New Essays in Women's History* (Toronto: University of Toronto Press, 1992); Mariana Valverde, *Sex, Power and Pleasure* (Toronto: Women's Press, 1985).

19. *Canadian Newspapers* (n. 3).

20. *Ibid.*

What is more Anglo or plain than Jane? It doesn't speak to age or culture or race or anything. Existing power structures are manifested in that.

Key Informant Jane Doe

She's white and middle class. Her social definers and issues are erased. She can't be a minority or a sex worker or a poor woman. Every time I see or hear about Jane Doe I think of the huge amount of fear it puts in place, they are images of fear.

Experiential Jane Doe

A little white woman, broken and pathetic, demolished, with bunched up Kleenexes in her hand. She's an object of pity and holds all the stereotypes of a hopelessly destroyed woman, emotionally mangled, who requires circling off and rescue.

Key Informant Jane Doe

Jane Doe is coded as white. Sort of a universal victim. All complexities are erased in a Jane Doe. She is young, 20–40. I think of her as being so individualized that she is just a thing. She exists outside of relationships, is probably single with no man to protect her.

Experiential Jane Doe

Racialized women are scarce or absent in our general understanding of women who are sexually assaulted. Their rapes are even further distanced from our consciousness if we hold to the descriptors above. On the other hand, the racial identities of raped women can be used purposefully to situate them in a negative light.

The same kind of breach of a publication ban occurs if the woman is identified as a sex worker. Every myth and judgment we hold about "those women" falls into place. Such violations not only subject the women involved to a greater potential for stigmatization and harm, they contribute to rape mythology that holds that some women cannot be raped, some are more subject to rape, or that men in their cultures are more prone to rape.

Currently, the convenient notion that some racialized women report their rapes less frequently than white women because they are more subject to shame, community censure, disbelief, and the fear of powerful men is common.[21] Although such strictures certainly exist, it is the nature and consequence of racism and systemic racist beliefs as well as stereotypes that further prohibit racialized women from reporting to the police or accessing the legal system.[22]

---

21. "Culture Clash: Ripples from a Sexual Assault," *Globe and Mail*, Editorial, September 30, 2007; Margaret Wente, "Why are we so afraid to offend?" *Globe and Mail*, September 29, 2007.

22. Y. Jawani, *Intersecting Inequalities: Immigrant Women of Colour, Violence and Health-care,"* (Vancouver: Freda Centre for Research on Violence Against Women

Indeed, we cannot separate race or racism from rape. How else can we explain the construction of Jane Does as white? We imbue raped women with character-istics with which we are comfortable, and when details of her race, geography, or trade become known, we isolate her, treat her as the "Other," and thus increase the likelihood that she will be denied presumptive protection.

In her 1992 social critique of print media coverage of sexual assault, Helen Benedict analyzed four sensational U.S. cases (that also led Canadian headlines) to conclude that sex crime coverage still privileges crimes against white women, while ignoring those against black women,[23] and still covers black men against white women rapes with an "exaggerated frequency, class prejudice and racist stereotypes."[24]

If our perception of Jane Doe/raped woman excludes racialized female identities why would First Nations women, black women, and women of color knowingly assume that location? The paper shield that the publication ban presents to white women is based on historical constructs of western female sexuality as delicate and in need of paternalistic protection, whereas racialized women, especially black and First Nations women, are understood as hypersexual and/or immoral, and therefore unable to be raped.[25]

D. Manipulating Jane

Ball of Confusion My survey resulted in some notable revelations: no one really understands the publication ban specific to sexual assault, not the lawyers, judges, antiviolence advocates nor the media, and certainly not the women to whom—or against whom—the publication ban is applied. Perhaps the specific-ity of the ban in sexual assault cases is also specific to the identity of the group that uses it. It has been documented in massive amounts of additional research internationally that rape mythology allows us to view women as causing sexual

and Children, 2001); Shahrzad Mojab, "Theorizing the Politics of 'Islamic Feminism,'" *Feminist Review* 69, no. 1 (2001):124–146; Sherene Razack, *Looking White People in the Eye: Gender, Race, and Culture in Courtrooms and Classrooms* (Toronto: University of Toronto Press, 1998).

23. In 2007 Amnesty International released "Maze of Lies: the Failure to Protect Indigenous Women from Sexual Violence in the USA." They report that Native women are raped at three times the rate of non native women and that there is an abysmal "failure to pursue" when the perpetrators are known to be nonnative men.

24. Helen Benedict, *Virgin or Vamp: How the Press Covers Sex Crimes* (New York: Oxford University Press, 1992), 251.

25. Donovan, Roxanne A. (2007). "To Blame or Not To Blame: Influences of Target Race and Observer Sex on Rape Blame Attribution," *Journal of Interpersonal Violence* 22, 6 (2007): 722–736; Joan Sangster, "Criminalizing the Colonized: Ontario Native Women Confront the Criminal Justice System, 1920–60," *Canadian Historical Review* 80, 1(1999): 32–60; Carolyn West, *Violence in the Lives of Black Women: Battered, Black, and Blue* (Binghamton: Haworth Press, 2003).

violence, lying about it, enjoying it, and making false allegations.26 If we are invested in those beliefs, why take the ban that seriously?

Grassroots Anonymity Women who work in community-based sexual assault centers (versus those who operate under the umbrella of legal, medical, and social work institutions and agencies) are in a unique position to comment on anonymity. They are often the spokeswomen for other women who have been sexually assaulted. As second wave feminists, many of them were directly involved in breaking the silence around rape. They fought and paid dearly for the Rape Shield Law and the publication ban. But the silence has returned; and only a feminist crack or two remains in the predominant discourse on violence against women today, and few workers are informed about the media ban.

With rape crisis centres like ours there is a public fear of our radicalism, that we are lesbians and man-hating. That understanding is alive and well.

Key Informant Jane Doe

Other Crisis Centre workers added,

Service providers often feel that they are helping and doing advocacy work when inadvertently we are taking women's power away. We will only speak on behalf of her if she asks us and we will look for ways to give her voice power. We want to reinforce that she has choices. The hard part is how do we know we are doing that?

Key Informant Jane Doe

When a woman loses her individuality and becomes anonymous there is an ability to speak to the larger systemic problem. It allows us to look at violence in a more theological and ideological way in order to analyze the impacts of gender inequity. Anonymity can help us do that. On the flip side the very act of removing individuality disables us from looking at that individual woman, her experience and needs. Women are not a homogenous group so how can anonymity speak to or serve all women? If you clump us all together you lose your consciousness of race, poverty, ability, all of the basic areas that affect how women are experiencing the crime.

Key Informant Jane Doe

The Media and Jane Doe What informs us most about the crimes of sexual assault and the women who experience them comes from mainstream media. It is

---

26. Canadian Association of Sexual Assault Centres, "Myths Mask the Facts About Rape," *Myths and Facts*, http://www.casac.ca/english/issues/(accessed September 30, 2007); N. Gavey and V. Gow, "'Cry wolf,' cried the wolf: Constructing the issue of false rape allegations in New Zealand media," *Feminism & Psychology* 11, no. 3 (2001): 341–360; Ontario Women's Directorate, "Sexual Assault: Dispelling the Myths," http://www.citizenship.gov.on.ca/owd/english/publications/sexual-assault/myths.htm (accessed September 30, 2007); Ontario Women's Justice Network (n. 7).

the "Fifth Estate" that defines the state of sexual assault to us, for us. In interviews with reporters from major dailies (one national and two local newspapers), I was informed that "rape sells," especially if it includes the can't-fail components of celebrity, sensation, and additional physical violence.

If it's juicy or more compelling, that's great, but there won't be a lot of coverage unless it is a serial rapist or the woman is left dead or a multiple number of attackers. It is the melodrama of life that most of us will not ever experience but we respond to it in our gut. I don't think there is anything intrinsically wrong in being interested in that sort of stuff—Scott Peterson versus Healthcare for instance. It resonates with us, the suspense, it's the same reason we read mystery novels.

Reporter Jane Doe

Sexual assault is a common crime. If we covered all of them there wouldn't be enough room in the newspaper. There has to be some other element to interest the paper. How it impacts the victim, the way it damaged or traumatized her. The general rule is if you report the crime you report the trial which takes a lot of man-hours so it needs to be compelling.

Reporter Jane Doe

When asked how they would feel, how their editors might react if women stopped using the name Jane Doe and, instead, used names of their individual choice, the following was explained to me:

Jane Doe is code for the longer story of sexual assault. It's a name that speaks the crime. It's like saying "Lolita" or even Karla Homolka, they are shorthand for an entire story or scene. I personally would continue to use Jane Doe in print even if rape victims chose other names. I think all reporters would.

Reporter Jane Doe

The Internet Unlike any other form of communication, the Internet offers the promise and possibility of anonymity, and has been utilized by women who have been sexually assaulted to share their experiences, to politicize, and to educate. Some women use their real names, sometimes in conscious defiance of a media ban they feel contributes to the stigma surrounding sexual assault. For instance, a woman whose rape is currently under investigation writes and signs with her own name:

I hope that I was able to create something positive out of such a horrific event in my life.

Facebook has become a gathering place for some women to speak about their rapes unmediated by the forced narrative of police, lawyers, advocates, or the media.[27] But the press is ever-hungry for a good rape story and mightily

27. Siri Agrell, "Sexual-assault Survivors Find Solace on Facebook," *Globe and Mail*, September 4, 2007.

conscious of the tempering of their constitutional rights as presented in a publication ban. A recent *Globe and Mail* article drew attention to the many Facebook sites in which women use their real names to discuss the sexual assaults that have been committed against them. The article prints some of those names. Has *The Globe* violated the publication ban in doing so? What about their own internal policies? Is it their decision to make? Are the Facebook women in violation of the legislation?

Unexpected Allies My literature review on the subject of the publication ban produced a host of unexpected allies who also question the benefits of anonymity for sexually assaulted women. Check any search engine or Google, "Jane Doe, anonymity, and sexual assault." Fathers' rights and men's groups who understand publication bans in rape trials as a method to support their own oppression are first to surface. The specter of false allegations, and the damage done to men by women granted use of media bans, are their reasons for condemning the Rape Shield Law and women's anonymity. In many instances, the vitriol and misogyny of their arguments allow for easy dismissal, but their political clout and media-friendly jingoism are not to be ignored. For example the article "Protection for Malicious Liars: The Supreme Court Upholds Anonymity for Women who Falsely Claim Sexual Assault"[28] addresses the court's decision in *Canadian Newspapers Co. v. Canada*[29] and contains sound bites such as "there's a war against men" and "these people are liars," which support the rape mythology and feminist backlash that surfaced in many of our institutions in the late eighties. In September of 2007, "FemCunts Are Angry"[30] waxed more graphic about "lying hags" and "bitches" whose identities are protected by a media ban.

Feminist advances that identified the systemic problems and nature of male sexual violence against adult women are also denied or at least missing in the mandates and directives of state-sponsored victims' rights groups. They embrace, instead, a law and order agenda that calls for bigger prisons and longer sentencing. Their initiatives present solutions that do not work in the best interests of women who experience the crime.[31]

Perhaps more than any other rape myth, the so-called "False Allegation"—also referred to by Toronto Police Sex Crimes investigators as "Alligators"[32]—is the

---

28. *Alberta Report* 23, no. 5 (1996): 24.

29. *Canadian Newspapers* (n. 3).

30. "FemCunts Are Angry," http://mensrightsblogs.com.

31. Mandy Bonisteel and Linda Green, *Implications of the Shrinking Space for Feminist Anti-Violence Advocacy*, (conference paper, Fredericton, New Brunswick, Canadian Social Welfare Policy Conference, June 16–18, 2005).

32. Christie Blatchford, "Crying Wolf: In a System That Assumes Children Don't Lie and Women Are Victims, False Allegations Happen with Alarming Regularity and Frequency," *National Post*, September 8, 2001.

most popular and damaging. Although police statistics themselves indicate that the occurrence of false allegations is no higher in sexual assault than in any other crime (only 5% of all those reported), false allegations can be manipulated to discredit all women who file charges.[33] Research has found that the 5% of false allegations stated by police also accounts for unfounded charges where 1) the woman is believed to have been raped, but there is not enough evidence to proceed to court; 2) the police do not believe her story; and 3) women have dropped the charges before they reach trial.[34] Nonetheless, thirty years after it was used in *R. v. Seaboyer* and *Canadian Newspapers Co. v. Canada* to attempt to disqualify women from the protection of the law, the False Allegation charge, or threat of it, contributes to a dismally low reporting rate of sexual assault nationwide.[35]

E. Living Jane Doe

Becoming Jane Doe Experiential Jane Does that I spoke with told me stories of judges who refused to allow them the choice of using their real names, as that would also identify their abusers or because they ruled that the legislation was mandatory—versus the mandatory right of the sexually assaulted woman to use it, or not.

> *I had the ban at first and then tried to have it removed before the trial ended but the judge completely patronized me. He said "we know what's good for you; there are laws in place to protect you. I don't believe you're prepared for the fall-out" and he said no.*

Experiential Jane Doe

> *Anonymity was not presented to me as a choice. The judge just put a stop on using my real name. There is an assumption that this is what you want, it is a rigid and non-flexible law.*

Experiential Jane Doe

On a personal level, I discovered during this research that if, for instance, I publish this paper under my real name, I would be breaching the ban and would be subject to criminal charges. Were I to flout the authority of the courts on this matter, I would be subject to penalties that can range from public confession and apology to a fine (plus court costs). The legal advisor with whom I spoke at Justice Canada also opined that given the notoriety of my case in the media,[36] it would be unlikely for the courts to overturn my ban.

---

33. Toronto Police Service, 2006 Annual Statistical Report, http://www.torontopolice.on.ca/publications/files/reports/2006statsreport.pdf (accessed September 30, 2007).

34. Ontario Women's Directorate (n. 26); Ontario Women's Justice Network (n. 7).

35. *R. v Seaboyer* [1991] 2 S.C.R. 577; *Canadian Newspapers* (n. 3).

36. *Jane Doe v Board of Commissioners of Police for the Municipality of Metropolitan Toronto* [1998] 39 O.R. 487.

Who knew that to be a Jane Doe could be a permanent choice? Or that the courts could appropriate my real name? Under law, the reasons my lawyers used (in the criminal and civil courts) to obtain my anonymity were that I would suffer shame and humiliation as a publicly named rape victim. To have my ban rescinded, I must say that those conditions do not exist for me anymore, and, by extension, for other women.

Many felt that the notion of protection afforded to them via a publication ban was just that—a notion, and a false one at that. Participants indicated that the ban only restricted the use of their name and likeness to media or public accounts, and did not offer them any safety or protection from identification in the courtroom.

So where's the privacy? Your real name is still being used in the courtroom. Classrooms of young boys and girls parade through looking at you. Anyone can.
Experiential Jane Doe

It should be noted that such protection is not the intent of the publication ban, and the woman's anonymity is far from total. It does not even begin until the trial stage, which on average is about two years after the offence.[37] Police officers are required to maintain sexually assaulted women's privacy during the investigation and in the interim, but are not bound to do so by law.[38] The fact that the ban does not cover the court proceedings is a source of considerable anxiety for women who must identify themselves, their address, and other highly personal information and history brought out in cross-examination in front of the accused and his family and friends (as well as a public gallery). Rapists, whether they are known to the woman whom they have raped, or unknown, often threaten women with serious reprisals if they report the rape to the police. Women are often misinformed or not informed enough about these limitations and assume protection when there is none.

Anonymity keeps you anonymous to anonymous strangers. Whoop di doo!
Experiential Jane Doe

Women located in nonurban settings told me that news of their reports of the crime traveled freely and quickly in small towns and communities, and that anyone or everyone seeking access to the legal proceedings had full knowledge of their identities.

It would appear that shoddy jurisprudence, intemperate jurists, the nature of the legislation itself, and uncertainty by all involved on the use of the publication ban—which does not actually, adequately, or completely protect women's identity or give them agency—undercut any perceived benefit the ban might offer.

---

37. Ontario Women's Justice Network (n. 7).

38. In Ontario, police officers are subject to charges under the Police Services Act should they breach anonymity. Police Services Act R.S.O. 1990 c. p.15.

I also asked women what impressions they had of Jane Does who appear on television. You've seen them—women who sit behind the shadows and pixilation commonly used to disguise raped women. Their voices are clear, although sometimes disguised, but their heads and torsos are in shadow or dissolved into an electronic mass. Sometimes we might see their hands or other truncated body parts.

When we see a Jane Doer on TV I think it allows us to impose all of our judgments and preconceived thoughts about who rape victims are. And I think that it is mostly negative, judgmental, always skeptical. Her disguise affects her credibility. I don't really see how she is being protected in that context or how her anonymity is making it safe for her.

Key Informant Jane Doe

A woman with whom I spoke did go public on TV, and told this story:

I felt most naked and vulnerable when I did TV. When any rape victim goes public, be it in the print media, the radio or TV, they are putting themselves out there to be judged by strangers. In the process, they hope to educate people and maybe even get folks to start asking questions. It's a very scary, risky business. I elected to allow strangers to see me as the "woman who sucked the priest's cock," to name but one of the crimes he committed. It is difficult to present yourself to strangers, never mind intimates, in this visual context. It's gross, icky, humiliating, but I believe the deleterious effects of the image of the named priest forcing his penis into a woman's mouth were more than humiliating to him and his church. I hope that this is the part of the picture that people will react to and remember most.

Experiential Jane Doe

My own experience was that, even with a media ban, the artist sketches of me that appeared on the TV news every night for weeks showed me from behind, or with a thin, black bar the size and shape of sunglasses covering my eyes. Even though my identity was protected, the sketches were remarkably like me, good enough that family members and acquaintances formerly unaware of my Jane Doe status were able to identify me. My voice, its quality and timbre, my physical size, skin, eye, and hair color were reported on. All clear violations of the publication ban.

10. Realities of Reporting There is immense institutional pressure on women to report sexual assault and most of us would prefer to. But here is some of what happens when we do and despite the stated intent of the publication ban to encourage others to come forward and to protect us from embarrassment and humiliation.

1. We are not believed.

There were a lot of letters to the editor about how horrible it was that this woman has lied and ruined his reputation and that I was hiding behind the ban.

Experiential Jane Doe

2. We are humiliated through public exposure of our personal lives in the courtroom, and misinformed by court officials.

I see the police utilize the threat of loss of anonymity all the time. It can be used as leverage to make women drop charges. They are told that for instance their case isn't strong and the judge won't grant them a ban or it will be made public if her attacker isn't found guilty and everyone will know what happened.

Key Informant Jane Doe

3. We are required to assume passive roles, cannot defend ourselves, and have no legal representation.

I see anonymity another way. I see it as a threat of exposure to women if they step outside of the victim role. It says "we are protecting you now but we will stop if you become problematic. We will take away this protection and you will be destroyed." It is another tool supposedly [designed] to protect women but used to diminish them.

Experiential Jane Doe

4. We are shunned by our friends, family, and community.

I lived in a small town and my name wasn't used so I thought I had some control. But word got around. My assailant was a doctor and someone in his office sent my name to another doctor I was seeing and he wouldn't treat me without someone else present. I was stunned. So shamed. It was a horrible experience.

Experiential Jane Doe

5. We cannot speak of our experience again unless it is in the context of trauma.

It's a lot of work to tell people you've been sexually assaulted, it's like telling people you are dying. Doing it in social or political circumstances is difficult. I think there is an amazing desire to keep the definition of sexual assault individualized or atomized. Anonymity assists with that.

Experiential Jane Doe

6. Our past histories can be used against us.

I have two divorces and was in a reform school for girls when I was young and a child I gave up for adoption. That and other stuff was brought up by his lawyer to describe my morals. It was in the paper. My name wasn't but lots of people knew anyway. I wish I had never done it.

Experiential Jane Doe

7. We can be charged ourselves.

A woman who was a Jane Doe spoke publicly about her case and the media started calling. The police told us that "we have not released her name yet as she is a victim, but if she goes forward with this political agenda we will charge her with public mischief and release her name.

Key Informant Jane Doe

Reclaiming Jane Many argue or suggest that the burden of shifting the negative constructions of rape victims is the responsibility of those very women who are burdened by it; that the use of anonymity only perpetuates the stigma—the thing women say they fear most. We are encouraged to rise up, break free from the shackles of shame and dishonor, and just use our real names. Do it for the team! If enough women used their own names it is argued, why before you know it, there would no longer be a rape problem. There is some truth in such ideology as the publication ban itself can be read to reinforce and endorse rape mythology.

There is this idea that to be shamed is the worst thing that can happen, as bad as the rape itself, but it is very Victorian and doesn't properly identify the harm of the assault.

Experiential Jane Doe

Some reporters also felt that it is the responsibility of individual women to renounce the publication ban in order to put a face to rape and to better address the crime.

Rape is not the worst crime. We play into the whole victim stain with anonymity. If she is anonymous we don't connect with her. If women would just be brave and do it, use their own name, then others would follow. If I were a victim I would far prefer that people know my name and know what had happened to me than to be put in a position where I am anonymous.

Reporter Jane Doe

Others disagreed:

Nothing would really change that much. It's not like the system would work differently or better [if women used their own names]. Reportage wouldn't change. We'd still go for the sensational, only it would have her real name on it.

Reporter Jane Doe

We must recognize that in supporting the "just say no to Jane Doe" response, we require women who have experienced crime to take a large and unknown risk without any safety net or reward—and to do it alone, without any institutional or social support. We forget that, despite the purported gains of some legislation, women's histories continue to be used to discredit them in court, and the most detailed accounts of their rapes are reported in local and national media. We disregard the rape myths that continue to inform our understandings of the crime. We negate the reality that few sexual assault trials end in convictions. We reduce the crime to a private matter and ignore its systemic and institutionalized nature and power.

One woman I interviewed who went public, but asked that her real name not be used here, wept when I suggested that for the duration of her trial (which took place during this writing process), all women adopt her real name to deflect the stigmatization to which she was subject.

> *That would have been amazing, I felt so alone. I couldn't look at anyone when I walked down the street. I was afraid to meet anyone I knew, even strangers who might know me from work, I kept thinking do they know? Do they know I'm her?*
>
> Experiential Jane Doe

What about reclaiming Jane Doe? Reconstructing "her" and what she signifies as honourableand heroic as opposed to rendering her tragic and hidden. Allotting her the respect and gratitude we would afford to any responsible citizen who, faced with incredible odds and hardship, enters the legal system and does what she thinks is the right thing and for the public good. Jane Doe it is then—all around.

II. CONCLUSION

There are a series of pros and cons in the issue of a woman's anonymity in relation to sexual assault and with dilemmas in all camps. Publication bans are seen by most as positive and convenient and to "improve the administration of justice." But in practice, they represent an enormous loss of power in a raped woman's circumstance—losses that are not accrued or tallied in other legal battles or for other anonymous persons, losses that are gender-based and intersected by race and social status. The relocation or appropriation of power the media ban represents is based on assumptions inherent in the belief, the reality (and the legislation) that being identified as raped results in public embarrassment and humiliation so great that women will not report at all if their privacy is not protected. But which comes first? Which impacts most, works best, and for whom? The presumption that she who has had something done to her or against her is the one who must guard against the ruination of her reputation (versus the perpetrator) is indicative of how turned-around we are on the subject of sexual assault.

We require that women protect themselves by limiting their actions before rape in order to prevent it and then hide themselves after rape to avoid shame, blame, and other retribution. We have organized a good/bad morality and racially based understanding of sexually assaulted women as defiled and suspect, without agency, choice, or activity of their own, so much so that their identities must be hidden, their names lost.

My interviews, however, revealed an entirely different picture of women who are vibrant, reflective, and informed.

16. LIFE IN THE FISH BOWL
Feminist Interrogations of Webcamming

JANE BAILEY*

"[A]ll women live in sexual objectification the way that fish live in water."[1]

I. INTRODUCTION

Inspired by, among other things, a coffee pot[2] and a fishbowl,[3] on April 14, 1996, Jennifer Ringley launched Jennicam. In a self-described "social experiment,"[4] whose diverse objectives included connecting with family and friends and challenging mainstream media images of women with "perfect hair and perfect friends,"[5] regularly refreshed still images of Ringley's home were uploaded to

---

* Thanks to Lisa Feinberg, Bridget McIlveen, and Sharon Marcushamer for their wonderful research and editorial assistance on this chapter, as well as to the students whose opinions and ideas have been inspirational in this and other projects, including Julie Shugarman, Louisa Garib, Brad Jenkins, Rafael Texidor Torres, and José Laguarta Ramirez. Thanks also to an anonymous peer reviewer and to my colleagues on the *ID Trail* project—George Tomlinson, Mary O'Donoghue, Shoshana Magnet, Ian Kerr, and Michael Froomkin for their extremely insightful commentary and suggestions on earlier versions of this chapter. All errors, of course, remain my own.

1. Catharine MacKinnon, *Feminism Unmodified: Discourses on Life and Law* (Cambridge: Harvard University Press, 1987), 149-150.

2. Peter S. Goodman, "Famous British Coffee Pot Webcam to go Dark," *The Ottawa Citizen*, B10, April 9, 2001, http://www.proquest.com.

3. Eric Meyer, *The Amazing Netscape Fish Cam* (2003), http://wp.netscape.com/fishcam.

4. Theresa M. Senft, "Camgirls: Webcams, Live Journals and the Personal as Political in the Age of the Global Brand" (Ph.D. Dissertation, New York University Department of Performance Studies, 2005), 198.

5. *Ibid.*, 12.

the web, where they were accessible (at least for some time) to anyone with an Internet-connected computer. Jennicam depicted everything from Ringley's empty couch to her cat to her working at her computer to her having sex with her boyfriend. It inspired considerable commentary and analysis, including among feminists struggling to understand the depth, breadth, meaning, and potential of voluntary personal exposure in this brave new networked world.

Jennicam is considered by many to represent the first of a growing number of "webcam girls" who are estimated by some to number in the hundreds of thousands.[6] Many of these "webcam girls" are young women determined to harness the power of new communication technologies, such as the Internet, in efforts to oppose socially imposed mainstream definitions of gender and sexuality.[7] They do so within the broader context of a societal turn toward exposure, micro-celebrity and "reality" television, and toward a contemporary flouting of the perceived puritanism of prior feminisms, feminisms that some have argued unnecessarily shamed women in relation to their sexuality and denied them the ability to explore and assert their sexuality as a form of social empowerment.[8] Directly raising long-standing unresolved tensions about identity, privacy, sexuality, and pornography, Jennicam and its ensuing iterations invite further debate and analysis within the feminist community. In this chapter, I will pursue these themes in three parts.

First, I will discuss the evolution of the Jennicam experiment with a focus on Ringley's own description of her project. Second, I will draw out the interlocking themes of identity, privacy, and pornography resonating within Anita Allen's 2000 analysis of various webcam experiments by women. Third, I will highlight some of the ways in which Allen's analysis both raises and invites further exploration of these historically contested themes in feminist work. In conclusion I suggest that technological moments such as these offer feminists fresh space for dialogue on these issues and for an interrogation of the continuing relevance of prior positions taken in relation to them. While remaining open to the idea that past insights may no longer carry the resonance that they once seemed to, we ought not to foreclose the possibility that aspects of them may continue to be relevant to the ongoing struggle for a lived social equality for women.

---

6. Solid numbers with respect to webcammers and webcam girls, in particular, are difficult to obtain. Estimates in the hundreds of thousands have been reflected both in print and television productions on the topic: Julie Szego, "Saturday Extra—Camgirls," *The Age*, February 1, 2003, http://www.factiva.com/; "Watch Me Generation," TV Documentary, *Canada AM*, January 3, 2003, http://www.factiva.com/.

7. For some examples of these efforts, see *Webcam Girls*, DVD (Vancouver: Producers on Davie Pictures Inc., 2004).

8. For views questioning the empowering nature of these efforts, see Shoshana Magnet, "Feminist sexualities, race and the internet: an investigation of suicidegirls.com" *New Media & Society* 9 (2007): 577; Ariel Levy, "Female Chauvinist Pigs" in *Female Chauvinist Pigs: Women and the Rise of Raunch Culture* (New York: Free Press, 2005); *Webcam Girls*, (n. 7).

II. EVOLUTION OF THE JENNICAM

Born on August 10, 1976, in Harrisburg, Pennsylvania, Jennifer Kay Ringley eventually went on to: skip her senior year of high school; score 1400 on her SATs; study economics and web design at Pennsylvania's Dickinson College; and work in web design and for a nonprofit social agency.[9] In 1996, intrigued by Netscape's FishCam[10] but convinced that watching people would be more interesting than watching fish,[11] Ringley conceived of the Jennicam—"a window into a virtual human zoo."[12] As for issues of privacy, Ringley's initial instincts were that "all the secrecy regarding what goes on 'behind closed doors' is doing more harm than good."[13]

In addition to the still images generated by the webcam set up in her home, the home page for www.jennicam.org featured options such as the "name that curve contest," email, photo galleries, journals, FAQs, and technological assistance.[14] Although she could have opted for a technology that would have allowed her to watch her watchers, Ringley rejected that option, a decision quite consistent with her perception of privacy:

> I don't feel like I'm giving up my privacy. Just because other people can see me doesn't mean it affects me. I'm still alone in my room, no matter what.[15]

Although she claimed that her webcam depicted her "life, exactly as it would be whether or not there were cameras watching,"[16] early in the life of Jennicam, Ringley would occasionally stage performances in garter belts and high heels.[17] She also reported spending hours responding to commonly asked questions in the FAQ section of her website as well as reading and answering some of the

---

9. Jennifer Ringley, interview by Ira Glass, *This American Life*, Chicago Public Radio, June 6, 1997, *This American Life Episode Archive*, http://www.thislife.org/Radio_Episode. aspx?sched=721.

10. FishCam features live shots of fish in an aquarium. It has been operating both before and after the Jennicam: Meyer, *Fish Cam*, (n. 3).

11. Jennifer Ringley, "Look@Me!!!" *The Australian*, February 21, 1998, http://www.factiva.com/.

12. *Reuters*, "Voyeur Website Jennicam to Go Dark," *CNN.com*, December 10, 2003, http://edition.cnn.com/2003/TECH/internet/12/10/jenni.cam.reut/.

13. Jennifer Ringley, "LOOK@ME," *The Australian*, January 24, 1998, http://www.factiva.com/.

14 Kristine Blair and Pamela Takayoshi, "Introduction: Mapping the Terrain of Feminist Cyberscapes" in *Feminist Cyberscapes: Mapping Gendered Academic Spaces*, ed. Kristine Blair and Pamela Takayoshi (Stamford: Ablex Publishing Corporation, 1999), 7.

15. Victor Burgin, "Jenni's Room: Exhibitionism and Solitude," *Critical Inquiry* 27 (2000): 78, http://www.jstor.org/.

16. *Reuters*, "Voyeur website" (n. 12).

17. Blair and Takayoshi, "Feminist Cyberspaces," 8 (n. 14).

hundreds of emails she received from viewers on a daily basis.[18] Nonetheless, in her mind, she maintained all the privacy she needed:

> [V]iewers can't phone me, fax me, they can't keep me from mercilessly over-sleeping. And until someone invents a plug-in that allows you to hear another person's thoughts via the web, I've got the most important privacy of all.[19]

> [A]s long as what goes on in my head is still private, I have all the space I need.[20]

Rejecting the idea that showing nudity automatically meant that her site was pornographic, Ringley argued that she "wasn't anywhere close to crossing the line," at least in terms of her own intentions.[21]

Ringley came to believe that her site offered a counter-point to beauty myths perpetuated in mainstream Hollywood media. "Enough with perfect, airbrushed models and starlets who refuse to be photographed eating because it is 'unbecoming,'"[22] Ringley declared, "real people are just as interesting and appealing as the people the media tells us we should like."[23] Representations of "real" people, she argued could be affirming for those whose bodies and images did not fit the Hollywood mould, noting that a sixteen-year-old girl had thanked her for demonstrating comfort with having a "fuller body."[24]

In 1997, with Ringley's cost of bandwidth escalating due to her site's increasing popularity,[25] Jennicam moved to a two-tier system of paying and nonpaying members. For an annual fee of $15, paying members were able to upload images every two minutes, while nonpaying members received images every twenty minutes.[26] On occasion, Ringley appeared contrite about her move toward commercialization.[27]

---

18. Ringley stated that men sent virtually all of the daily 700 emails she received in 1996. Though many requested private pictures, Ringley interpreted only one to be sufficiently threatening to close down her website for several days: Jennifer Ringley, interview by Ira Glass, (n. 9).

19. Ringley, "LOOK@ME," (n. 11).

20. Jennifer Ringley, "Frequently Asked Questions," *JenniCam*, Internet Archive Wayback Machine, January 24, 1998, http://web.archive.org/web/19990420213308/www.jennicam.org/faq/general.html.

21. Ringley, "LOOK@ME," (n. 11).

22. *Ibid.*

23. *Ibid.*

24. Jennifer Ringley, "Why I Star in My Own *Truman Show*," *Cosmopolitan* 25 (1998): 76.

25. Senft, "Camgirls," 229 (n. 4).

26. Krissi M. Jimroglou, "A Camera with a View: JenniCAM, visual representation, and cyborg subjectivity," *Information, Communication & Society* 2, no. 4 (1999): 440, http://www.EBSCOhost.com.

27. Burgin, "Jenni's Room," 78 (n. 15).

In 1998, after moving to Washington, D.C., Ringley increased the number of cameras in her residence and changed her operating system to be "much faster and more reliable than the old method [she] was using. And more secure."[28] Between 1998 and 2003, Ringley made a number of aesthetic and content changes to her website. In 1998 she added a copyright notice, later followed by the addition of a trademark.[29] In 1999 she uploaded professional photographs of herself, including some in which she posed semi-nude.[30] Later that year, she added a definition on her home page:

JenniCam:

1. A real-time look into the real-life of a young woman. 2: An undramatic photographic diary for public viewing especially via the Internet.[31]

For several days in 2000, her home page was modified to show a picture of her behind the camera—an image that reappeared on her site from 2001 onward.[32] By 2003, in keeping with an escalating air of commercialization, the website featured advertising and a detailed layout of the cameras located in her California home.[33]

Later in 2003, Ringley shut down Jennicam. Some have speculated that the shutdown resulted from PayPal's cancellation of her account due to its concerns about online nudity on her site.[34] The experience of other women involved in 24/7 webcamming would suggest that Ringley's decision could simply reflect the fatigue associated with maintaining the homecamming system and consistently being in front of the camera.[35]

---

28. Ringley, "Frequently Asked Questions," (n. 20).

29. Jennifer Ringley, *JenniCam*, Internet Archive Wayback Machine, December 2, 1998, http://web.archive.org/web/19981202112602/http://jennicam.org/; Jennifer Ringley, Internet Archive Wayback Machine, April 18, 1999, http://web.archive.org/web/19990418100201/http://www.jennicam.org/.

30. Jennifer Ringley, "Jennifer's Picture Album," *JenniCam*, Internet Archive Wayback Machine, January 25, 1999, http://web.archive.org/web/19991013001942/jennicam.org/~jenni/pics/picsmain.html.

31. Jennifer Ringley, *JenniCam*, Internet Archive Wayback Machine, October 12, 1999, http://web.archive.org/web/19991012055007/http://jennicam.org/.

32. Jennifer Ringley, "JenniCam Command Central," *JenniCam*, Internet Archive Wayback Machine, October 18, 2000, http://web.archive.org/web/20001018022108/http://jennicam.org/.

33. Jennifer Ringley, "The Set," *JenniCam*, Internet Archive Wayback Machine, January 29, 2003, http://web.archive.org/web/20030129010133/http://jennicam.org/.

34. Peter Howell, "Without a Net: Jenni's Public Life Unplugged," *The Toronto Star*, December 14, 2003, D1, http://www.proquest.com.

35. For a sense of the significant amount of work and expense associated with maintaining a webcam, see discussions by Ducky Doolittle and Ana Voog in *Webcam Girls* (n. 7).

Jennifer Ringley, the embodied person, seems now to have very successfully slipped into the obscurity of an unwebcammed existence.[36] Tellingly—or perhaps only interestingly—Ringley maintained that she was neither a feminist nor engaged in a feminist project.[37] Nonetheless, the digital vestiges left by her experiment along with the era of voluntary personal disclosure-cum-exposure[38] that her project foreshadowed have reawakened controversial issues within feminisms.

III. ALLEN'S ANALYSIS: CYBERSPACE AND SELF-INVASION

Many authors, including those who identify as feminists[39] and those who do not, have analyzed Jennicam.[40] I have chosen to focus on self-identified feminist analysis in order to exploit an opportunity to work through issues such as identity, privacy, and pornography, which have long been contested subjects among those working toward the common goal of a lived social equality for women. It is my hope that issues raised by technologies like Jennicam might, through the relative "newness" of their contexts, open up a safe space for dialogue for those with differing visions on how women's lived social equality might be achieved. My aim is not to suggest that feminists must shirk from or resolve their substantive differences, but to suggest that some aspects of both

36. In an interview posted online in 2007, Ringley reported that after years of being so "over-exposed," she no longer had a website or even a MySpace page and was really enjoying her privacy: "Behind the Scenes with Jennifer Ringley," WebJunk TV (posted 18 March 2007), online: http://images.google.ca/imgres?imgurl=http://upload.wikime-dia.org/wikipedia/en/thumb/e/eo/Jennicam_o2.jpg/3oopx-Jennicam_o2.jpg&imgrefurl=http://en.wikipedia.org/wiki/JenniCam&h=225&w=3oo&sz=21&hl=en&start=11&um=1&tbnid=5dwhueB6yGXteM:&tbnh=87&tbnw=116&prev=/images%3Fq%3D%2Bjennifer%2Bringley%2Bcat%26um%3D1%26hl%3Den%26sa%3DN.

37. Senft, "Camgirls," 108–109 (n. 4).

38. Blogging and social networking trends involve millions in exposing their own personal information online: Alessandro Acquisti and Ralph Gross, "Imagined Communities: Awareness, Information Sharing and Privacy on the Facebook," *Privacy Enhancing Technologies Workshop* (2006): 1, http://www.heinz.cmu.edu/~acquisti/papers/acquisti-gross-facebook-privacy-PET-final.pdf.

39. I use the term "feminist" to refer to those dedicated to the objective of a lived social equality for women. In this particular context, I am focusing on those whose work strives to analyse and understand the potential contribution of the webcamming phenomenon to this lived social equality.

40. Burgin, "Jenni's Room," (n. 15); Jimroglou, "A Camera with a View," (n. 26); Hille Koskela, "Webcams, TV Shows and Mobile phones: Empowering Exhibitionism," *Surveillance & Society* 2, no. 2 (2004): 199, http://www.surveillance-and-society.org/articles2(2)/webcams.pdf.

past and current approaches may be more effective than others in forming strategies aimed at achieving meaningful social change.[41]

Three years before the final curtain fell on Jennicam, Anita Allen reflected on the continuing relevance of the pre-cyberspace feminist position on privacy set out in her 1988 book *Uneasy Access*.[42] In 1988, Allen had presented privacy as a condition of inaccessibility to others. She argued that the problem for women was that they had enjoyed too much of the wrong kinds of privacy (in the forms of modesty, isolation, chastity, and domestic violation) and too little of the right kinds, including "opportunities for replenishing solitude and independent decision making."[43]

Allen characterized her analysis in *Uneasy Access* as a feminist analysis with a liberal orientation.[44] It was feminist in that it accepted the idea that men and women had traditionally occupied separate spheres and the idea that the traditional liberal focus on keeping the state out of the private sphere—the sphere primarily occupied by women—had often disbenefited women by allowing various forms of domestic oppression to remain unchecked.[45] At the same time, Allen acknowledged the liberal orientation of her approach. Rather than suggesting that privacy was unlikely to *ever* materially advance the feminist project, Allen argued in favour of finding ways to ensure that the kinds of privacy traditionally enjoyed by individual men (such as "opportunities for replenishing solitude and independent decision making") were extended equally to individual women.[46]

Writing in 2000, Allen reflected on the fact that women's economic and social positions had changed significantly since the publication of *Uneasy Access*, leaving many women more centrally located in the public sphere than ever before. Even so, she noted that this existence within the public sphere carried other privacy-related burdens unique to women—including exposure to sexual harassment and more restrictive standards of modesty.[47]

When she approached the question of the relevance of cyberspace to her analysis, Allen concluded that themes raised by feminists in real space, such as objectification, subordination, violence, and isolation, were mapping themselves

---

41. Fraser and Nicholson suggest the importance of examining the helpful critiques that so-called feminist and post-modern positions can offer one another: Nancy Fraser and Linda Nicholson, *Social Criticism Without Philosophy: An Encounter Between Feminism and Postmodernism* (New York: Routledge, 1990), 20.

42. Anita L. Allen, *Uneasy Access—Privacy for Women in a Free Society* (New Jersey: Rowman & Littlefield, 1998).

43. Anita L. Allen, "Still Uneasy: Gender and Privacy in Cyberspace," *Stanford Law Review* 52 (2000): 1179.

44. *Ibid.*, 1182–1183.

45. *Ibid.*, 1177, 1182.

46. *Ibid.*, 1183.

47. *Ibid.*, 1180.

onto cyberspace.[48] Further, she argued that women's privacy was *more* at peril in cyberspace than men's, because there was a disrespect shown both for women and for the forms of privacy and intimacy most valued by women.[49] Allen identified voluntary self-exposure as a key abrogator of privacy in cyberspace and suggested that it created an expectation of the virtually unlimited accessibility of the female body.[50] Cyberspace practices, like voluntary webcamming in the home, she argued, directly raised the question of whether it was possible to invade one's own privacy, invoking the need for a liberal society to do more than simply criticize and tolerate.[51]

Allen suggested elsewhere that liberal thinkers might well be moved to support legislation that limited individuals' control over their own personal information on the basis that "people are choosing to give up more privacy than is consistent with liberal conceptions of the person or the liberal way of life."[52] She argued for recognition of the moral limits on the individual choice to give up personal information through self-disclosure and self-exposure.[53] In this way, Allen posited a vision that accepted the moral agency of individuals, but recognized occasions of incompatibility between the individual choice to waive control over personal information and a broader societal interest in maintaining personally and socially beneficial forms of privacy.[54]

Working from this perspective, Allen analyzed a number of examples of privacy-abrogating activities by women online—everything from posting mastectomy surgeries and live births online to egg selling, online communities, and fetishism. In relation to these examples, Allen stated,

> For better and sometimes for worse, in my opinion, these women repudiate expectations of female modesty, chastity and domestic seclusion.[55]

Nestled prominently among Allen's examples of repudiation was Jennicam. Allen acknowledged that in her project, Ringley made decisions "that represent a sharp break with the past and its expectations of domestic privacy and female modesty."[56] However, even as Allen recognized Ringley's rejection of the "wrong kinds of privacy," she expressed concern about the project's appeal to the same

48. *Ibid.*, 1184.

49. *Ibid.*, 1179.

50. *Ibid.*, 1184.

51. *Ibid.*, 1185.

52. Anita Allen, "Privacy as Data Control: Conceptual, Practical, and Moral Limits of the Paradigm," *Connecticut Law Review* 32 (2000): 871.

53. *Ibid.*, 871. She later more fully articulated this perspective in Anita Allen, *Why Privacy Isn't Everything: Feminist Reflections on Personal Accountability* (Boulder & New York: Rowman & Littlefield Publishers, Inc., 2003).

54. *Ibid.*

55. Allen, "Still Uneasy," 1187 (n. 43).

56. *Ibid.*, 1191.

male voyeuristic tendencies that have dominated women's experience in real space:

> Jenni's use of the cyber-world is playful and inventive, but it also replicates the condition of women in the real world—women are objects or commodities, and they are available on demand to men with "needs."[57]

Allen suggested Ringley's project was unlikely to advance women's interests, in that it appealed primarily to the "prurient interests" of men to see a strange woman's body.[58] She contrasted Jennicam with body-exposing projects of other women online, projects that she viewed as educational and, therefore, perhaps valuable enough to warrant the trade-off of privacy that was necessarily entailed in the exposure. Allen argued that access to information such as the reality of breast cancer through online streaming of a woman named "Patti's" double mastectomy and reconstructive surgeries brought to light essential issues that have been historically withheld from public view and discourse to the detriment of women's health.[59] In her comparison of Patti's double mastectomy with Jennicam, Allen acknowledged that "[s]ome feminists would applaud Jenni no less loudly than they would applaud Patti." However, Allen concluded, "If Patti is a teacher, Jenni is a call girl."[60]

IV. RECURRING THEMES: PRIVACY, IDENTITY AND PORNOGRAPHY

Allen's analysis acknowledges that flouting privacy could be freeing for women, especially if the trade-off involves access to other social goods for women, such as education. However, she remains cautious about the risk that such flouting may reinforce patriarchal notions about men's access to the bodies of women that they do not know. Others have suggested that traditional understandings of private and public spaces and strangers and intimates may not map onto multi-media projects such as Jennicam, which involve numerous forms of mediated interaction between the watcher and the watched.[61]

Further, one might wish to consider whether projects like Jennicam present other potential benefits not taken into account by Allen. Not only might Ringley's choice to occasionally display her naked body constitute an individually empowering rejection of the regime of shame surrounding women's bodies, a collective benefit may flow. Waivers like Ringley's may offer images that counter often-unrealistic, Hollywoodized versions of beauty and sexuality that undermine the

---

57. *Ibid.*, 1191.
58. *Ibid.*, 1191.
59. *Ibid.*, 1188.
60. *Ibid.*, 1191.
61. Senft, "Camgirls," 213 (n. 4).

confidence and self-perception of many girls and women.[62] One might also argue that the moments of Ringley's bodily exposure should be viewed in the context of her project as a whole, a context in which multiple identities of "woman" were performed—student, cat-lover, web designer, patient, sleeper, daughter, and girlfriend, to name a few. Otherwise, we may too easily dismiss the potential meaning of projects such as this to the sum of their sexually explicit moments, indirectly reinforcing patriarchal constructions through our acceptance of the interpretations of the voyeuristic male consumer. On the other hand, it seems irresponsible for feminists to posit the potential for the realization of the dream of women as powerful agents over their own identities, including with respect to their sexuality, without referring to the stark reality of patriarchal constructions that continue to interfere with the realization of this agency.

To my mind, experiments like Jennicam and analyses such as Allen's raise some of the central tensions among feminists and within feminisms. I propose to address two of them here: (a) privacy's usefulness (or uselessness) in achieving the project of a lived social equality for women; and (b) defining "woman" by reference to pornography.[63]

A. Privacy's "Usefulness" in the Social Equality Project

When Ringley turned the webcam onto her home life, making it accessible to all of those with an Internet connection, she contradicted (however consciously or unconsciously) a long-standing western societal presumption that what goes on inside the home is private. When she went further to transmit sequences of her in various states of undress and in sexual activity, her acts flew in the face of another such presumption—that women's naked bodies and sexual activity are private. Whether the privacy norm itself and explicit female rejections of interpretations thereof should be considered beneficial to the feminist struggle for equality has been a matter of some disagreement within feminist communities.

Allen remains committed to the idea that privacy is essential in promoting the objectives of a liberal society and can still be useful to women, provided that they are accorded access to the "right" kinds—privacy in service of "replenishing solitude and independent decision making," for example. Feminists ought not to throw away privacy because of its checkered past. Rather, they ought to seek access to the benefits of privacy that have long been enjoyed by men.[64]

---

62. For further analysis, see Naomi Wolf, *The Beauty Myth* (Toronto: Random House of Canada Limited, 1990), 185–186.

63. The term "pornography" is used quite differently by various feminists and, as will be discussed in detail in sub-part B below, these different approaches to the definition of pornography contribute significantly to the differences of opinion as to its social meaning and potential as a tool for effecting social change.

64. Allen, "Still Uneasy," 1182–1183 (n. 43).

In contrast, feminists like Catharine MacKinnon have questioned whether privacy is so steeped in a negative, individualistic history of protecting "private" male violence against women from public scrutiny and sanction that it is, at minimum, useless to and, more likely, harmful to the pursuit of a lived equality for women.[65] What Martha Nussbaum once referred to as a primary tool in defending the "killers of women,"[66] MacKinnon characterized as follows:

> This epistemic problem explains why privacy doctrine is most at home at home, the place women experience the most force, in the family, and why it centers on sex . . . For women the measure of the intimacy has been the measure of the oppression. This is why feminism has had to explode the private. This is why feminism has seen the personal as political. The private is public for those for whom the personal is political. In this sense, for women there is no private, either normatively or empirically.[67]

MacKinnon, therefore, has urged against a feminist strategy that involves primary reliance on "privacy," at least as it is predominantly understood within the western legal tradition. The issue, from this perspective, is not whether women have enough of the right kinds of "privacy," but whether privacy could ever be an effective tool in a state of inequality, where women are regularly placed within or associated with the private domain and men within the public. Privacy, under these conditions, it is argued, simply reinforces men's freedom to dominate women.

Critical race scholar Patricia Williams, on the other hand, has expressed more optimistic ideas about privacy's utility in struggles for social justice. Reflecting on the historic inability of blacks, and in particular of black women, to assert any meaningful right to privacy, Williams suggested that a better strategy was to redefine and redistribute privacy in a socially meaningful way "so that privacy is turned from exclusion based on self-regard into regard for another's fragile, mysterious autonomy."[68]

B. Defining "Woman" by Reference to Pornography

When Ringley performed in high heels and garter belts or had sex with her boyfriend in front of her webcam, did she waive her privacy in exchange for reinforcing the pornographic stereotype of women's sexual accessibility to men?

---

65. MacKinnon, *Feminism Unmodified*, 101 (n.1); Martha C. Nussbaum, "Is Privacy Bad for Women?" *Boston Review* (April/May 2000), http://bostonreview.net/BR25.2/nussbaum.html.

66. Nussbaum, *ibid.*

67. Catherine MacKinnon, *Toward A Feminist Theory of the State* (Massachusetts: Harvard University Press, 1989), 191.

68. Patricia Williams, *The Alchemy of Race and Rights: Diary of a Law Professor* (Cambridge: Harvard University Press, 1991), 164–165.

Allen's analysis seems to suggest so. In contrast, others have asked why one would zero in on those relatively few occasions in order to define Ringley, her project, and its purposes and, better yet, if one did so, why one would not envision Ringley's project as a liberating one.[69] These differing visions of the social meaning of sexually explicit imagery of women long predate Jennicam, and have animated feminist debate since at least the 1980s when Catharine MacKinnon and Andrea Dworkin sought to define pornography as an act of sex discrimination and a primary component of inequality between men and women. MacKinnon asserted,

> [P]ornography, with the rape and prostitution in which it participates, institu-tionalizes the sexuality of male supremacy, which fuses the eroticization of dominance and submission with the social construction of male and female. Gender is sexual. Pornography constitutes the meaning of that sexuality. Men treat women as whom they see women as being. Pornography constructs who that is. Men's power over women means that the way men see women defines who women can be. Pornography is that way.[70]

Dworkin conceptualized pornography under male supremacy as "the subordi-nation of women perfectly achieved [as] the access to [women's] bodies as a birthright to men.[71]

The arguments that the identity "woman" is socially constructed primarily in terms of sexual accessibility and submission to men, and that pornography is instrumental in creating and maintaining this sexual and gender hierarchy, stirred intense controversy in the feminist community. It is a controversy that seems, at least in some senses, to be reflected in feminist analyses of Jennicam. Allen maintained that Jennicam simply resulted in a waiver of privacy, of Ringley's modesty, in exchange for a supply of further sexualized images that reinforce the social construction of "woman"as she who is sexually accessible to men. Another approach, however, shares more in common with feminist critiques of Dworkin and MacKinnon's position. These critiques have arisen from feminists variously labeled as writing from "pro-sex" and "postmodern" positions—positions with which the so-called third wave of young feminist women is said to identify.[72] Differences in view have centered on what is meant by "pornography," and whether

---

69. Senft, "Camgirls," 199, 240 (n. 4).

70. MacKinnon, *Feminist Theory*, 197 (n. 67).

71. Andrea Dworkin, "Against the Male Flood: Censorship, Equality and Pornography" in *Feminism & Pornography*, ed. Drucilla Cornell (New York: Oxford University Press, 2000), 27.

72. For further analysis, see Jennifer Baumgardner and Amy Richards, *Manifesta—Young Women, Feminism and the Future* (New York: Farrar, Straus and Giroux, 2000); Bridget J. Crawford, "Toward a Third-Wave Feminist Legal Theory: Young Women, Pornography and the Praxis of Pleasure," *Michigan Journal of Gender and Law* 14 (2007): 99.

new forms of pornography could meaningfully counter and undermine the stereotypical constructions emanating from the materials addressed by Dworkin and MacKinnon.

Wendy Brown criticized MacKinnon's approach primarily on the basis that it mirrored the very system that it purported to criticize—heterosexual pornography.[73] Two of Brown's insights seem particularly pertinent in the context of the Jennicam debate. First, she argued that the Dworkin and MacKinnon theory erroneously converted "woman"—as discriminated against by virtue of her status as the sex object of man—into a universal truth from a temporary, particularized moment in history.[74] Brown suggested that pornography's role in the sexualized social construction of gender described by MacKinnon was primarily the product of a lack of sites of gender production and gender effects, which allowed a male heterosexual perspective to produce the binaries male and female that enhanced male dominance.[75] By presenting women's subjectivity as completely encompassed by the sexualized definition offered by mainstream heterosexual pornography at that moment,[76] Brown suggested that MacKinnon and Dworkin's approach offered no possibility for change—no possibility for the sexual emancipation of women.[77]

Brown then suggested that the moment in history described by MacKinnon and Dworkin has been shifted materially through representations of gender, sex, and sexuality that defy the male/female binary essential to their theory. Brown argued that it is through the profusion of sexualized images offering a multiplicity of gender and sexual identities that confining social constructions of mainstream heterosexual pornography can be undone.[78] She asserted that social orders are constructed in multiple sites and that women, as a class have the capacity to engage in subversive resignification—to seek sexual emancipation

---

73. Wendy Brown, "The Mirror of Pornography" in *Feminism & Pornography*, ed. Drucilla Cornell (New York: Oxford University Press, 2000), 198–217.

74. *Ibid.*, 207.

75. *Ibid.*

76. I find this aspect of Brown's analysis to be somewhat stilted and overreaching. The possibility of an erotic literature—such as that proposed by Audre Lorde ("Uses of the Erotic: The Erotic as Power" in *Sister Outsider: Essays & Speeches* (California: The Crossing Press, 1984), 53)—is not foreclosed by the Dworkin and MacKinnon analysis. Admittedly, however, where the sex or fantasies involved replicate the theme of female submission at the behest of male dominance, their analysis would certainly suggest the strong possibility of a false consciousness in women who claim to take pleasure in those roles. In other words, under their analysis, it becomes difficult to tell where what one woman thinks and feels ends and what she has been trained to think and feel begins.

77. In this regard, Brown notes, "MacKinnon's analysis is bound to its oft-noted theoretical closures and political foreclosures. 'There's no way out' is among students' most frequent responses to her work": Brown, "The Mirror of Pornography," 211 (n. 73).

78. *Ibid.*, 214.

on their own terms. The resignification process could even, Brown suggested, lead to the conclusion that some women consciously express and experience pleasure through submission. She proposed for feminism the task of articulating what she described as "more extravagant and democratic" analyses than that of Dworkin and MacKinnon.[79]

The idea that pornography, the erotic, and sexuality in general are susceptible to being reconfigured and redefined in more empowering ways for women is also reflected in the work of Angela Davis, Drucilla Cornell, and Candida Royalle. Davis, who suggested the problem lay in "our contemporary ideology of pornography [that] does not encompass the possibility of change, as if we were the slaves of history and not its makers,"[80] advocated for pornography depicting sexuality as part of broader social contexts involving healthy relationships with others.[81]

Like Davis, Cornell held out hope for a redefinition of sex and sexuality not through legal restrictions on pornography, but through support for more egalitarian productions that refute the gender stereotypes presented in mainstream heterosexual pornography.[82] Rather than working from the premise that the identity "woman" carved out in mainstream pornography defines all women for all time, necessarily compelling retreat from sexuality in order for women to be equal, Cornell suggests opening up production of imagery that allows women to explore their "imaginary domain"—"the moral and psychic space we as sexuate beings need in order to freely play with the sexual persona through which we shape our sexual identity, whether as man or woman, straight, gay, lesbian or transgender."[83] She argued that cinematic presentations of the fantasies of women characters, such as those depicted in Candida Royalle's work, presented hope for transformative visions of sexuality.[84]

Royalle—both an actor in pornography and a producer of it—prides herself in the production of erotic materials in which the working conditions allow those

---

79. Brown, "The Mirror of Pornography," 198 (n. 73).

80. Angela Davis, "Polemical Preface: Pornography in the Service of Women" in *Feminism & Pornography*, ed. Drucilla Cornell (New York: Oxford University Press, 2000), 527.

81. *Ibid.*, 539.

82. Drucilla Cornell, "Pornography's Temptation" in *Feminism & Pornography*, ed. Drucilla Cornell (New York: Oxford University Press, 2000), 553. The distinction between heterosexual pornography and gay and lesbian pornography is one made by authors like Brown and Cornell that has been powerfully contested by authors such as Christopher N. Kendall, *Gay Male Pornography: An Issue of Sex Discrimination* (Vancouver: UBC Press, 2004) and Janine Benedet, "Little Sisters Book and Art Emporium v. Minister of Justice: Sex Equality and the Attack on R. v. Butler," *Osgoode Hall Law Review* 39 (2001): 187.

83. *Ibid.*, 554.

84. *Ibid.*, 565. In this regard, the ideals behind Royalle's work seem to address many of the features of the male gaze identified as problematic by Mulvey in her analysis of film: Senft, "Camgirls," 75 (n. 4).

presented as submissive to be in control.[85] Concerned that women have been robbed of an aspect of their selves and their power by being told not to explore or to trust their sexual fantasies, Royalle insists on productions in which it is clear that the representations in play reflect the acting out of the fantasies of the woman rather than the man.[86] Further, her work strives to incorporate sexuality within the social context of other aspects of human interaction.

As the work of critical race scholars such as Sherene Razack and Kimberle Crenshaw reminds us, however, sexual emancipation for *all* women requires counter-narratives to far more than the dominant male/submissive female binary. Representations of sexuality frequenting much mainstream pornography also interlock with racist stereotypes. Whereas Caucasian and Asian women are stereotypically represented as submissive in mainstream pornography, Aboriginal[87] and black[88] women are frequently presented as hyper-sexualized predators, constantly sexually accessible to men. These myths are then used to stereotype women and even to justify sexual violence against them—from the typecast submissive white and Asian women caricatured as too modest either to consent or dissent, to mythical, hyper-sexualized Aboriginal and black women stereotyped into a constant state of consent. These insights make clear that sexual emancipation through woman-centered representations of sexuality depends upon much more than simply combating imagery of gendered dominance and submission.

If one extracts some of the key messages playing out in the feminist debates relating to privacy and pornography, one sees how aspects of Allen's analysis fit within the broader debate, and also how some of the key aspects and observations of the larger debate appear to apply directly to Jennicam. With respect to privacy, one fundamental question is whether privacy is a right or value that is strategically worth attempting to assert and enforce in order to improve women's social position—and to recognize that it is not equally accessible to all women. With respect to pornography, one fundamental question[89] is whether it is possible to transform pornography and its meanings by reshaping it in a manner that counters the aspects of mainstream pornography that constrain the identity "woman" with stereotyped presumptions of sexuality constructed not only in

---

85. Candida Royalle, "Porn in the USA" in *Feminism & Pornography*, ed. Drucilla Cornell (New York: Oxford University Press, 2000), 546.

86. *Ibid.*, 542, 546.

87. Sherene Razack, "Gendered Racial Violence and Spatialized Justice: The Murder of Pamela George," *Canadian Journal of Law and Society* 15, no. 2 (2000): 99.

88. Kimberle Crenshaw, "Mapping the Margins: Intersectionality, Identity Politics, and Violence Against Women of Colour," *Stanford Law Review* 43 (1991): 1241.

89. Another perhaps more fundamental question is whether it is a normatively useful exercise to attempt to breathe equality-affirming life into a form that has for so long been premised upon and drawn its power from inequality.

relation to gender but to interlocking axes of discrimination such as race. For those who believe that the resignification project is worth the effort, critical factors would appear to include the offering of sexual imagery that refutes raced and gendered stereotypes premised on dominance and submission present in mainstream pornography, the presentation of sex within the broader context of human interaction, the offering of imagery challenging dualistic sexes and sexualities, and the offering of imagery over which and in which women maintain control.

C. Thinking Strategically

Is flouting "privacy" a viable feminist strategy? Jennicam arguably flouted traditional notions of privacy in at least two senses. First, Ringley introduced a camera into what is traditionally viewed as the "private" sanctum of the home and made that content publicly accessible. Second, within the content that was released, Ringley included images of herself in various states of undress and engaged in various sexual activities. Could flouting these aspects of privacy constitute part of a viable feminist strategy and, if so, how?

To the extent that Ringley's exposure of the goings-on in her home could be characterized as transgressing notions of white, upper-middle-class feminized domesticity—rejecting the "a woman's place is in the home" tradition, it could well contribute to a demystification of the sanctity of the "home" that has been central to sheltering, among other things, male violence from social scrutiny.

At the same time that the privacy of the home has played a central role in sheltering male violence from state intervention, it can equally play a role in sheltering women in marginalized communities from the glare of public surveillance. Moreover, as the work of authors such as Williams suggests, the significance of a right to privacy may be much more easily dismissed by those of us in communities historically vested with the privilege of even asserting such a right to begin with. Given the somewhat duplicitous role that the "home" can play in women's lives and the social situatedness of having the privilege to "reject" privacy, it seems at least prudent to question whether a general "flouting" of the privacy of that "place" by a white, upper-middle-class, college-educated woman is likely to prove strategically useful to women who are not as comfortably situated.

With respect to flouting notions of what women are supposed to be doing in the private spaces of the home, it is possible to imagine situations in which a webcam might help to dispel sexualized or domesticized mythologies about what women are actually doing in their homes. The 24/7 nature of Jennicam presented an interesting prospect for doing this by allowing for the reality of the plain old mundane monotony that characterized much of the (in)action in Ringley's home. Unsurprisingly, however, it seems to have been the promise of the moments of sexual display that motivated many of her mainly male "fans" to tune in regularly.

Similarly, Ringley's flouting of the shroud of modesty cast around women's bodies might be seen as an empowering move—particularly insofar as she described one of the ends of her project to be speaking back to the beauty myths perpetuated in mainstream media. However, the very nature and existence of any such shroud is contentious due to the strangely duplicitous standards that seem to operate in western culture around the issue of women's naked bodies. In fact, the partially clad and unclad bodies of women permeate western culture and media—everything from cars to computers are eroticized through imagery of the naked or semi-naked female stranger. In contrast to what Allen argued about access to strange women's bodies, I would suggest that western culture is quite comfortable with the idea of having access to strange women's bodies. What we are more uncomfortable with is the concept of seeing the naked bodies of women with whom we are familiar as well as those thought to depart too significantly from the "norm."[90]

If one takes into account another author's suggestion that what happens in situations like Jennicam is the development of a sort of strange intimacy between the watcher and the watched,[91] it becomes difficult to tell whether Ringley was flouting convention by flashing her neighbors or actually behaving perfectly consistently with it by flashing strangers. One thing, however, seems certain. By having placed the camera in her home and chosen to turn it on and keep it on, Ringley flouted that aspect of convention that places the *initial* power of exposure in the hands of the other (the magazine, newspaper, and television producers for example).

As a result, it seems perfectly plausible to argue that projects like Jennicam have at least a limited potential to flout unhelpfully controlling conceptions of privacy as enforced domesticity and modesty by presenting an unromanticized and persisting insight into one woman's domestic sphere. Presentation of nudity as part of this context, particularly of a body distinct from conventional media standards of beauty as assessed by the individual woman herself, might also be conceptualized in this way. How far exposure of a white, middle class, blonde-haired woman's body takes us in terms of transgressing that norm is, however, certainly open to legitimate question. The more troubling aspect of Jennicam, and webcamming more generally, is the capacity of the audience to isolate imagery from its context and employ it in service of more mainstream messages affirming male entitlement to continuing access to women's bodies. Similar concerns arise in relation to pornographic meanings.

Can camgirl camp[92] destabilize the mainstream pornographic meaning of "woman"? The idea that the genders male and female are socially constructed

---

90. The "norm" is defined and confined by interlocking axes of discrimination, including race, ethnicity, sexual identity and ability.

91. Senft, "Camgirls," 213 (n. 4).

92. Senft, "Camgirls," 240 (n. 4).

and that pornography plays a central role in that construction are premises broadly accepted by many feminists.[93] Two contentious issues stem from these premises, however. First is the question of whether we would be freer if gender identities were left behind altogether. Second is the question of what role a different approach to pornography might play in the abandonment or reshaping of mainstream constructs.

Jennicam, shaped as it was by her mainstream, white, upper-middle-class existence, hardly presented possibilities for transgression with respect to sexual identities. The sexual imagery that Ringley presented largely played to the heterosexual male fantasy that animates mainstream pornography. However, the way in which Jennicam allowed us to see sexuality and gender being performed in daily life opened up a practical space in which concepts like performativity and the multiplicity of gender can be more easily grasped.

Jennicam, too, represents the opening up of a medium within which women might begin to gain greater access to a means of producing erotic imagery to counter mainstream pornography and its stereotypical messaging. However, when one considers the specifics of Jennicam, the criteria attached to visions of the subversive potential of a woman-centered reshaping of pornography seem to be lacking. First, staged heterofantasmic sexualized performances seem difficult to characterize as subversive of mainstream stereotypes—particularly where the performer is aware of, and perhaps strangely intimate with, the watcher, but not certain whether he is there or what exactly it is he is doing. These performances and other sexual activity that arose in the ordinary course of events in Ringley's life were part of an ongoing presentation of the broader social context of her life. In that way, Ringley's experiment presented the possibility of a pornography that integrates sex into the broader context of human interaction. The initial production was something over which Ringley asserted a degree of control,[94] serving both as a subject and object of the webcam. Problematically, however, ultimate control over the images, once released to the Internet, was placed in the hands of the watchers—some of whom chose to excerpt the sexual from its context in order to recreate material that shares many of the features of voyeuristic mainstream pornography.

In the case of Jennicam, the potential for subversive resignification is arguably undermined by the medium itself, insofar as it permits reversion of the content both to fit the traditional pornographic mould and to tell the same old story about the accessibility of women's bodies. Whether emerging Web 2.0 technologies will offer new potentialities for overcoming this particular bug is likely to be

---

93. However, the question of whether sex is the sole determinant of gender remains heavily contested.

94. However, Ringley certainly did not control the cinematic angling and shots or consciously script them in the way that Royalle suggested was essential to affirmation: Royalle, "Porn in the USA," (n. 84).

significantly affected by the features of the technologies themselves—and perhaps to an even greater extent on their accessibility to persons whose bodies do not coincide with those constructed as the "norm."

V. CONCLUSION

For me, what is perhaps the most important message arising from my thinking about Jennicam, the differing feminist responses to it, and the deeper theoretical contests lying below those differences, is the importance of direct feminist-to-feminist dialogue on issues of privacy, identity, and pornography. A key historic stumbling block has been in defining the terms of inter-feminist engagement in a way that promotes understanding and dialogue even as it fails to promote anything approaching unanimity.[95]

As feminists, we should consider the strategic benefits to the overall project of lived social equality for women of opening up to ideas inconsistent with our own, however deeply held. "New" technologies (as webcamming once was) present us with fresh terrain that allows us to assess the "truths" to which many of us have become quite attached in an atmosphere that doesn't require admitting that we may have gotten a few things wrong. Similarly, they invite a sharing of wisdom and thinking between contested feminisms and generations of feminists within new contexts that provide opportunities for recognizing that those who went before may also have gotten a few things right.

Experiments like Jennicam allow us to revisit the potential for individual transgression in the face of powerful social constructions and to reconsider concepts like privacy and pornography as tools for advancing the quest for a lived equality for women. Although, at the end of the day, Ringley's experiment itself was probably of limited utility in relation to this quest, the potential of future experiments with future technologies remains a theoretically open question. As these experiments and technologies unfold, I look forward to productive feminist dialogues unfolding along with them.

95. Unanimity is neither a practical nor a desirable goal. Disagreement about our views offers each of us the opportunity to clarify what it is we are really saying and to recognize strengths and weaknesses that may lead us to productive and empowering modifications in our thinking.

17. UBIQUITOUS COMPUTING, SPATIALITY, AND THE CONSTRUCTION OF IDENTITY
Directions for Policy Response

DAVID J. PHILLIPS

I. INTRODUCTION

This chapter argues that ubiquitous computing has the potential to profoundly affect our ability to inhabit and create our identities. Thus the infrastructure of ubiquitous computing—the symbiotic interrelations of laws, techniques, economic arrangements, and cultural practices that structure its use—is a profoundly important object of public policy.

Briefly, I argue that identity is the negotiated performance of meaningful relationships. Identity is always social. We are always and only who we are with respect to others.

Performances and enactments of identity call on a variety of resources. Among them are reciprocal techniques of visibility and concealment, ideals and genres of engagement, and tact. Spatiality is implicated in at least two ways. First, the architectures of lived space afford possibilities for visibility or concealment. They shape the ways in which we may see or be seen. Second, spaces themselves are socially meaningful. Certain roles and interactions are appropriate or not in certain spaces. Genres of performance create, sustain, and are supported by genres of place.

Ubiquitous computing—the embedding of networked sensing, calculating, and responsive machines throughout spaces—alters both these architectures of visibility and the ability to negotiate the sense and meaning of spaces. Because it affects the structures that mediate social relations, ubiquitous computing is an appropriate subject for public policy or regulatory intervention. However, most current approaches to such regulation have focused on protecting personal autonomy or privacy. Semiotic democracy, or the equitable distribution of the resources for social meaning making, provides a more productive framework for understanding the potential risks and benefits of ubiquitous computing.

Principles of telecommunications regulation may be effectively applied to the infrastructures mediating ubiquitous computing to more ethically design and distribute access to that infrastructure.

II. IDENTITY AND SOCIAL PERFORMANCE

Identity is the sharing, creating, and performing of socially meaningful relationships. As Erving Goffman put it in his classic *The Presentation of Self in Everyday Life*,

> to *be* a given kind of person . . . is not merely to possess the required attributes, but also to sustain the standards of conduct and appearance that one's social grouping attaches thereto. A status, a position, a social place is not a material thing, to be possessed and then displayed; it is a pattern of appropriate conduct, coherent, embellished, and well-articulated . . . It is something that must be enacted and portrayed, something that must be realized.[1]

Identity is social not merely in the sense of being relational; it is also social in that it is negotiated. Identity is both internal and external, simultaneously projected and imposed.[2] We do not stride into the social world as wholly formed individuals. Nor are we putty in the hands of the collective. Instead, we become who we are in relation to others, as others become themselves in relation to us. We realize who we are by noticing how we are treated, and we demand to be treated as the person we sense ourselves to be. Thus identity is a process, a becoming. It is the "systematic establishment and signification, between individuals, between collectivities, and between individuals and collectivities, of relationships of similarity and difference."[3] It is work.

Just because identity and social relations are continually coconstructed, doesn't mean that anything goes. These performances and negotiations occur in particular settings and call upon a variety of resources. These include, among others, a) resources structuring mutual awareness, b) shared vocabularies, grammars, or genres of identity, and c) tact.

Goffman uses the dramaturgical metaphors of front stage and backstage to discuss the negotiation of mutual awareness and visibility.[4] For example, to successfully enact a social role, individuals retreat to "back regions" to prepare for later performances before audiences in the "front region." In these back regions, performers collaborate with other team members in their preparations.

---

1. Erving Goffman, *The Presentation of Self in Everyday Life* (New York: Doubleday, 1959), 75.

2. Richard Jenkins, *Social Identity*, 2nd Ed. (New York: Routledge, 2004).

3. Jenkins, *Social Identity*, 5 (n. 2).

4. Goffman, *The Presentation of Self in Everyday Life* (n. 1).

Should the audience penetrate those back regions and become aware of those preparations, the front region performance loses some of its credibility. Therefore barriers are erected to control communication. In Goffman's work, these tend to be physical barriers such as doors or curtains.[5] Yet cultural codes, in-jokes, or shibboleths can also act as discriminating techniques, directing meanings and conversations among groups.[6]

Meaningful relations and identities are not created anew. Culturally shared ideal identities—waiter, crofter, man, woman—are called upon and reenacted in performance. These ideal identities are useful as shared cognitive frames, as paths of least resistance, and as ready-made symbolic resources. Successful performance can be understood as a command of these idioms and genres of identity.[7]

But these idioms and genres are themselves the result of complex and historically embedded social interaction. In a process of structuration,[8] the performances both call upon and create enduring patterns and genres of identity, relationship, and interaction. Bourdieu's concept of habitus describes this process.[9] The habitus, according to Bourdieu, is a set of dispositions, or "generative schemata of cognition, perception, evaluation etc."[10] Shared perspectives on normalcy, propriety, value, and sameness or difference may all be understood as aspects of habitus. While the habitus may be seen as the internalization of social structures, it also informs the practices which, in turn, reproduce social structures.[11] Thus the habitus "is the dynamic intersection of structure and action, society and the individual."[12] Familiar patterns and genres of identity are the product of the interactions they facilitate.

---

5. *Ibid.*, 106–140.

6. David J. Phillips, "From Privacy to Visibility: Context, Identity, and Power in Ubiquitous Computing Environments," *Social Text* 23, no. 2 (2005): 95–108.

7. Judith Butler, "Imitation and Gender Insubordination," in *The Lesbian and Gay Studies Reader*, ed. H. Abelove, M. A. Barale, and D. Halperin (New York and London: Routledge, 1993), 307–320; Goffman, *The Presentation of Self in Everyday Life* (n. 1).

8. Anthony Giddens, *The Constitution of Society: Outline of a Theory of Structuration* (Berkeley: University of California, 1984).

9. Pierre Bourdieu, *Distinction: a Social Critique of the Judgment of Taste* (London: Routledge, 1984).

10. Nicos Mouzelis, "Habitus and Reflexivity: Restructuring Bourdieu's Theory of Practice," *Sociological Research Online* 12, no. 6 (2007), par 1.1, http://www.socresonline.org.uk/12/6/9.html.

11. Mouzelis, "Habitus and Reflexivity: Restructuring Bourdieu's Theory of Practice," (n. 9).

12. C. Calhoun, E. LiPuma, and M. Postone, "Introduction: Bourdieu and Social Theory," in *Bourdieu: Critical Perspectives*, ed. C. Calhoun, E. LiPuma, and M. Postone (Cambridge: Polity Press, 1993), 4.

Finally, performances call upon tact. They call upon an audience willing to go along, to negotiate a mutually acceptable definition of identities, relationships, and situations.[13] The tact, the degree of play that one can rely upon, varies enormously. For example, unusual gender performances notoriously call forth intransigence, as can attest anyone who has tried to live a queer identity.

At stake in these negotiations is neither autonomous decision-making nor the protection of any core self, but the structure of rights, resources, and power. As Goffman put it, an identity claim is an effort to control the conduct of others toward oneself, a demand to be treated in a certain way, as a certain sort of person.[14] And as Eliza Doolittle put it, "The difference between a flower girl and a lady is not how she behaves, but how she is treated."[15]

In assessing these negotiations in terms of social justice, we might look at where power lies in these negotiations. Whose definitions of situations, whose identity claims, whose strategies of performance, count? As we intervene in these negotiations, either through policy or technology, we might look specifically to new practices and structures that alter visibilities, meaning-making, or tact. Who is able to see or conceal what, and in what conditions? Who is able to influence schemas of cognition and evaluation? How rigid are these structures? How much leeway is granted, and how great is the cost of transgression?

III. IDENTITIES AND PERFORMANCES IN SPACE

As Dourish and Bell put it, "the organization of space [is] an infrastructure for the collective production and enactment of cultural meaning."[16] Spatiality is implicated in identity negotiation in at least two ways. First, and most obviously, spatial arrangements structure resources of visibility and copresence. Goffman's notions of front and back stages are inherently spatial and architectural. People retire behind closed doors before they drop one role, one set of social demands, and take on another. Curtains, one-way mirrors, street lighting, and ha-ha's all shape the interactions between individuals and their audience.

Second, though, spatial organization permits different possibilities for the "mutual coordination of actions" and so for collective meaning-making.[17] Certain

---

13. Goffman, *The Presentation of Self in Everyday Life*, 9 (n. 1).

14. Goffman, *The Presentation of Self in Everyday Life*, 3 (n. 1).

15. George B. Shaw, *Pygmalion* (Baltimore: Penguin Books, 1951), 99.

16. Paul Dourish and Genevieve Bell, "The Infrastructure of Experience and the Experience of Infrastructure: Meaning and Structure in Everyday Encounters with Space," *Environment and Planning B* 43 (2007): 414–430, 415.

17. Dourish and Bell, "The Infrastructure of Experience and the Experience of Infrastructure: Meaning and Structure in Everyday Encounters with Space," 419.

settings carry expectations of appropriate actions and exchanges; certain roles and relations are easier to sustain in certain places.

Yet the logic of space does not precede the logic of interaction. Again in a process of structuration, settings themselves are negotiated and created along with the performances, the roles, and the identities that they support. Space is produced by the actions it mediates. Standards of appropriate activity, and hence the meaning of spaces, are under constant renegotiation. Dodge and Kitchin refer to this as "transduction"—"the constant making anew of a domain in reiterative and transformative practices."[18]

As with the negotiation of identity, the negotiation of space calls upon genres of interaction. Spaces are "negotiated through learnt, relational, or familiar practice."[19] They are given meaning, they inform action, with respect to habitus. Individual decisions, informed by habitus, take on a "collective logic."[20] That collective logic is expressed in patterns of spatial organization. Thus although space is produced in improvised interactions, those improvisations conform to learned and familiar genres and idioms, and spaces tend to coalesce into relatively stable and recognizable places, neighborhoods, or regions. Certain places become more attractive to people of shared habitus. This "clustering of people of similar habitus" produces what Parker et al. refer to as "class places."[21]

This recursive construction of habitus and place is itself structured by laws, economics, and cultural norms. Berlant and Warner, for example, talk of how zoning laws that relegate erotic bookstores and clubs to unpopulated areas deeply impacts the street life of urban neighborhoods and hence the opportunities for queer interactions, identities, and visibilities.[22] The boundaries of tact and the potential for practical ambiguity are imbricated with economic interests and physical structures. The strategic ambiguity of department store windows, for example, provides opportunities legitimately to dawdle and tarry (and perhaps, covertly, to flirt).[23]

---

18. Martin Dodge and Rob Kitchin, "Code and the Transduction of Space," *Annals of the Association of American Geographers* 95, no. 1 (2005): 162–180, 162.

19. Dourish and Bell, "The Infrastructure of Experience and the Experience of Infrastructure," (n. 17), 420.

20. Roger Burrows and Nick Ellison, "Sorting Places Out? Towards a Social Politics of Neighborhood Informatization," *Information, Communication, & Society* 7, no. 3 (2004): 321–336, 331.

21. Simon Parker, Emma Uprichard, and Roger Burrows, "Class Places and Place Classes: Geodemographics and the Spatialization of Class," *Information, Communication, & Society* 10, no. 6 (2007): 902–921, 905.

22. Lauren Berlant and Michael Warner, "Sex in Public," *Critical Inquiry* 24 (1998): 547–566.

23. George Chauncey, *Gay New York: Gender, Urban Culture, and the Making of the Gay Male World, 1890–1940* (New York: Basic Books, 1994), 187–205.

IV. SURVEILLANCE, UBIQUITOUS COMPUTING, AND IDENTITY NEGOTIATION

Two cultural shifts are causing deep structural changes to the negotiations of space and identity. The first is the increasing prevalence of surveillance as a mode of knowledge production. Although Lyon has described surveillance as "any collection and processing of personal data, whether identifiable or not, for the purposes of influencing or managing those whose data have been garnered," I wish to think of surveillance as a very particular form of the collection and processing of data and the management of populations.[24]

In this idealized form, surveillance individualizes each member of the population, and permits the observation and recording of each individual's activities, then collates these individual observations across the population. From these conglomerated observations, statistical norms are produced. These norms are then applied back to the subjected individuals, who are categorized and perhaps acted upon according to their relation to the produced norm. Thus surveillance produces both discipline (that is, conformity to the norm), and the disciplines (regulated fields of knowledge and expertise).[25] It alters both the structures of visibility and the structures of meaning making. It renders us visible—it identifies us—in relation to the norms it produces.

This model of knowledge production operates every day, usually silently and without notice, in computer-mediated communication systems. A paradigmatic example is the *Wall Street Journal Online*. The system uses "cookies" to uniquely identify individual users, then to monitor and track their traversal of the site. The information thus gathered is statistically analyzed to place each user in one of eight categories (car buffs, consumer techies, engaged investors, health enthusiasts, leisure-minded, mutual-fund aficionados, opinion leaders, or travel seekers). This categorical identification then becomes the knowledge guiding the treatment of each individual, as different advertisements are served to members of different classes.[26]

Surveillance as a technique of knowledge production and population management is becoming a central organizing principle of modern institutions. It is being adopted in more and more institutional settings. It is especially important in the understanding and management of populations in space.

---

24. David Lyon, *The Surveillance Society: Monitoring Everyday Life* (Buckingham: Open University, 2001), 2.

25. Michel Foucault, *Discipline and Punish: The Birth of the Prison* (New York: Pantheon Books, 1979).

26. Nat Ives, "Online Profiling, Separating the Car Buff from the Travel Seeker, Is a New Tool to Lure Advertisers," *The New York Times*, June 16, 2003, C10.

Geodemographics is the "codification and spatial mapping of habitus."[27] Geodemographic systems correlate residential data with personal data, including credit card purchases, subscription data, and public records, to produce statistical identity categories. These categories include, for example, "Blue Blood Estates" ("The nation's second-wealthiest lifestyle,. . . characterized by married couples with children, college degrees, a significant percentage of Asian Americans and six-figure incomes . . .") and "Shotguns and pickups" (". . . young, working-class couples with large families . . . living in small homes and manufactured housing"). These lifestyle clusters are associated with particular neighborhoods. Subscribers to geodemographic services can then choose a neighborhood and discover the prevalence of particular lifestyles within that neighborhood. As one of these services puts it, "You are Where You Live."[28]

These categorization techniques work. They seem to be correlate both with the observations of ethnographers and with the subjective perceptions of inhabitants. Thus they can be seen as one mechanism of normativity, entrenchment, and stabilization in the cocreation of identities and places.[29]

The second deep structural shift in the resources of identity negotiation is the development of ubiquitous computing. Also known as ambient intelligence or pervasive computing, this is the trend toward distributing computing systems throughout space. Sensors, computation devices, and responders are being embedded into everyday objects and linked in networked communication to create an environment that is itself "perceptive, interpretive, [and] reactive."[30]

Ubiquity implies spatiality; ubiquitous computing mediates our awareness of places and our ability to create, engage, and use those places. It "modulates space by significantly altering the conditions through which space is continually beckoned into being."[31] It mediates the practices of "locating and hailing people and things."[32]

Like zoning laws, the infrastructures of ubiquitous computing and surveillance become resources in the mutual construction of habitus and place. Corporations and police agencies have been particularly vocal about their interest in using them

---

27. Parker et al., "Class Places and Place Classes: Geodemographics and the Spatialization of Class," 905, (n. 21).

28. Claritas Inc. 2008. "Customer Segmentation > 66 PRIZM Marketing Segments, Claritas Customer Segmentation," http://www.claritas.com/claritas/Default.jsp?ci=3&si=4&pn=prizmne_segments (accessed March 4, 2008).

29. Parker et al., "Class Places and Place Classes: Geodemographics and the Spatialization of Class," (n. 21).

30. Anne Galloway, "Intimations of Everyday Life," *Cultural Studies* 18, no. 2/3 (2004): 384–408, 388.

31. Dodge and Kitchin, "Code and the Transduction of Space," 178 (n. 18).

32. Mike Crang and Stephen Graham, "Sentient Cities: Ambient Intelligence and the Politics of Urban Space," *Information, Communication & Society* 10, no. 6 (2007): 789–817, 794.

to normalize places and the activities that constitute them. With ubiquitous computing, physical stores hope to mimic the classificatory and responsive actions of online sites such as the *Wall Street Journal*.[33] RFID tags (small tags that emit short, unique identifiers) or iris scanners might recognize return shoppers, or infer genres of behavior from a new shopper's actions, and respond accordingly. Perhaps the system will automatically send an enticing message to the shopper's PDA. Perhaps the security cameras will be automatically trained on a suspected shoplifter.

Some in the U.S. military have advocated for a "Manhattan project" to develop pervasive identification and tracking, especially in urban areas. The goal would be to identify the abnormal from a background of normalcy. This is a project of "anticipatory seeing," extending codes of normativity from the past into the future.[34]

It is important to remember first that ubiquitous computing does not necessarily imply surveillance as we have defined it here, and second that the knowledge produced in surveillance is not necessarily oppressive. All individuals and groups call on norms and genres to make sense of themselves and the world, if only to question their position relative to those norms and genres. The question is not how to stop the expansion of ubiquitous computing and surveillance. Rather, the question is how that expansion will be regulated and structured to allocate access to the resources that ubiquitous computing and surveillance provide.

The time for this is ripe. Although the technologies exist for the aforementioned scenarios, the "commercial logics" of these networks—mutually agreeable technical and economic arrangements among those who would provide, transport, and manipulate data—are unstable.[35] Intervention at the level of policy, especially policy that addresses these nascent commercial logics, might now determine whether ubiquitous computing and surveillance are useful mostly for the replication, reentrenchment, and amplification of existing power relations, or whether the infrastructure might be available for novel, even transgressive and transformative, coalitions.

V. POLICY RESPONSES

Privacy has been a common response to the changes in visibility that ubiquitous computing entails. But, for several reasons, privacy fails as an antidote to

---

33. Jerry Kang and Dana Cuff, "Pervasive Computing: Embedding the Public Sphere," *Washington and Lee Law Review* 62 (2005): 93–146, 106–107.

34. Crang and Graham, "Sentient Cities: Ambient Intelligence and the Politics of Urban Space," 803 (n. 32).

35. *Ibid.*, 795.

surveillance.[36] In general, privacy law is geared toward protecting the autonomy and dignity of the individual. It offers a naive treatment of the relation between the individual and society, in that it understands individual awareness and cognition as preceding social interaction. Especially in the United States, privacy law is profoundly ambivalent and even inept in its approach to the effects of technical mediation. For example, it offers no legal distinction between face-to-face visual monitoring and 24-hour video recording of the workplace.[37] Moreover, the extent of privacy law's protection is inextricably linked to an essentialist definition of the space one inhabits at the moment. That is, activities in a private place are private; activities in a public place are public. Hence it is difficult to apply privacy principles to ubiquitous computing as a technical mediation of public space. New legal theories interpreting privacy as the protection of "contextual integrity"[38] offer some hope here, but so far that work has failed to adequately address context not as merely the container of activities, but as the product of activities.

Data protection is often conflated, both administratively and conceptually, with privacy protection. It is important, though, to carefully disentwine the two. Data protection both narrows and broadens the scope of privacy protection. Unlike privacy law, it is concerned only with the creation, storage, and transfer of information about individuals. However, it explicitly expands privacy interests beyond physical spaces, and recognizes that new forms of technological mediation require new forms of regulatory principles and practice.

The principles of data protection require that information relating to identifiable individuals be collected only with notice and consent and for an explicit purpose. The information is to be used only for that purpose, and to be retained only as long as is necessary for that purpose. The data holder is responsible for the accuracy, completeness, and security of the data. Data subjects have the right to access and correct data held about them. These principles are generally enforced by government commissions with oversight authority.[39]

These are certainly useful principles for structuring access to the resources of ubiquitous computing. In theory, transparency and consent are essential to exercising meaningful decisions. In order to translate Goffman's back and front regions to the world of ubiquitous computing, one must know what systems of data gathering are in operation and one must be able to consent to that gathering. In practice, though, these principles become not only difficult to enforce, but

---

36. Felix Stalder, "Privacy Is Not the Antidote to Surveillance," *Surveillance & Society* 1, no. 1 (2002): 120–124.

37. *Vega-Rodriguez v Puerto Rico Tel. Co* [1997] 110 F. 3d 174 (US 1st Cir).

38. Helen Nissenbaum, "Technology, Values, and the Justice System: Privacy and Contextual Integrity," *Washington Law Review* 79 (2004): 119–157.

39. Colin Bennett and Charles Raab, *The Governance of Privacy* (Cambridge: MIT, 2006), 12–13.

problematic in themselves. As anyone who has set their browser to inform them whenever they accept a "cookie" can attest, it is in fact impossible to consider and consent to each instance of pervasive data gathering.

Just as consent becomes more and more impracticable, so does the obligation to hold data only for specified purposes. Not only are there countless exceptions to this requirement, but the requirement itself is construed so broadly that virtually any "legitimate business purpose" is considered sufficient.[40]

Finally, protection is limited to data relating to a personally identifiable individual. But often the purpose of surveillance and ubiquitous computing is to discover or create usable patterns in vast amounts of data, rather than to isolate or act upon any particular individual. Any social, rather than personal, implications of that sort of knowledge production are orthogonal to the principles' intent. Recently, though, an EU policy team has recommended that data be subject to protection if it "is used to determine or influence the way in which [a] person is treated or evaluated."[41] This would certainly seem to cover, for example, mobile carriers supplying marketers with anonymized locational data that would nevertheless permit the marketers to deliver location-specific messages to mobile phones. However, the recommendations specify that the data be used to influence a "person," and it is not clear that it would apply to the wholesale use of large quantities of anonymized locational data if that information were used in ways that affected the lives of many people (for example, in siting billboards or roadblocks), so long as none of them were targeted individually.[42]

Some recent trends in intellectual property law might have some bearing on ubiquitous surveillance. These trends attempt to extend intellectual property to aboriginal or tribal artifacts or knowledge in order to protect not merely the economic value of the artifact, but the cultural identity of its producers. The harm to be addressed is inauthentic cultural representation, resulting in a "misrecognition" that is "demeaning or contemptible."[43] At first glance, insofar as geodemographic models or other typifications of place,

40. Oscar H. Gandy, Jr., "Legitimate Business Interest: No End in Sight? An Inquiry into the Status of Privacy in Cyberspace," *The University of Chicago Legal Forum* 77 (1996): 77–137.

41. European Union. 2005. *Working document on data protection issues related to RFID technology.* Working Party on the Protection of Individuals with Regard to the Processing of Personal Data. Brussels. WP 105 (19 January 2005), http://ec.europa.eu/justice_home/fsj/privacy/docs/wpdocs/2005/wp105_en.pdf (accessed August 15, 2007).

42. David J. Phillips, "Locational Surveillance: Embracing the Patterns of Our Lives," in *Handbook of Internet Politics*, ed. P. Howard and A. Chadwick (London: Routledge, in press).

43. Madhavi Sunder, "Intellectual Property and Identity Politics: Playing with Fire," *Journal of Gender, Race & Justice* 4 (2000): 69–98, 69–72, quoting Charles Taylor, "The Politics

identity, or activity can be seen as cultural representations, an approach aimed at protecting their authenticity might seem to hold promise. But in fact, these models and typifications are often, by any objective measure, authentic. As previously mentioned, geodemographic categories capture fairly well the lived sense of place, nor are they obviously demeaning or contemptible. The problem is not their authenticity, but the reentrenchment and reenactment of very particular, predictable, manageable types of authenticity. Just as the protection of "contextual integrity" as a privacy principle ignores the emergent qualities of context, so does the protection of "authentic cultural representation" ignore the emergent qualities of culture. Cultural identity is always a work in progress, "a matter of 'becoming' as well as 'being.'"[44] Protecting "authenticity" adds a perhaps unwanted and stultifying restraint to this process of becoming.

None of these policy frames—the protections of privacy, data integrity, or cultural representation—specifically address that process of becoming. None of them focus on the equitable distribution of the resources necessary for the cultural production of identity. We are not concerned merely with protection from the excesses of administrative management. Instead, we want to facilitate active engagement in the cocreation of the informational/geographic/social landscape. The question is not how to protect our privacy; it is how to be public, how to engage in public life, how to figure out one's situation, identity, and desires *in community*. To turn in that direction, we might look again to current work in intellectual property law to borrow and extend the idea of "semiotic democracy," or common sense making.[45]

The phrase, "semiotic democracy," was first coined by John Fiske in 1987.[46] Fiske used the term to refer to the process of returning to audiences the power to recode cultural symbols to express meanings divergent from the intent of their creators. More recently, it has been taken up by legal activists in their fight against exclusive ownership of meaningful cultural icons.[47] While many of these scholars deploy the ideal of semiotic democracy in specific legal battles over the right to use industrially produced cultural symbols such as Barbie or Mickey Mouse, it has also been more generally referenced in what Benkler refers to as

> the capacity and need to observe a cultural production and exchange system and to assure that it is as unconstraining and free from manipulation

of Recognition," *Multiculturalism*, ed. Amy Guttmann (Princeton: Princeton University, 1992): 25–73, 25.

44. *Ibid*, 86, quoting Stuart Hall, "Cultural Identity and Diaspora", in *Identity: Community, Culture, Difference*, ed. Jonathan Rutherford (London: Lawrence & Wishart, 1990): 223–240, 225.

45. Madhavi Sunder, "IP3," *Stanford Law Review* 59 (2006): 257–332, 279.

46. John Fiske, *Television Culture* (London: Routledge, 1987).

47. For example, Lawrence Lessig, *Free Culture* (New York: Penguin, 2004).

as possible. We must diagnose what makes a culture more or less opaque to its inhabitants; what makes it more or less liable to be strictly constraining of the conversations that rely on it; and what makes the possibility of many and diverse sources and forms of cultural intervention more or less likely.[48]

When we imagine cultural production and exchange as not merely the traffic of symbolic artifacts, but instead as the creation and interpretation of patterns of lived, embodied interactions in space, then the ambit of concern about semiotic democracy extends well beyond intellectual property. What we seek to protect and nurture is the project of "world-making,"[49] the possibilities for "new genres of communication, new styles of contestation, new solidarities or enmities, and new settings for interaction,"[50] by providing for "space[s] of entrances, exits, unsystematized lines of acquaintance, projected horizons, typifying examples, alternate routes, blockages, [and] incommensurate geographies."[51] As Noveck puts it, people "com[e] together, not just to create content, but also to create power."[52]

Crang and Graham, among others, offer visions for ubiquitous computing practices that might "reenchant and reanimate" cities, "destabiliz[e] space," decenter subjectivity, and enable new social performances and new public identities.[53] They suggest three things that ubiquitous computing must provide to enable this generative sociality. First, the environment's coding must be "transparent and/or aesthetically problematic."[54] Ubiquity need not imply invisibility or seamlessness. Indeed, Ratto has outlined the ethical problems of "seamlessness":

. . . the seams between systems provide the most opportunity for extending, troubling, and repurposing infrastructures . . . If the infrastructures themselves hide these seams from view, we are left with little recourse to the kinds of actions, behaviors, and identities infrastructures presuppose . . . By removing our knowledge of the glue that holds the systems that make up the infrastructure together, it becomes much more difficult, if not impossible,

48. Yochai Benkler, *The Wealth of Networks* (New Haven: Yale University Press, 2006), 298–299.

49. Berlant and Warner, "Sex in Public," 558 (n. 22).

50. Mustafa Emirbayer and Mimi Sheller, "Publics in History," *Theory and Society* 28 (1999): 145–197, 164.

51. Berlant and Warner, "Sex in Public," 558 (n. 22).

52. Beth Simone Noveck, "A Democracy of Groups," *First Monday* 10, no. 11 (2005), under "The Wisdom of Crowds," http://firstmonday.org/issues/issue10_11/noveck/index.html.

53. Galloway, "Intimations of Everyday Life," 397 (n. 30); Crang and Graham, "Sentient Cities: Ambient Intelligence and the Politics of Urban Space," 806, 812 (n. 32).

54. Crang and Graham, "Sentient Cities: Ambient Intelligence and the Politics of Urban Space," 806 (n. 32).

to begin to understand how we are constructed as subjects, what types of systems are brought into place (legal, technical, social, etc.) and where the possibilities for transformation exist.[55]

Second, the ubiquitously coded environment should admit of plural authorship, folksonomies, lay classifications, and community mapping.[56]

Finally, the infrastructure should promote "new practices of direct contact and association."[57] Coded, aware, and responsive environments can provide opportunities for new kinds of gaming, new modes of interactive art. For example, Kang and Cuff discuss an urban artscape where inhabitants anonymously relay biometric information such as heartbeat or respiration to a central server, where it is aggregated and used to control a light display, publicly visualizing the city's "mood."[58]

All of these are structural prerequisites for nonnormative play, for "ephemeral . . . and fugitive" acts of world-making, for space that is "public in the sense of accessible, available to memory, and sustained through collective activity."[59] We might look to telecommunications policy for ways to sustain these structural prerequisites. The most obvious reason for this is that telecommunications companies and services in fact permeate the infrastructures that mediate ubiquitous computing. For example, telecommunications companies own the backbones that transport IP traffic. They own many of the ISPs through which households access the backbone. They are the first holder of the locational data generated through their mobile systems. They control access between mobile users and services through contract agreements with each.[60] They own or have financial interests in informational content—from directories to sports teams to movies. They care deeply about the demographic, cultural, and economic composition of the markets for these services. Because ubiquitous computing has the potential to reconfigure those markets, and the means of their construction, telecom companies have complex and contradictory interests in providing interconnections to the services and devices that comprise ubiquitous computing.

55. Matt Ratto, "Ethics of Seamless Infrastructures: Resources and Future Directions," *International Review of Information Ethics* 8, no. 8 (2007): 20–27, 25; http://www.i-r-i-e.net/inhalt/008/008_5.pdf.

56. Crang and Graham, "Sentient Cities: Ambient Intelligence and the Politics of Urban Space," 806 (n.32).

57. *Ibid.*

58. Kang and Cuff, "Pervasive Computing: Embedding the Public Sphere," 144 (n. 33).

59. Berlant and Warner, "Sex in Public," 561–562 (n. 22).

60. David J. Phillips, "Texas 9–1–1: Emergency Telecommunications, Deregulation, and the Genesis of Surveillance Infrastructure," *Telecommunication Policy* 29, no. 11 (2005): 843–856; Larry Magid, "Global Positioning by Cellphone," *New York Times*, July 19, 2007, C7.

316 DAVID J. PHILLIPS

Telecommunications policy has a rich history of addressing this complexity through sophisticated synthesis of industrial, technical, and social policy. Although the trend for the past two decades has been to abandon that sophistication in favor of a no-holds-barred grab for territory and power, it is nevertheless instructive to remember and resurrect the traditional theories and mechanisms of telecommunications policy.

Historically, telecommunications policy has, to one degree or another, approached information and communication infrastructure as a public resource. Its objective has been to provide universal access to the communication services that are deemed essential to social and political participation. Not only is service to be universally available, it is to be amenable to all sorts of content without public censorship or private gatekeeping.[61] This approach and these goals are increasingly crucial political tenets as communication, information, networks, geography, sociality, identity, and political power become more intimately interdependent.

In recognition of this interdependence, especially between physical and informational spaces, policy should address the concern that monopoly ownership of physical space can be leveraged to colonize information space. For example, Kang and Cuff suggest that mall owners can manage the information space of malls by providing WiFi access, but requiring registration and imposing filters. Telecommunications policy can thwart this colonization by supporting the development of broad range, high bandwidth data services. If these are offered under common carriage requirements, then jamming or filtering (for example, by mall operators) would constitute unlawful interference with radio signals. Thus the private space of the mall might be overlaid with a mosaic of information spaces, and the information infrastructure can support positions apart from the mall from which to negotiate its meaning and the interactions it affords.[62]

This then shifts the concern over filtering and jamming to the carriers themselves. How can policy structurally prevent telephony operators, with their complex economic interests, from shaping access to the information space to advance those interests? In the past, in the United States, this was accomplished through the strict structural separation of economic interests in content and conduit. AT&T may have been the only phone company in the country, but (in theory at least) they could deny access to no one, and they could only make money by carrying other people's content. So, again at least in theory, their sole

61. For a comprehensive set of desiderata for advanced telecommunication in the public interest, see Amelia Potter and Andrew Clement, "A Desiderata for Wireless Broadband Networks in the Public Interest," 35th Research Conference on Communication, Information and Internet Policy (Arlington, VA, 2007).

62. Kang and Cuff, "Pervasive Computing: Embedding the Public Sphere," 140 (n. 33).

economic incentive was to promote as much communication as possible, regardless of the content or among whom that content flowed.

Since the mid'90s, and again especially in the United States, the structural walls between content and conduit have vanished, and their return is extremely unlikely. This policy trend in telecommunications has supported an industrial configuration with intrinsic tendencies toward closure, gatekeeping, and control. This trend is not total, however. The Federal Communications Commission, under pressure from a coalition of equipment manufacturers and service providers, recently ruled that licensees in some wireless spectrums must use that spectrum for open platform services.[63] The debate over net neutrality, requiring nondiscriminatory access to network capacity, is far from over.

VI. CONCLUSION

I have argued in this chapter that ubiquitous computing alters the resources available for the construction and embodiment of social identities. I have outlined some of the activities entailed in that construction and embodiment, and suggested how ubiquitous computing, as mediated by industrial arrangements, potentially restructures those activities. I have offered "semiotic democracy" as a unifying frame for policy responses to ubiquitous computing, and I have laid out a palette of existing regulatory principles and practices that might be creatively synthesized to formulate new regimes that simultaneously address economic, social, and technical structures as an organic whole.

However, I have two final suggestions, only peripherally related to information policy.

Tact was mentioned earlier as one of the primary social resources in the negotiation of identity. There must be some leeway, some willingness to go along, some balance of power before anything like negotiation can occur. This resource is under severe pressure in a political and social environment almost obsessively concerned with security and engaged in an apparently unending "war on terror" that itself produces and depends on a climate of fear and distrust. This social and political climate nurtures the kinds of technical and policy decisions that relish the production of the normal and the fear and punishment of deviancy. Until we find a way to counteract the political rhetoric of "good guys vs. bad guys," policies supporting nonnormative cultural production and exchange are pie-in-the-sky.

---

63. Stephen Labaton, "Airwaves, Web Power At Auction," *The New York Times*, January 22, 2008, C1.

Finally, we need to put good ethnographic work on an equal footing with policy analysis. Networked, ubiquitous, and pervasive computing infrastructures are transforming interactions, spaces, places, identities, and relations that we used to take for granted. New practices are altering the ways in which we get along in the world. We must look at how we actually do get along. Because we *do* get along. In myriad ways and every day, we act *ourselves*. We get out of each other's way, we mind our own business, we live and let live, we are strategically intransigent, we watch our backs. I suggest we look carefully at the conditions and resources that permit us to do so, try to discover how the information environment is implicated in those activities, and so develop new paradigms for democracy, sociability, and self-determination.[64]

---

64. For an excellent treatment of user and group centered analysis, modeling, and visualization of social, physical, and informational overlays, see Jeni Paay, Bharat Dave, and Steve Howard, "Understanding and Representing the Social Prospects of Hybrid Urban Spaces," *Environment and Planning B* 34 (2007): 446–465.

the historical cynic of the same name (who, you might recall, once suggested to a fawning Alexander the Great that the greatest honor the king could grant him was that of moving a little to the side so that he could continue to soak up the sun's rays). Our fictitious Diogenes is strongly driven by the lead of impulse and completely ignores any inhibiting social conventions. In a way that might remind a dog owner of her lovable companion (recall the etymology of "cynic"—the original Greek κυνικος means "like a dog"), Diogenes makes no attempt to hide whatever inclinations and appetites he happens to find coming his way, satisfying them whenever and wherever he can. Bodily functions that we would normally consider to be deeply private he carries out in full view of whoever happens to be in his presence. He says whatever comes to mind, regardless of who it might happen to offend or of how it might make him appear to others. Simply put, Diogenes lets it all hang out, always.

It seems that we can say three things about Diogenes. First, he remains quite capable in a fundamental sense of acting with dignity, should he so choose. He regularly does not choose, led as he is by the drive of impulse, but this does not remove his basic capacity to do so. Second, his behavior is massively lacking in dignity: his life consists of one undignified act after another. Third, Diogenes has little or no dignity. And this last point is not merely another way of putting the previous one: it is rather to say that, precisely because of his undignified behavior, we are inclined to say that he has no dignity.

A further distinction drawn from a virtue-theoretic approach to ethics may help more fully to resolve the seeming paradox in our ascriptions of dignity. In the second book of his *Nicomachean Ethics*, Aristotle argues that the virtues cannot be considered mere capacities because, unlike capacities, they are acquired by a process of repeated practice—habituation—and not simply bestowed on us by nature. "Nature gives us the capacity to acquire them," he writes, "and completion comes through habituation."[3] Part of being human is being capable of virtuous activity. But, Aristotle reasons, it is neither the capacity nor the activity of which virtue consists. It cannot be the activity itself, because we often appeal to the possession of virtue to explain the occurrence of virtuous activity. The reason why someone acts with sensitivity, for example, might very well be that she is a sensitive person—has the virtue of sensitivity. Nor can virtue be identified with the capacity to act virtuously, for in that case all humans would be born virtuous and have no need of the right sort of habituation to acquire it. Moreover, we often praise an individual for her possession of a virtue, but we do not typically praise her merely for the possession of a capacity that she was naturally given. (This even though we may value her possession of the capacity, very highly.) The virtues, Aristotle concludes, are thus best thought of as deepseated *dispositions* to virtuous activity—that is, firmly entrenched features of one's

---

3. Aristotle, *Nicomachean Ethics*, tr. R. Crisp (Cambridge: Cambridge University Press, [c. 350 BCE] 2000), II.i, 1103a18–26.

psyche that incline one toward doing the right thing with the right sort of motivation in the relevant context of action.

The practice or habituation by which such dispositions are acquired amounts to repeated performance of the relevant virtuous activity in the relevant context of action. The more the right activity is performed with the right sort of motivation, the more the inclination so to perform it becomes dispositionally ingrained in her as second nature; the less it is performed with the right motivation, the less the inclination and, typically, the less the degree of virtue.[4]

The dispositional nature of the virtues thus distinguishes them from mere capacities for virtuous activity. It is also what makes them, unlike capacities, the sort of things that can be acquired, lost, diminished, and increased, depending on what sorts of activities one engages in, that is, on one's practice of virtue. I suggest that similar points can be applied to human dignity. Sometimes when we talk of human dignity, we talk of the basic human capacity for dignified action; at other times, we talk of a disposition toward dignified action, and at other times yet we talk of digni-fied action itself. In the first sense—call it "natural dignity"—we refer to something that is both inalienable and nongradational. All humans who are capable of acting at all have natural dignity, regardless of their circumstance, condition, or behavior. (This applies even to the severely impaired: the range of actions open to them may be very different from the range open to others, but with respect to the actions that are open to them, they remain as capable of acting with dignity as anyone else.) In the second sense, which I'll call "robust dignity," we denote something that is both alienable (indeed, that may never be had at all) and gradational, as with the "practical dignity" of the third sense. And, as in the case of the virtues conceived along the lines suggested by Aristotle, the degree of one's dignity in the second sense will be largely a function of the degree of dignity in the third sense—a function of how much practice at dignity one has had.

The distinction between natural, robust, and practical dignity, then, allows us more fully to resolve the aforementioned puzzle. And it explains the intuition that Diogenes, while remaining capable of dignified action, is nonetheless not possessed of dignity, where this means something more than the indignity of his behavior. Diogenes has natural dignity, but he has little or no robust dignity, as is made manifest by his massive lack of dignity along practical lines.

III. PRACTICAL DIGNITY AS SELECTIVE SELF-PRESENTATION

Natural and robust dignity are conceptually parasitic upon practical dignity. To understand them more fully, then, we would do well to turn our attention to the latter. What is it for an individual to act with dignity?

---

4. Aristotle, *Nicomachean Ethics*, II.i, 1103b8–24 (n. 3).

One account may be derived from Dworkin's approach to the right to dignity.[5] An individual's right to dignity, he suggests, is best thought of as "the right that others acknowledge his genuine critical interests: that they acknowledge that he is the kind of creature, and has the moral standing, such that it is intrinsically, objectively important how his life goes."[6] Dignity itself as a feature of individuals, then, on Dworkin's approach, would seem to be the condition of having this sort of acknowledgment or recognition from others. We may sum up this sort of acknowledgment by calling it a form of *respect*. Although respect has to do with valuing, not just any valuing counts. I may value my car, my computer's processing power, and the plentiful supply of food in my region of the world, but it would be odd to say that I *respect* such things. I do, however, respect my wife, my family, and my friends. In the one sort of case, the value is of an instrumental sort, where the objects of value are valued insofar as they serve as instruments for the acquisition of other things of value. In the other sort of case—that of respect—the value is intrinsic. And I may be said to respect the actions of others to the extent that I value them as a result of the respect that I have for others as the agents of action. On the Dworkin-inspired "respect account," accordingly, an individual's practical dignity consists of her acting in ways that are respected by others.

It is surely correct that dignity is importantly related to respect. The etymology of the term itself suggests this, with the original Latin *dignitas* meaning the quality of being worthy of respect. But there is a large gap between being worthy of respect (respectability) and actually being respected (respectedness). The respect account tells us, in effect, that the respectability of actions supervenes on their respectedness—that the feature in virtue of which actions are worthy of respect is simply their being respected.

To see the implausibility of this claim, consider a society that is largely populated by extreme cynics such as our fictitious Diogenes. Not only do most members of this society typically let it all hang out, they are further driven instinctively to preserve the social conditions for doing so by constantly denigrating and ridiculing the actions of those very few members of their society who do not share their cynical lifestyle. Imagine now one such noncynic, Xanthippe. Xanthippe's life in cynical society is far from easy, but she remains steadfast in her conviction about the importance of living a dignified life, and does her best to act accordingly. Are her efforts doomed? Can she act in a largely respectable, dignified manner? On the respect account, the answer is "no," but this just seems wrong. Xanthippe can act with respectability and dignity, difficult as it may be to do so on a regular basis, despite the fact that her actions are not respected by her fellow citizens.

---

5. R. Dworkin, *Life's Dominion: An Argument about Abortion, Euthanasia, and Individual Freedom* (New York: Alfred A. Knopf, 1993).

6. Dworkin, *Life's Dominion*, 236 (n. 5).

Feinberg[7] suggests[8] an alternative account of practical dignity that attempts to locate the respectable character of dignified action not in considerations of actual respect, but rather in its connection to the business of claiming one's rights. Feinberg asks us to imagine a world without rights, "Nowheresville." Nowheresville could, he stresses, be a world that is saturated with such valuable things as benevolence, sympathy, and the recognition that it is in some sense fitting to praise, blame, reward, and punish people for certain sorts of behavior. But it would not be a world in which anyone could legitimately *claim* their just deserts. To claim that something is one's just desert is to do more than merely point out that it is fitting for one to have it and that it would be benevolent of others to provide it; it is further to assert that it is fitting for one to have it because not having it amounts to a wrong. It may be fitting and benevolent to award an employee with a gratuity for excellent work, but it is not wrong to withhold the gratuity in the way that it would be wrong to refuse agreed upon wages for work performed. With Nowheresville's absence of rights, Feinberg argues, its inhabitants can at best appeal to the benevolence or sense of fittingness of others to get what they want, in cases where the getting requires the others' say-so. What the inhabitants of Nowheresville cannot do is properly claim what they want from others.

The absence of rights in Nowheresville implies the absence of legitimate claims, according to Feinberg. But this in turn, he suggests, implies that no one is worthy of respect in such a world, however much they are valued. Where no legitimate claims are possible, no one has the capacity to make such claims, and in Feinberg's view the capacity to make them is what being worthy of respect is all about.[9] And so it turns out that the inhabitants of Nowheresville have no dignity.

If this is what dignity as a basic capacity is—the capacity to claim one's rights—then practical dignity would seem on this "claimant account" to amount to acting so as to claim one's rights. The account at least has the virtue of being able to explain why it is that Xanthippe can act with dignity in a society full of Diogeneses. However much the other members of her society fail to respect her actions, Xanthippe surely retains those fundamental moral entitlements we call her rights. And as long as she continues to claim those rights, difficult as it may be in the hostile environment in which she finds herself, she can properly be

---

7. J. Feinberg, "The Nature and Value of Rights," *The Journal of Value Inquiry* 4 (1970): 243–57.

8. I say "suggests" because Feinberg does not explicitly offer an account of practical dignity itself. What he offers is an account of what I have called natural dignity, that is, an account of the basic capacity to act with dignity. The suggested account of practical dignity is drawn out by inference from this account of natural dignity.

9. Feinberg, "The Nature and Value of Rights," 252 (n. 7).

said to be acting with dignity. What the claimant account gets right and the respect account gets wrong, in other words, is that the dignity of an individual's behavior is not contingent upon the approbation of others.

Even so, the claimant account seems to go too far in identifying practical dignity with the claiming of one's rights. Although dignified action can in various instances involve claiming one's rights, there are other instances in which claiming one's rights is a distinctly undignified matter, as can be seen in Meyer's apt example of the "bumptious man." The bumptious man "has a strong tendency to claim his rights too vehemently and at all the wrong times, seemingly asserting that people are always on the verge of denying him his rights."[10] He is in the constant business of claiming his rights. On the claimant account, then, it should turn out that his behavior is among the most dignified in the world. But it is not. Indeed, the behavior of the bumptious man is highly undignified. His constant claiming of his rights is motivated by an overwhelming fear that others do not really respect him, and where it is manifestly motivated in this sort of way, the activity of claiming one's rights, however proper in and of itself, is the very paradigm of indignity.

Moreover, acting so as to claim one's rights does not even seem to be necessary for practical dignity. Meyer provides a further example to illustrate. Suppose that a member of a town's racial minority encounters the town schnook, whose well-known, pathetic habit it is to wander around insulting everyone he encounters. In the face of the schnook's offensive racial insults, the member of the racial minority might understandably be tempted to react in just the way he would react when confronted with the town's bigots. Yet, whereas to protest the insults of the bigots—and thereby claim his rights—might be precisely what dignity requires, a similar protestation against the schnook's insults might well be *beneath* his dignity: "It is quite possible that he chooses what he sees as the dignified expression: to control his anger and ignore the dolt."[11]

Perhaps the counterexamples that Meyer raises provide an important clue as to the nature of practical dignity. What is striking about the bumptious man is that he is severely lacking in self-control: his behavior is largely determined by the overwhelming fears and worries that grip him. The dignified member of the racial minority, by contrast, is very much self-controlled: despite the understandable temptation to silence the schnook's sad behavior, he keeps his anger in check and does not allow it to overwhelm him. In the case where there is a lack of self-control, we find undignified action; in the case where self-control is present, we find dignified action. Thus Meyer proffers a "self-control account" of practical dignity,[12] where to act with dignity is to act in a self-controlled manner, that is, to act in such

---

10. Meyer, "Dignity, Rights, and Self-Control," 525 (n. 2).

11. *Ibid.*

12. Meyer, "Dignity, Rights, and Self-Control," 526–527 (n. 2) and "Dignity, Death, and Modern Virtue," 51ff. (n. 2).

a way that one's action is not the result of being dominated by any of one's own internal fears, appetites, or impulses, or by the external influence of others.

The self-control account has much to be said for it. It has an undeniable historical appeal, as it reflects a nascent strand of thinking about dignity that runs throughout Renaissance humanism, Enlightenment rationalism, and twentieth-century existentialism. Compare Pico's famous suggestion that human dignity derives from the distinctly human capacity for self-determination—for being a "self-shaper" of one's nature[13]—, Kant's claim that autonomy, or the capacity for self-legislation, is "the ground of the dignity of human nature and of every rational creature,"[14] and Sartre's exposition of the existentialist insight that, for humans, "existence precedes essence"[15]; that is, proper human function is not predetermined but, rather, set only by what humans find themselves doing after they make an appearance in this world. Moreover, the account not only yields the intuitively correct verdict in the cases of the bumptious man and dignified member of a racial minority; it further provides a compelling explanation of why our fictitious Diogenes virtually never acts with dignity, and of why Xanthippe can so act despite finding herself surrounded by a society of disrespectful Diogeneses. Diogenes's behavior is massively lacking in dignity, according to the self-control account, because it is not self-controlled; it is rather controlled by whatever impulses he happens to find coming his way. And, despite the lack of respect from her fellow citizens, Xanthippe distinguishes herself from them precisely by not giving in to the heteronomy of impulse that largely governs their behavior.

Still, I think that the self-control account fails to recognize a central feature of dignified action that both the respect account and claimant account, for all their drawbacks, do: dignified action is an essentially social phenomenon, in the sense that for one to act with dignity is for one's behavior to be importantly related to others. On the self-control account, no significant relation to others is implied at all by acting with dignity, because self-controlled behavior can be a socially isolated occurrence.

Suppose, for example, that while on a solitary hiking expedition in the wilderness I joyously sing my way through Manrico's lines in Verdi's *Il Trovatore*. I revel in the emotional release of imitating the likes of Giuseppe di Stefano, and of imagining Maria Callas's moving replies. Consonant with my abilities, the singing is awful. But I do not care; there is no one around to hear me, after all. However self-controlled

---

13. G. Pico della Mirandola, "Oration on the Dignity of Man," tr. E. Livermore in *The Renaissance Philosophy of Man*, ed. E. Cassirer et al. (Chicago: University of Chicago Press, [1486] 1948), § 3.

14. I. Kant, *Groundwork of the Metaphysic of Morals*, tr. H.J. Paton (New York: Harper & Row, [1785] 1964), 103.

15. J.-P. Sartre, *Existentialisme est un humanisme* (New York: Philosophical Library, 1947).

my behavior is in this situation, I think it would be odd to say that it is a manifestation of dignity. And even if it is a matter of great abandon, the very paradigm of a temporary lack of self-control, it would be just as odd to say that my behavior is undignified. To say that it is undignified implies that I bear the wrong sort of relation to others by engaging in it, just as to say that it is dignified implies that I bear the right sort of relation to others by so doing. Yet such relational conditions are not satisfied, because I'm all by myself.

So even if practical dignity does involve a form of self-control, not just any self-controlled action counts. It must be self-controlled action with a social face—a "performance" in Goffman's famous sense[16]—because it must involve a significant relation between the agent of the action and other individuals. I want, accordingly, to propose a new account of practical dignity that preserves its essentially social face. On what I will call the "selective self-presentation account,"[17] to act with dignity is to present aspects of oneself to others in a selective manner, that is, to reveal information about oneself to different individuals, in different contexts, in accord with one's considered convictions about the appropriateness of doing so. That the presentation of aspects of oneself is selective—effected in accord with one's considered convictions—is what makes dignified action a kind of self-control. But because on the selective self-presentation account it is only self-presentation—action that involves the epistemic relation of revelation of aspects of oneself to others—that has the potential to be evaluated from the point of view of dignity, not just any self-controlled action is relevant to dignity concerns, and practical dignity turns out to be an essentially social phenomenon.

In this light, the selective self-presentation account provides a good explanation of why my solitary vocal behavior in the wilderness is at most a case of nondignified action—neither dignified nor undignified. The singing does not involve the presentation of aspects of myself to others, and hence, regardless of the amount of self-control with which I effect it, it is not a candidate for being evaluated positively or negatively from the point of view of dignity. Moreover, when it comes to the sorts of cases that proved problematic for the respect and claimant accounts, the selective self-presentation account seems to fare quite well. The member of the racial minority who declines to dignify the town schnook's insults with a

---

16. E. Goffman, *The Presentation of Self in Everyday Life* (New York: Doubleday & Co., 1959).

17. For the language of "self-presentation," as well as for the initial inspiration to think of the connection between dignity and self-presentation, I am particularly indebted to a very engaging discussion of what is involved in our sense of shame in J. D. Velleman, "The Genesis of Shame," *Philosophy and Public Affairs* 30 (2001): 27–52. In my view Velleman quite rightly connects our sense of shame with our interest in being self-presenting creatures, though he seems to me to underemphasize the essentially social (or public) nature of self-presentation.

response is acting with a great deal of dignity, because, by presenting only a calm exterior, he refuses to give the schnook the satisfaction of knowing anything about the extent to which he is upset by the inane gibberish. The bumptious man acts in a highly undignified manner because he engages in acts of self-presentation that are not selective: he reveals to others on a regular basis just how strongly he is gripped by the sorts of fears and anxieties that drive his rights-claiming behavior. Xanthippe manifests dignity in her behavior, in contrast[18] with undignified behavior of the Diogeneses who surround her, because, unlike them, she does not allow her acts of self-presentation to be determined simply by whatever impulses happen to come her way.

The selective self-presentation account also affords us a useful explanation of how the invasion of privacy can amount to an assault upon one's dignity. Simply put, on the selective self-presentation account, invasions of privacy can in various contexts transform an individual's behavior from the nondignified to the undignified by altering the epistemic relations carried by the behavior.

This can be seen by adding to the *Il Trovatore* scenario a busybody who roams the area in search of scandalous tidbits about individuals who believe themselves to be alone in the wilderness. Having spied my initial entry into the woods, he follows my path until eventually discovering the spot where I have stopped to devote my full vocal energies to a favorite part in Manrico's lyrics. Surprised but highly amused that anyone with such poor abilities would attempt such a difficult vocal feat, even in private, the busybody begins recording my behavior with his zoom-lens, long-range-microphone audio-video recorder. I continue on with great vigor, unaware that a substantial portion of my performance is being captured for purposes of my eventual humiliation before an audience of the busybody's friends and family.

The busybody has obviously invaded my privacy. And there is a strong intuition that he has, ipso facto, impugned my dignity. In some way, his covert action has rendered my vocal behavior of negative value on the dignity scale. How so? Prior to encountering me, my singing bore no significant epistemic relations to any others, and was thus outside the scope of dignity evaluation.

---

18. One might suggest that Diogenes's actions (like those of most of his fellow citizens) turn out to be dignified on the selective self-presentation account—the idea being that he simply has different (much more liberal, say) standards of selective self-presentation, that is, unusual considered convictions about the appropriateness of revealing things about himself in different contexts to different individuals. That, however, is not how Diogenes was meant to be taken in Section I. It is not that he is merely possessed of very liberal standards of selective self-presentation, but rather that he has (for whatever original philosophical motivations) given up on the whole business of selective self-presentation. Compare the individual who gains a large amount of weight due to purposeful overeating (a Sumo wrestler, e.g.) with the individual who gains excessive weight as a result of abandoning any attempt at diet-monitoring and allowing unhealthy gustatory impulses to drive the show. Diogenes is more like the latter than the former individual.

With the busybody's intrusion into my privacy, however, that activity becomes, unbeknownst to me, an exercise in self-presentation: I now reveal a lot about my vocal abilities, attitudes, and emotional states—to him, at the very least, and potentially to the wider audience of his friends and family. And the self-presentation that he forces on me is not effected in accord with my considered convictions about the appropriateness of revelations of this sort. Indeed, were I to be made aware of the busybody's intrusion, I would surely protest both his observation and recording. His invasion of my privacy thus transforms my singing from something that is neither dignified nor undignified to something that is positively undignified—from something that is not an exercise in self-presentation at all to an exercise in nonselective self-presentation. He renders my behavior deficient in practical dignity.

When discussing the respect account of practical dignity, I noted that dignity does seem to be importantly tied to respectability, if not actual respect as the respect theorist would have it. Does the selective self-presentation account that I have here offered accommodate this insight? How does selective self-presentation relate to respectable action?

For an action to be respectable in the relevant sense of being worthy of respect by others, it must be such that others are able to see the agent of the action as a person—as an autonomous individual capable of self-control. But this in turn requires that others have reason to believe that the agent is capable of self-controlled action. And the connection between selective self-presentation and respectable action emerges plainly when we consider that it is precisely in acts of selective self-presentation that others acquire reason to see an individual as capable of self-controlled action. Self-controlled actions alone will not do the trick, for, as we have seen, such actions can take place in isolated contexts where they effect no significant relations between others and the agent of action. If *all* of my self-controlled actions were like my singing of *Il Trovatore*, others would never have reason to believe that I am self-controlled, because they would never bear the epistemic relations to me whereby they come to know that my actions are not merely driven by my internal fears, appetites, or impulses, or by the external influence of other people. It is in this sense, then, that practical dignity on the selective self-presentation account stands as a necessary condition on respectable action: absent acts of selective self-presentation on her part, others would have no reason to believe that an individual is self-controlled, and would thus have no grounds for seeing her as a person.

IV. THE NATURE AND VALUE OF NATURAL AND ROBUST DIGNITY

With the selective self-presentation account of practical dignity now before us, we have a clear way of spelling out the nature of the other two forms of dignity mentioned in Section II. If practical dignity amounts to selective self-presentation, then natural dignity turns out to be the characteristically human capacity for selective self-presentation, and robust dignity the disposition toward selective self-presentation.

Moreover, the value of natural and robust dignity, on the selective self-presentation account, can be drawn out in connection with respectability as a person. Practical dignity, as we have seen, is required in some measure to have even a minimal degree of respectability as a person. Because natural dignity is also so required—a being with no capacity whatsoever for selective self-presentation is one whose behavior could never amount to acts of selective self-presentation— its value stems, at least in part, from its role as a necessary condition on the possession of even a minimal degree of respectability as a person.

But of course, we also value degrees of respectability beyond the minimal, and it is in light of this fact, I think, that the value of robust dignity emerges on the selective self-presentation account. Practical dignity, together with the natural dignity it requires, is necessary for the set of reasons that others have for seeing one as a person to be nonempty. The value of robust dignity stems from its tendency to populate that set with a large and varied number of elements. The more one is disposed to acts of selective self-presentation, the more one's behavior in the presence of others will involve acts of selective self-presentation. And the more such acts one performs, the greater the number and variety of reasons that others will have for seeing one as a person. Thus, natural dignity is valuable because without it, there would be no respectability of the person at all. Robust dignity is valuable because of the part it plays in making for robust respectability of the person.

V. DIGNITY, DEPERSONALIZATION, AND AUTOMATED HUMAN IDENTIFICATION SYSTEMS

There is a strong intuition that the use of certain information systems in the networked society carries a depersonalization effect for individuals within the systems. In this closing section, I want to draw attention to the way in which the selective self-presentation account of dignity that I have presented helps us to make sense of this intuition.

To illustrate what I have in mind when I talk of a "depersonalization effect," consider Goffman's classic discussion of the ways in which "total institutions"— institutions such as prisons, concentration camps, and asylums, where virtually every aspect of an individual's location, social life, and behavior is strictly governed so as to accord with a general plan aimed at fulfilling the putative aims of the institution—carry out a "mortification of the self" on the institutionalized individual.[19]

---

19. E. Goffman, *Asylums: Essays on the Social Situation of Mental Patients and Other Inmates* (New York: Anchor Books, 1961).

The mortification involves a diminishment of the individual's respectability as a person insofar as it decreases the ability of others (e.g., other inmates, institutional employees) to see her as a person, and it constitutes a paradigm example of depersonalization. Chief among the ways in which it is carried out in the context of total institutions is by the entrenchment of deeply privacy-invasive techniques, which include stripping the individual of "identity kits" (e.g., sets of cosmetic aids and distinctive clothing whereby, outside of the institution, she might have exercised some measure of control over certain aspects of her appearance), depriving her of personal spaces wherein she might have concealed various intimate activities, forcing her to reveal sensitive facts about her relationships to others, and rendering futile her attempts to distance herself from proscribed actions that she has performed.[20]

The privacy-invasive techniques entrenched in the institutions have the effect of rendering the institutionalized individual's activities largely exercises in *nonselective* self-presentation: "On the inside," those activities no longer tend to reveal aspects of herself to others in accord with *her own* considered convictions about the appropriateness of revelation, but rather in accord with *institutional* convictions and standards. The privacy-invasive techniques thus lead to a diminishment of the institutionalized individual's practical dignity on the selective self-presentation account.

Recall now the point that robust dignity requires the right sort of practice, which in turn requires ample opportunities to act with dignity. The privacy-invasive techniques of the total institution drastically reduce this set of opportunities, and thereby serve as a barrier to the institutionalized individual's development of robust dignity. Because robust dignity is, as I have argued, the central means whereby the individual's respectability as a person is expanded, the depersonalization of the institutionalized individual that occurs in a total institution can thus be said to affect her respectability as a person in a very deep way: it cuts the practical lifeline whereby she might hope to develop robust respectability as a person.

My suggestion is that the intuition of depersonalization by means of inclusion in certain information systems of the networked society can be explained along similar lines. For purposes of the present discussion, I will take an *information system* to be an organization of people and technologies aimed at the acquisition and management of information of a certain type, where the relevant type helps to distinguish the sort of information system in question.[21] A *human identification system* is an information system that is primarily aimed at the

20. Goffman, *Asylums*, 20–38 (n. 19).

21. I take this characterization to be broadly consistent with standard definitions in information systems theory. Cf., B. Langefors, *Theoretical Analysis of Information Systems, Vol. 1.* (Lund: Studentlitteratur, 1966), 143; and J. Laudon & K. Laudon, *Essentials of Management Information Systems, 4th ed.* (Upper Saddle River, NJ: Prentice-Hall, 2001), 7.

acquisition and management of identifying information about a subset of the people involved in the system. Talk of "identifying information" may here be construed quite broadly, as any empirical information about the identities of specific persons. Because the identities of specific persons are various and multifaceted,[22] this will include large swaths of information about (for example) the names, behavior patterns, locations, addresses, social connections, political affiliations, medical conditions, and financial statuses of specific persons.

The networked society is particularly well-suited to facilitate the use of *automated human identification systems*, where these are to be distinguished from the historically more common *manual human identification systems*. In a manual human identification system, the acquisition of identifying information about individuals within the system depends centrally on those individuals engaging in regular acts of what Davis has called acts of "reflexive identifying," that is, on those individuals voluntarily exposing identifying information about themselves to others on a regular basis through the use of certain technologies within the system.[23] Consider, for example, the "old-fashioned" use of verifying artifacts—picture ID cards, birth certificates, passports, passwords, and the like—for the authentication of legitimate access to various places or goods. This involves an organization of people (e.g., the bearers of the artifacts, those to whom the artifacts are presented) and technologies (e.g., the artifacts themselves) aimed at the acquisition and management of identifying information about a subset of people involved (viz. the bearers of the artifacts). But the acquisition of that information depends centrally on those in the subset voluntarily exposing the relevant identifying information about themselves: By presenting the artifacts, they generate various bits of identifying information about themselves within the system, for example, that they have legitimate access to the goods or places in question, that they did in fact access them at certain times, and so on; by withholding presentation, they prevent the acquisition of such information by the system.

In an automated human identification system, by contrast, the acquisition of identifying information about individuals within the system depends centrally not on those individuals engaging in regular acts of reflexive identifying, but rather on regular occurrences of automatic nonreflexive identifying, that is, on the identification of those individuals by automated technologies that form integral elements of the system. Radio-frequency human identification systems ("human RFID systems") serve as primary examples of the sort of human identification system. In human RFID systems, individuals have digitally encoded microchip-transponders attached to (or implanted within) their bodies for the

---

22. Cf. G. Marx, "Identity and Anonymity: Some Conceptual Distinctions and Issues for Further Research," in *Documenting Individual Identity*, ed. J. Caplan & J. Torpey (Princeton: Princeton University Press, 2001), 311–327.

23. S. Davis, "The Epistemology of Identifying and Identification," unpublished manuscript, 2007.

purpose of tracking their locations, movements, and activities, relative to a networked set of radio-frequency "decoders" or "readers." The point of such systems is precisely to acquire identifying information about those individuals without having to rely on their engaging in regular, voluntary acts of reflexive identifying: the "chips," in effect, do the individuals' identifying for them.

To some, the automation of identification carried by automated human identification systems represents the latest welcome convenience of the networked society. Kerr's firsthand experience with individuals involved in the implementation of one such system provides a nice illustration. Many "[saw] the [RFID] chip as original," Kerr reports. "They [saw] it as convenient. They [saw] it as the future."[24] Other reactions are much less enthusiastic, however, and serve to highlight the intuition of depersonalization on which I wish to focus. Consider, for example, the strong reaction of civil liberties groups to the 2004 decision of the Brittan Public School District in northern California to implement a human RFID system for purposes of monitoring student activity. "The monitoring of children with RFID tags is comparable to the tracking of cattle, shipment pallets, or very dangerous criminals in high-security prisons," protested Cédric Laurant, Policy Counsel with the Electronic Privacy Information Center. "[C]ompelling children to be constantly tracked with RFID-trackable identity badges breaches their right to privacy and dignity as human beings."[25] And the dominance of this sentiment among students themselves was captured in a joint letter to the Brittan Board of Trustees from representatives of the American Civil Liberties Union, the Electronic Frontier Foundation, and the Electronic Privacy Information Center. "Indeed," the letter notes, "one parent told us that his child came home from school, threw the badge down on the table, and said 'I'm a grocery item, a piece of meat. I'm an orange.'"[26]

The intuition of depersonalization here expressed finds a compelling basis in the same sorts of considerations that ground the intuition brought out in Goffman's discussion of total institutions, and the selective self-presentation account of dignity helps make these considerations explicit. The automation of identification within automated human identification systems—where what would be acts of reflexive identifying outside the system become acts of nonreflexive identifying

24. I. Kerr, "Not So Crazy about the Chips," *Innovate Magazine* (Center for Innovation Law and Policy), Spring (2004): 35.

25. Electronic Privacy Information Center, "Parents and Civil Liberties Groups Urge School District to Terminate Use of Tracking Devices," press release (February 8, 2005), http://epic.org/privacy/rfid/prs_rls-020705.html (accessed March 5, 2008).

26. American Civil Liberties Union, Electronic Frontier Foundation, & Electronic Privacy Information Center, "Letter to Mr. Don Hagland, Brittan Board of Trustees. Re: Safety and Civil Liberties Implications of Including Radio Frequency Identification Tags in Student Identity Badges" (February 7, 2005), http://epic.org/privacy/rfid/brittan-letter.pdf (accessed March 5, 2008).

within the system—amounts to a set of privacy-invasive procedures similar in kind, if not in degree, to the privacy-invasive techniques of the total institution, which tend to transform the activities of individuals within the system into exercises in *nonselective* self-presentation. Within an automated human identification system, in other words, the monitored individual's activities tend to reveal different things about her in accord with the *system's* standards of revelation, as contrasted with the standards set by *her own* considered convictions about appropriate revelation (which can be more closely followed in manual human identification systems). The automation thus leads to a diminishment of the individual's practical dignity on the selective self-presentation account. And this in turn—bearing in mind the point that robust dignity itself depends upon ample opportunities for dignified action—makes for a significant barrier to the individual's development of robust dignity. The selective self-presentation account thus brings out the depth of justification behind the intuition about the depersonalization of monitored individuals within automated human identification systems. The systems threaten to depersonalize in the sense of removing the central practical means whereby those individuals can develop robust dignity and expand—rather than shrink—the sets of reasons that others have for seeing them as persons.

19. THE INTERNET OF PEOPLE?

Reflections on the Future Regulation of Human-Implantable Radio Frequency Identification*

IAN KERR

Convincing people to put computer chips in their bodies is a hard sell. Subcutaneous silicon has both the ozone smell of cyberpunk dystopia and the cornpone reek of the end-times Mark of the Beast.

   .   .   .

Still, for all its shortcomings, VeriChip's bold appearance on the public stage gives me a subcutaneous itch. I never imagined I'd want such a thing, but I'm seriously thinking about getting one. Not for the cumbersome medic-alert features or theatrical security clearances, but as the 21st century's first genuinely transgressive cyberpunk fashion statement.
—Bruce Sterling[1]

I remember sitting at the back of the Baja Beach Club in Barcelona's famous Olympic Port in July 2004 with twenty-five global law students on a "field trip" of sorts.

 * This chapter emerged from ID Trail's 2006 Paris Workshop. The author wishes to extend his gratitude to Angela Long for her research assistance in preparation for the Workshop. A hearty thank-you, as well, to Latanya Sweeney, Jena McGill, David Matheson, Valerie Steeves, Carole Lucock, Jason Millar, and Hillary Young for the excellent suggestions for improvement that they so generously offered. Special thanks are owed to Katie Black for all of her extraordinary efforts and for the high quality of research assistance that she so regularly and reliably provides.
 1. Bruce Sterling, "Go Ahead, Chip Me," *Wired Magazine*, October 2007, http://www.wired.com/wired/archive/13.10/posts.html?pg=7.

After paying for our meal, we were ushered into the VIP lounge to hear Baja's proprietor offer up a very strange sales pitch. In the weeks leading up to our visit, my class had studied the implications of emerging technologies on privacy and identity. Would my students seriously consider getting chipped? What did they think were the broader social implications of human-implantable radio frequency identification?

The proprietor's proposition was straightforward: become a VIP, get a Veri-Chip™, and you will not have to pay for drinks. Well, at least not one at a time. The 12 mm × 2 mm radio frequency identification (RFID) tag jammed into your triceps through a six-gauge needle might smart for a couple of weeks, but once implanted, it would enable an automated authentication scheme allowing easy access to the VIP lounge and a replenishable, cashless payment system for buying booze at the bar.

For most of my students, the allure was exactly the "transgressive cyberpunk fashion statement" described by Bruce Sterling at the outset of this chapter. Or, as Conrad Chase (the proprietor) put it to us that day in the VIP lounge, "the VIP chip takes body piercing to the next level." Numbed by an exponentially increasing array of new and emerging technologies introduced during the course of their short adult lives, my students predicted that this was yet another techno-fad doomed to the electronic trash-bin—the next "carbolic smoke ball."[2] I believed otherwise, and expressed my concern that chipping people might actually become a mainstream practice.

Only a few years later, with reported 2006 annual sales in the order of 1.7 million for human implantable chips and a projected increase through at least 2010,[3] Applied Digital Solutions Inc. seems to have found a way to make Bruce Sterling's hard sell easy, not just in nightclubs but in hospitals, too. The scheme is not much different from that of the Baja Beach Club. But instead of authenticating a patron's identity in order to link it to her bar tab, the implantable chip is linked to an electronic health record. As such, the chip enables the automated identification of incapacitated or disoriented individuals to facilitate health care delivery in the event of an emergency.

In this chapter, I examine some of the legal and ethical implications of human-implantable radio frequency identification (RFID). I commence Part I with a brief account of RFID technologies. In Part II, I examine the existing regulatory environment for RFID, suggesting in Part III that our current control and consent model of privacy and autonomy provides inadequate protection against an RFID-enabled Internet of things. In Part IV, I consider the broader implications of human-implantable RFIDs and their role in what I call the

---

2. Carbolic Smoke Ball Company Inc., "Carbolic Smoke Ball: Will Positively Cure," http://www.directly2u.co.uk/carbolic/index.htm.

3. Siobhan Morrissey, "Are Microchip Tags Safe?" *Time Magazine*, October 18, 2007, http://www.verichipcorp.com/news/1192716360.

"human-machine merger." I conclude in Part V by suggesting that, rather than giving up core principles and values just because they are in tension with RFID and other emerging technologies, we must (i) rethink the appropriate application of these principles, and (ii) determine whether there is sufficient justification for moving forward with human-implantable RFID, ubiquitous computing, and the Internet of things.

I. RFID TECHNOLOGIES

A. What Is an RFID?

RFID tags enable the remote and automatic identification of physical entities by way of radio signals that operate in the unlicensed part of the broadcast spectrum. RFID systems usually incorporate three main components: (i) a tag (transponder), which emits a unique identifier through radio waves; (ii) an interrogator (scanner), which receives the signal and identifies the object; and (iii) an associable database.[4]

Composed of a coupling element (the antenna) and an integrated circuit (also known as microchip), tags are classified as either passive or active depending on their power source requirements when emitting their identifying signal. Active tags rely on energy from a battery to power its antenna, giving it a long radio range. Passive tags do not require a power source, remaining dormant until activated by the proximate signal from an RFID scanner. It is the scanner's signal that powers the tag, enabling it to emit a radio signal of its own, though the radio range of a passive tag is thus shorter than an active tag. Passive tags, however, can be made smaller, more cheaply, and longer-lasting than their active counterparts.[5] Tag size also varies dramatically with tag memory and with speed and range of transmission. Active tags can be as large as a book, whereas the smallest commercially available passive tag, Hitachi's mu-chip—less than 0.4 mm wide—can be embedded in a piece of paper.[6] Antennas are either coiled or flattened to further reduce their size. At the time of writing, Mojix, a start-up company based in Los Angeles, recently announced a passive ultrahigh-frequency (UHF) RFID tag that can be read up to 600 feet away. Their readers can cover 2,500 square feet, providing users with three-dimensional location information.[7]

---

4. K. Finkenzeller, *RFID-Handbook*, 2nd ed., trans. R. Wadding (Chichester: Wiley & Sons, 2003), 7.

5. *Ibid.*, 8; Simson Garfinkel and Henry Holtzman, "Understanding RFID Technology," in *RFID: Applications, Security, and Privacy*, eds. Simson Garfinkel and Beth Rosenberg (Upper Saddle River, NJ: Addison-Wesley, 2005), 15–17.

6. See Hitachi's mu-chip at Hitachi, "The World's Smallest RFID IC," http://www.hitachi.co.jp/Prod/mu-chip/ (accessed July 22, 2008).

7. Mark Roberti, "Mojix Takes Passive UHF RFID to a New Level," *RFID Journal*, April 14, 2008, http://www.rfidjournal.com/article/articleview/4019/1/1/.

Information is stored on the RFID tag as strings of memory either burned into the chip in advance (read-only) or assigned later as read/write memory using a reader.[8] The signal of "promiscuous," or "dumb," tags can be read and understood by *any* RFID scanner within proximity. This possibility raises obvious privacy and security concerns. "Secure," or "smart," tags, on the other hand, incorporate authentication and encryption elements to prevent having their signal read without a key.[9] Tags featuring a kill switch can be deactivated, thus preventing future communications.[10]

RFID scanners are the eyes and ears of the system, ranging in size from a desktop computer to a handheld pricing gun and even smaller. Readers operate by constantly emitting radio waves until a tag is detected. When within range, the tag's antenna amplifies the signal and emits the chip's stored information back to the reader. The read range depends on the power, efficiency, and data integrity requirements of both the tag and the reader.[11]

If the reader functions as the eyes and ears, then the database to which the RFID is linked is the brain. To interpret data emitted from the tag, most readers need to link that information to other information, usually stored in a database. Using the human-implantable VeriChip as an example, the chip itself does not contain any medical information. It merely emits a unique 16-digit verification number when activated by a VeriChip scanner. The patient's medical record is made available only after the identification number has been entered into the password-protected Global VeriChip Subscriber (GVS) Registry. The VeriChip functions as an "access control" for the database, thereby limiting patient health information to the patient and authorized health care professionals. It is up to the patient to determine what information to provide, ranging from a list of the patient's medical conditions and medications, to the names and coordinates of the family physicians, to a PDF of the patient's living will. Because the passive RFID inside the VeriChip is always on, it will "speak on [the patient's] behalf"[12] to *any* scanner[13] in its read range—even if the patient is unconscious or otherwise incapacitated. This enables access to vital health information in emergency situations, and, in the case of unauthorized scanners, it offers valuable health information to identity thieves and other third-party information vendors who gain database access.

8. Garfinkel and Holtzman, "Understanding RFID," 18 (n. 5).

9. *Ibid.*

10. This is an important privacy-enhancing feature, as it enables RFID assistance in the supply chain without interfering with consumer rights after the point of sale.

11. Garfinkel and Holtzman, "Understanding RFID," 24 (n. 5).

12. VeriMed Patient Identification System, "Patients: For Patients, Caregivers, and Loved Ones," VeriMed, http://www.verimedinfo.com/for_patients.asp (accessed July 18, 2008).

13. This includes unauthorized scanners, because the VeriChip is a passive, unencrypted chip.

To fully understand the social implications of RFID, it is crucial to distinguish this technology from other radio frequency devices, such as the Electronic Article Surveillance systems (EAS) used to prevent shoplifting. RFID technology can be distinguished from EAS by virtue of its smaller size and, more importantly, its capacity to enable objects to announce their *presence* and their *unique identities*.[14] The latter set of capacities is significant. For example, consider having a scanner that indicates an unidentified "tagged object" is hidden in a knapsack (perhaps setting off an alarm after passing through the threshold of the door of a library or retail store). Now consider having a scanner tell you that the tagged object in the knapsack is a 1-kg bag of fertilizer (EPC# 016 37221 654321 2003004000), which was bought at the Home Depot store on Merivale Road in Ottawa on September 26, 2009, at 09:06:17 by CIBC credit card holder # 4408 0412 3456 7890 and is hidden in the knapsack beside Ottawa Library book call # 662.2014 B679 (titled: *Explosives*) signed out by Library cardholder # 11840003708286 on September 20, 2009, along with call # 921 H6755 (*Mein Kampf*), call # 320.533 H878 (*Les skinheads et l'extrême droite*), and call # 296.65 Kad (*Synagogues*).

When linked to databases and communications networks,[15] the amount of descriptive information associated with an RFID chip becomes practically limitless. Consequently, basic radio signals emitted from the tag can potentially provide incredibly descriptive information as they permeate clothing, knapsacks, body parts, and even buildings to communicate with RFID scanners and databases some distance away.

B. RFID Applications

Although the focus of this chapter is on human-implantable chips, RFID technology offers a wide range of applications across various segments of society. In the commercial sector, it is predicted that RFIDs will transform supply-chain management, allowing manufacturers, distributors, and retailers not only to increase their efficiency but, perhaps one day, to track individual items in the supply chain in real time from the point of production to the point of sale and beyond.[16] If achievable, item-level tagging could facilitate much greater coordination between supply and demand in a way that would allow warehouse space to be maximized, theft between production and sale to be minimized, and greater

---

14. Garfinkel and Holtzman, "Understanding RFID," xxv–xxvii (n. 5).

15. Such as Verichip's Verimed Patient Registry online database, which links a sixteen-digit RFID identifier to a patient's medical records; see VeriMed, "Patient Identification System" (n. 12).

16. See W. O. Hedgepeth, *RFID Metrics: Decision Making Tools for Today's Supply Chains* (Boca Raton, FL: CRC Press, 2007) and Jonathan Whitaker, Sunil Mithas, and Mayuram Krishnan, "IBM: A Field Study of RFID Deployment and Return Expectations," *Production and Operations Management* 16, no. 5 (2007): 599–612.

customer satisfaction to be achieved through the avoidance of delivery errors and lowered product costs.[17]

Likewise in the public sector, governments are using RFID technology to increase administrative efficiency and to track equipment. In 2003, the U.S. Department of Defense mandated that all suppliers must become RFID enabled by January 2005.[18] Aside from its use in product tracking,[19] supply-chain management,[20] and asset management,[21] RFIDs are being employed in numerous other government and commercial contexts, including passports, contactless payment systems, transportation payments, authentication systems, library management, baggage control, and health care applications. A number of hospitals, for example, are now using RFID-based systems used to "identify, locate and protect people and assets."[22]

Should it ever be realized, a universalizable item-level tagging combined with the capacity to track those items in real time is not merely another "disruptive" technology; it is predicted to be the precursor to something truly transformative, enabling what some people have called "the internet of things."[23] Adam Greenfield refers to this incredible technological capability as *everyware*, which he describes as follows:

[A]ll of the information we now look to our phones or Web browsers to provide becomes accessible from just about anywhere, at anytime, and is delivered in a manner appropriate to our location and context.

. . . the garment, the room and the street become sites of processing and mediation. Household objects from shower stalls to coffee pots are reimagined

---

17. John A Wolff, "RFID Tags: An Intelligent Bar Code Replacement" (IBM White Paper, IBM Global Services, June 2001), http://72.14.205.104/search?q=cache: Xg4_N35wPhYJ:ftp://ftp.software.ibm.com/software/pervasive/info/tech/gsoee200.pdf +RFID+Tags:+An+Intelligent+Bar+Code+Replacement&hl=en&ct=clnk&cd=2&gl= ca&client=firefox-a (accessed July 18, 2008).

18. Matthew Broersma, "Defense Department Drafts RFID Policy," cnet News.com, October 24, 2003, http://www.news.com/2100-1008-5097050.html (accessed July 18, 2008).

19. The Canadian Cattle Identification Agency started replacing barcodes with RFID tags in order to identify the origin of bovine herds. See Canadian Cattle Identification Agency (CCIA), "RFID and the Canadian Cattle Industry," CCIA, http://www.canadaid. com/ (accessed July 18, 2008).

20. Wal-Mart requires its top 100 suppliers to employ RFID labels in all shipments; see Wolff, "RFID Tags" (n.17).

21. Wise Track, "What Is Wise Track," http://www.wisetrack.com/ (accessed July 18, 2008).

22. VeriChip Corp., "VeriGuard Security Suite: RFID Security Never Before Possible" (working paper, VeriChip Corp.): 2, http://www.verichipcorp.com/files/VeriGuard(web). pdf (accessed July 18, 2008).

23. See International Telecommunications Union, *The Internet of Things, 2005*, 7th ed. (Geneva: ITU New Initiatives Programme, 2005).

as places where facts about the world can be gathered, considered and acted upon. And all the familiar rituals of daily life—things as fundamental as the way we wake up in the morning, get to work, or shop for our groceries—are remade as an intricate dance of information about ourselves, the state of the external world, and the options available to us at any given moment.[24]

With human-implantable RFIDs, it is even possible to add people to the mix.

C. Human-Implantable RFIDs

The VeriChip human-implantable RFID that debuted at the Baja Beach Club is now available in U.S. hospitals.[25] At the time of writing, VeriChip claims that its RFID technology is used by more than five thousand installations worldwide, crossing health care, security, government, and industrial markets.[26] More than 900 hospitals in the United States have signed agreements with VeriChip, and 230 have implemented its protocols.[27] The VeriChip operates in much the same manner as other passive, unencrypted tags except that it is encased in glass and coated with a proprietary substance, known as biobond, that attaches the chip to connective tissue in the triceps in order to prevent migration within the body once implanted.[28] Each microchip contains a unique identifier that health care providers can scan and read to immediately identify patients and access personal health information.

VeriChip does not currently support an automated payment system for medical providers;[29] however, other automated payment systems are being tested, linking the chip to credit card information through a database. Consequently, it is not difficult to envision a day when payment for medical services takes place when a patient is scanned upon entering the hospital. Such a system would simply link the sixteen-digit identifier with the patient's health insurance plan or credit card number. It is likewise easy to imagine the chip's unique identifier being used for

---

24. Adam Greenfield, *Everyware: The Dawning Age of Ubiquitous Computing* (Berkeley, CA: New Riders, 2006), 1.

25. PR Inside.com, "VeriChip Corporation Adds More Than 200 Hospitals to Its VeriMed Patient Identification System at the American College of Emergency Physicians (ACEP) Conference, Far Surpassing Last Year's Enrollment," *Business Wire*, October 11, 2007, http://72.14.205.104/search?q=cache:MsuL9WtVjy8J:www.pr-inside.com/verichip-corporation-adds-more-than-r241908.htm+Verichip+900+hospitals&hl=en&ct=clnk&cd=1.

26. VeriChip, "Frequently Asked Questions," http://72.14.205.104/search?q= cache:Cng9ZrvpVNkJ:www.verichipcorp.com/content/company/corporatefaq+5,000+ins tallations+worldwide+VeriChip&hl=en&ct=clnk&cd=1 (accessed July 19, 2008).

27. *Ibid.*

28. Biobond introduces complications to the subsequent surgical removal of the chip should it be compromised or otherwise revoked.

29. VeriChip, "What Does VeriChip NOT Do," http://www.verichipcorp.com/ content/company/corporatefaq#g9 (accessed July 18, 2008).

secondary purposes, such as paying for groceries or expediting passage through a security system in an office or airport.

Given that current VeriChip applications employ passive RFID technology, the read range of the chip is at present only a few inches. This perhaps accidental privacy-enhancing feature is thought by some to be a bug, giving rise to the rapid increase in RFID scanning ranges and the coming RFID/GPS merger. The Mojix external passive chip, for example, can be read at 600 feet, and the Identec Solutions external GPS tag employs "satellites in combination with RFID to chart its route and movement."[30] As such, although the current VeriChip lacks an implantable transponder of appropriate size and specificity for such distance tracking, various commercial drivers in the logging industry[31] and elsewhere[32] will likely enable the development of an implantable version of these forms of technology in the near future. A GPS-enabled implant would allow people to be tracked in real time. It would add *everybody* to Greenfield's *everyware*; the supply chain could also become a kind of *human supply chain*, the Internet of things becoming an infrastructure for an "Internet of people."

It is interesting to think about the concept of an Internet of people in the context of more recent VeriChip developments, which include at least two new forms of implants.[33] Unlike its current ID chip, the newer biosensor devices offer diagnostic functions compatible with human biology. The first development is a biothermal temperature-sensing implantable RFID microchip, which can be used remotely to detect changes of temperature in a biological organism. Although the current use is geared toward early warning systems for avian flu in poultry farms,[34] human health applications have also been contemplated, such as "monitoring the location and medical condition of at-risk patients."[35]

---

30. Identec Solutions Inc, "Identec Solutions Develops Satellite Assisted RFID Tag Technology, June 2007," http://72.14.205.104/search?q=cache:SCzsQo8pqgoJ:www.identecsolutions.com/265%2BM5ef65d289bc.html+RFID+GPS+tag&hl=en&ct=clnk&cd=2 (accessed July 24, 2008).

31. Claire Swedberg, "Loggers Use Tags to Track Trucks, Timber: Papermakers and Sawmills Deploy RFID Systems in Forests to Facilitate the Loading, Weighing and Unloading of Logging Trucks," *RFID Journal*, November 28, 2005, http://www.rfidjournal.com/article/articleview/2007/1/1/.

32. Darren Murphy, "Fujitsu Unveils GPS Receiver with Integrated RFID Tag," *ENGADGET*, December 27, 2006, http://www.engadget.com/2006/12/27/fujitsu-unveils-gps-receiver-with-integrated-rfid-tag/.

33. These devices remain in the research and development phase and would require separate FDA approval for use in humans. See Digital Angel, "Bio-sensing: Miraculous Medical Potential," http://www.digitalangel.com/biosensor.aspx (accessed July 18, 2008).

34. Ephraim Schwartz, "Could Chips in Chickens Track Avian Flu?" *PC World*, December 6, 2005, http://www.pcworld.com/article/123845/could_chips_in_chickens_track_avian_flu.html.

35. Matt Hayden, "DEFA14A Filing: "Medical Advisory Systems' Stockholders to Vote on Digital Angel Merger on March 18, 2002," SEC Info, http://72.14.205.104/

The second development is a self-contained implantable RFID glucose-sensing chip.[36] Still in early stages of development, this device aims to provide artificial means for treating patients with diabetes.[37] Once contained in a biostable device with a biocompatible interface, this chip will interoperate with an electronics compatible signal transduction unit to create an "implantable, externally readable glucose sensor."[38] Current research and development is focused on a stable, self-contained glucose-sensing system that is contained in a selectively porous, biocompatible membrane. This "biostable sensing component will be incorporated into a millimeter scale signal transduction and RFID enabled communication device."[39]

Technological integration and interoperability of RFID with automated payment systems, GPS, and, in particular, biosensors will certainly enable implantable chips to transcend their original function as mere patient identification systems. They will become full-fledged medical devices providing therapeutic outcomes that restore and possibly even enhance biological function. It is the combination of these multifarious functions, however, that raises significant issues with regard to the appropriate regulatory environment for human-implantable RFID.

II. THE CURRENT REGULATORY ENVIRONMENT FOR RFID

Many law and policy makers around the world are just barely beginning to contemplate the appropriate regulatory environment for RFID—even less so for human-implantable RFID. Still, a number of existing laws already apply to RFID and more are likely on the way. These include municipal, provincial, federal, national, and international laws, regulations, and directives regarding such things as (a) communications, (b) electronic waste, (c) health and safety, and (d) privacy. My aim in this part is not to provide an exhaustive account of existing laws or their application. Instead, my brief explication aims to set the stage for Part III, where I claim that current approaches are too narrow and will fall short in protecting our privacy and autonomy interests if implantable RFID becomes part of the infrastructure of the so-called Internet of things.

search?q=cache:-mShO9SRctIJ:www.secinfo.com/dsvRq.3k4.htm+bio-sensor+digital+angel&hl=en&ct=clnk&cd=8 (accessed July 18, 2008).

36. Robert E. Carlson, Scott R. Silverman, and Zeke Mejia, "Development of an Implantable Glucose Sensor" (white paper, Digital Angel, April 12, 2007), http://www.digitalangel.com/documents/articles/GLU_120407.pdf (accessed July 19, 2008).

37. VeriChip, "VeriChip News: VeriChip Corporation's and Digital Angel Corporation's Self-Contained Implantable RFID Glucose Sensing Microchip, December 5, 2007," VeriChip, http://www.verichipcorp.com/news/1196870556 (accessed July 19, 2008).

38. Carlson, Silverman, and Mejia, "Implantable Glucose Sensor," 2 (n. 36).

39. *Ibid.*, 3.

A. Communications

Because RFID tags communicate with scanners and network databases by broadcasting signals on the electromagnetic spectrum, they are subject to communications regulations and standards set by bodies such as the U.S. Federal Communications Commission (FCC),[40] Industry Canada,[41] and the European Telecommunications Standards Institute (ETSI).[42] Generally speaking, these regulatory regimes aim to prevent interference and disruption of licensed spectrum services. Some parts of the spectrum are controlled for military use and public safety announcements. Others are for commercial services, including television, cellular phones, and broadband Internet. Regulatory bodies prevent interference and disruption of such services by prescribing and enforcing various technical, operational, and design requirements. RFID manufacturers must comply with these. In addition to standards aimed at coordinating proper allocation and use of the broadcast spectrum, some jurisdictions, such as Canada, set additional regulations aimed to prevent harmful emissions to human health.

B. Electronic Waste

In addition to health concerns generated by RFID emissions, bodies such as the European Union have published directives that protect against health concerns generated by electrical and electronic equipment waste (WEEE).[43] These directives require manufacturers of electrical and electronic equipment to establish an infrastructure for collecting WEEE in an ecologically friendly manner, such that users of electronic products can return them for disposal free of charge. RFID manufacturers are subject to these requirements.

---

40. See US Communications Act of 1934 ch 652 (US) s 302 and regulation made by the Federal Communication Commission pursuant to the Federal Communications Commission Authorization Act of 1988 (US).

41. See Canadian Radio Standards Specifications (RSS) and Radio Standards Procedures (RSP) at Industry Canada, "Spectrum Management and Telecommunications," http://www.ic.gc.ca/epic/site/smt-gst.nsf/en/h_sf01841e.html#guidelines; ministerial authority is conferred by Radiocommunication Act R.S. 1985 c. R-2 (Canada) s 5.

42. See ESTI, "Telecommunications and Internet Converged Services and Protocols for Advanced Networking (TISPAN): Overview of Radio Frequency Identification (RFID) Tags in the Telecommunications Industry" (ETSI TR 102 449 VI.I.I, January 25, 2006), and ESTI, "Electromagnetic Compatibility and Radio Spectrum Matters (ERM); Short-Range Devices" (ESTI EN 300 220-1, 2000).

43. Council Directive (EC) 2002/95 of the European Parliament and of the Council of 27 January 2003 on the restriction of the use of certain hazardous substances in electrical and electronic equipment [2003] OJ L037: 19-23, and Council Directives (EC) 2002/96 of the European Parliament and of the Council of 27 January 2003 on waste electrical and electronic equipment (WEEE)—Joint Declaration of the European Parliament, the Council and the Commission relating to Article 9 [2003] OJ L037: 24.

C. Health and Safety

The more typical means of regulating the health implications of implantable RFID, however, are through provisions in food and drug laws.[44] Through these laws, bodies such as the U.S. Food and Drug Administration (FDA) or the Canadian Therapeutics Product Directorate (TPD) determine whether the RFID application in question is a "medical device" within the meaning of their guiding legislation and, if so, which category of device it falls into, depending on the degree of patient risk and the corresponding controls required to ensure safety and effectiveness. The core function of such regulation is to preclude and prevent the marketing of medical devices that are unhealthy or unsafe. Neither the FDA nor the TPD is charged with making broader determinations about the social implications of a proposed new medical device. For example, the FDA *did not* consider patient privacy or autonomy in its 2004 decision to approve the VeriChip as a Class II medical device.[45] The central issue was merely whether the device met basic health and safety requirements.[46]

Unlike its U.S. counterpart, Canada has not yet approved the VeriChip as a medical device. Although the regulations associated with Canada's Food and Drugs Act[47] contain a definition of "medical device" extremely similar to the one stipulated in U.S. legislation,[48] the two differ significantly in their application.

---

44. In Canada, this is done by the Food and Drugs Act R.S. c. F-27 and its associated regulation made pursuant to s. 30 of the Act. In the United States, this is done by the 1938 Food, Drug, and Cosmetic Act Title 21 ch 9 s 361.

45. U.S. Department of Health and Human Services, Food and Drug Administration, "Medical Devices; Classification of Implantable Radiofrequency Transponder System for Patient Identification and Health Information" (Docket No. 2004N-0477, December 10, 2004), http://www.fda.gov/ohrms/dockets/98fr/04-27077.htm.

46. The FDA may not have succeeded in this, as there are a number of recent reports indicating a link between implantable RFID and cancer. See Le Calvez et al., "Subcutaneous Microchip-Associated Tumours in B6C3F1 Mice: A Retrospective Study to Attempt to Determine Their Histogenesis," *Experimental and Toxicologic Pathology* 57 (2006): 255-265; Vascellari, Melchiotti, and Mutinelli, "Fibrosarcoma with Typical Features of Postinjection Sarcoma at Site of Microchip Implant in a Dog: Histologic and Immunohistochemical Study," *Veterinary Pathology* 43 (2006): 545–548; see also Katherine Albrecht, ed., "Microchip-Induced Tumors in Laboratory Rodents and Dogs: A Review of the Literature 1990–2006" (CASPIAN Consumer Privacy, 2007), http://www.antichips.com/cancer/index.html#Research_Article_Tables; Applied Digital disputes this claim. See William Wustenberg, "Effective Carcinogenicity Assessment of Permanent Implantable Medical Devices" (white paper, AlterNetMD Consulting, Farmington, MN, September 27, 2007), http://72.14.205.104/search?q=cache:jnOqeQdaIsUJ:www.verichipcorp.com/files/RodentSarcomagenesis092807Wustenberg.pdf+Effective+Carcinogenicity+Assessment+of+Permanent+Implantable+Medical+Devices&hl=en&ct=clnk&cd=1&gl=ca&client=firefox-a.

47. Food and Drug Act s 2 (n. 44).

48. Federal Food, Drug, and Cosmetic Act s 201(h) (n. 44).

Both refer to "medical devices" as implements involving diagnostics, treatment, mitigation of disease, restoring health, modifying bodily function, and the like. But Canadian regulators seem to employ a stricter definition of what constitutes a medical device. It is, therefore, plausible that the TPD would refuse an application from VeriChip because it is not an instrument of diagnosis or treatment, it does not mitigate or prevent diseases, and it plays no role in restoring, correcting, or modifying body function or structure.[49]

From a broader social perspective, not that much is riding on the legalities surrounding the appropriate statutory interpretation. After all, such legislation regulates only how VeriChip can and cannot be marketed. If it is not a medical device, then the regulation does not apply at all. Food and drug laws merely stipulate that medical devices on the market must meet basic health and safety requirements. Even on the assumption that VeriChip meets these standards,[50] the more important paucity in existing regulations, from a health and safety perspective, pertains to who can implant them, under what conditions, and for what purposes.

This became an issue in Canada for the first time in 2006 when the *Kitchener Record* reported that Jesse Villemaire implanted VeriChips into the hands of four students who drove up from Lockport, New York, for the procedure.[51] Leaving aside concerns about cancer and toxic shock,[52] the intricate connective tissues between the index finger and thumb do not render it an ideal location for the implantation of a VeriChip, which may be why the four sought out the well-known Cambridge tattoo artist and body-piercer to do this work rather than a licensed physician.

Although many jurisdictions have statutes regulating who can perform surgical acts, most do not specifically contemplate subdermal radio-emitting chip implants. In some Canadian provinces such as Ontario (where Jesse Villemaire resides), performing a procedure on the tissue of another person below the dermis is a regulated activity.[53] Not just anyone can do it. Subject to a limited

---

49. The yet-to-be-approved glucose and biothermal chips might one day, however, have therapeutic capabilities.

50. Recall that this is a contentious claim; see Albrecht, "Microchip-Induced Tumors" (n. 46).

51. Melinda Dalton, "Under Their Skin; Local Piercer Tries His Hand at Implanting Microchips;" *The Record*. Kitchener, February 4, 2006: A.1, http://64.233.167.104/search ?q=cache:E1Un1HZfOqQJ:idtrail.org/files/The%2520Record%2520Archive.pdf+Kitchen er+Record+Jesse+Villemaire+Chip&hl=en&ct=clnk&cd=1; Anna Bahney, "High Tech, Under the Skin," *New York Times*, February 2, 2006, http://www.nytimes.com /2006/02/02/fashion/thursdaystyles/02tags.html.

52. See V.P. McCarthy, "Toxic Shock Syndrome after Ear Piercing," *Pediatric Infectious Disease Journal* 7, no. 10 (1988): 741–742.

53. Regulated Health Professions Act S.O. 1991 c 18 (Ontario, Canada) s 27(2).

number of exemptions, one must be a licensed health professional.[54] Because implanting an RFID is a subdermal procedure, it is necessary in Ontario to determine whether a non-authorized person falls within the narrow range of exemptions set out in 8(1)–(4) of the Controlled Acts Regulations.[55] These include (i) acupuncture; (ii) ear or body piercing for the purpose of accommodating a piece of jewelry; (iii) electrolysis; and (iv) tattooing for a cosmetic purpose. Although "body piercing" is explicitly exempted, it is crucial to note that the exemption is strictly limited to piercing that accommodates jewelry.

The regulations nowhere define "piercing" and "jewellery." Ordinarily, the aim of ear or body piercing is to decorate the body by placing jewelry through a hole created for that purpose. Such ornamentation is usually visible to an onlooker. So while Baja Beach Club's Conrad Chase viewed the VeriChip as a next-generation body piercing,[56] the more plausible account is that a computer microchip is *not* jewelry or a piercing within the meaning of the regulations. Imbedded underneath the skin, the VeriChip is not a visible ornamentation, nor is its primary function decorative. This very likely means that the VeriChip and other RFIDs can be implanted in Ontario only by authorized health professionals. Even if the implantation of RFID chips is regulated in Ontario insofar as who can implant them, they are for the most part unregulated in terms of their use once implanted. The same is true for most jurisdictions.

D. Privacy and Autonomy

It requires little imagination to see how the implementation of human-implantable RFID systems could create serious risks to personal privacy and autonomy. As one journalist speculated, "it would be an interesting feature of an employee's first day: sign a contract, fill out a W-2 and roll up your sleeve for your microchip injection."[57]

---

54. *Ibid.*, s 27(1)(a); under s 40(1) of the Act, the consequences of performing such a procedure without the legal authority are not more than $25,000 in fines or imprisonment for a term of not more than one year or both for a first offense. This increases to $50,000 for all subsequent offenses.

55. Controlled Acts Regulations O. Reg 107/96 1991 (Ontario, Canada) ss 8(1)–(4), made pursuant to the Regulated Health Professions Act (n. 53).

56. Ian Kerr, "Not So Crazy about the Chips," *Innovate Magazine*, Spring 2005, http://www.idtrail.org/files/innovate%20-%20not%20so%20crazy%20about%20the%20chips%20%28may%202005%29.pdf.

57. Orr Shtuhl, "California Could Become Third State to Ban Forced Microchip Tag Implants (RFID), January 12, 2008," GlobalResearch.ca, http://64.233.167.104/search?q=cache:U2dcSe_njOcJ:www.globalresearch.ca/index.php%3Fcontext%3Dva%26aid%3D7781+It+would+be+an+interesting+feature+of+an+employee%E2%80%99s+first+day:+sign+a+contract,+fill+out+a+W-2+and+roll+up+your+sleeve+for+your+microchip+injection&hl=en&ct=clnk&cd=1&gl=ca&client=firefox-a (accessed July 21, 2008).

In response to the mere possibility of this scenario,[58] a handful of U.S. states have proposed, and some have passed, legislation that would ban the coerced implantation of RFIDs. Wisconsin was first to ban involuntary chipping.[59] Violators are subject to forfeiture not exceeding US$10,000. California[60] and North Dakota[61] quickly followed suit. Laws passed in Georgia[62] and New Hampshire[63] recently mandated expert study of the consumer privacy implications of RFID technology and the development of policy recommendations.

The central underpinning of these state laws is to ban implantation where there is a lack of consent on the part of the implantee. Like any other surgical procedure or medical "treatment," consent is a crucial prerequisite to implantation. But it does not end there. In the case of RFID implants, the issue of consent is ongoing, not only because of medical treatment laws, but also because of privacy law. From the perspective of informational privacy and data security, it is generally important to ensure knowledge and consent whenever there is a collection, use, or disclosure of information about an identifiable individual.[64]

The question about how to ensure that RFID complies with the consent principle and other fair information practices has occupied the minds of the Data Commissioners' community around the world for several years. For example, in Europe, the Article 29 Data Protection Working Party (Working Party) released its "Working Document on Data Protection Issues Related to RFID Technology" in January 19, 2005.[65] To the extent that RFID systems are used to collect, share,

---

58. HR-BLR.Com, "Ohio Employer First to Implant Employee Microchips, April 10, 2006," HR-BLR.Com, http://64.233.167.104/search?q=cache:OoCUcauGgzIJ: hr.blr.com/news.aspx%3Fid%3D17924+Ohio+employer+forced+chipping&hl=en&ct=cl nk&cd=1&gl=ca&client=firefox-a.

59. 2005 Wisconsin Act 482 Assembly Bill 290, May 30, 2006 (Wisconsin, US).

60. An Act to Add Section 52.7 to the Civil Code, Relating to Identification Devices, Senate Bill 362 ch 538, June 19, 2007 (California, US).

61. Senate Bill No. 2415 ch 12.1-15 of the North Dakota Century Code, 2 (North Dakota, US).

62. Bill No.: H.B. 203 (Georgia, US), introduced on April 12, 2005, creates a Joint House and Senate Emerging Communications Technologies Study Commission.

63. New Hampshire House, HB 686-FN—As Amended by the House March 18, 2008 (New Hampshire).

64. Consent is, of course, only one of a larger set of privacy-protecting principles sometimes known as "fair information practice principles." See, e.g., Organisation for Economic Cooperation and Development, Guidelines Governing the Protection of Privacy and Transborder Flows of Personal Data, Annex to the recommendation of the Council of 23 September 1980, http://www.oecd.org/document/18/0,3343,en_2649_34255_1815186 _1_1_1_1,00.html and the Personal Information Protection and Electronic Documents Act (PIPEDA) S.C. 2000 c 5 (Canada) s 7.

65. This Working Party was set up under Article 29 of Council Directive (EC) 95/46 of the European Parliament and of the Council of 24 October 1995 on the protection of individuals with regard to the processing of personal data and on the free movement

and store personal data, they must conform to the principles set out in the European Community Data Protection Directive[66] and the directive on privacy and electronic communications.[67] In its interpretation of the EU data protection law, the Working Party expressed concern "about the possibility for some applications of RFID technology to violate human dignity as well as data protection rights."[68] Specifically, the Working Party expressed unease regarding the possibility of government, business, and individual use of the technology to "pry into the privacy sphere of individuals. The ability to surreptitiously collect a variety of data all related to the same person; track individuals as they move into public places . . . [and] enhance profiles."[69]

The Working Party held that unambiguous consent "will be the only legal ground available to data controllers to legitimize the collection of information through RFID."[70] Further, they held that data controllers must provide data subjects with information as to the "identity of the controller, the purposes of the processing as well as, among others, information on the recipients of the data and the existence of a right of access."[71] In particular, they noted that "data controllers should be very clear in informing individuals that the presence of such devices enables the tags to broadcast information without individual engaging in any active action" and that the data subject should be informed about the RFID-garnered information's intended use, "including (a) the type of data with which RFID information will be associated and (b) whether the information will be made available to third parties."[72] In its ultimate conclusion, the Working Party was clear that RFID manufacturers must ensure that the technology is privacy compliant.[73]

Similarly, the Privacy Commissioner of Canada has recognized that certain uses of RFID are subject to federal regulation in Canada.[74] This legislation adopts

---

of such data [1995] OJ L281: 31. It is an independent European advisory body on data protection and privacy.

66. *Ibid.*

67. Council Directive (EC) 2002/58 of the European Parliament and of the Council of 12 July 2002 concerning the processing of personal data and the protection of privacy in the electronic communications sector (Directive on privacy and electronic communications) [2002] OJ L201: 37–47.

68. Article 29 Data Protection Working Party, *10107/05/EN: Working Document on Data Protection Issues related to RFID Technology* (Luxemburg: Article 29 Data Protection Working Party, January 19, 2005), http://ec.europa.eu/justice_home/fsj/privacy/docs/wpdocs/2005/wp105_en.pdf.

69. *Ibid.*, 2.

70. *Ibid.*, 10. Note, however, that consent may not be required as foreseen by Article 7 of the Data Protection Directive (n. 57).

71. Article 29, "Working Document," 10 (n. 58).

72. *Ibid.*, 10.

73. *Ibid.*, 12.

74. PIPEDA (n. 54).

a version of the fair information practice principles similar to those first set out in the OECD Guidelines and implemented in the EU Data Protection Directive. According to the Privacy Commissioner of Canada:

1. If the chip has had the personal information of the individual written to it, then it is a repository of personal information;
2. If the tag is unique, and can be associated with an individual, it becomes a unique identifier or proxy for that individual; and
3. Information about possessions or purchases, which can be manipulated or processed to form a profile, is personal information, whether gathered through multiple visits to a facility or organization, or through access to the data base of RFID purchase information.[75]

Consequently, the Commissioner has noted that RFID systems can raise numerous privacy concerns, such as (i) the surreptitious collection of information; (ii) the ability to track an individual's movements; (iii) the ability to profile individuals; (iv) the ability to reveal secondary information about individuals; and (v) the capacity for massive data aggregation.[76]

The Ontario Information and Privacy Commissioner (OIPC) has also been a thought leader on this subject, producing the first ever set of best practices to ensure privacy compliance.[77] In addition to applying Canada's ten privacy principles to RFIDs, the OIPC offers three guiding principles: (i) focus on RFID information systems, not technologies; (ii) privacy and security must be built in at the design stage; and (iii) maximize individual participation and consent. In a white paper released January 2008,[78] the OIPC expressed concern about the use of RFID in the health care context, recognizing that RFIDs linked to people are governed by provincial legislation[79] because they implicate "organizations and individuals involved in the delivery of health care services in both the public and private sectors."[80] In highlighting its potential benefits, the OIPC found that if the

---

75. Office of the Privacy Commissioner, "Fact Sheet: RFID Technology," http://www.privcom.gc.ca/fs-fi/02_05_d_28_e.asp.

76. Ibid.

77. Ontario Information and Privacy Commissioner (OIPC), Privacy Guidelines for RFID Information Systems (RFID Privacy Guidelines) (Toronto: OPIC, 2006), http://www.ipc.on.ca/images/Resources/up-rfidgdlines.pdf.

78. Ontario Information and Privacy Commissioner (OPIC), RFID and Privacy: Guidance for Health Care Providers (Toronto: OPIC, 2008), http://www.ipc.on.ca/images/Resources/up-rrfid_HealthCare.pdf.

79. Personal Health Information Protection Act (PHIPA), 2004, S.O. 2004, c 3 (Ontario, Canada).

80. Ontario Information and Privacy Commissioner Ann Cavoukian, "RFID and Privacy: Guidance for Health-Care Providers on RFID" (lecture, MaRS Centre, Toronto, 2008), OPIC, http://72.14.205.104/search?q=cache:JDTnfWCsCigJ:www.ipc.on.ca/

. . . RFID patient identification program responds to a defined problem or issue in a limited, proportional and effective manner, and is deployed in a way that minimizes privacy and security risks, at least as effectively as any alternative solution, then in principle there should be few privacy concerns with the program.[81]

The OIPC, however, expressed concern about human-implantable RFID, recognizing that there are "complex legal and ethical questions" invoked by RFID "implants in the human body."[82] Stressing the importance of informed consent, the use of patient autonomy as the yardstick consent, and the need for the utmost transparency of its use in the health care context, the OIPC referred to the 2007 report issued by the U.S. Council on Ethical and Judicial Affairs (CEJA)[83] and the 2005 report by the European Group on Ethics (EGE) in Science and Technology to the European Commission.[84] Both reports held "that implantable RFID devices may compromise people's privacy and security because it is yet to be demonstrated that the information in the tags can be properly protected."[85]

In the United States, VeriChip is not directly subject to U.S. health privacy laws,[86] as VeriChip and its parent company are not health care providers, a health plan, or a health care clearinghouse.[87] However, both companies are bound to the extent that their contractual relationships with health care providers make them responsible for the protection of personal health care information. Applied Digital has, as a result, developed a policy to enable Health Insurance Portability and Accountability Act (HIPAA) compliant business associate agreements.[88] Moreover, VeriChip operates under Federal Trade Commission (FTC) oversight because the technology is governed by consumer protection regulation. To this end, the FTC will enforce promises made by businesses with regard to the use, control, and protection of personal information.

---

images/Resources%255C2008-03-05-HPRFIDCanada.pdf+RFID+Canada+implantable&hl=en&ct=clnk&cd=4&gl=ca&client=firefox-a.

81. OIPC, "RFID and Privacy," 29 (n. 78).

82. *Ibid.*, 30.

83. Robert M. Sade, "Report of the Council on Ethical and Judicial Affairs," *CEJA Report* 5 (2007), http://www.ama-assn.org/ama1/pub/upload/mm/369/ceja_5a07.pdf.

84. Rafael Capurro, "Ethical Aspects of ICT Implants in the Human Body," European Group on Ethics in Science and New Technologies (EGE) de la Comisión Europea: EGE Opinion (March 16, 2005), http://64.233.167.104/search?q=cache:jGz9zgxN-PAJ:www.capurro.de/talca.ppt+European+Group+on+Ethics+(EGE)+in+Science+and+Technology+to+the+European+Commission+Report+RFID+2005&hl=en&ct=clnk&cd=6.

85. See Ann Cavoukian, "RFID and Privacy Lecture" (n. 80).

86. E.g., Health Insurance Portability and Accountability Act of 1996 (HIPAA) 42 USC 201.

87. *Ibid.*, s 1172(a).

88. VeriChip Corp, "S-1/A SEC Filing, January 9, 2007," Edgar, http://sec.edgar-online.com/2007/01/09/0001193125-07-003171/Section16.asp.

Because the whole point of the VeriChip is to provide a unique identifier associated with a particular individual, and given the passive, promiscuous nature of the unencrypted VeriChip, there is little doubt that fundamental privacy principles are implicated whenever an implantee comes within the read range of a scanner. The key difference between RFID and traditional forms of identification (such as presenting a health card or medical history) is that the RFID identification process is entirely automated. When one considers that the design of VeriChip was meant to identify the implantee and collect information unbeknownst to that person (e.g., while unconscious or disoriented), one realizes the ease with which surreptitious collection of information becomes possible and the consequent challenges of obtaining meaningful consent.

It is tempting to think that the consent issue for human-implantable RFID is no different from other RFIDs, which can also be easily associated with an identifiable individual. In fact, Applied Digital and a number of other providers offer many kinds of less invasive forms of associable RFIDs, such as bracelets. The key differences are the potentially coercive elements around implantation and the fact that the current human-implantable RFIDs are read-only, not easily removed, and not encrypted, and they do not have an "on-off" switch. A read-only chip that is not easily removed is problematic in circumstances where the personal identifier in the chip becomes compromised. Because it is not possible to rewrite data to the current chips, it is not possible to "revoke" the identifier without physically removing the chip. This problem is compounded by the fact that the chip is purposefully unencrypted.[89] This makes the VeriChip entirely vulnerable from an information security perspective. It has been easily hacked and cloned, with the method for doing so widely available on the Internet.[90] Given its insecurity and the inability to revoke and rewrite new identifiers, its inability to be turned "off," compounded by the need to surgically remove the chip if compromised or no longer desired, it is unclear why anyone who wants the chip for anything other than a "transgressive cyberpunk fashion statement" would consent to its implantation in the first place.

VeriChip's only attempt to address these problems seems to be the addition of a password requirement for access to the portion of its database with which a given chip is associated. Ironically, this element undermines any need for the chip itself, because the rather weak form of authentication that a password affords is really all that is on offer. As a number of information security experts

---

89. It is has been said that the fact that human-implantable RFIDs are unencrypted is a feature rather than a bug; allowing the personal identifier to be easily intercepted prevents wrongdoers from using more coercive means of extracting the information on the chip. See John Halamka, et al., "The Security Implications of VeriChip Cloning," *Journal of American Medical Informatics Association* 13, no. 6 (2006): 601–607.

90. Jonathan Westhuese, "Demo: Cloning a VeriChip," http://cq.cx/verichip.pl (accessed July 23, 2008).

(including the Harvard Medical School's CIO, who implanted himself with the VeriChip) have clearly stated, "[t]he VeriChip should serve exclusively for *identification* and not *authentication* or access control."[91]

III. THE INTERNET OF THINGS AND THE NOT-SO-LONG ARM OF THE LAW

Setting aside VeriChip's current privacy and security concerns, the broader challenge with RFID will be its future collision course with the consent principle. RFIDs are subject to a "network effect."[92] Like the Internet itself, the so-called Internet of things will reach its true potential only if it is (near-) ubiquitous; the only way to derive the maximum benefit of an automated identification system is to make it pervasive and automatic.

Such a system would completely undermine the consent/control model of privacy, which is premised on the possibility that individuals can determine for themselves when, how, and to what extent information about them is communicated to others. To illustrate, let us continue with Greenfield's description of *everyware*, mentioned briefly in Part I.B:

> You close the door to your office because you want privacy, and your phone and IM channel are automatically set to "unavailable." You point to an unfamiliar word in a text, and a definition appears. You sit down to lunch with three friends, and the restaurant plays music that you've all rated highly.[93]

In order for the world to truly work like this, one would have to abandon altogether the requirements, recommendations, and guidelines set out by the European Working Party, the Privacy Commissioner of Canada, and the OIPC. In a world laced with RFIDs—a world many if not most network aficionados think inevitable—it will no longer be feasible to obtain individualized consent (or, for that matter, even individual waivers of privacy) for each informational transaction resulting in collection, use, or disclosure of personal information. The OIPC's excellent and important guideline to ensure "maximal individual participation and consent" is fundamentally at odds with a system geared toward pervasive and automated information transactions.

---

91. Halamka, "Security Implications of VeriChip," 601 (n. 89).

92. A network effect (sometimes called a "network externality") is an attribute by which the value of a good or service becomes dependent on its broad adoption by others. VeriChip would not provide a valuable emergency service if only one doctor, one hospital, or one patient used it. See John Halamka, "Straight from the Shoulder," *New England Journal of Medicine* 353 (2005): 331–333; in general, the only way to achieve ubiquity is a low unit cost for RFID, which itself requires mass adoption.

93. Greenfield, *Everyware*, 26–27 (n. 24).

Whether for personalized jukeboxes or emergency health services, such automated systems would instead require that all or almost all individuals opt in by way of *blanket-consent*: offering up, in advance and without limitation, a host of unforeseeable, unpredictable, and often unintended personal information collections, uses, and disclosures. In what meaningful sense could this be called "consent"? And if the goal of the Internet of things truly is ubiquitous efficiency, then there will be little or no opportunity to opt out of the system in any meaningful way—much like trying to live as an adult without a credit card, drivers license, or passport in contemporary North American or European society. In an RFID-enabled network society (not to mention RFIDs seamlessly integrated into human bodies), the nature of collection, use, and disclosure of information becomes what designer Naoto Fukasawa once spoke of as "design dissolving in behaviour." It is a system so well designed and so effortless for those who use it that the collection, use, and disclosure of personal information "effectively absconds from awareness."[94]

Whatever else remains unclear, it seems obvious that our current regulatory model—premised on control and consent—would provide a not-so-long arm of the law in an RFID-enabled Internet of things.

IV. THE HUMAN-MACHINE MERGER

To better grasp the potential shortcomings of our current regulatory environment, it is important to recognize that human-implantable RFIDs are just one drop in the bucket-load of implantable devices being developed as part of a growing trend in medicine that seeks to merge human bodies with machine parts. Mechanical and biomechanical implants and devices are not completely new to the health agenda.[95] To offer a few examples, cochlear implants have been available for several years to restore or enhance hearing.[96] Wireless sensors and pumps have been implanted to deliver insulin to patients with diabetes who lack a fully

---

94. *Ibid.*, 26.

95. Ray Kurzweil and Terry Grossman, *Fantastic Voyage: Live Long Enough to Live Forever* (Emmaus, PA: Rodale Press, 2004); Ian Kerr and James Wishart, "A Tsunami Wave of Science: How the Technologies of Transhumanist Medicine Are Shifting Canada's Health Research Agenda," *Health Law Review* (forthcoming); Ian Kerr and Timothy Caulfield, "Emerging Health Technologies," in *Canadian Health Law and Policy*, 3rd ed, eds. Jocelyn Downie, Timothy Caulfield, and Colleen Flood (Toronto: Butterworths, 2007): 509–538.

96. National Institute on Deafness and Other Communication Disorders, "Cochlear Implants, May 2007," http://www.nidcd.nih.gov/health/hearing/coch.asp (accessed July 17, 2008).

functioning pancreas.[97] Totally implantable artificial hearts have undergone extensive clinical trials and have extended life significantly for some patients with congestive heart failure and no hope for a transplant.[98]

In addition to these well-known examples, there are a number of interesting cybernetic implants and network devices that will interoperate with the human body. For example, RedTacton is a "human area networking" technology that uses the surface of the human body as a high-speed network transmission path. According to its corporate profile, RedTacton will enable "ubiquitous services based on human-centered interactions that are more intimate and easier for people to use."[99] RedTacton integrates communications with ordinary bodily functions and activities, providing greater control than implantable RFID: for example, "touching, gripping, sitting, walking, stepping and other human movements can be the triggers for unlocking or locking, starting or stopping equipment, or obtaining data."[100]

It is practically impossible not to marvel at the possibilities of this kind of innovation in the near future. Not *that* long ago (the year of my bar mitzvah), the famous philosopher and cognitive scientist, Daniel Dennett, dreamed in sci-fi prose of "mainlining Brahms" directly into his brain, which, he speculated, would be "an unforgettable experience for any stereo buff."[101] Are we not now on the precipice of Apple iTunes traveling wirelessly from a miniature implantable or wearable device across our skin and into cochlear implants that are "mainlined" directly to our auditory systems?

To show that this technological possibility is not far-fetched, consider a second example. Cybernetics professor Kevin Warwick has implanted a neural transducer, a device that allows him to "hook [his] nervous system up to the Internet."[102] Through direct links between the neural transducer and nerve fibers in his arm, he is able to transmit radio signals from a computer to the neural transducer implant and download them onto his nerve fibers and vice versa. Warwick and

---

97. Robert F. Service, "Can Sensors Make a Home in the Body?" *Science* 297, no. 5583 (2002): 962–963.

98. Wray Herbert, "The Artificial Heart: Not Just a Pump," *Scientific American Body*, February 2008, http://www.sciam.com/article.cfm?id=not-just-a-pump; Emily Singer, "An Artificial Heart That Doesn't Beat," *Technology Review*, September 21, 2006, http://www.technologyreview.com/read_article.aspx?id=17523&ch=biotech&pg=1.

99. RedTacton, "What's RedTacton?," http://www.redtacton.com/en/info/index.html (accessed July 17, 2008).

100. RedTacton, "Three Features," http://www.redtacton.com/en/feature/index.html (accessed July 17, 2008).

101. Daniel C. Dennett, "Where Am I?" in *Brainstorms: Philosophical Essays on Mind and Psychology*, ed. Daniel C. Dennett (Boston: MIT Press, 1981), 6, http://www.cs.umu.se/kurser/TDBC12/HT99/Dennett.html (accessed July 17, 2008).

102. Kevin Warwick, "Cyborg Morals, Cyborg Values, Cyborg Ethics," *Ethics and Information Technology* 5 (2003): 135–137, 135.

his research team have investigated the signals corresponding to his bodily movement. For example, when he moves his finger, some of the electronic signals from his nervous system that caused his muscles and tendons to operate are also transmitted to the computer, where they are then stored as a sequence. The team found that they can play back those same signals and thereby re-create much of the original movement. Likewise, Warwick's brain and central nervous system have successfully received and made sense of signals from external ultrasonic sensors and transmitters used in mobile robots. Warwick's "cyborg experiments" may seem like an eccentric exploration of an over-funded academic, but there is much hope within medical and bioengineering communities that such applications will soon become mainstream cures for paralysis and other physical impairments. In fact, many hope that such devices will one day enhance physiological function and capability *above and beyond* species-typical norms.

At the same time, reflecting upon the broader implications of radio frequency implants and other human-machine mergers, Professor Warwick has noted that this is not merely a question about enhancing human capabilities but also "a completely different basis on which the . . . brain operates in a mixed human, machine fashion."[103] According to Warwick, the human-machine merger implicates individual identity and personal autonomy. As he put it,

> . . . a human whose nervous system is linked to a computer not only puts forward their individuality for serious questioning but also, when the computer is part of a network or at least connected to a network, allows their autonomy to be compromised.[104]

V. THE INTERNET OF PEOPLE

When we think about human-implantable RFID in the context of the Internet of things and the human-machine merger, we see that the issues are much more profound than the perceived pros and cons of the current VeriChip. Our existing regulatory approaches provide some measure of protection against RFID and the misuse of the electromagnetic spectrum, improper disposal of electronic waste, and the dishonest marketing of unsafe medical devices. But in most North American and European jurisdictions, our laws are insufficient to deal with what devices can be implanted, by whom, and under what circumstances. Although existing data protection regimes currently afford individuals some measure of autonomy and control over the personal information transactions generated by today's *one-off* RFID applications, the suggested approaches and guidelines discussed above in Part II are premised on an ability to obtain meaningful

---

103. *Ibid.*, 136.
104. *Ibid.*, 132.

consent and individual participation. These approaches do not adequately contemplate the obfuscation and automation of information collection, use, and disclosure likely to occur should our world move closer to an integrated and ubiquitous Internet of things.

Here is how the International Telecommunications Union framed the problem back in 2005:

> When everyday items come equipped with some or all of the five senses (such as sight and smell) combined with computing and communication capabilities, concepts of data request and data consent risk becoming outdated. Invisible and constant data exchange between things and people, and between things and other things, will occur unknown to the owners and originators of such data. The sheer scale and capacity of the new technologies will magnify this problem. Who will ultimately control the data collected by all the eyes and ears embedded in the environment surrounding us?[105]

Consent is a serious bug in the code of automation.

Of perhaps even greater concern, technologists, physicians, and their regulators have yet to adequately consider what to do about the fact that human-implantable RFID and other innovations are adding humans to this ubiquitous network. Although the benefits that these innovations promise are considerable if not revolutionary, do we have *any* idea how humanity might change when the emerging Internet of things likewise becomes an Internet of people?

If we are to remain committed to fundamental principles and values such as consent, personal privacy, and autonomy, we will need to seriously rethink their application in light of RFID and other emerging network technologies. Given the paucity of an appropriately accommodating regulatory environment—*and, rather than giving up these bedrock values simply because they seem "outdated"*—we also need to continue thinking carefully about whether there is sufficient justification for moving forward with human-implantable RFID, ubiquitous computing, and the Internet of things. We must ensure that today's rather primitive specter of the VeriChip automatically enabling collection, use, or disclosure of the identity and health records of the somnambulist patient does not become the dystopic metaphor for the place of people in tomorrow's Internet of things.

---

105. ITU, *ITU Internet Reports 2005: The Internet of Things Executive Summary* (Geneva: ITU Strategy and Policy Unit (SPU), 2005): 15, www.itu.int/dms_pub/itu-s/opb/pol/ S-POL-IR.IT-2005-SUM-PDF-E.pdf.

20. USING BIOMETRICS TO REVISUALIZE THE CANADA–U.S. BORDER

SHOSHANA MAGNET*

I. THE LONGEST UNDEFENDED BORDER IN THE WORLD: MAINTAINING THE BOUNDARY BETWEEN THE UNITED STATES AND CANADA

Stretching between the two countries for more than 5000 miles, the boundary between the United States and Canada is described as the longest undefended border in the world. More than 200 million people cross the border annually, making it the world's largest trading relationship.[1] Bilateral trade between the two countries is valued at close to $680 billion Canadian dollars. More than $1.5 billion dollars is exchanged across the border on a daily basis.[2] Extensive partnerships between the United States and Canada govern this border. From the Free Trade Agreement (FTA) and North American Free Trade Agreement (NAFTA) to North American Aerospace Defense Command (NORAD) and North Atlantic Treaty Organization (NATO) military accords, the list of bilateral initiatives between the two countries is extensive.

* The author would like to thank Robert Smith, Celiany Rivera-Velazquez, Amy Hasinoff, Aisha Durham, Himika Bhattacharya, Helen Kang, Carolyn Randolph, Jillian Baez, Kent Ono, C. L. Cole, Paula Treichler, Ian Kerr, Jane Bailey, Daphne Gilbert, and the anonymous reviewers for their helpful suggestions.

1. U.S. Department of State, "Canada: Security Assistance," (2007), http://www.state.gov/t/pm/65290.htm.

2. Government of Canada, "Securing an Open Society: Canada's National Security Policy," Privy Council Office (2004), http://www.pco-bcp.gc.ca/docs/information/Publications/natsec-secnat/natsec-secnat_e.pdf.

This "special friendship" between the United States and Canada is not free of stress, nor has it been historically as issues of industrialization, social policy, natural resources, power, and pollution have taxed—and continue to tax—the relationship between the two countries. Disputes over the U.S.–Canada boundary were common in the nineteenth century. In particular, disagreements over boundaries within maritime regions gave rise to the War of 1812. Originally set along the 45th parallel, the U.S.–Canada border moved several times as a result of a series of nineteenth-century border disputes. In 1818, the Canada–U.S. boundary was reestablished at the 49th parallel.[3] By the 1870s, relations between the two countries had become increasingly peaceable. In 1871, only four years after Canadian confederation, the Treaty of Washington officially recognized the borders of the Dominion of Canada,[4] and relations between the two countries improved.[5] All remaining boundaries between the two nations were settled nonviolently by 1903 when the Alaska boundary was resolved.[6]

In an attempt to avoid future border disputes repeating the near-conflicts that had occurred in the nineteenth century, Canada and the United States established the International Boundary Commission (IBC) in 1908, cementing a friendship through a bilateral border initiative. Initially designed to address boundary disputes between the two countries through the clarification of the boundary line between the United States and Canada, the IBC was made a permanent institution in 1925. Today, it is the IBC that maintains the 6-metre swath between the two countries, keeping the border clear of brush and vegetation, and maintaining the boundary markers and buoys that demarcate the U.S.–Canada border. Until recently, the IBC's tasks have "been reasonably specific and technical in nature, a fact that kept its operation relatively free of controversy and public debate."[7]

The IBC shares its boundary maintenance obligations with a second bilateral commission, the International Waterways Commission. The border between the United States and Canada is one-third water. Thus, determining the coordinates of the liquid boundary that traverses the Great Lakes and the St. Lawrence River is of paramount importance. This task was the responsibility of the International Waterways Commission, now the International Joint Commission (IJC).[8] Although the relationship between the United States and Canada is not free from bilateral tensions, a boundary open to cross-border

---

3. John Herd Thompson and Steven Randall, *Canada and the United States: Ambivalent Allies* (Athens: University of Georgia Press, 1994).

4. Thompson and Randall, *Canada and the United States*, 40 (n. 3).

5. Norman Hillmer, Canada's Relations with United States, *The Oxford Companion to Canadian History* (Oxford: Oxford University Press, 2004).

6. Thompson and Randall, *Canada and the United States*, 40 (n. 4).

7. *Ibid.*, 73.

8. *Ibid.*, 74.

trade has been the hallmark of the long and primarily friendly relationship between the two countries.[9]

II. THE POST-9/11 U.S.–CANADA BORDER

The events of September 11, 2001, prompted a significant change in U.S.–Canada border relations. Previously represented as the "longest undefended border in the world," the border newly came to be understood instead as a reified line between the two countries, and openness was represented as a "luxury" that the United States could no longer afford.[10] The United States ceased to understand Canada as its "friendly neighbor" and as the "Great White North." Instead, U.S. understandings of Canada shifted to highlight the dangers to the United States of Canada's "permissive" immigration and refugee policy. One incident in particular highlighted this transformation of Canada in the U.S. cultural imaginary: the persistence of the rumor that the 9/11 hijackers entered the United States from Canada.

III. RUMORS THAT THE 9/11 HIJACKERS CAME FROM CANADA

The shifting place of Canada in the U.S. national imaginary began immediately following the attacks on the World Trade Center and the Pentagon on September 11, 2001. Within days of the attacks, several major U.S. newspapers claimed that a number of the hijackers had entered the United States across the Canadian border. On September 13, 2001, an article in the *Boston Globe* suggested that investigators were "seeking evidence [. . .] that the hijackers responsible for Tuesday's attacks had slipped into the United States from Canada."[11] A day later, on September 14, the *Washington Post* asserted that two of the suspected

---

9. Of course, key differences between U.S. and Canadian national policies have historically and continue to tax their "special" relationship. One famous example is the tension between the two countries as a result of the Vietnam War, in which Canada repeatedly voiced concerns over U.S. military policy. Tensions between the two countries escalated over the course of the war when Canada accepted more than 50,000 draft resisters from the United States (Thompson and Randall, 2002: 230). More recently, Canadian resistance to American military policy surfaced in Canadian refusal to engage with the U.S. Star Wars plan for missile defense. Canada also refused to send troops to fight in Iraq, although Canada's support for the war in Afghanistan makes it clear that the ambivalence that has historically plagued the relationship between the two countries remains.

10. Blas Nuñez-Neto, "Border Security: The role of the U.S. border patrol" (2005), http://www.fas.org/sgp/crs/homesec/RL32562.pdf.

11. Colin Nickerson and Ellen Barry, "Attack Aftermath/Looking for Answers to the Hunt: Seeking Trail of Suspects across Borders," *Boston Globe* (September 13, 2001).

9/11 hijackers definitely had entered the United States across the northern boundary: "Two suspects in Tuesday's terrorist attacks in the United States crossed the border from Canada with no known difficulty at a small, border entry in Coburn Gore, Maine, which is usually staffed by only one border inspection officer, a U.S. official said today."[12] Although this claim quickly was disproved, it nonetheless continued to circulate.

Both immediately and over the next several years, the continuing persistence of this and other mistaken beliefs concerning Canada's role in allowing terrorist access to the United States led the Canadian government to take steps to dispel a number of falsehoods about Canada's connection to terrorism. In 2004, the government of Canada launched a website called CanadianAlly.com, designed specifically to reassure Americans that their neighbor to the north remains a friendly one. The website provided a number of facts about the relationship between the United States and Canada, including a "debunking the myths" section that roundly denounced original and persistent rumors that the 9/11 terrorists had entered the United States from Canada:

True or False: Some of the 9–11 Hi-jackers (sic) entered through Canada:

FALSE

This is simply not true. In fact, they had all been legally admitted to the United States, as has been confirmed by senior American officials.[13]

IV. THE RECONFIGURATION OF CANADA IN THE U.S. IMAGINARY: FROM FRIENDLY NEIGHBOR TO TERRORIST HAVEN

Despite these and other attempts by the Canadian government to dispel this mistaken belief, fears that Canada is a "terrorist haven" have continued to circulate. Since 2001, U.S. politicians ranging from Democratic Senator Hillary Clinton to Republican Senator Conrad Burns have repeated the story. Given that the mistaken claim that the 9/11 hijackers came from Canada was disproved almost immediately, why has this claim about Canada persisted?

Canada-as-terrorist-haven has served as a justification for U.S. attacks on Canadian immigration and refugee policy. Thus, U.S. congressional representatives repeatedly have "blasted Canada as an unwitting haven for a large number of terrorists, blaming soft immigration laws."[14] Shortly after 9/11,

---

12. DeNeen Brown and Ceci Connolly, "Suspects Entered Easily from Canada; Authorities Scrutinize Border Posts in Maine," *Washington Post* (September 13, 2001).

13. Government of Canada, "Did you know? Facts about Canada and the US" (2007), http://www.canadianally.com/ca/news-en.asp.

14. Beth Gorham, "Wilson not worried about U.S. troops guarding border," *Globe and Mail* (March 24, 2006).

U.S. members of the Foreign Service already were claiming that "Canada's political asylum laws have helped make the country a 'safe haven' for foreign extremists."[15] Making clear that the perils of Canadian immigration were connected to the racialization of those crossing the border, a commentator in the *Los Angeles Times* argued that "security controls are famously lax in Canada because politically correct Canadians do not differentiate between 76 year old Madame Dupont coming to visit her grandchildren and bearded young men from Islamic countries."[16] Voicing the same problematic views about immigrant and refugee newcomers to Canada, Douglas Mackinnon, former press secretary to Bob Dole, argued that "the Canadian government not only willingly allows Islamic terrorists into their country, but does nothing to stop them from entering our nation [the United States]."[17] Unpacking the durability of the myth of the 9/11 hijackers makes clear the ways that the border between the United States and Canada is undergoing transformation. After September 11, Canadian bodies are imagined to be newly suspect. This understanding of Canada underlies the need to make the U.S.–Canada border and unreliable Canadian bodies newly visible. Learning to see Canadian bodies as othered is a project to which biometric identification technologies are essential. Identifying what were problematically referred to as "homegrown" suspects is no easy task. Biometric technologies are represented as able to sharpen the edges of a border zone made soft by an historical understanding of the border as an unmilitarized zone separating special friends.

---

15. Brown and Connolly, "Suspects Entered Easily from Canada; Authorities Scrutinize Border Posts in Maine," (n. 12).

16. Editorial cited in Peter Andreas, *The Rebordering of North America: Integration and Exclusion in a New Security Context* (New York: Routledge, 2003), 454.

17. Douglas MacKinnon, "Oh, no, Canada." *Washington Times* (December 16, 2005). Although it is beyond the scope of this paper, it is important to note that the United States is not alone in its attacks on Canadian immigration and refugee policies. Canadians rushed to join the United States in blaming newcomers to Canada for terrorism. Regressive changes to Canadian immigration policies began pre 9/11; Sunera Thobani, "Nationalizing Canadians: Bordering Immigrant Women in the Late Twentieth Century," *CJWL/RFD*, 12 (2000). However, connecting the 9/11 terrorists to immigrants and refugees expedited increasingly draconian reforms to Canada's immigration policy. Thus, the bilateral *Smart Border Declaration*, signed in December 2001, included stipulations for a *Safe Third Country Agreement*, which would "harmonize" Canadian policies with those of their southern neighbor. This agreement, in prohibiting refugees who had filed a claim in the United States from filing in Canada, has succeeded in dramatically reducing refugee claims filed in Canada; Kent Roach, *September 11: Consequences for Canada* (Montréal: McGill-Queen's University Press, 2003). Refugee claims from some countries, including many in Latin America, have been reduced even further. For example, refugees from Colombia have been reduced almost to zero since the *Safe Third Country Agreement* was signed.

V. MAKING THE U.S.–CANADA BORDER VISIBLE

> The United States wants to better secure its border with Canada, but it might have trouble finding it in some areas, an official with the agency that maintains the border said. "If you can't see the boundary, you can't secure it."

> —Dennis Schornack, U.S. commissioner of the International Boundary Commission (IBC), the intergovernmental agency responsible for maintaining the U.S.–Canada border."[18]

Canada's immigration and refugee policy was not the only part of the idea of the "Great White North" to come under post-9/11 US scrutiny. The U.S.–Canada border itself was the object of American anxiety with regard to the risks posed by Canada. Earlier, I noted the role of the International Boundary Commission in ensuring that the border between Canada and the United States be clearly defined as a recognizable "six-metre-wide swath" between the two countries. The IBC currently operates with a budget of $1.4 million from the United States and $2 million from Canada.[19] This budget is extremely modest in comparison with the overall budget for border security. For example, Canada alone has earmarked $368 million U.S. for border security in 2007–2008.[20] The goal of the IBC is to ensure that even those persons who accidentally stumble across the border cannot fail to note its existence—a challenge colloquially referred to by border officials as the "moron test."[21] Despite its identification as a simple undertaking, finding the U.S.–Canada border has proven to be no easy task.

The border is long. It runs through changing physical terrain, including territory that is remote and hard to access. In 2006, the *Ottawa Citizen* noted, "The United States is eager to install a battery of surveillance towers, motion sensors and infrared cameras to monitor the Canada–U.S. border. Now if only they can find it."[22] Old maps drawn in the 1930s and thorny vegetation up to four meters tall (12 feet) provide significant challenges to locating the border. Even those places that have been cleared on a regular basis quickly become

---

18. David Sharp, "U.S.–Canada Border Security Choked with Weeds," *Dessert News* (October 1, 2006).

19. D. Bowermaster, "Blaine couple fight to retain backyard wall near Canada border," *Seattle Times* (April 11, 2007). This budget is contentious, as the United States and Canada are supposed to share equally in IBC funding.

20. Stockwell Day, "Canada's New Government invests over $430M for smart, secure borders" (June 14, 2007), http://www.cbsa-asfc.gc.ca/media/release-communique/2007/0112windsor-eng.html.

21. Sheldon Alberts, "Where, Oh Where Has the Border Gone?" (April 27, 2006), http://forum.blueline.ca/viewtopic.php?p=174897&sid=abb4abe8115ad391a8a22bfc3e4f18c7.

22. *Ibid.*

overgrown with trees, brush, and snow, making the boundary hard to locate. In a 2006 article, the Associated Press documented that "The U.S. and Canada have fallen so far behind on basic maintenance of their shared border that law enforcement officials might have to search through overgrown vegetation for markers in some places."[23] This inability to find the border causes serious consternation among the border officials of both countries.

Concerned border officers have expressed their apprehension about being charged with the difficult task of securing an invisible border. During his tenure with the IBC, Dennis Schornack, the former U.S. Commissioner of the International Boundary Commission, worried that the agency had not been able to physically locate the border in a number of places, asserting anxiously, "I can send you places where you just can't find the border."[24] As he said: "If you can't see the boundary, then you can't secure it."[25] Schornack feared "real diplomatic dispute" between the two countries as a result of the border's ambiguous location. Border officials responsible for guarding the boundary with renewed post-9/11 fervor found themselves playing a game of hide-and-seek—a game that highlights the tension over the paradoxical process of making the border visible.

The hard work of cutting down hedges to locate the border has failed to attract the attention and excitement of funders to the IBC in the face of sexier tech-nological solutions. "I've talked and talked, and we don't seem to be getting anywhere," stated Schornack, additionally making reference to the fact that weed whackers no longer suffice in the manufacturing of the border. Schornack's comments highlighted the tensions endemic to the process of making the U.S.–Canada border visible. New technologies have come to play a complicated role in this post-9/11 context. Deemed essential to the fraught process of uncovering the material edge between the United States and Canada, these technologies introduce poorly understood ideological issues.

VI. BIOMETRICS AND BORDERING

In order to address both the physical difficulty of locating the border and the need to consider which bodies should be allowed and which denied access into the United States, innovative ways to make both Canada and Canadians newly visible needed to be identified. In this context, biometrics have risen to prominence in the post-9/11 spotlight. Biometric technologies have become an

---

23. Associated Press, "Canada–U.S. border obscure in places: Commission" (2006), http://www.ctv.ca/servlet/ArticleNews/story/CTVNews/20060930/canada_us_border_060930?s_name=&no_ads=.

24. Associated Press, "Canada–U.S. border obscure in places," (n. 23).

25. Alberts, "Where, Oh Where Has the Border Gone?" (n. 21).

essential component of the identification and application of the U.S.–Canada border, represented as able to locate and enforce the border through the inspection and classification of individual bodies.

The first major indication that biometrics would become central to post-9/11 border management occurred shortly after the attacks in December 2001. At that time, the United States and Canada entered into the Smart Border Declaration and an accompanying 32-point Action Plan. Biometrics featured centrally in this post-9/11 border accord. The very first point of the Smart Border Declaration action plan concerned the use of biometric technologies:

#1 BIOMETRIC IDENTIFIERS

The United States and Canada have agreed to develop common standards for the biometrics that we use and have also agreed to adopt interoperable and compatible technology to read these biometrics. In the interest of having cards that could be used across different modes of travel, we have agreed to use cards that are capable of storing multiple biometrics.

The Smart Border Declaration has given rise to a number of subsequent border initiatives. Each of these initiatives has continued to feature biometrics as central to their security strategies. One example is the NEXUS-Air pass. The third point of the Smart Border Action Plan called for the development of a program designed to expedite "pre-approved, low-risk travelers" across the border.[26] NEXUS-Air was designed to allow precleared travelers to bypass scrutiny by customs agents so long as they agreed to have their identity verified by biometric iris scanners instead. The fourth point of the Smart Border Action Plan subsequently gave rise to a Statement of Mutual Understanding. This agreement harmonized the Canadian and U.S. processing of refugee and asylum claims. The "harmonization" is partially accomplished through the cross-border sharing of applicants' biometric information, including both face- and fingerprints.[27]

Biometric passports were also the subject of continuing discussion and development. Although the Smart Border Declaration had given rise to discussions concerning mandatory biometric travel documents for Canadians entering the United States, Canadian passport holders continued to be exempt from the 2004 U.S.-VISIT rules requiring biometric passports.[28] Changes resulting from the U.S.-sponsored Western Hemisphere Travel Initiative (WHTI) for the first time required both Canadians and Americans to present passports if they

26. Foreign Affairs and International Trade Canada, "Smart Border Action Plan Status Report," (2004), http://geo.international.gc.ca/can-am/main/border/status-en.asp.

27. Ibid.

28. Passport Canada, "Biometrics in the International Travel Context" (2004), http://www.pptc.gc.ca/newsroom/news.aspx?lang=e&page=/newsroom/20040201.aspx.

wished to enter the United States, rather than other identifying documents such as driver's licenses. Further to the WHTI, those traveling by air or sea were required to present a passport by January 8, 2007, while those traveling across land borders were required to present a passport by December 31, 2007[29]— a date that was deferred to June of 2009. It remains unclear when and how Canada will comply with the WHTI by developing biometric passports— although as early as 2005, Canada had commenced trials of biometric passports that contained digitized photos.

At the same time, the U.S. attempt to racialize risk through the biometric classification of Canadians can be noted in the advisory issued by Ottawa notifying Canadian residents born in Iran, Iraq, Libya, Sudan, and Syria that they must be biometrically fingerprinted at the U.S. border."[30] Although the United States retracted the decision to target these Canadians in particular, it reserved the right to interrogate Canadians depending on "where they had traveled and if they were traveling on another country's passport."[31]

Given the number of border initiatives that rely on biometrics, their role in the reimagining of the post-9/11 U.S.–Canada border is significant. One example that well illustrates how biometric technologies facilitate the remaking of the northern boundary between the United States and Canada is their role in outsourcing the U.S.–Canada border away from the territorial edges of the state.

VII. OUTSOURCING THE BORDER

Biometrics are regularly identified as the most effective border technology. In large part, this is because Canada–U.S. border agreements discursively represent biometric technologies as able to fulfill one of the new features of a post-9/11 security environment—moving the border as far away from the edge of the nation-state as possible. In a 2005 report, the Canadian Senate Committee on National Security and Defense suggested that securing the border required that "threats" to Canadian security be identified as far away from North America as possible. This assertion was illustrated by the following diagram:

---

29. Krista Boa, "Biometric Passports: A response to the Western Hemisphere Travel Initiative?" (2006), http://www.anonequity.org/weblog/archives/2006/08/biometric_passports_a_response_1.php.

30. CBC News, "Some Canadians may be Photographed, Fingerprinted at U.S. Border" (October 30, 2002), http://www.commondreams.org/headlines02/1031-08.htm.

31. *Ibid.*

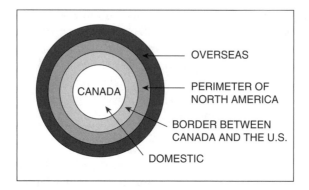

FIGURE 1. OUTSOURCING THE BORDER[32]

The Senate Committee's recommendation and its recognition that, with the United States it securitize the broader entity of North America, is consistent with what Didier Bigo describes as state attempts to extend their spheres of control by delocalizing their borders.[33] Acting as a North American geopolitical entity, both Canada and the United States are attempting to "outsource" their borders. By "outsourcing the border," I am referring to specific techniques that a state may use to deterritorialize their boundaries. In the Statement of Mutual Understanding (2003) between the United States and Canada, the primary way to secure the state is described in the following way:

> The best way to secure our borders is to identify and intercept persons posing security risks as early as possible, and as far away from our borders as possible.

> Information sharing supports the Multiple Borders Strategy, which focuses control on measures overseas, where potential violators of citizenship or immigration laws are intercepted prior to their arrival to the United States or Canada.[34]

Biometrics is one of the primary technologies used to achieve the out-sourcing of the border. This helps to explain the proliferation of biometrics programs used to test individuals before they leave their point of origin. As part of

---

32. Senate Committee on National Security and Defence, "Borderline Insecure: Canada's land border crossings are key to Canada security and prosperity. Why the lack of urgency to fix them? What will happen if we don't?" *An Interim Report by the Senate Committee on National Security and Defence* (June 2005).

33. Didier Bigo, "Security and Immigration: Toward a Critique of the Governmentality of Unease," *Alternatives* 27, no. 1 (2002).

34. Citizenship and Immigration Canada, "Statement of Mutual Understanding on Information Sharing" (2003), http://www.cic.gc.ca/english/policy/smu/smu-ins-dos.html.

Canada's $3.5 million program to screen immigrants before they arrive on Canadian soil, the Canadian government is opening an office in Singapore to collect biometric information from immigration applicants. The biometric information will be used to determine "the identity of immigrants, although how this will be done is not clear."[35]

Rather than continuing to understand the U.S.–Canada border as a one-dimensional dotted line along a surface, biometrics now are deployed discursively to represent the U.S.–Canada border in 3D, as "effective border management requires governments to treat the border as more than a single line at which threats can be intercepted."[36] In this way, the border is multiplied endlessly outward, replicating itself such that no one line may be identified. Thus, we understand that

> Canada and the United States are pursuing a regional approach to migration based on the Multiple Borders Strategy. The Multiple Borders Strategy views the border not as a geo-political line but rather a continuum of checkpoints along a route of travel from the country of origin to Canada or the United States. At every checkpoint along the travel continuum—visa screening; airport check-in; points of embarkation; transit points; international airports and seaports; and the Canada–United States border—there is an opportunity for the participants to link the person and the document and any known intelligence.[37]

This linking of "person and document" is facilitated through biometric inspection.

Moreover, the U.S.–Canada border is not only outsourced to other nation-states in order to prescreen "risky travelers." New technologies additionally are deployed to "insource" the U.S.–Canada boundary onto Canadian territory. The Smart Border Declaration declared that most major Canadian airports—including those in Vancouver, Edmonton, Calgary, Winnipeg, Toronto, Ottawa, and Montreal—would now have U.S. customs screening located in Canada rather than in the United States, precluding the admission of those deemed dangerous rather than requiring their expulsion.[38] As biometric passports are implemented, the screening of travelers to the United States will be outsourced to Canada so that the traveler's biometric identity will be determined before they cross the U.S. border.

---

35. Canadian Biometric ID Documents Public Forum, "FAQ" (2006), http://www.ferenbok.com/biometricIDforum/webcast.html.

36. Government of Canada, "Securing an Open Society," 41 (n. 2).

37. Citizenship and Immigration Canada, "Statement of Mutual Understanding on Information Sharing," (n. 34).

38. Foreign Affairs and International Trade Canada, "Smart Border Action Plan Status Report," (n. 26).

Biometrics thus are central to the outsourcing of the U.S. border as they allow it to be exported. What formerly was understood to be just "a coastline, or a line on the ground between two nations" is now understood to be composed of the individual "bordered" bodies that make up the "line of information in a computer, telling us who is in this country, for how long, and for what reason."[39]

VIII. BIOMETRIC FAILURE

Despite the growth in reliance on biometric technologies in a climate of particular attention to race, ethnicity, and religious identification, biometrics often are described as technologies able to provide both "mechanical objectivity"[40] and race-neutrality. The claim that biometrics can automate inspection suggests that these technologies are able to replace the subjective eye of the customs inspector with the neutral eye of the scanner. In this way, biometric technologies are represented as able to circumvent racism—imagining the Canada–U.S. border as a race-neutral space. Biometric technologies are held up as bias-free technologies that will objectively and equally scan everyone's bodily identity. The director of corporate communications for Visionics, a leading U.S. manufacturer of biometrics systems, asserted that the corporation's newly patented iris scanning technology "is neutral to race and color, as it is based on facial features recognized by the software."[41] This understanding finds more than a little resonance in public opinion. In an online discussion surrounding the implementation of iris scanners at the U.S.–Canada border, one respondent claimed he would much prefer to present himself to "race-neutral" biometric technologies than to potentially racist customs border officials:

> If I was a member of one of the oft-"profiled" minorities, I'd sign up for sure. Upside—you can walk right past the bonehead looking for the bomb under your shirt just because of your tan and beard . . . In short, I'd rather leave it up to a device that can distinguish my iris from a terrorist's, than some bigoted lout who can't distinguish my skin, clothing or accent from same.[42]

Biometrics are being mustered in the fight to identify suspect Canadian bodies at the border, a deeply problematic task. It is not surprising, therefore,

---

39. Citizenship and Immigration Canada, "Statement of Mutual Understanding on Information Sharing," (n. 34).

40. I take this phrase from Peter Daston and Lorraine Galison, "The Image of Objectivity," *Representations* 40 (1992).

41. Zelazny cited in Saumya Roy, "Biometrics: Security Boon or Busting Privacy?" *PC World*, 32 no. 4 (2002).

42. "Airport Starts Using Iris Screener" (2005), http://www.vivelecanada.ca/article.php/20050715193518919.

that when biometric technologies are used to accomplish this task they fail easily and often. What is most interesting about biometric failures are the specific ways in which they do not work. As biometrics are deployed to make Canadian bodies visible, they regularly break down at the location of the intersection of the body's class, race, gender, and dis/abled identity. In this way, biometrics fail precisely at the task that they have been set—to identify newly othered bodies.

As biometric technologies are developed in a climate of increased anxiety concerning suspect bodies, stereotypes around "inscrutable" racialized bodies are technologized. That is, biometric technologies consistently are unable to distinguish the bodies of persons of color. For example, research on the use of biometric fingerprint scanners resulted in the conclusion that some "Asian women . . . had skin so fine it couldn't reliably be used to record or verify a fingerprint."[43] Tests of biometric iris scanners also have revealed that they perform differently on racialized bodies. In some cases, it seemed as if W. E. B. Dubois's "color line" was being technologized: the darker the skin color, the greater the likelihood of technological failure.

> Answering a question on whether it regarded the rates (of failure) as satisfactory, the Home Office replied: "It is true to say that at times in the past some difficulties have been experienced in successfully recording the iris images of people with very dark skin (on some iris systems). The difficulty lay in the ability of the system to successfully locate irises against a darker skin tone."[44]

John Daugman is the scientist who invented the mathematical algorithms upon which all iris scanning technologies depend. He consistently has found that these technologies perform differently on brown and black eyes than they do on blue, green, or hazel eyes—a problematic finding given the connection of eye color to racialization. These biometric failures result, in part, from their reliance on outdated and erroneous biological understandings of race. There are a multitude of biometric studies that assume that the faces of different "races" will give rise to clear and different (race specific) biometric scans. One example is the troublingly titled study "Facial Pose Estimation Based on the Mongolian Race's Feature Characteristic."[45] The suggestion underlying this biometric identification technology—that race is a stable, biological entity that reliably yields common measurable characteristics—is deeply problematic. Such conclusions are repeated in a number of articles that claim to classify "faces on the basis of

---

43. W. Sturgeon, "Law & Policy Cheat Sheet: Biometrics" (2004), http://management.silicon.com/government/0,39024677,39120120,00.htm.

44. Kablenet, "More Accurate on the Eye," *The Register* (2006), http://www.theregister.co.uk/2006/04/05/iris_scan_tech_improving/.

45. Yadong Li, Ardeshir Goshtasby, and Oscar Garcia. "Detecting and Tracking Human Faces in Videos," *IEEE* (2000): 807–810.

high-level attributes, such as sex, 'race' and expression."[46] Although the scare quotes around the word "race" would suggest that the authors acknowledge that race is not biological, they still proceed to program the computer to identify both gender and race as if it were so. This task is accomplished by scanning a facial image, and then identifying the gender and race identity of the image for the purposes of programming the computer, until they claim the computer is able to classify the faces itself. Not surprisingly, error rates remain high. Neither gender nor race is a stable category that consistently may be identified by the human eye, nor by computer imaging processes. Thus, much of the scientific research underlying biometrics serves as a disturbing reminder of the racial science that provided the foundations of earlier identification technologies including the passbook system used under apartheid in South Africa.[47]

These assumptions concerning the dependence of biometric performance on racial and ethnic identity can also be noted in the locational differences in hypotheses around race and biometrics that are specific to the site of several of the studies. In the United States, biometric technologies failed to distinguish "Asian" bodies. In the United Kingdom, biometric technologies had difficulty distinguishing "black" bodies. In Japan, one study posited that it would be most difficult for biometrics to identify "non-Japanese" faces, beginning with the premise that race is biological and that there may be an "other race effect": "[M]ost people report finding it difficult to recognize the faces of people of other races." Asserting that there were few mixed-race individuals in Japan, the author concluded that facial recognition technology could distinguish more reliably between "Japanese" faces than between "non-Japanese" faces.[48]

Nor does the technological fallibility of biometrics end with hi-tech racism. Biometric technologies consistently were unable to identify those who deviated from the "norm" of the young, able-bodied male. In general, studies showed that "one-size-fits-all" biometrics technologies did not work. For example, biometric facial recognition technology was shown to work poorly with elderly persons and failed more than half the time in identifying those

---

46. Michael J. Lyons, Julien Budynek, Andre Plante, and Shigeru Akamatsum, "Classifying Facial Attributes using a 2-D Gabor Wavelet Representation and Discriminant Analysis," *Fourth IEEE International Conference on Automatic Face and Gesture Recognition* (2000).

47. In their book *Sorting Things Out* (1999), Leigh Star and Geoff Bowker document the impossibility of classifying race given its socially constructed nature through their analysis of the race-based passbook system in South Africa.

48. Kenichi Tanaka, Kazuyuki Machida, Shingo Matsuura, and Shigeru Akamatsu, "Comparison of Racial Effect in Face Identification Systems based on Eigenface and Gaborjet," *SICE Annual Conference in Sapporo* (2004).

who were disabled.⁴⁹ Other studies on biometric iris scanners showed that the technologies were particularly bad at identifying those with visual impairments and those who are wheelchair users.⁵⁰ New demands for biometric forms of identification served to manipulate and extend the definition of disability. Thus, those who had rare skin diseases such that they did not have fingerprints became the newly disabled. In California, an individual teacher was unable to work because he could not be fingerprinted.⁵¹

Class also became a factor. Those persons with occupations within the categories "clerical, manual, [and] maintenance" were found to be difficult to biometrically fingerprint.⁵² Biometric iris scanners failed to work with very tall persons,⁵³ and biometric fingerprint scanners could not identify 20% of those who have nonnormative fingers: "One out of five people failed the fingerprint test because the scanner was 'too small to scan a sufficient area of fingerprint from participants with large fingers.'"⁵⁴ Any kind of bodily breakdown could give rise to biometric failure. "Worn down or sticky fingertips for fingerprints, medicine intake in iris identification (atropine), hoarseness in voice recognition, or a broken arm for signature" all gave rise to temporary biometric failures while "[w]ell-known permanent failures are, for example, cataracts, which makes retina identification impossible or [as we saw] rare skin diseases, which permanently destroy a fingerprint."⁵⁵

Moreover, in addition to having technologized problematic assumptions around the comprehensibility of difference, biometric technologies discursively are deployed in ways that continued to target specific demographics of suspect bodies. For example, biometric facial recognition technology requires Muslim women who wear the hijab to remove it in order to receive new forms of ID cards, where older forms of identification such as the photos on driver's licenses only required their partial removal.⁵⁶ In this way, biometric technologies are

---

49. "Black Eye for ID Cards," (2005), http://www.blink.org.uk/pdescription. asp?key=7477&grp=21&cat=99; BBC News, "ID cards scheme dubbed 'a farce'" (October 17, 2005).

50. Karen Gomm, "U.K. Agency: Iris recognition needs work," News.com, (October 20, 2005).

51. David Lyon, *Surveillance as Social Sorting: Privacy, Risk, and Digital Discrimination* (New York: Routledge, 2003).

52. UK Biometrics Working Group, "Biometrics for Identification and Authentication - Advice on Product Selection" (2001), http://www.idsysgroup.com/ftp/Biometrics%20 Advice.pdf.

53. Gomm, "U.K. Agency: Iris recognition needs work" (October 20, 2005).

54. "'Black Eye' for ID Cards," (n. 49).

55. Bioidentification, "Biometrics: Frequently asked questions," (2007), http://www. bromba.com/faq/biofaqe.htm.

56. "ID Card and You" (2004), http://www.idcardandyou.co.uk/racism.html.

literally deployed to further the invasion by the state of the bodily privacy of Muslim women.

Given the specific anxieties that biometric technologies are discursively represented as able to allay, their failure rates are not surprising. Significant failures of the technology have occurred in Virginia Beach and Tampa, Florida.[57] In Florida, the biometrics system was eventually abandoned altogether due to its failure to identify even one person correctly.[58] In a test of facial recognition technology at Logan Airport in Boston, biometric technology worked only 50% of the time in situations of compromised lighting.[59] As it is unlikely that terrorists would stop to pose for well-lit photographs, this is a serious failing. The ease with which hi-tech biometric technologies can be hacked also calls their security into question. Researchers at Yokohama National University revealed that biometric fingerprint readers can easily be deceived by artificial gelatin fingers onto which a real print from either an actual finger or from another surface such as glass had been dusted.[60] This ease of falsely replicating fingerprints was confirmed by Marie Sandström in her 2004 Master's thesis in which she tested nine different fingerprint recognition systems and found that all could be deceived by an artificial gelatin imprint. In Germany, a community of hackers called the Chaos Communication Camp gathered to figure out how to hack the new technologies. The many ways in which they were able to hack biometric information further emphasized biometric fallibility. In a 2007 presentation at a biometric industry conference, Samir Nanavati of the International Biometrics Group asserted that spoofs of biometric technologies generally have been ignored, and then proceeded to demonstrate a number of techniques that continue to work to violate the security of biometric identification technologies.

The inaccuracies, misplaced and racist assumptions, and easy penetrability of biometric technologies seriously calls into question their use in the definition of the U.S.–Canada border, as well as their reliability in distinguishing and identifying those bodies entitled to pass through the border from those threatening or otherwise inappropriate bodies who must be excluded. Biometric technologies are being used to discursively construct new categories based on

57. Kelly Gates, "Our Biometric Future: The social construction of an emerging information technology," PhD Thesis, Institute of Communications Research, Urbana-Champaign, University of Illinois at Urbana-Champaign (2004).

58. *Ibid.*

59. ACLU, "Three Cities Offer Latest Proof That Face Recognition Doesn't Work, ACLU Says" (2003), http://www.aclu.org/privacy/spying/14872prs20030902.html.

60. T. Matsumoto and H. Matsumoto, "Impact of Artificial Gummy Fingers on Fingerprint Systems," *Proceedings of SPIE - Optical Security and Counterfeit Deterrence Techniques IV* (2002).

biometrificability—categories that have significant consequences for personal mobility, and ones that mimic imaginary racial categories.

IX. CONCLUSION

As previously noted, the boundary separating Canada from the United States is regularly described as the longest, undefended border in the world. However, the relationship between the two countries historically has not been free from stress. Moreover, although the border between Canada and the United States was described as separating "special friends" in the years leading up to September 11, 2001, this friendship underwent a shift after the attacks on the Pentagon and World Trade Center. In particular, the persistence of the rumor that the hijackers responsible for the attacks came from Canada made evident the post-9/11 shift to representing this border as newly porous— leaking suspect threats from north to south. Through the inaccurate connection between terrorist threats and Canada's supposedly "permissive" immigration and refugee policy, Canadian bodies were rendered newly dangerous. As a result, technologies able to visualize these threats and to distinguish them from the bodies of Americans were needed.

Biometric technologies drew increased attention in the post-9/11 political environment. Represented as able to identify newly threatening bodies and thus to allow for their exclusion, biometrics were identified as the leading border technology in all of the border accords signed after September 11, 2001. Biometric technologies also were represented as able to meet new needs to move the border away from the material edge of the United States—to "outsource" the border. In doing so, biometrics were deemed central to the process of identifying Canadians, as they were imagined to be able to visualize newly suspect Canadian bodies. In this way, biometric technologies are key to contemporary projects of identification—a bureaucratic process central to the modern state. As both Canada and the United States try to determine who belongs to the state and who must be expelled, biometric technologies are mustered as one of the tools allowing the state to make bodies legible to state institutions. In this way, the biometric inspection becomes a ritual of identification key to contemporary rationalities of governing.

The use of biometric identification technologies at the U.S.–Canada border has been shaped by a discourse of technological neutrality and efficiency. This narrative of efficiency and security needs to be interrogated given the ways in which it allows for and encourages the scrutiny of certain bodies, particularly immigrants and refugees, at the same time as it eases the passage of others. Although the biometric industry claims that these new technological tools are identity-neutral, we must call these claims into question as biometric technologies depend upon the classification of race, class, and gender identities in order to function. Given the reliance of biometric technologies on outdated, biological understandings of race, the objectivity and race-neutrality of biometrics must be interrogated and their widespread use at the U.S.–Canada border reconsidered. A new narrative is needed that works to identify the border in ways that are not based on principles of exclusion or claims to "mechanical objectivity." Rather, we need policies based on principles of inclusiveness and which facilitate substantive claims to equality at the U.S.–Canada border.

21. SOUL TRAIN
The New Surveillance in Popular Music*

GARY T. MARX

Videos are watching me
But dat is not stopping me
Let dem cum wid dem authority
An dem science and technology
But Dem can't get de Reggae out me head.
—Zepaniah

Under the spreading chestnut tree
I sold you and you sold me:
There lie they, and here lie we
Under the spreading chestnut tree
—The Chestnut Tree, 1984

Most analysis of information technology uses printed words and numbers, and considers structures and behavior. As important as historical, social, philosophical, legal, and policy analyses are, they are insufficient for broad understanding. We also need cultural analysis to understand how surveillance is experienced.

Contemporary surveillance methods and popular culture are both distinctive kinds of *soul training*. The title of this chapter plays off of Michel Foucault's study of modern means of training the person to be compliant.[1] It also reflects popular rhythm and blues and disco musical culture. "Soul Train" was a 1970s song title and a popular TV musical program. In connecting these two markedly disparate uses of the term, I call attention to the close links between surveillance and culture, and control and entertainment.

---

* This article draws from *Windows into the Soul: Surveillance and Society in an Age of High Technology*, University of Chicago Press, forthcoming, and related materials at garymarx.net.

1. M. Foucault, *Discipline and Punish: The Birth of the Prison* (New York: Vintage, 1977).

In considering soul training, Foucault was primarily discussing the emerging modern organizational forms of control in the prison, workplace, and school. Popular culture as entertainment and recreation might seem very far from the sober, hard worlds of surveillance and control.[2] However, music along with television, film, literature, and advertisements can also serve as a kind of soul training along with the more familiar formal organizational structures.[3] Such cultural forms may also serve to undermine surveillance. Media depictions, humor, and visual art may do the same.

This chapter looks at surveillance in popular music over the last fifty years. In contrast to most studies of music lyrics, in which the focus is on a genre such

---

2. Here we see the blurring and/or merging of entertainment and surveillance. Note video games with implicit morality tales. Or consider the camera that delivers crime and social control events to the six o'clock news. The video can serve as a means of both surveillance and communication (most frequently sequentially, but sometimes simultaneously, as with "live" helicopter video images of car chases. News footage also figures prominently in many music videos.

However, these are not the same as Orwell's "telescreen," which simultaneously brought the "news" and also watched. Yet over time the difference for some forms is one of degree (note cable TV systems that monitor viewer behavior and can collect other data from sensors in the home, including visual images for security purposes). Surveillance data feed the mass media's appetite. This in turn can reinforce cultural beliefs about crime and control and strengthen public support for surveillance as a result of the need demonstrated by the "news" (T. Mathiesen, "The Viewer Society," *Theoretical Criminology* 1 (1996): 215–234; D. Altheide, *Creating Fear: News and the Construction of Crisis* (New York: Aldine de Gruyter, 2002); A. Doyle, *Arresting Images* (Toronto: University of Toronto Press, 2003)). Mass media communication about surveillance may serve to "normalize" behavior through morality tales of what happens to those caught by panoptic mechanisms. Yet when documenting abuses, it can also serve to arouse public indignation, and fear of exposure may modulate practices. Beyond overlapping functions we can note parallels in the ease of mass application of both. Rule notes twentieth-century developments permitting both mass surveillance and mass communication (J. Rule, "1984— The Ingredients of Totalitarianism," in I. Howe (ed.), *1984: Totalitarianism in Our Century* (New York: Harper & Row, 1983).

These are increasingly joined by precisely targeted forms that may, ironically, increase choice as well as the ability to be controlled.

As Leman-Langlois argues, the discourse of surveillance can also be changed by technology beyond literal impacts. See S. Leyman-Langlois, "The Myopic Panopticon: The Social Consequences of Policing through the Lens," *Policing and Society* 13 (2002): 43–58.

3. Marx suggests a number of categories for classifying aspects of surveillance (e.g., distinguishing between subjects and agents (and among the latter) organizations and individuals, conditions of use, kinds of technology, and goals; see G. Marx, "Surveillance and Society," *Encyclopedia of Social Theory* Vol. II (California: Sage Publications, 2004). Two goals reflected in other music not considered here that are treated in the forthcoming book involve surveillance as protection (as with a loving God or partner to look after the subject) and the search for true love. (New York: Vintage, 1977)

as country and western, teen pop, or rap,[4] my emphasis is on a particular kind of lyric expressed across a variety of genres. I view the musical themes as a window into knowledge about surveillance and society.

In identifying songs, I drew on my own observations and others' suggestions and searched the Internet for songs with words such as "surveillance," "watching," "police," "FBI," "DEA," "video," "spying," "big brother," and "privacy." In this chapter, I will discuss three major themes in the music: warnings from a male singer watching a love object, accounts of those who are watched, and protests against surveillance. I will conclude by considering some implications. Let us first consider songs by agents of surveillance applying it for personal ends.

I. SUSPICION-DRIVEN SURVEILLANCE

The theme of suspicion-driven surveillance is reflected in early rhythm and blues and rock and roll music. It involves boasting about the lover's super-surveillance powers to discover unfaithfulness. Such songs contain an implicit threat and may be intended to deter. This is an individual form rather than a government or private sector organizational form.

In 1956, in "Slippin' and Slidin'," Little Richard has been "peepin' and hidin'" to discover his baby's jive, and as a result he "won't be your fool no more." Bobby Vee sings that "the night has a thousand eyes" and that these eyes will see "if you aren't true to me." If he gets "put down for another" or told lies, he warns, "I'll know, believe me, I'll know." The Who more directly imply the possession of extrasensory powers when they sing, "There's magic in my eyes." The singer knows he has been deceived because he sings, "I can see for miles and miles and miles and miles and miles." Hall and Oates sing about the inability to escape my "Private Eyes," which, while "looking for lies," are "watching you. They see your every move." The Doors sing about "a spy in the house of love" who "can see you and what you do" and who knows your dreams and fears, and "everywhere you go, everyone you know."

The Alan Parsons Project makes direct use of technology to discover lies and to tell the deceiving lover to "find another fool" because "I am the eye in the sky looking at you I can read your mind."

The classic song of this type is "Every Breath You Take," written by Sting, who reports that it is about "the obsessiveness of ex-lovers, their maniacal possessiveness"—written after a divorce. While Sting reports that he reads Arthur Koestler, who wrote about the dangers of totalitarianism,[5] he says his song is personal, not political. The female is warned that her faked smiles,

---

4. P. Vannini and S. Myers, "Crazy about You: Reflections on the Meanings of Contemporary Teen Pop Music," *Electronic Journal of Sociology* 6, no. 2 (2002), www.sociology.org/content/vol006.002/.

5. A. Koestler, *Darkness at Noon* (New York: Bantam, 1984).

and broken bonds and vows, will be observed by the singer. The song is about surveillance, ownership, and jealousy.[6]

Although the song does not mention technological supports for the omnipresent and omnipotent surveillance it promises, it is easy to connect it with contemporary tools. One can hear the song to suggest an encyclopedic list of the means that were coming into wider use in the 1980s:

Every breath you take [breath analyzer]
Every move you make [motion detector]
Every bond you break [polygraph]
Every step you take [electronic monitoring]
Every single day [continuous monitoring]
Every word you say [bugs, wiretaps, mikes]
Every night you stay [light amplifier]
Every vow you break [voice stress analysis]
Every smile you fake [brain wave analysis]
Every claim you stake [computer matching]
I'll be watching you [video]

Songs about watching by individuals contrast with those about the watching of organizations. In Tom Paxton's haunting and threatening "Mr. Blue" we hear from the all-knowing "we":

Good morning Mister Blue, we've got our eyes on you. The evidence is clear, that you've been scheming. You like to steal away; and while away the day. You like to spend an hour dreaming. What will it take, to whip you into line? A broken heart? A broken head? It can be arranged.

The song "The Chestnut Tree," at the start of this chapter, begins on a discordant note on the telescreen in the 1984 version of the film 1984 as Julia and Winston come to betray each other.

Let us next turn to the point of view of surveillance subjects. I will first discuss songs that express resignation, and then those of a protest nature.

II. SUBJECT CHRONICLES: THERE IS NO ESCAPE

In contrast to the songs in which surveillance agents brag of their prowess and process, and even threaten, are chronicles of organizational surveillance that subjects experience. There is often resignation and an implied moral directive here. The singers, while hardly apostles of law and order and maximum security, conclude that resistance is likely to be futile and that the best response is to follow the rules.

---

6. *Rolling Stone Magazine*, March 1, 1984.

In "I Fought the Law" Sonny Curtis of the Crickets sings

Breakin' rocks in the hot sun
I fought the law and the law won

Or consider the instructions of Ice-T in "Pain":

Jail cells know me too damn well
Seems like I've built on earth my own personal hell
No matter how high I climbed, somehow I always fell
I guess a lot of players got this story to tell
. . . Custody haunts my dreams, nightmares of capture
Paranoid of surveillance, phobia of cameras
My banks bigger, but so are my fears
. . . No matter who you trust, you simply cannot win
It's always fun in the beginning
But it's pain in the end

Nelly, in "Utha Side," similarly tells a dealer in trouble:

I heard your clientele is doin well
I see you boomin out the S-T-L . . .
Now the feds knocking at your door, you took the bait
They got taps on your mobile phone
They do surveillance all around your home
Now ya pawnin' everything ya own
Calling on your partners for a loan
No more slip and sliding on the chrome
Your good days have come and gone
I tried to tell you

Judas Priest, in "Electric Eye," sings of the awesome power of the technology, from which "There is no true escape": "There's nothing you can do about it." It is unlikely that these heavy metal pioneers are advocates of such surveillance, but the satire—if that it is—is all too muted.

Ja Rule in "Watching Me" asks, "Are ya watching me? They be watching, niggas they be watching, keep watching. . . And hustlers ya'll keep slanging. We stuck in the game wit not a lot to gain but everything to lose."

The pessimistic note of resignation of the subjects in these songs contrasts with a more optimistic tone of songs more clearly of a protest nature, which are considered next.

III. WARNINGS ABOUT AND RESISTANCE TO SURVEILLANCE

Protest is a rich—often veiled—theme in popular culture. The field hollers and shouts of slaves contained encoded messages of resistance, and their connotations of biblical words in hymns have often been noted. The labor songs of Woody Guthrie and Pete Seeger and groups such as The Almanac Singers and the Weavers were more direct.

Much surveillance involves inequalities in power and can serve to sustain and strengthen a contested status quo. In broad outline, as Ray Charles sang, "those that get are those that got." Yet in societies with civil liberties and a market economy, there are forms of resistance and unintended consequences. The situation is more complicated than a reductionist, zero-sum power perspective suggests. Music can serve as a form of cultural neutralization in offering ideas that rationalize and call forth resistance.[7] These are aided by the ambiguity of language.

Such music can inspire and sustain commitment. Songs such as "We Shall Overcome" and "I Shall Not Be Moved," and more recent songs, such as "Oh Freedom" and "Blowin' in the Wind" were vital to the civil rights movement.

In the protest songs considered next, the voice is not that of the surveillance agent claiming omnipotence, making veiled threats or offering a morality tale. Rather, we hear from the individual subject of surveillance, or a third party telling about it. A central theme is, "They are watching us and it's wrong." It can be wrong for a variety of reasons.

The songs are concerned with threats to liberty, racism, injustice (especially with respect to false accusations and lack of due process), inequality, and the chilling effects of being spied upon and the loss of privacy.

Judas Priest in "Electric Eye" offers an analytic summary of key aspects of the new surveillance involving omnipresence, omnipotence, accuracy, invisibility, and uninformed and involuntary subjects. Surveillance watches "all the time," probing "everything you do" and "all your secret moves," while offering "pictures that can prove." The song links knowledge with power: "I feed upon your every thought and so my power grows." People think they have private lives, but they should "think nothing of the kind."

Jill Scott in "Watching Me" offers varied examples that suggest the comprehensiveness of contemporary observation:

Satellites over my head
Transmitters in my dollars
Hawking, watching, scoping, jocking
Scrutinizing me
Checking to see what I'm doing

---

7. The idea of neutralization was first applied to culture by Sykes and Matza as they asked how cultural messages helped individuals rationalize rule breaking; see G. Sykes and D. Matza, "Techniques of Neutralization: A Theory of Delinquency," *American Sociological Review* 22 (1957): 664–670. Music can be an important source for such countermessages. Eleven behavioral techniques of neutralization used to thwart the collection of personal information are identified in G. T. Marx, "A Tack in the Shoe: Neutralizing and Resisting the New Surveillance," *Journal of Social Issues* 59, no. 1 (2003): 369–390.

Where I be
Who I see
How and where and with whom I make my money
What is this??
. . . Se-cur-i-ty
Video cameras locked on me
In every dressing room
On every floor
In every store
. . . Direct TV
Am I watchin' it or is it watchin' me

Siouxsie and the Banshees, in "Monitor," sing of a "monitor outside for the people inside" that offers both a "prevention of crime, and a passing of time."

The duality of surveillance as control and entertainment is reminiscent of Orwell's 1984, in which a video device linked mass surveillance with mass communication. Having no control over being seen or over what they see, individuals are doubly controlled.

Narcissism, exhibitionism, and voyeurism can be joined with video technology. Fish, in "The Voyeur," sings of "private lives up for auction," information overload, and living vicariously through the mass media. As in Peter Sellers, role in the film *Being There*, the individual's persona is formed by reflecting back what is seen on television. Negative reactions to video invasions of personal space are very much tempered by the allure of being seen. The narrator identifies with media stars and fantasizes that he is also a celebrity. Rather than privacy lost, here we have "hey ma look at me."

I like to watch as my face is reflected in blank TV screens
The programmes are over, I like to pretend that that's
Me up there making headlines, camera close-ups
Catching my right side I don't care if it's only a moment
As long as it's peaktime, just as long as all of
My friends and family see me, the world
Will know my name–come on down.

Yet concerns over lost privacy are also common. In "Fingerprint File," the Rolling Stones complain about "feeling followed, feeling tagged," and "it gets me down"; also, in a rare direct attack, "There's some little jerk in the F.B.I. a' keepin' paper on me ten feet high." Concern is expressed over "listening to me on your satellite," informers who will sell out and testify, and "electric eyes." Listeners are urged to be suspicious, lie low, and watch out. The song ends in a whisper: "These days it's all secrecy, no privacy."[8]

---

8. Here we see a common confusion. These are not necessarily opposed. Secrecy can be involved in protecting privacy when the very existence of a type of information is not

Rockwell feels "like somebody's watching me and I have no privacy." "Somebody's Watching Me" begins with a synthesized voice asking, "Who's watching me?" The narrator is just an average man who works "from nine to five," and all he wants "is to be left alone in my average home." The listener is led to ask, "Why would anyone want to monitor him?" Ordinary people there is no reason to suspect become targets, not simply those who "deserve" to be sur- veilled. Is this an out-of-control system, incompetence, or a logic of random application to create deterrence through uncertainty?

Anyone can be watched or a watcher. He asks if the watchers are neighbors, the mailman, or the IRS. These realistic questions give rise to paranoia. He won- ders if the persons on TV can see him, and he is afraid to wash his hair—"cause I might open my eyes and find someone standing there."

Nor does Sy Kahn in "Who's Watching the Man" understand why he is a target, because he pays taxes and doesn't vote or criticize. He reports a truck with a telephone company sign next to his house, which has no phone, and new wires on his roof. He wonders about three men in his barn "trying to read my electric meter through a telescope" and about someone living in his TV set. Kahn poses a classic endless regress issue for social control theory in asking, "Who is watching the man who's watching the man who's watching me?"

In the songs discussed above, subjects are watched for no reason. In other songs there is a reason, but it is viewed as illegitimate. Surveillance is based only on general stereotypic characteristics associated with lower status. Bob Dylan's "Subterranean Homesick Blues" offers an early example of categorical searching based on age profiling. Youth are watched, regardless of whether they have actually done anything wrong. Given covert surveillance involving a "man in a trench coat," microphones planted in the bed, and telephone taps, a warning is offered: "look out kid, no matter what you did." To avoid surveillance, they are told not to wear sandals and to try to be a success.

Rather than discriminatory targeting, the protest may involve the goal. "Spy in the Cab" by Bauhaus protests meters recording the driving behavior of truckers. "Hidden in the dashboard the unseen mechanized eye" with "a set function to pry," brings a "coldly observing" twenty-four-hour "unblinking watch."

In "The Smoke Police" The Intended sing

Undercover smoke police
sulk in holes and corners

---

known or the key to accessing information is secret (e.g., a password). Yet the secrecy of covert surveillance can also be a means of invading privacy. Whether something is secret refers to the empirical status of information—whether it is known or not known. As such it is adjectival in a way that private is not. That is, information can be private in the sense of being normatively subject to the control of the person to whom it refers. If the person chooses to release it or if it is discovered, it ceases to be secret, even though it retains its normative status of being private information.

they do not warn you openly
like a cop in uniform does . . .
Who knows if they will ask to smoke,
thus hoping to entrap you?

Plainclothes enforcement is seen as sneaky. There is no warning and there is
the danger of entrapment. In addition, the song reflects knowledge of the organizational process of goal displacement (e.g., as seen in parking enforcement in
which a strong latent goal is revenue) when it asks, "will they make a busybody
cause into a city cash cow?"

Concern over social control is a major theme in rap songs. Yet, as with graffiti
wall art, the emphasis is most likely to be on direct coercion, harassment, and arrest
at the hands of uniformed patrol officers, rather than with the more subtle forms of
surveillance. N.W.A. in "Fuck Tha Police" calls attention to age and style:

Fuckin with me cuz I'm a teenager
With a little bit of gold and a pager
Searchin' my car, lookin' for the product
Thinkin every nigga is sellin narcotics . . .

For Anti-Flag in "Police Story" it is race and age:

Patrol man cruising in his car at night
Just looking for some homeys he can rough up in a fight
Pulled over 3 kids in a total rage . . .
The cops they did it just cause those kids color and their age

Trick Daddy in "Watch the Police" adds targeting by dress style and location
to age and race. Unlike some rap songs where the emphasis is on not getting
caught for drug dealing and related activities, here it is on not being framed.

Watch the police when I'm rolling through the projects
My pants sag so I'm labeled as a suspect
Who be the boys in blue, the authority
To arrest me cause I live in a minority . . .
Watch the police
In my hood, they'll pull you over
And put dope on you and bring you to jail

In "The Men in Blue" Prince Paul talks of corrupt police, informing, and
faked evidence:

New York's largest crew, it's the Men in Blue
we stick together like glue and make lies come true . . .
if we make this connection,
I'll give you protection . . .
'cause I plant what I want on any crime scene
I keep my hands clean, you know what I mean

In the early rock and roll song "Framed," the Robbins offer a first-person account of victimization by an informer rather than the police. The lead singer is put in a police lineup and realizes he is a victim of "someone's evil plan. When a stool pigeon walked in and said, 'That's the man.'" In the political and commercial climate of the 1950s, it was easier to talk of betrayal by an informer than by police.

Other songs go beyond bringing the news about potential abuses and urge active resistance. As Rakaa Iriscience bluntly puts it:

> No questions
> I pledge resistance to the grass
> That hides the snakes of America
> so they watch it, now I walk with caution . . .
> Under heavy surveillance
> They might call you a traitor if you want something greater

In "Del's Nightmare," Del the Funky Homosapien observes,

> . . . They give us a white Jesus to appease us.
> We talk among ourselves and hope nobody sees us . . .
> The slave master watching over you,
> But ain't nothing gonna stop me and my crew!

Tupac Shakur in "All Eyez on Me" will do what he desires in spite of being scoped:

> . . . Live my life as a Boss playa (I know y'all watching)
> (I know y'all got me in the scopes)
> Live my life as a Thug nigga
> Until the day I die

Black Bomb, in "Police Stopped da way," notes that social control exists for the body and the mind, and it will be resisted:

> Police for everything . . .
> Police for da crimes . . .
> Police for da mind
> Stop da way
> When you think I'll surrender
> You get it wrong
> I will not stay in you shit
> When you think you'll get my mind
> You get it wrong
> I prefer to start a fight
> You get it wrong

Jill Scott in "Watching Me" illustrates the neutralization moves of refusal and blocking in singing:

Excuse me miss
May i have your phone number and your social security?
Who me?
When all i came to do is buy my double or triple a batteries
Please
I decline!!!
. . . I'm gonna build me a lead house
Keep them satellites out

With respect to drug testing, Mojo Nixon applies Nancy Reagan's "Just say no" to his defiant "I Ain't Gonna Piss in No Jar" (1987). He can be fired from his job, but something more important can't be robbed: "my freedom and my liberty." He urges everybody to go to Washington. If "they want our piss we ought to give it to 'em. Yeah, surround the White House with a urinary moat."

Eric Carmen in "Lost in the Shuffle" is reminiscent of philosopher Herbert Marcuse's critique of what is seen as the illusion of freedom in ostensibly democratic countries.[9]

You know you pay your taxes and you work all day
But you better watch out for the CIA
'Cause they're putting together a dossier on you
And now I'm glad I'm livin' in the land of the free
Where I can speak my mind if I don't agree
But it seems like it really doesn't matter
What I say or do
'Cause I feel I'm lost in the shuffle

Anti-Flag, in "Police State in the USA," also suggests that things are not as they seem. Anti-Flag responded to the fall of communism by observing similarities between elite control in the East and the West:

Politicians from the West claim the police state's dead
But what of the police state in the West? . . .
The government controls everything you do
With police and fed watching over you . . .
It's a big brother state it's the same as the East
The cops protect the rich and corporate elite
Police State in the U.S.A.

In "Privacy Invasion," Exploited draws a parallel between physical and mental invasion and pessimistically suggests it's too late.

You're led to think we're free, a democratic race
Told of equal rights well that's just not the case . . .
Too late to shut your curtains they've caught you unaware

9. H. Marcuse, *One-Dimensional Man* (New York: Routledge, 2002).

388 GARY T. MARX

They're not at your window man, they're sitting in your chair
A privacy invasion of the head

In an uncommon juxtaposition, Dead Prez expresses the traditional bourgeois concern with privacy, as well as noting the role of surveillance in sustaining inequality. In "Police State" we hear

FBI spying on us through the radio antennas
And them hidden cameras in the streetlight watching society
With no respect for the people's right to privacy
I'll take a slug for the cause like Huey P . . .
And the jobs don't ever pay enough
So the rent always be late.
Can you relate?
We living in a police state

In The Broadways' "Police Song" we see the counterintuitive suggestion that social control may threaten rather than protect public safety, and attention is called to the parallels between control in prison and in society more broadly:

. . . Tell me is this security, do we need protection from the police?
we need to reassess the power vested in authority
and social control threatens public safety do you feel safe?
. . . I had a dream that my whole town had turned into a prison
a cop on every corner but I don't feel too safe
feels like I'm in jail

Similarly, in "Bang Bang" Young Buck asks, "Why you mad at me? The Government's the Drug Dealers."

Jill Scott in "Watching Me" her watching song suggests that surveillance is misplaced:

You busy watching me, watching me
That you're blind baby
You neglect to see
The drugs coming into my community
Weapons in my community
Dirty cops in my community
And you keep saying that I'm free

A few satirical songs make a joke of surveillance, perhaps de-clawing it for some listeners in the process. In "Talkin' John Birch Paranoid Blues," Bob Dylan parodies the surveillant's search for communist conspiracies. The problem is not surveillance, but the supposed cleverness of the communists in evading detection. This cleverness necessitates extreme investigative means. In a social process endemic to the truly paranoid, the failure of strong measures to find subversives proves the need for even stronger measures. Communists are looked for "under my bed," "in the sink and underneath the chair," "up my chimney hole" even "deep down inside my toilet bowl," "in my TV set," "the library," and among "all the people that I knowed."

The 1985 film *Spies Like Us* is based on incompetent CIA aspirants who get caught cheating on the entrance exam.[10] They are then hired to be unknowingly used as bait against the Russians. In the film's theme song, Paul McCartney sings,

> Hey don't feel afraid
> Of an undercover aid
> There's no need to fuss
> There ain't nobody that spies like us

IV. SOME IMPLICATIONS

We didn't have any answers, but at least we brought up the questions.
—David Crosby of Crosby, Stills and Nash

In the first instance, these songs literally or symbolically speak for themselves. As with a good meal, the value comes from the experience. Consuming is an end in itself. In the case of music, for example, maternal and religious surveillance songs such as "Lullaby and Good Night" can be uplifting and transcendent, and the evocative and clever poetry of love, or protest lyrics, are just there. Experiencing them communicates on a level beyond academic analysis. In that sense questions about representative samples, hypotheses, and social theory are beside the point.

The material might even be profaned by shining a too bright and probing scholarly beam on it. Yet it has meaning beyond the individual consumer. However, rather than deductively straining these materials through varieties of available explanatory theory, I will proceed inductively and indicate some implications for understanding surveillance and society.

Social scientists generally draw too rigid a line between their data and the offerings of the artist. Artistic creations can significantly inform us about surveillance and society. They can be approached from the standpoint of the sociology of knowledge, and we can ask about the message conveyed, how this has changed, and how it correlates with the characteristics of the context, the creator, and the audience. Here art is treated as a dependent variable. But the materials

---

10. Consider also the theme music associated with the Pink Panther series and the misnamed Maxwell Smart in the 1960s sitcom *Get Smart*. As a bumbling secret agent working for CONTROL, Smart demonstrated a profound ineptitude. The sole of his shoe was a telephone that frequently dialed the wrong number, and his jet shoes propelled him into the roof.

can also inform us about broader societal issues, and we can speculate on their social impact as independent variables.

Artistic statements, unlike scientific statements, do not have to be defended verbally. But the social scientist can ask about their social antecedents and impacts. Do they move the individual? Do they convey the experience of being watched or of being a watcher? Do they create indignation or a desire for the product? Do they make the invisible visible?

The treatment of surveillance in popular culture—whether music, television, cinema, cartoons, literature, or advertisements—brings the news. These cultural forms may educate by offering descriptions and moral messages. They inform the audience about what surveillance can do, or is presumed to be able to do. Like some science fiction, they may offer a view of what could, or may, happen. Because they are not bound by specific empirical cases, such cultural forms can bring us the big picture and push conventional boundaries of thought and image.

Life may imitate art, as things based on the imagination of the artist later come to exist. An early example is the 1936 film *Modern Times*, in which Charlie Chaplin's private reverie, smoking a cigarette in the bathroom at work, is shattered by the sudden appearance of his boss on a wall-sized video screen gruffly saying, "Hey, quit stalling and get back to work." The boss has a two-way video camera. H. G. Wells, Dick Tracy, Spider-Man, Wonder Woman, James Bond, and *Star Trek* are other familiar examples.[11] Popular culture treatments of surveillance can help us "see" and understand (whether emotionally or cognitively) new developments in surveillance. Visual and auditory artistic expressions offer an alternative way of knowing relative to words—whether fiction or nonfiction. For example, we can more readily understand electronic data and microscopic DNA sequences when they are transformed into images through artistic representations. The blurry line between the human and the nonhuman—robots, cyborgs, implants—is more easily grasped when we see the results through artists' imaginary creations, or hear an electronically generated voice or weird sounds.

Songs such as "Watching Me" by Jill Scott or Judas Priest's "Electronic Eye," in bringing together so many different aspects, can help us grasp the scale, totality, comprehensiveness, and simultaneity of the new forms of surveillance across multiple dimensions. We can more easily "see" or better comprehend this in our "mind's eye." The above songs are the equivalent of a *New Yorker* cartoon by Fradon (June 29, 1987), "Joe's Drive-Thru Testing Center," which offers motorists tests for emissions, drugs, intelligence, cholesterol, blood pressure, and the polygraph. Note also the equivalence between the human and the machine on the assembly line Charlie Chaplin created in *Modern Times*.

---

11. The originator of Wonder Woman went on to help develop the polygraph and a Spider-Man comic inspired a New Mexico judge to implement the first judicial use of electronic location monitoring equipment.

The meaning of authoritarianism, repression, domination, intolerance, and spying is likely to be different when experienced vicariously through seeing and hearing, as against reading and quantifying. The traditional role of the artist, in making the unseen visible (or what might be possible, imaginable), can be observed in some songs.

Art can educate in a distinctive and perhaps more profound sense than can the traditional written text. For example, a popular protest song that periodically enters consciousness will likely have a much wider, more enduring, and in some ways different, impact than an op-ed article or pamphlet on the same topic. Labor organizer and singer Joe Hill reportedly observed that a pamphlet, no matter how good, is read only once. A melody, rhyme, or rhythm may insinuate itself into consciousness (although the extent to which this comes with comprehension of the words is an open question).

Attention to the kinds of issues the music of a given period treats can help chart change, just as the analysis of news stories or research articles on a topic can. Contrasting song titles and lyrics over time and across settings can reveal the archaeological stratum of a culture as it influences, and is influenced by, social and technical change. Consider how song's concerns have evolved as the technology has.

Bessie Smith in her 1923 rendition of "Ain't Nobody's Business" offered a libertarian plea consistent with the Warren and Brandeis (1890) emphasis on the importance of a right to privacy that involves being "let alone":

If I go to church on Sunday
And I honkytonk all day Monday
Ain't nobody's business if I do

In contrast, in the early 1950s, Hank Williams in "Mind Your Own Business" complained about misuse of the telephone and about other individuals, rather than governments or corporations, invading privacy:

Oh, the woman on our party line's the nosiest thing
She picks up her receiver when she knows it's my ring
Why don't you mind your own business

By the 1990s REM, in "Star 69," sings about the ability to trace the last telephone number dialed in what could almost be an ad for the phone company's call trace service:

You don't have to take the bar exam to see
What you've done is ignoramus 103
. . . I know you called, I know you called, . . .
I know you hung up my line
Star 69

Popular culture, of course, reflects developments in technology. Paul Simon in the 1960s said of "Mrs. Robinson," "We'd like to know a little bit about you for our [presumably manual] files" and in "America" sang of the spy in a gabardine suit whose "bow tie is really a camera." Several decades later he was writing about, "lasers in the jungle" and "staccato signals of constant information" in "The Boy in the Bubble." Still later songs are concerned with DNA and micro-chips. Compare Tom Paxton's singing in 1967 about abstract concerns over an Orwellian dystopia to his more concrete songs in the early 2000s about "Homeland Security."

In a period of rapid technological change, the songs risk being quickly dated and having their shocking, humorous, or satirical punch undermined by reality (e.g., songs from the 1970s and 80s suggesting that the TV one watches could be looking back at the watcher). Now, with systems for monitoring television viewing, webcams, and video-phones, this is science, not fiction. While still far from being able to know "everything I am thinking," technologies for reading emotions and assessing truth telling from facial expressions, eye movements, and brain wave patterns are under development. Consider also seat cushions that measure wiggling as signs of attentiveness.[12]

V. MUSIC CONTENT: SOCIALIZATION FOR CONFORMITY OR RESISTANCE?

Artistic materials can educate and politicize by telling us what is happening and by offering warnings. They can bring the news to broader audiences and may use potentially more powerful and poignant means of conveying their messages. Which news is brought and the impact of that news vary—by its own properties and the social order in question.

Karl Marx, Antonio Gramsci, and Michel Foucault stress the links between power and culture. Dominant groups and individuals have disproportionate con-trol over the means of culture creation and distribution and the ability to censor. Glorification, spin, obfuscation, and censorship are prominent features of the mainstream media. Escapist media may call attention away from social issues.

The religious and children's songs and those of suspicious male lovers con-sidered support the established order. These songs may inspire confidence and reassure, although they may also intimidate.

The case for conformity and the status quo are clearly heard. Beyond the reas-surance offered by protection, their message is, "you are not alone and you can't get away with it." As with the implicit morality of the fairy tale, the dominant figure knows what the child (or adult) is up (or down) to. Rewards and punishment will flow from that knowledge.

---

12. Marx considers this along with a variety of emerging unobtrusive techniques designed to illicit personal information in controlled settings; see G. Marx, "Surveys and Surveillance" in F. Conrad and M. Schrober (eds.), *Envisioning the Survey of the Future* (Hoboken, NJ: John Wiley & Sons, 2008).

The music may accustom the child to being watched by benign-appearing (sometimes unseen), all-powerful authority figures. This encourages internalization of the dominant society's standards, just as playing with surveillance toys does.

Children may come to look at themselves through the eyes of presumably loving authority figures that have their best interests at heart. The message carries over into adulthood as they become watchful and watched citizens and workers.

Songs with humorous or satirical components may suggest that there is nothing to worry about. The entertainment quality may be beguiling. If surveillants are simply Keystone Cop bunglers, or have magical and exaggerated powers far beyond what the technology can presently do, then there is little to worry about (at least for now). Their incompetence makes them incapable of doing harm, in spite of their technology, or the technology is depicted so unrealistically as to be unworthy of concern. Such songs, along with those that simply fold the technology into other themes, hardly inspire vigilance.

Even some songs from the point of view of those watched, though not meant to be supportive or reassuring, may encourage conformity by suggesting that resistance is futile.

Yet, in spite of fashionable concerns about capitalist cultural hegemony, we can also note capitalist irony and complexity. There is much space for counter-messages even if they are in the minority, or not found equally in all communications media (the Internet, for example, opens up vast new opportunities for those previously unable to own a printing press or a radio or television station). Whatever the disproportionate influence of the dominants (sounds like the name of a rock group), this influence is far from total. Factors undercutting dominant voices can be identified.

A counterview offered by the pluralist perspective, while not claiming that all messages or images are equal, observes that a free market economy with civil liberties offers opportunities for opposing voices.

Dominant groups are hardly homogeneous in their interests and values. The interest of elites in ideological hegemony may conflict with the profit motive of some segments (consider record companies profiting from selling anti-establishment materials—whether Columbia Records' early endorsement of folk music or the current establishment marketing of rap music).[13]

Marked discrepancies between the claims of the dominant world view and the observable empirical world may generate critiques and alternative views. Sometimes reality wins.

---

13. In a related example the advertisements that accompany protest (and other lyrics) on the Web must cause a smile in even the most jaded social critic. Note advertisements to "Send [name of singing group] polyphonic ringtone to your cell phone" or a moving target under the banner "SHOOT THE PAPARAZZI! Get Your FREE Sony PSP or Nintendo DS."

Ideological systems may contain contradictory and inconsistent elements. Belief systems are rarely clearly specified and their inherent ambiguity, particularly as applied to a given case, also supports alternative views.

There may be dialectical processes in which what is dominant calls forth its opposite, which in turn calls forth opposites in an enduring chain. Woody Guthrie's "This Land Is Your Land" was written in response to "God Bless America." The hegemonic lesson in "I fought the law and the law won" was eventually matched by the Dead Kennedys, "Drinkin' beer in the hot sun I Fought the Law and I Won." In spite of a large number of antiwar songs in response to Viet Nam, the most popular record of the period was "The Ballad of the Green Berets." The abundance of 1960s and 1970s songs criticizing establishment ways, encouraging protest, and supporting countercultural life styles was met by tunes such as Merle Haggard's "An Okie from Muskogee"—"a place where even squares can have a ball . . . wave Old Glory down at the courthouse And white lightnin's still the biggest thrill of all . . . and the kids still respect the college dean."[14]

The idea of the all-knowing surveillant carries the threat to conform to the standards of the watcher, or face the consequences. Where there is a high degree of consensus about rules, this is not an issue, but with contested norms (e.g., involving work monitoring, drugs, life style, or the legitimacy of political and other elites) critical artistic expressions are likely. The protest songs reflect cultural neutralization and a kind of socialization for rejection. Bringing the news about the bad things "they" are doing may encourage questioning and call forth resistance.

The means of expressing a cultural message, as well as its content, varies depending on whose interests are served. Views in opposition to the mainstream are not found equally across types of expression, media, or performers. They seem more likely to appear in popular music, in cartoons, and on Web sites than in television, major studio films, or newspapers. The degree of corporate control and the resources needed for expression are likely relevant factors here. Performers from less privileged backgrounds appear more likely to offer criticism than those from dominant groups.

The music and other artistic expressions can be seen as part of a broader political struggle over the meaning of surveillance technology and how it ought to be judged. Is surveillance best seen as benevolent protection or malevolent domination, and when? This involves conflicts over symbols and words. Cultural

---

14. There is a paper here waiting to be birthed exploring surveillance in country and western music. It appears to be more self-pitying, self-blaming, or blaming other individuals than focusing on a social order seen to be unjust. The watching often involves seeing another man taking the singer's woman, dog, or truck, or police showing up at the scene of some misfortune that has befallen the singer. State surveillance agencies may be mentioned as offering no help in finding one's true love. Conservative religious themes involving an observant, knowing, and justice-dispensing God and watching over a love object also seem more common.

communications and political interests are often linked, and the conflict over symbols and words is about something more.

Each side has its preferred outlets and audience. For governments, manufacturers, and surveillance vendors, communications tend to be directed to potential consumers rather than mass audiences. There are no songs praising political surveillance, drug testing, informing, video surveillance, and work monitoring (although in Japan company songs might encourage conformity with the latter two).[15] Apart from the religious songs appreciative of sacred and parental protective surveillance, there are almost no songs honoring government, corporate, and employer surveillance. Instead print media—speeches, professional publications, and advertisements—are the preferred outlets for views stressing surveillance as protection, order, and security.

Employers and merchants generally say much less about their means of control, although signs may inform subjects about video cameras, searches, and drug tests. This display is for legal reasons and for deterrence.

In contrast, artistic expression is a prime means for expressing criticism, and this tends to be addressed to a mass audience. The songs offer a mix of the real and fantasy and are more likely to exaggerate than to underestimate the power of current technology (although here, as we note, they may be correct in the longer run in anticipating what it will be possible to do).

Plato wanted poets to be controlled by the state—and with good reason, from an establishment perspective. Cartoonists, popular songwriters, and artists often demystify, expose, and delegitimate surveillance. As the related forms of rap and folk music suggest, they are more likely to express a bottom-up view in taking the role of the watched, controlled, or victimized.[16]

Reduced to essentials, the artists tend to view technology as the enemy or the problem—as something that profanes and from which we need to be protected—while control agents and those who provide surveillance resources view it as the solution, bringing salvation. The sides are mirror opposites. It is an interesting exercise to fill in the other half of the story. The various means of communication are as revealing for what they say as for what they do not say.

In generally bringing a single message, the songs are one-sided against the richness of social life. Perhaps the medium's form (limited time, short and repetitive phrases) does not lend itself as well to this richness as the written word does.

---

15. But contrast the propaganda efforts on behalf of informing seen in the USSR. The young boy who informed on his father's bourgeois sentiments was made a national hero. Note also efforts to encourage the use of hotlines for reporting everything from littering to bad drivers to suspicious persons increasingly seen in the United States.

16. There is, of course, variation within musical genre; thus religious and country and western music are, in general, supportive, and folk, alternative, and rap music, more critical. There are many country and western songs about "big brother," but these are always about an elder sibling.

Just whose message gets across most successfully, under what conditions and to what audiences, is a topic for quantitative research and goes far beyond the literal words of a song.

Frank Zappa observed, "there are more love songs than anything else. If songs could make you do something we'd all love one another." In considering the impact of a song's words, we must be humble and tentative and not assume that they will be uniformly heard and understood, or lead to feelings or actions that might be desired by the artist or sponsors.

Competing messages can make individuals cynical and questioning. The flood of efforts to convince may make for suspicion. In this sense, rather than "seeing [or hearing] is believing," it may mean not believing. In communicating the fragmented and movable quality of the "realities" we perceive, such cultural materials may lead to a healthy skepticism—or an immobilizing paranoia.

There is great variety among listeners, contexts, music, and time periods. Lyrics can be analyzed for their presumed intended meaning (whether by the creator, performer, or promoter), or with more confidence, their meaning to a given listener. A song's origins, assumptions, and connections to other songs and things happening in the society can be analyzed. But in most cases it is a leap from there to broad generalizations about the meaning of a song to mass, highly variegated audiences. However, song content can be considered with respect to some broad factors involving the contemporary sociology of surveillance.

Lyrics and music need to be disentangled. A song's effect may stem from more than the meaning of its words. The interaction of lyric, musical structure, and instrumentation on the listener is a topic for a musicologist, rather than an amateur listener. But here we can at least note that certain chords, rhythms, and instruments are heavy and somber and that others communicate lightness and seem upbeat. One need not know how to read musical notation to read music. Consider John Williams's work for *Star Wars* and other films, or the warning viewers experience when a film's music suggests doom and dread, or the uplift when the music suggests that victory is at hand. The harsh sounds accompanying some rap music may bolster images of violence and angst.

Yet words may say one thing even as the melody communicates something very different. We hear through our bodies as well as through our ears. Thus Little Richard in "Slippin' and Slidin'" is behaving badly in spying on his girl-friend, but the song has a toe-tapping, upbeat rhythm that makes one want to dance and ignore the content. Compare the infectious rhythms of this song to the somber, threatening feeling generated by Queensryche's equivalent voyeuristic song "Gonna Get Close to You" with different instrumentation and slow rhythm. The words to Sting's "Every Breath You Take" suggest a massive invasion of privacy, yet the song is often heard as a love song because of its melody. Consider also songs in a different language whose words are not generally understood, but that become popular because of a familiar melody. Nor are words necessary—note Jimi Hendrix's protest version of the national anthem at Woodstock in 1968 in which the guitar simulates the sounds of guns, sirens, and screams.[17]

This article began by suggesting that contemporary surveillance methods and popular culture are interwoven and can both serve as kinds of soul training.

But the story is complex. There is no sole form or impact. Using both hard and soft means, powerful forces may seek to reduce the soul to an object like a shoe sole that is worn down and expendable. But other forces resist and push toward a more soulful view of humans.

Settings are diverse and fluid. Certainly there are unsavory elites using doubtful means for nefarious ends. But they are often opposed by those favoring more communal and democratic means and goals. And individuals act back, frequently in ways unanticipated by professional soul trainers. The latter themselves have imperfect tools and a variety of (often conflicting) goals. This makes for a messy and un-utopian (if not fully dystopian) society, but one that muddles through.

I have tried, as singer David Crosby suggests, to bring the questions and to suggest some possible answers. Of course, whether (and under what conditions) music and other aspects of popular culture serve as soul training for compliance or as soulful messages encouraging resistance and dignity is a topic for more systematic empirical research. Music can also be more systematically contrasted to other surveillance message bearers such as cinema, jokes, literature, art, and advertisements.

---

17. Performers may also encourage social and political change through concerts that seek to raise funds and increase awareness in which most, or all, of the songs performed lack a protest message (e.g., Farm Aid).

22. EXIT NODE REPUDIATION FOR ANONYMITY NETWORKS

JEREMY CLARK, PHILIPPE GAUVIN,
AND CARLISLE ADAMS

I. INTRODUCTION

Recruiting volunteers to act as node operators in anonymity networks can be a daunting task. Although setting up a network node is becoming a simpler task, there remains the serious question of liability for the forwarding of unlawful communications such as terrorist threats, child pornography, or hate speech. In cryptography, repudiation means disclaiming responsibility for an action.[1] Cryptographers have proposed anonymity network protocols that would allow network node operators to avoid undue liability for illegal communications that have been anonymized by the network.[2] However, current research only allows the owner of a node to prove that he or she is not the originator of the message *if asked*. Given the ease with which digital evidence can be destroyed, it is unlikely that investigators would ask a suspect node operator for his or her cooperation.

---

1. Alfred J. Menezes, Paul C. van Oorschot and Scott A. Vanstone, *Handbook of Applied Cryptography* (Boca Raton: CRC Press, 1997), 4.

2. P. Golle, "Reputable mix networks," *Fourth Workshop on Privacy Enchancing Technologies: Proceedings of PET 2004*, in *Lecture Notes in Computer Science*, volume 3424 (Berlin: Springer-Verlag, 2005): 51–62.

It is much more probable that a warrant for the search, and possibly the seizure, of the node will be acquired without the knowledge of the node operator. It is therefore imperative that network designers understand the circumstances under which a warrant will be issued and how networks could be designed to avoid the disincentive of seized servers.

By their nature, data sent through an anonymity network will appear to have originated from the last server in the chain—the exit node. This situation illustrates two salient problems with online anonymity: it can deter or prevent law enforcement from identifying users who behave unlawfully online, and it creates liability issues for the innocent operator of the exit node who could be erroneously accused of being the perpetrator.

These problems have a seemingly easy solution: the anonymity network could simply reveal the identity of the sender. Before considering the plausibility of this, one must understand how anonymity networks of this type work. We present an overview of online anonymity and demonstrate that the decentralized structure of anonymity networks complicate this simple solution. Furthermore, we consider whether anonymity networks in theory should be able to reveal the sender's identity and what unintended consequences may result from this. We focus our attention on a solution to the second of the two problems—that the threat of a long legal process and equipment seizure is a deterrent to voluntarily operating a server in an anonymity network. We examine the legal protections against unreasonable search and seizure afforded by the Canadian Charter and laws in other jurisdictions, and propose a legally informed cryptographic protocol to allow exit nodes to repudiate any data originating from a different Internet protocol address than its own. In essence, we propose to allow exit nodes to prove, in addition to not knowing the identity of the sender and without the need for the node owner to intervene, that they are not themselves the originators of a communication.

II. PRELIMINARIES

A. A Technical Definition of Anonymity
Anonymity can mean different things in different contexts. In the field of security and privacy, anonymity requires two necessary conditions that together are sufficient for anonymity:

P1: an anonymous action is not linkable to the identity of the actor, and P2: two anonymous actions performed by the same actor are not linkable to each other.

If the proposition P1 is false, actions are associated with the actor's identity, and the identifier is considered veronymous (a Latin portmanteau for "true name"[3]).

3. Carlisle Adams, "A classification for privacy techniques," *University of Ottawa Law & Technology Journal: special issue on anonymity, privacy, and identity* 3, no. 1 (2006): 35–52.

In this case, two disparate actions performed by the same actor would be linkable to the actor's identity and are thereby linkable to each other. This implies that proposition P2 is false whenever P1 is. If P1 is true and P2 is false, then actions can be linked to a common identifier that is not the actor's true identity. This is referred to as pseudonymity ("alternate name"). P1 is necessary for pseudonymity.

We now consider what "the identity of the actor" is in an online world. Pseudonymous identifiers are pervasive online. A self-assigned identifier is a digital pseudonym used to access features on a Web service (i.e., a screen name, user name, or e-mail address). A server-assigned identifier is a unique identifier used to monitor users (i.e., a cookie or spyware). The anonymity afforded by anonymity networks does not extend to either of these categories of identifiers. Rather, it deals with transport-layer identifiers—specifically Internet protocol (IP) addresses. When a device is online, it is reachable through its unique IP address. An IP address does not necessarily correspond to a single computer; it could, for example, identify the gateway to a network of computers. At best, IP addresses tie actions from this device together, and, therefore, could be considered pseudonymous. However, if the holder of an IP address is revealed (e.g., through self-disclosure in the holder's traffic or by the holder's Internet service provider), then the IP address could become a veronymous identifier. Anonymity networks unlink a user's actions from her IP address.

The anonymity afforded by an anonymity network is important even if the user does not reveal her full identity during communications. An IP address can be augmented with other personally identifiable information (PII), such as a search query for a relative or the revelation of a postal code, and aggregating enough information can be used to reduce the user's privacy and possibly uncover her true identity. Datamining and geo-location[4] are examples of this privacy threat.

B. An Analogy of an Anonymity Network

In order to illustrate how an anonymity network works, consider Bob who is very flattered when he realizes that someone has left him an anonymous valentine. His secret admirer, Alice, knew that leaving the note on Bob's desk was too risky—she might be seen—so she decided to ask her trustworthy friend, Charlie, to assist her. The initial idea was that Alice would give Charlie the valentine, and Charlie would leave it on Bob's desk. In this case, Charlie is acting as a proxy for Alice, and Charlie decides to announce publicly that he will be acting as a

---

4. Venkata N. Padmanabhan and Lakshminarayanan Subramanian, "An investigation of geographic mapping techniques for internet hosts," *Proceedings of SIGCOMM 2001*, in *ACM SIGCOMM Computer Communication Review* 31, no. 4 (2001): 173–185. See also James A. Muir and P. C. van Oorschot, "Internet geolocation and evasion," *TR-06-05* (Carleton University: Technical Report, 2006): 1–22, http://cs.smu.ca/~jamuir/papers/TR-06-05.pdf.

go-between for anyone wanting to send anonymous valentines. To Charlie's surprise, a large number of co-workers emerge to take him up on the deal. Alice is also happy with this news. She knows that if she is seen giving Charlie a valentine, she will be just one in a large group of potential senders.

There are a few complications, though. If Alice is seen giving the valentine to Charlie, someone could later recognize it when it is in Bob's possession. To prevent this, Alice hides the valentine in an envelope, and Charlie, in the privacy of his office, opens the envelope and accordingly forwards the valentine found inside it. However, Charlie must also be careful in the order in which he distributes the valentines he has received. For example, if, immediately upon receiving a sealed envelope from a sender, Charlie ducks into his office and then promptly places a valentine on someone's desk, it is easy to deduce who is sending a valentine to whom. Instead, Charlie spends the day collecting a batch of envelopes, and then at the end of the day, he takes them all out of their envelopes, shuffles them, and distributes them in a different order than he received them.

This process works if Charlie is trustworthy. However, trust can also be distributed to more than one person. For example, Alice could put her valentine to Bob in an envelope and write another trusted co-worker's name on it. She could then put this envelope in a second envelope with Charlie's name on it. She gives the package to Charlie, who opens the first envelope and learns that the envelope should be given to Deborah. Deborah opens the second envelope and finds the valentine for Bob. In this case, neither Charlie nor Deborah know that Alice is sending a valentine to Bob. Charlie knows that Alice sent a valentine to someone care of Deborah, and Deborah knows that Bob received a valentine from someone care of Charlie. As long as they do not collude with each other, no one can link Alice and Bob together.[5] This model can be expanded with an arbitrary number of proxies, and the only requirement for anonymity is that at least one is trustworthy.

C. Anonymity Networks

Online, the role of Charlie and Deborah are played by nodes, which forward Internet data between a user and a recipient. Many Web sites log the IP addresses of users who visit their site, and the use of a proxy server hides the user's IP address from the Web site. However, an IP address is not hidden if someone sees the traffic before it reaches the proxy server. In this case, the eavesdropper knows the source of the packets (the user), the destination (the proxy server), and if they open the packets, they can learn the ultimate destination (the recipient). An example of an entity who could easily log this information is an Internet service provider (ISP). This privacy threat is plausible: in June 2006 Canadian

---

5. It is possible for Charlie to open both envelopes, but this is a shortcoming of the analogy, not the technology: opening digital envelopes requires a secret key that only the intended recipient possesses.

ISP Bell Sympatico announced to its customers, in response to expectations that the federal government would revive an Internet surveillance bill, that it may "monitor or investigate content or your use of your service provider's networks and to disclose any information necessary to satisfy any laws, regulations or other governmental request."[6]

To protect the final destination of data from an eavesdropper, the destination can be placed into a digital "envelope" by using cryptography. Some proxy servers offer an encrypted channel to their users using the transport layer security (TLS) protocol.[7] This prevents an eavesdropper, like an ISP or someone with access to a user's network, from discovering the final destination based on the content of the message. However, if the eavesdropper could see both the traffic entering and leaving the proxy server (an entity with access to both ISP and Web site logs), they could link messages using simple timing analysis. For example, if every time an unreadable encrypted packet comes in from a given user and immediately a packet is sent from the proxy to a certain recipient, it can be reasonably deduced what recipient a user is communicating with. To prevent this, the proxy can take a batch of data from multiple users and reorder it before forwarding it. By sending traffic through a chain of such mix proxies, no one proxy will know both the original source and the final destination of the data. Every proxy server in the chain would have to collude to break the sender's anonymity, and as the sender herself could operate one of these servers, she can guarantee her own anonymity without trusting anyone else.

Mix proxies that use a random permutation to remove order-based correspondence between an input and output message set and cryptography to remove content-based correspondence were first proposed in 1981 by David Chaum.[8] A network of mix nodes is shown in Figure 1. Many modern anonymity networks are based on the idea of sending traffic through several of these specialized servers, although variations on how the servers work exist. Anonymity networks have been proposed to anonymize email[9] and Web traffic.[10]

---

6. M. Hammond, "Big brother watching you surf?" *The Globe and Mail*, June 27, 2006.

7. Or its predecessor, secure sockets layer (SSL).

8. David Chaum, "Untraceable electronic mail, return addresses, and digital pseudonyms," *Communications of the ACM* 24, no. 2 (1981): 84–88.

9. George Danezis, Roger Dingledine, and Nick Mathewson, "Mixminion: design of a type III anonymous remailer protocol," *Proceedings of the 2003 IEEE Symposium on Security and Privacy* (2003): 2–15.

10. Roger Dingledine, Nick Mathewson, and Paul Syverson, "Tor: The second-generation onion router," in *Proceedings of the 13th USENIX Security Symposium* (2004): 303–320. *Also see* O. Berthold, H. Federrath, and S. Köpsell, "Web MIXes: a system for anonymous and unobservable internet access," *Proceedings of Designing Privacy Enhancing Technologies: Workshop on Design Issues in Anonymity and Unobservability*, in *Lecture Notes in Computer Science* 2009 (2001): 115–129.

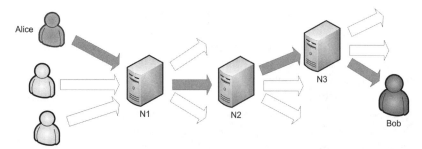

FIGURE 1. ALICE SENDS AN ANONYMOUS MESSAGE TO BOB THROUGH A NETWORK OF THREE MIX NODES. TO BOB, IT APPEARS THE MESSAGE ORIGINATED FROM THE EXIT NODE AND NOT FROM ALICE.

D. Revisiting the Motivating Problem

A seemingly simple solution to the problem of determining the originator of unlawful anonymous messages would be for the final node to reveal from whom it received the data, and law enforcement could iteratively trace the data back to the original sender. However, this would require the servers to store server logs, and server logs have no inherent integrity—they can be easily modified or forged. A further complication is that anonymity networks deliberately stretch across multiple countries. Even if server logs were reliable, an international effort would be required to subpoena the required data.[11] Alternatively, anonymity networks could be legally compelled to encrypt the identity of all participants and leave the decryption key to this information in escrow with law enforcement. However, the political viability of this situation seems dismal, as it closely parallels the proposed Clipper chip in the United States during the 1990s, which was met with a political backlash that ensured it was never adopted. Concern has also been raised that provisions created to facilitate the prosecution of heinous online crimes, like the distribution of child pornography, could also be used for

---

11. International law enforcement agreements already exist. As stated in "Searching and Seizing Computers and Obtaining Electronic Evidence in Criminal Investigations" (July 2002) Computer Crime and Intellectual Property Section, Criminal Division, United States Department of Justice, http://www.justice.gov/criminal/cybercrime/searching.html#searchmanual:

> "To secure preservation, or in emergencies when immediate international assistance is required, the international Network of 24-hour Points of Contact established by the High-tech Crime Subgroup of the G8 countries can provide assistance. This network, created in 1997, is comprised of approximately twenty-eight member countries, and continues to grow every year. Participating countries have a dedicated computer crime expert and a means to contact that office or person twenty-four hours a day. See generally Michael A. Sussmann, The Critical Challenges from International High-Tech and Computer-Related Crime at the Millennium, 9 Duke J. Comp. & Int'l L. 451, 484 (1999)."

anti-democratic purposes in prohibitive nation-states or in less clear-cut situations, such as civil disputes over copyright infringement.

The situation forces us to choose between the right to online anonymity and the efficacy of criminal prosecution. It is not an easy decision. Although we have focused thus far on the costs to society, online anonymity has benefits as well. It offers privacy protection to whistle-blowers, victims of abuse, political advocates in oppressive nation states, military and intelligence agencies, individuals seeking information in confidence, or simply citizens concerned with how easily personal data can be aggregated in an online world. It is our expectation that public opinion on online anonymity will converge to a position similar to that of cryptography—that the benefits outweigh the danger.

In the meantime, we turn our focus to the perhaps secondary but more imminent legal concern for anonymity networks: server operators in anonymity networks could face anything from the seizure of equipment to the threat of criminal prosecution as a result of unlawful data they did not originate. German police have recently seized Tor servers that (presumably unwittingly) served to anonymize a child porn ring's communications.[12] It is important to understand the circumstances under which a lawful seizure can be instigated before constructing technical measures to prevent such seizures.

III. COMPUTER-RELATED SEARCH AND SEIZURE

Even if server operators are not the originators of "bad" communications, this does not resolve the basic fact that once a server is seized in an investigation, it may take well over a year before the judicial system processes the evidence and exonerates the server operator. To avoid the stress, hassles, and expense of a seized computer, the designers of anonymity networks should be concerned with search and seizure procedures along with exonerating node operators from guilt.

A. Constitutional or Supra-Statutory Protections

The Supreme Court of Canada in *R. v. Genest* discussed the balancing of interests involved in the state's right of search and seizure versus an individual's right to privacy:

> The privacy of a man's home and the security and integrity of his person and property have long been recognised as basic human rights, enjoying both an impressive history and a firm footing in most constitutional documents and international instruments. But much as these rights are valued they

---

12. John Oates, "German police seize Tor servers," *The Register*, September 11, 2006, http://www.theregister.co.uk/2006/09/11/anon_servers_seized/.

cannot be absolute. All legal systems must and do allow official power in various circumstances and on satisfaction of certain conditions to encroach upon rights of privacy and security in the interests of law enforcement, either to investigate an alleged offence or to apprehend a lawbreaker or to search for and seize evidence of crime. The interests at stake are compelling. On the one hand the security and privacy of a person's home and possessions should not be invaded except for compelling reasons. On the other hand society, represented by its organised institutions, also has an undeniable and equally powerful interest in effectively investigating crime and punishing wrongdoers. The task of balancing these conflicting interests is a matter of great importance and of considerable difficulty; but it must be attempted, and so far as possible, for the health of civil liberty and law enforcement alike, satisfactorily performed.[13]

Such a balance is struck, at least nominally, in most western nations. Section 8 of the Canadian Charter of Rights and Freedoms stipulates, "Everyone has the right to be secure against *unreasonable* search and seizure" (emphasis added).[14] Section 8 not only provides the basic rights of individuals, but also serves as a constraint against unreasonable search and seizure by the state. Not only does it restrain agents of the state, but, due to the constitutional nature of the Charter, it also protects against the erosion of Canadian civil liberties through the enactment of privacy invasive legislation.

The United States also provides constitutional protections against search and seizures by the State through the Fourth Amendment to its Constitution:

The right of the people to be secure in their persons, houses, papers, and effects, against *unreasonable searches* and seizures, shall not be violated, and *no Warrants shall issue, but upon probable cause*, supported by Oath or affirmation, and particularly describing the place to be searched, and the persons or things to be seized [emphasis added].[15]

In Europe, similar protection is accorded through Article 8 of the European Convention on Human Rights, which states the following:

1. Everyone has the right to respect for his private and family life, his home and his correspondence.
2. There shall be no interference by a public authority with the exercise of this right except such as is in accordance with the law and is necessary in a democratic society in the interests of national security, public safety or the

---

13. *R. v Genest*, (1989), 45 CCC (3d) 385 (SCC) at 388, citing Polyvios G. Polyviou, *Search and Seizure: Constitutional and Common Law* (London: Duckworth, 1982) at vii.
14. Part I of the Constitution Act, 1982, being Schedule B to the Canada Act 1982 (.K), 1982, c. 11. (the "Charter").
15. U.S. Const. am. 4.

economic well-being of the country, for the prevention of disorder or crime, for the protection of health or morals, or for the protection of the rights and freedoms of others.[16]

Doubt as to the meaning of "correspondence" was eliminated in the Charter of Fundamental Rights of the European Union,[17] which provides that everyone has the right "to respect for his or her private and family life, home *and communications* [emphasis added]."[18]

These European Union documents do not, in and of themselves, ensure the protection of Member States' citizens. They have, however, been implemented by most Member States with the European Commission taking enforcement action against those that have lagged behind.[19] Although not all European nations have a written constitution in which to implement these rights, some, such as the United Kingdom, have nevertheless provided "enhanced protection" to privacy with reference to European Convention on Human Rights.[20]

B. Search and Seizure

The definition of a "search" is simple enough. The Supreme Court of Canada,[21] for example, noted in *R. v. Wise*, "If the police activity invades a reasonable expectation of privacy, then the activity is a search."[22] One has to keep in mind, however, that the Charter only applies to governmental entities, as espoused in Section 32 of the Charter. Private individuals may be found to be acting as state agents in certain situations. In *R. v. M. (M.R.)*, the Supreme Court considered

---

16. Convention for the Protection of Human Rights and Fundamental Freedoms, Rome 4 November 1950 as amended by Protocol 11.

17. [2000] OJ C 364/8, 18 December 2000.

18. *Ibid.* art. 7.

19. For more on this topic, see Douwe Korff, *EC Study on Implementation of Data Protection Directive: comparative summary of national laws* (Cambridge: Human Rights Centre, September 2002).

20. *Ibid.* 8–9.

21. Due to space constraints, we, being Canadian, have focused our analysis on the Canadian situation. We note, however, that search and seizure legal schemes are substantially similar in other free and democratic jurisdictions. In the United States, for example, if government conduct does not violate the "reasonable expectation of privacy," it does not constitute a "search," and warrants are issued upon the establishment of "probable cause." (*Illinois v Andreas*, 463 U.S. 765, 771 (1983).) Unfortunately, in some jurisdictions it may not be possible to avoid the risk of search and seizure or even imprisonment for the hosting or use of anonymizing networks. Some would argue that the United States is such a jurisdiction since the passing into law of the Protect America Act of 2007, which allows for the warrantless wiretapping of international communications. We offer no opinion other than the fact that our proposed solution would render such wiretapping unreasonable, as the information sought by the State would be unavailable in properly configured nodes.

22. *R v Wise* [2002] 70 CCC (3d) 193 (SCC).

whether a school vice-principal conducting a search of a school student in the presence of a police officer was in fact a "state agent" bound by the Charter. The court formulated a test to be followed in determining whether someone is a state agent under section 8 of the Charter: "Applying the test to this case, it must be determined whether the search of the appellant would have taken place, in the form and in the manner in which it did, but for the involvement of the police."[23] As the primary purpose of the search was enforcing school discipline, the majority found that the vice-president was not a state agent in this case. There was no violation of Section 8 of the Charter in this case. This case is important as it means that an employer seizing an employee's computer, or an ISP conducting its own investigation of suspicious communications as per their user agreement may not be bound by the Charter (or similar legislation in other countries).

In seeking to obtain a warrant, enforcement agencies in Canada must, in addition to clearly defining what is sought by the warrant, establish that "there are *reasonable grounds* to believe [that what is sought by the warrant] *will afford evidence* with respect to the commission of an offence, or will reveal the where-abouts of a person who is believed to have committed an offence"[24] (emphasis added). A prudent anonymity network designer will therefore wish to ensure that the server will not produce any information that would have probative value with respect to the commission of an offence. The easiest way would be to give the police the ability to confirm for themselves whether or not the node is the originator of a communication. If the node is not the originator and the network does not allow the collection of evidence with respect to the whereabouts of the suspect, it may be unreasonable for the police to seize the server. This is precisely the design approach we will take in the next section.

IV. EXIT NODE REPUDIATION (ENR)

In this section, we propose a protocol that allows exit nodes in an anonymity network to prove that the traffic that they forward on behalf of other users does not originate from their IP address. We term our solution *exit node repudiation* (ENR).

---

23. *R. v M. (M.R.)* [1998] 129 CCC (3d) 361 (SCC).

24. An Act respecting the criminal law, R.S.C. 1985, c. C-46, as amended, art. 487 (1) (b). Similarly, law enforcement officers must, in the United States, draft a sworn statement that explains the basis for their belief that the search is justified by probable cause that that contraband, evidence, fruits, or instrumentalities of crime exist in the location to be searched. See "Searching and Seizing Computers and Obtaining Electronic Evidence in Criminal Investigations" (July 2002), Computer Crime and Intellectual Property Section, Criminal Division, United States Department of Justice, http://www.justice.gov/criminal/cybercrime/searching.html#searchmanual.

Previous technical research on the issue of dealing with unlawful messages has predictably forked between providing traceability for messages and providing measures that allow the anonymity network to prove it did not originate the messages without revoking anonymity. A representative work on the traceability side[25] presents a scheme that allows for the selective tracing of a single message in an anonymity network without revealing the origin of other messages. Alternatively, mathematical proofs can be constructed to prove that an output set of an anonymity network is a perfect random bijection of the input set without revealing the permutation,[26] a property termed *robustness*, which indirectly proves that the servers are not responsible for any data in the output set unless if they contributed a message to the input set. However, robustness proofs are burdensome and not very practical.

A. Defining Exit Node Repudiation

Phillipe Golle suggests a weaker but computationally feasible form of robustness termed *near-reputability*:

> An anonymity network is near-reputable for demarcation function f, batch output B, and set of players P_B if there exists a subset of the batch output $f(B) \subseteq B$ such that each message in $f(B)$ can be proven to have originated from some player $p \in P_B$ without revealing which one.[27]

We expect legal enforcement action to be levied against the exit nodes of an anonymity network and not the anonymity network as a whole. As a result, we prefer a definition of a near-reputable exit *node*. However, it is not sufficient for a node to have near-reputability by extension of operating in a near-reputable network. If all the nodes behave correctly and the exit node is in P_B, then this definition will suffice; but these assumptions are too strict. First, a major incentive to operating a node is the ability to mix in your own traffic (this way, you can ensure that one node in the network operates correctly), and so requiring the set of exit nodes to be disjoint from P_B is not ideal. Second, we expect some nodes will not behave correctly, whether maliciously or as a result of unintentional data corruption. Thus, we must consider the case that a message is not in $f(B)$ (i.e., is in $B - f(B)$). Such a message may have originated from the exit node in question, or it may have originated from any other node in the network.

---

25. Luis von Ahn and others, "Selectively traceable anonymity," *Sixth Workshop on Privacy Enchancing Technologies: Proceedings of PET 2006*, in *Lecture Notes in Computer Science* 4258 (Berlin: Springer-Verlag, 2006): 208–222.

26. Markus Jakobsson, Ari Juels, and Ronald L. Rivest, "Making mix nets robust for electronic voting by randomized partial checking," *Proceedings of the 11th USENIX Security Symposium* (2002): 339–353.

27. Golle, "Reputable mix networks," 55 (n. 2).

The situation is ambiguous and offers plausible deniability to all nodes. We have chosen to tighten definition 4.1.2 so that the consequent can be affirmed:

An exit node is g-reputable for batch output **B**, demarcation function **g**, and subset of all players **g(P)⊂P** if every message can be proven to have originated from a player in **g(P)** without revealing which one. Exit node repudiation (ENR) is the further condition that the only player in **P − g(P)** is the exit node itself.

ENR divides the set of all players into two subsets: the exit node in question, and everyone else. Our proposed solution will query an algorithm to determine if a message originated from the set of "everyone else." If the algorithm returns true, the message is proven to not have originated from the exit node. If the algorithm returns false, the message is proven not to have originated from the exit node. This definition is perfectly precise and resolves any ambiguity over the exit node's actions. If accused of originating a message, the message is either repudiable or nonrepudiable. This definition presumes that the anonymity network will only output messages if they properly conform to a protocol and drop everything else. It also excludes the exit node from serving as an exit node for its own anonymous messages; however, it can still originate anonymous messages and serve as an entrance or intermediary node to ensure the integrity of the chain.

B. A Nonmathematical Overview of ENR

We will consider the following participants in our solution: Alice who wishes to send an anonymous message to Bob through three nodes in an anonymity network (the exit node we refer to as **N₃**), and an issuing authority who we will call Justine. The ultimate goal of this protocol is to provide **N₃** with the ability to prove that Alice's message did not originate from its own IP address. To accomplish this, we will employ digital credentials that were proposed by Stefan Brands for identity management.[28] Digital credentials are similar to a digital certificate in that they enclose attributes in a signed document. However, these attributes can be selectively hidden or disclosed in a fine-grained manner. Moreover, the presentation of a digital credential cannot be linked to its issuance on the basis of the issuer's signature or other cryptographic materials contained in the credential.

The protocol begins with Alice contacting Justine for a digital credential that encloses her IP address. We allow law enforcement, for whom the proofs are ultimately intended, to assume the role of Justine or delegate it to an entity it trusts. Justine is free to choose the most trustworthy method she is aware of for

---

28. Stefan A. Brands, *Rethinking public key infrastructures and digital certificates: building in privacy* (Cambridge, MA: MIT Press, 2000), http://www.credentica.com/the_mit_pressbook.html. See also Stefan Brands, "A technical overview of digital credentials," (February 20, 2002), http://www.cypherspace.org/credlib/brands-technical.pdf.

verifying Alice's IP address. Verifying the integrity of an IP address is a nontrivial problem; however, it persists even if law enforcement is given the ability to trace a message as that message will be traced to an IP address that will need to be resolved to an identity.

Justine creates the credential in cooperation with Alice. Both Alice and Justine use private keys in this protocol: Justine to sign the credential and Alice to ensure that she will be the only person able to use the credential. During the interactive creation of the credential, Alice can blind the credential—a process that makes it unrecognizable to Justine without destroying the integrity of the IP address in the credential or Justine's signature on the credential. Later, Alice will show her credential to N_3 and Bob without fully revealing the attribute inside it. Either can use Justine's public key to verify that the credential was issued by her and is intact. However, because of the blinding process, N_3 or Bob can show Alice's credential to Justine, and Justine will not be able to determine that it is the same credential she issued to Alice. Therefore Alice is anonymous to N_3 and Bob due to the properties of the anonymity network, and she is anonymous to Justine due to the properties of the digital credential.

With Alice's digital credential alone, any attribute in it cannot be determined by anyone unless Alice actively participates in a showing protocol. To reveal an attribute, Alice claims that the credential contains a certain value, and then proves it does by showing a mathematical relationship that depends on her private key and on a random challenge (chosen by a publicly verifiable method). This proof is unforgeable by anyone without Alice's secret key, and because it is in response to a random challenge, the credential and proof cannot reused together.

To complete the protocol, Alice appends her credential and a proof to her messages. The proof does not reveal the attribute in the credential, Alice's IP address, as this would break her anonymity. Instead it proves a property of her credential: that it is not equal to the exit node's IP address. The scheme is shown in Figure 2.

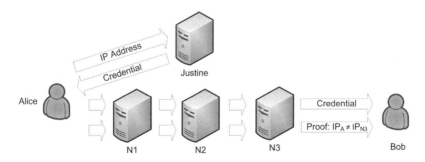

FIGURE 2. EXIT NODE REPUDIATION USING DIGITAL CREDENTIALS: ALICE IS ISSUED AN ANONYMOUS CREDENTIAL AND OFFERS A SIGNED PROOF THAT HER IP ADDRESS IS NOT EQUAL TO THE EXIT NODE'S IP ADDRESS. THIS CAN BE VERIFIED BY THE EXIT NODE AND BY THE RECIPIENT.

The remainder of this section will detail the cryptographic nature of the solution. It is included for completeness and is intended for computer scientists. It may be skipped over by those without knowledge of cryptographic primitives, as the high-level description above should suffice for understanding the design of the system.

C. Key Generation

The key generation protocol run by Justine to establish her public and private key is shown in Algorithm 1. Note that all algorithms are derived from the work of Stefan Brands.[29]

Algorithm 1: Key Generation for J

Input: Public parameter p.
Output: Private key $\langle s_1, s_2 \rangle$ and public key $\langle g_0, g, h \rangle$.
1   **J should:**
2   Choose random secrets $s_1, s_2 \leftarrow_r \mathbb{Z}_p$.
3   Choose random generator $g_0 \leftarrow_r \mathbb{G}_p$.
4   Compute $g = g_0^{s_1}$ and $h = g_0^{s_2}$.
5   **end**

Public parameter **p** is a suitably large prime number (e.g., 1024 bits), and $\mathbb{G}_p$ is the set of primitive roots in $\mathbb{Z}_p^*$. Justine's public key is $\langle \mathbf{g_0, g, h, p} \rangle$, and $\mathbf{s_1}$ and $\mathbf{s_2}$ are retained as her private key. Note that $\mathbf{s_1}$ and $\mathbf{s_2}$ cannot be recovered from the knowledge of the parameters in the public key without computing a discrete logarithm, a problem assumed to be computationally infeasible for large **p**.

D. The Issuing Protocol

The issuing protocol is shown in Algorithm 2. The key generation algorithm produces public parameters **g** and **h**, which are arranged by Alice into a credential of form $\mathbf{g^x h^\alpha}$ where **x** is Alice's IP address. This credential can be thought of as having secret key α applied to an encrypted attribute **x**. For every value of **x**, there is a unique value of α that will produce the same value for the credential. Thus if α is unknown, the value of **x** is perfectly hidden.

In Algorithm 2, Alice creates the credential, **I**, and Justine provides a signature certifying that is correct. Note that Justine never sees the value of **I** itself, so she cannot recognize **I** when Alice uses it. The signature on the credential, $\langle \mathbf{c, r} \rangle$, is more properly a private key certificate;[30] however, we refer to it as a signature for convenience. Once again, Justine does not see , only a blinded version of the values: $\langle \tilde{\mathbf{c}}, \tilde{\mathbf{r}} \rangle$. The protocol employs a hash function $\mathcal{H}$ that is assumed to be publicly known and cryptographically secure with an output space less than **p**.

---

29. Brands, *Rethinking*, 91 (n. 28).
30. Brands, *Technical Overview*, footnote 3 at 17 (n. 28).

Alice employs the hash to send a function of her credential, c, to Justine who calculates a suitable response using the value of x. Should Alice's credential not contain the same value of x that Justine uses in her response, the signature will not hold.

Algorithm 2: Issuing Protocol

Input: Public Key $\langle g_0, g, h, p \rangle$, A's IP address x, and (known only to J) Private Key $\langle s_1, s_2 \rangle$.
Output: Credential I and signature $\text{sig}(I) = \langle c, r \rangle$.

1   **A should:**
2   Choose random secret $\alpha \leftarrow_r \mathbb{Z}_p^*$.
3   Compute $I = g^x h^\alpha$.
4   **end**

5   **J should:**
6   Choose random secret $w \leftarrow_r \mathbb{Z}_p$.
7   Compute $z = g_0^w$ and send to A.
8   **end**

9   **A should:**
10   Choose random secrets $\beta_1, \beta_2 \leftarrow_r \mathbb{Z}_p$.
11   Compute $c = \mathcal{H}(I, (g^x h)^{\beta_1} \cdot g_0^{\beta_2} \cdot z)$.
12   Blind c by computing $\tilde{c} = (c + \beta_1) \bmod p$ and send to J
13 **end**

14 **J should:**
15   Compute $\tilde{r} = (\tilde{c}(s_2 + xs_1) + w) \bmod p$ and send to A.
16 **end**

17 **A should:**
18   Verify $z = g_0^{\tilde{r}}(g^x h)^{-\tilde{c}}$.
19   Unblind r by computing $r = (\tilde{r} + \beta_2 + c\alpha) \bmod p$.
20 **end**

E. The Showing Protocol

Algorithm 3 demonstrates how Alice can generate a signed proof that the attribute in her credential x is not the same as another attribute y. In this case, x is her IP address and y is the IP address of the exit node. The IP address of the exit node must be known by Alice. Although it is more efficient if she knows it a priori, it is possible for N_3 to send its IP address back through the anonymity network to Alice. In anonymity networks like Tor, Alice can choose her own exit node and thus know its IP address.

The showing protocol is based on a challenge-response, where the challenge requires nonce n. The nonce is used to ensure that the credential is not used by anyone other than Alice (i.e., only by those who know the secret key α). If the protocol were not challenge-response, the credential and proof could be replayed together by someone who observed Alice using a credential. We suggest that the nonce be a hash of the message, Bob's IP address, which both N_3 and Bob know, and a large random number collaboratively generated by the nodes in the anonymity network—the latter being published with a timestamp and periodically updated. This does not completely prevent replay attacks, but it severely limits

---

Algorithm 3: Signed Proof $(x \neq y)$

Input: $\langle g_0, g, h, p \rangle$, I, x, N_3's IP address y, and nonce n.
Output: $\langle a, r_2, r_3 \rangle$.

1   **A should:**
2   Choose random secrets $w_1, w_2 \leftarrow_r \mathbb{Z}_p$.
3   Compute $a = I^{-w_1} g^{yw_1} h^{w_2}$.
4   Compute $c_1 = \mathcal{H}(a, I, y, n)$.
5   Compute $\varepsilon = y - x$.
6   Compute $\delta = \varepsilon^{-1}$.
7   Compute $r_2 = c_1 \delta + w_1$.
8   Compute $r_3 = c_1 \alpha \delta + w_2$.
9   **end**

---

them to the same message and same receiver in the same window of time. This small cost is outweighed by the benefit of a standardized public nonce: Alice can compute the value of the nonce a priori and can create her response without having to exchange any information with N_3.

The proof itself is based on the observation that if **x** (Alice's IP address) and **y** (N_3's IP address) are different, their difference is nonzero and thus invertible within an appropriate group such that $(x - y)(x - y)^{-1} \equiv 1 \bmod p$. If **x** and **y** are the same, the difference is zero, which is noninvertible, leaving δ uncalculated (or zero if the inverse of zero is so defined). However, in the case that $\delta = 0$, then r_2 and r_3 would equal w_1 and w_2, respectively, and the verification procedure in Algorithm 4 would fail.

Algorithm 4: Verification Algorithm

Input: $\langle g_0, g, h, p \rangle$, $\langle I, c, r, a, r_2, r_3 \rangle$, y, n.
Output: TRUE or FALSE.

1   N_3 **should:**
2   Verify $c = \mathcal{H}(I, g_0^{r_0}(Ih)^{-c})$.
3   Compute $c_1 = \mathcal{H}(a, I, y, n)$.
4   Verify $I^{r_2} a = g^{r_2 y - c_1} h^{r_3}$.
5   **end**

The complete package that Alice delivers to N_3 is $\langle I, c, r, a, r_2, r_3 \rangle$. There are three distinct parts to this package: I is the credential; c and r are used to verify Justine's signature on the credential; and a, r_2, and r_3 are Alice's signed proof that **x** is not equal to **y**. This verification should be performed by N_3 before releasing the message to Bob. If either verification fails, the circuit should be destroyed. The package can also be forwarded to Bob, who also has all the information needed to verify the correctness of the credential. This is important because it allows law enforcement to satisfy themselves of ENR without requiring any *ex post* interaction with N_3.

The credentials can be independent of what anonymity network Alice wants to use or what message she will send; in fact, they could be used for any online purpose where Alice wants to prove some property about her IP address.

Furthermore, Alice can be issued a large quantity of credentials in bulk, each unique but with the same attribute, at some time prior to using an anonymity service as long as the issuing authority's public parameters are still known when she uses the credential. This changes the efficiency of the issuing protocol from a marginal cost to a fixed overhead cost.

One criticism of our proposed ENR protocols is the validity of x in the credential. For example, it is possible for a credential to be issued to a user at one IP address and then used by the same user to send a message from a different IP address. It would also be possible to use a proxy server to interact with credential issuer, so that the proxy server's IP address is encoded into the credential instead of Alice's. In response to this criticism, we note several things. First, Alice has no incentive to try to obscure her IP address from the credential issuer. The only property of her IP address that will be revealed is that it is not equal to N_j's, and any further proofs about x or its properties require Alice's private key. Second, lending and borrowing credentials is the equivalent of using someone else's computer—something that is possible independent of whether an anonymity network is even used. Third, lists of known proxy servers could be compiled and checked against. Finally, as noted previously, the legal alternative to ENR is traceability, and this problem applies equally to it. If a message is traced through an anonymity network to a supposed sender's IP address, there is no guarantee that the IP address is actually the sender's and not that of a proxy server or compromised machine.

V. CONCLUDING REMARKS

Recruiting server operators for anonymity networks is of primary importance to the functionality of the network. Network node servers must therefore not only be easy to set up but there must also be low risks for the node operators themselves for the dissemination of unlawful communications. Evading liability is of little comfort, however, if the node operator's computer is seized by police forces. The anonymous capability of the receiver to verify that the last communicator is not the originator of a message, without revealing the originator's IP address, could actually increase the network's anonymizing capability. Indeed, the threat of breaking the privacy of lawful communications for the purpose of uncovering unlawful ones would decrease.

We note that in Canada, a computer may be seized only if "there are *reasonable* grounds to believe [that the articles] will afford evidence with respect to the commission of an offence, or will reveal the whereabouts of a person who is believed to have committed an offence"[31] (emphasis added). It will be much harder to convince a judge that seizing an exit node will afford evidence of a crime if the

---

31. Criminal Code of Canada 487 (1) (b).

exit node can prove, without the node owner's knowledge or intervention, that it did not originate the communication and does not harbor information that could be linked to the sender.[32] Exit node repudiation provides a method of retaining the anonymity of the sender while presenting a response to the pertinent question of legal liability for the exit node as well as the practical hassles of equipment seizure. We hope this innovation is helpful in preserving the legality of anonymity networks and decreasing the aversion to volunteer as operators of servers in these networks.

---

32. This approach is also consistent with the need to establish "probable cause" in preparing a warrant to search and seize a computer under U.S. law. "Probable cause" has been defined by the U.S. Supreme Court as the establishment of "a fair probability that contraband or evidence of a crime will be found in a particular place." (*Illinois v Gates* [1983] 462 U.S. 213 at 238).

23. TRACKMENOT: RESISTING SURVEILLANCE IN WEB SEARCH

DANIEL C. HOWE AND HELEN NISSENBAUM[*]

TrackMeNot (TMN) is a Firefox browser extension designed to achieve privacy in Web search by obfuscating users' queries within a stream of programmatically generated decoys. Since August 2006, when the initial version of TMN was made publicly available free of charge, there have been over 350,000 downloads. TMN protects Web users against data profiling by simulating HTTP search requests to search engines with queries extracted from the Web. In an attempt to mimic users' search behavior, this basic functionality is augmented with several technical mechanisms: dynamic query lists (with RSS-based initialization),

* Many individuals and institutions have contributed in essential ways to this paper. For critical feedback on earlier versions of this paper, we thank audiences at the Haifa Center of Law and Technology Conference on Law of Search Engines (2006); the Conference on Computer Ethics: Philosophical Enquiry (2007); the Annual Meeting of the American Association, Eastern Division (2007); the A2K2 Conference, Information Society Project, Yale University (2007),; the Poynter Center, Indiana University, Bloomington (2007); and the Santa Fe Institute (2007). Additional thanks to Jinyang Li, Robb Bifano, the Mozilla foundation, MissingPixel™, and the NYU Media Research Lab. Thanks also to the reviewer for this volume, who guided us toward several key improvements. We are indebted for help with TrackMeNot itself to innumerable users around the world who cheered us, critiqued us, and generously offered marvelous tips. We extend a special thanks to Michael Zimmer for all these contributions, and more. Support for this project came from the NSF award CCR-0331542: *Sensitive Information in a Wired World* (or PORTIA: Privacy, Obligations, Rights in Technologies of Information Assessment). The idea for TrackMeNot was hatched in a series of stimulating conversations with PORTIA colleagues at a project retreat.

real-time search awareness, live header maps, burst-mode queries, and selective click-through. We describe each of these mechanisms, evaluate its strengths and weaknesses, and demonstrate how the consideration of values directly informed design and implementation. In the discussion section we conceptualize TMN within a broader class of software systems serving ethical, political, and expressive ends. Finally, we address why Web search privacy is particularly important and why TMN's approach, for the present, is both legitimate and necessary.

I. INTRODUCTION

In August 2005, public awareness of the ubiquitous practices of logging and analyzing users' Web search activities was heightened when front-page articles in the mainstream press revealed that the United States Department of Justice (DOJ) had issued a subpoena to Google for one week's worth of search query records (absent identifying information) and a random list of one million URLs from its Web index. These records were requested in order to bolster the government's defense of the constitutionality of the Child Online Protection Act (COPA), then under challenge. When Google refused the initial request, the DOJ filed a motion in a federal district court to force compliance. In March 2006, swayed by Google's arguments that the request imposed an unreasonable burden and would compromise trade secrets, undermine customers' trust in Google, and have a chilling effect on search activities, the court granted a reduced version of the first motion, ordering Google to provide a random listing of 50,000 URLs, and denied the second motion seeking the query records. One year later, however, the illusion that our Web searches are a private affair was further eroded when a news investigation revealed that in anonymized search query logs provided to the research community, the identities of certain searchers had been extracted from personal information embedded in search terms.[1] Other media reports followed detailing how the major search companies (Yahoo!, AOL, MSN, and Google) log, store, and analyze individual search query logs.

Setting aside the details of these two highly publicized cases, a few disquieting facts are evident: one, that search queries are systematically monitored, scrutinized, and indefinitely stored by search service providers; two, that for all we know, they are shared with third parties; and three, that policies governing these practices are unilaterally set by search companies with little indication,

---

1. Saul Hansell, "Marketers Trace Paths Users Leave on Internet," *New York Times*, September 15, 2006; Michael Barbaro and Tom Zeller, Jr., "A Face Is Exposed for AOL Searcher No. 4417749," *New York Times*, August 9, 2006.

or control, provided to individuals about what is done with their search records.[2] Since then, interest in the issue of search privacy has greatly expanded, drawing attention from citizens and advocacy organizations, scholars, and government agencies in the United States and beyond.[3] Responding to concerns surrounding the handling of search-query logs, search companies have offered several compromises, few of which, with the possible exception of those offered by Ask.com, have proved adequate or fully transparent. We believe these policies and practices challenge foundational moral and political principles of our society.

In Western liberal democracies, freedom of expression and of association are among a set of core values protected directly through laws (for example, the U.S. Constitution) and indirectly in the design of public institutions. Protection of liberties is also extended to activities considered supportive of these values, such as education, research, reading, and communication. As many of these activities have moved online, so the recognition has grown that robust civil rights protections are required online as well. It is no great leap to compare the role of public libraries and town squares in promoting core freedoms with that of the Web, functioning as it does not only as a repository of information, but also as a public and personal medium for communication and association. Just as we expect freedom and autonomy in the former, "brick and mortar" venues, so we should in the latter, digital electronic version. Information search and retrieval behaviors are part and parcel of these activities, profoundly reflecting who we are, what we care about, with whom we associate, and how we live our lives. For dealing with behaviors that open a window to the personal and political commitments of individuals, existing practices and policies of search engine companies seem clearly inadequate. Less clear, however, is how to pursue reforms to achieve necessary levels of protection, and who should or will lead the way.

Among potential agents of reform, the evident structure of incentives indicates that two with the greatest power to effect change—government, by pursuing new laws and regulations, and search companies, by revising internal policies—would be the least likely to support such change. Intransigence and inaction in the face of early challenges has borne this expectation out. For the first potential source of reform, government, search logs are an obvious and potentially important repository of information about individuals' interests and transactions, a valuable component of the vast stockpile of personal information assembled under the more lenient terms governing the collection and uses of

---

2. For example, court documents indicate that AOL, Yahoo!, and Microsoft had not been issued subpoenas because they had complied with the government's request.

3. See, for example, Michael Zimmer, "*The Quest for the Perfect Search Engine: Values, Technical Design, and the Flow of Personal Information in Spheres of Mobility*" (*unpublished dissertation, New York University, 2007*); "Privacy Issues and Behavioral Advertising," (Federal Trade Commission Town Hall Meeting, Washington, D.C., November 1–2, 2007).

information by the private sector.[4] Actions that might constrain access to such information or limit its availability are not likely to be attractive.

As for the second potential source of reform—search engine companies—we predicted that they would be unlikely to welcome external restraints on how their logs are treated and used. For a start, there is the general suspicion corporate actors hold for any imposition of third-party regulation. With their interests best served by as little oversight as possible, search companies attempt to mollify worried users and regulators by insisting that unconstrained access to and use of query data is an essential necessity for running their businesses, as, for example, explained by Eric Schmidt, CEO of Google: "the data helps us to improve services and prevent fraud."[5] Although there is no reason to doubt this explanation, it masks a story that is never front and center in search companies' public rhetoric, but lies behind concerns of critics and privacy advocates, namely, the ways unconstrained assembly and use of detailed search query logs factor into the massive profit engine of personalized advertising.

A third possible source of reform is new government regulation or legislation steered by direct citizen action or advocacy organizations such as the Electronic Privacy Information Center, Privacy International, the Center for Democracy and Technology, and the Electronic Frontier Foundation.[6] Although this approach has already borne fruit—see, for example, the widely publicized report "A Race to the Bottom"[7]—it will require an orchestrated effort of diverse parties, including many (government actors, search companies, advertisers, etc.) with a stake in maintaining unrestricted access to search logs. Ultimately, however, this is our soundest hope for lasting change, with measurable success most likely a long-term prospect.

TrackMeNot (TMN), a lightweight Firefox browser extension designed to ensure privacy in Web search by obfuscating a user's actual searches amidst a stream of programmatically generated decoy searches, represents a fourth alternative. Since August 2006, when the first version of TMN was made publicly accessible free of charge, there have been over 350,000 downloads.[8] Overcoming some

---

4 Michael D. Birnhack and Niva Elkin-Koren, "The Invisible Handshake: The Reemergence of the State in the Digital Environment," *Virginia Journal of Law & Technology* 6 (2003): 1–57.

5. "Eric Schmidt on Global Privacy Standards," *Peter Fleischer: Privacy . . . ?* September 19, 2007, http://www.peterfleischer.blogspot.com/ (accessed January 2, 2008).

6. Electronic Privacy Information Center, http://www.epic.org; Privacy International, http://www.privacyinternational.org; The Center for Democracy and Technology, http://www.cdt.org; Electronic Frontier Foundation, http://www.eff.org.

7. Privacy International, "A Race to the Bottom: Privacy Ranking of Internet Service Companies," http://www.privacyinternational.org/article.shtml?cmd[347]=x-347-553961 (accessed December 30, 2007).

8. TrackMeNot (http://trackmenot.org) may be downloaded from the Web site http://mrl.nyu.edu/~dhowe/TrackMeNot/ or from the Mozilla add-on Web site https://addons.mozilla.org/en-US/firefox/addon/3173.

of the obstacles inherent in similar software, TMN offers control directly to those most motivated to seek reform, providing a relatively near-term if imperfect solution. The hope, too, is that alternatives like TrackMeNot will bring reluctant parties into meaningful dialogue about search privacy.

II. DESIGN CONSTRAINTS

The constraints of technique, resources, and economics *underdetermine* design outcomes. To account fully for a technical design one must examine the technical culture, social values, aesthetic ethos, and political agendas of the designers.[9]

Our approach to the development of TrackMeNot builds on prior work that has explicitly taken social values into consideration in software design.[10] Throughout the planning, development, and testing phases, we have integrated values-oriented concerns as first-order "constraints" in conjunction with more typical engineering concerns such as efficiency, speed, and robustness. Specific instances of values-oriented constraints include transparency in interface, function, code, and strategy; personal autonomy, where users need not rely on third parties; social protection of privacy with distributed/community-oriented action; minimal resource consumption (cognitive, bandwidth, client and server processing, etc.); and usability (size, configurability, ease-of-use, etc.). Enumerating values-oriented constraints early in the design process enabled us to iteratively revisit and refine them in light of the specific technical decisions under consideration.[11] Where relevant in the following section, we discuss ways in which TMN's technical mechanisms benefited from this values-oriented approach.

III. TECHNICAL MECHANISMS

TrackMeNot, written in Javascript, C++, and XUL, is a Firefox browser extension designed to hide users' Web searches in a stream of decoy queries. Query-like phrases are harvested by TMN from the Web and sent, via HTTP requests, to search engines specified by the user. To augment this basic functionality and

---

9. Bryan Pfaffenberger, "Technological Dramas," *Science, Technology & Human Values* 17, no. 3 (1992): 282–312.

10. Batya Friedman, Daniel C. Howe, and Edward Felten, "Informed Consent in the Mozilla Browser: Implementing Value Sensitive Design," *Proceedings of the 35th Annual Hawaii International Conference on System Sciences* 8 (2002): 247; Mary Flanagan, Daniel C. Howe, and Helen Nissenbaum, "Values at Play: Design Tradeoffs in Socially-Oriented Game Design," *Proceedings of the SIGCHI Conference on Human Factors in Computing Systems* (2005): 751–760.

11. Flanagan, Howe, and Nissenbaum, "Values at Play" (n. 9).

frustrate attempts by search engines to distinguish between actual and generated queries, a range of mechanisms were implemented to simulate users' actual search behaviors more effectively. These mechanisms and the design constraints informing their implementations are described in the following sections.

A. Dynamic Query Lists

To keep control in the hands of users TMN operates solely on the "client," with no dependence on centralized servers or third-party sites during its operation. To support this design constraint while maintaining unique query lists for each instance of TMN's operation, we employed a mechanism we called *dynamic query lists*, which functions as follows. When downloaded, each instance of TMN is equipped with two mechanisms for creating an initial seed list of query terms: (1) a set of RSS feeds from popular Web sites (e.g., the New York Times, CNN, Slashdot) and (2) a list of popular queries gathered from publicly available lists of recent search terms.

When TMN is first enabled, an initial query list is constructed from both the results of requests to the RSS feeds and the list of popular terms.[12] From this list of seed terms (100 to 200 per client, as illustrated in Figure 23.1), TMN issues its initial queries. As operation continues, individual queries from this set are randomly marked for substitution. When a marked query is sent, TMN intercepts the search engine's HTTP response and attempts (nondeterministically) to parse a suitable "query-like" term from the HTML returned. If, according to a series of regular-expressions tests, the substitution is successful, this new term replaces the original query in the query list and the substitution mark is removed. This new term is now a member of the current query list (visible to users via the options panel described later) and included as a potential future substitution candidate. Additionally, each time the browser is started, a randomly selected RSS feed is queried and some subset of its terms are substituted into the seed list in the same manner. Over time, each client "evolves" a unique set of query terms,

```
fashion, tv guide, barbie, neopets, bit torrent, xbox, angelina jolie, nin-
tendo, jennifer lopez, jennifer aniston, local weather, anime, jokes, reci-
pes, music lyrics, games, iraq, global warming, north korea, hillary clin-
ton, barack obama, dick cheney, zodiac, music and lyrics, bone cancer, lena
katina, iran, canada, veronica mars, lost, the constitution, valerie
plame, karl rove, halliburton, Iceberg, global warming, world map, earth
day, southern cross, spiderman 3, 300 movie, borat, shrek, bill of rights,
ghost rider, Hawaii, dubai, mexico, freedom of speech, Chelsea, London,
kurt vonnegut, shaha riza, yuri Gagarin, knut, Virginia tech, wellness,
copyright law, health, yoga, fishing, golf, Israel, Syria, Iraq, Pakistan
```

FIGURE 23.1 SAMPLE FROM A TMN SEED LIST

12. The default list of popular search terms is included primarily for the rare case where some or all of the RSS feeds may be unavailable.

Turning carbon dioxide into fuel, Online Student Services, free essential software, business globalization solutions, National Pasta Association, Share your life with friends, Demand Financial Suite, este calitatea produselor, Chicago Symphony Orchestra, This film contains violence, Expects below Average, Emergency Contact, bodies have been established, residential real estate, American Heritage Month, Manhattan Athletic Club, healthcare support occupations, people cannot realize their dreams, green chemistry breakthroughs, Free online versions, Also find tools, Hope Press

FIGURE 23.2 SAMPLE FROM AN "EVOLVING" QUERY LIST

based in part on the random selection of queries for substitution, in part on the nondeterministic query extraction from HTML responses, in part on new terms gathered from continually updating RSS feeds, and in part on the continually changing nature of Web search results (generally yielding different results for the same search on different days). Figure 23.2 shows examples from the query list of Figure 23.1 after several weeks of TMN operation. With dynamic query lists, TMN is able to avoid the use of any central or shared (and necessarily trusted) repository of query terms while still frustrating the filtering schemes to which a static list is vulnerable.

B. Selective Click-Through

"Click-through" refers to the behavior of following one or more additional links on a results page after an initial search query. Although versions of TMN with this functionality were tested from early on, we chose not to release any until we were confident we could minimize potential impacts on existing business practices, specifically on those advertisers who paid search engines on a per-click basis. Current versions of TMN (since 0.6), however, employ what we call *selective click-through*, in which a series of regular-expression tests are used to identify and avoid potentially revenue-generating ads. Clicks are then simulated on one or more of the remaining links on the results page—either a "more results" button, a returned link to an external Web site, or a link internal to the search engine (e.g., "news" or "images"). Assuming that the search engines continue to format ad-related links in a relatively consistent manner, this appears to be an adequate solution for the time being.

C. Real-Time Search Awareness

Real-time search awareness (RTSA) is a second mechanism developed to improve TMN's capacity to mimic searchers' actual behavior. As TMN evolved, it became clear that it would need to "know," in real-time, when a user had initiated a search at one of the engines the user had selected. To facilitate this, the RTSA module examines each outgoing request from the browser and, via a series of regular expressions unique to each search engine, alerts TMN when the user is initiating a search. This feature has proved increasingly important, by enabling the development of several other mechanisms (described later) that require knowledge of the user's current behavior, whether it be initiating a search, performing a series of searches, or engaging in other, nonsearch activities.

D. Live Header Maps

Initially, development efforts focused on simulating the behavior of searchers in general. In later versions, however, several features were introduced that enabled TMN to adapt to the behavior of specific users. In addition to the *TMN Control Panel* (described later), which allows users to manually configure TMN to more closely mimic their own search behavior, *live header maps* operate automatically to adapt TMN-generated queries to specific data sent by the client browser. This data generally varies according to browser version and operating system, as well as the search habits of specific users. To facilitate this adaptive behavior, TMN maintains a set of variables (per search engine) representing the header fields and URLs for the search most recently issued by the browser (see Figure 23.3). These dynamically updating variables allow TMN to reproduce, in its own requests, the exact set of headers the browser last used.

Similarly, the specific URL last used to access a search engine is maintained, so that, for example, if one user searches via the Google toolbar and another via the Google home page, TMN requests will mimic the header values for each. The RTSA module facilitates this functionality by allowing updates to these variables only when the user is initiating a new search at one of the selected engines.

E. Burst-Mode Queries

Another functionality enabled by RTSA is termed *burst-mode querying*. In initial versions of the software, semi-random intervals were used to temporally space TMN requests, with the average of these intervals set by the user. To more closely mimic actual user behavior, burst mode triggers a batch of queries within close proximity to an actual user search (as detected by RTSA). By using this mode in

```
Url -> http://www.google.com/search?hl=en&client=firefox-
a&rls=org.mozilla%3Aen-US%3Aofficial&hs=nxM&q=hello&btnG=Search
User-Agent -> Mozilla/5.0 (Windows; U; Windows NT 5.1; en-US;
rv:1.8.1.11) Gecko/20071127 Firefox/2.0.0.11
Accept -> text/xml, application/xml, application/xhtml+xml,text/html;
q=0.9, text/plain; q=0.8, image/png, */*; q=0.5
Accept-Language -> en-us,en; q=0.5
Accept-Encoding -> gzip, deflate
Accept-Charset -> ISO-8859-1, utf-8; q=0.7, *; q=0.7
Keep-Alive -> 300
Connection -> keep-alive
Referer -> http://collection.eliterature.org/1/
```

FIGURE 23.3 AN EXAMPLE OF A HEADER MAP FOR A GOOGLE WEB SEARCH

conjunction with randomized intervals, users can "blend" the two behaviors, employing more or less of each as desired. Further, by limiting bandwidth and processing use (for both client and search engine) while dynamically adjusting to the use patterns of the individual user, burst-mode operation allows TMN to meet another design constraint, namely, lowered client (and network) resource-use. To further mimic user behavior, a subset of burst-mode queries are selected as variants on a "search theme." Specifically, a longer query is selected and permuted into a set of smaller, related queries constituting a "burst." For example, a search from a recent RSS feed, "dancing with the stars," was permuted into the following set of queries: "dancing," "stars," "dancing with," "with the stars," and "dancing with the stars"—all of which were sent sequentially over the course of a 60-second burst.

F. TMN Control Panel

The Control Panel provides a range of user-configurable parameters allowing users to customize TMN's behavior further (see Figure 23.4). These include options to enable/disable TMN itself, the status bar display, query bursting, and RSS feed management. Additionally, users may select which search engines

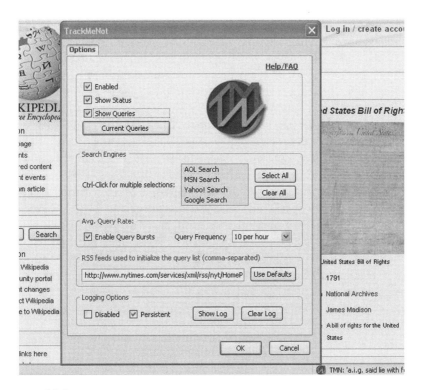

FIGURE 23.4 THE TRACKMENOT CONTROL PANEL

they wish to target, select an average query frequency, and manage TMN's logging options. Finally, the Control Panel features buttons enabling users to view the current query list and action logs within the browser itself and to access the TMN Web site for additional information.

The capacity for direct, real-time access to system operation (logs and query lists) was directly informed by the design constraint of transparency. Further, TMN was released as free and open-source under a Creative Commons license[13] with all source files included (in plain-text format) in every download, allowing technically sophisticated users to examine the inner workings of the code and verify that it has functioned as described. Similarly, our intentions and the specific technical decisions made to realize them are included in straightforward, nontechnical language on the TMN Web site (accessible directly from within the software itself).

IV. EVALUATION: STRENGTHS AND WEAKNESSES

Evaluation of TMN was performed iteratively throughout development and relied on solicited and unsolicited feedback from a range of groups, including users, developers, software reviewers at Mozilla (where TMN is cohosted), and a range of privacy and security advocates. Although the question of whether TMN in fact "worked" seemed at first, a simple one, we soon noticed how users' behaviors, goals, expectations, and perceived risks shifted the meaning of the question. Analysis of feedback was thus often a two-part process: first determining the users' orientations and then examining their feedback in light of their respective goals, concerns, and other priorities. Through such analysis we were able to identify at least four distinct groups of users, although individuals often identified with more than one group.

One group was interested in TMN's ability to cloak a searcher's identity and thus prevent all search activity from being traced back to the user. We recognized that there were at least four mechanisms through which a search could be identified: (1) identifying information included in search queries (name, zip code, phone number, Social Security number, etc.), (2) IP addresses linking searches across sessions, (3) explicit login to search engines (often for mail or other services), and (4) persistent cookies linking any of the preceding items to users' search activities.

Although various prototype versions of TMN had included code to generate arbitrary personal information to mask actual identifying information, this strategy was not energetically pursued. This was largely because TMN was not designed to mask IP addresses and thus could not prevent identification via the

---

13. Creative Commons, http://creativecommons.org/.

IP addresses logged by search engines with every query, or those maintained by users' ISPs. We pointed users interested in such capabilities to various proxy-based solutions[14] linked from the TMN FAQ. Contrary to the assertions of some critics,[15] TMN was presented not as a lightweight replacement for proxy-style solutions, but rather as a very different approach (with a distinctive set of strengths and weaknesses). For one thing, proxies generally require users to grant some degree of trust to a third party, whether a centralized server or some "exit node" representing the last hop in a "distributed" solution. In the past, such exit nodes have been abused for a variety of purposes, or simply blocked by those not wishing to receive their traffic (Google and Wikipedia being prime examples).[16] Although specific TMN users could also easily be blocked once they were identified by a search engine (at least for the duration of the activity connected with their IP address), it would take a very different kind of effort to block all such users. With Tor, for example, the identification of a single proxy node could result in the blocking of many thousands of user requests.

While a full discussion of the relative strengths and weaknesses of proxy-based solutions (including problems with internationalization and potential vulnerabilities to traffic analysis attacks[17]) is beyond the scope of this chapter, it is worth noting the relative "user-friendliness" of such solutions in comparison with TMN. At least at the time of this writing, proxy-based solutions have been notoriously difficult for nonexperts to set up, configure, and use. They generally involve multiple components (e.g., a local executable and a browser plug-in) that must be installed and configured to communicate correctly, at which point it is

---

14. Tor: Anonymity Online, http://www.torproject.org/.

15. Schneier on Security, http://www.schneier.com/blog/archives/2006/08/trackmenot_1.html.

16. In September 2007 Dan Egerstad, a Swedish security consultant, revealed that he had intercepted usernames and passwords for a large number of e-mail accounts by operating and monitoring Tor exit nodes. On November 15, 2007, he was arrested on charges stemming from discovering and publishing this information. As Tor does not, and by design cannot, encrypt the traffic between an exit node and the target server, any exit node is in a position to capture any traffic that is not encrypted at the application layer (e.g., by SSL). Although this does not inherently violate the anonymity of the source, it affords more opportunities for data interception by self-selected third parties, greatly increasing the risk of exposure of sensitive data by users who are careless or who mistake Tor's anonymity for security. From http://en.wikipedia.org/wiki/Tor_(anonymity_network). See also http://www.boingboing.net/2006/09/07/google-blocking-priv.html, by Cory Doctorow, discussing Google's blocking of Tor nodes, and http://simple.wikipedia.org/wiki/Wikipedia:Bans_and_blocks, regarding Wikipedia's policy of blocking all requests from anonymizing proxies (including Tor).

17. See Steven J. Murdoch and George Danezis, "Low-Cost Traffic Analysis of Tor," *Proceedings of the 2005 IEEE Symposium on Security and Privacy* (2005): 183–195, http://dx.doi.org/10.1109/SP.2005.12.

often still unclear exactly what the proxy is doing. This situation has been considered serious enough that privacy advocates (and third-party companies) have begun providing versions of popular software already containing, say, a Tor configuration to eliminate these difficulties for users.[18] This differs noticeably from TMN's one-click-and-restart installation and subsequent transparency of operation.

Of course, there is no reason these different approaches cannot be used together to additive effect. In fact, we believe this to be a rich area for future research. On the other hand, there are difficulties faced by Web users that are equally troublesome for all proposed solutions. An example is the increasingly common occurrence where a user wishes to search the Web while being explicitly logged on to a search engine, say for its free e-mail services. Here none of the proposed solutions, TMN, proxy server, or any other, offers much help.

Another group of users were worried about being targeted in connection with "hot-button issue" searches, that is, stigmatized or taboo subject descriptors such as "anarchy," "HIV," or "drug-use." To protect such users adequately, TMN would need to generate a range of similarly "hot" query terms, a capability with which we experimented throughout development, and that showed particular promise with the addition of dynamic queries in version 0.4. Having found that dynamically evolved queries tend to stay within general topic areas, we reasoned that with hot terms in the initial seed list, TMN would generate some number of extreme, or at the very least unwelcome, surprises—potentially offensive or NSFW (not safe for work) queries, for example, which would be displayed publicly in the browser's status bar. An open question, since the release of version 0.6, is whether, and to what extent, users in this group will be able to customize their RSS feeds (via the options panel) to maintain a query list with a significant number of "hot" queries. It would seem that such users could find, or even create, one or more RSS feeds matching the types of "hot" queries in which they were interested, though how such a list would "evolve" is unclear. Although a similar tactic has worked quite well for moving between languages (e.g., the queries in a French user's list will tend to stay in French as they evolve, assuming that their initial RSS feeds are in French), it will require significantly more testing before we can claim the same for "hot-button" queries.

The same issue was of concern to users in a third group, who instead wanted TMN to avoid hot-button issues entirely, citing worries relating to social stigma, job loss, and even potential arrest. This group, preferring generic and innocuous noise, was primarily interested in TMN as a way to mask the true nature of their online searches in order to avoid wholesale aggregation and profiling,

---

18. See OperaTor, a preconfigured bundle including the Opera Browser, Tor, and Privoxy, http://archetwist.com/opera/operator, and the XeroBank Browser, a Firefox derivative with an integrated Tor configuration, http://xerobank.com/xB_browser.html.

advertising and marketing purposes being the most salient. This clash between groups 2 and 3 is evident in the following two excerpts:

> Some of them would have to have HIV, some of them would have to be contemplating suicide, some of them would have to be anarchists, etc. Maybe you wouldn't want to have pedophiles and terrorists in the mix . . . or people growing hydroponic marijuana? (anonymous user from group 2)

> I downloaded and installed the plug-in you developed. I just turned it off when I noticed that the search term it had generated was "free russian porn boys." I'm a little confused. I understand the rationale of TrackMeNot, or I thought I did, but how does associating my IP with searches for gay porn fit in? If my employer logged this search, it could put my job at risk. (anonymous user from group 3)

The concerns of a fourth group of users stemmed from potential civil rights violations due to Web search monitoring. Although, like the third group, they also worried about the logging and aggregation of search queries for the purpose of profiling, they were interested in TMN mainly as a disruptive tool for protecting citizens against agents of government who might be engaged in various search surveillance and aggregation practices.

As we saw these groupings emerge and considered how they might guide the iterative process of feedback and development, it was clear (as per the popular saying) that "you can't please all the people all the time." Accordingly, it made sense to focus on what we believed to be TMN's greatest strength, that is, providing protection against aggregation and profiling of individual search queries. This meant anticipating various ways that TMN-generated queries might be detected and filtered, a process in which we were aided greatly by the helpful feedback of critics and enthusiasts alike who volunteered their insights and pointed out potential weak links. We conjecture, in large part due to the many iterations of the software emerging from such discussions, that considerable effort is now necessary to "defeat" TMN and successfully filter user queries from TMN queries. We further surmise that such filtering efforts would require significant resources and would still be likely to generate a number of false positives, that is, user queries mistakenly judged to be TMN generated.

The critiques we considered drew attention to various ways in which TMN queries could be different enough from user queries to inform a filtering algorithm able to distinguish between the two. We have worked most recently to address variations of this critique based on three aspects of TMN's operation: query timing, click-through behavior, and query term analysis. Timing-based critiques have argued that the timing patterns of TMN's queries, even when randomized, were different enough from those of human-generated queries to be detectable. Our solution to this critique was to add burst-mode querying so that TMN queries can occur only when users are actually searching at a targeted engine.

"Click-through" critiques pointed out that TMN queries were never followed by clicks to outgoing links on a search results page. The current version of TMN, however, implements "selective click-through" for nonadvertising links, as described previously. Yet even with this mechanism in place, a search company might be able to identify real users whenever an ad link *was* clicked. However, while one might "know" that queries leading to click-throughs on ads were user generated, inferring the converse—that queries yielding either unclicked results or those with click-throughs to non-ad pages were TMN generated—would surely result in a significant number of false positives (user-generated searches discarded along with those generated by TMN). Missing user queries of this type might be particularly costly to search companies aiming to improve their performance through personalized query log analysis.

A final version of the filtering argument focused on the nature of the query terms themselves, claiming that these were not "real" enough to fool a sophisticated learning algorithm with access to the vast amounts of data that search engines have already collected. Although dynamic query generation from actual Web pages has clear virtues, it is difficult to state how effective this strategy would be if search engines were willing to allocate significant resources to overcoming it. It is possible that a machine-learning algorithm focusing on query content, perhaps in conjunction with other factors, could be trained to identify a high percentage of TMN users, possibly even a high percentage of specific user queries themselves. The primary obstacles to defeating TMN are the costs of human and material resources (engineers, hardware, software), the cost of false positives (discarded user queries), potential costs to one's reputation (as a result of user and/or media outcry), and the potentially increasing maintenance costs necessary to handle past and future versions of TMN equipped with different behaviors. Although the extent of such costs are difficult to assess, especially in light of the vast resources available to search companies, we hope they are high enough to make other collaborative, trust-oriented compromises more attractive.

Unfortunately, we have little insight into the countermeasures that may be taken by targeted search engines. Unlike tactics such as URL format changes or IP address blocking, which will be readily apparent, approaches such as the filtering strategies discussed earlier might go unnoticed. We have thus far benefited from the "many eyes" of the developer and open-source communities, which have prodded us to consider such countermeasures, as well as from the evaluations of users and critics.

V. POLITICS THROUGH TECHNOLOGY

Conceiving of technologies as forms of political action builds on an intellectual tradition that includes figures such as Langdon Winner and Bruno Latour, who have argued that technical devices and systems may embody political and moral qualities. Lawrence Lessig and others[19] have explored these ideas in the context of information technologies and digital networks. Allied with this academic tradition, though not necessarily in direct dialogue with it, activist designers, software developers, and digital artists have leveraged the malleability of IT and the openness of network protocols to develop utilities that are expressive of particular political commitments or that mediate transactions in politically charged ways.[20]

The placement of control in the hands of users, which we adopted as one of TMN's design constraints, is not the only thing that makes it political. Its political character stems also from the way it enters into and attempts to reshape a particular aspect of individuals' relationships with social actors far more powerful than themselves on nearly every measurable dimension—including wealth, mastery over technology, and access to power. TMN, by allowing individuals to set limits on the flow of personal information, belongs in a class of technical tools that serve as amplifiers of social resistance or political voice. Relying on neither the largesse nor the permission of others, most notably those with potentially clashing interests, TMN provides for some users a means of expression, akin to a political placard or a petition. For others it provides a practical means of resistance similar to that described by Gary T. Marx, where individuals take advantage of the blind spots inherent in large-scale systems of surveillance.[21]

VI. IS TRACKMENOT MORALLY DEFENSIBLE?

In previous sections we addressed some of TMN's technical limitations, many drawn to our attention by critics. Here we will discuss challenges to TMN's moral standing. Those we will *not* discuss, however, are accusations that TMN makes life easier for the likes of pedophiles and terrorists by enabling them to hide from public view. Although these are important concerns, we believe they call attention to the more general challenge of living in a free society where protecting the rights of speech, association, and action inevitably creates space for exercising these liberties in ugly and hurtful ways. In order to remain free,

---

19. Friedman, Howe, and Felten, "Informed Consent in the Mozilla Browser," 247 (n. 9); Lucas Introna and Helen Nissenbaum, "Shaping the Web: Why the Politics of Search Engines Matters," *Information Society* 16, no. 3 (2000): 186–189.

20. Examples include GNU, http://www.gnu.org/; Creative Commons tools, http://creativecommons.org/; P3P, http://www.w3.org/P3P/; Adrian Ward's AutoIllustrator, http://www.medienkunstnetz.de/works/autoillustrator/; Wikipedia, http://www.wikipedia.org/; and the Radical Software Group's Carnivore, http://r-s-g.org/carnivore/.

21. Gary T. Marx, "A Tack in the Shoe: Neutralizing and Resisting the New Surveillance," *Journal of Social Issues* 59, no. 2 (2003): 369–390.

a society strives to minimize or prevent the hurt and ugliness without diminishing the relevant liberties. Thus, this is not a problem related to TMN only, nor is it one that we can make progress on here.

Instead we focus on criticisms addressing specific features of TMN. One such criticism accuses TMN of being no different from "spamware" or "denial of service" (DoS) attacks, generally wasting network bandwidth and clogging the servers of search engines. Naturally, we resist these critiques. By invoking rhetorical terms such as "spam" and "DoS" critics seek to cast doubt on our efforts and intentions by associating TMN with activities generally deemed reprehensible; we see these accusations, however, as question begging. After consulting numerous sources, we are confident that TMN fits no reasonable, commonly accepted definition of either DoS or spamware. In Wikipedia, for example, a "denial of service" attack is defined as "an attempt to make a computer resource unavailable to its intended users. Typically the targets are high-profile Web servers, and the attack attempts to make the hosted Web pages unavailable on the Internet."[22] And spam is defined as "the abuse of electronic messaging systems to send unsolicited bulk messages, which are generally undesired."[23] Neither is applicable to TMN.

Behind the rhetoric of DoS and spam, however, lies a question that deserves attention: the extent of TMN's impact on servers and bandwidth. This concerns us as well, as we had set forth with the principle of minimizing resource consumption as a design constraint, as stated earlier. The relevant facts are that TMN's resource usage is relatively low—tiny, in fact, compared with common components of Web traffic such as animations, music, and video—and consequently it is unlikely to have any appreciable effect on network bandwidth. It is conceivable, however, depending on the number of users and their use patterns (e.g., the mode and frequency settings they select), that TMN might have an impact on search engine performance by placing additional demands on server processing and bandwidth. Our intention and our expectation, based on the current usage and trajectory, is that the impact on search engines will be minimal. Universal deployment is not the goal of the project; our intention is to offer a degree of protection to individuals who may feel threatened and to afford such users a voice in the evolving debate over Web search privacy. We are confident that search companies will take steps to address user dissatisfaction long before TMN usage reaches significant proportions.

We still have not addressed a key driver of this critique that TMN "wastes" bandwidth and server resources. We know, both from anecdotes and through search statistics aggregated by Google Zeitgeist, the Lycos 50, and other such services,[24] that people search the Web for a vast range of items of information.

---

22. Wikipedia, http://www.wikipedia.org (accessed March 29, 2007).

23. Wikipedia, http://www.wikipedia.org (accessed March 29, 2007).

24. Google Zeitgeist, http://www.google.com/press/zeitgeist.html; Lycos 50, http://50.lycos.com/.

Judging by perennial favorites—the likes of "Britney Spears," "Paris Hilton," and "Pokemon"—we conclude that most search subjects are not terribly weighty. Further, people and enterprises download and distribute large video, music, and image files with no apparent socially redeeming value, and search companies constantly seek out new customers and markets with the hope of enticing to their services millions of new users from all over the world. All these activities use bandwidth and place heavier and heavier burdens on servers and services, but they are generally not criticized for wasting network and server resources. Why is this? These patterns reveal an underlying presumption about what constitutes proper use of the network; the aforementioned uses, however trivial, are assumed to be legitimate, whereas TMN-generated traffic is not. We challenge this assumption. Because adequate privacy protection is incorporated into neither the technology of search engines nor the policies governing it, steps taken by individuals to protect themselves do constitute a legitimate draw on resources, certainly no less legitimate than the myriad of others drawing on these resources. In this regard, we place TMN in a category along with uses of encryption technologies for securing transactions and proxies for anonymization (e.g., Tor). Despite the latter's incremental draw on resources, these additional burdens are generally understood as warranted and at times necessary. The same goes for TMN.

Another critique charges that TMN is morally indefensible because it violates search engines' terms of service (ToS) forbidding access by automated means such as scripts and Web crawlers (e.g. http://www.google.com/accounts/TOS). Although the legal enforceability of Web site ToS is a broader question than concerns us here, the active debates surrounding it provide valuable input.[25] Since the very beginnings of the Web, a complex and constantly evolving system of social norms, derived from a combination of law, morality, and affordances of architecture, has formed the background against which online actions and transactions are evaluated. Terms of service can be controversial because they unilaterally impose obligations on users that go beyond those implied by the background norms—in particular, a ToS designed to control users' experiences of a Web site or service. To be sure, Web site owners' preferences in setting the terms of engagement deserve consideration, but these expressed preferences do not automatically imply moral obligations, particularly ones that society needs to honor and defend. Owners' preferences need to be weighed against a range of other considerations.

---

25. The authors acknowledge the limitations of their perspective on legal issues, formed exclusively with reference to the United States legal system; Dan L. Burk, "The Trouble with Trespass," *Journal of Small and Emerging Business Law* (1998): 3; Maureen A. O'Rourke, "Is Virtual Trespass an Apt Analogy?" *Communications of the ACM* 44, no. 2 (2001): 98–103; Orin S. Kerr, "Cybercrime's Scope: Interpreting 'Access' and 'Authorization' in Computer Misuse Statutes," *NYU Law Review* 78, no. 5 (2003): 1596–1668.

One such consideration is efficiency. Legal discourse cautions that enforcement of the arbitrary preferences of Web site owners "for this or that type of usage,"[26] subjecting users to exclusions and exceptions, would result in the need for users to pick their way cautiously through the Web. Such a requirement would degrade the efficiency and positive externalities of the Web.[27] A Web requiring such cautious engagement represents a sadly diminished alternative to the Web extolled for its provision of freewheeling access to vast repositories of information goods and services.

Fairness is another consideration. Since search engines are able to generate value by skimming information off the Web by means of crawlers, thereby benefiting from the willingness of others to place informational resources online with no strings attached, it is unfair to prevent others from doing the same. Fairness precludes making an exception of oneself, imposing arbitrary restrictions on how others may use the resources one has placed on the open Web, while taking full advantage of the norms of open access embraced by others. Legal scholar Dan Burk argues that granting Web site owners overly strong exclusionary rights would make it possible for them "to free-ride upon the benefits of the network, while at will avoiding contribution of such benefits to others."[28]

Although efficiency and fairness are important considerations, they do not necessarily trump the claims of search engines (expressed in ToS) against any and all automated access. Essential to TMN's defense is its role in promoting the morally legitimate ends of user privacy and autonomy in Web searching and, ultimately, freedom of expression, association, and inquiry. Also relevant is TMN's relatively low imposition on resources. In other words, even if a case could be made for favoring the preferences of search engine developers, as expressed in ToS, in opposing *some* forms of automated query (e.g., ones that are frivolous and seriously undermine performance), fairness and efficiency considerations should place the burden of proof on the search companies; in the case of TMN, we believe, they ought not prevail.

VII. FUTURE WORK AND CONCLUSION

TMN provides individuals a means of both expressing and asserting a commitment to privacy in Web searches without having to depend on the largesse or intervention of third parties. Although it is fully functional, TMN is best

---

26. Burk, "The Trouble with Trespass," 3 (n. 24).

27. Some, like Orin Kerr, have argued that only those ToS expressible in "code" should be enforceable. We imagine such protocols as robots.txt would qualify, but the question is a larger, more general one than can be adequately addressed here.

28. Burk, "The Trouble with Trespass," 3 (n. 24).

considered a prototype, a proof of concept for a particular approach to privacy, that is, privacy through obfuscation. As discussed, TMN's greatest potential lies in its capacity to protect individuals against profiling, and its greatest challenge is to stay abreast of evolving search services themselves. Beyond the challenges of simply keeping up, there are challenges of providing rigorous, scientific assessments of performance as well as of improving the system in several ways.

A scientific means of evaluating TMN's performance, or the performance of any system adopting this approach, needs to address at least one key question, which we are not equipped to answer: what measure one employs to confirm that user-generated searches have been successfully obfuscated by TMN-generated searches. To be efficacious, TMN needs to introduce into the set of user search queries not only sufficient noise, and not only noise in the correct format, but noise of the right kind in relation to the type of protection being sought and the information being mined. Such needs are likely to turn not only on the statistical analysis of signal-to-noise ratios, but also on a practical understanding of how search query data is actually mined and how users are profiled.

Future work on TMN will focus on making various improvements to the search query terms. One alternative is to incorporate into TMN further mechanisms that effectively generate hot-button and identifier queries. As mentioned in an earlier section, after going some distance along this path, we chose not to follow it. A second avenue for future work is to explore P2P approaches to generating both search queries and timing patterns as a possible alternative to current mechanisms. A central challenge is to develop a system that meets functional criteria as well as the design constraints discussed early in this paper, such as usability and independence from third parties (i.e., central servers or potentially untrustworthy third parties.) We are not sure this is practically achievable.

We conclude with a philosophical point. TrackMeNot operates in an environment that is not only technologically complex, as we have tried briefly to demonstrate, but is also socially complex. Search engines provide an important service in a volatile and competitive marketplace in which search query logs are a valuable resource and source of revenue. For individuals, however, whether or not they view their discrete acts of search and retrieval as sensitive, patterns recorded over time potentially open a window into their lives, interests, and ambitions. Thus, such faculties are not only a source of individual vulnerability, but they could interfere with the rights to free and autonomous inquiry, association, and expression that are essential to sustaining a healthy democratic society. Consequently, there remains a tension in the relationship between individual users, important political values, and search service providers. In a better world, this tension would be resolved in a transparent, trust-based mutual accommodation of respective interests.

Instead, users who are concerned with privacy in searching perceive little transparency and few credible assurances in the policies of search engine companies that privacy will ever trump pursuit of direct profit as a priority. In light of this, trust-based mutual accommodation of necessity gives way to an adversarial relationship. TMN, a tool for *this* world and *this* relationship, gives users a say in shaping the terms of engagement with search companies. Although obvious measures of TrackMeNot's success include impenetrable camouflage and 100 percent adoption, we would prefer a world in which TMN is not needed.

PART III

ANONYMITY

Building on our investigation of the various concepts and technologies pertaining to identity and identification in Part II, Part III offers a snapshot of the laws governing our ability or inability to be anonymous. Scholars from five North American and European jurisdictions—Michael Froomkin from the United States; Carole Lucock and Katie Black from Canada; Ian Lloyd from the United Kingdom; Simone van der Hof, Bert-Jaap Koops, and Ronald Leenes from the Netherlands; and Giusella Finocchiaro from Italy—survey the place of anonymity across the legal domain and assess the law as it currently stands in each country. Although each survey can be read in isolation, it is interesting to consider some of the similarities and differences among and between them.

No "right to anonymity" is explicitly protected by any of the five jurisdictions' constitutions or human rights provisions. However, anonymity may enjoy limited protection as an acknowledged component of another right or freedom, in particular, privacy, freedom of expression, restrictions on state search and seizure, and provisions related to protecting liberty and life. In fact, it would seem that there is no coherent or integrated approach to anonymity in any jurisdiction. Rather, the law has developed piecemeal in a number of disparate public and private law areas. Consequently, the meaning of anonymity is contextually situated and may vary from one area of law to another.

All in all, each jurisdiction reports scant protection of anonymity, a preference for identifiability, and an increasing encroachment on areas of de facto anonymity that the law, to date, has not protected. Each author discusses the law's specific responses to the network society along with descriptions of existing approaches to anonymity in a broad range of areas within their jurisdictions. Despite differences, there is a great deal of similarity to the legal approach in each country, aided perhaps by adherence to or influence of international agreements, treaties, and directives. In addition, legal protections for anonymity in all five jurisdictions appear to be shrinking, as the focus on safety and security has repeatedly trumped the call or justification for anonymity.

For example, each jurisdiction has considered a requirement to carry a national identity card, and this has created prominent debate in most. The introduction of an all-purpose identity card is a significant change that promises to have a chilling effect on anonymity. This has been presaged in some jurisdictions by judicial decisions that have lowered the threshold of the legal grounds necessary for law enforcement personnel to detain persons and to require them to identify themselves. Even when a national identity card has not been introduced, a number of jurisdictions have added biometrics and radio frequency identification chips to "smart" drivers' licenses, in effect turning them into de facto identity cards.

Apart from a general requirement to identify oneself to the state, each jurisdiction reports instances in which identification is statutorily required. Examples include producing a driver's license when using public highways and providing identifying information in order to conduct banking transactions. Courts and tribunals have similarly upheld requirements that individuals identify themselves for certain commercial purposes such as obtaining a refund or exchanging goods. In all jurisdictions, there has been an increase in these calls for context-specific mandatory identification and a consequent reduction in the ability to transact or enter commercial or noncommercial relations anonymously.

The use of surveillance in public spaces, particularly video surveillance, is clearly increasing in all jurisdictions. The de facto anonymity once enjoyed in these spaces has, as a consequence, diminished, and to date the law seems to be enabling the deployment of technologies of surveillance rather than protecting anonymity.

The appropriate role of and the degree of control over the providers of communications services, especially Internet service providers, is another area in which the law in currently in flux. The combined interests of law enforcement agencies and the private sector in ensuring that identity can be revealed on demand has resulted in significant pressure to require service providers to collect and maintain records for identification purposes and, in some countries, to allow identifying information to be disclosed to authorities without judicial preauthorization or oversight.

Although there are remarkable similarities in approach among the five jurisdictions, there are also some interesting differences. For example, the United States reports that a strong adherence to the open court principle has limited the use of a pseudonym in criminal and private law proceedings. This is in stark contrast to other jurisdictions where the use of a pseudonym is supported both by the courts and by legislation as a means to protect and promote the pursuit of legal claims. Although in these jurisdictions the use of a pseudonym and a publication ban does not usually shield facts or the identity of witnesses from an accused, there are exceptions. In Canada, undercover operatives may have their identity concealed, and in the United Kingdom, recent legislation now permits the granting of witness anonymity orders to protect the witness's anonymity. Interestingly, Canada also reports that permission to use a pseudonym to protect privacy may now be given to those persons who have used an online pseudonym to enable them to continue to use it in court.

Other differences are equally noteworthy. The UK law enforcement DNA database has been particularly controversial, especially given its size and the wide set of circumstances that allow the government to add information to it. Although other jurisdictions have similar databases, the restrictions on information inclusion and use appear far more stringent. The Netherlands reports growing concerns over electronic voting, including the use of the Internet for remote balloting. As other jurisdictions contemplate or implement e-voting, many wonder how the traditional protection of voter secrecy and the assurance of system integrity and accountability will be preserved and protected. Italy reports a number of interesting provisions that legally protect the right to be anonymous in some circumstances, including entering a detoxification center, seeking help for social problems, and protecting the name of the mother at the time of childbirth.

Each author expresses a general concern as to the direction the law is taking and calls for greater attention to and protection of anonymity as a necessary component of protecting valued human rights such as liberty, dignity, and privacy.

24. ANONYMITY AND THE LAW IN THE UNITED STATES

A. MICHAEL FROOMKIN

INTRODUCTION

Surveys suggest that the public is increasingly concerned about privacy issues, but post-9/11 concerns have motivated the federal government, in particular, to develop a number of initiatives that lessen the scope for anonymous communication and behavior in the United States. Some of the core protections, however, rest on pre-9/11 constitutional foundations, and the courts are only beginning to hear challenges to these new statutes and programs. That there has been a lurch against anonymity since September 2001 is indisputable; how great a lurch and for how long major parts of it will last remains uncertain and is, in fact, deeply contested.

Underlying this contest is the lack of a consensus as to when and whether anonymity is good, at least outside the realm of core political speech. Anonymity has both valuable and harmful consequences, and different persons weigh these differently. Some, focusing on anonymity's contribution to many freedoms, argue that anonymity's benefits outweigh any likely harms it may cause, or that the harms (e.g., censorship, lack of privacy) associated with trying to ban anonymity are not worth any benefits that could ensue. Others, perhaps focusing on the harmful actions that can be accomplished anonymously (libel, spamming, massive copyright violations), look at anonymity and see dangerous license. Their conclusion is that at least some forms of anonymity should be banned.

Generalization about U.S. law regulating anonymity is difficult because U.S. law treats it in a patchwork fashion, owing to the nation's constitutional and federal structure. At present, U.S. law enjoys a strong, reasonably well-entrenched core constitutional protection for anonymous political speech, and this seems likely to endure. As one moves away from this core and includes speech that cannot so easily be characterized as political or religious, legal protection for anonymity generally becomes less clearly protected as the law begins to accumulate some uncertainty. The public law regulation of anonymity is mediated through a mix of federal and occasionally state constitutional provisions, and also a growing patchwork of state and federal legislation. The private law regulation of anonymity is even more decentralized, as it shares all the sources of the public law regulation, albeit sometimes in an attenuated fashion, but also frequently involves state statutes and court decisions.

I. BASELINE PROTECTION OF ANONYMITY IN (FEDERAL) CONSTITUTIONAL LAW

The U.S. Constitution does not guarantee a right to be anonymous in so many words. The First Amendment's guarantees of free speech and freedom of assembly (and whatever right to privacy exists in the Constitution) have, however, been understood for many years to provide protections for at least some, and possibly a great deal of, anonymous speech and secret association.

A superficial examination of the recent decisions of the U.S. courts might fail to disclose much ambiguity. On the surface, the Supreme Court's recent decisions evince a strong, repeated endorsement of the legitimate role of anonymity in political discourse. The cases are replete with references to the close relationship between the right to anonymous association and the role that anonymous communication legitimately plays in political discourse. Anonymity has basked in its association with good causes, including the civil rights movement[1] and, as described below, both religious liberty and civic activism.

Game, set, match? Not at all.

Balancing—and in time perhaps overbalancing—these legal protections for anonymity are a number of countervailing legal initiatives and even trends, notably a vast increase in the technical and legal capability to monitor electronic communications at home and abroad, and legal developments suggesting that

---

1. *NAACP v Alabama ex rel. Patterson*, 357 U.S. 449 (1958).

communication intermediaries must assist the governments and others who seek to discover the identity of anonymous authors. The Bush administration has not been shy about suggesting that it needs the broadest access to communications intelligence for national security, and too few have gainsaid that viewpoint. Meanwhile, a number of traditional civil law doctrines, applied in a doctrinally predictable fashion, combine to provide considerable powers for civil litigants to demand, usually upon the showing of good cause, the disclosure of the identity of otherwise anonymous speakers in a variety of legal settings. And the Supreme Court's most recent relevant decision, although somewhat equivocal as to the details, did uphold a state requirement that persons identify themselves to police officers armed with "reasonable suspicion" when asked to do so.

The Supreme Court has repeatedly noted the existence of a "profound national commitment to the principle that debate on public issues should be uninhibited, robust, and wide-open."[2] Political speech receives the highest constitutional protection because it "occupies the core of the protection afforded by the First Amendment"[3]; other types of speech, notably "commercial speech," sometimes receive a reduced level of First Amendment protection. Core political speech need not center on a candidate for office, but can affect any matter of public interest—especially if it is an issue in an election.[4]

The leading case on anonymous political speech is *McIntyre v. Ohio Elections Commission*.[5] In 1988, Margaret McIntyre distributed some leaflets outside the Blendon Middle School in Westerville, Ohio. Indoors, the superintendent of schools was discussing raising the school tax, which would require approval in a referendum; Ms. McIntyre opposed it. Some of the leaflets had her name; others were signed "Concerned Parents and Taxpayers." The unsigned leaflets violated a section of the Ohio Code that required any general publication designed to affect an election or promote the adoption or defeat of any issue or to influence voters in any election to contain the name and address of the person responsible for the leaflet. After a complaint by school officials, lodged five months later, Ms. McIntyre was fined $100 by the Ohio Elections Commission, and this fine provided the occasion for all that followed. Ms. McIntyre died while the case was wending its way through three levels of Ohio state courts, but her husband, as executor of her estate, appealed the adverse decision of the Ohio Supreme Court to the U.S. Supreme Court, which issued its decision in 1995, some seven years after the imposition of the fine.

In tone, the *McIntyre* opinion is a ringing affirmation of the right to anonymous political speech; arguably the defense of anonymity might be stretched

---

2. *New York Times Co. v Sullivan*, 376 U.S. 254, 270 (1964).
3. *McIntyre v Ohio Elections Comm'n*, 514 U.S. 334, 346 (1995).
4. See *First Nat. Bank of Boston v Bellotti*, 435 U.S. 765, 776–777 (1978).
5. *McIntyre v. Ohio Elections Commission*, 514 U.S. 334 (1995).

even further. "Under our Constitution," Justice Stevens wrote for seven members of the Court, "anonymous pamphleteering is not a pernicious, fraudulent practice, but an honorable tradition of advocacy and of dissent."[6] Thus, "an author's decision to remain anonymous, like other decisions concerning omissions or additions to the content of a publication, is an aspect of the freedom of speech protected by the First Amendment" and "the anonymity of an author is not ordinarily a sufficient reason to exclude her work product from the protections of the First Amendment."[7] To those, like Justice Scalia in dissent, who worried that anonymous speech might be abused, Justice Stevens replied that "political speech by its nature will sometimes have unpalatable consequences" but "our society accords greater weight to the value of free speech than to the dangers of its misuses."[8]

Similarly, in *Watchtower Bible and Tract Soc. of New York, Inc. v. Village of Stratton*,[9] the Supreme Court struck down a village ordinance requiring all door-to-door solicitors and canvassers—whether religious or commercial—to register with the village, and to disclose their identities and the reason for which they wished to go door-to-door. The Watchtower Bible and Tract Society (known also as Jehovah's Witnesses), a religious group that wished to go door-to-door in Stratton in order to proselytize, challenged the ordinance as unconstitutional. The Supreme Court agreed, holding that the "breadth and unprecedented nature of this regulation" meant that it violated the First Amendment: "Even if the interest in preventing fraud could adequately support the ordinance insofar as it applies to commercial transactions and the solicitation of funds, that interest provides no support for its application to petitioners, to political campaigns, or to enlisting support for unpopular causes."[10]

Despite these ringing words, how broad a right one has to be anonymous in the United States remains somewhat unclear, as difficult cases are precisely those in which exceptions are made to fit facts that sit uncomfortably within the rules that apply "ordinarily."[11] To date, the Supreme Court has addressed the easy cases such as broad prohibitions of anonymous political speech. As a result, it is now clear that ordinances prohibiting all anonymous leafleting, like the one in *McIntyre*, are an unconstitutional abridgment of free speech.[12] Thus, in

---

6. *Ibid.*, 357.

7. *Ibid.*, 341.

8. *Ibid.*, 357.

9. *Watchtower Bible and Tract Soc. of New York, Inc. v Village of Stratton*, 536 U.S. 150 (2002).

10. *Ibid.*, 168.

11. For a contrary view that "*McIntyre* will prove to be dispositive" in providing First Amendment protections to anonymous political speech, see Richard K. Norton, Note, "*McIntyre v. Ohio Elections Commission*: Defining the Right to Engage in Anonymous Political Speech," *North Carolina Law Review* 74 (1996): 553.

12. *Ibid.*; *Talley v California*, 362 U.S. 60 (1960).

McIntyre Justice Stevens found the state's "interest in preventing fraudulent and libelous statements and its interest in providing the electorate with relevant information" was insufficiently compelling to justify a ban on anonymous speech that was not narrowly tailored.[13] And in *Watchtower*, the Court found the village's attempt to justify the ordinance on grounds of "protecting the privacy of the resident and the prevention of crime" to be unconvincing, given the facts.

There is no doubt that the Supreme Court has been solicitous in considering the need of dissidents and others to speak anonymously when they have a credible fear of retaliation for what they say. Thus, the Supreme Court has struck down several statutes requiring public disclosure of the names of members of dissident groups.[14] But the Court has consistently left the door open to finding a compelling state interest which would justify overcoming the right to privacy in one's political associations and beliefs—if state interest is evident. Nothing in *McIntyre* or *Watchtower* really changes this. In *McIntrye*, Justice Stevens carefully distinguished earlier cases upholding statutes that sought to preserve the integrity of the voting process.[15]And indeed, in earlier cases the Supreme Court sometimes upheld more targeted restrictions on anonymous political speech and association, such as the Federal Regulation of Lobbying Act 2 U.S.C. § 267, which requires those engaged in lobbying to divulge their identities.[16] As a constitutional matter, therefore, the anonymity issue remains far from resolved even for the most highly protected category of speech.

To be sure, there are doctrinal grounds for near-absolutist protection for anonymity. In *Tattered Cover, Inc. v. City of Thornton* the Colorado Supreme Court interpreted both the state and federal constitutions to "protect an individual's fundamental right to purchase books anonymously, free from governmental interference."[17] It thus required a "heightened showing" by law enforcement officers before they would be allowed to execute a search warrant seeking customer purchase data from an innocent bookstore. As the Court explained,

> When a person buys a book at a bookstore, he engages in activity protected by the First Amendment because he is exercising his right to read and receive ideas and information. Any governmental action that interferes with the willingness of customers to purchase books, or booksellers to sell books, thus implicates First Amendment concerns. Anonymity is often essential to the

---

13. *McIntyre*, 348 (n. 5).

14. See *Brown v Socialist Workers' 74 Campaign Comm.*, 459 U.S. 87, 91 (1982) (holding that the "Constitution protects against the compelled disclosure of political associations"); *Shelton v Tucker*, 364 U.S. 479, 485–487 (1960) (holding invalid a statute that compelled teachers to disclose associational ties because it deprived them of their right of free association).

15. *McIntyre*, 344 (n. 5).

16. *United States v Harriss*, 347 U.S. 612, 625 (1954).

17. *Tattered Cover, Inc. v City of Thornton*, 44 P.3d 1044, 1047 (Colo. 2002).

successful and uninhibited exercise of First Amendment rights, precisely because of the chilling effects that can result from disclosure of identity."[18]

Given that the book in question was a "how to" book on operating a methamphetamine lab, and that drug cases are notorious for their tendency to bend constitutional rights to the breaking point,[19] this demonstrates the extent of judicial solicitude for the right to remain anonymous.

In practice, however, many state interests are routinely found to be sufficiently compelling to justify restrictions on First Amendment rights, and it is from the First Amendment that the right to anonymity derives. For example, the state interest in applying sufficiently targeted measures to forbidding discrimination in places of public accommodation has been held to be sufficiently compelling to overcome the First Amendment associational privacy rights of property owners and club members.[20] Similarly, in *Buckley v. Valeo*,[21] the Supreme Court upheld a statute forbidding donations of more than $1,000 to a candidate for federal office, and compelling disclosure to the Federal Election Commission of the names of those making virtually all cash donations.[22] Because the Court in the same decision essentially equated the expenditure of money in campaigns with the ability to amplify political speech,[23] the decision appears to say that, given a sufficiently weighty objective and a statute carefully written to minimize the chilling or otherwise harmful effects on speech, even political speech can be regulated.[24] Similarly, in *First Nat. Bank of Boston v. Bellotti*,[25] the Supreme Court struck down a state requirement forbidding corporations from making political contributions except for ballot measures directly affecting its business; but it contrasted the unconstitutional state law with others that it suggested would surely be acceptable: "Identification of the source of advertising may be required

---

18. *Ibid.*, 1052.

19. See Steven Wisotsky, "Crackdown: The Emerging 'Drug Exception'"to the Bill of Rights," Hastings Law Journal 38 (1987): 889.

20. See *Bd. of Directors of Rotary Int'l v Rotary Club of Duarte*, 481 U.S. 537, 544 (1987); see also *New York State Club Ass'n v City of New York*, 487 U.S. 1, 13 (1988) (stating that freedom of expression is a powerful tool used in the exercise of First Amendment rights); *Roberts v U.S. Jaycees*, 468 U.S. 609, 617–19 (1984) (recognizing that an individual's First Amendment rights are not secure unless those rights may be exercised in the group context as well).

21. *Buckley v Valeo*, 424 U.S. 1, 143 (1976).

22. *Ibid.*, 23–29, 60–84.

23. *Ibid.*, 19.

24. *Cf. Los Angeles v Taxpayers for Vincent*, 466 U.S. 789 (1984) (upholding ban on posting any signs, including political ones, on utility poles). Justice Stevens held, however, that the utility poles were not public fora, *id.* suggesting that the court might not extend this idea to public fora and that *Vincent* may come to be seen as simply a decision upholding a particular time, place, and manner restriction.

25. *First Nat. Bank of Boston v Bellotti*, 435 U.S. 765 (1978).

as a means of disclosure, so that the people will be able to evaluate the arguments to which they are being subjected."[26]

In sum, anonymous speech—especially speech about political or religious matters—enjoys a privileged position under the U.S. Constitution. However, no form of speech is completely immune from regulation. Even political speech can be regulated, given sufficient cause, especially if the regulation is content-neutral, as a regulation on anonymous speech would likely be. What the cases demonstrate is that any regulation of anonymous speech, especially any rule that threatens to touch the most protected types of speech, will require a particularly strong justification to survive judicial review.

II. CRIMINAL LAW/NATIONAL SECURITY LAW

The criminal law and national security arenas exhibit a patchwork of anonymity regulation, and, at present, the law in this area is somewhat fluid. By enabling much greater surveillance on a much lower evidentiary basis, post-9/11 enactments have significantly eroded the capability of citizens to remain anonymous. On the other hand, in specific circumstances, the law clearly upholds the right to anonymity. There may be some tension between the Fourth Amendment's prohibition of unreasonable search and seizure—which is understood to require the government to seek advance court approval for most searches and wiretaps in domestic law enforcement—and the 2008 amendments to the Foreign Intelligence Surveillance Act that expands the government authority to intercept U.S. citizens' and residents' telephone and e-mail communications without a warrant.[27]

Exactly how this plays out in identity/anonymity issues is somewhat up for grabs. The most recent relevant Supreme Court decision, the *Hiibel*[28] case, upheld a state statute requiring persons to identify themselves to police when the investigating officer's demand is "based on reasonable suspicion"[29] that the person may have committed a crime. Even so, the Court upheld the self-identification requirement on the understanding that "the statute does not require a suspect to

---

26. *Ibid.*, 792(n. 32). The Supreme Court again noted the communicative importance of the identity of a speaker, albeit in a different context, in *City of Ladue v Gilleo*. 512 U.S. 43, 56–57 (1994) (noting that a poster in front of a house associates speech with the identity of the speaker).

27. Foreign Intelligence Surveillance Act of 1978 Amendments Act of 2008, Pub. L. No. 110–261, 122 Stat. 2436 (2008).

28. *Hiibel v Sixth Judicial Dist. Court of Nevada, Humboldt County*, 542 U.S. 177, 183 (2004).

29. *Ibid.*, 184.

give the officer a driver's license or any other document"[30] and reserved for a future day the Fifth Amendment question of what rule would apply if disclosure was self-incriminatory.[31] *Hiibel* thus stands for the proposition that the state may demand your identity if it has reason to do so, while also signaling some wariness in the Supreme Court about the issue.

That wariness may be tested as post-9/11 cases begin to wind through the courts. The original law-enforcement investigatory power legislation passed in the wake of the 2001 terrorist attack on the World Trade Center, the Patriot Act,[32] had a very limited effect on the right to anonymity. Congress did not attempt to impose any new limits on the legal right to possess and use the cryptographic tools that make Internet anonymity possible. But the Patriot Act was only a first step. More recent enactments, such as the revised Foreign Intelligence Surveillance Act, empower both data mining and wide-spread surveillance of phone calls and e-mails between the United States and a foreign location. The Act allows dragnet surveillance without requiring the government to make any showing to a court and with almost no judicial oversight, removing any obligation to demonstrate whether the communication has anything to do with terrorism or any threat to national security.[33]

Meanwhile, the U.S. government is widely reported to have stepped up its domestic communicative surveillance efforts, including the much-touted, perhaps even over-hyped, Carnivore system. And, even before all this, the exercise of the right to the anonymous exchange of information was under substantial pressure, primarily from commercial interests who seek to know exactly who is accessing digital content in order to be able to charge for it. The United States has also begun to amass biometric data banks and related databases for law enforcement purposes that could be used to identify formerly anonymous persons if DNA evidence of their identity can be collected.

Lest this seem fanciful, consider that the Bush administration has suggested that the Espionage Act of 1917 Act might be used against investigative reporters to get them to reveal their sources. The Act makes it a crime to transmit or receive national defense information, and the administration apparently views it as a tool to be used against leakers and whistle-blowers. As it is, courts traditionally have possessed, and have not feared to use, contempt power to get reporters to reveal anonymous sources, and in the past decade a number of journalists have chosen to be jailed rather than disclose them.

Conversely, it is important to note what has *not* changed in the wake of 9/11. There has, for example, been no serious attempt by either Congress or the

---

30. *Ibid.*, 185.

31. *Ibid.*, 90–191.

32. Providing Appropriate Tools Required to Intercept and Obstruct Terrorism (USA PATRIOT ACT) Act of 2001, Pub. L. No. 107–156 (2001).

33. Foreign Intelligence Surveillance Act of 1978 Amendments Act of 2008, Pub. L. No. 110–261, 122 Stat. 2436 (2008).

administration to impose any new limits on the legal right to possess and use the cryptographic tools that make Internet anonymity possible. And, at least until further notice, the constitutional protections for anonymous discourse remain in force.

It is also important to note that some doctrines that have the effect of making anonymity difficult as a practical matter—notably the so-called third-party doctrine—long predate 9/11. Under the third-party doctrine, any time a person discloses information to a third party, the disclosing party waives all Fourth Amendment rights in the data revealed.[34] In short, there is no reasonable expectation of privacy in any information disclosed to a third party: absent common-law or statutory evidentiary privileges such as attorney-client and priest-penitent, anyone who knows of a speaker's identity can be forced to reveal it if the police know to ask.

Anonymity of Witnesses

The right to hear and see one's accuser in an open courtroom has been a hallmark of American criminal law. For example, the Confrontation Clause of the Sixth Amendment provides that "[i]n all criminal prosecutions, the accused shall enjoy the right . . . to be confronted with the witness against him."[35] This imposes severe limits on the anonymity of witnesses at trial, as the clause is understood as a safeguard to ensure the reliability of evidence presented at a criminal trial by subjecting it to adversarial testing. As one authority aptly summarizes the situation,

> American courts have rarely allowed even minor exercises of anonymity. In *Alford v. United States*, 282 U.S. 687, 692 (1931), the Supreme Court held that disclosure of a witness' identity and address were unequivocally required in a criminal trial, reasoning that "prejudice ensues from a denial of opportunity to place the witness in his proper setting and put the weight of his testimony and his credibility to a test." Using dicta in *Smith v. Illinois*, some lower courts have loosened this requirement and refined it to allow witness anonymity in situations where the prosecution can show actual threat to the witness exists and fully discloses such threats to the trial judge. In these courts, the trial judge must weigh the value of disclosure with witness safety. Other trial courts remain fastened to the holding of Alford.[36]

Indeed, courts have struggled with the degree of protection owed even to witnesses whose lives might be endangered by testifying. In *Alvarado v. Superior*

---

34. For a defense of this justly criticized doctrine, see Orin Kerr, "The Case for the Third-Party Doctrine," *Michigan Law Rev* (forthcoming, 2009): 107, http://papers.ssrn.com/sol3/papers.cfm?abstract_id=1138128.

35. U.S. CONST. amend. VI.

36. Nicholas W. Smith, "Evidence and Confrontation in the President's Military Commissions," *Hastings Constitutional Law Quarterly* 33 (2005): 83, 96.

Court[37] the Supreme Court of California held that the Confrontation Clause prevents witnesses from testifying anonymously at trial, if their testimony was crucial to the prosecution's case. On occasion, however, judges have allowed undercover and intelligence agents to testify in disguise so as to protect their identities.[38]

The use of hearsay from anonymous witnesses before the status review tribunals held at Guantanamo has been heavily criticized. One federal court, reviewing a decision based entirely on the hearsay testimony of three absent witnesses, contemptuously characterized the government's defense of the military tribunal's reliance on such poor evidence as equivalent to the line in Lewis Carroll's "Hunting of the Snark": "what I tell you three times is true."[39]

In like vein, U.S. law generally requires open trials. In criminal cases other than those dealing with classified material, there are few mechanisms that allow judges to exclude the public (as opposed to sequestering other witnesses whose testimony might be tainted). Although courts may sometimes issue gag orders to participants and their lawyers, it cannot muzzle the press or the general public. Despite the very rare attempt, successful publication bans such as those found in the UK or Canada are unknown in the criminal and civil courts. Closed hearings, however, do occur in the civil courts (especially for family court matters), and it is possible to seal evidence pertaining to trade secrets and other confidential matters. There is a presumption of openness, although actual practice varies by state and sometimes within them.

In *Waller v. Georgia*[40] the Supreme Court stated that to close a proceeding: (1) the party seeking closure must advance an "overriding interest that is likely to be prejudiced"; (2) the closure must be "no broader than necessary to protect that interest"; (3) the court must consider "reasonable alternatives" to closure; and (4) the court must "make findings adequate to support the closure."[41] This rule applies in the main to child witnesses as it does to adults, all of whom ordinarily must testify in open court.[42] In addition, both the press and the public enjoy a qualified First Amendment right of access to criminal trial proceedings.[43]

---

37. *Alvarado v Superior Court*, 5 P.3d 203 (Cal. 2000).

38. E.g., *United States v Martinez*, 2007 WL 2710430 (S.D.N.Y. 2007), in which the court allowed an undercover officer to testify in disguise, "but without dark glasses so that the Defendant and jury can observe his eyes, his facial reactions to questions, and his body language." *Ibid.* at *3.

39. *Parhat v Gates*, 532 F.3d 834, 848–49 (D.C. Cir. 2008).

40. *Waller v Georgia*, 467 U.S. 39 (1984).

41. *Ibid.*, 48.

42. See *United States v Thunder*, 438 F.3d 866 (8th Cir. 2006) (holding that closure of courtroom during testimony of allegedly abused children violated defendant's Sixth Amendment right to public trial).

43. *Globe Newspaper Co. v Superior Court for the County of Norfolk*, 457 U.S. 596, 603 (1982).

Anonymity of Defendants

There are at least as strong restrictions precluding the anonymity of criminal defendants. The trial courts in southern and central Florida, for example, experimented with a system in which some cases involving defendants believed to be particularly dangerous were kept in a secret docket that was not made part of the public record. This practice was severely criticized by the court of appeal, which said that it violated the First Amendment right of the public, a right that extends to the docket sheets themselves.[44]

Anonymity of Jurors

Under the modern rule, a district court may empanel an anonymous jury in any case in which "the interests of justice so require."[45] The first reported use of an anonymous jury in federal court was in a 1977 trial.[46] Courts have warned that anonymous juries are a "drastic" measure.[47] Nevertheless, since 1977, "significant numbers of federal and state courts throughout the country have utilized the procedure to protect jurors, prevent jury tampering and limit media influence."[48] The court must mitigate the potential prejudicial effects of an anonymous jury by conducting a careful voir dire designed to uncover juror bias and provide the jurors with plausible, nonprejudicial reasons for their anonymity.

The traditional rule that criminal trials should be fully public so that justice can be seen to be done turns out to have accumulated some exceptions, but these are still limited. While post-9/11 pressure may spur further growth, at present, anonymity in any part of a criminal case remains a source of discomfort and as a result this growth will likely remain limited.

III. ANONYMITY IN CIVIL ACTIONS

Protection of anonymity is, in principle, significantly less in the context of U.S. private law than public law. Although it is true that a lawsuit invokes the state's power, and thus in some cases can be seen as a form of state action, the private lawsuit is ordinarily seen as something invoked by a private party, and based on private rights. As a result, constitutional protections designed to limit the state's power over the individual often do not apply, or apply in a more attenuated fashion.

---

44. See *United States v Valenti*, 987 F.2d 708, 715 (11th Cir. 1993) (holding that "dual-docketing system" or "sealed docket" violated the press and public's First Amendment right of access to criminal proceedings, and declaring it facially unconstitutional). See also *United States v Ochoa-Vasquez*, 428 F.3d 1015 (11thCir. 2005).

45. 28 U.S.C. § 1863(b) (7) (2008).

46. See *Ochoa-Vasquez*, 428 F.3d 1015, 1033–34 (11th Cir. 2005).

47. *United States v Ross*, 33 F.3d 1507 (11th. Cir. 1994).

48. *Ibid.*

We see this principle in action as regards plaintiffs, defendants, third parties, and also reports of decisions. Like the criminal law, the civil law begins with the presumption that all proceeding, evidence, and decisions will be public. However, in civil cases this presumption can be displaced for good cause somewhat more frequently than in the criminal arena, and nowhere more so than in state family court matters relating to adoption, divorce, or related issues.

Anonymity of Plaintiffs

The Federal Rules of Civil Procedure contain no provision contemplating fictitious or anonymous parties. Federal pleading presumes the disclosure of the names of adult parties, and the courts rarely allow anonymous (or pseudonymous) plaintiffs, except in special circumstances. Nevertheless, both Jane and Robert Doe and Roe appear with some frequency in the casebooks as plaintiffs, and more rarely as defendants. In all cases, however, proceeding without using one's true name requires leave of court.

On an application a court may permit a "John Doe" plaintiff if the party can show a substantial privacy right that outweighs the presumption of openness in judicial proceedings.[49] Among the factors weighing in the balance are the following:

- Whether plaintiff challenges a government activity
- Whether prosecution of the lawsuit would compel the plaintiffs to disclose very intimate information (thus, for example, the most famous pseudonymous U.S. court case, *Roe v. Wade*[50])
- Whether the plaintiff would be compelled to admit his intention to engage in illegal activity and therefore subject himself to criminal liability
- Whether plaintiff would be subjected to physical harm if identified
- What prejudice the defendant would suffer if plaintiff is permitted able to proceed anonymously[51]

A party's age is also a relevant factor. The Federal Rules contemplate a form of pseudonymity, as they permit a party making a filing to replace the name of a person known to be a minor with the minor's initials.[52] Actual anonymity is rarer, but it is possible with leave of court.[53] Countervailing factors against anonymity include whether the plaintiff has illegitimate ulterior motives, the extent of the public interest in knowing the identity given the subject matter,

---

49. See 5A Charles Alan Wright & Arthur R. Miller, Federal Practice and Procedure § 1321 (3d ed. 2004).

50. 410 U.S. 113 (1973).

51. See 5A Charles Alan Wright & Arthur R. Miller, Federal Practice and Procedure § 1321 (3d ed. 2004).

52. Fed. R. Civ. P. 5.2(a) (3).

53. See 5A Charles Alan Wright & Arthur R. Miller, Federal Practice and Procedure § 1321 (3d ed. 2004)

or the status of the plaintiff as a public figure.[54] In addition, some states have legislated against so-called SLAPP (Strategic Lawsuits Against Public Participation) suits that may provide anonymous parties some protections against John-Doe-as-defendant suits that are actually designed to discover their identity.

Using Legal Process to Identify Defendants

Holders of rights in digital intellectual property have been particularly assiduous in seeking to use the U.S. court system to identify persons they believe to have infringed copyrights via online file-sharing. In a large number of recent cases, a rights holder has brought suit seeking to compel an intermediary, usually an ISP, to disclose the name of a customer whom the plaintiffs believe engaged in unlicensed file-sharing.

In the first wave of such cases, plaintiffs sought to invoke the Digital Millennium Copyright Act[55] (DMCA) to subpoena ISPs for the identities of alleged file-sharers. The DMCA offered copyright holders an expedited means of securing subpoenas directed against the information-holder. Subpoena practice under the DMCA is rapid, because the civil order does not require judicial approval. Warrants in a criminal investigation require that affidavits be submitted to a judge who must sign the order; routine civil discovery requires a series of time-consuming steps that give the subject actual notice and an opportunity to block the discovery by seeking a protective order from the court. In contrast, the DMCA allows the plaintiff to file a short-form request with the clerk of court and the subpoena automatically issues.[56] As a practical matter, the third-party subjects of these requests rarely have a chance to object before the information is disclosed. However, in a 2003 decision that has become the leading case, the D.C. Circuit held that this expedited method was only available in cases where the plaintiff alleged that the infringing material was stored on the ISP's own servers.[57]

Thus, when seeking to find the identities of parties sharing files via peer-to-peer networks, rights-holders must now file a lawsuit against "John Doe" defendants, then use ordinary court discovery procedures to learn their names. This is slower, more expensive, and ordinarily means that the third party will receive actual notice before the subpoena is enforced. Armed with this notice, the third parties can and have contested the issuance of the subpoena—although with rather mixed success.

---

54. *Ibid.*

55. Digital Millennium Copyright Act, Pub. L. No. 105–304, 112 Stat. 2860 (1998) (codified in scattered sections of 17 U.S.C.).

56. 17 U.S.C. § 512(h) (2008).

57. *Recording Indus. Ass'n of America, Inc. v Verizon Internet Servs., Inc.*, 351 F.3d 1229 (D.C. Cir. 2003).

Alleged file-sharers have not generally fared that well in their attempts to block court-ordered disclosure of their identities, but other parties in similar procedural postures have tended to fare much better. In particular, courts have tended to be careful to protect the rights of persons engaged in anonymous online First Amendment activities such as criticism of corporations and politicians. Many states now use some version of the so-called *Dendrite* principles:

> . . . when faced with an application by a plaintiff for expedited discovery seeking an order compelling an ISP to honor a subpoena and disclose the identity of anonymous Internet posters who are sued for allegedly violating the rights of individuals, corporations or businesses [, t]he trial court must consider and decide those applications by striking a balance between the well-established First Amendment right to speak anonymously, and the right of the plaintiff to protect its proprietary interests and reputation through the assertion of recognizable claims based on the actionable conduct of the anonymous, fictitiously-named defendants.

> . . . when such an application is made, the trial court should first require the plaintiff to undertake efforts to notify the anonymous posters that they are the subject of a subpoena or application for an order of disclosure, and withhold action to afford the fictitiously-named defendants a reasonable opportunity to file and serve opposition to the application . . .

> The court shall also require the plaintiff to identify and set forth the exact statements purportedly made by each anonymous poster that plaintiff alleges constitutes actionable speech.

> The complaint and all information provided to the court should be carefully reviewed to determine whether plaintiff has set forth a prima facie cause of action against the fictitiously-named anonymous defendants . . .

> Finally, assuming the court concludes that the plaintiff has presented a prima facie cause of action, the court must balance the defendant's First Amendment right of anonymous free speech against the strength of the prima facie case presented and the necessity for the disclosure of the anonymous defendant's identity to allow the plaintiff to properly proceed.[58]

Courts faced with a disclosure request thus demand that plaintiffs provide something more substantial than a form recitation; armed with this

---

58. *Dendrite Int'l, Inc. v John Doe*, No. 3, et al., 342 N.J. Super. 134, 141–42 (App. Div. 2001).

information they seek to balance the relevant interests. As courts give substantial weight to First Amendment and privacy values, in cases about controversial speech (as opposed to file-sharing) they are proving to be far from a rubber-stamp for identity disclosure requests.

Even though copyright law is federal, California has made extra efforts to protect the interests of rights holders against anonymous file-sharers by, in 2005, making it a misdemeanor for anyone located in California to "knowingly electronically" disseminate all or most of a commercial recording or audiovisual work to more than ten other people "without disclosing his or her email address, and the title of the recording or audiovisual work . . . [while] . . . knowing that a particular recording or audiovisual work is commercial."[59]

Legal Process to Reveal the Identity of Third Parties

The situation regarding disclosures of identity by and about third parties is also complicated. U.S. civil cases begin with a presumption that the parties should be allowed wide-ranging discovery in order to get at the truth. Working against that presumption are a number of evidentiary privileges (e.g., doctor-patient), and some constitutional issues, including the First Amendment right to speak anonymously (discussed above).

The situation in state court is complex, not only because rules vary from state to state but also because the docket of state courts more commonly includes family law, adoption, and other matters where courts traditionally are more willing to view the private interest in privacy as outweighing the public interest in disclosure. Even in Florida, where a state constitutional provision mandates access to most public records[60] (it is indeed the "sunshine state" for matters of public record as well as weather), the family courts in particular are willing to seal records and protect the identity of parties, especially minors. Similarly, in family-related matters it is sometimes possible to get an order that protects the identity of third parties such as other family members from being disclosed.

Compared to courts hearing criminal cases, judicial tribunals hearing civil matters are significantly more willing to consider claims that parties or witnesses may have legitimate reasons to remain anonymous. Nevertheless, with the

---

59. Cal. Penal Code § 653aa (a) (West 2008).

60. Florida Constitution, Art. I, section 24(a) states that "Every person has the right to inspect or copy any public record made or received in connection with the official business of any public body, officer, or employee of the state, or persons acting on their behalf, except with respect to records exempted pursuant to this section or specifically made confidential by this Constitution. This section specifically includes the legislative, executive, and judicial branches of government and each agency or department created thereunder; counties, municipalities, and districts; and each constitutional officer, board, and commission, or entity created pursuant to law or this Constitution." The state legislature can create exceptions to this rule only by a two-thirds vote. *Ibid.* at sec. 24(c).

possible exception of the family courts, where a greater solicitude for privacy interests sometimes reigns, the presumption remains strong that plaintiffs and witnesses should be identified. As regards attempts to use the court's powers of compulsion to force third parties to reveal the identities of persons whom plaintiffs would make defendants, the law appears to be settling toward treating these discovery requests with significant solicitude for legitimate third-party rights (if, perhaps, not so much solicitude for unlicensed file-sharing). It is perhaps not yet completely clear where the balance will tilt, but it is increasingly clear that courts have no intention of becoming rubber stamps for anonymity-piercing requests.

Data about persons who are neither witnesses nor parties in civil litigation often emerges in responses to civil discovery requests or to government subpoena—and sometimes these groups are huge. Lawsuits against ISPs or search engines in which plaintiffs demand data about the behavior of large groups threaten the privacy and functional anonymity of tens of thousands, even millions, of users. (Users in these cases are not in the main anonymous to the ISPs or search engines, but are commonly functionally anonymous to the rest of the world.) Firms have demonstrated an inability to anonymize data sufficiently to foil reconstruction efforts.[61] Some courts have demonstrated solicitude to third-party privacy interests by limiting discovery requests or insisting on strong anonymization before release,[62] but the initial (and much-criticized) response elsewhere has been to dismiss privacy concerns as unwarranted.[63] At present it is unclear if legislation will be needed to define companies' and courts' duties in this area.

IV. ANONYMITY IN OTHER CITIZEN-GOVERNMENT RELATIONSHIPS

The right to anonymity in public (or lack thereof) becomes even less clear in the context of citizen-government relationships outside the courtroom and the criminal justice system. In spite of the strong constitutional protections for free speech and against unreasonable search and seizure discussed above, there are a number of circumstances in which citizens are required to identify themselves to the State beyond the obvious cases of citizens who seek government permits or government benefits such as pensions, disability benefits, welfare, or medical benefits. For example, all U.S. states other than North Dakota require voters to register in order to vote.[64] States with voting rolls

---

61. See Anita Ramasastry, FINDLAW, Privacy and Search Engine Data: *A Recent AOL Research Project Has Perilous Consequences for Subscribers*, http://technology.findlaw.com/articles/00006/010208.html.

62. See *Gonazales v Google*, 234 FRD 674 (ND Cal. 2006).

63. See *Viacom Intern. v Youtube*, 2008 WL 2627388 (July 2, 2008).

64. Lillie Coney, *A Call for Election Reform*, 7 J. L. & Soc. Challenges 183, 186 (2005).

treat them as publicly accessible records, usually including the voter's party identification. These records are "routinely shared with political parties, candidates and for non-election related purposes."[65] The anonymity of the vote itself is protected when exercised at a poll, but that guarantee of anonymity becomes less easy to police as voters in many states increasingly vote by mail in advance of election day.

The Lobbying Disclosure Act[66] requires that organizations or firms register their paid employees as lobbyists if they seek to influence most federal executive or legislative branch activities. However, these registration rules do not apply to citizens acting on their own. Many states also have rules requiring paid lobbyists to register, but as the *McIntyre* case holds, citizens retain a right of anonymity when engaged in unpaid political advocacy.

For every donor making (cumulative) donations of $200 or more, the Federal Election Campaign Act[67] (FECA) requires candidates for federal office to make their best efforts to collect and publicly disclose on a financial report the donor's name, address, occupation, and employer, as well as the date and amount of the contributions. Contribution information is reported quarterly to the Federal Election Commission, which publishes it online and makes it widely available. The Supreme Court upheld FECA's public disclosure provisions in *Buckley v. Valeo*,[68] a decision that remains controversial; critics argue that making donations public may chill contributions to potentially unpopular or controversial causes and may even invite retaliation by employers or others.[69]

Most states also require disclosure of political donations, although the details vary widely.[70] Many cities and counties also have their own local rules.[71]

---

65. *Ibid.*, 198.

66. Lobbying Disclosure Act of 1995, Pub. L. No. 104–65, 109 Stat. 691 (1995), *codified at* 2 U.S.C. §§ 1601–1612 (2008), as amended by Honest Leadership and Open Government Act, Pub. L. No. 110–81, 121 Stat. 735 (2007).

67. Federal Election Campaign Act, Pub. L. No. 92–225, 86 Stat. 3 (1972) (codified as amended at 2 U.S.C. § 431 (2008)).

68. *Buckley* (n. 21).

69. For a critique, see, e.g., William McGeveran, "McIntyre's Checkbook: Privacy Costs of Political Contribution Disclosure," *U. Pa. J. Const. L.* 6 (2003): 1.

70. "States generally did not adopt legislative conflict of interest or ethics laws until much later than the federal government did. New York, considered an 'early leader' in ethics regulation, adopted its statute in 1909 and did not enact comprehensive state ethics legislation until 1954. Other states began comprehensive ethics reform in the 1970s." Rebecca L. Anderson, "The Rules in the Owners' Box: Lobbying Regulations in State Legislatures," *Urban Lawyer* 40 (2008): 375, 379.

71. A 2002 survey by the National Civic League found that 135 city and county governments in eighteen states and the District of Columbia had adopted their own campaign finance laws. *National Civic League, Local Campaign Finance Reform* (Feb. 2002).

In addition, the U.S. Constitution requires a decennial census.[72] Participation is formally mandatory,[73] although there appear to have been few if any prosecutions for failing to participate since 1976 when Congress reduced the maximum penalty from 60 days imprisonment to a $100 fine. The primary purpose of the census is to enumerate populations for the purpose of congressional apportionment, but the government also uses it to collect demographic and statistical information. These data are supposed to be anonymized before being released, but questions have been raised as to whether census tracts are now so small, and the information collected of such great granularity, that it would be possible to de-anonymize the data.

Law and tradition say that personally identifiable information disclosed in the census should not be used for any other government function. These rules were skirted, and perhaps breached, both during WWII and in the aftermath of 9/11. Amidst allegations that it may have disclosed even more, the Census Bureau admitted that after 9/11 it provided "specially tabulated population statistics" on Arab Americans to the Department of Homeland Security, including ZIP-code-level breakdowns of Arab-American populations, sorted by country of origin. The Census Bureau also admits to providing a similar "compilation" about Japanese Americans during World War II.[74]

The extent to which reported census data is anonymous is in any case open to serious question. One study demonstrated that public so-called anonymous data from the 1990 census permitted 87 percent of the U.S. population to be uniquely identified by just three data: their five-digit ZIP code, their gender, and their date of birth.[75]

Although their right to anonymity is protected in the context of political and religious rights, U.S. citizens are required to identify themselves in a wide range of other encounters with their government. Identification is required for one to receive almost any recurring government benefit, to vote, to make substantial campaign contributions (but not independent expenditures), and to lobby for pay. The decennial census is mandatory, and although the census is supposed to safeguard personal data, there is ground to fear both intentional and unintentional release of personally identifiable information.

---

72. U.S. Const. art I, sec 2, cl. 3.

73. Failure to participate is grounds for a $100 fine; willfully giving false information can cost $500. 13 U.S.C. § 221 (2008).

74. Lynette Clemetson, "Homeland Security Given Data on Arab-Americans," *New York Times* July 30, 2004, http://query.nytimes.com/gst/fullpage.html?res=9d02e4d b113df933a05754c0a9629c8b63.

75. Latanya Sweeney, "Uniqueness of Simple Demographics in the U.S. Population," (2001), http://privacy.cs.cmu.edu/dataprivacy/papers/LIDAP-WP4abstract.html.

V. DISCLOSURE OF IDENTITY REQUIREMENTS IN DAILY LIFE

Beyond the realms of criminal investigations and civil litigation, U.S. law does not at present have a coherent approach to disclosure of identity requirements—which is consistent with its inconsistent and patchwork approach to privacy. Certain regulated industries are required to ascertain and disclose the identity of customers. In general, however, the law imposes few constraints on identity collection and disclosure in either the context of private economic relations or non-economic relations.

Regulated Industries

Certain, primarily financial, regulated industries are subject to rules requiring them to request and in many cases verify their customers' addresses. Many other firms do so by choice, and there is rarely any legal rule preventing it.

Banks and other financial intermediaries are subject to "know your customer" rules designed to deter money laundering and facilitate its prosecution.[76] Any financial transaction involving $10,000 may trigger a reporting requirement in not just the financial industry but also a range of other businesses. Depending on the circumstances, however, the sending of much smaller sums of money by wire—even as low as $250—may trigger reporting requirements. Furthermore, any income-generating activity requires disclosure of a social security number. All active and most passive income-generating activities also trigger tax-reporting requirements on the payer.

Under the Patriot Act, banks and other financial firms are also responsible for ensuring that their customers are not on any lists of suspected terrorists or money launderers maintained by the federal government, such as the Office of Foreign Assets Control's Specially Designated Nationals list.[77] This list contains thousands of entries and is updated at least monthly. In order to perform this check, firms must know the customer's real identity.

Protection of Identity Requirements

A very small number of federal statutes impose limits upon the sharing of private transactional data collected by persons not classed as professionals.

---

76. For example, the Bank Secrecy Act of 1970, Pub. L. No. 91-508 (as amended, codified at 12 U.S.C. §§ 1829(b), 1951–1959 (2000), and 31 U.S.C. §§ 5311–5330 (2002)), requires most financial institutions to report suspicious transactions. See, e.g., 31 U.S.C. § 5318(g). The Bank Secrecy Act and other post-9/11 laws and regulations also require financial institutions to make a "due diligence" effort to identify their customers.

77. The list is available from the U.S. Dept. of Treasury, Office of Foreign Assets Control, SDN List, http://www.ustreas.gov/offices/enforcement/ofac/sdn/index.shtml.

The most important is the Fair Credit Reporting Act.[78] In addition to imposing rules designed to make credit reports more accurate, the statute also contains rules prohibiting credit bureaus from making certain accurate statements about aged peccadilloes, although this restriction does not apply to reports requested for larger transactions.[79]

There are few statutory federal privacy-oriented restrictions on the sale of commercial data. The Cable Communications Policy Act of 1984 forbids cable operators and third parties from monitoring the viewing habits of subscribers. Cable operators must tell subscribers what personal data is collected and, in general, must not disclose it to anyone without the subscriber's consent.[80] The "Bork Bill," formally known as the Video Privacy Protection Act, also prohibits most releases of customers' video rental data.[81]

As noted above, both state and federal law contain a number of evidentiary privileges that protect priests, lawyers, doctors, and some others from having to disclose the identity of penitents or clients, although it should be noted that some evidentiary privileges, and especially those available to psychiatrists and other therapists, vary by state. The federal Health Insurance Portability and Accountability Act (HIPAA)[82] imposes restrictions on data-sharing by health care providers, health care plans, and health care "clearinghouses" (processors of data created by another), but to the extent that a patient's anonymity enjoys protection, the primary protections lie in medical ethics and evidentiary privileges rather than anything in HIPAA.

Anonymous Online Communication

U.S. law imposes no direct bar to the running and use of anonymous remailers. This in effect creates opportunities to enjoy anonymous speech in the online context. Arguments have been advanced that a remailer operator might be subject to some sort of contributory liability for bad acts committed by arms-length users, but at present there is no support in the case law for this assertion.

However, U.S. law does impose significant restrictions on the export of encryption technology and also on the provision of technical assistance relating

---

78. 15 U.S.C. §§ 1681–1681s. (2008).

79. See *ibid.* § 1681(c).

80. See 15 U.S.C. § 551.

81. 102 Stat. 3195 (1988) (codified as 18 U.S.C. § 2710 (1999)). The act allows videotape rental providers to release customer names and addresses to third parties so long as there is no disclosure of titles purchased or rented. Customers can, however, be grouped into categories according to the type of film they rent. See *ibid.* § 2710(b)(2)(D)(ii).

82. Health Insurance Portability and Accountability Act ("HIPAA") of 1996, Pub. L. No. 104-191, § 261, 110 Stat. 1936 (1996), codified at 42 U.S.C. § 1320d (2000) et seq.

to the use of such technology. The U.S. export regime has become somewhat more liberal than in the past, with DES exports now decontrolled, and the export of substantially stronger encryption allowed for selected industries such as banks. Despite the occasional trial balloon,[83] the United States does not have mandatory key escrow to enable the state to ensure it has the means to unlock encrypted digital communications without great effort.

Anonymous online communication therefore remains legal in most cases, and indeed as noted enjoys substantial legal protection. But the practical obstacles to anonymous communication remain substantial, especially online. The most prevalent obstacle is that most home and office Internet users have IP numbers that are either fixed or, if variable, are almost certainly logged by employers or ISPs. These numbers thus can easily be traced and linked back to the user. In addition, every internet-capable device has a unique and consistent MAC number, which is emitted by machines using the IPv6 protocol unless altered by a technically savvy user.

Moreover, purely anonymous transactions with untraceable e-cash have yet to make it off the drawing board in any meaningful way. As noted above, cash transactions of any size are likely to trigger reporting requirements. There is thus, in practice, little scope for licit anonymous commerce in the United States beyond small cash transactions.

On the other hand, some areas have free publicly accessible wifi. Public libraries in many communities offer free public internet access, although frequently they require patrons to display a library card or other identification in order to use a machine.

National ID Cards

A particularly hot issue in the American context has been the call for national identity cards.[84] The United States does not currently have national ID cards as such. Every state, however, licenses drivers, and because cars are a practical necessity for most adults living outside the largest cities, the state-issued drivers licenses are gradually becoming de facto national ID cards. This status was semiformalized in the REAL ID Act of 2005,[85] in which the federal government sought to impose standards on states relating to what information they must include on licenses or other ID (and in what format), what documentation states must demand before issuing the credential, and how states should share data. Implementation of REAL ID has been controversial, with some states vowing not to participate. The federal government has delayed the effective date of some

---

83. See A. Michael Froomkin, "It Came From Planet Clipper," *University of Chicago Legal Forum* 15 (1996).

84. Ian Kerr, *Lessons from the Identity Trail: Anonymity, Privacy, and Identity in a Networked Society* (New York: Oxford University Press, 2009), Chapter 14.

85. REAL ID Act of 2005, Pub. L. No. 109-13, 119 Stat. 231 (2005).

of the most controversial aspects, and repeal or modification of the statute remains possible.

Anonymity in Public

The baseline rule in the United States with regard to anonymity in public is that there is no right to privacy in public places with respect to anything open to public view or voluntarily revealed.[86] With the exception of certain government facilities, anyone may take photographs in public; state laws vary, however, as to the consent required for sound recordings. Thus, for example, a newspaper that published a photo of persons lining up for unemployment benefits was not liable to an identifiable complainant who claimed the photo violated his privacy.[87] There are some limits on the publication of photographs for advertising and publicity purposes, although these do not apply to the reporting of news. Indeed, the only significant constraints on photographic news reporting are (1) some state anti-paparazzi statutes that impose limits on photography from public areas of activities taking place on private property[88] and (2) state law rules restricting intrusion into private areas.

Thus, in *Shulman v. Group W Productions*, the California Supreme Court allowed two people injured in a car accident to sue a TV station for the tort of intrusion based on a cameraman's recording of emergency roadside care given in a rescue helicopter, holding that there was no right of privacy regarding the images at the accident scene prior to being moved to the helicopter, but there was one inside it even if the patients could be overheard.[89] The court also held that there was a triable issue as to whether "by placing a microphone" on one of the victims "amplifying and recording what she said and heard, defendants may have listened in on conversations the parties could reasonably have expected to be private."[90]

---

86. States make an exception to this rule for so-called upskirt photos. To the extent that they even bother to try to explain it, cases suggest that the general rule may not apply to an indecent and vulgar intrusion that would be embarrassing to an ordinary person of reasonable sensitivity. See Restatement (Second) of Torts § 652B (1977); Jeffrey F. Ghent, Annotation, *Waiver or loss of right to privacy; Matters in public view; photographs*, 57 A.L.R. 3d 16 at § 8 (1974 & 2008 supp.).

87. *Cefalu v Globe Newspaper Co.*, 391 N.E.2d 935 (Mass. App. Ct. 1979).

88. Cal. Civ. Code § 1708.8(b), (e) (West 2008), perhaps the model, limits the offense to invasions offensive to a reasonable person, where there was already a reasonable expectation of privacy. See *generally* Andrew D. Morton, "Much Ado About Newsgathering: Personal Privacy, Law Enforcement, and the Law of Unintended Consequences for Anti-Paparazzi Legislation," *U. Pa. L. Rev.* 147 (1999): 1435.

89. 955 P.2d 469, 486–490 (Cal. 1998).

90. *Ibid.*, 491.

SUMMARY AND CONCLUSION

That the U.S. approach to the regulation of anonymity seems patchwork should not surprise anyone prepared to look past the leading Supreme Court cases. Despite the Court's repeated, ringing endorsements of the role of anonymous advocacy and proselytizing, protection of anonymity is of a piece with the overall protection of privacy in the United States, which is to say that there is no fundamental consensus or coherent national policy. The mish-mash is less the result of neglect than the product of a clash between conflicting strongly felt policies and imperatives interwoven with a federal structure. As a result, at present U.S. policy toward anonymity remains primarily situational, largely reactive, and is slowly evolving.

On the one hand, the courts tend to interpret the protections of speech and assembly and other fundamental rights in ways friendly to anonymity as against the government, and friendly to privacy from government more generally. On the other hand, the courts remain open to governmental demands for identification when the grounds seem sufficiently compelling. And compelling demands have come from varied sources: It may be constitutional norms relating to open trials or the legislature seeking to regulate campaign finance or voter registration; it may be the police investigating a possible crime armed with probable cause; it could be the intelligence services (and police) seeking access to communications in the hunt for terrorists and criminals; it may be businesses seeking to use the court's power to compulsion to force others to divulge the identity of file-sharers. In each of these cases the countervailing case lacked sufficient force to carry the day—although the campaign finance issue in particular remains controversial.

In other cases, such as the attempt by private parties to use the courts to get the identities of political and corporate critics, the demands have seemed insufficiently compelling, and anonymity prevailed. Although it can be overcome for sufficiently good cause, the background norm that the government should not be able to compel individuals to reveal their identity without real cause retains real force.

The picture is quite different when two legitimate private interests come into conflict. Then the capitalist presumption of free contract (or open season) tends to be the background norm. Legislatures and regulators seem reluctant to intervene to protect privacy, much less anonymity, from what are seen as market forces. Thus the government imposes few if any legal obstacles to the domestic use of privacy-enhancing technology such as encryption and remailers. Conversely, and excepting a few special cases such as the Video Privacy Protection Act, the law generally requires little more than truth-in-advertising for most privacy-destroying technologies—firms must not lie about what they are doing because that would violate general consumer protection law. Absent actual lies and misleading statements, even duties to disclose tend to exist only in highly regulated industries such as the financial sector.

But as surveillance cameras proliferate and facial recognition software improves, it is increasingly hard to be lost in a crowd in real life; as virtual tracking tools improve, the same is even more quickly becoming true online. In the future it is likely to matter little who operates the recorders, as data is easily stored and sold to both private and public buyers. This and other technological changes suggest a possible convergence between de facto public and private sector anonymity destruction—a change that will necessitate a policy debate that has hardly yet begun.

25. ANONYMITY AND THE LAW IN CANADA

CAROLE LUCOCK AND KATIE BLACK

I. INTRODUCTION

Anonymity can be understood as not being named or identified or as not having identity connected with certain pieces of information. Anonymity thus broadly covers the "availability or unavailability of various kinds of information that may be known or identified about persons"[1] and includes the ability of others to reveal identity.

In Canada, there is no general right to anonymity. Rather, the law focuses on the circumstances and conditions under which a person's identity may or must be revealed or hidden from view. As such, this chapter discusses limited, rather complete, anonymity and examines the contexts and conditions under which the law supports a person not being named or known.

Although anonymity is often associated with the right to privacy, this chapter distinguishes anonymity from privacy. It only touches on privacy principles when they are directly relevant to the discussion of anonymity in Canadian law. As it relates to privacy, anonymity is often viewed as a mechanism for enhancing privacy.

---

1. G. Marx, "What's in a Name? Some Reflections on the Sociology of Anonymity," *The Information Society* 99, 15:2 (1999): 19.

Canada's legal system is jurisdictionally complex due to its operation within Canada's federated landscape. Legislative power is constitutionally divided between the federal government and ten provincial governments.[2] Given this complexity, we provide a cursory overview of Canadian laws pertaining to anonymity citing jurisdictional legislation and case law as examples. In general, we have tried to capture newer legal developments to illustrate that social and technological changes have had an impact on anonymity and its support in law. Some instances reveal that there has been an erosion of what would have been de facto anonymity, for example, unrecorded transactions, travel, or presence in a public space. Other instances demonstrate there has been a greater willingness to shield identity, for example, the identity of parties and witnesses in criminal and civil law suits, the requirement of the anonymization of data to be used for research purposes, and the disclosure of identity in access to information requests.

II. CONSTITUTIONAL PROVISIONS

A. Knowledge of Citizens Contemplated: Vital Statistics, Citizenship and Census

Canada's founding constitutional documents, the Constitution Act of 1867[3] and the Charter of Rights and Freedoms,[4] clearly permit and arguably require some state knowledge of citizens and noncitizens within Canadian jurisdiction. As such, the constitution cannot be said to have contemplated or provided for complete state-related anonymity.[5]

The Constitution Act divides the powers of citizen knowledge and information collection between the provincial and federal governments. The power and responsibility for citizenship[6] and census[7] taking rests with the federal government. The provinces have control over other primary registration systems (such as birth registrations), other vital statistics, as well as mandatory personal naming systems.[8]

---

2. The Constitution Act, 1867 (U.K.), 30 & 31 Victoria, c. 3, ss 91 & 92. Note that Canada also has three territories that constitutionally are under the jurisdiction of the federal government but in practice have powers akin to those of the provinces. The governance of specific areas of activity can be complicated and involve both levels of government. Legislation relating to the protection of privacy (with an indirect impact on the topic of anonymity) in the private sector is a good illustration of this.

3. *Ibid.*

4. The Constitution Act, 1982, being Schedule B to the Canada Act 1982 (U.K.), 1982, c. 11, Part I, The Canadian Charter of Rights and Freedoms.

5. Library and Archives Canada, Canadian Genealogy Centre, "Civil Registration," http://www.collectionscanada.gc.ca/genealogy/022-906.006-e.html; and Statistics Canada, "History of the Census of Canada," http://www.statcan.ca/english/census96/history.htm.

6. Constitution Act s 91(25) (n. 2).

7. *Ibid.* s 8, s 51, s 91(6).

8. *Ibid.* s 92(13), (16).

Requirements for these registration systems dovetail as the provincial birth certificate is typically used to confirm identity and rights for "most government documents and services, including health cards, drivers' licences, passports and social benefits."[9]

B. Charter of Rights and Freedoms: Limited Anonymity Related to Constitutional Rights

The Charter guarantees specified rights and freedoms by preventing all levels of government from placing limits on the enumerated rights and freedoms unless such limits can be demonstrably justified in a free and democratic society.[10] Although the Charter does not address anonymity directly, a number of sections are indirectly concerned with protecting it in certain circumstances. With the exception of provisions related to the criminal law, addressed in section 3, these sections are canvassed below.

Section 2(b): The Protection of Freedom of Expression Including Freedom of the Press[11] Although freedom of expression has been recognized by the courts as an important democratic right,[12] the role of anonymity in facilitating the exercise of this right has not been established. Indeed, the lower court in *Harper v. Canada*,[13] the one case that expressly considered whether anonymity is a value protected by s.2 (b) of the Charter, limited its findings to attribution requirements for third party advertisers in election advertising finding that "while this argument should not be foreclosed upon . . . s. 2(b) does not guarantee anonymity for third party advertisers or contributors in the circumstances of this case. Elections in general, and specifically election financing, are highly regulated activities and third parties can have no expectations of anonymity."[14] The court noted that "the concerns for public information outweigh citizens' ability to participate."[15] In finding against a right to anonymous political advertising, the court notably confined the decision to the facts of this case and additionally implied that a right to Charter protection of anonymous speech might be found at a later date,[16] as anonymity may either curtail or enhance the right to freedom of expression depending on the nature

---

9. For example, in order to obtain a passport, see Passport Canada, "Proof of Canadian Citizenship," http://www.ppt.gc.ca/cdn/section4.aspx?lang=eng.

10. Charter s.1 (n. 4). See also *R. v Oakes* [1986] 1 S.C.R. 103.

11. *Ibid.* Charter s 2(b), which provides that everyone has the fundamental freedoms of thought, belief, opinion, and expression, including freedom of the press and other media of communication.

12. See, for example, *R. v Keegstra* [1990] 3 S.C.R. 697at 763–764; and *Edmonton Journal v Alberta (Attorney General)* [1989] 2 S.C.R. 1326 at 1336.

13. *Harper v Canada (Attorney General)* [2001] A.J. No. 808 (Q.B).

14. *Ibid.* para. 186.

15. *Ibid.* para. 109.

16. *Ibid.* para. 186, where Justice Cairns' intimates that s.2(b) of the Charter might protect some privacy or anonymity rights.

of the circumstances. On appeal of this decision, and despite not addressing the issue of anonymity, the Supreme Court of Canada finds that overriding considerations of trust in the integrity of the electoral system, election fairness, and transparency are sufficiently important to justify the infringement of freedom of expression in the case of third-party advertising.[17]

One circumstance in which the salutary effects of anonymity can be seen is the expression of otherwise unpopular or socially repressed ideas.[18] Although American jurisprudence has provided robust protections for this type of anonymous expression, Canadian courts have not followed suit. To date, our courts have not acknowledged that anonymous speech may, in some instances, be essential to the exercise of freedom of expression.

In relation to the freedom of the press, jurisprudence engaging the role of anonymity clearly tends to focus on its deleterious ability to stifle transparency in the judicial process. In both the civil and criminal contexts,[19] many such cases concern the need for openness of the courts. Often at the behest of the press, attempts to curtail this transparency by granting limited anonymity to parties or witnesses are interrogated. Anonymity in the judicial process has thus been limited to very specific circumstances, including protecting the vulnerable and promoting the prosecution of claims and crimes.

Section 7: Right to Life, Liberty and Security of the Person[20] Section 7 of the Charter of Rights and Freedoms has been found to contain and protect a right to privacy.[21] This finding, however, has primarily been limited to the criminal law context (which is discussed below). Beyond this, there are some cases that recognize section 7 as protecting a right not to be identified or the right to limited anonymity as a component of the right to privacy.[22] *Cheskes*[23] exemplifies this protection. The case involved a recent challenge to new Ontario adoption legislation retroactively and nonconsensually disavowing birth parents and adoptees of their anonymity by opening the adoption record. The court found that the retroactive provisions infringed upon section 7 and were therefore of no force and effect, suggesting that section 7 protects anonymity, as incorporated in a right to privacy, beyond the criminal law context. As such *Cheskes* opens up section 7 anonymity protections and contextualizes the earlier limits placed on them in

---

17. *Harper v Canada (Attorney General)* [2004] 1 S.C.R. 827 at paras 136–139 and 142–146.

18. See, for example, C. Keen, "Anonymity and the Supreme Court's Model of Expression: How Should Anonymity be Analysed Under Section 2(b) of the Charter," *Canadian Journal of Law and Technology* 23, 2:3 (2003): 1671.

19. See sections III.A and IV.A.

20. S. 7 provides that "Everyone has the right to life, liberty and security of the person and the right not to be deprived thereof in accordance with the principles of fundamental justice."

21. *R. v O'Conner* [1995] 4 S.C.R. 41.

22. See *Cheskes v Ontario Attorney General* [2007] 87 O.R. (3d) 581 (S.C.)

23. *Ibid.*

Canadian AIDS Society v. Ontario.[24] In this case, public health legislation that required the reporting of blood donors' HIV seropositive status was challenged, specifically when blood samples taken before the HIV/AIDS test was available were retested. Here, the court found that the donors' section 7 right to security of the person was infringed. The legislative measures were upheld, however, because they accorded with the principles of fundamental justice due to the over-riding public health considerations and public health officials' requirements to maintain reported information in confidence.

Section 3: Right to Vote[25] The Canada Elections Act[26] and provincial election acts, such as Ontario's Election Act,[27] recognize the role that anonymity plays in ensuring meaningful and free participation in the elections process. They have incorporated a number of provisions that deal with identification during the registration process, proof of elector identification when obtaining ballots at polling stations, anonymity in the actual voting process to ensure the secrecy of a person's vote, disclosure of campaign contributions, and disclosure of campaign advertising.[28]

Although voting eligibility requirements have always mandated that voters demonstrate their identity by providing their name and address in exchange for a ballot, for example, the new federal Canada Elections Act requires voters to provide physical identification at polling stations.[29] Voters are not, however, required to produce photo ID, and there are mechanisms to allow persons who are unwilling to show their faces to demonstrate their identities.[30]

Once elector identity has been confirmed, the Canada Elections Act ensures voting anonymity. The vote is to be secret[31] as a rule of absolute public policy that cannot be waived.[32] The identity of the elector can no longer be ascertained after the ballot has been provided to them.[33] Moreover, the Act obligates all in attendance at a polling station or at the counting of votes to maintain this secrecy.

---

24. (1995), 25 O.R. (3d) 388 (Gen. Div).); affirmed (1996), 31 O.R. (3d) 796 (C.A.).

25. Section 3 provides that "Every Citizen of Canada has the right to vote in an election of members of the House of Commons or of a legislative assembly and to be qualifies for membership therein."

26. Canada Elections Act SC 2007, c. 21.

27. Election Act RSA 2000 c. 9 s. 6.

28. Also see *Harper* (n. 17), which upholds the constitutionality of the latter two.

29. Canada Elections s 143(1) (n. 26) and clarified by The Chief Electoral Officer to include one piece of government issued photo ID containing name and address, two pieces of ID containing name and address, or to have another eligible voter vouch for a person's identity. Press Release, Elections Canada, http://www.elections.ca/content.asp?section=med&dir=spe&document=sep1007&lang=e&textonly_false.

30. *Ibid.*

31. *Ibid.* s 163.

32. *Walsh v Montage* [1888] 15 S.C.R. 495 (S.C.C.).

33. Canada Elections s 144.1 (n. 26).

Only an elector requiring assistance may reveal his or her vote to another.[34] This right to secrecy is also mirrored within provincial election legislation.[35]

III. CRIMINAL LAW

Anonymity is engaged throughout the criminal justice system. It concerns the concealment or disclosure of identity as well as methods and techniques of investigation, surveillance, and evidence gathering of such things as fingerprints or DNA.

A. Disclosing and Concealing Identity

General Requirement for Identification There is no general requirement that persons carry identification or identify themselves to law enforcement officers.[36] When law enforcement authorities have no reasonable grounds to detain or arrest an individual, that individual is provided a limited degree of anonymity by common-law principles and Charter guarantees of the right to be free from arbitrary detention[37] and the right to remain silent.[38] No law, however, prevents law enforcement officers from stopping people to ask questions. Courts have upheld the brief detention of people by officers as lawful for investigative purposes in a crime under investigation.[39] Reasonable grounds for the detention based on a reasonable suspicion of involvement must exist in such cases. Even though persons are not *required* to identify themselves when detained, there is nothing to prevent them from volunteering this information when questioned by law enforcement personnel.[40] Although refusing to answer such questions will not constitute a charge of obstructing justice, the provision of a false identity will.[41] If a person feels compelled to provide identifying information because of the circumstances of their physical or psychological detention, the use of obtained identifying information may be considered a Charter infringement of the right to be free from unreasonable search and seizure.[42] This is especially so if the identifying information is used to search law enforcement databases.

---

34. *Ibid.* S. 164(1)–(2).

35. For example, *Elections Act*, R.S.A., 2000, c. E-1, s. 93.

36. *R. v Mann* [2004] 3 S.C.R. 59, see also, *R. v Legault* [1998] 54 C.R.R. (2d) 155 and *R. v Greaves*, [2004] 189 C.C.C (3d) 305 (BCCA).

37. Charter s 9 (n. 4).

38. *Ibid.* S 7 has been held by the courts to contain the right to remain silent. See, for example, *R. v Hebert* [1990] 2 S.C.R. 151 (SCC).

39. *Mann* at para 17 (n. 36).

40. *Greaves* at 47–48 (n. 36).

41. *Ibid.* at 49–51.

42. *R. v Harris* [2007] 87 O.R. (3d) 214 (On CA).

Nonetheless, this sphere of limited anonymity is very restricted. It does not apply once a person has been charged with an offence[43] or arrested,[44] or when there is a legal duty to identify oneself—for example, as exists in the Highway Traffic Acts.[45] Proposals to introduce a National Identification Card threaten to further restrict, if not obliterate, the limited anonymity currently enjoyed in Canada.[46]

Concealing Identity: Informants, the Accused, and Witnesses In the judicial process, the concealment of identity generally arises during criminal trials. It may relate to disclosing all information to the accused for the purposes of making a full defense or the placement of publication bans on the names of the accused, victims, or witnesses. Generally, when bans are issued, the person is known under a pseudonym in publications and in reported legal decisions of the case.

Informants There is a long-standing common-law rule preventing the disclosure of police informants' identities on the grounds that it is important for people to assist the police without fear of retaliation.[47] Informer privilege has been extended to more recent programs such as "Crime Stoppers." This program encourages people to report potential crimes to the police on the understanding that their identities will be concealed.[48] Informer privilege is not absolute, and identity may be revealed in certain limited circumstances relating to trial fairness and the rights of the accused.[49] Even here, there is a preference for providing nonidentifying information to the accused.[50]

The Accused Generally, the identity of the accused is not concealed or subject to publication restrictions. This adheres to the general policy of court openness prevalent in the Canadian criminal justice system. Young offenders represent an exception to this general rule. In most cases, the Youth Criminal Justice Act[51] prohibits the publication of the identity of a child[52] or young person[53]

---

43. *R. v Beare* [1988] 2 S.C.R. 387.

44. *Moore v The Queen* [1978] 43 CCC (2d) 83 (SCC). See also Criminal Code, R.S.C. 1985, c. C-46 s 495(2)(d)(i).

45. For example, Highway Traffic Act RSO 1990, c H.8, s 33, s 104.1(4)) and s 218.

46. See, Privacy Commissioner of Canada, "Appendix A: The National Identity Card Debate" in *Identity, Privacy and the Need of Others to Know Who You Are: A Discussion Paper on Identity Issues* (Ottawa: Privacy Commissioner of Canada, September 2007), http://www.privcom.gc.ca/information/pub/ID_Paper_e.asp.

47. *R. v Leipert* [1997] 1 S.C.R. 281.

48. *Ibid.*

49. *R. v Scott* [1990] 3 S.C.R. 979, see also, *R. v Rodney Appleby* (2006), [2007] 263 Nfld. & P.E.I.R. 262.

50. *Scott* (n. 52) per Cory, J.

51. S.C. 2002, c 1.

52. A person who is or appears to be less than 12. *Ibid.* s 2(1).

53. A person who is or appears to be older than 12 but younger than 18. *Ibid.* s 2(1).

accused of a crime.[54] Exceptions to this general prohibition concern treating the accused as an adult for the purposes of the Act,[55] disclosure of identity for the purposes of the administration of justice,[56] disclosure of identity when required to apprehend the young person or if the young person is a danger to others,[57] and at the request of the person to whom the disclosure prohibition applies.[58]

A more limited exception exists to protect the reputation of the accused when there is some doubt about the laying of charges and the accused's reputation in a small community may be severely damaged as a result of the charges.[59]

Witnesses The strong presumption of open courts, supported by the Charter protection of freedom of the press, generally requires the identity of witnesses to be known and subject to publication. However, their identities may be concealed for a variety of policy reasons.[60] Crimes such as extortion or sexual offences may go unprosecuted or become underreported if victims are not permitted to conceal their identity.[61] The identity of child and youth victims and witnesses are concealed under both the Criminal Code[62] and the Youth Criminal Justice Act.[63] Police informants, undercover operatives, and persons subject to witness protection schemes[64] may be harmed if their identities become known. Consequently, publication bans will often be granted in these cases.[65]

---

54. *Ibid.* s 110.

55. *Ibid.* s 110(2)(a) and (b).

56. *Ibid.* s 110(2(c).

57. *Ibid.* s 110(4).

58. *Ibid.* s 110 (3) and (6).

59. *In the matter of an application by an unnamed person for an Order banning the publication of his name* [2005] 249 Nfld. & P.E.I.R. 233 citing as authority for permitting the ban *Dagenais v Canadian Broadcasting Corporation* [1994] 3 S.C.R. 835 at paras 87–88, which recognized the privacy of the accused and his or her family as a factor to consider in granting a publication ban.

60. *Ibid. Dagenais,* which articulates the factors to be taken into consideration when considering whether to grant a publication ban; *A.G. (Nova Scotia) v MacIntyre* [1982] 1 S.C.R. 175 (protecting the innocent), *R. v O.N.E,* 2001 SCC 77 and *R. v Mentuck,* 2001 SCC 76 (proper administration of justice and protection from harm). S 486.5(1) of the Criminal Code (n. 44) encapsulates much of the common law with respect to whether to grant a publication ban in the interests of the proper administration of justice.

61. Criminal Code s. 486.4(1) (n. 44) lists a number of offences where a nonpublication order may be issued. Generally, the issuing of an order is discretionary; however, s 486.4(2) provides that a complainant must be informed of this section and non-publication order *must* be issued if an application is made. See also *Canadian Newspapers Co. v Canada (Attorney General)* [1988] 2 S.C.R. 122 and *R. v Seaboyer* [1991] 2 S.C.R. 577.

62. *Ibid.* Criminal Code s. 486.4(2).

63. Youth Criminal Justice s 111.(1) (n. 51).

64. Witness Protection Program Act, S.C. 1996 c.15.

65. *O.N.E.* and *Mentuck* (n. 60).

B. Investigation, Surveillance, and Evidence Gathering

Reasonable Expectation of Privacy Section 8 of the Charter[66] guarantees the right to be free from unreasonable search or seizure and has thus been used to determine the constitutionality of law enforcement methods of investigation and evidence gathering. The Supreme Court of Canada, in *R. v. Dyment,* [67] articulated what is of concern and why, as follows: "The restraints imposed on government to pry into the lives of the citizen go to the essence of a democratic state."[68] Anonymity is here engaged more in the sense of being left alone by the state and not having information collected and known, rather than identity being revealed per se.

The threshold question for engaging the protections accorded by section 8 is whether, in the circumstances, a person has a reasonable expectation of privacy. If not, then a search is considered to have not occurred for constitutional purposes; section 8 remains unengaged.[69] Many of the cases consequently center around whether there was a reasonable expectation of privacy in the context of specific state activity. If a search is found to have taken place, thereby engaging section 8, the specific activity is scrutinized by asking: was the activity authorized by law and is that law reasonable? For the most part, courts expect to see judicial authorization (generally a warrant) for the activity.

Some authorization requirements are found in legislation. The Criminal Code, for example, contains a general provision concerning the need for a warrant in certain circumstances[70] as well as specific reference to such things as the interception of private communications[71] and the use of video surveillance.[72] General provisions for the warrant state that it is necessary when the activity would constitute an unreasonable search and seizure if not authorized.[73] This implies the necessity of a warrant when there is a reasonable expectation of privacy.

As noted, a key question in the jurisprudence is whether, in the circumstances, there is a reasonable expectation of privacy. The 2004 *Tessling*[74] case summarizes the law in this regard as well as the impact of the use of newer methods of surveillance on the reasonable expectation of privacy. In synthesizing the law, the court notes three realms of privacy subject to a reasonable expectation: personal, territorial, and informational.[75] Personal privacy is accorded the greatest protection.[76]

---

66. Charter (n. 4).
67. [1988] 2 S.C.R. 417.
68. *Ibid.* Para 17.
69. *R. v Tessling,* [2004] 3 S.C.R. 432 at para 18.
70. Criminal Code s.487.01 (n. 44).
71. *Ibid.* s.184.
72. *Ibid.* s.487.01(4).
73. *Ibid.* s. 487.01(1).
74. *Tessling* (n. 69).
75. *Ibid.* Para 20.
76. *Ibid.* Para 21.

Territorial privacy, especially as it relates to the home or dwelling place, is also given a high degree of protection.[77] Informational privacy is accorded the lowest degree of protection, and authorization for its collection is only required with respect to a "biographical core of personal information."[78] This core includes "information which tends to reveal intimate details of the lifestyle and personal choices of the individual."[79]

In many instances, a reasonable expectation of privacy may not be found as a consequence of the privacy hierarchy and judicial authorization will not be required, especially if the context is characterized as concerning informational privacy. These contexts include information that is in public view, information that has been abandoned, and information that is not subject to customer confidentiality (for example, electricity records).[80] In *Tessling*, it included images of heat emanating from a building captured by a forward-looking infrared camera installed in a plane that flew over the building. To determine whether a reasonable expectation of privacy existed, the *Tessling* court looked at the "totality of the circumstances" taking into account subjective expectations of privacy and whether these are objectively reasonable.[81] The Supreme Court stated that technology should be considered in light of its current capabilities and noted that advances in surveillance capabilities and the diminished subjective expectation of privacy that might ensue should not lower the constitutional protection given. Simply put, Binnie J. wrote "expectation of privacy is a normative rather than a descriptive standard."[82]

Somewhat contentious are the spaces that may entail some, albeit a diminished, expectation of privacy. For example, schools,[83] lockers in bus stations,[84] hotel rooms,[85] airports, and motor vehicles.[86] The law continues to develop as to the standards of search which they require. Two recent cases concerning the permitted uses of sniffer dogs to detect illegal drugs have destabilized the law to some degree because the Supreme Court was divided on a number of points, in

---

77. *Ibid.* Para 22, which recognizes privacy interests in a number of places beyond the home including places of work, private cars, and prisons.

78. *Ibid.* Para 25 citing *R. v Plant* [1993] 3 S.C.R. 281. A recent Supreme Court decision has clarified that if information fails to meet the 'core biographical' test it will not necessarily be without protection, citing wire tapping as an example. See *R. v A.M.*, 2008 SCC 19 at para 68.

79. *Tessling* para 25 (n. 69).

80. *Plant* (n. 78).

81. *Tessling* paras 34–62 (n. 69).

82. *Ibid.* para 42.

83. *R. v M. (M.R.)* [1998] 3 S.C.R. 393 and *R. v. A.M* (n. 78).

84. *R. v Buhay* [2003] 1 S.C.R. 631.

85. *Ibid.*, at para 22.

86. *R. v Wise* [1992] 1 S.C.R. 527.

particular, whether or not there was a reasonable expectation of privacy in the circumstances and the standard to be used to allow sniffer dogs to investigate.[87]

Biometric Banks The collection and use of fingerprints and DNA foreclose anonymity in cases in which this information has been added to databases that are made available for law enforcement purposes. Indeed, courts have accepted that persons convicted of designated, serious offences lose their expectation of privacy and anonymity. The Supreme Court in *Rogers* wrote "can persons convicted of designated offences . . . reasonably expect to retain any degree of anonymity *vis-à-vis* law enforcement authorities after their conviction?"[88] The court concluded that "a person convicted of a designated offence would reasonably expect the authorities to gather and retain identifying information, such as fingerprints, distinctive body markings, or eye color. The bodily sample here is simply another form of identification." Mr. Rodgers consequently lost

> any reasonable expectation of privacy in the *identifying information* derived from DNA sampling in the same way as he . . . lost any expectation of privacy in his fingerprints, photograph or any other identifying measure taken under the authority of the Identification of Criminals Act.[89]

The collection and use of fingerprint information for identification purposes has long been accepted in common law and more recently held to be constitutional[90] along with the collection and use of DNA for similar purposes.[91] Legislation, such as the Identification of Criminals Act[92] (dealing with fingerprints and photographs) and the DNA Identification Act,[93] provides for the collection of information and its use. Generally, collection is only permitted in connection with serious offenses, and use is restricted to the purpose of identification. The constitutionality of the DNA Identification Act and provisions in the Criminal Code relating to the collection of DNA has been upheld, in part, on the basis that the use of DNA information is restricted to identification and that the collection of DNA information generally occurs under judicial authorization.[94]

Addressing Newer Technologies Anonymity may be enhanced by the use of new technologies, particularly in an electronic or online environment. This is of particular concern to law enforcement and national security agencies seeking to ensure that a link is maintained between individuals and their activities.

---

87. *R. v Kang-Brown*, 2008 SCC 18 and *R. v. A.M* (n. 78).

88. *R. v Rodgers* [2006] 1 S.C.R. 554 at para 43. See also, *R. v. S.A.B.*, [2003] 2 S.C.R. 678, 2003 SCC 60.

89. *Ibid. Rogers.*

90. *Beare* (n. 43). See also The Identification of Criminal Act, RSC 1985, c. I–1.

91. *Rogers* (n. 88).

92. R.S.C. 1985, c. I–1.

93. S.C. 1998, c. 37. See also Criminal Code ss 487.04–487.092 (n. 44).

94. *Rogers* (n. 88).

For a number of years, the federal government has attempted to introduce legislation that would require telecommunications service providers, such as cell phone and Internet service companies, to provide identifying information under certain terms and conditions.[95] These legislative initiatives are ongoing[96] and may result in legislative change. Questions remain regarding the necessity of the change,[97] the sufficiency of existing law enforcement access to identifying information, and if change is required, the nature of the judicial oversight and grounds for authorizing the provision of identity information.

Encryption technologies, although helpful in enabling secure online interactions, communications, and anonymity, also pose a challenge to law enforcement and security agencies. At present, there are few legal controls concerning the use of encryption technologies.[98] This may change, however, due to growing opposition mounted by government agencies to their unregulated employment and development. The main concern raised involves the ability of encryption to frustrate counterterrorism and law enforcement initiatives by impeding law enforcement access to information.

In October 1998, Industry Minister John Manley confirmed that Canada's Cryptography Policy established Canadians' freedom "to develop, import and use whatever cryptography products they wish."[99] Concurrently, he also committed the government to "[giving] law enforcement agencies and national security agencies the legal framework they need to ensure public safety." [100] This included "making it an offence to wrongfully disclose private encryption key information and to use cryptography to commit or hide evidence of a crime."[101] He continued,

---

95. Proposed legislation has been hotly contended by privacy and civil liberties groups. See Canadian Internet and Public Policy Clinic, *Lawful Access* (updated June 2, 2007), http://www.cippic.ca/projects-cases-lawful-access/ for a discussion of the history and links to relevant information.

96. In the fall of 2007 a consultation paper was released by Public Safety Canada and Industry Canada; see Public Safety Canada, *Customer Name and Address Information Consultation*, http://securitepublique.gc.ca/prg/ns/cna-en.asp.

97. For example, Criminal Code s. 430(1.1) (n. 44) creates the offence of mischief for willfully obstructing, interfering, or denying access to data to any person who is entitled to it.

98. For example, the Export and Import Permits Act, R.S.C. 1985, c-E–19, and the United Nations Act, R.S.C. 1985, c.U–2 limit the export of technologies such as methods of encryption to a limited number of countries and groups and were implemented to minimize the threat that such technologies would be used against Canada in conflict. The Security of Information Act, R.S.C. 1985, c. O–5, s.1; 2001, c.41, s.25; (updated by the Anti-terrorism Act, R.S.C. 1985, c.O–5, s.1; 2001, c.41, s.25) makes the possession of any "device, apparatus or software useful for concealing the content of information or for surreptitiously communicating, obtaining or retaining information," enumerated in the act, an offence ss.22(1)(e).

99. Industry Canada, Canada's Cryptography Policy (October 1, 1998), http://e-com. ic.gc.ca/epic/internet/inecic-ceac.nsf/en/gv00119e.html.

100. *Ibid.*, policy, 6th point.

101. *Ibid.*

"we also need to make it clear that warrants and assistance orders also apply to situations where encryption is encountered—to obtain the decrypted material or decryption keys."[102]

IV. PRIVATE LAW

A. Legal Proceedings

Parties and Witnesses As with criminal law, legal proceedings in court are generally open, parties and witnesses are known, and their identities are subject to publication. Children and youth involved in child protection or adoption proceedings,[103] the innocent in need of protection,[104] and those who may be subject to harm[105] present the main exceptions to this general rule. A gray area concerns when the likelihood of suffering embarrassment, shame, or humiliation will suffice to tip the scales in favor of permitting the concealing of identity. By and large, courts are reluctant to allow these as grounds for shielding identity; yet, exceptions have been made for some plaintiffs, letting them proceed under a pseudonym.[106]

Traditionally, courts have shown a reluctance to permit the shielding of identity on a simple claim of privacy. This may be changing, however, especially in circumstances in which the plaintiffs wish to uphold a previously established pseudonym. A recent case suggests that pseudonyms will be upheld in cases in which identity was already shielded behind a pseudonym prior to the civil action; at issue (in part) was the revelation of the identities of individuals using pseudonyms during peer-to-peer music file sharing.[107]

Although courts clearly favor openness and disclosure of identity, this is not the case for all decision-making bodies. For example, the federal private sector

---

102. *Ibid.*

103. These provisions are generally specified in legislation. See, for example, The Child and Family Services Act, RSO, 1990 c. C11 s 45.

104. *A.G. (Nova Scotia) v MacIntyre* [1982] 1 S.C.R. 175 at pp. 186–187. This exception usually applies to children; however, in *T.H. v C.D.G* (Man QB 1997), 7 W.W.R. 318, 120 Man. R. (2d) 11, a case of alleged sexual abuse by clergy, the alleged perpetrator, and institution were permitted to proceed under a pseudonym.

105. Concealing identity because harm may ensue is more common in criminal cases; however, discrimination may be considered a sufficiently compelling ground to permit pseudonym use. For example in cases concerning HIV/AIDs, see *A.(J.) v Canada Life Assurance Co.* (Ont HCJ 1989), 66 O.R. (2d) 736.

106. See, *T. (S.) v Stubbs* (Ont Gen Div 1998), 38 O.R. (3d) 788 and *B. (A.) v Stubbs* (Ont Gen Div 1999), 44 O.R. (3d) 391, where, based on similar facts (a penis enlargement operation that did not go well) different decisions were rendered concerning permitting the use of a pseudonym.

107. *BMG Canada Inc. v John Doe* [2004] 3 F.C.R. 241, affirmed in result but, in some instances, on different grounds [2005] 4 F.C.R. 81 (CA).

privacy legislation contemplates an ombudsperson approach to dispute resolution, which includes the publishing of case summaries without the names of parties.[108]

Revealing the Identity of Potential Defendants The identity of potential defendants may be known by third parties but not by the party seeking to pursue a claim. Before the widespread use of pseudonyms in the online environment, legal tests had been developed to determine when such third parties would be required to divulge identity. With the expanded use of pseudonyms, and the relative anonymity they provide, there have been a number of cases that have addressed the conditions under which third parties such as Internet service providers (ISPs) will be compelled to reveal identity. Outlining the legal test for this purpose, the case of *BMG*[109] requires first that a bona fide claim be made out and, second, that factors mitigating in favor of and against disclosure be considered. The ability to pursue the claim is the chief factor in favor of disclosure. Factors mitigating against disclosure are less clear but center on a number of interests including privacy, competing public-interest considerations (such as freedom of speech), and the nature of the relationship between the party whose identity has been concealed and the identity of the revealing party. In refusing to permit disclosure, the court in *BMG* took into consideration the lack of reliability of the information linking identity to pseudonym, the implied desire for privacy as a result of pseudonym use, and the contractual agreement of privacy between the user and the ISP.

B. Anonymous Transactions

In theory, many transactions, including contracts, can be executed anonymously, especially if these are simple transactions requiring a single instance of mutual exchange, such as the purchase of a product or service for cash. The scope for anonymity is limited in practice. Contracts contemplating an ongoing relationship that are reduced to writing require identity information of the parties.[110] Simple exchanges often use cash substitutes such as credit or debit cards, which could be used to track the identity of a person. Vendors of various goods and services collect identity information for a variety of purposes including advertising and customer service. The return or exchange of a product may require the provision of identity information if a refund is to be provided. The provision of specific services may entail the provision of identity information. Provided that the collection of identity information is considered reasonable in the circumstances, it will not be in contravention of private sector privacy legislation restricting the collection of personal information.[111]

---

108. Personal Information Protection and Electronic Documents Act, S.C. 2000 c 5 (PIPEDA).

109. *BMG* (n. 107). See also *Irwin Toy v Doe* (Ont SCJ 2000), 12 C.P.C. (5th) 103).

110. For example, the Statute of Frauds, R.S.O. 1990, c S19 requires that certain types of contracts be reduced to writing and signed by the parties.

111. For example, Privacy Commissioner of Canada, PIPEDA case summaries # 361 (refund or exchange of goods), #288 (provision of cell phone services), and #280 (preventing signal theft).

In addition to the collection of identity information being considered reasonable and therefore permissible under private sector privacy legislation and the requirements of the heavily regulated financial and securities sectors, other legislation, such as the Pawn Brokers Act[112] and the Proceeds of Crime (Money Laundering) and Terrorist Financing Regulations,[113] may expressly require the collection of identity information before transactions are permitted.

Identity is also connected to signature in the electronic environment, where legislation enabling the use of electronic signatures also contemplates a link to identity information.[114] In such environments, where there is an increased opportunity for the collection and use of identity information and therefore fewer opportunities for anonymity, the Privacy Commissioner of Canada has called for making the right to anonymity the norm.[115]

C. Surveillance

The Personal Information Protection and Electronic Documents Act[116] and companion provincial private sector privacy legislation[117] govern the collection and use of personal information in the private sector, including the collection of information using surveillance technologies. The use of technologies such as video surveillance is generally not prohibited. However, guidelines produced by the Office of the Privacy Commissioner of Canada[118] as well as findings related to surveillance[119] indicate, among other things, that the use of such technology will be reasonable (and hence lawful) if:

1. There is a compelling reason engage in surveillance[120]
2. It is deployed only if less privacy-invasive measures are inadequate
3. Surveillance is not used in highly private areas such as washrooms
4. Notice of the deployment of surveillance cameras is given

---

112. For example, Pawnbrokers Act RSO 1990 c P.6 s 9.

113. Proceeds of Crime (Money Laundering) and Terrorist Financing Regulations, S.C. 2000, c 17, s 6.1, S.O.R. 202–184 s 53.

114. PIPEDA (n. 108).

115. Privacy Commissioner, Identity, Privacy at 16–17 (n. 46).

116. PIPEDA (n. 108).

117. Alberta, British Columbia, and Quebec have private-sector privacy legislation that has been found to be substantially similar to PIPEDA. See Privacy Commissioner of Canada, "Substantially Similar Provincial Legislation," http://www.privcom.gc.ca/legislation/ss_index_e.asp.

118. Office of the Privacy Commissioner of Canada, *Guidelines for Overt Video Surveillance* (Office of the Privacy Commissioner of Canada: Ottawa, 2008), http://www.privcom.gc.ca/information/guide/2008/gl_vs_080306_e.asp.

119. *Eastmond v Canadian Pacific Railway*, (2004), 16 Admin. L.R. (4th) 275 (FC) at para 127; Privacy Commissioner of Canada, PIPEDA Case Summaries #114, #268, #269, #273, #279, #290, #379.

120. Examples given include bank machines and high-crime areas.

Other legislation will also have an impact on what techniques of surveillance are permitted. For example, the Criminal Code makes it an offence to intercept telecommunications,[121] and consequently this type of surveillance activity is curtailed.

In the employment context, video surveillance of employees for performance purposes is generally frowned upon and disallowed.[122] Provided that surveillance is being conducted for legitimate purposes such as theft prevention or detection, the inadvertent capture of employee information might not be problematic so long as its subsequent use is in compliance with PIPEDA.[123] When used for legitimate purposes, other technologies that have a surveillance component, such as global positioning devices and voice print biometrics, have also been found to be consistent with PIPEDA.[124]

D. Data Mining

Privacy legislation protects personal information that is connected to an identifiable individual. Consequently, information with identifiers removed is not protected under privacy law. As such, the commercial and health care setting displays a great deal of latitude for the unimpeded use of de-identified information. Apart from the questions surrounding the efficacy of techniques used to de-identify personal information—is the information truly anonymous?—thorny questions concerning whether consent is needed *prior to* anonymization have yet to be discussed or answered by courts or policy makers.

E. Special Areas Permitting or Requiring Anonymity

Copyright Law Copyright legislation provides authors and creators of works with the right to remain anonymous with respect to attribution, including the right to use a pseudonym.[125]

Adoption and Reproductive Technologies Rules surrounding adoption and the use of donor gametes hold that the anonymity of all concerned is the general rule.[126] Nonidentifying and useful information such as health information is generally available to children who have been adopted or were conceived through the

---

121. Criminal Code s. 184 (n. 44).

122. This is a very complex topic and only very briefly touched on here. See Eastman (n. 119) at paras 126–173.

123. *Ibid.* See, for example, Privacy Commissioner of Canada, Case Summary #290. Case Summary #279 strongly suggests that the use of video surveillance solely for performance monitoring would be contrary to PIPEDA. Note that even covert surveillance has been found to be acceptable provided that it meets the strict standards of the legislation; see Case Summary #379.

124. See, for example, Privacy Commissioner of Canada, Case Summaries #351 and #281.

125. Copyright Act, R.S.C. 1985, c. C–42, s. 14.1(1).

126. For example, Child and Family Services Act, R.S.O. 1990, c. C.11.

use of donor gametes. In the case of adoption, there are also significant provisions to allow parties to connect when the child reaches maturity. Additionally, some Canadian jurisdictions show a move toward more open adoptions, allowing parties to contact each other more easily and with fewer constraints.[127] Over time, the social policies favoring the support of anonymity in this context have given way to a greater emphasis on the provision of at least nonidentifying information as well as promoting the provision of identity information to facilitate contact.

V. ANONYMITY IN PUBLIC

The cumulative effect of government and industry deployment of technology, particularly systems of surveillance, has resulted in a loss of the de facto anonymity once enjoyed in public spaces.[128] The increased deployment of surveillance by government[129] has a clear impact on individuals seeking anonymity in public places.

There is no clear answer as to how the law will limit the use of generalized surveillance, that is, surveillance that is not time-limited and targeted to a particular person, circumstance, or event. However, there are a number of reasons to believe that there are some legal limits placed on government before generalized public surveillance systems are deployed.

An influential 2002 legal opinion[130] suggests that the use of generalized video surveillance for law enforcement purposes violates the public sector Privacy Act[131] and section 8 of the Charter.[132] Although this opinion makes a strong case, it is not definitive, and a number of other developments suggest that although deployment may be controlled, it will nonetheless be permitted.

A number of jurisdictions have put forth guidelines concerning the deployment of video camera surveillance by the government that restrict deployment on the basis of provisions of the public sector privacy legislation regulating the collection and use of personal information by government. This includes law enforcement agencies. These guidelines express concern about the increased deployment of generalized surveillance and seek to limit it to situations in which deployment is a last resort measure.

---

127. See note 23 and accompanying text.

128. Ian Kerr, *Lessons from the Identity Trail: Anonymity, Privacy, and Identity in a Networked Society* (New York: Oxford University Press, 2009), Chapter 5.

129. Office of the Privacy Commissioner of Canada, *OPC Guidelines for the Use of Video Surveillance of Public Places by Police and Law Enforcement Authorities* (Office of the Privacy Commissioner of Canada: Ottawa, 2006).

130. Opinion by Justice Gérard La Forest, April 5, 2002, Privacy Commissioner of Canada, http://www.privcom.gc.ca/media/nr-c/opinion_020410_e.asp.

131. R.S.C. 1985, c. P–21.

132. Charter (n. 4).

Regrettably, the promulgation of guidelines and their content indicates that there is no anticipated bar on this form of government activity. Moreover, a number of formal findings concerning the deployment of generalized surveillance for law enforcement or security purposes suggest that private sector privacy legislation will not be violated if properly justified with sufficient safeguards in place.[133] An example that bodes poorly with respect to establishing limits is the special report of the Information and Privacy Commissioner of Ontario. The report focused on the use of generalized surveillance in Toronto's mass transit system.[134] The commissioner found that the deployment of video surveillance and its ability to provide information to law enforcement authorities was in compliance with public sector privacy legislation.

The criminal law section above noted that surveillance for law enforcement purposes is somewhat constrained and curtailed. In order to determine whether the deployment of generalized video surveillance[135] is constitutionally sound and free from section 8 Charter infringements, one must determine the "status" of public space with respect to the reasonable expectation of privacy.

The jurisprudence in this area is far from clear. Although there are strong statements to the effect that unrestricted video surveillance on the part of the state could annihilate privacy,[136] other statements recognize that some spaces and circumstances are not likely to be found to have a reasonable expectation of privacy.[137] Until this matter is squarely before the courts, it is not possible to state definitively that the deployment of generalized video surveillance by the government for law enforcement purposes would be found to be constitutionally sound.

---

133. See section IVC.

134. Office of the Information and Privacy Commissioner of Ontario, *Privacy and Video Surveillance in Mass Transit Systems: A Special Investigative Report* (March 2008).

135. Particularized surveillance of a specific individual or event would be subject to the normal legal tests.

136. For example, *R. v Wong* [1990] 3 S.C.R. 36 "The notion that the agencies of the state should be at liberty to train hidden cameras on members of society wherever and whenever they wish is fundamentally irreconcilable with what we perceive to be acceptable behaviour on the part of government. As in the case of audio surveillance, to permit unrestricted video surveillance by agents of the state would seriously diminish the degree of privacy we can reasonably expect to enjoy in a free society. There are [. . .] situations and places which invite special sensitivity to the need for human privacy. Moreover . . . we must always be alert to the fact that modern methods of electronic surveillance have the potential, if uncontrolled, to annihilate privacy."

137. For example, *Tessling* (n. 69) found that there was no reasonable expectation of privacy in images of heat emanating from a building that were captured by a plane using FLIR camera and, in discussing the lesser protection afforded informational privacy, suggests that if generalized surveillance in public places is characterized as "informational" and is not seen to contain core biographical then it may well be consistent with section 8 of the Charter (n. 4).

Although technically within the "private realm," shopping malls, stores, and buildings with general public access may well be considered by those using them to be quasi-public and similar to public spaces such as streets and parks. Although the deployment of surveillance in these spaces was discussed above, here it is important to take stock of the cumulative impact that surveillance in these and public spaces has on the overall ability to remain anonymous outside the home. Apart from the "feeling" of being surveilled and the impact that this may have on behavior, there is also the fact of significant data collection concerning activities in these spaces, which, if recorded, may be used in combination for a variety of purposes, including law enforcement purposes.

VI. CONCLUSION

Anonymity is a complex topic and one that the law has dealt with in a piecemeal rather than coherent fashion. As a result, the impact on the de facto anonymity once enjoyed in Canada of information collection practices, information consolidation, and general surveillance has not been fully appreciated or addressed. The existing social climate is one that is marked more by concerns related to security than concerns related to lessening opportunities for anonymity. The current legal structure has not proved sufficiently able to preserve and protect what might be considered a somewhat fragile "right" of anonymity. Although it is extraordinarily difficult to hold back the juggernaut of surveillance, information collection, and consolidation on the part of government and industry, it is the authors' view that more robust protections for anonymity should be explicitly considered and adopted in order to preserve fundamental elements of what it is to be human.

26. ANONYMITY AND THE LAW IN THE UNITED KINGDOM

IAN LLOYD

I. INTRODUCTION

The wartime British Prime Minister Winston Churchill famously described the government of the Soviet Union as a "mystery wrapped inside a riddle inside an enigma." Attempts to tease legal meaning from the concept of anonymity arouse similar sentiments, and hypothesizing any answers tends merely to give rise to further questions. Like its conjoined sibling privacy, anonymity very seldom enjoys the luxury of dealing in absolutes, and a balancing act has constantly to be struck between competing interests. Trends in social and political thinking also fluctuate over time with greater or lesser stress being placed upon the rights of individuals as opposed to broader claims such as those relating to national security and the prevention and detection of crime. "My right to swing a stick," it is suggested, "stops at the point where it hits your head!" In a similar vein, my right to act under conditions of anonymity becomes at least qualified when my conduct impacts upon other people. Anonymity—or at least the ability to operate under a range of false identities—is frequently used by those who wish to make multiple and false claims for social benefits. Data sharing and identity management techniques may be effective in reducing fraud but at the cost of requiring everyone involved to surrender a considerable degree of anonymity.

Increasingly, issues of national security have come to dominate discussion in the field of anonymity in comunications. There is no denying the challenges that modern communications technologies pose for law enforcement agencies.

Encryption tools are available to everyone today at a strength that would have been unimaginable to the largest organizations a decade ago. The volume of text and e-mail messages is such as to swamp any form of real-time interception on the part of law enforcement and national security agencies. Within the United Kingdom, the response has tended to be to require service providers to retain details of all electronic communications for periods considerably beyond those that might be justified by their own operational requirements.

It is difficult to challenge the emotive nature of national security claims. Images of the September 2001 attacks and the more recent bombings in Madrid and London continue to traumatize the Western world. In many respects, the prospects for explicit recognition of a right of anonymity appear bleak, and the current trend is to take away from, rather than add to, rights in this area. The cry "if you have done nothing wrong, you have nothing to hide" is heard with increasing stridency. Warning voices, however, are also being raised. The United Kingdom's Information Commissioner has warned repeatedly against the dangers of "sleepwalking into a surveillance society," and in June 2008 the House of Commons Select Committee published a report on the same topic warning, in particular, of dangers linked to the forthcoming system of identity cards.

II. ANONYMITY AND PRIVACY

The relationship between the concepts of privacy and anonymity is a complex one, and there is a considerable degree of overlap. It might be suggested, however, that the predominant element in any claim regarding privacy is that an individual does not want others to know details of what he or she has been doing. The person striving for anonymity predominantly seeks the freedom to move through public spaces without others knowing who he or she is. Typically, actions alleging breach of privacy are brought by those who might be described as the "rich and famous" whose activities may be of intrinsic interest to many people. Examples include the action brought by the supermodel Naomi Campbell[1] against a newspaper that had published a photograph of her leaving a drug addiction support group meeting and the more recent action brought by the motor racing supremo Max Mosely[2] concerning publicity given by a newspaper about his participation in a sadomasochistic sex session. These cases almost invariably involve a balancing act between the rights of privacy and freedom of expression, with the common complaint made by the media that giving excessive weight to privacy allows the rich and famous to conceal evidence of misdeeds. For most of us, unless we are fortunate or unfortunate enough to enjoy or endure a Warholian

---

1. *Campbell v Mirror Group Newspapers* [2004] UKHL 22.
2. *Mosely v News Group* [2008] EWHC 1777 (QB).

15 minutes of fame, most of our activities are of limited interest to any other person other than perhaps our nearest and dearest.

III. WHEN IS AN INDIVIDUAL IDENTIFIABLE?

The question of when an individual can be identified—that is, loses anonymity—is one that assumes great importance in the context of data protection legislation. The United Kingdom's Data Protection Act 1998, which is intended to implement the European Data Protection Directive,[3] confers a variety of rights on data subjects and obligations upon data controllers when data relating to a "living, identifiable individual" is processed. If an individual cannot be identified from the manner in which data is collected, processed, or used, there can be no significant threat to privacy and no justification for the application of at least the Data Protection Act—although there may well be rights under other legal headings such as the law of contract or the concept of breach of confidence. The case of *R. v. Department of Health ex parte Source Informatics Ltd.*[4] constitutes an illustration of such a situation. The case involved a challenge to the legality of guidance issued by the Department of Health to general practitioners and pharmacists to the effect that information that had been provided by a patient in confidence was not to be disclosed without the consent of the patient. For the applicant, who was trying to persuade practitioners and pharmacists to allow them to collect anonymous data about prescribing habits, it was argued that the guidance confused the notions of privacy and anonymity. An obligation of confidence, it was argued, could apply only where there was a threat to an individual's privacy, and the applicant argued that the data would be obtained and processed in a manner that would secure anonymity.

The High Court was not convinced. Although it was accepted that most patients would be unconcerned about the use of their data if anonymity was assured, others would be concerned either on the basis of doubts as to the effectiveness of the assurance of anonymity or on the ground that their data should not be used for the commercial advantage of others. In these circumstances, the proposed transfer would constitute the tort of breach of confidence. The Court of Appeal,[5] however, took a different view. Accepting that the data would be transmitted in a form in which they could not be further processed in order to identify individuals, it was held that the purpose of the law was "to protect the confider's personal privacy." The patients did not own the data constituting their prescriptions and in

---

3. Directive 95/46/EC of the European Parliament and of the Council of October 24, 1995 on the protection of individuals with regard to the processing of personal data and on the free movement of such data OJ 1995 L 281/ 31.

4. *R. v Department of Health ex parte Source Informatics Ltd* [1999] 4 AllER 185.

5. [1999] EWCA Civ 3011.

the absence of anything that might affect their privacy (or anonymity), could have no legal basis to object.

In the case in which data is linked to a named person, there can be no question that the individual is identifiable. A wide range of other identifiers can, however, be envisaged with the European Data Protection Directive stating that:

> an identifiable person is one who can be identified, directly or indirectly, in particular by reference to an identification number or to one or more factors specific to his physical, physiological, mental, economic, cultural or social identity.[6]

Neither the Directive nor the Act provide any definition as to when data relates to an identifiable individual, but the point has been considered extensively by Article 29 Working Party,[7] initially in respect to the privacy implications arising from the use of RFID chips and more specifically to the nature of personal data.[8]

In its initial work, the Working Party suggested that "data relates to an individual if it refers to the identity, characteristics or behaviour of an individual or if such information is used to determine or influence the way in which that person is treated or evaluated."[9]

Developing this concept in 2007, the Working Party identified three elements that may indicate that data relates to a particular individual. These are referred to as content, purpose, and result elements. The distinction between the elements may be complex on occasion, but the Working Party stresses that only one element needs to be present in order to justify a finding that data relates to a particular individual. The content element will be satisfied when information is about an individual. A medical or personnel record, for example, will fall within this category. The purpose element applies when the data is intended to be used to determine the manner in which an individual is treated. Data may, for example, be recorded by an employer of the Web sites accessed from workplace computers. The purpose may be to take disciplinary action against employees who violate Internet usage policies. Finally, a result element applies when the use of data, even though not collected originally for that purpose, is likely to have even a minor impact upon an individual's rights and interests. Further guidance produced by the United Kingdom's Information Commissioner emphasizes similar criteria suggesting that:

> Data which identifies an individual, even without a name associated with it, may be personal data where it is processed to learn or record something

---

6. Article 2(a).

7. The Article 29 Working Party was established under that article of the directive and is effectively a committee of all national data protection supervisory agencies.

8. Working Paper 4 of 2007.

9. Working Party document No WP 105: "Working document on data protection issues related to RFID technology," adopted on 19.1.2005, p. 8.

about that individual, or where the processing of that information has an impact upon that individual.[10]

Once again the Article 29 Opinion identifies a wide range of potential situations and provides extensive guidance. Linking data to a name is an obvious form of identification, although especially in the case of a common name such as Smith or McDonald, this may not sufficient. Use of an identification number may aid identification. In other cases an individual may be identifiable indirectly. The example might be posited of a closed circuit television camera (CCTV) operator instructing an undercover police officer to "detain the person wearing a Glasgow Rangers' football shirt and carrying a can of lager sitting slumped in the doorway of 27 Hoops Street Glasgow." No name is given, but the individual is readily identifiable. Again ISPs and possibly employers may maintain records of Internet use associated with particular computers and from these to the individuals behind the computers.

The work of the Article 29 Working Party is significant and illustrates well the blurring of divisions between privacy and anonymity. Given the increasing sophistication of data processing technologies, the individual's sense of anonymity may be compromised even in cases in which identification by name is not possible.

IV. RECOGNITION OF ANONYMITY AS A HUMAN RIGHT?

The European Convention on Human Rights has had a direct effect in the United Kingdom since the enactment of the Human Rights Act 1998. Effectively, any person can claim before a court that rights established under the Convention have not been respected and demand that the court provide a remedy.

The Convention, in common with almost every national and international instrument, makes no specific reference to a right of anonymity. Neither, it might be noted, does it establish a specific right of privacy. Instead recognition of rights can be seen as implicitly recognized in a number of articles of the Convention, principally although not exclusively, articles 2, 3, and 8.

Article 8 is of the most direct relevance and requires respect for an individual's private and family life, home, and correspondence. This is frequently referred to, not least in the dicta of the European and national courts, as conferring a right of privacy, although this is only one component of what has been accepted as a very broad-ranging right.

---

10. "Determining Personal Data—Quick Reference Guide," Available from <www.ico.gov.uk/upload/documents/library/data.../160408_v1.0_determining_what_is_personal_data_-_quick_reference_guide.pdf>.

This provision has been at issue before the United Kingdom and European courts on many occasions. Two cases are of particular significance to the present chapter. In *Peck v. United Kingdom*, the claimant had been seen by the operators of a local authority's CCTV system walking in the streets in a distressed condition and carrying a large knife. The police were alerted and discovered the claimant in the act of attempting to cut his wrists. The incident was reported in the local authority's newsletter as evidence of the success of the CCTV system, and subsequently a number of broadcasters sought copies of the footage. Although it appears that the authority obtained a verbal undertaking that the claimant's features would be masked when the material was broadcast, this did not take place. Failure to ensure anonymization of the data was held by the European Court of Human Rights to constitute a breach of the claimant's Article 8 rights.

The decision in *Peck* came from the European Court of Human rights and was delivered prior to the implementation of the Human Rights Act within the United Kingdom. The recent decision of the Court of Appeal in the case of *Murray v. Big Pictures*[11] provides an illustration of the application of these principles under domestic law. At issue were a number of photographs taken surreptitiously of the well-known author J. K. Rowling, her husband, and infant son walking (or in the case of the son, being pushed in a buggy) along a public street. An action raised on behalf of the child sought an order, based on rights conferred by Article 8 of the Convention, that the photographs be handed over. At trial, the action failed, in large part because the judge assumed that the claim being raised on behalf of the child was merely a smoke screen for an attempt to protect the mother in circumstances in which she would have no actionable right to privacy, as all aspects of the case had taken place on a public street. The Court of Appeal was more sympathetic. As in so many aspects of life, context was critical. If a photograph had been taken as a "street scene" and subsequently published, there could have been no cause for complaint. In the present case, however, the defendant had deliberately sought to capture the image secretly and with the intention of profiting from its use. Although any publication of an image must carry the risk that someone will identify the individuals portrayed, the key element of the Court's decision would appear to be that when anonymity is deliberately destroyed without due cause, an action will lie under Article 8.

In addition to Article 8, account has to be taken also of a number of other provisions of the European Convention on Human Rights, in particular, Articles 2 and 3. These provide respectively that:

Everyone's right to life shall be protected by law. No one shall be deprived of his life intentionally save in the execution of a sentence of a court . . . No one shall be subjected to torture or to inhuman or degrading treatment or punishment.

---

11. *Murray v Big Pictures* [2008] EWCA Civ 446.

The major case on this point is that of *Venables and Thompson v. News Group Newspapers and Others.*[12] Here, the claimants had a number of years previously been convicted of the murder of a young child. At the time they were both ten years old. Although their identities had been concealed during the trial, subsequent to their conviction the judge directed that their names and some of their background should be made public. Injunctions were also issued, however, prohibiting the publication of further information in order to facilitate the possibility that the individuals might be rehabilitated and reintegrated into society.

By 2000 the claimants were reaching eighteen years old, and the initial injunctions would have expired on their birthdays. The likely date of their release from custody was expected to be in 2001, and arrangements were in hand to provide the claimants with new identities. Proceedings were brought by them seeking continuance of the injunctions in perpetuity out of fear that, once released into the community, their lives would be at very real threat should their identities be disclosed.

The murder in question had been a particularly horrific one, and evidence indicated that feelings within the public at large (and relatives of the deceased in particular) still ran very high. A variety of media reports were put before the court. One entitled "Throw Away the Key" suggested that:

> . . . if Venables and Thompson returned to Liverpool they would be lynched—and nobody would shed a tear. The pair of them should stay inside for the rest of their natural lives. They took a baby's life. So why should they be allowed a life of their own?[13]

Faced with such evidence the court was driven to the

> . . . inevitable conclusion . . . that sections of the Press would support, and might even initiate, efforts to find the claimants and to expose their identity and their addresses in their newspapers.[14]

The media claim to publish information under the protection of Article 10, therefore, could not compete with Article 2 and 3 protections. Injunctions were granted prohibiting, *inter alia*, the publication of any information likely to lead to the identity of the claimants.

In some respects this case is an exceptional one, and in only one other case[15] has a similar injunction been issued. The issue of publication or retention of details of criminal convictions is a rather broader one, and significant publicity has attended attempts by some media outlets to publish details of the name and

---

12. *Venables and Thompson v News Group Newspapers and Others* [2001] EWHC QB 32.

13. Part D para 12.

14. At Part E para 4.

15. *X (A Woman Formerly Known As Mary Bell) & Anor v O'brien & Ors* [2003] EWHC 1101 (QB).

current address of persons convicted of sexual offences involving children. In a recent case,[16] the Information Tribunal has ruled that the retention by the police of details of minor convictions many years in the past contravenes the requirement of the Data Protection Act that data should not be retained beyond a reasonable time.

V. ANONYMITY IN THE CRIMINAL JUSTICE SYSTEM

The previous discussion has concerned the possibility that convicted criminals may be afforded a measure of anonymity in order to rehabilitate themselves into society. The issue of anonymity is currently a matter of major controversy at an earlier stage of the criminal justice process with debate concerning the possibility that witnesses in criminal cases may be permitted to give evidence under conditions of anonymity. The recent decision of the House of Lords in the case of *R v. Davis*[17] has generated massive publicity and the enactment of emergency legislation by parliament to overturn most aspects of the decision.

The principle that all aspects of court proceedings should be conducted in public has been a fundamental tenet of the United Kingdom's criminal justice system for centuries. In a number of high-profile cases of serious crime or terrorism, difficulty has been encountered in persuading witnesses to give evidence out of fear of the consequences should they be identified by defendants or their associates, and measures have been taken by the courts under common-law powers to preserve the anonymity of witnesses.

In *R v. Davis*, the appellant had been accused of murder. A number of potential witnesses had indicated to the authorities that they would fear for their lives should they be identified as giving evidence. To induce them to testify, the trial judge, exercising common-law powers, made a series of orders under which they could give testimony under pseudonyms and shielded from the sight of the public and of the accused and his legal advisers, that their voices should be electronically modulated, and that the accused or his counsel should not be permitted to know details of the witnesses or to ask any questions in cross examination that might lead to their identification.

Following trial, the accused was convicted. The conviction was upheld by the Court of Appeal but overturned by a unanimous decision of the House of Lords. Delivering the leading judgment, Lord Bingham restated the principle that an accused was entitled to be confronted by his accusers in open court "in order that he may cross examine them and challenge their evidence."[18]After surveying a

---

16. *Chief Constable of Humberside and Others v Information Commissioner*, 21 July 2008, http://www.informationtribunal.gov.uk/Decisions/dpa.htm.

17. *R v Davis* [2008] UKHL 36.

18. At para 5.

wide range of authorities from a number of common-law jurisdictions and recognizing that exceptions had validly been made to this principle in cases—for example, when a witness had died prior to trial—Lord Bingham concluded that the level of anonymity granted to the witnesses had unlawfully deprived the appellant of his right to a fair trial. Although some limited exceptions to the general requirements of openness might be acceptable in specific cases, the grant of absolute anonymity contravened the principles of common law. Accordingly the conviction was quashed with clear signals sent to the government that if this result was seen as unsatisfactory, it was for Parliament to change the law rather than for judges to violate basic tenets of common law.

Change did follow after dire predictions from law enforcement agencies concerning the number of serious crimes that could not realistically be prosecuted unless witnesses could be assured of anonymity. Up to forty convicted criminals, it was suggested, might also be able to appeal their convictions.[19] The Criminal Evidence (Witness Anonymity) Act received the Royal Assent on July 21, 2008, only thirty-three days after the decision of the House of Lords. The Act repeals all common-law powers regarding the grant of anonymity[20] and provides for the making of "witness anonymity orders."[21] These may be made by a court when it is considered appropriate and when they effectively provide for measures similar to those considered unacceptable in Davis.

VI. SURVEILLANCE AND THE DEMISE OF ANONYMITY

A range of statutes provides the legal basis for surveillance in the United Kingdom. The Regulation of Investigatory Powers Act 2000 is the major statute, but this has to be considered in conjunction with the Anti-Crime and Terrorism Act of 2001, the Intelligence Services Act 1994, and the Security Services Acts of 1989 and 1996. The combined statutes provide legal sanction for a wide range of covert information-gathering activities as well as for access to a wide range of communications data. The Regulation of Investigatory Powers Act provides for the issuance of warrants legitimizing covert surveillance. These extend beyond interests of national security or even serious crime and may be invoked by a range of organizations including local authorities.

A recent survey conducted by the Press Association asked ninety-seven local authorities for details of their use of surveillance powers. Forty-six authorities responded, describing 1,343 uses of the powers. Most surveillance was directed against instances of suspected fraud, but there was also evidence of the use

---

19. "Police Chief Fears Witnesses Rule," BBC News Channel, June 21, 2008, http://news.bbc.co.uk/1/hi/uk/7466946.stm.

20. Section 1(1).

21. Section 2.

of powers to detect persons allowing their dogs to foul public areas, who left litter in the streets, or misused parking spaces marked for the use of disabled persons.[22]

Activities such as those previously cited constitute a worrying indication of how widespread are the use of powers permitting surveillance activities in respect to what may be regarded as minor infractions of the law. It is at this level that we again see the complex relationship between notions of privacy and anonymity. Monitoring of everyday activities such as dog walking goes beyond concepts of privacy, which are concerned primarily with bringing unusual or noteworthy conduct into the public arena. We cannot expect to walk a dog in a public place without being noticed, but the sense that the activity (or any other act taking place in public) is the subject of targeted observation instills a sense of disquiet in many people, relating more to a sense of loss of anonymity than to privacy. This is the case even though we may not be identified by name. As was discussed above in the context of data protection, identity is about much more than names.

A. Use of CCTV as a Surveillance Tool

Although many of the instances of surveillance carried out under the Regulation of Investigatory Powers Act make use of human agents, this form of activitity is expensive, especially in terms of the number of watchers required. Increasingly, surveillance technologies are being automated. Perhaps the most noticeable and extensive surveillance tool is the closed circuit television camera (CCTV). It is a rare high street or even shop that does not have one or more cameras. It is estimated that there are approximately 4.2 million CCTVs in the United Kingdom. With a population approaching 60 million, that equals one camera for every fourteen inhabitants of the country. Two million motorists are fined each year as a result of being caught by speeding cameras. In general it is estimated that the average person can expect to be "caught" on camera around 300 times a day.[23]

Traditionally, CCTV systems have relied upon images being viewed and assessed by human operators. In at least some instances, this is no longer the case. A nationwide system of Automatic Number Plate Recognition cameras is being installed on the United Kingdom's roads and is scheduled for completion in 2008, at which time about fifty million number plates will be recorded each day.[24] The cameras will capture images of car number plates and compare these with records maintained by the Driving and Vehicle Licencing Agency and motor insurance companies to identify vehicles that are not taxed or insured.

---

22. "Spy Law Used in 'Dog Fouling War,'" BBC News Channel, April 27, 2008, http://news.bbc.co.uk/1/hi/uk/7369543.stm.

23. "Britain is 'Surveillance Society,'" BBC News, November 2, 2006, http://news.bbc.co.uk/1/hi/uk/6108496.stm.

24. "Your Life in Their Lens," Telegraph, November 3, 2006, http://www.telegraph.co.uk/news/main.jhtml?xml=/news/2006/11/02/nspy202.xml.

The system will also link with police databases to flag the appearance of any vehicle recorded as being of interest to the police.[25]

VII. ANONYMITY IN ELECTRONIC COMMUNICATIONS

A walk down any street will evidence the fact that for many people, electronic communications have become an indispensible part of life. Although use of mobile phones in public places affords very little privacy (either for the caller or for others in the vicinity!), there is normally the sense of anonymity. Additionally, e-mail has to a very large extent supplanted the postal system as a means of communication.

The Regulation of Investigatory Powers Act 2000 empowers a senior police officer to require a communications provider to disclose any communications data in its possession when this is considered necessary in the interests of national security, the prevention or detection of a crime, or a number of other situations.[26] The term "communications data" is defined broadly to include any data relating to a communication other than the contents of the communication itself. Thus details of numbers called (whether answered or not), time and duration of calls, e-mail addresses, and the URL's of Web sites visited are consider communications data. Also included is "location data," in the form of information relating to the location (and movements) of a mobile phone.[27]

The procedures to be followed in requesting or requiring disclosure are laid out in a Code of Practice on the Acquisition and Disclosure of Communications Data, which was brought into force by the Regulation of Investigatory Powers (Acquisition and Disclosure of Communications Data: Code of Practice) Order 2007.[28]A wide range of public authorities can lawfully access communication data—from the police through to the Department of Transport (DoT). It has been stated by the Home Office that "Law enforcement

---

25. Details of the system and its possible uses are given in a document, "ANPR Strategy for the Police Service 2005–8" produced by the Association of Chief Police Officers and available from www.acpo.police.uk/asp/policies/Data/anpr_strat_2005-08_march05_12x04x05.doc.

26. Section 22.

27. See "Mobile Phones Expose Human Habits," BBC News, June 4, 2008, http://news.bbc.co.uk/1/hi/sci/tech/7433128.stm.

28. SI 2007 No. 2197. for an interesting account of the use of location data to track the movements of 100,000 mobile users (under conditions of anonymity) as part of research work designed to identify the nature of human movements. One conclusion was that the majority of people seldom moved more than 10 kilometres from home.

agencies make roughly half a million requests for communications data annually."[29]

Under the 2000 Act there was no obligation upon service providers to retain traffic data, and indeed the Data Protection Act 1998 requires that data be retained for no longer than is necessary for the purpose for which it was first processed.[30] The extent of time might vary depending upon the nature of the communication and the nature of the communications provider's relationship with the user. In a situation in which a mobile phone was supplied under a contract providing for bills to be sent each month, it would be reasonable for the provider to retain the data until the bill had been accepted as accurate by the customer and payment received. For prepaid customers, it would be difficult to justify retention for more than a very short period of time.

A further statute, the Anti-Crime and Terrorism Act of 2001, was rushed through parliament in the aftermath of September 11 and provided power to the Secretary of State to issue a code of practice defining the length of time that service providers might lawfully retain traffic data for the purposes of the Regulation of Investigatory Powers Act.[31] Such a code was issued in 2003,[32] and its Appendix A specifies the periods of time that various forms of data might lawfully be retained. In most cases a period of six months is laid out, but in the case of Web activity logs (restricted to the first page of a Web site) the period is reduced to four days.

The 2003 code legitimized rather than mandated data retention. This situation changed upon the implementation of the European Directive "on the retention of data generated or processed in connection with the provision of publicly available electronic communications services or of public communications networks"[33] (the data retention directive). This directive, which was introduced in the aftermath of the Madrid and London bombings in 2004 and 2005, respectively, provides in Article 5 that service and network providers are to be required to retain a very wide range of items of communications data relating to the source and destination of telephone calls, e-mails, and Internet access. The directive provided that member states might opt out of applying its provisions to all the forms of communications listed and the United Kingdom, along with a number of other states issued a declaration to the effect that

> it will postpone application of that Directive to the retention of communications data relating to Internet access, Internet telephony and Internet e-mail.[34]

29. "Communications Data," Home Office Security, http://security.homeoffice.gov.uk/ripa/communications-data.

30. Fifth data protection principle. Schedule 1.

31. Section 102.

32. Available from http://security.homeoffice.gov.uk/ripa/communications-data/retaining-data.

33. OJ 2006 No L105/54.

34. *Ibid.*

The periods for which items of data are to be retained are to be specified by member states within the range of sixmonths to two years. The directive was implemented in the United Kingdom by the Data Protection (EC Directive) Regulations 2007,[35] which entered into force on October 1, 2007. Regulation 5 requires that communication data must be retained for a period of twelve months.

VIII. ANONYMITY AND THE INTERNET

The Internet is frequently, although erroneously, touted as a haven for anonymity. As with any other environment, the Internet can be used for lawful or for unlawful purposes. An example of the latter might be forms of file sharing that constitute infringement of copyright in musical or other works. Again, individuals may use the apparently anonymous nature of the Internet to post comments that are defamatory of another person. In the event that legal proceedings ensue, posters may discover that anonymity is more apparent than real.

In *Totalise v. Motley Fool Ltd.*[36] a company, Interactive Investor, operated a business providing financial information to individual investors. The information was made available via a Website. Included in the Website was a bulletin board facility allowing users to post views and comments.

In order to access the Website, users had to register and indicate acceptance of the operator's terms and conditions. These contained a data protection notice to the effect that the provider would not pass personal data on to any other parties.

One user, operating under the pseudonym "Zeddust," posted comments that were defamatory of the claimant company. The latter complained to Interactive, who removed the positing and suspended the user. Totalise then requested provision of information identifying the poster in order to initiate proceedings for defamation. This was refused by Interactive, who stated that the supply of personal data would place it in breach of its terms and conditions and also of the requirements of the Data Protection Act 1998.

Procedurally the case involved complex questions as to costs and turned on whether the defendant had acted unreasonably in refusing to divulge the identity of its users without need for the claimant to obtain a court order. The Court of Appeal held that the behavior was not unreasonable. The issues involved, it was ruled, were complex, especially with the addition of the Human Rights Act 1998 to the UK statute book. A balance had to be struck between the interests of the claimant in being able to secure a remedy and the respect for the private life of

---

35. SI 2007 No 2199.
36. *Totalise v Motley Fool Ltd* [2001] EWCA Civ 1897, [2002] 1 WLR 1233.

the individual. In such a situation, it was not unreasonable for a party to refuse to hand over the information on a voluntary basis in the absence of consent from the individuals concerned. The issue could reasonably, it was held, be left to the court to decide, with the Web site owner taking what was referred to as a "neutral" position with regard to the claimant's demands.

Further consideration was given to these issues in the case of *Sheffield Wednesday Football Club Ltd. and Others v. Hargreaves.*[37] The claimants here were parties connected with the management of a less-than-triumphant English football club. The defendant operated a supporters' Web site that allowed for the posting of comments on matters concerned with the club. A number of comments (published pseudonymously) were considered to have been defamatory of the claimants, who brought an action before the courts seeking an order that the Web site owner identify the individuals responsible (users were required to register with the site owner before being allowed to post comments).

The basis for the action (as was also the case under *Totalise v. Motley Fool*) lay under the doctrine laid down by the House of Lords in the case of *Norwich Pharmacal Co. v. Commissioners of Customs and Excise.*[38] This established the doctrine that a party to potential litigation could seek disclosure of information held by a third party that might identify others against whom a claim could be made if three conditions could be satisfied:

- A wrong had arguably been committed against the claimant by a third party whose identity was not known to the claimant.
- Identification of the third party is necessary to allow proceedings to be instituted.
- The party against whom the action is brought must be in a position to identify the wrongdoer.

Although these conditions will normally be met in a case involving Internet bulletin boards, it was emphasized that the court retained the discretion whether to make such an order. As is common in discussion groups devoted to participants' enthusiasms, many of the postings in question, although technically defamatory, were insulting rather than damaging. The judge described several of the comments as being "trivial" or amounting to no more than "saloon-bar moaning about the way in which the club is managed." In these cases, the court declined to order the identification of the posters. In other instances, complaints centered on allegations of financial impropriety, and in these cases it was held that disclosure should be made.

Once again, a balancing act has to be performed between notions of free speech and the interests of the subject of material not to have their reputation or

---

37. *Sheffield Wednesday Football Club Ltd and Others v Hargreaves* [2007] EWHC (QB) 2375.

38. *Norwich Pharmacal Co v Commissioners of Customs and Excise* [1973] 2 AllER 943.

financial interests damaged. The approach of the court in *Sheffield Wednesday* is to be welcomed in recognizing that the full might of the law should not be used against those who engage in what might be regarded as robust criticism in a forumin which this can cause little genuine harm to the subject. In other cases, matters may take a different aspect. In 2008, an agreed award of £100,000 damages, possibly the largest award in a case of Internet defamation, was made in respect to the activities of a Web site, Dads Place. In a statement to the court it was recounted that

> this group were responsible for the publication of a seriously defamatory, abusive and scurrilous anonymous website at www.dadsplace.co.uk . . . Over a period of two years from April 2004 to about mid-July 2006, from behind their cloak of anonymity, Dads Place used their publications and in particular the Website to conduct a malicious, unpleasant and relentless campaign of libel and harassment.[39]

It appears that the Website was established by one of the defendants, a property developer, to pursue a personal and professional vendetta against a rival company and its managing director. Few could argue in support of a right to anonymity when conduct is so malignant in nature and, as indicated in court, had such damaging consequences for the personal and professional lives of those targeted.

A rather different aspect of Internet-based activities concerns the attempts by parties to monitor these activities through placing devices commonly referred to as "cookies" on users' computers. Cookies can take a variety of forms and persist for periods of time ranging from seconds to, potentially, centuries. Effectively, cookies store data relating to browsing activity and pass this data to their controller. At one level, cookies might be used by e-commerce Web sites to allow them to recognize previous customers and to personalize the data presented to them; in other cases the intention may be to build a profile of an individual's or (perhaps more accurately) an individual computer's browsing habits.

European and United Kingdom legislation applies to the use of cookies with the European Communications Data Privacy Directive,[40] providing that the use of cookies should be lawful only when this occurs with the consent of users. The major difficulty may well be that the default setting of Internet browsers such as Microsoft Explorer is set to accept cookies. In many cases even if the user changes the setting either to require notice of and approval for the placing of a cookie or to refuse to accept any cookies, the effect will be to render access to many Websites difficult or even impossible. For users the choice may be between accepting cookies or doing without access to a site. In such cases consent might not be considered either informed or freely given.

---

39. www.gentoogroup.com/pdf/Statement_in_Open_Court.pdf.
40. Directive 2002/58/EC.

IX. USE OF BIOMETRIC BANKS FOR LAW ENFORCEMENT PURPOSES

The United Kingdom operates what is reported to be the world's largest DNA database used for law enforcement purposes. As of December 31, 2007, data relating to almost five million individuals was held,[41] with this figure increasing by around 700,000 every year[42]. The database per se has no statutory basis, but a range of statutes dating back some ten years has increased both the range of situations in which the police are entitled to take DNA samples and the use to which these may be put. Essentially in England and Wales, samples may be (and are) taken whenever an individual is arrested for a "recordable offence." This covers all but the most minor offences. Once taken the DNA may be retained on the database without limit of time, even when no conviction is subsequently secured. The situation differs in Scotland, where DNA must be destroyed in the event that the individual is acquitted of the charge in respect of which the sample was taken. The conformity of the English practice with the requirements of Articles 8 and 14 (prohibition against discrimination) was tested before the courts in the case of *R v. Chief Constable of South Yorkshire Police ex parte LS and Others*[43] and was upheld by a majority of the judges in the House of Lords. Delivering the leading judgment for the majority, Lord Steyn endorsed the comments of Lord Justice Sedley in the Court of Appeal. Considering the application of Article 8, he commented that:

> The purposes of retention—the prevention of crime and the protection of the rights and freedoms of others to be free from crime—are four-square within Article 8(2), and retention is provided for by law.[44]

As regards the Article 14 claim, the argument was that there was discrimination between those who had been charged but not convicted of an offence (and therefore had to be presumed innocent) and those other innocent persons who had not come to the notice of the police. This claim was also rejected. First it was accepted that any difference in treatment was a result of history rather than status. An analogy was drawn with a person who may have suffered a broken leg and had x-rays taken in a hospital. The fact that these might be retained would not be compromised by the fact that individuals who had not suffered similar misfortune would not have had their details recorded. Rather more contentiously, Lord Steyn also failed to overturn a further argument put forward by Lord Justice Sedley in the Court of Appeal to the effect that:

> The line between those unconvicted people who have faced charges and those who have not, while not a bright line, is not arbitrarily drawn. It does

---

41. House of Commons Select Committee on Home Affairs, May 20, 2008.

42. http://www.publications.parliament.uk/pa/cm200607/cmhansrd/cm070510/text/70510w0019.htm.

43. *R v Chief Constable of South Yorkshire Police ex parte LS and Others* [2004] UKHL 39.

44. [2002] EWCA Civ 1275 at para 69.

not tarnish the innocence of the unconvicted in the eye of the law. But it recognises that among them is an indeterminate number who are likelier than the rest of the unconvicted population to offend in the future or to be have found to have offended in the past.[45]

It has recently also been reported that:

Primary school children should be eligible for the DNA database if they exhibit behaviour indicating they may become criminals in later life, according to Britain's most senior police forensics expert.[46]

The notion that there are categories of innocence seems to contradict basic tenets of the law to the effect that an individual is presumed innocent until found guilty. Following the maxim that there is no smoke without fire may be appropriate for a writer of crime fiction but should have no place in a mature legal system.

Given the current scale of the DNA database and its claimed utility[47] as a tool for crime detection, there is pressure from some sources for further expansion. There seems no doubt that a disproportionate percentage of persons from disadvantaged backgrounds and areas have their DNA currently held. Perhaps paradoxical argument is that the present system of partial coverage is discriminatory against such persons and that a system of universal inclusion, perhaps from birth, should be instituted. When such a solution was advanced by Lord Justice Sedley, the government response was that "we are broadly sympathetic to the thrust of what he has said."[48] Once again we see the dilemmas that flock to every facet of the topic. Universal DNA testing may well prove an effective tool for the purposes of criminal investigation. Selective testing involving loss of anonymity for some but not others is difficult to defend conceptually. Perhaps the major flaw in the UK system is that, as noted at the start of this section, the DNA database has grown in an ad hoc fashion with very little in the way of parliamentary discussion, let alone legislation.

X. CONCLUSIONS

In the Bible, we are told "vanity, vanity, all is vanity." The term "inconsistency" could well be substituted for "vanity" in the present context. Different interests

---

45. [2002] EWCA Civ 1275 at para 86.

46. "Put Young Children on DNA List, Urge Police," *The Observer*, March 16, 2008, http://www.guardian.co.uk/society/2008/mar/16/youthjustice.children.

47. It is claimed (*The Independent*, September 5, 2007) that 3,500 matches are provided to police forces each month. It has also been claimed that although only 14% of cases of burglary are solved by traditional policing methods, the figure rises to 48% when DNA evidence is obtained at the scene of crime.

48. "Judge Wants Full DNA Base," Manchester Evening News, September 5, 2007, www.manchestereveningnews.co.uk/news/s/1015525_judge_wants_full_dna_database.

and people have different expectations, and it is perhaps fair to suggest that most of us display internal inconsistencies. We claim to value privacy and anonymity, yet millions of British householders have signed up for store loyalty cards, which provide a key to link massive amounts of personal data relating to our shopping patterns. Again, millions of people voluntarily disclose personal information to social networking Web sites either unaware or uncaring of the consequences, which may follow them for the rest of their lives. Law can only do so much. It is fair criticism that too little has been done to create a framework for a right of anonymity, but all too often people fail to take even the most elementary steps to protect themselves.

27. ANONYMITY AND THE LAW IN
THE NETHERLANDS

SIMONE VAN DER HOF, BERT-JAAP KOOPS, AND
RONALD LEENES

I. INTRODUCTION

Anonymity is important in current society. The feeling that anonymity is disappearing has raised the question of whether a right to anonymity exists, or whether such a right should be created given technological and societal developments. In this chapter, we address this question from a Dutch legal perspective. Our analysis of the hypothetical legal right to anonymity in the Netherlands may contribute to the overall research into the status and importance of a right to anonymity in contemporary society.

The core of this chapter consists of an overview of relevant areas in Dutch law where a right to anonymity may be found, construed, or contested. Section 2 discusses anonymity in constitutional law. Sections 3 and 4 explore the status of anonymity in criminal law and private law, respectively. Section 5 provides an overview of anonymity in public spaces. In section 6, we focus on anonymity in citizen-government relationships: service delivery, e-voting, anonymized case-law, and naming and shaming. Finally, we draw conclusions regarding the right to anonymity in current Dutch law—something that turns out to be only piecemeal, and rather weak. The chapter concludes with a reflection on these conclusions: should a right to anonymity (or, at least, a more powerful right than the current one) be created in Dutch law?

II. ANONYMITY IN CONSTITUTIONAL LAW

A right to anonymity in the Dutch Constitution (Grondwet, hereafter: DC)[1] could be construed in several ways: as a general right to anonymity (i.e., as a separate constitutional right), or as a right subsidiary to or included in other constitutional rights, such as the rights to privacy, secrecy of communications, and freedom of expression. In the following, we explore the DC; the scope of this chapter does not allow us to discuss the equally important *European Convention on Human Rights* (ECHR)[2] as a source of constitutional rights.

A. A General Right to Anonymity
There is no general right to anonymity in the DC, and it is unlikely that one will be created in the foreseeable future. Anonymity was discussed in the late 1990s in relation to the amendment of Art. 13, DC (confidential communications).[3] After the amendment floundered in the First Chamber, the Dutch government decided to investigate a broader update of the fundamental rights in the Constitution in light of information and communications technologies.

To this aim, the Committee on Fundamental Rights in the Digital Age was instituted to advise the government. The Committee, surprisingly, considered a right to anonymity as an alternative to the right to privacy. Predictably, this was not found to be a sound alternative, anonymity being further-reaching than privacy and therefore requiring more exceptions.[4] The Cabinet, in its reaction, agreed, adding that a right to anonymity is unnecessary to substitute or complement the right to privacy. Art. 10, DC (the general right to privacy), provides sufficient protection even if anonymity were considered to be a starting point in society.[5] Moreover, the cabinet stated that knowability rather than anonymity is the norm in society, and although there is sometimes a need for anonymity, this need does

---

1. An English version of the Dutch Constitution is available at http://www.minbzk.nl/contents/pages/6156/grondwet_UK_6-02.pdf.

2. European Convention on Human Rights, (November 4, 1950).

3. Dutch Constitution, 1983 (*Grondwet*), Art. 13. See generally Bert-Jaap Koops and Marga Groothuis, "Constitutional Rights and New Technologies in the Netherlands," in *Constitutional Rights and New Technologies: A Comparative Study*, eds. Ronald Leenes, Bert-Jaap Koops, and Paul de Hert (The Hague: T.M.C. Asser Press, 2008), 159.

4. Committee on Fundamental Rights in the Digital Age, "Grondrechten in het digitale tijdperk" (Fundamental Rights in the Digital Age), *Kamerstukken II* 27460, 2000/01, no. 1, p.125 (appendix), http://www.minbzk.nl/actueel?ActItmIdt=6427.

5. *Ibid.*, 20.

not warrant safeguards at a constitutional level.[6] This view generally reflects academic literature.[7]

B. Anonymity as Part of Other Constitutional Rights

Although the DC lacks a proper right to anonymity, the government holds the view that anonymity often goes hand in hand with privacy and data protection.[8] (Art. 10, DC). Furthermore, other rights can "shelter" anonymity, such as the right to confidential communications (Art. 13, DC) and the right to freedom of expression (Art. 10, ECHR).[9] For example, the anonymity of a whistleblower can be protected by a journalist's right to protection of sources.[10]

In light of the "shelter" provided by these constitutional rights, there seems to be no need to establish a separate right for anonymity. However, it is unclear how far this protection stretches, for conditions for sheltering are lacking. Presumably, these conditions will be fairly strict, in light of the repeated statement by the government that identification rather than anonymity is the norm in current society:

> [A]gainst a certain desirability of anonymity, there is the fact that the functioning of our society is based, rather, on identifiability. In order to meet obligations and for law enforcement, knowability is appropriate and necessary in order to adequately protect the interests of third parties. In these frameworks, it is important that the responsibility for acts can be attributed to identifiable persons.[11]

Also, in Dutch academic literature there is little support for explicit constitutional protection of anonymity, even though anonymity itself is seen as important. The subsumption of anonymity under other constitutional provisions seems sufficient, freedom of expression being a more likely candidate than the right to privacy or the right to secrecy of communications.

---

6. *Kamerstukken II* 27460, 2000/01, no. 2, p. 44 (n. 3).

7. For an extensive discussion on the constitutional grounds for anonymity in public speech, see A. H. Ekker, *Anoniem communiceren: van drukpers tot weblog* (Den Haag: Sdu, 2006).

8. The General Right to Privacy, Dutch Constitution, 1983 (*Grondwet*), Art. 10.

9. Dutch Constitution, 1983 (*Grondwet*), Art. 13; European Convention on Human Rights, Art. 10.

10. Explanatory Memorandum, p. 5, from Letter from the Minister, October 29, 2004, with a Draft Bill and Explanatory Memorandum to amend Art. 10 Dutch Constitution (n. 8), and the advice of the Council of State, http://www.minbzk.nl/aspx/get.aspx?xdl=/views/corporate/xdl/page&VarIdt=109&ItmIdt=101328&ActItmIdt=12755; see *Voskuil v The Netherlands* ECHR November 22, 2007, for a case in point.

11. *Ibid.*, 4. Unless otherwise stated, all translations in this chapter are the authors'.

III. ANONYMITY IN CRIMINAL LAW

Anonymity plays a clear role in criminal law enforcement. First, anonymity is of interest when reporting a crime. Generally, reporting a crime is done in writing or orally, put to paper by an officer and signed by the person reporting (Art. 163 Dutch Code of Criminal Procedure (hereafter: DCCP)).[12] Signing implies identification that negatively affects people's willingness to report crimes. To stimulate crime reporting by people who fear retribution, an anonymous reporting system, "M.," was introduced in 2002; its catch-phrase, "Report Crime Anonymously" (*Meld Misdaad Anoniem*), is actively promoted in the media.[13] M. is a toll-free number (0800-7000) that can be called to report serious crimes that will then be forwarded to the police or other law-enforcement agencies with a guarantee of anonymity. The reporting system is likely to be supplemented by anonymous reporting by victims—of intimidation, for example. This requires changes in the DCPP in order for anonymous reports to be admissible as evidence in court.[14]

Second, and more important, witnesses can remain anonymous in specific situations. *The Witness Protection Act* of 1994 has introduced the concept of "threatened witness" (*bedreigde getuige*)—a witness whose identity is kept secret during interrogation at the court's order (Art. 136c, DCCP).[15] The court first has to determine whether a witness really requires anonymity, something judged to be the case only if there is reasonable fear for the life, health, security, family life, or social-economic subsistence of the witness, and if the witness has declared his or her intent to abstain from witnessing because of this threat (Art. 226a, DCCP).[16] If anonymity is granted, the witness is heard by the investigating judge (who knows the witness's identity but makes sure that the interrogation safeguards anonymity, Art. 226c, DCCP), if necessary in the absence of the defendant, attorney, and prosecutor (Art. 226d, DCCP).[17] The judge investigates and reports the witness's reliability (Art. 226e, DCCP).[18] The Act also provides a witness-protection program.[19]

---

12. Dutch Code of Criminal Procedure (*Wetboek van Strafvordering*), Art. 163.

13. See http://www.meldmisdaadanoniem.nl/ (in Dutch), http://www.meldmisdaadanoniem.nl//article.aspx?id=203 (English). C.f., *Gerechtshof*[Court of Appeal] Amsterdam, February 7, 2005, LJN AS5816.

14. http://www.nu.nl/news/1118441/14/rss/Ministers_werken_aan_anonieme_aangifte_bij_politie.html.

15. Witness Protection Act (*Wet getuigenbescherming*) of November 11, 1993, *Staatsblad* 1993 (Netherlands) 603, entry into force February 1, 1994. The provision is included in the Dutch Code of Criminal Procedure as Art. 136c.

16. Dutch Code of Criminal Procedure (*Wetboek van Strafvordering*), Art. 226a.

17. Dutch Code of Criminal Procedure (*Wetboek van Strafvordering*), Art. 226c and 226d.

18. Dutch Code of Criminal Procedure (*Wetboek van Strafvordering*), Art. 226e.

19. See Art. 226f, DCCP, the Witness Protection Decree (Besluit getuigenbescherming), and the Ruling on the Witness Protection Police Register (*Reglement politieregister getuigenbescherming*). Note that the latter implies that many identifying data of threatened

A recent change in the DCCP enables intelligence officers to testify anonymously as a "shielded witness" (*afgeschermde getuige*, Art. 136d, DCPP) in criminal court proceedings.[20] The identity of a shielded witness is kept secret in a way similar to that of a threatened witness if interests of state security or a considerable interest of the witness or another party so requires (Art. 226g and 226h, DCPP).[21] Only the Rotterdam investigating judge is authorized to hear shielded witnesses (Art. 178a(3), DCCP).[22] Testimony reports should contain no information that undermines the interests of the witness or the state and are only shown to the defense and included in the case records if the witness consents (Art. 226j(2) and (3), and 226m, DCCP).[23] A result of these far-reaching provisions is that the defense has limited possibilities to question the evidence given by intelligence officers. Here, the right to anonymity as a safeguard of state security seems to prevail over the right of the defendant to a fair trial.

A right to anonymity for suspects is absent in Dutch law. Fingerprinting suspects to facilitate identification is deemed lawful on the basis of the Police Act (Art. 2, Police Act).[24] Recent "measures in the interest of the investigation" go even further to identify anonymous suspects. They are "indirect means of coercion to force the suspect to reveal identifying data himself."[25] Among other measures, Art. 61a DCCP allows the police to take photographs and fingerprints, bring about a witness confrontation, conduct a smell-identification test, and cut hair or let it grow.[26] To facilitate identification, these measures can only be used in cases involving crime allowing custody. Anonymous suspects who are stopped or arrested can also be asked for their social-fiscal number and frisked (Art. 55b DCPP), and suspects may be held for interrogation, with the purpose of determining their identity, for a maximum of 6 to 12 hours (Art. 61, DCCP).[27]

Parties in criminal proceedings have very limited rights to remain anonymous.

In contrast, law-enforcement agencies have abundant powers to collect identifying data that bear on the overall picture of anonymity in Dutch law.

---

witnesses can be registered by the police, including old and new identity, address, description and photograph, birth data, and transport and communication data, in order to execute the witness-protection program.

20. Shielded Witnesses Act (*Wet afgeschermde getuigen*), Staatsblad 2006, 460 (Netherlands), in force since November 1, 2006.

21. Dutch Code of Criminal Procedure (*Wetboek van Strafvordering*), Art. 226 and 226h.

22. Dutch Code of Criminal Procedure (*Wetboek van Strafvordering*), Art. 178a(3).

23. Dutch Code of Criminal Procedure (*Wetboek van Strafvordering*), Art. 226j(2) and (3), and 226m.

24. Police Act (*Politiewet*), Art. 2.

25. According to the legislator, as quoted in C. P. M. Cleiren and J. F. Nijboer, *Tekst & Commentaar Strafvordering*, 2nd edition (Deventer: Kluwer, 1997), note 1 to Dutch Code of Criminal Procedure, Art. 61a.

26. Dutch Code of Criminal Procedure (*Wetboek van Strafvordering*), Art. 61a.

27. Dutch Code of Criminal Procedure (*Wetboek van Strafvordering*), Art. 55b.

As of January 1, 2006, a broad range of data-production orders have been put in place allowing any investigating officer to order the production of identifying data in case of any crime (although not misdemeanors),[28] provided that the data are processed for purposes other than personal use (Art. 126nc, DCCP). The production order can also be given in case of "indications" of a terrorist crime— a lower standard than the "probable cause" normally required for investigation (Art. 126zk, DCCP).[29] Identifying data that are processed for personal use (e.g., a citizen's address book) can be ordered by a public prosecutor for a crime for which preliminary detention is allowed (Art. 126nd).[30]

A separate rule with similar conditions (Art. 126na, 126ua, and 126zi, DCCP) allows the identification of telecommunications data, such as IP addresses.[31] Separate powers provide for the identification of prepaid-card users, because even telecom providers do not know their identity. A mandatory registration and identification scheme for prepaid-card buyers was briefly considered in the 1990s, but, this being considered too extensive, two less infringing measures were taken instead. Art. 126na(2), DCCP, allows providers to be ordered to retrieve the phone number of a pre-paid card user by means of data mining if the police provide them with two or more dates, times, and places from which the person in question is known to have called.[32] To make sure that providers have these data available, a three-month data retention obligation is in place.[33] If data mining by the telecommunications provider is impossible or overly inefficient, the police can also use an IMSI catcher—a device resembling a mobile phone base station that attracts the mobile phone traffic in its vicinity (Art. 126nb and 126ub, DCCP, Art. 3.10(4), Telecommunications Act).[34] An IMSI catcher may only be used to collect an unknown telephone number (or IMSI number), not to collect traffic data or to listen in on communications.

---

28. Or in cases of planned organized crime, on the basis of the Dutch Code of Criminal Procedure (*Wetboek van Strafvordering*), Art.126uc.

29. Dutch Code of Criminal Procedure (*Wetboek van Strafvordering*), Art. 126zk.

30. Or in cases of planned organized crime (Dutch Code of Criminal Procedure (*Wetboek van Strafvordering*), Art. 126ud) or of 'indications' of a terrorist crime (Dutch Code of Criminal Procedure (*Wetboek van Strafvordering*), Art. 126zl).

31. Dutch Code of Criminal Procedure (*Wetboek van Strafvordering*), Art. 126na, 126ua, and 126zi.

32. Dutch Code of Criminal Procedure (*Wetboek van Strafvordering*), Art. a126na(2).

33. Art. 13.4(2) Telecommunications Act (*Telecommunicatiewet*) juncto Decree on Special Collection of Telecommunications Number Data (*Besluit bijzondere vergaring nummergegevens telecommunicatie*), Staatsblad 2002, 31, in force since March 1, 2002. Note that the Data Retention Directive, 2006/24/EC, has not yet been implemented in Dutch law. This directive requires electronic-communications providers to store traffic data for a period of 6 to 24 months. A bill is pending in Parliament with a retention period of 12 months.

34. Dutch Code of Criminal Procedure, Art. 126nb, 126ub; Telecommunications Act (*Telecommunicatiewet*), Art. 3.10(4).

IV. ANONYMITY IN PRIVATE LAW

A. Civil Proceedings

Identification is the cornerstone of the enforcement of citizens' rights in civil proceedings. Serving a summons, for example, is very difficult if a person's identity, including his or her address, is unknown.[35]

Anonymity is, however, not a priori excluded in the Dutch Civil Procedure Code (DCPC). Under exceptional circumstances (e.g., in case of genuine fear of retaliation), anonymous witness statements are admissible in civil proceedings.[36] In these cases, the identity of the witness is unknown to the other party in the proceedings but is known to the court. Statements of anonymous witnesses differ from those of regular witnesses but produce the same result; it is up to the court to weigh them in the case at hand.

Another example concerns summonses to quit vacant properties, which can be given to anonymous persons under certain conditions.[37] First, such a summons must relate to (a part of) real estate. Second, the name and the place of residence of the person(s) concerned must not be able to be identified with reasonable effort. This case obviously applies to squatters, whose identity can only be retrieved with great difficulty—if at all. Their anonymity cannot be maintained in appeal; by then, their identity must be known.

Internet Service Providers (ISPs) may be requested to identify subscribers in civil proceedings as a result of the Dutch Electronic Commerce Act.[38] In civil proceedings, the court may order ISPs to disclose the identity of users who post information on sites hosted by the ISPs.[39] The Dutch High Court confirmed this position in *Lycos v. Pessers.*[40] It decided that ISPs may have a duty to provide a third party with identity information, the non-observance of which may amount to tort,[41] even if the allegations on that person's Web site are not prima facie illegal or unjust. The following considerations are relevant:

- The possibility that the information is unjust and damaging to a third party is sufficiently reasonable.
- The third party has a reasonable interest in receiving the identity information.

---

35. See Dutch Civil Procedure Code (*Wetboek van Burgerlijke Rechtsvordering*), Art. 45(2).

36. See Dutch Civil Procedure Code (*Wetboek van Burgerlijke Rechtsvordering*), Art. 165ff.

37. See Dutch Civil Procedure Code (*Wetboek van Burgerlijke Rechtsvordering*), Art. 45(3) and 61.

38. Dutch Electronic Commerce Act (*Aanpassingswet elektronische handel*).

39. *Kamerstukken II* 28197, 2001/2, no. 3, p. 28. See also Art. 15(2) of Directive 2000/31/EC on e-commerce (which was, however, not implemented into Dutch law).

40. *Hoge Raad* [Dutch High Court] November 25, 2005, LJN AU4019. (LJN refers to the publication number at the Dutch official case-law publication Web site, http://www.rechtspraak.nl).

41. See Dutch Civil Code (*Burgerlijk Wetboek*), Art. 6:162.

- It is reasonably certain that less invasive possibilities of obtaining the information do not exist.
- The third party's interests carry more weight than those of the ISP and the Web site owner (if known).

In the 2006 case *Brein v. UPC*, the court added as a further requirement that the person whose identity information is requested must be, beyond reasonable doubt, the person who conducted the allegedly illegal activities.[42] In the same year, the court ruled in *Stokke v. Marktplaats* that online marketplaces do not have to provide their users' identifying information to third parties unless withholding such information would be unreasonable.[43]

B. Contract Law

Contracting parties are free to stipulate the conditions of a contract, which means they can decide not to exchange identifying information or to remain mutually anonymous. Anonymity can be purposeful, even instrumental, to the transaction process, as witnessed by the popularity of online marketplaces and brokers remunerated for the matching of the orders and offering contracts that guarantee buyer and seller anonymity (even as the broker knows the identity of both).

Anonymity in contract law is often restricted for practical and legal purposes. From a practical perspective, identity information may be required to perform contractual obligations, such as when physical delivery or payment of the products is involved (there are limited possibilities for delivering or paying anonymously). Moreover, identity information plays a role in building trust; the perceived trustworthiness of an identified business partner appears to be greater than that of an anonymous one. The risks and importance of a transaction determines the required level of assurance regarding the provided identity information. If payment is made up front, there may be no need to know the buyer's identity. In other cases, a check of the trade register will suffice. And yet, in others, digital certificates may be required to build a high level of trust. Identity data is also collected for the purpose of personalizing services and in determining the value of customers. And, furthermore, identity data is nowadays considered economically valuable—a business asset that provides businesses with incentives to not do business anonymously, even though they could.

From a legal perspective, the identity of a defaulting party may be necessary to be able to hold the party accountable. There are also legal obligations requiring

---

42. *Rechtbank Amsterdam* [District Court], August 24, 2006, LJN AY6903. Note that Ekker, *Anoniem communiceren* (n. 7), offers some recommendations to shape the right to anonymity in legislation, with a procedure for providing identifying data in civil proceedings and a provision in the Telecommunications Act, Ch. 10.

43. Rb. Zwolle, May 3, 2006, LJN AW6288.

online businesses to provide identity information.[44] "Identity" in this respect means the name of the natural person or of the business providing the online service.[45] In the case of businesses, the identity of the owner need not be disclosed on the Web site; this information can be obtained for a marginal fee from the trade register, something that was established long ago to provide data about businesses in order to facilitate trust in commerce.

Dutch contract law is ruled by the principle of consensualism (see Art. 3:37(1), DCivC), yet, in some instances, a certain form (e.g. a signed writing) is required, without which a contract may be void or annulled. Because, according to Dutch case law, signatures are constituted by individualization and identification under Dutch law, signed writings undercut anonymity; a cross, drawn picture or a stamp (unless equivalent to the hand-written signature) are not considered legally valid signatures.[46]

Electronic signatures are legally valid. The DCivC defines an electronic signature as data in electronic form that are attached to or logically associated with other electronic data and that serve as a method of authentication. Authentication does not necessarily mean identity authentication but may be restricted to data (e.g., the contents of the contract) authentication. In our view, the law, therefore, does not necessarily require an electronic signature to fulfill the identification function. Hence, signing electronically (contrary to what is legally allowed in respect to hand-written signatures) can be done anonymously, although possibly bringing with it less legal certainty about the evidential value such a signature holds in court.[47] The court may consider nonidentifying electronic

---

44. See Art. 7:46c(1a), Dutch Civil Code (*Burgerlijk Wetboek*). In this respect, this provision overlaps with the Dutch Civil Code (*Burgerlijk Wetboek*), Art. 3:15d(1a), although these provisions address different kinds of information to be provided by online businesses. Another difference between these provisions is the scope of application: the Dutch Civil Code (*Burgerlijk Wetboek*), Art. 7:46c, is not restricted to online consumer contracts but covers distance contracts more generally.

45. *Kamerstukken II* 28197, 2001/02, no. 3, p. 38.

46. S. M. Huydecoper and R. E. van Esch, *Geschriften en handtekeningen: een achterhaald concept?*, ITeR Series, Vol. 7 (Alphen aan den Rijn: Samsom Bedrijfsinformatie, 1997).

47. The principle of contractual freedom, however, also allows contracting parties to determine the evidential value of an electronic signature between them in a probative contract; see also Dutch Civil Code (*Burgerlijk Wetboek*), Art. 3:15a(6), and consideration 16 of Directive 1999/93/EC. Moreover, the law expressly leaves room for such signatures, which may, nonetheless, be legally equivalent to handwritten signatures so long as the method of authentication is sufficiently reliable in view of the purpose for which the electronic signature was used, and of all other circumstances (see Dutch Civil Code (*Burgerlijk Wetboek*), Art. 3:15a(1)). This is also called the functional approach. Compare Art. 7 of the UNCITRAL Model Law on Electronic Commerce of 1996, which also takes a functional approach with respect to electronic signatures but expressly requires a method for identifying the signer.

signatures less reliable than identifying electronic signatures or secure identifying electronic signatures.

Directive 1999/93/EC on e-signatures, on which the Dutch Electronic Signature Act is based,[48] explicitly permits the use of pseudonyms, yet both the Dutch act and the explanatory memorandum to the act are silent on this point.[49] The principle of contractual freedom also allows parties to agree to use pseudonymous certificates in their transactions. If the law stipulates a specific form of contract encompassing identified parties, pseudonymous digital certificates are not allowed, unless the identity of the certificate's holder can be obtained from the CSP when necessary. Pseudonym use may also be restricted as a result of the aforementioned information obligations regarding online services. In light of the lack of case law in the area of electronic signatures, the legal status of pseudonymous certificates and identification requirements is not entirely clear.

The identification of the signer is one of the basic requirements of advanced and qualified electronic signatures,[50] which provide strong and nearly conclusive evidential value, respectively, in court.[51]

Identification of the parties is a requirement in the regulation concerning the equalization of written and electronic contracts (see Art. 7: 227a(1d), DCivC). This provision requires the identity of the parties to be determinable with sufficient certainty. The requirement also has to be interpreted with respect to the reason why a written contract is obligatory in a certain case. If a written document is required solely to provide evidence of the contents of the document, and not identification of the parties, then identification in an electronic environment is not required (as in the offline world).

V. ANONYMITY IN PUBLIC

In recent years, the ability to move anonymously in public spaces has decreased as a result of a combination of legal and *de facto* technological developments.

Until January 1, 2005, the *Compulsory Identification Act* contained identification obligations only in special circumstances (such as during soccer matches and in public transport, when boarding without a ticket). After this date, a general identification obligation applies: Dutch citizens aged 14 and older have to show

---

48. Which is (mainly) incorporated in the Dutch Civil Code (*Burgerlijk Wetboek*).

49. The Dutch Minister of Justice has pointed out that special attention to the identification of individuals in an electronic environment is necessary in view of, among other considerations, identity fraud risks and the expected development of anonymous and pseudonymous interaction on the Internet. See *Kamerstukken II* 27400 VI, 2000/01, no. 2, p. 8.

50. See Dutch Civil Code (*Burgerlijk Wetboek*), Art. 3:15a(2b).

51. See Dutch Civil Code (*Burgerlijk Wetboek*), Art. 3:15a(2) and (3).

an official ID when ordered by a police officer or a public supervisor, provided this is necessary to fulfill the police task (Art. 2, Compulsory Identification Act *juncto* Art. 8a, Police Act 1993).[52] Failure to comply is punishable with a fine of up to €3,350 (Art. 447e, Dutch Criminal Code, henceforth DCC). The extended compulsory identification was somewhat controversial when introduced; for example, the group ID Nee ("ID No") campaigned against it. This group also runs an Identification Abuse Hotline.[53] Nevertheless, Parliament accepted the act without much opposition. The effect of the general compulsory identification on public safety has not been empirically studied so far, but there are indications that the law is often used to fine people committing banal offenses, or found in apparently "suspect" circumstances. For example, the police ordered a man who sat idly on the window ledge of a post office to show his ID.[54]

Although less omnipresent than in the UK, CCTV surveillance is constantly increasing. Different laws apply to camera surveillance depending on the context in which it is used and the person or organization responsible. According to Art. 151c, Municipal Act, the city council can authorize the mayor to decide upon camera surveillance in public areas for purposes of public order for a specified period of time.[55] In case of a justified interest (protection of employees, customers, and property), private parties, such as employers and shop owners, may also install cameras for surveillance at the work place, in stores, and so on, so long as these do not cover public areas (e.g., a whole street or public square) and do not infringe upon privacy interests (e.g., by monitoring private places). Camera surveillance at the work place requires the consent of the employees' council (Art. 27(1l), Employees' Councils Act).[56] In all instances, camera surveillance must be clearly indicated at the respective locations. Secret camera surveillance of individuals in public and private places is illegal pursuant to Art. 441b and 139f, DCC respectively.[57]

The public prosecutor can order camera surveillance without the recording of confidential information (monitoring) in criminal investigations on suspicion of a crime (Art. 126g(3), DCCP).[58]

In addition to camera surveillance, other anonymity-decreasing technologies are used or experimented with in different areas. For example, shopping areas in Amsterdam and Utrecht are experimenting with facial recognition technologies aiming at identifying shoplifters. The city of Groningen and the Netherlands

---

52. Compulsory Identification Act (*Wet op de identificatieplicht*). Extended Compulsory Identification Act (*Wet op de uitgebreide identificatieplicht*), *Staatsblad* 2004, 300.

53. See http://www.id-nee.nl/English.html.

54. *Algemeen Dagblad* March 2, 2007, see http://www.id-nee.nl/Actueel.html#499.

55. Municipal Act (*Gemeentewet*), Art. 151c.

56. Employees' Councils Act (*Wet op de ondernemingsraden*), Art. 27(11).

57. Dutch Criminal Code (*Wetboek van Strafrecht*), Art. 441b and 139f.

58. Dutch Code of Criminal Procedure (*Wetboek van Strafvordering*), Art. 126g(3).

Railways, amongst others, have installed systems to detect aggressive behavior. Soccer club ADO Den Haag has introduced a crowd control system to help locate hooligans (relying on facial recognition at the entrance and in the stadium and microphone detection of aggressive or otherwise undesirable speech).

Furthermore, a public transport chipcard (OV-chipkaart) is being introduced in the Netherlands that facilitates massive tracking and tracing of travelers throughout the country. The card scheme allows for anonymous and personalized cards. The former option is more expensive and excludes card usage for age discounts, season tickets, and so on.

VI. ANONYMITY IN CITIZEN-GOVERNMENT RELATIONSHIPS

A. Service Delivery

Citizens do not have an explicit right to anonymity with respect to public service delivery, but the rule of law requires the government to have specific legal grounds to oblige citizens to identify themselves. If there are no such legal grounds, citizens actually have a right to be or stay anonymous in their relationship with the government, or at least have no obligation to identify themselves.

Irrespective of the requirement for legal grounds, identification plays a key role in government-citizen relationships regarding service delivery, because entitlement to particular services is sometimes hard to establish without having access to personal data contained in government records. This requires identification of the individual.

Anonymous interaction with the government is increasingly difficult. A recent research report discusses two important causes: the use of new technologies (CCTVs, data-mining, data-sharing, and data-linking) and the ongoing informatization of government (and private-sector) administrations. As a result, new kinds of personal information are collected and used, and on a bigger scale than before.[59] Although the report focused on the impact of trends in criminal investigations and national security on ordinary (nonsuspect) citizens, similar patterns can be expected in public service delivery. The newly introduced biometric passports, which allow automatic identity verification, may spur more obligations to identify for services. Personal data is increasingly linked in order to detect fraudulent use of government benefits, for optimizing children's aid, and for providing proactive and personalized public services.

A crucial aspect of the public sector identification web is likely to be the recently introduced Citizen Service Number (Burger Service Nummer; hereafter CSN), which will be used in all communications between citizen and public

---

59. A. Vedder et al., *Van privacyparadijs tot controlestaat? Misdaad—en terreurbestrijding in Nederland aan het begin van de 21ste eeuw* (The Hague: Rathenau Instituut, February 2007), available at http://www.rathenau.nl/showpage.asp?steID=1&item=2097.

administration. After decades of opposition to a unique identification number for citizens in the Netherlands tracing back to the aftermath of World War II, the legislature adopted the CSN with little discussion in July 2007.[60] The name CSN is a misnomer, because it is a registration number rather than an instrument to improve service delivery for citizens. The CSN facilitates the sharing and linking of personal data across the public sector and may turn out to be an important inhibiter of anonymity. The CSN consists of the existing social-fiscal number but may be used by many more public entities and in fact replaces other sector-specific numbers.

Most public services, especially transaction services, require citizens to prove their identity, whether actively (by showing an ID card or using a digital identifier called DigiD) or passively (by, for example, using their postal address as recorded in the Municipal Registry). Information services can usually be obtained anonymously, although even in this sector numerous instances exist in which individuals have to identify themselves in order to receive public-sector information. The Dutch Government Information (Public Access) Act 1991 embraces the principle that public information should be public to all.[61] In practice, public-sector information is sometimes disclosed selectively (e.g., for scientific purposes only), implying the identification of the requester.[62]

From an identification perspective, conventional and electronic communications, in principle, should adhere to the same requirements.[63] The emerging electronic identification infrastructure for electronic public service delivery and the potential for the eNIK (an electronic national identity card, which was expected to be deployed in 2008 but the status of which is presently unknown) to introduce advanced electronic signatures therein will likely promote secure identification in public service delivery.[64] Because of the limited possibilities for using pseudonymous digital certificates, these ID schemes could increase citizen identification.

---

60. *Staatsblad* 2007, 288.

61. Dutch Government Information (Public Access) Act 1991 (*Wet openbaarheid van bestuur*).

62. S. van der Hof et al., *Over wetten en praktische bezwaren, Een evaluatie en toekomstvisie op de Wet openbaarheid van bestuur* (Tilburg: Tilburg University, 2004), 19.

63. Electronic communications between citizens and government are regulated by the Act on Electronic Government Communications (*Wet elektronisch bestuurlijk verkeer*), which has amended the General Administrative Law Act (*Algemene Wet Bestuursrecht*). Pursuant to this law, electronic messages should be as reliable and confidential as conventional communications can be (functional approach). Additionally, the electronic signature provisions in the DCivC apply to electronic communications within the public sector.

64. C.f. B. J. Koops, H. Buitelaar, and M. Lips, eds., *D5.4: Anonymity in electronic government: a case-study analysis of governments' identity knowledge*, FIDIS report, May 2007, available at http://www.fidis.net.

B. e-Voting

Anonymity in voting is closely related to secrecy of the vote, which is an important principle in Dutch democracy. Public elections should reflect the voters' choices and should be free from undue influence. Secrecy and privacy are, therefore, essential characteristics of public elections. Secrecy of the vote is established in Art. 53(2), DC, and is further detailed in the Voting Act for the different Dutch types of casting votes: ballot boxes (Art. J 15), voting machines (Art. J 33), and postal votes (Art. M 7).[65]

Although voting secrecy could be seen as optional—the voter may opt to vote anonymously—it is usually taken as a strict mandatory lawful duty, meaning that voter anonymity has to be guaranteed (by the state) for all voters.[66] The effect is that voters may tell anyone whom they voted for without being able to prove their claims.

Interestingly, voting secrecy is traditionally guaranteed by social control. The polling station officials observe that voters enter the voting booth alone, where they can cast their vote without anyone looking over their shoulder. The ballot paper is subsequently deposited in an opaque box.

Electronic voting machines have been in operation in Dutch polling stations since the early 1980s. The voting secrecy is safeguarded in the same manner as for paper ballots. These electronic voting machines have recently caused controversy. The machines leave no paper trail, nor is their software open (or certified), which basically means that only the manufacturer knows what the machines actually count.[67] Also a group of concerned people, WijVertrouwenStemcomputersNiet ("We don't trust voting machines"), have proven that the votes cast in the machines used in the Netherlands can be remotely monitored through interception of residual screen radiation, which undermines the secrecy of the vote and therefore affects the anonymity of the voting process.

Voter anonymity is even more problematic in postal and Internet voting. Postal voting is an option for Dutch nationals living or residing abroad at the time of general elections (Art. M 1 Voting Act).[68] The voter can be coerced, and the voting ballot inspected, before being sent to the election officer. Furthermore, the vote can be linked to the voter because it is sent with a separate letter stating that the voter personally cast her vote. Therefore, voter anonymity depends on the election officers who receive the postal votes.

---

65. Dutch Constitution (*Grondwet*), Art. 53(2); Voting Act (*Kieswet*), Art. J 15, J 33 and M 7.

66. See H. Buchstein, "Online Democracy, Is It Viable? Is It Desirable? Internet Voting and Normative Democratic Theory," in *Electronic Voting and Democracy—A Comparative Analysis*, eds. N. Kersting and H. Baldersheim (London: Palgrave, 2004).

67. See http://www.wijvertrouwenstemcomputersniet.nl/English.

68. Dutch Voting Act (*Kieswet*), Art. M 1.

Since the late 1990s, the Dutch government has actively pursued the introduction of Internet voting. Experiments with Internet voting for expatriates were conducted during the Dutch elections for the European Parliament in 2004 and the November 2006 general elections. Internet voting is even more problematic than postal ballots are. Not only is family-voting unavoidable, but also the voting process itself is highly opaque. An interesting question regarding postal ballots and Internet voting is whether the European Court of Human Rights will sanction them if challenged in the light of Art. 3, protocol 1, of the *European Convention on Human Rights* (secrecy of the vote).[69]

C. Anonymized Case-Law and "Naming and Shaming"

Anonymity, for privacy and data-protection reasons, features in administrative law regarding the publishing of court cases. The official court cases Web site, www.rechtspraak.nl, generally anonymizes cases by replacing names with neutral indications such as "plaintiff" or "defendant." Names of professionals (such as judges, lawyers, interpreters, and expert witnesses) are not, however, anonymized. Names of legal persons, such as companies, are also published, unless these are directly linkable to individual persons.[70]

However anonymous the cases thus published may be, there are several legal provisions that require complete publication of a case, which may be viewed as a form of "naming and shaming." Examples are

- Fines or penalties delivered in competition cases (implying that a case is open for inspection at the Dutch Competition Authority (NMa)) must be published in the official journal *Staatscourant* (Art. 65, Competition Act);
- The Netherlands Authority for the Financial Markets (AFM) can publish the names and addresses of people fined for violating financial-market legislation (see, for example, Art. 48m, Stock Trade Supervision Act). Moreover, the AFM can, in order to "promote compliance with the Act," apart from imposing possible fines, publish facts that violate the Act (Art. 48n);
- The yearly publishing in the *Staatscourant* of a list of companies who have submitted insufficient emission rights in the context of environmental-law obligations (Art. 18.16p(1), Environmental Protection Act).[71]

Whereas these "naming sanctions" largely affect legal persons, a similar provision affecting citizens can be found in criminal law. The publication of a criminal sentence can be ordered in criminal cases as an additional

---

69. L. Pratchett, *The implementation of electronic voting in the UK* (London: Local Government Association, 2002).

70. See http://www.rechtspraak.nl/Over+deze+site/ under "Anonimiseringsrichtlijnen."

71. Competition Act (*Mededingingswet*), Art. 65; Stock Trade Supervision Act (*Wet toezicht effectenverkeer*), Art. 48m; Environmental Protection Act (*Wet milieubeheer*), Art. 18.16p(1).

sanction (Art. 9(1)(b)(3) DCC) or as an alternative sanction (Art. 9(1)(b)(3) *juncto* Art. 9(5), DCC); this is also possible with economic offences (Art. 7(g), Economic Offences Act).[72] Whether publishing a criminal verdict with the name of the convicted person is justified depends on the kind rather than the seriousness of the crime. For example, it may be a useful response to convictions for selling health-threatening food, death by neglect in official functions, embezzlement, or fraudulent bankruptcy. The sanction of publishing is, however, hardly ever given in practice.[73]

VII. CONCLUSION

A. Does a Right to Anonymity Exist in Dutch Law?

Our overview clearly shows that no general right to anonymity exists in Dutch law. Rather, identification is the default. In criminal law, this is unsurprising in light of the obvious importance of identification in crime detection and prosecution. In civil and administrative law, however, anonymity might have been expected to be more important than it actually is. After all, there is often no intrinsic need to know the identity of someone engaged with in a legal act.

In today's society, however, with its pervasive ICT infrastructures that increasingly facilitate the performance of legally relevant acts at a distance, the trust that often used to come with face-to-face relationships must be reconstructed by other means. Identification is a prime tool for re-establishing trust between unfamiliar parties who often lack other indicators of the other party's likelihood of keeping his or her part of the deal. This may at least partially explain why anonymity currently does not feature in the legal framework for e-commerce and e-government.

On the contrary, powerful identification infrastructures are built in the private sector, with e-signatures and PKIs, and even stronger ones in the public sector, with the Citizen Service Number and the eNIK. Furthermore, the legal frameworks for these infrastructures are far from sympathetic to anonymity: the possibility of pseudonymous e-signature certificates is not embedded in Dutch law (and is even prohibited in e-government relationships), and the CSN will be used across all areas of government. Moreover, identification duties are on the rise, with recent laws requiring e-commerce providers and—most importantly—citizens aged 14 and older, in general, to identify themselves when requested by an officer. Another significant detail is that many "naming and shaming" provisions, particularly in

---

72. Dutch Criminal Code (*Wetboek van Strafrecht*), Art. 9(1)(b)(3) and Art. 9(1)(b)(3) *juncto* Art. 9(5); Economic Offences Act (*Wet op de economische delicten*), Art. 7(g).

73. C. P. M. Cleiren and J. F. Nijboer, *Tekst & Commentaar Strafrecht* (Deventer: Kluwer, 2000); Dutch Criminal Code (*Wetboek van Strafrecht*), Art. 9 (n. 3).

administrative law, were introduced over the past years, adding to the significance that modern society apparently attaches to identification in public.

This is not to say that anonymity is non-existent in Dutch law. There are various legal fields in which forms of anonymity rights exist. Occasionally, anonymity is the default (in voting, and official case-law publication) or a strong right (in relation to freedom of expression). More often, however, a right to anonymity is the exception to the rule: threatened witnesses, both in civil and criminal cases, can testify anonymously—a right which, ironically, can be claimed both by organized criminals and by intelligence officers—and contracts can be concluded anonymously.

The rationale underlying these anonymity rights is diverse. An intrinsic reason for protecting anonymity clearly seems absent. In all fields where some form of anonymity right exists, this right is instrumental in furthering the purpose of the law and policy in those fields. Anonymity is an important tool for fair voting procedures, for stimulating the public exchange of (unpopular) ideas to enhance the freedom of expression and of thought, and, sometimes, for protecting the life and limb of persons at risk. Anonymity thus is a servant to several masters.

Altogether, we conclude that in Dutch law, there is merely a very piecemeal and rather weak right to anonymity. Only in some very specific areas of law is there a strong claim to anonymity, but the default position in Dutch law is that identification is preferred and, increasingly, mandated.

B. Should a Right to Anonymity Be Created in Dutch Law?

If a substantial right to anonymity does not exist, should it be created? After all, the discussions in the Netherlands about anonymity (for example, in the debate over digital constitutional rights) indicate that there is some reason to cherish anonymity in the current, ICT-pervaded society—if only to a certain extent.

The key questions are whether the need for anonymity is significant enough for a full-bodied right to anonymity, and if so, how and to what extent such a right should be defined. We think there is insufficient reason to answer the first question, generally, in the affirmative. There is some need for anonymity in numerous situations, and this need is perhaps growing, but the contexts in which anonymity plays a part are so diverse, that speaking of "a" right to "anonymity" is hardly justified as such. Instead, the question should be asked in terms of which contexts, sectors of society, and legal areas there exists a substantial need to protect anonymity nowadays.

Ekker, for example, has pleaded for a right to anonymous communications, which should take the form of a procedure for providing identifying data in civil proceedings and a provision in the Telecommunications Act.[74] Much pleads in favor of this suggestion, for (tele)communication is nowadays a crucial enabler for almost all activities. People increasingly generate traces when communicating

---

74. Ekker, *Anoniem communiceren* (n. 7).

via ICT—not only on the Internet, but also with mobile telecommunications, which increasingly have to be stored as a result of regulation such as the Data Retention Directive. The variety of parties that can somehow access, legitimately or unlawfully, these traces, combined with the deficit of data-protection law to effectively limit the wide-scale processing of personal data in practice, warrants the conclusion that privacy is slowly disappearing.[75] To stop this process, a right to anonymity, rather than reliance on data-protection law only, could be a valuable add-on in an integral effort to save privacy. A right to anonymous communications would also foster other rights, not least the freedom of expression in an online environment. Naturally, such a right could and should not be absolute: it would only be relative to certain parties and could be infringed when sufficient interests required identification. But the important added value would be that the default position would be reversed: rather than the current assumption of identification, there would be an assumption of anonymity, revoked only when necessary.

A right to anonymous communications—something worthy of much more elaboration than we may present here—is one example of an area in which a right to anonymity makes sense. When surveying the developments currently taking place in ICT, and also in DNA fingerprinting and bio-banking, we see that large-scale identification infrastructures are being built.[76] Experience shows that infrastructures persist: they can be adapted or rebuilt, but they are rarely removed. This means that we should carefully analyze the consequences of large-scale identification, for these will become the norm in the coming decades. A result may well be that in situations where previously people used to act anonymously, identification will be a standard instead, whether mandatorily (because of legal obligations) or in practice (because technology just happens to implement identification). And because anonymity used to be taken for granted in such situations—buying groceries in a supermarket, walking in another city, travelling by train, visiting a soccer match—there is no history of a "right to" anonymity in these cases: if something is natural, there is no need to protect it by law. Now that the world is changing, with anonymity no longer a matter of course, it is time to consider embedding the protection of anonymity in law for those areas of social life that entail no intrinsic need for identification.

Although anonymity hardly has a history as a right, it may well have a future as a right, and in many more fields than is the case today. It is perhaps one of the

---

75. See B. J. Koops and R. E. Leenes, "'Code' and the Slow Erosion of Privacy," *Michigan Telecommunications & Technology Law Review* 12, no. 1 (2005): 115–188, http://www.mttlr.org/voltwelve/koops&leenes.pdf.

76. See also Koops, Buitelaar, and Lips, *Anonymity in electronic government*, 76–77 (n. 42).

few available "tools of opacity"[77] that ensure an acceptable balance between the powerful and the power-poor in today's technology-pervaded, identification-driven society.

---

77. See S. Gutwirth and P. de Hert, "Privacy and Data Protection in a Democratic Constitutional State," in *D7.4: Implications of profiling practices on democracy and rule of law*, eds. M. Hildebrandt et al., FIDIS report, September 2005, available at http://www.fidis.net, 11–28.

28. ANONYMITY AND THE LAW IN ITALY

GIUSELLA FINOCCHIARO

I. INTRODUCTION

In a technological society where everyone leaves traces in both the digital world and the material world—often without being aware of it—there is an increased interest in the problem of anonymity from a legal viewpoint. One only has to think about traces left by mobile phones, video surveillance cameras, and Internet connections to realize that anonymity seems impossible nowadays.

This *de facto* statement, however, has legal consequences. This chapter examines the legal understanding of anonymity in Italy. In it, I argue that data that is not anonymous is defined as personal data under Italian and European law; therefore, personal data protection law applies. I also suggest that the definition of anonymity is a relative one that depends on the legal context in which anonymity is sought.

II. ANONYMITY UNDER ITALIAN LAW

A. Anonymity Defined

Defining anonymity is not a simple task. The Oxford English Dictionary's definition of "anonymous" as "of unknown name"[1] evokes an absolute concept. By definition, anonymity excludes the identity of the subject to which it refers—it is faceless and without identity. Anonymity is a concept that evokes an absolute lack of connection between a piece of information or an action and a person.

---

1. "Anonymous," OED online, http://www.oed.com.

Upon closer examination, however, anonymity is often relative to specific facts, subjects, and purposes. A written composition, for instance, may be anonymous to some, but not necessarily to others, depending upon whether or not a person is able to recognize its author. Anonymity, therefore, can be defined in many different ways, something that affects the legal definition and experience of the right to anonymity.

In the Italian context, the concept of anonymity does not belong to public or private law but is more of a general concept. The definition of anonymity is found in the Italian Personal Data Protection Code (in force since January 1, 2004) and applies to both private and public entities.[2] The Code explicitly defines "anonymous data" as data that, in origin or after being processed, "cannot be associated with an identified or identifiable data subject."[3] There is no distinction made between electronic and non-electronic data in the definition.

Data can be anonymous as soon as it is collected or can be processed to make it anonymous. The key question is whether or not the data can be associated with the data subject. In which cases can it be deemed that data cannot be associated with a subject? Must this be a physical or a technological impossibility? The latter question has been clarified by the Council of Europe Recommendation on medical data protection, which states that information cannot be considered identifiable if identification requires an unreasonable amount of time and manpower.[4] In cases in which the individual is not identifiable, the data is referred to as anonymous.

In contrast, the Code defines "personal data" as "any information relating to natural or legal persons, bodies or associations that are or can be identified, even indirectly, by reference to any other information including a personal identification number."[5] In like vein, the European directive defines "personal data" as follows:

[A]ny information relating to an identified or identifiable natural person ("data subject"); an identifiable person is one who can be identified, directly or indirectly, in particular by reference to an identification number or to one or more factors specific to his physical, physiological, mental, economic, cultural or social identity.[6]

Both definitions include not only data that refers to a data subject but also data that may possibly be connected to a data subject. However, the likelihood of making this connection is measured in relation to the time, cost, and technical means necessary to do so. The value and sensitivity of the information is also

---

2. Italian Personal Data Protection Code Legislative Decree no. 196 of June 30, 2003.

3. *Ibid.*

4. Council Recommendation (EC) R97/5 of February 13, 1997, on the protection of medical data.

5. Italian Personal Data Protection Code (n. 2).

6. EU Directive (EC) 95/46, The Data Protection Directive.

taken into account. The technical threshold at which medical data, for example, will be considered identifiable is lower, because the data is sensitive and therefore warrants a high level of protection. The question of whether or not data is personal or anonymous is a relative one that depends on the type of data and the uses to which it is put. Personal data can legally be processed only for specified purposes by authorized persons, and data can be anonymous to certain people under pre-defined conditions. In other words, data can be anonymous in some contexts, but not in others. Therefore, anonymity in the processing of personal data is not an absolute concept but rather a relative concept, tied to the use to which the data is put and protected by the reasonableness of the technical efforts that would be required to identify it.

This latter point is illustrated by Recital 26 of the Directive on the Protection of Personal Data. The recital explicitly refers to reasonableness when it states that "to determine whether a person is identifiable[,] account should be taken of all the means likely [to be reasonably] used either by the controller or by any other person to identify the said person."[7] As pointed out by the recent Opinion 4/2007 on the concept of personal data, adopted on June 20, 2007, by the Article 29 Data Protection Working Party[8] the determination of the reasonableness of the means likely to be used should, in particular, take into account factors such as the cost of identification, the intended purpose, the way the processing is structured, the advantage expected by the controller, the interests at stake for the individuals, and the risk of organizational dysfunctions and technical failures.

Interestingly, reasonableness is not a civil law principle, but a common law principle. Therefore, anonymity is not a black-or-white concept—one cannot simply state that anonymity exists or does not exist. Rather, there are degrees of anonymity as well as degrees of identifiability, and the determination of whether each piece of data is anonymous must be made in context. This is particularly true in a digital world.

For example, the Article 29 Data Protection Working Party directive states that the test of identifiability is a dynamic one that should consider state-of-the-art technology at the time of processing.[9] Although it may be possible to quantify anonymity in the future, given computer science research on k-anonymity,[10]

---

7. EU Directive (EC) 95/46, The Data Protection Directive R 26.

8. Article 29 Working Party Opinion on the Definition of Personal Data, Opinion 4 of June 20, 2007.

9. *Ibid.*

10. On the technological side, see Pierangela Samarati and Latanya Sweeney, "Protecting Privacy When Disclosing Information: k-Anonymity and Its Enforcement through Generalization and Suppression," *Proceedings of the Symposium on Research in Security and Privacy* (1998): 384–393; Latanya Sweeney, "Achieving K-Anonymity Privacy Protection Using Generalization and Suppression," *International Journal of Uncertainty, Fuzziness and Knowledge Based Systems* (2002): 571–588; Latanya Sweeney, "K-anonymity: a model for protecting privacy," *International Journal on Uncertainty, Fuzziness and*

at this point, anonymity is a relative concept that depends upon context, and that must therefore be evaluated on a case-by-case basis.

B. Does a Right to Anonymity Exist under Italian Law?

Italian law does not provide for an explicit right to anonymity.[11] There is no general legal right, in the digital world or in the real world, for a subject to be anonymous, to not be identified, to refuse to disclose information, or to refuse to reveal himself or herself.

If the right to anonymity under Italian law cannot be affirmed in general terms—that is, as the right to forbid the connection among facts, acts, and data and a subject, in relation to any information and to any circumstance—it does not mean that a right to anonymity is not contemplated by the Italian legal system. Anonymity has been protected in the context of particular needs. Therefore, the picture for the Italian jurist is inevitably fragmentary.

There are three ways to ground the right to anonymity in Italian law. First, the right to anonymity is recognized under Italian law for certain subjects, in predefined circumstances, and for specific occasions, as specified by the law. We will return to this in the sections of this chapter dedicated to private law, public law, and criminal law.

The second way of grounding the right to anonymity in Italian law is by using the principle of minimization. As a general principle, applying to private and public law, as well as to criminal law, Art. 3 of the Personal Data Protection Code provides for the principle of minimization in data processing.[12] It states that information systems and software shall be configured to minimize the use of personal data and identification data in such a way as to rule out their processing if the purposes sought in the individual cases can be achieved either by using anonymous data or by making arrangements suitable to allow for the identification of data subjects only in cases of necessity, respectively.[13] Therefore, according to this principle, when possible, personal data should be processed as anonymous data.

Knowledge-based Systems (2002): 557–560; Fosca Gianotti and Dino Pedreschi, eds., *Mobility, Data Mining and Privacy* (Berlin-Heidelberg: Springer, 2008); Jaideep Vaidya, Chris Clifton, Michael Zhu, *Privacy Preserving Data Mining* (Berlin-Heidelberg: Springer, 2006).

11. The right to anonymity has not been much explored by Italian doctrine. Among the rare works exploring the concept of anonymous in legal terms, it is worth mentioning the following: CANDIAN, *Anonimato (diritto all')*, in *Enciclopedia del diritto* (Milan, 1958): 499–502; CORSO, *Notizie anonime e processo penale* (Padova, 1977): Chapter VI, §§ 2 and 3, 148–155; PIOLETTI, *Il concetto di "scritto anonimo" è diverso e più vasto di quello di "non sottoscritto,"* in *Rivista penale* (1935): 1214–1219, G. FINOCCHIARO, ed., *Diritto all'anonimato* (Padova, Italy: Cedam, 2008).

12. Italian Personal Data Protection Code, Art. 3 (n. 2).

13. *Ibid.*

Third, the right to anonymity can be seen as instrumental to the effective exercise of the personal data protection right or to the effective exercise of the right to privacy. The personal data protection right and the right to privacy have a general constitutional basis in Art. 2 of the Italian Constitution.

I examine each of these avenues in turn.

C. Anonymity in Constitutional Law

The Italian Constitution does not provide for a right to anonymity. In certain cases, however, anonymity can be seen as instrumental to the effective exercise of the right of personal data protection or the right to privacy.

The Right to Privacy There is no explicit right to privacy in the Italian constitution. However, a privacy right was created by Italian jurisprudence in the first half of the last century.[14] There is no single unifying notion of this right. To date, Italian courts have used it to protect the original historical meaning of privacy as the right to exclude others and to prevent the disclosure of information concerning the private personal and familial life of a person. The most recent meaning ascribed by the courts has been privacy as informational self-determination. The right to privacy has therefore been considered by Italian doctrine as a unique right and also as a plurality of rights.

The Right to Personal Data Protection The right to personal data protection is the right of a subject to exercise control over information regarding himself or herself. This general right includes, for example, the right to obtain information as to whether or not personal data concerning oneself exists, the right to be informed about the source of such data (as well as the purposes for and methods of their processing), and the right to know the entities to whom the personal data may be communicated. The data subject is also entitled to require that the data be updated or corrected, and that data processed unlawfully be deleted. Moreover, the data holder must certify that the required corrections have been made and that the data holder has notified the entities to whom the data was communicated.

---

14. Among the first Italian authors who have studied the right to privacy are Adolfo Ravà, *Istituzioni di diritto privato* (Padova, Italy: Cedam, 1938); Francesco Carnelutti, "Il diritto alla vita privata," *Rivista trimestrale di diritto pubblico* (1955): 3–18; Giorgio Giampiccolo, "La tutela giuridica della persona umana e il c.d. diritto alla riservatezza," *Rivista trimestrale di diritto e procedura civile* (1958): 460; Adriano De Cupis, *Teoria generale, diritto alla vita e all'integrità fisica, diritto sulle parti staccate del corpo e sul cadavere, diritto alla libertà, diritto all'onore e alla riservatezza* (Milano, Italy: Giuffrè, 1959); Adriano De Cupis, *I diritti della personalità* (Milano, Italy: Giuffrè, 1959–1973); Giovanni Pugliese, "Il diritto alla riservatezza nel quadro dei diritto della personalità," *Rivista di diritto civile* (1963): 605–627; Pietro Rescigno, "Il diritto all'intimità nella vita privata," in *Studi in onore di F. Santoro Passarell* 4(Napoli, Italy: Jovene, 1972); Michele Giorgianni, "La tutela della riservatezza," *Rivista trimestrale di diritto e procedura civile* (1970); Stefano Rodotà, *Elaboratori elettronici e controllo sociale* (Bologna, Italy: Il Mulino, 1973).

The right to personal data protection is regulated by the Personal Data Protection Code. Because, as previously discussed, the definition of personal data is very broad, the right to personal data protection is also construed broadly. According to the code, everyone is entitled to the protection of his or her own personal data. This right is to be distinguished from the right to privacy or confidentiality. The former—the right to the protection of personal data—concerns information about natural or legal persons and is not necessarily relevant to the private or family life of an individual. The latter concerns the protection of an individual's private life. Both rights are provided for in the Italian system in general and by the code in particular. The right to the protection of personal data is also different from the right to personal identity, which includes, for example, the right not to have one's social image misrepresented.

The right to personal data protection was recognized in 2000 as an autonomous right by the Charter of Fundamental Rights of the European Union.[15] It is mentioned in Art. 8 and is considered a right of freedom.

Anonymity Anonymity can be seen as a method to advance either the right to personal data protection or the right to privacy. The first is a "positive liberty" that allows the exercise of control on the part of the individual, whereas the second is a "negative liberty" that ensures that the individual has the power to exclude others from a personal and private sphere. The personal data protection right is a "freedom to." The right to privacy is a "freedom from." Because both rights are connected to liberty—one positively, the other negatively—anonymity can be seen as part of "diritti della personalità,"[16] or the right of personality. Anonymity may therefore gain more prominence in the digital world than in the "material" world, because anonymity as a way of exercising liberty in the digital world in order to guarantee a sphere of freedom is instrumental to the expression of personality.

The constitutional foundation of the right to privacy and of the right to personal data protection is in Art. 2 of the Italian constitution, which states that

> [T]he republic recognizes and protects all human beings' fundamental rights, for individuals by themselves as well as in the social contexts where their personality is developed, and also requires them to carry out their duties of solidarity in the political, social and economic fields.[17]

---

15. The Charter of Fundamental Rights of the European Union (EC), December 7, 2000.

16. The category of "*diritti della personalità*" is a category elaborated by the Italian doctrine. It partially matches with the category of "personal rights" defined by Francesco De Franchis, *Dizionario giuridico-Law Dictionary* 2 (Milano, Italy: Giuffrè, 1996), as non-patrimonial rights, as the right to reputation, and as the right to physical integrity. It also partially matches with the category of "fundamental rights" defined by the Black's Law Dictionary, 6th ed. (St. Paul, MN: West Publishing Co., 1990) as "those rights which have their source, and are explicitly or implicitly guaranteed, in the federal Constitution."

Because of the incomplete correspondence with other categories such as "fundamental rights" and "personal rights," the definition in Italian will be maintained.

17. Italian Constitution, Art. 2.

The expression used by Art. 2 of the Italian constitution—fundamental rights—constitutes the basis for other rights that can be implied or explicitly stated in another constitutional provision, such as the liberty of expression.[18]

New rights would be "implied" and included in the content of more extensive rights explicitly recognized in the constitution. There are also "instrumental rights" that can be invoked because, in case of their absence, other rights would be deprived of their effective meaning or not sufficiently guaranteed.[19]

D. Criminal Law

Introduction The first argument against a possible right to anonymity is the need for security; nowadays, anonymity is usually considered only as a danger.

In criminal law, the opposition between anonymity and security is more evident.

As previously stated, anonymity in and of itself is not a right under Italian law—this is especially true in the criminal law.

In some cases, anonymity is denied. Identification seems to be the necessary basis for fighting and preventing certain crimes. Anonymity thus seems to be a source of social insecurity, particularly as regards antiterrorism legislation, money laundering legislation, and tax evasion.

On the other hand, in some cases Italian penal law protects anonymity, either as instrumental for the protection of other rights or as part of a data protection right.

Cases in Which Identification Is Required Starting from the cases in which identification is required, it is worth remembering that part of Italian criminal legislation is characterized as "emergency legislation." It dates back to the 1970s and was enacted to counteract internal terrorism. An example is the duty of real estate owners to identify and promptly report to the police their tenants' names and other data useful for personal identification.[20] More recently, emergency legislation has been passed to combat tax evasion, money laundering, and recent forms of terrorism.[21] Some laws have been enacted to allow tax officers access to people's bank accounts.[22] A strict duty to inform public authorities about clients who are suspected of money laundering has also been enacted.[23]

---

18. See Antonio Baldassarre, *Diritti della persona e valori costituzionali* (Torino, Italy: Giappichelli, 1997), 60; Augusto Barbera, "Commento all'art. 2," in *Commentario della Costituzione*, Giuseppe Branca and Antonio Scialoja, eds. (Bologna-Roma, Italy: Zanichelli, 1975), 80.

19. See Antonio Baldassarre, *Diritti della persona*, 59 (n. 7).

20. D. l. 21.3.1978, n. 59, Art. 12.

21. D.l. 27.7.2005, n. 144 enforced with law 31.7.2005, n. 155.

22. Among others, d.l. 30.12.1991, n. 413, and d.p.r. 29.9.1973, n. 600.

23. See d. lgs. 20.2.2004, n. 56, modified by Art. 21 l. 25.1.2006, n. 29, and d.m. 10.4.2007, n. 601.

The police have powers to identify people. False declaration is punished by articles 495, 496, and 651 of the Italian Penal Code.[24] Moreover Art. 349, § 2 *bis* of the Italian Procedural Criminal Code states that the police, if authorized by the public prosecutor (*pubblico ministero*), can coercively take hair or saliva from a person under investigation or from a person who has refused to declare his or her identity or from anyone who seems to have declared a false identity.[25]

However, it must be emphasized that legislation concerning a DNA database to assist in criminal investigations has yet to be passed, although it is now under discussion. Any new law must ostensibly comply with data protection standards.

Owners of public Internet access nodes have a duty to identify persons who access the Internet over their systems and register their names according to anti-terrorism laws.[26] Moreover, the same laws suspend Personal Data Protection Code rules concerning data retention, providing cancellation of traffic data, until December 12, 2008.[27]

Anonymity as an Aggravating Circumstance In some cases, anonymity is seen as an aggravating circumstance. Examples include cases of menace, violence, or resistance towards a public officer.[28] In other cases, anonymity is an essential element of the criminal case—in the case of slander and false self-incrimination, for instance.[29] Anonymity is also considered instrumental in legislation for the protection of witnesses, which allows a witness at risk to be admitted to a special protection program in order to obtain a new formal identity (name, surname, date and place of birth, etc.).[30]

Anonymity as a Form of Protection of Privacy and of Personal Data In other cases, anonymity is seen as a form of protection of privacy and of personal data. Article 734 *bis* of the Italian Penal Code protects the victims of sexual crimes by prohibiting the publication of their name or picture without their consent. Article 167 of the Personal Data Protection Code criminally punishes the illegal processing of personal data in certain cases when the offense causes effective damage to the victim.[31] A special kind of malice is also necessary: the perpetrator of the offense has to have acted maliciously, with the purpose of causing such damage or of gaining profit from his or her conduct.

E. Private Law

Contractual Regulation In a contract, there are no obstacles to anonymity or pseudonymity, which are a mere fact, unless the contract is a formal contract

---

24.
25.
26. L. 31.7.2005, n. 155.
27. Term recently postponed by l. 28.2.2008, n. 31.
28. Italian Criminal Code, Art. 339, 610, 611, 612.
29. Italian Criminal Code, Art. 368–370.
30. L. 29.3.1993, n. 119.
31. Italian Personal Data Protection Code, Art. 167 (n. 2).

(deed) or the identity of the party is essential to the contract. The name in this case is functional to other interests—ensuring payment, for instance. From a theoretical point of view, the contract can be anonymously concluded and performed.

There are, however, some provisions that require an identification of the contractual parties. Among these are certain provisions contained in the "*Codice del consumo.*"[32] Specifically, in contracts concluded at a distance, Art. 52, par.1, lett. a of the Code states that the supplier has to be identified and has the duty to give the consumers information about his or her identity. In the case of deceptive advertising, Art. 26 of the Code provides that the Antitrust Authority can require the advertising operator to give information about the client in order to identify him or her.[33] Another provision requiring identification is found in Art. 55 of the Electronic Communications Code,[34] which states that companies have to provide the Ministry of the Interior with a list of subscribers and a list of the buyers of prepaid cards that are identified at the time of the activation of the service.

Copyright law Italian law recognizes the right of the author to be anonymous and to use a pseudonym as well as the right to reveal his or her identity. Originally this right was not explicitly stated but recognized as implied;[35] in latter years, the right has been explicitly recognized.[36] Current copyright laws provide an author with the right to publish a work anonymously or with a pseudonym, if included in the contract with the publisher. The author has the right to reveal himself at anytime in any circumstance.[37] It is a moral right—a "*diritto della personalità*"—a right of personality that can be exercised towards anybody.

It should also be noted that the pseudonym has the same protection in Italian law as a name if it is well known, according to Art. 8 of copyright law, or if it has the same importance as the name.[38]

Electronic Signature The legislation in force, known as the Digital Administration Code or CDA ("*Codice dell'amministrazione digitale*"),[39] was recently amended.[40] The Digital Administration Code has replaced previous legislation concerning electronic signatures. In essence, it introduces two types of signatures—the "*elettronica*," or electronic (Art. 1, § 1, lett. q), and the "*qualificata*," or qualified (Art. 1, § 1, lett. r). The former corresponds to the electronic signature of the directive, and the latter to the advanced signature with a qualified certificate created by a secure signature–creation device. The Digital Administration Code also

---

32. Consumers' code, d. lgs. 6.9.2005, n. 206.
33. Consumers' code, Art. 26 (n. 32).
34. Electronic Communications Code, d.lgs.1.8.2003, n. 259.
35. L. 25.6.1865, n. 2337.
36. R.d.l. 7. 11.1925, n. 1950.
37. This is provided by Art. 21 of the l. 633/1941.
38. According to Civil Code, Art. 9.
39. D. lgs. 82/05.
40. D. lgs. 159/2006; the technical rules in force are contained mainly in d.p.c.m. of January 13, 2004.

sets forth norms concerning the so-called *"firma digitale,"*—digital signature (Art. 1, § 1, lett. s)—which is a type (the only one at present) of qualified signature and which is based on PKI, its private key embedded in a smart card issued by selected certification service–providers who have to comply with strict rules regarding their economic robustness and trust requirements.

Although Italian law allows for the use of pseudonyms,[41] an electronic certificate may not be anonymous.

Duty of the Internet Service Provider Internet service providers (ISPs) do not have a general obligation to monitor the information that they transmit or store; neither do they have a general obligation to actively seek facts or circumstances that indicate illegal activity.[42] Art. 156 *bis* of Italian copyright law compels the defendant to disclose the identity of people supposedly engaged in intellectual property violations whenever the plaintiff's complaints appear reasonably grounded.[43]

On August 19, 2006, and September 22, 2006, the Tribunal of Rome upheld two orders on a complaint filed under this provision by the German music label Peppermint Jam Records GmbH, ordering an Italian ISP to disclose the identification data of 3,636 Internet users. The said users were allegedly involved in copyright infringement, performed through the BitTorrent and eMule applications. This was the beginning of the largest legal case ever in Italy in this field.

Peppermint had received the IP and GUID codes of these users from a Swiss company, Logistep, which was engaged in a massive scan of Internet traffic and subsequently built a collection of personal data on behalf of the plaintiff. For that purpose, Logistep used a specific software application simulating P2P file-sharing activities. Circumstances suggested that the 3,636 infringement cases constituted only a fraction of the actual users' data collection. This led many experts to define it as an impressive profiling operation.

On February 9, 2006, the same Tribunal of Rome issued another order of disclosure regarding a complaint filed by the abovementioned German music label. On May 18, the Italian Data Protection Authority communicated that it would enter as a party in the trial,[44] for all necessary assessments with respect to the correct application of legislation on data protection.

On July 16 and 17, the Tribunal of Rome issued two new decisions overruling its previous ones. This time, the complaints of Peppermint-Logistep and Techland (a Polish company) were dismissed on the basis that they were not compliant with data protection legislation. The Tribunal found that Art. 156 *bis* was not applicable to the case at hand, for several reasons, the most relevant one

---

41. If clearly indicated as such in the certificate as provided in Art. 28, § 1, lett. d.

42. According to the legislative decree 70/2003, implementing the directive 2000/31 on electronic commerce.

43. Art. 156 *bis* of Italian copyright law implements the directive 2004/48/EC.

44. According to Italian Personal Data Protection Code, Art. 152, § 7 (n. 2).

being the incorrect balance of rights. Data protection and freedom of communication are recognized by the Italian Constitution in Articles 2 and 15 and, as such, can be overcome only for superior public interests or in case of protection against attacks to ICT systems.[45]

Although these decisions do not technically affect the previous ones, it is believed that they will set the trend in Italy for future court cases.

Minors According to the Code of self-regulation "Internet and minors, which was approved on November 19, 2003, anonymity of users is allowed, but the identification of the users from the information society service providers is required. Therefore, the user may be anonymous to other users, but the provider has to know his or her identity. The provider has also to inform the user that it is possible that unauthorized third parties may identify the user through abusive data processing.[46]

A specific protection concerning minors in cases of data processing by journalists was provided in 2006 by the updating of *"Carta di Treviso"*—the code of conduct concerning the right to information and minors.[47]

Health Data There are a number of explicit provisions regarding health data that require the anonymity of data.[48] Health data cannot be published or disseminated[49] and must also be encrypted and kept separate from other data.[50] More generally, sensitive or judicial data has to be given a form of relative anonymity so that the data is temporarily unintelligible to the entities authorized to access them, but that also allows the data subject to be identified, although only in case of necessity.

The protection of the identity of the patients affected by HIV is provided for by Art. 5 of the Italian Personal Data Protection Code, and the protection of the identity of the women who have practiced abortion is provided for by Art. 11[51]

Debtors In the past, the need to guarantee the privacy of a debtor was raised in order to respect his or her particular situation of poverty;[52] nowadays, however, a debtor's anonymity is not generally guaranteed. However, the Personal Data Protection Code and the Code of Conduct and Professional Practice Applying

---

45. For more information on this case, and for the text of the decisions, see *Diritto dell'Internet*, (2007): 461.

46. See, among other things, the following decisions issued by the Italian Data Protection Authority: http://www.garanteprivacy.it, decision 11.10.2006, doc. web. n. 1357845; decision 6.4.2004, doc. web. n. 1091956; decision 10.3.2004, doc. web. n. 1090071.

47. The *"Carta di Treviso"* has also been published at http://www.garanteprivacy. it, doc. web. n. 1357821.

48. For example, Art. 87 of the Italian Data Protection Code, concerning prescriptions, and Art. 93, concerning the right of anonymity of the mother at the time of childbirth.

49. Italian Personal Data Protection Code, Art. 23, § 8 (n. 2).

50. *Ibid.*, Art. 22, § 6 and 7.

51. L. 5.6.1990, n. 135; l. 22.5.1978, n. 194.

52. For example, by l. 10. 5. 1938, n. 745.

to Information Systems Managed by Private Entities with Regard to Consumer Credit, Reliability, and Timeliness of Payments, which became effective on January 1, 2005, provide limits to accessing information regarding the debtor's financial position. In particular, as far as this research is concerned, the right to oblivion of the debtor has been specifically guaranteed. Many decisions of the Italian Data Protection Authority have been issued in this field.[53]

Publication of Decisions Data that is somehow related to a trial, may be anonymized. This is provided by Art. 734 *bis* of the Italian criminal code, which forbids the publication of the name or picture of a victim of sexual crime without his or her consent. Art. 50 of the Personal Data Protection Code forbids the publication of data concerning minors involved in any kind of trial. In accordance with Art. 13, § 5 of the law 23.2.1999, n. 44, the public prosecutor has to adopt any possible protection in order to protect the identity of the victims of crimes of extortion and usury.

Art. 52 of the Personal Data Protection Code provides that a party may require the court to omit his or her identification data from the decision when it is published in legal reviews or data banks.[54] It also provides that the publisher has the duty, when the decision is published, to omit data that identifies minors and the parties, if the decision concerns family relations and status.[55] This provision could also be applied to journalists, but examining this problem would require a separate paper.[56]

It must be noted that the parties are not de-identified in the trial and that the official decision has the names of the parties. The above-mentioned provisions merely apply when the decision is published in legal reviews.

Other Special Provisions of Private Law Anonymity is recognized as a right by some special legislation. For instance, it is recognized in the case of a drug addict when he or she enters detox.[57] In this instance, the patient can ask to remain anonymous while at the hospital, with doctors and with personnel. Patients also have the right to ask that their medical file contain no identifying data.

Mothers may ask not to be named in the birth file should they not want to reveal their identity at the time of childbirth.[58] This right can conflict with the child's right to know the identity of his or her birth mother. If the child has been adopted, he or

---

53. See, among other things, the following decisions issued by the Italian Data Protection Authority: http://www.garanteprivacy.it, decision 31.7.2002, doc. web. n. 621342; decision 9.1.2003, doc. web. n. 1067798.

54. Italian Personal Data Protection Code, Art. 52.

55. *Ibid.*

56. See, among other things, the following decisions issued by the Italian Data Protection Authority: http://www.garanteprivacy.it, decision 30.10.2001, doc. web. n. 42188; decision 21.10.1998.

57. In this case, the right to ask for anonymity is provided by Art. 120 of the d.p.r. 9.10.1990, n. 309.

58. Art. 30 of d.p.r. 30.11.2000, n. 396.

she does not have the right to know the name of his or her mother because of the mother's right to anonymity.[59] According to the court, this guarantees the mother the right to access hospital care and to avoid having an abortion. Therefore, according to the court, in this case, anonymity is a way to protect maternity.

The right to anonymity of the mother is denied in cases of assisted procreation.[60] In other cases, the legal system imposes a duty of anonymity. When organs or bone marrow are donated, for example, administrative and medical personnel have to guarantee the anonymity of the donor as well as the anonymity of the recipient.[61]

F. Anonymity in Public Spaces

Anonymity in public spaces is not a right, but rather a fact. It is not explicitly guaranteed, but it was taken for granted in the past. In recent years, with video surveillance systems, anonymity has become more and more difficult to achieve.

On April 29, 2004, the Italian Data Protection Authority issued an act regarding video surveillance in public space.[62] This provision has been applied on many occasions by the Italian Data Protection Authority.[63] The basic principles stated in the act are that the processing of personal data has to respect principles of legality, minimization, proportionality, and purpose. The reasons for adopting a video surveillance system, and the criteria for processing and retaining such data, should be indicated in a specific act. The potential data subjects should be informed.

Art. 137 of the Italian Data Protection Code, which regulates data processed by journalists, provides for the processing of data concerning circumstances or events that have been made known either directly by the data subject or on account of the latter's public conduct. However, it is doubtful that "private" (as opposed to "public") is a concept related to the location and the place instead of the particular fact photographed.[64]

G. Anonymity in Public Law

In many cases, the state or the public administration interacts with citizens electronically; in these cases, anonymity is not guaranteed. On the other hand, there is a specific need for the identification of citizens.

---

59. This has been recently confirmed by the Italian Constitutional Court in decision 25. 11. 2005, n. 425; also published in www.cortecostituzionale.it.

60. See l.19.2.2004, n. 40.

61. See l. 1.4.1999, n. 91.

62. http://www.garanteprivacy.it, doc. web. n. 1003482.

63. See, among other things, the following decisions issued by the Italian Data Protection Authority: http://www.garanteprivacy.it, decision 23.2.2006, doc. web. n. 1251535; decision 27.10.2005, doc. web. n. 1246675; decision 23.11.2005, doc. web. n. 1202254; decision 21.7.2005, doc. web. n. 1150679; 19.12.2001, doc. web. n. 40085; 28.9.2001, doc. web. n. 39704; decision 7.3.2001, doc. web. n. 30947; decision 28.2.2001, doc. web. n. 40181.

64. This thesis was already presented by Giorgio Giampiccolo, *La tutela giuridica*, 460 (n. 5).

The Electronic Identity Card (EIC) and the National Services Card (NSC) are instruments provided by Public Administrations to citizens as a means of identification in online communication. They are therefore essential tools for the development of higher value-added e-government services, which require certainty and security (e.g., for access to customized databases or transactions). The EIC card is issued by local authorities.[65]

The National Services Card (NSC) is a card issued by Public Administrations that contains an embedded microprocessor having the same features as the EIC and an identical running software.[66] It differs from the latter only in that it lacks the additional security elements of the EIC, such as laser bands, holograms, and such like. Therefore, the NSC does not work as an ID document accepted on sight. The NSC does not bear a photo of the owner and is not subject to special security constraints regarding its plastic material. However, although the NSC is not accepted on sight, it does work in ICT-based services as an instrument of entity authentication.

It should also be noted that the NSC can be used to sign electronic documents with a qualified signature. In fact, it contains not only an entity authentication certificate but also a qualified signature certificate.[67]

Tax Law A recent law[68] guarantees citizens and companies the right to be anonymous vis-à-vis the tax administration when they return capital that was illegally sent abroad. This provision and the guarantee that data will be not communicated to the tax administration have constituted an incentive to bring back capital that was illegally sent abroad. This right to remain anonymous can only be exercised in accordance with specific circumstances and conditions (for instance, capital must be maintained by an authorized intermediary who will tax them) and is not a general freedom from questioning by the tax administration.

III. CONCLUSIONS

Italian law does not have a uniform approach toward anonymity. Legal provisions cover the gambit, sometimes negating any right to anonymity and other times protecting it. Sometimes anonymity is instrumental to the actual and concrete

---

65. The EIC was introduced by the l. 15.5.1997, n. 127. Technical rules for the issuing of the card have been first supplied by d.p.c.m. 22.10.1999, n. 437 and by d.m. 19.7.2000. Other relevant norms can be found in the law of June 16, 1998, and in d.m. 2.8. 2005, n. 191 (decree of the Ministry of Internals).

66. The most relevant legal sources for the NSC are the D.p.r. March 2, 2004, No. 117, and the CDA.

67. According to Art. 64, § 3 of CDA, beginning on December 31, 2007, access to e-government services provided by Public Administrations using tools other than EIC and NSC will no longer be allowed.

68. L. 23.11.2001, n. 409.

exercise of another right; in others, it is considered irrelevant in law; in still others, it is protected as a right.

I suggest that anonymity should be considered not only instrumentally, but also as a form of exercising the right to privacy and the right to data protection. It is a form of control of personal data and is also a form of excluding others from the private sphere of an individual. It may be a form of exercising both a positive and a negative liberty.

Anonymity constitutes a space of liberty for the individual, something becoming more and more essential in a digital world. Nowadays, we leave traces everywhere—it is virtually impossible not to. The difference between privacy and data protection now compared with privacy and data protection twenty years ago is that now, we always leave traces and information records.[69] In fact—which is very important—the right to data protection has been defined as a freedom in the Charter of Fundamental Rights of the European Union. As control becomes more and more diffuse and easily realized, anonymity becomes a way to guarantee privacy and data protection. Thus, in this way, anonymity is essential. It should be guaranteed in order to allow individuals a space of liberty. Anonymity should be seen as a purpose.

However, as a form of exercising the right to privacy and the right to data protection, the right to anonymity has to be continuously balanced with other fundamental rights. Because anonymity cannot be absolute, space should also be left to forms of "sustainable," "protected," or "reasonable" anonymity.

It could be useful to express this solution clearly in a specific legal provision, for instance by making more general the provisions on data minimization contained in Art. 3 of the Italian Data Protection Code.

After the law has established an appropriate balance between anonymity and other rights, technology should implement the rules. The effectiveness of a right to anonymity must be guaranteed using technology,[70] and technology should provide for the protection of different degrees of anonymity.

---

69. Bruce Scheneier, paper presented at the Conference *Terra Incognita*, held in Montreal on September 25–28, 2007.

70. Joel R. Reidenberg, paper presented at the Conference *Terra Incognita*, held in Montreal on September 25–28, 2007, and at the Conference *Reinventing Data Protection?*, held in Brussels on October 12–13, 2007.

INDEX

Note: An italicized *t* after a page number refers to a table on that page, and an italicized *f* after a page number refers to a figure.